SUMMERTIME

SUMMERTIME

GEORGE GERSHWIN'S
LIFE IN MUSIC

RICHARD CRAWFORD

W. W. NORTON & COMPANY
Independent Publishers Since 1923

Frontispiece: George Gershwin's self-portrait in checkered sweater, 1936.

Copyright © 2019 by Richard Crawford

All rights reserved
Printed in the United States of America
First Edition

Photographs from the Ira and Lenore Gershwin Trusts.

For information about permission to reproduce selections from this book, write to
Permissions, W. W. Norton & Company, Inc., 500 Fifth Avenue, New York, NY 10110

For information about special discounts for bulk purchases, please contact
W. W. Norton Special Sales at specialsales@wwnorton.com or 800-233-4830

Manufacturing by LSC Communications, Harrisonburg
Book design by Marysarah Quinn
Production manager: Julia Druskin

Library of Congress Cataloging-in-Publication Data

Names: Crawford, Richard, 1935– author.
Title: Summertime : George Gershwin's life in music / Richard Crawford.
Description: First edition. | New York : W. W. Norton & Company, [2019] |
Includes bibliographical references and index.
Identifiers: LCCN 2019015000 | ISBN 9780393052152 (hardcover)
Subjects: LCSH: Gershwin, George, 1898–1937. | Composers—United States–Biography.
| LCGFT: Biographies.
Classification: LCC ML410.G288 C73 2019 | DDC 780.92 [B]–dc23
LC record available at https://lccn.loc.gov/2019015000

W. W. Norton & Company, Inc., 500 Fifth Avenue, New York, N.Y. 10110
www.wwnorton.com

W. W. Norton & Company Ltd., 15 Carlisle Street, London W1D 3BS

1 2 3 4 5 6 7 8 9 0

Penelope Ball Crawford
Companion nonpareil

The fact is that in the Gershwin years there was nothing more thrilling than to hear George play the piano. It heightened the sense of being alive.

—S. N. BEHRMAN

CONTENTS

PART II

IRA COMES ABOARD

PART III
_____

COMPOSER IN CHARGE

INTRODUCTION

A SONGWRITER AND PIANIST who became an honored composer, George Gershwin (1898–1937) brought a blend of originality and musicianship unique to America's musical landscape. His success, embracing both popular and classical spheres, has made him a figure well known to posterity. Over the years his biographers, some two dozen strong, have served him well.

Their effort began with scholar Isaac Goldberg's study of Gershwin's life and music, published in 1931 on the composer's thirty-third birthday. Goldberg wrote knowledgeably about a matchlessly talented young pianist and composer whose parents and siblings—especially Ira Gershwin, elder brother and collaborator—played key roles in the author's portrait of George. In 1973, marking the seventy-fifth anniversary of George's birth, two consequential biographies appeared. *The Gershwins* by Robert Kimball and Alfred Simon—a scholar and a pianist, respectively—appeared in a coffee-table-book format, mixing historical narrative, personal comments and recollections, and photographs plus lists of data relevant to the authors' research. Both men knew Ira Gershwin firsthand, and their story was grounded in what he could reveal to them.

George, who had died in 1937, is portrayed here within America's culture of artistry and entertainment, and a number of the Gershwins' friends and contemporaries are quoted generously. Another book from that anniversary, *The Gershwin Years*, by Edward Jablonski and Lawrence Stewart, a biographer and an academic collaborator, also relied heavily on the accumulation of material in Ira Gershwin's Beverly Hills abode. Their book, too, was filled generously with pictures and facsimiles of documents. More recently, by 2005 musicologist Howard Pollack had researched *George Gershwin: His Life and Work* rigorously, producing a singular account of a prominent American composer's music and its history, and of his artistic accomplishments. Pollack's impressive tome covers its subject's work in detail, while mostly steering clear of the life Gershwin led as a force in America's cultural landscape.

These books stand as a substantial core in a roster of biographies with varied qualities. Thanks in part to them, and to the efforts of other writers, Gershwin's achievements are well known today. Most of all, the verve and panache of his music has won a place for it in the world's soundscape. But what justifies the appearance of a new Gershwin biography now, eighty-two years after his death? The answer lies in the perspective of the story told here: an academic scholar's account of Gershwin's life in music during the composer's own time.

Who is that author, and how did this book come to be written?

THE AUTHOR of *Summertime: George Gershwin's Life in Music* has specialized in the study of America's music. Growing up in Detroit in a family that encouraged piano lessons, and where public schools offered instrumental instruction and organized ensembles, I spent much of my youth making music. Though awkward at the keyboard, I took lessons for several years from a piano teacher whose tutelege, grounded in European masters from Bach to Schumann, guided me through the variety and challenge of a pianistic zone that my technique could negotiate, more or less. As a saxophonist in bands and orchestras, too, I played pieces ranging from marches and dance music to classical overtures and tone poems. During those years, I also sang in school choruses and a church choir: groups where singers—sopranos aside—learn the satisfactions of making harmony. At the same time, thanks to the phonograph, I learned that jazz was the music I was most drawn to hear and to perform. Playing sax for several years with friends in a jazz-based quintet opened the door for me to the art of improvising. And thanks to a diligent leader who fashioned an infrastructure for us, we played for dances and other functions for pay. In retrospect, it could be said that my youthful years were lived to a soundtrack of music from Bach to Brubeck: an aural spectrum rich in moments that could bring a tickle to the spine and a lump to the throat.

I began college in 1953 with engineering in my sights to prepare for a life in the family's foundry business. But by the second year, stepping up my listening, and finding plenty of music-making on the University of Michigan campus, I discovered plenty to engage with, especially classical concert-going. Soon my saxes—alto and tenor—were consigned to the closet, for Ann Arbor already had enough decent sax players to handle the work available. (In those days jazz music was *verboten* in the halls of the university's School of Music.)

By my third year in college I knew I was a musician at heart, if far from a skilled maker of music. So I looked into a transfer to the School of Music. I learned that the curricula most appealing to me were for budding composers and performers, neither of whose skills fit my capacities. That year found me accepting an invitation to conduct a group of friends in a choral competition, but the university offered no program in conducting. A course of study in music literature, history, and criticism was also described in the catalogue. That approach struck a note appealing to a reader of books about the composers and the music that I was learning to love. But the program gave no hint of a postgraduate future. And with three siblings in the Crawford family to be schooled after me, that option wouldn't fly. Thus the field of music education, training music teachers for elementary and high schools, proved to be my sole sensible option. That curriculum included two years of courses in both music history and music theory, plus participation in an ensemble, but little else that intrigued me. Nevertheless, I'd never been schooled in either of the "core" subjects required, and the music education program would lead to a job. So I applied to transfer from Engineering to the School of Music and was accepted as a music education major.

By the time I won a bachelor's degree in music ed, followed by a master's in music literature, history, and criticism in 1959, I had figured out that my future lay in a field called musicology: the scholarly and historical study of music. The Michigan graduate school offered both human and institutional assets in that field that enabled me to find a course to a future that I never could have anticipated.

AMONG THE TEACHERS in the University of Michigan's Rackham Graduate School were two scholars, both inveterate lovers of music, whose varied approaches left me with enough freedom to lead to an unorthodox path. Prof. Hans T. David, German-born and -educated, and known for his writings on the music of Johann Sebastian Bach, brought to his students a deep understanding of Western music history from the Renaissance through the time of Haydn and Mozart. In seminars, leading us through the workings of master composers, he preached that the quality of our musical knowledge would depend on our command of language, both oral and written. Professor David's English, not his mother tongue, was clear, nimble, and unpretentious. And the literary models he recommended to his students—the King James Version of the Bible, and the *New Yorker* magazine—urged us to steer our written voices toward economy, power, and grace rather than academic formality. (The first paper I wrote for Professsor David earned a B-minus, with copious comments in green ink citing lapses in the writer's self-scrutiny.)

I also had the good fortune to work with Prof. H. Wiley Hitchcock of the School of Music. A veteran of World War II and an accomplished musician, Hitchcock dispensed clear, learned, and often inspired teaching. His research centered on French and Italian Baroque vocal music. The courses he taught centered on realms of Western music history outside the core of the school's curriculum: music of the medieval and Renaissance eras, twentieth-century classical music, and a one-semester survey of music in the United States. Beyond the scope of his classroom assignments, Professor Hitchcock also convened an informal group of students (the "Camerata"), who gathered to sing and play, for our own pleasure and edification, music from lesser-known repertories, from the 1500s to the present.

Beyond life-changing encounters with Professors David and Hitchcock, the environment I discovered at Michigan included an asset of another kind: one that opened for me an unexpected door in the hall of musicology. The William L. Clements Library, a scholarly hideaway devoted to early Americana, had been built on the campus in 1923, and by the latter 1950s had collected a substantial amount of printed musical material and music. Much of that material pertained to American Protestant sacred music-making, grounded in British practices of congregational singing.

To explain: by the 1760s books of psalm and hymn tunes were being compiled and printed in North America's British colonies, chiefly for the use of "singing schools." These gatherings, led by "singing masters," taught fundamental vocal technique and introduced the "scholars" to musical notation: both skills put to use in the worship of God. By 1770 tunebooks from local presses were adding to the British repertory fresh psalm and hymn tunes composed by local musicians, most notably William Billings, a Boston tanner by trade. The Clements Library's shelves, I soon discovered, held dozens of American tunebooks of eighteenth-century vintage.

As a student drawn to choral conducting—a master's "thesis" I wrote had centered on Handel's oratorios—I'd given little thought to what in that realm might be the subject of the Ph.D. dissertation I would need to write. But at this moment a message from Professor Hitchcock reported that the Clements Library had recently acquired a sizable collection of documents pertaining to an American musician: Andrew Law, a singing master from Connecticut. Figuring that it might interest me, he suggested that I check out the new acquisition.

What I discovered on my visit to the Clements manuscript reading room were hundreds of letters, written to and by Andrew Law (1749–1821), a prolific singing master of the latter 1700s and early 1800s. Not a composer himself, Law had taught choral singing and compiled sacred tunebooks to serve classes of singers that he had assembled. He was a devout Christian and an educated man (Rhode Island College, Class of 1775) who had devoted his life, I learned, to peddling his wares as he taught the art of singing sacred music from the printed page.

During my academic life so far I had felt no particular inclination to study American music as a field distinct from the legacy of European music-making, where the roots of musicology lay. Nor did music as plain as the New Englanders' psalm and hymn tunes hold particular artistic attraction for me. But the Clements Library's Andrew Law Papers, I realized, comprised a vast collection of materials documenting a career carried on in a historic American domain ripe for musicological study. Law's correspondence, memorabilia, and printed output held the key to observing an "early" American musician at work in a tradition whose norms and accomplishments, I was learning, had won only meager scrutiny from scholars.

Thus Professor Hitchcock's heads-up message marked a decisive turn in my academic path: the moment when a scholar-in-the-making chooses the subject of his or her Ph.D. dissertation. By now a married man with a family to feed, and feeling lucky to have encountered the Law Papers on local turf, I sensed after a week or so in the Clements Library's archive that the musical life and output of Andrew Law, Connecticut singing master, could be the subject of my dissertation.

Reflecting more than half a century later on how I came to be a musicological Americanist—a breed rare in 1961—I've come across a statement that embodies my process's faith in a blend of luck and intuition. The statement is said to have emerged from the brain of a professional athlete: Lawrence Peter "Yogi" Berra, a nonpareil catcher for the New York Yankees baseball team during the post–World War II era. Over the years, Berra won a reputation as a sage of sorts: a maker of remarks you can't forget. (One example was the plaintive question he posed about the situation of a batter preparing to face a hard-throwing pitcher: "How can I *think* and *hit* at the same time?") Recalling the confidence I had felt during my first days with the Andrew Law Papers in the summer of 1961, I remembered that Berra had also voiced a *faux* axiom guaranteed to draw a smile and a shrug from a fan like me, whenever I thought about the academic choice I had made so cavalierly. But nowadays, when I recall the snap decision that might then have seemed to turn me away from the artistic riches of my chosen discipline's core in Europe, I've come to grasp the spirit of that professional about-face by channeling another nostrum from the arsenal of Yogi Berra: "When you come to a fork in the road, take it."

WORK ON MY PH.D. dissertation began with gathering information in the Law Papers' documents, while serving as a teaching assistant in courses taught by School of Music faculty. By 1963 I'd made my way through the Law manuscripts, integrated his printed material into the chronology I was assembling, and begun to write the story of Andrew Law's life and work. Professor David had declined an invitation to serve on my dissertation committee, but his advice that savoir-faire as a writer would enhance a scholar's authority had made me a believer. And Professor Hitchcock had moved eastward by then, settling in eventually at the City University of New York, to become a leading figure in the study of American music. I was hired to teach music history classes for undergraduates in the School of Music, and I also took over Hitchcock's American music class. My dissertation on Andrew Law was completed by the summer of 1965.

During that year a political decision was made in Washington, D.C., that proved fortunate for the course I was taking. The U.S. Congress passed legislation enacted "to promote progress and scholarship in the humanities and the arts in the United States." To meet this goal two grant-making agencies were created: the National Endowment for the Arts (NEA) and the National Endowment for the Humanities (NEH). The latter's enrichment of financial support for scholarly work in the humanities proved also to be an investment in the study of music in America, and in American music. Between 1965 and the Bicentennial of the American Revolution in 1976, interest in American music rose steadily in the field of musicology, as both experienced scholars and new ones found academic opportunity in fresh forays into music made in the United States. The notion of funding for such ventures now had a government agency on its side. Indeed, I wondered at the time if that shift in attitude had anything to do with Northwestern University Press's publication of my dissertation as *Andrew Law: American Psalmodist* (1968).

As my research on Protestant church music during the 1700s and early 1800s continued, that field and other strains of early American music-making were winning more attention from graduate students. And the years approaching the Bicentennial celebration in 1976 brought a surge of scholarly interest to the study of American composers, past and present.

Dominant among composers "discovered" in this moment was Charles Ives. Born in 1874 in Connecticut, schooled in composition at Yale College, and successful as a businessman who had fashioned, more or less in obscurity, a flow of compositions in a uniquely American style, his music now came to the fore. As Ives's own hundredth birthday drew nigh, he was studied and lauded as an idiosyncratic and luminary figure: a radical maker of American artistry.

A fresh generation of American composers followed. Born around the turn of a new century, many among them sought training in Europe, finding varied ways to sustain careers on America's musical scene when they returned. As twentieth-century artists, they were touched by varied manifestations of modernism. Beyond composing and tending to their musical output, these artists also exercised their talents as performers; some took on varied teaching opportunities, while others wrote and lectured about their music and that of their contemporaries. As for vernacular music outside the church, musicologically trained scholars and students came forward who performed or fancied band music, blues music, jazz music, rock and roll, or other varied emanations of this country's entertainment industry. For them, America was now offering a near-boundless arena in which scholarly curiosity was free to roam.

GEORGE GERSHWIN, born in New York in 1898, belonged to that generation: a composer whose command of the realm of melody, success in popular songwriting, assimilation of a jazz-based idiom from black pianistic colleagues, and passion for learning about his art enabled him to stand apart from his contemporaries. Bringing to his work a compositional voice appealing to listeners on both sides of the purported classical/popular divide, Gershwin was a unique figure on the Amrican scene. But as the teacher of a one-semester course on America's music, I was slow to perceive him as a major figure in that history. I believed in his talent, for jazz musicians, whose imagination and skills I esteemed, included Gershwin songs in their repertory of "standards." Which I took to mean that he had composed melodies and harmonic plans good enough to invite solo improvisors and arrangers to invent their own versions of his music. Nevertheless, and for whatever reason, I was slow to warm up to his "classical" triumphs: the *Rhapsody in Blue* (1924), *Concerto in F* (1925), and *Porgy and Bess* (1935).

The incident that brought Gershwin into my purview in 1972 was a strike by African American students at the University of Michigan, insisting that their numbers on campus be boosted substantially. Faculty members sought ways to support their cause. And the School of Music faculty decided to convene a panel on the subject of black American music. I volunteered to participate, but time was short. As I looked for a subject it occurred to me that *Porgy and Bess*, America's best-known opera, was a tale about African Americans, and sung by them. What did it mean, I wondered, that an acclaimed folk opera about black people was the work of a white Southern novelist, Dubose Heyward, and a white Jewish songwriter from New York, George Gershwin?

As noted, time was short, and a title for my talk was needed. Learning that questions had been raised in the past about the legitimacy of white creators of black characters in studies of *Porgy and Bess*, I concocted a flashy title referring to one of the opera's most famous songs. Hinting (unjustifiedly) that racial argument would loom large in my remarks, though I had yet to think that matter through, I decided to title my talk "It Ain't Necessarily Soul: Gershwin's *Porgy and Bess* as Symbol." It was no problem to find enough information about the opera to justify my place on the panel, for *Porgy and Bess* offers compelling stories on many levels. And the talk I gave was well enough received. In fact, requests for encore readings followed, which I accepted, but only after further research had strengthened my grasp of the subject.

This event taught me that, unlike my experience with early American psalmody, if George Gershwin was announced as the subject of an academic talk, an audience was likely to appear, primed for enjoyment. Nevertheless, through the rest of the 1970s and 1980s the core of my scholarly effort continued to abide in the fields of early New England sacred music. That endeavor culminated in an 798-page tome—*Early American Sacred Imprints (1698–1810): A Bibliography*, by Allen P. Britton, Irving Lowens, and Richard Crawford (Worcester, MA, 1990)—plus an edition of the 101 favorite psalm and hymn tunes of that era. But once the music-making of George Gershwin had visited my atelier, so to speak, I discovered that the more I listened, and the more I learned about him and his music, the greater the respect I gained for the public's opinion of both. And I was being asked for more articles related to him, including the George Gershwin entry in the *New Grove Dictionary of American Music* (1987).

In 1985, delivering a series of six Bloch Lectures at the University of California at Berkeley under the heading *The American Musical Landscape*, I decided to assign one of those lectures to Gershwin. To outline the historical sweep from the 1700s into the 1900s, I had devoted four of those lectures to the work of American composers prominent in their time: in the 1700s William Billings; in the 1800s George Frederick Root; and in the 1900s Duke Ellington, before closing the series with a song by Gershwin. The song I chose, "I Got Rhythm," from the Broadway musical comedy *Girl Crazy* (1930), had come to be a favorite of jazz musicians, who had also transformed it into a thirty-two-bar improvisatory structure ("Rhythm Changes"), minus the Gershwin brothers' words and melody. When the Bloch Lectures appeared in print as *The American Musical Landscape* (1992), the piece on George Gershwin's music-making served as the book's last chapter. Nine years later, initiated by the publisher, *America's Musical Life: A History* (2001), appeared in print, enabling me to chronicle in forty chapters what I had learned about five centuries of music-making in America.

In 2003 I retired from the classroom, having decided, in the wake of writing a historical panorama, that my next project would center on George Gershwin, the American composer whose life in music had come to intrigue me the most. Perhaps the notion of adding another Gershwin biography to a roster already well served would make that choice seem redundant. But I figured that the breadth of my experience of America's music would help to guide me, once I knew more about what had made my subject's musical talents tick. So, as with Andrew Law decades ago, I compiled a chronology of George Gershwin's life and work. Reporting the full contents of the documents available—letters and notes, articles and reviews, contracts and other written items—my chronology, together with evidence from biographies already accessible, provided a more than ample supply of data to mull over as I studied and savored the sound of Gershwin's music.

The making of the chronology led me to understand that, in the course of telling the story of George Gershwin's life in music-making, my assignment would center on tracing the path he had discovered to claim his unique place on the Western world's musical stage. How had Gershwin marshaled his talents to compose music so successful at engaging both "the many and the few"?

While completing this Introduction I grew increasingly mindful of a source that, had I recognized its import earlier, might have brought the theme of collaboration to the surface of my story more emphatically. That source, helpful even so, had been given to me as a gift during the 1960s. I had visited it during the 1980s for reference.

But I'd found no reason to dig further into its contents then; for, light on narrrative, it's an anthology of versified lyrics. More specifically, *Lyrics on Several Occasions* (1959) consists of a selection of song lyrics, with the author's comments about each one. And who was the author? The title page, cast in the antique mode of seventeenth- and eighteenth-century Great Britain, reveals that fact, and a good deal more, if the reader takes the time to pay attention:

A Selection of Stage & Screen Lyrics Written for Sundry Situations; And Now Arranged in Arbitrary Categories. To Which Have Been Added Many Informative Annotations & Disquisitions On Their Why & Wherefore, Their Whom-For, Their How; And Matters Associative.

By IRA GERSHWIN *GENT.*

Here, then, was a book by Ira Gershwin about his own work, written long after the death of George, who had composed much of the music for which Ira had written the words. In fact, I had already quoted Ira's book in *The American Musical Landscape*, explaining how the song "I Got Rhythm" had been made. (In that entry Ira described the difficulty he'd faced while seeking the best rhyme scheme for a harmonized melody fashioned by George. And he was able to cite more than one of the attempts he had tried out and then abandoned.) As a Gershwin biographer-to-be by 2003, I knew that a figure as famous as George would require thorough and meticulous research, which my chronology would underlie. But the heart of a biography depends, too, on how effectively the subject's persona can be revealed. And on that front I figured that it would be impossible to find a witness of George Gershwin's talent and modus operandi more observant and reliable than Ira Gershwin, his elder brother and regular collaborator.

Lyrics on Many Occasions, the only book Ira Gershwin ever wrote, was published twenty-two years after the death of George, who had composed the music for sixty-nine of the 104 songs that Ira had chosen. (Other composers who worked with Ira after George died include Harold Arlen, Vernon Duke, Jerome Kern, Harry Warren, and Kurt Weill.) After a three-page Foreword announcing the half-dozen subjects to be represented comes the table of contents. Here the titles of the songs are listed, divided into groups according to their subject matter. The 104 entries follow, with full texts of the numbers the author has written. Each is then introduced by its associations: the show in which the song first appeared and its date, its composer, the number's style or tempo direction, and the names of the original performers, plus a line or two indicating the background or situation in which the number is sung. Almost all the entries conclude with data pertaining to the song, ranging from a few lines to as many as three or four pages. Collectively, Ira's book amounts to a storehouse of insightful essays, each with its own emphasis and flavor, and showing a lyricist at work with his brother, or with one of five other leading composers.

Ira's Foreword comes to an end with a graceful postscript, marking with a gentle twist the gap between his craft and that of a poet:

> P.S. Since most of the lyrics in this lodgment were arrived at by fitting words mosaically to music already composed, any resemblance to actual poetry, living or dead, is highly improbable.

And the text concludes, in Ira's one-page Afterword, with songful forces competing with each other. In fact, this definition has been borrowed from the *Encyclopedia Britannica*, for Ira had discovered "no better way to conclude what much of his book has been about":

> SONG is the joint art of words and music, two arts under emotional pressure coalescing into a third. The relation and balance of the two arts is a problem that has to be resolved anew in every song that is composed.

Finally, written from the heart as well as the brain, the last two paragraphs of Ira's text, revisiting his own collaboration with DuBose Heyward on numbers for *Porgy and Bess*, dwell on Ira's awe for George's preternatural talents. "These many years," he writes, "and I can still shake my head in wonder at the reservoir of musical inventiveness, resourcefulness, and craftsmanship George could dip into."

> He takes two simple quatrains of DuBose's, studies the lines, and in a little while a lullaby called "Summertime" emerges—delicate and wistful, yet destined to be sung over and over again.

And later on, "out of the libretto's dialogue," he continues, George "takes Bess's straight, unrhymed speech" and finds music that enables him to transform these words into "a rhythmic aria."

Ira Gershwin's last paragraph revisits the standard layman's query about whether, in any given song, the words or the music came first. Limiting that question's relevance to the experience of the Gershwin brothers, here, minus the examples he cited, is Ira's reply:

> If I have stumbled into the field of the musicologist without being a musician, all I'm trying to say is that George could be as original and distinctive when musicalizing words . . . as when composing music which later will require words. . . . Regardless of which procedure was used, the resultant compositions sang so naturally that I doubt if any listener, lacking the mentions in this note, could tell which came first—the words or the music.

In describing the work of George, the exacting wordsmith Ira avoids the word "genius." But his testimony offers a revelation that his brother and collaborator owned a genius for breathing life, as well as sound, into the words that Ira had chosen.

PART I

COMPOSER TO THE FORE

THE GERSHWINS:
MORRIS AND ROSE AND FAMILY

GEORGE GERSHWIN'S PARENTS were part of the tide of immigrants that hit American shores between 1880 and the outbreak of World War I. More than two million Jews immigrated to the United States during those years, many of them fleeing anti-Jewish pogroms that followed the assassination of the Russian czar Alexander II in 1881. A majority came from the stetl—the near-impoverished rural communities of eastern Europe where Yiddish was spoken and the omnipresence of God assumed. Those people's westward journey, the Gershwin parents included, ended in New York City. There, during the three decades before 1910, the Jewish population grew more than tenfold. Many of the new arrivals settled on the Lower East Side, where urban crowding and the scarcity of decent-paying work complicated the struggles of recent stetl-dwellers to make their way in the New World.

By the time Morris Gershovitz and Rose Bruskin married on July 21, 1895, however, their adjustment to life in America was well under way. Born and bred in the Russian capital St. Petersburg, Morris came from urban stock. A leather-cutter by trade, he was the grandson of a rabbi and the son of a mechanic who had provided technical support to the czarist artillery. When forced military service loomed, he left Russia for the United States, arriving on August 14, 1890.[1] Rose, also a St. Petersburg native and the daughter of a furrier, likely immigrated with her family early in 1892.

Morris made his ocean crossing with an essential piece of information written on a slip of paper and kept in his hatband: the address of his mother's brother, "Greenstein the tailor," who lived somewhere in the New York area. But after a gust of wind blew the hat overboard just before the ship docked, Morris was cast alone into a teeming city with no money, no address, and no knowledge of the English language. Yet the culture in which he found himself left him unintimidated. Locating a pool hall with a game in progress, he won enough cash to pay for a bed in a Bowery flophouse. And he met speakers of Russian and Yiddish, who steered him to the Brownsville section of Brooklyn, where many immigrants lived. Within hours of his arrival there, he found his uncle Greenstein.[2]

Rose had already caught Morris's eye back in St. Petersburg, and by some turn of events he located her after the Bruskins arrived in New York. At the time of their wedding, Morris was a foreman in a shoe factory, designing fancy women's shoes and earning $35 a week. Immigrant families could live on half that amount or less. "Compared to most of us," observed lyricist Yip Harburg, who also grew up on the Lower East Side, "the Gershwins were affluent."[3]

The name "Gershwin," inscribed in the annals of America's culture by the couple's second son—to replace Gershovitz, or its variants Gershwine or Gershvin—points to George and his brother Ira, who wrote the words for most Gershwin songs.[4] But first and foremost, "the Gershwins" signifies a family—Morris and Rose, Ira, George, Arthur, and their sister Frances—who shared a household until 1929, long after both George and Ira, at thirty-one and thirty-three, had won fortune and fame in show business. The family spent much of their lives in each other's company. While Morris and Rose did little to encourage their sons' artistic leanings, they did not oppose them either. But from the time George began to make his mark in the music business, the lives of his parents and siblings grew more affluent.

During the years before 1916, the Gershwins occupied twenty-eight different residences, owing to Morris's preference for living within walking distance of his place of business, which changed often.⁵ His post–shoe-business ventures included a cigar store, a bakery, a billiard parlor, a Turkish and a Russian bath, and a succession (even a small chain) of restaurants, not to mention a brief stint as a bookmaker at the Belmont Park racetrack. They reveal the range of possibilities that existed for a man like him in the commercial life of New York City. Ira worked for a time as cashier in Morris's Turkish bath business, an experience that provided fodder for the diary he began on September 3, 1916, under the title "Every Man His Own Boswell." "From what I have seen thus far of the Turkish Bath business," he wrote in October,

> the "season" is always starting next month. Excuses for bum business / When outside it is a beautiful day—"can't expect business today everybody wants to be out on a day like this." / When it is a dreary, rainy, dismal day, "can't expect business today—nobody wants to leave home." / Very Cold Day, "can't expect etc.— 'stoo cold." / [Very] "Warm—'stoo hot." / or "Can't expect much this month—everybody's away." . . . [Or "Can't expect much this] year—Presidential Year."⁶

Against a background in which financial security was far from guaranteed, impermanent living arrangements must sometimes have unsettled family harmony. Avoiding banks—Ira was tasked with pawning and redeeming Rose's diamond ring through the course of Morris's varied ventures, each time raising around $400— changing occupations, and moving a lot, the Gershwins seemed to place little value on domestic stability.[7] George and Ira's lives and destinies were left mostly in their own hands.

As a musician, George was not formally trained in standard fashion, but neither was he self-educated. Rather, he was taught by a succession of private teachers, most of whom he hired himself. Hungry for knowledge, he showed a keen sense of what he needed to know, how to obtain it, and from whom. At age fifteen, he left school for a job as a song seller on Tin Pan Alley. Unlike Ira, George possessed an independent drive that resisted the learning environment of the schoolroom. Nor did the Gershwins show themselves more than casual practitioners of their Jewish faith; only Ira had a bar mitzvah. For a latter-day observer in search of patterns in George's early life, his lack of experience in being socialized under institutional authority looms large.

What we know about Morris and Rose has come most directly through their offspring, especially Ira and George. Arthur, a shadowy figure, did not weigh in on the subject of family life. Frances, the only daughter, did so with a bang—but only in the 1950s, after her mother had died, when she began to challenge the outlook of Ira, who had emerged over the years as the family's chief spokesman. The Gershwin saga according to George took shape during the 1920s. Its main source was the celebrity interview, a journalistic form he mastered early in life.[8] Anticipating interviewers' questions, he could be counted on to offer a few words about his parents (Russian immigrants, not musicians, with a dad engaged in "business") and his musical training, plus an early encounter or two with music as an enthralling force. Rose's purchase of a piano in 1912, when George was thirteen or fourteen, marked the pivotal point in his story, for, as he often said, its presence in the house changed his life. But beyond that decisive moment, family history was almost never on his interviewers' minds, nor was it on George's mind unless an anecdote happened to occur to him.

As the lesser-known partner of what came to be a luminary

songwriting team, Ira was seldom interviewed. Nevertheless, he was a reliable source of information: a keen observer who took words seriously and enjoyed keeping accurate written records. (The first Gershwin scrapbooks date from Ira's teenage years, which also found him involved with school newspapers.) Circumspect and seemingly born with an antigossip gene, Ira placed a high value on privacy—that of others as well as his own. Virtually from boyhood to old age, he lived by the principle that when he had nothing positive to say on a subject, nothing is what he would pass on. His studied avoidance of negative judgments, especially where family members and friends were concerned, made him a discreet keeper of the flame. Ira's philosophy of information-keeping set the guidelines for Gershwin biography during his lifetime. Not until after his death did Frances go public about her own struggle growing up in the Gershwin household.

Gershwin's first biographer, Isaac Goldberg, who was able to observe the family firsthand, detected overlap between George's sense of humor, fundamental to his personality, and the social manner of his father, in whom the author found "a strange combination of fun without humor." On one occasion, when somebody questioned the stature of the *Rhapsody in Blue*, Morris shot back: "Of course it's a great piece! Doesn't it take fifteen minutes to play?"[9] From the mid-1920s on, "Papa" Gershwin stories in this vein circulated in the Gershwins' social circle. Friends eager for more were known to greet George with "What's the latest?" Goldberg came to believe that Morris had passed on something of his unintended humor to his second son. (No one seems to have questioned that Ira's humor was always the intended kind.)

A family friend, journalist and playwright S. N. Behrman, characterized Morris as an eccentric with a gift for saying "that final thing beyond which there is nothing to be said."[10] Pianist and composer Oscar Levant felt, like Goldberg, that "Papa" Gershwin's "gift for oblique thinking and apparently irrelevant simplicity was not unlike certain attitudes of George."[11] There was a strong emotional bond between father and son as well, for Morris's pride in George's accomplishments was palpable. And surely it was Morris—who appreciated opera, enjoyed singing, whistled with flair, and was known to "coax music out of the silliest contraptions, such as combs and clothespins and pencils"—who passed his feeling for music on to his offspring.[12]

At age sixty-one, Ira published an anthology of his song lyrics that included comments his father had made about several of them. One was "Embraceable You" from *Girl Crazy* (1930). When company was present, he recalled, Morris sometimes asked George to " 'play that song about me.' And when the line 'Come to papa—come to papa— do!' was sung, he would thump his chest, look around the room, and beam."[13] "Fascinating Rhythm" offered another example of the odds Morris faced in making sense of the English language. For he was known to request this song by a title—"Fashion on the River"—that, however distant from the song's literal meaning, never dampened his love for it.[14]

Rose Gershwin was the boss of the family, not her husband. Though she avoided close involvement in her children's activities, George described her as "very loving": set on their being educated and ready to enter a respectable line of work—which, in the spring of 1914, did not include making music. When the fifteen-year-old George declared his intent to become a musician, Rose balked at the idea. But when he proposed leaving New York's High School of Commerce for a $15-a-week salary at Remick's publishers, Rose saw the advantages of a job in hand, and her resistance crumbled.

It is fair to say that two views about the Gershwins exist, both with roots in the family and each true in its own way. According to Ira, the family was significant only insofar as it produced a musical genius, whose work could speak for itself. But Frances Gershwin Godowsky, the family member most openly aggrieved by the influence of Rose, held that as the cradle of extraordinary talent, the family was fundamental to the Gershwin story. As Frances saw it, the lovable Morris's feckless tendencies and Rose's dominating selfishness created an unsupportive, emotionally precarious environment for the children, leaving marks not only on Ira, Arthur, and especially on her, but on George too, the family genius—who, it must be noted, dedicated his magnum opus, *Porgy and Bess*, "To My Parents."

If sorting out the personal relationships behind Gershwin's artistry affects the way his music is understood, then Frances's perspective contributes to the context for his musical achievements. As a humanizing force, love in the Gershwin household seems to have been in limited supply. Yet there is no denying that the parents' laissez-faire attitude gave both George and Ira freedom to find their own way. As things worked out, each chose a fiercely competitive line of work with a slim chance of success, and each beat the odds spectacularly.

A PIANO IN THE HOUSE, AND ELSEWHERE

WHEN GEORGE GERSHWIN first became known to the public, he referred to himself as a native New Yorker. As his fame grew, however, he made it a point to specify Brooklyn, across the East River from the borough of Manhattan. And that is where Jacob Gershwine was born, on September 26, 1898, twenty months after Ira. The family's Brooklyn address was 242 Snediker Avenue, and sixty years later Ira was able to reach back in memory to that time.[1] "We must have lived there . . . two or three years because I was old enough to be aware of the two-story house with trees on each side, and a fenced-in yard where grapes grew; and to remember that until I was five I wore starched dresses and long golden curls. Not sissy, this. My mother told me years later it had been quite the style for little boys."

Six weeks after George's birth, Morris left his $35-a-week job in the shoe trade and embarked on a career in business, moving his family back to the Lower East Side as part owner of a Turkish bath at Broome and the Bowery. "We now lived on Christie Street," Ira continued, where I went to kindergarten (short pants, no curls), which was most likely in 1901. Then we moved to a flat at Forsyth and Delancey. . . . Several schools later, I found myself uptown in one on 125th Street. The Turkish bath, no bonanza, had been given up by my father and Uncle Harry for a restaurant on Third Avenue near 129th, a block or so from the Harlem River. . . . At the age of nine [1905–06] I was back again at P.S. 20, because the Harlem restaurant had been given up for one on Forsyth, between Hester and Grand Streets.[2]

When questioned about his own personal history, George would begin with a musical epiphany he had at age six, when the family lived in Harlem. "I stood outside a penny arcade listening to an automatic piano leaping through Rubinstein's Melody in F. The peculiar jumps in the music held me rooted. To this very day I can't hear the tune without picturing myself outside that arcade on One Hundred and Twenty-fifth Street, standing there barefoot and in overalls, drinking it all in avidly."[3] Another such moment occurred some years later, while attending Public School 25 on the Lower East Side. In this case, George heard a schoolmate at an assembly—Maxie Rosenzweig, later Max Rosen—play Dvořák's "Humoresque" on the violin. Struck by the beauty of what he had heard, George sought out the young musician, and the boys became friends.[4] Before he met Maxie, George thought that "there was something radically wrong with youngsters who went in for music. To scrape away at the fiddle, to wear out one's fingers on piano keys, was to be a 'little Maggie,' a sissy."[5] By making friends with a violin-playing boy, George was also making room for music in his own consciousness.

These two memories stand out in contrast with the rest of what we can learn about Gershwin's pre-piano boyhood. Ira, a self-defined introvert who liked to stay home and read, remembered George as his opposite: always outside playing, getting into fights and known to come home with a black eye. Yip Harburg, a schoolmate and life-long friend of Ira's, identified ethnic rivalry as a driving force in the lives of youngsters who grew up on the Lower East Side.

> When I was about seven, we moved to Eleventh Street and Avenue C, a sort of borderline between the Irish and the Italians that was just becoming Jewish. Among the kids there was plenty of friction. The enmity was supposedly residential—block by block—but we Jews were always aware that the goyim were after us. Since they came in gangs we formed gangs too. We fought the 14th Street-ers who were Italian, we fought the Irish—and both of them fought the Jews.

In neighborhoods like these, Yiddish-speaking parents and their English-speaking offspring were likely to drift apart. "The street, not the home, was your life," Harburg recalled. To be a street kid meant to grow up in an urban world ruled by a sense of danger, and by peer pressure.[6] Because of that pressure, boys, at least, were not encouraged to like or take much interest in school.

Both Ira and Harburg remembered the day the new family piano was delivered in 1912—startlingly, George already knew how to play it. In their telling, the change is instantaneous: a street urchin sits down at the piano and is magically transformed into a musical prodigy, like a frog turned into a prince. (George explained that he had been "fooling around" on a player piano at a schoolmate's house.)[7] The surprise for Ira was not just that George could play but that his playing was good enough to sound like vaudeville. Given the importance of this tale in Ira's memories, it is worth noting that George himself never told any such story.

As soon as the Gershwins had their piano and George had decisively taken it over, a Miss Green, who lived nearby, was engaged as his teacher. Once he had learned what Miss Green had to teach him, he moved on to another neighborhood teacher, and then to yet another.[8] At that point, Gershwin crossed paths with a musician named Goldfarb, who impressed him by playing "with great gusto and with a barrel of gestures." Learning that Goldfarb's teacher, one Von Zerly, had led operetta and a band in Hungary, Gershwin signed on as Von Zerly's student, at the "stiff price" of $1.50 an hour. Rather than assigning exercises and little piano pieces, the teacher started him out on excerpts from grand operas; in six months, George was tackling the Overture to *William Tell*. Whatever their musical delights, arrangements like these were not standard fare for a novice seeking to establish a solid piano technique.[9]

As 1912 came to an end, the erstwhile street kid was behaving like a true lover of music. George started a scrapbook of articles about musicians that he clipped from newspapers and magazines, and programs from concerts he heard. During the three-month period from December 1912 to March 1913, the fourteen-year-old attended eight concerts in various New York venues, enthusiastically embracing orchestral and chamber works by Beethoven, Handel, Liszt, Mascagni, Mendelssohn, Rossini, Rubinstein, Saint-Saëns, Schubert, Tchaikovsky—Joseph Lhevinne playing the Piano Concerto No. 1—and Wagner, and piano works by Bach/Liszt, Balakirev, Brahms, Chopin, Godowsky, Grieg, Liszt, and Schumann, among others. With music in his ears, Gershwin began to consciously cultivate a habit of intensive listening in his earliest teens. "I listened not only with my ears," he explained to Goldberg, "but with my nerves, my mind, my heart. I had listened so earnestly that I became saturated with the music. . . . Then I went home and listened in memory. I sat at the piano and repeated the motifs."[10]

At this moment, however—most likely late in 1912 or early in 1913—George stood on the brink of another breakthrough. Through Jack Miller, a young pianist who played with a community ensemble called the Beethoven Symphony Orchestra, he began lessons with Miller's accomplished teacher, Charles Hambitzer. George remembered vividly the first time he played for Hambitzer.

"I rubbed my fingers and dived into the Overture to *William Tell*. Hambitzer said nothing until I had finished. 'Listen,' he finally spoke, getting up from his chair. 'Let's hunt out that guy and shoot him—and not with an apple on his head, either!'"[11]

By all accounts an extraordinary musician, Hambitzer is remembered today only because he was Gershwin's teacher. Yet he turned out to be unusually well suited to introduce the gifted youngster to the world of music in which he would make his way.[12] Born of Russian ancestry, probably in 1881, Hambitzer grew up in a midwestern city, Milwaukee, known for its German heritage. He became a versatile composer, player of several orchestral instruments, teacher of some of them, and a stalwart in the pit of Milwaukee's Pabst Theatre.

After moving to New York in 1908, Hambitzer joined the orchestra at the Waldorf-Astoria Hotel, led by Joseph Knecht—playing viola, oboe, bassoon, cello, and organ, but never piano there, according to his student Nathaniel Shilkret. Hambitzer's friend Edward Kilenyi, soon to be Gershwin's harmony teacher, described the Milwaukeean as a talented musician who wore his accomplishments lightly: "On his viola or cello, in his jolly way, he could play concertos as if performing a trick, to the pleasure of his colleagues." Shilkret remembered a colleague challenging Hambitzer to show that he actually knew how to play the piano. After pleading that he was out of practice, Hambitzer sat down and performed one piece after another. "He could play any number we suggested. He was the most natural pianist I ever heard—barring no one—and his memory was phenomenal. Bach, Beethoven, Mozart, Schubert, Chopin, Schumann, Liszt. . . . Pieces just poured out of him flawlessly."[13]

Though endowed with talent, technique, generosity, and good humor, Hambitzer managed only spotty success in his life and career. An early marriage into which a dishonest woman supposedly lured him was followed by a second, happier one that produced a child, but ended with his wife's early death from tuberculosis. His operetta *The Love Wager* was performed on a road tour but never produced on Broadway. As for why Hambitzer's pianistic career failed to thrive, Shilkret believed that he simply had no interest in concertizing. Yet as word got around of Hambitzer's abilities at the piano and interest in teaching, he became "the busiest teacher in New York."[14] He died of tuberculosis in 1917 or 1918, at age thirty-seven.[15]

What we know about Gershwin's experience with Hambitzer comes chiefly from its beginning. Hambitzer wrote his sister in Milwaukee not long after George's lessons began: "I have a new pupil . . . who will make his mark in music if anybody will. The boy is a genius, without a doubt; he's just crazy about music and can't wait until it's time to take his lesson. No watching the clock for this boy!" Though the young genius had his own thoughts about what he wanted to learn, Hambitzer, a classically trained artist with plenty of experience in public entertainment, had a clear view of what he needed to know. "He wants to go in for this modern stuff, jazz and what not," the teacher wrote his sister. "But I'm not going to let him for a while. I'll see that he gets a firm foundation in the standard music first."[16]

It was Hambitzer who introduced Gershwin to Chopin, Liszt, and Debussy. Gershwin credited his teacher too with making him "harmony-conscious. . . . I was crazy about that man. I went out, in fact, and drummed up ten pupils for him."[17] He learned to play with a loose wrist that allowed for plenty of endurance, which would serve him well during his youthful stints as a song demonstrator and rehearsal pianist. And in Hambitzer he found a teacher who, surely rare in that day, shared his own sense that the goals of learning classical piano technique and exploring modern popular music could be complementary: "I have listened to him playing classics with great rhythmic extemporizing, and I have not discouraged him," said Hambitzer.[17] In that approach lay the heart of the young musician's lifelong commitment to the musical present. By continually exercising his creative fancy as a performer, Gershwin was affirming his identity as a musical modernist.

During the summer of 1913, fourteen-year-old George landed his first paying job as a musician in the Catskill Mountains, a resort area north of New York City, earning $5 a week.[18] Back in the city for the fall, he started another year of school, now at New York's High School of Commerce. His parents were of different minds about his musical obsession. Morris apparently supported it. Rose, who chose the school, insisted, though, that he also learn account-ing.[19] But George did not flourish there. Indeed, the only informa-tion surviving from his last academic year has to do with music. Barely fifteen, he wrote his first two compositions: a popular song and a "ragged" piano classic—"Ragging the Träumerei," an embel-lishment of Schumann's famous character piece with rhythms from popular music.[20] He also gave his first documented public perfor-mance, on March 21, 1914, at a meeting of the Finley Society of the City College of New York, a student literary club set up by Ira, now a student at the college. The program lists "George Gersh-vin" as both player of a piano solo and accompanist for a singer named Charles Rose. (Gershwin revealed in 1931 that the solo was a tango written for the occasion, a piece he could still remember and was even willing to play when he was in the mood.) Two months later, George left school, apparently before the semester was offi-cially over.

As George would later tell Goldberg, he had a friend, Ben Bloom, who introduced him to an older musician named Mose Gumble, of the Jerome H. Remick music-publishing firm. Gumble auditioned the lad in May 1914 and hired him to demonstrate songs for $15 a week.[21] Yet by the testimony of Irving Berlin, who knew Ben Bloom in those days, Gershwin's first job for Remick was not as a pianist but as a delivery boy who helped Bloom haul copies of Remick-published songs to venues around New York for $5 a week.[22] During the summer of 1914, George returned to the Catskills, this time playing duets at a hotel with a violinist named Jack Diamond, and again earning $5 a week.[23] It is easy to imagine him, newly liberated from formal education in 1914, trading a $5-a-week delivery job that summer for a playing job at the same rate; it is harder to imagine that having become a salaried song demonstrator in May, he temporarily left that new post for an out-of-town summer engagement that paid only one-third as much.[24] It appears that in the late summer of 1914, though, Gershwin *was* hired by Remick's "professional" department, joining a corps of pianists who labored to promote songs created by staff composers and lyricists. For the next two and a half years, he earned his keep by presiding over a Remick piano room.

The music-publishing district called Tin Pan Alley had been the nation's chief popular music marketplace since the 1890s. Performers searching for new songs went there to find them. Publishing representatives in turn courted singers and paid them to sing their interpolated songs in shows. A catchy song performed in a musical comedy, variety, or minstrel show was the ultimate "plug" for boosting its popularity, and could trade on the performer's charisma. When Gershwin went to work for Remick's, the firm occupied roomy quarters at 219–221 West 46th Street, with the various departments geared to distributing songs as an industrial-style product.[25] The departments were: shipping (where Gershwin likely started, as Ben Bloom's sidekick), band and orchestra (where standard voice-and-keyboard settings were adapted for instrumental ensembles), sales and publicity, slides (where visual images were created to illustrate performances), and the arranging department (where songs were dressed up for a variety of performances, including medleys). The piano rooms in the "professional" department were cubicles in which the pianists pushed numbers created by Remick staff.

As well as being practiced sightreaders, pluggers tried to choose numbers that matched a customer's talent and personality as well as voice. They learned to teach songs from scratch if necessary, and they worked to inspire clients' confidence so that they could put them over to an audience. A song demonstrator also had to learn transposition, fitting the key of a song to the singer's range. Gershwin was expected at the piano every morning at nine. Few, if any, headliners dropped in; instead, "colored people used to come in and get me to play 'God Send You Back to Me' in seven keys."[26] But combined with other skills, an infectious sense of rhythm could turn any piano-room session into an artistic encounter. Gershwin's personality and talent enabled him to master such basics quickly.[27]

Moreover, by "writing a tune now and then," as Ira offhandedly put it, the young Gershwin began a lifetime involvement in the enterprise of creating music to entertain listeners. He quickly learned that the industry's creative standards stood well within his capabilities, and he kept writing songs after the Remick firm— which drew a clear distinction between its staff of pluggers and songwriters—rejected his first attempts.[28]

Not long after he joined Remick's, he realized that there was something special about the work of Irving Berlin and Jerome Kern.[29] The "martial rhythms" of Berlin's 1911 hit "Alexander's Ragtime Band" got into his blood during those years, or perhaps even before. As for Kern, in the spring of 1915 Gershwin had an epiphany at an aunt's wedding, after hearing the orchestra play two songs from *The Girl from Utah*—"You're Here and I'm Here" and "They'll Never Believe Me." Kern, said Gershwin, "was the first composer who made me conscious that most popular music was of inferior quality and that musical-comedy music was made of better material." As a result of this experience, "I paid him the tribute of frank imitation and many things I wrote at this period sounded as though Kern had written them himself."[30]

Reports from those who knew Gershwin during his early years on Tin Pan Alley describe an idealistic young man who was learning that the art of music could be an encompassing, exacting master. One such report comes from Harry Ruby, later a leading Broadway and Hollywood songwriter, but then a song plugger with the publisher Harry Von Tilzer. It seems that in a competitive push, some time before Gershwin's nineteenth birthday, various publishers sent their pluggers to Atlantic City. One evening, with the day's work finished, they gathered at a restaurant on the Boardwalk to talk shop. Ruby was struck by George's eagerness, "his intense enthusiasm for his work, his passionate interest in every phase of the popular-music business." When Gershwin "spoke of the artistic mission of popular music, we thought he was going highfalutin'. The height of artistic achievement to us was a 'pop' song that sold lots of copies, and we just didn't understand what he was talking about." His view of music "was a completely different musical world from ours, and we did not completely understand it at the time, though we all reacted to it instinctively. I am also sure we were all jealous of him too."[31]

More evidence comes from Irving Caesar, who became a successful lyricist on Tin Pan Alley and Broadway and met Gershwin after he began dropping in at the Remick office. "There was nothing modest about him . . . he had self-confidence, and rightly so. . . . When George sat down at the piano, there was no one who could move you as George would. . . . It was very difficult to put your finger on his talent because it lapsed over into the serious field."[32] George liked having him around, Caesar said, because "he wanted his tunes wedded to words," adding that in those days composers on Tin Pan Alley outnumbered lyricists by far.[33] "I used to make up titles just to have him sit down and go up and down the keys and see what he could strike from them, and he could work wonders. I wrote very fast and he wrote very fast. . . . George wrote with chords. His chordation was so interesting, so modern and remarkable, and out of his chordation came the melodies."[34] Between 1916 and 1923, the two men collaborated often on songs, from an unpublished antimilitary number, "When Armies Disband" (1916), to "Swanee" (1919), their first big hit.[35]

But of all the acquaintances Gershwin made at the Remick firm, none had more direct professional significance than Fred Astaire, who wrote about their early meetings in his autobiography. Astaire and his sister Adele, natives of Omaha, Nebraska, formed a song-and-dance act as child performers in vaudeville, traveling the circuit with their mother as early as the century's first decade. Later, when in New York, Fred made the rounds of music publishers looking for material, and met George at Remick's in 1915. The two teenagers hit it off, even to the point of comparing some keyboard tricks. "He was amused by my piano playing and often made me play for him," Astaire recalled. "I had a sort of knocked-out slap left hand technique and the beat pleased him. He'd often stop me and say, 'Wait a minute, Freddie, do that one again.'" But beyond their mutual involvement with show business and the piano, the two shared a dream. "I told George how my sister and I longed to get into musical comedy. He in turn wanted to write one. He said, 'Wouldn't it be great if I could write a musical show and you could be in it?'"[36] The two youngsters could not have known how "great" great could be.

In November 1915, Gershwin began a new exercise for skills he had been developing at Remick's. Crossing the river to East Orange, New Jersey, he appeared at the studio of the Standard Music Roll Company to make the first of many rolls for player piano in which he was involved over the next decade. By 1926, some 140 Gershwin performances had been issued in this form, starting at $5 per roll, or $35 for six.[37] By all indications, Gershwin thought of piano rolls as work for hire, in which not much of his artistic self was invested. Yet the rolls identify music that he came to know as a young professional, as well as examples of his own music as he chose to present it in those years. Like the older harmonium or reed organ, the player piano was air-powered, relying on the vacuum created when foot-operated pedals pushed air out of the player mechanism. The agent determining the sound was a roll of paper with perforations that corresponded to musical notation, scrolled through the mechanism at a steady speed. When passed over a "tracker bar"—a metal device with a hole for each note on the keyboard—the perforations were "read" in a way that, through air pressure, responded to every hole with a musical sound of the specified pitch and duration.[38] Gershwin's job was to sketch out at the keyboard musical "maps" of performances, indicating when keys and pedal were depressed and released, which company personnel then turned into finished products.

Gershwin's early piano rolls preserve in mechanical facsimile a gifted player's rendering of Tin Pan Alley performance style in the mid-1910s. By the time George was born in 1898, the African American–influenced style called ragtime was already making an impact on the music of Tin Pan Alley, and Broadway as well. Its signal traits included a rock-solid beat, foursquare phrase structure, and pervasive syncopation. When played on a piano, as notated in sheet music, rhythmic and harmonic duties are assigned to the left hand, with the right hand playing the melody, usually syncopated and often supported by harmonic filling-in. Many of Gershwin's piano rolls from 1915–17 reflect ragtime's influence, as can be heard in five numbers reconstructed and issued on CD in the early 1990s: "Kangaroo Hop," by Melville Morris (January 1916); "Chinese Blues," by Oscar Gardner and Fred Moore (May 1916); "Arrah Go On I'm Gonna Go Back to Oregon," by Bert Grant, Sam Lewis, and Joe Young (May 1916); "Pastime Rag No. 3," by Artie Matthews (June 1916); and "Rialto Ripples," by Gershwin and Will Donaldson (September 1916).[39] To a modern ear, the general impression left by this sound is of a sophisticated, lighthearted music with a measured, sometimes herky-jerky way of moving that reflects the mechanized quality of the instrument.

But there was a true advantage to the medium: the illusion of a midregister third hand. Between the boom-chuck pattern in the bass and the busy treble melody, the Gershwin piano roll adds a conjunct line in quarter notes that knits the registers together in a three-part texture. Once his songs began to appear in print, some of them also boasted midregister melodies (playable by a two-handed pianist) that filled out the texture and harmony in a similar way. Here was a young song-seller from Remick's who was already playing with countermelody.

IN HIS TIME and ours, Gershwin has often been portrayed in group settings, usually as the center of attention. Recognized before age thirty as a famous musician and man about town, he was seen by cultural commentators as part of a postwar "Jazz Age" generation that was putting its stamp on the American scene. And he showed every sign of savoring his niche in the social circles of New York City. A standard trope of Gershwin biography holds that when he attended a gathering and the room included a piano, he would surely be asked to play it. There is no record of him resisting any such invitation.

Less often noted is that his custom of blending sociability with artistry seems to date back to his Tin Pan Alley years—the fruit of a social connection that began in the workplace. While still in his middle teens, George befriended Russian-born Herman Paley, a senior colleague at Remick's, who had studied composition with Edward MacDowell at Columbia University, harmony and theory with Edward Kilenyi, and piano with Charles Hambitzer.[40] Paley invited George into a group of friends and relatives who gathered regularly at his apartment on 112th Street and Seventh Avenue, not far from the Gershwin residence at 108 West 111th Street. The group welcomed the young man warmly, offering him friendship and the attention of a sophisticated, intellectually lively company. In 1917, George introduced Ira to Herman's younger brother Lou, an English teacher who in 1918–19 would write lyrics for a number of George's songs. It was through Lou's girlfriend—and wife from 1920 on—Emily Strunsky, a student of German literature at Hunter College, that Ira would meet *his* future wife, Emily's sister Leonore.

George blossomed in the Paley circle. "The atmosphere was different than at George's parents'," explained Emily Paley, "and he liked that—he breathed in the surroundings and atmosphere," which she described as "very easy, full of young people and music and literature." It may have been in that environment that his custom of entertaining at the piano first took root, maybe as early as 1915. Some years later, after Lou and Emily married and moved downtown to Greenwich Village, they held regular Saturday night gatherings that often included George and sessions at the keyboard. "This was during Prohibition and we served tea, cookies and lichee nuts and played Twenty Questions." Among the purported regulars over the years were songwriters (Milton Ager, Phil Charig, Vernon Duke, Vincent Youmans), playwrights (S. N. Behrman, Morrie Ryskind), lyricists (Irving Caesar, Buddy DeSylva, Howard Dietz), comedians (Groucho and Harpo Marx, Fanny Brice, said to be "a good friend" of the Strunsky sisters), Oscar Levant, and classical pianist and critic Samuel Chotzinoff.[41] Behrman "knew from the first Saturday night at the Paleys' that I was having the best time I'd ever had in my life." Drawn together by age, common interests, and heritage—most were Jewish—the regulars and their friends made up a group akin to a salon.

At informal gatherings like these, George showed an uncanny gift for sitting down at the piano and pouring out a continuous flow of music whose appeal seems to have been nearly universal. Mabel Pleshette, a niece of the Paley brothers and herself a pianist whom George had recruited as a Hambitzer student, was a frequent witness to such moments. She recognized that spontaneity was what made George's playing special. "When he sat down at the piano, he not only played what was written—he was improvising all the time. George could make the piano laugh, he could make it sad, he could make it do anything. And when he made it laugh he chuckled and you would chuckle with him. You just had to laugh. I never saw such piano playing, such an approach."[42] The Paleys' belief in his genius, and the unconditional friendship they offered, surely fed Gershwin's confidence, and would benefit all three as long as he lived.

REMICK'S REJECTED his first songwriting efforts, but Gershwin was not an easy person to discourage. When he and a collaborator, Murray Roth, finished a song they judged worthy, called "When You Want 'Em, You Can't Get 'Em (When You Got 'Em, You Don't Want 'Em)" they found another publisher—Harry Von Tilzer, one of the trade's most influential figures in that decade—who offered a royalty of half a cent per copy.[43] While Roth received an advance of $15, Gershwin "waivered an advance, wanting my royalties—glamorous word!—in a lump sum. After some time I went to Von Tilzer and asked him for a little cash on the song. He handed me five dollars. And I never got a cent more from him."[44]

Gershwin's collaboration with Roth not only produced his first published song, but led to his first professional contact with the theater. He and Roth wrote another number, "The Runaway Girl," that they imagined in the kind of show favored at the Winter Garden Theater: the flagship venue for the brothers Lee and J. J. Shubert, two of Broadway's leading producers. "After several tries," Gershwin said,

> we got to play the piece for Mr. [Ernest R.] Simmons, of the Shubert office. He was evidently impressed, because he, in turn, had me play it for Sigmund Romberg, who was then the chief composer for the Shuberts. Romberg had me meet him at the Hotel Majestic, where he lived, and suggested that we collaborate on some tunes for the next Winter Garden attraction. I was naturally delighted and excited with this chance to break into Broadway musical society.

For several weeks I brought ideas to Romberg, and when the show opened I was represented with one little two-four number called Making of a Girl.[45]

Born in Hungary and trained in Vienna, Sigmund Romberg had arrived in New York in 1909, where he gained attention as a pianist and orchestra leader in upscale restaurants. By 1914, he was writing scores for the three or four revues the Shuberts produced each year. Romberg wrote much of the music for these shows, but he also farmed some out to others, and kept his ear open for numbers that could be interpolated. "Making of a Girl," with words by another Shubert stalwart, librettist and lyricist Harold Atteridge, was published by G. Schirmer and interpolated into *The Passing Show of 1916*, which ran at the Winter Garden from June 22 to October 21.[46] This song evidently netted Gershwin about $7 in royalties.

By March 1917, the songs he was playing for Remick customers having begun to "offend" him, Gershwin decided he wanted to write "production music" for Broadway shows, following the lead of Jerome Kern. One reason he found himself at odds with Tin Pan Alley's anti-intellectual tone lay in his sustained stake in the classics, though no longer as a student of Hambitzer. He had experienced the scramble, excitement, and present-mindedness of Tin Pan Alley, but also the grace of a Kern stage song; the formality and timelessness of the concert hall; the infinite colors of a symphony orchestra's sound palette; the technical or aesthetic challenges of a piano work by Liszt or Debussy; and the process of study that enables musicians to strengthen their skills. Even as he sold songs to customers, his awareness of music's scope continued to grow.

Around this time, Gershwin began lessons in harmony with Hungarian-born Edward Kilenyi, on Hambitzer's recommendation. "The boy is not only talented," he told Kilenyi, "but is uncommonly serious in his search for knowledge of music. The modesty with which he comes to his piano lessons and the reverence with

which he approaches instruction impress me, in fact, touch me."
Kilenyi brought strong credentials to the task. Having begun music
studies in his native Hungary, he continued them briefly in Rome
with Pietro Mascagni and then at the Cologne Conservatory. Emi-
grating to the United States, he settled in New York and attended
Columbia University, where he was taught by Daniel Gregory
Mason.[47] He then worked as a private teacher, scholar, violinist, and
an orchestra conductor in local theaters. His publications, all from
the 1910s, attest to academic seriousness, including a pair of articles on Arnold Schoenberg's *Harmonielehre* and another on modern
Hungarian music.[48] From the mid-1920s on, Kilenyi was based in
Hollywood, where he worked in the film industry as a composer
and conductor.

While the start of Gershwin's lessons cannot be dated exactly,
Ira's diary toward the end of March 1917 notes that "Geo. gave up
job at Remicks, Sat. 3/17/17 in order to be able to study unhin-
dered by time taken at Remicks."[49] The notion of a song plugger
resigning to pursue further musical study would have baffled the
denizens of Tin Pan Alley. As Kilenyi got to know his new student, he too was struck by Gershwin's love for learning, reflected
in the young man's enthusiasm when he grasped an idea that had
previously eluded him. When Gershwin wondered whether exercises with figured bass were really necessary, for example, Kilenyi
explained that they develop skills in writing music in much the
same way that scales prepare one to perform it. And neither of these
foundational practices are "meant for public hearing." Once Gershwin understood that, Kilenyi recalled, he completed the figured
bass exercises "carefully and patiently": evidence, he decided, that
the talented young student Hambitzer had sent him was revealing
himself as a wise student too.[50]

3

A SONGWRITER EMERGES (1917–18)

SHORTLY AFTER LEAVING the Remick firm in 1917, Gershwin suffered a professional humiliation that haunted him for years. At the Fox City Theater on 14th Street, he got a $25-a-week job filling in at the piano for the orchestra—at the so-called supper show—while its members broke for their evening meal. This was apparently Gershwin's first stint as an accompanist in vaudeville, and he took the assignment seriously:

> Happy to be working, I attended the Monday morning rehearsal and sat beside the pianist, watching the acts go through their routine. I also sat through the first show (matinée) eagerly watching the music and the acts to make sure I'd make good. The supper show began. I got along fine with three or four acts. I was especially good with a turn that used Remick songs.

The next act, however, featured a juvenile male lead, a soprano, six chorus girls, and a "terrible" comedian. Its music, cobbled together from varied sources, was in manuscript form.

You know the cryptic condition of those theatrical manuscript scores. I started to play the opening chorus and seemed to be getting along fine, when suddenly I found myself playing one thing and the chorus girls singing another. Evidently I had missed a couple of cues. After all it was my first day at the new job, and aside from nervousness I was as yet unfamiliar with all the musical terms you find in such music.

Gershwin soldiered on, managing to struggle through the first number. But the worst was yet to come: later on, he again seemed to be playing something the soprano was definitely not singing. "I tried to find the right cue, but failed and gave up trying to play." Another cast member saw an opportunity. "The comic—I can still see his leering face—came down to the footlights and began to jeer at me. 'Who told you you were a piano player?' he bawled out. 'You ought to be driving a truck.' The audience howled, the chorus girls giggled and I died a thousand deaths." After the show ended, Gershwin informed the box office cashier, "I was the piano player here this afternoon and I'm quitting," and left without picking up his pay ($3.13) for the evening's work. A certain measure of vindication came thirteen years later, when the Fox movie studio in Hollywood offered the Gershwin brothers $100,000 to write music for a movie called *Delicious*. When it came time to sign the contract, George "changed the figure to read $100,003.13 and when eyebrows were raised I told the story. 'You see I've got an eighth of a week's salary coming,' . . . and the revised figure was solemnly agreed to."[1]

Although the incident left no perceptible mark on the course of Gershwin's career, it surely left an emotional one: a rare example of professional failure and ridicule. Gershwin was not in the habit of discussing scars on his memory, and it is hard to think of another incident in his life whose telling centers so fully on his emotions. To fail on musical grounds wounded him unforgettably.

Not sure where to turn, he sought help from a friend—Will Vodery, a "colored arranger" who had worked on several editions of the *Ziegfeld Follies*. Vodery seems to have opened the right door, for before the summer's end Gershwin was accompanying rehearsals for a new Ziegfeld revue: *Miss 1917*, coproduced by Charles Dillingham, another eminent figure in musical comedy. The show boasted a score by Victor Herbert and Jerome Kern, with lyrics by P. G. Wodehouse—three luminaries of the trade he hoped to practice himself.[2] In Vodery, Gershwin had chosen a unique figure as a confidant: a well-schooled African American musician with connections to the upper echelon of the (white) Broadway theater. Although a composer, Vodery was respected most for his arranging, orchestrating, conducting, and coaching.[3] It is not clear when the two men met, but Vodery's new prominence in Gershwin's life points to the matter of how the young composer was drawn to jazz music.

More than most of his white colleagues, he was drawn to music made by black Americans, and he had some contact with three other illustrious black musicians before 1920. All were pianists older than he, and all wrote scores for musicals: James Hubert ("Eubie") Blake, Charles Luckeyeth ("Luckey") Roberts, and James P. Johnson. They were by profession "ticklers": pianists who held forth at saloons, cabarets, dance halls, ballrooms, sporting houses, and joints of other kinds that comprised the bedrock of New York's black entertainment and show business. Their job was to attract customers and keep the music going through the long hours that such places maintained, especially before Prohibition. A successful tickler had to have the right blend of personality and musicianship, and as Johnson saw it, another virtuoso pianist, Willie ("the Lion") Smith, whom Gershwin came to know a few years later, struck that balance better than anyone else. These four were but a handful of the dozens of skilled pianists who moved through the city's black entertainment venues during the 1910s. Few, however, matched their combination of talent, creativity, and access to the means of preserving and disseminating music.

One undocumented report has Roberts and Johnson telling Blake as early as 1916 about a recent arrival in the city, a "very talented ofay [white] piano player at Remick's . . . good enough to learn some of those terribly difficult tricks that only a few of us could master."[4] If Gershwin was indeed able to execute dazzling piano tricks akin to those of his black compatriots, it is hard to imagine where, other than directly from them, he could have learned them. Roberts claimed Gershwin as his student more than once, but never while the composer was still alive.[5]

In these years, Gershwin was living in upper Manhattan with his parents and siblings, first on West 111th Street and then farther north, on West 144th Street. The city's black neighborhoods were then close to midtown Manhattan, from the West 20s to the 50s and 60s. Only after the country's entry into World War I in April 1917 did the black population move north to the point that Harlem became home to the city's African American culture. After Prohibition began in 1920, nightlife there came to include high-toned "black and tan" clubs, where the entertainers were black and the clientele white. Indications are that Gershwin, who was making a mark on Broadway by then, visited such places to listen to the music.

Bert Williams, the gifted actor, singer, and comedian, is another African American stalwart who noticed Gershwin's talent before he was famous. In 1914, the year George began to work for Remick's, the firm published "The Darktown Poker Club," a song with music attributed to Vodery and Williams. It's possible that Gershwin took a hand in making the piano arrangement, or in plugging the number after it was published, and he likely accompanied Williams at least once. During *Miss 1917*'s Broadway run, cast members gave concerts on Sunday nights in the Century Theater, which otherwise would have been dark. Gershwin, as rehearsal pianist, served as an accompanist for these Sunday Evening Concerts. The first one, which took place on November 11, boasted a stellar cast that included Williams along with Eddie Cantor, George White, Ann Pennington, and Fanny Brice.[6]

Gershwin met James P. Johnson in 1920, when both were making piano rolls for the Aeolian Corporation. Each excelled in his own milieu—Johnson in the world of the black cabaret, Gershwin in that of Broadway songwriting—while cultivating talents beyond their specialty. Gershwin by this time had written the score for a successful Broadway musical comedy and had logged at least a year of study with Edward Kilenyi. Johnson was beginning to dream of "conducting symphony orchestras in large concert halls, playing his works based on native Afro-American musical themes."[7] Within the decade, each man would make a major statement along the lines Johnson was imagining.

FEW MUSICALS of the World War I era left a mark on history. The so-called Princess Theatre shows, beginning in 1915—among them *Very Good Eddie, Leave It to Jane, Oh, Boy,* and *Oh, Lady, Lady*—are considered landmarks for their modest scale (the theater held only 299 seats), the catchiness of their songs (music by Kern, lyrics by Wodehouse), and the deft coordination between music and books (many of the latter by Guy Bolton).[8] The popular *Ziegfeld Follies,* a series of annual variety shows—"revues"—are remembered for their emphasis on glamour and spectacle, and on muscle as a box-office draw.[9] Operetta, a distinctive European genre, flourished as well: Sigmund Romberg's *Maytime* (1918) enjoyed a Broadway run of 492 performances.

Miss 1917, another Bolton–Wodehouse collaboration, proved to be a flop, opening on November 5 and closing after only seventy-two performances. Given the credentials of the creative team and the talented cast, the outcome must have surprised many.[10] Aside from Herbert and Kern, producers Dillingham and Ziegfeld both had records of success; the director, Ned Wayburn, was famous for his work with theatrical dancers; Viennese-born Joseph Urban, Ziegfeld's favorite designer, did the sets. Moreover, the cast boasted such headliners as veteran comedian Lew Fields, female impersonator Bert Savoy, dancers Irene Castle and Ann Pennington, singer Vivienne Segal, and dancer and future producer George White. But the writers and the producers were seldom on the same page. As Bolton and Wodehouse claimed fancifully long after the fiasco, the principals—"three classical dancers, three acrobatic dancers, a Spanish dancer, forty-eight buck and wing dancers, two trained cows, a performing seal and Harry Kelly and his dog Lizzy"— posed obstacles for Bolton, whose job it was to invent a plot for them all. Meanwhile, Wodehouse labored to write words for a number that featured no fewer than a dozen dancing girls, each with a different costume:

> On arriving at the theater in the morning, the sensitive poet [Wodehouse] was handed a pile of costume designs. One would represent a butterfly, another the Woolworth Building, a third a fish, a fourth a bird, a fifth a fruit salad and the others the Spirit of American Womanhood, Education Enlightening the Backward South, Venus Rising from the Sea, and so on, and Mr. Ziegfeld says will you please have it ready for tomorrow's rehearsal, as the girls are threatening to walk out because they have nothing to do. . . . When the bard had finished twelve refrains, cunningly introducing the butterfly, the Woolworth Building, the Growing Unrest in the Balkans and Venus Rising from the Sea, the management decided that they didn't want to use those costumes after all, and handed him another batch.[11]

The show turned out to be so large and lavish that, even with full houses, it stood to lose almost $4,000 a week. Luckily for Bolton and Wodehouse, "The boy who played the piano at rehearsals was a young fellow named George Gershwin."[12]

The young rehearsal pianist found Broadway's environment far superior to that of Tin Pan Alley: more musically ambitious and more varied in the challenges it offered. Capital flowed more freely too: he earned $35 a week. Drawing on his own improvisatory bent, Gershwin took to his new position with grace and panache. "After I got to know the music of the show," he told a *Billboard* interviewer in 1920, "I started to put little frills and furbelows into it. This made a hit with the chorus girls and Ned Wayburn found they worked better when I played for them." The rehearsals for *Miss 1917* alerted Jerome Kern to Gershwin's talent, especially his unusual gift for improvisations and arrangements. Hearing Gershwin launch into an impromptu session at the piano after one rehearsal, Kern was so impressed that he arrived the next day with his wife so that she might hear "this young man who is surely going to go places."[13] Director Wayburn kept Gershwin on the payroll after the show opened, which made him available for a succession of Sunday Night Concerts.

Between the end of those concerts in December and the early days of February, Gershwin held no steady employment, but he still managed to find work as a pianist. When a nightspot called the Coconut Grove, on the roof of the Century Theatre, staged an all-Spanish revue featuring the music of Quinito Valverde, a composer for the popular stage in Spain, Gershwin played piano in the orchestra for about half the thirty-three performances. In a November Sunday Evening Concert at the Century, he accompanied Vivienne Segal, a star from the *Miss 1917* cast. A classically trained singer, Segal was by 1917 a poised trouper with the clout to choose two songs by her even younger accompanist. After singing "There's More to the Kiss Than the X-X-X" and "You-oo Just You," both with lyrics by Irving Caesar, she brought Gershwin out for a bow. Segal's performance may have marked the first time a New

York theater audience had heard a Gershwin song with the composer at the piano.

Caesar and Gershwin liked what they had accomplished in "You-oo Just You" enough to seek out a publisher. Remick's was their first choice, and they set their sights on making $25 each from the song. At the audition, Fred Belcher of the professional department listened while Caesar sang and George played. Caesar recalled:

> When we stopped Belcher asked, "Well, boys, how about $250?" We were speechless. We both thought he was telling us we would have to pay him that to see the song in print. Belcher took our silence to mean we were not satisfied. He said, "OK, I'll give you $500." We were so excited that we ran all the way uptown to where George lived. We told his parents the great news. Many years have passed since that day but I've never forgotten what Rose said: "Morris," she told her husband. "Send a lawyer to help them. These boys will be eaten up."[14]

"You-oo Just You," Gershwin's third published song, and his first with a text accompanied by blackface images, projects a mood of tenderness. The song's grounding in minstrel-show conventions is unmistakable, from the colloquial diction ("Evenin' comes and my work is thru-oo") to the southern plantation frame. It was thus with Caesar that Gershwin, an advance of $250 in his pocket, got his first taste of the moneyed side of the business he hoped to break into. By late 1917, he was collaborating with three other lyricists: Ira's friend Ben Praskins, Lou Paley, and Ira himself. And by February, Ira, then working at the B. Altman department store, had written around ten songs with George.

Miss 1917, in addition to offering Gershwin the opportunity to work with leading lights of musical comedy, provided an even more important breakthrough. Harry Askins, the show's manager, having observed the competence and flair with which Gershwin carried out his duties, recommended him to Max Dreyfus, the head of T. B. Harms music publishers.[15] Born in Germany and trained in the European classical tradition, Dreyfus had worked as a song plugger on Tin Pan Alley and was a composer as well. But his genius lay in his ability to spot talent, to choose and market songs, and to run a business. Dreyfus focused his attention on the theater, recruiting leading theatrical composers to the Harms staff, with a salary plus a royalty on songs the firm published. One of the first to receive this treatment was Jerome Kern, followed over the years by an impressive roster of relatively young men at or near the beginning of their careers, among them Rudolf Friml, Sigmund Romberg, Vincent Youmans, Richard Rodgers, and Cole Porter. By the late 1920s, under Dreyfus's direction, approximately 90 percent of Broadway stage music being published, from show songs in sheet music format to vocal scores, was issued by Harms.[16]

Dreyfus was careful about whom he recruited, and he could be a forbidding figure, as Rodgers discovered in 1922. When a neophyte producer named Lawrence Schwab was looking for someone to score a new musical and Rodgers offered him a batch of songs, Schwab proposed that his "good friend" Max Dreyfus judge his efforts; but Dreyfus found "nothing of value" in the tunes. Three years later, however, when two shows with scores by Rodgers and his lyricist Lorenz Hart were running simultaneously on Broadway, Rodgers received "the royal summons" to visit Dreyfus again. This time, when he walked into the office, "Dreyfus rose solemnly from his desk, greeted me warmly and immediately got down to business. Not only did he want to publish the songs from *Dearest Enemy*, he also wanted Larry and me to sign with his company as staff writers," an offer he did not refuse. At the end of the meeting, "he put his arm around my shoulder, and I suddenly realized what it meant to be one of Max Dreyfus' boys. 'There's one thing I want you to promise me,' he said. 'If you ever need money, I don't want you to go to anyone else but me. From now on, don't ever forget that I'm your friend.'" And Rodgers never did.[17]

In Gershwin's case, the anointing took place early in 1918, when Harry Askins offered to introduce him. Dreyfus

> asked me to play for him and I played four of my songs. When I finished, he said, "Come and see me next Monday." At this I laughed inwardly, for it had a familiar sound by that time. . . . I didn't consider Mr. Dreyfus's invitation to call again very seriously. You can judge of my surprise then, when on going to see him the next Monday, he said, "Gershwin, I believe you've got the stuff in you. I'm willing to back my judgment by putting you on the salary list."[18]

Ira's diary for February 10 added more details: "Geo. has been placed on the staff of T. B. Harms Co. . . . He gets $35 a week for this connection, then $50 advance & 3c royalty, on each song of his they accept. This entails no other efforts on his part than the composing, they not requiring any of his leisure for 'plugging' nor for piano-playing. Some snap." From this moment in his twentieth year until the end of his life, Gershwin was never without a ready source of income.[19]

The new Harms staff composer continued to work as a pianist in vaudeville. On February 25, Gershwin and singer Louise Dresser opened at New York's Riverside Theatre, the first engagement in a four-city tour. Their program included five songs—apparently interwoven with personal anecdotes by the singer, who had a personal connection to at least four. Foremost among them was "My Gal Sal" (1905), with words and music by Indiana native Paul Dresser, brother of novelist Theodore Dreiser, said to have been written specifically for Louise. Born Louise Kerlin in Evansville, Indiana, she apparently took the name Dresser because of her link to the song. (Paul adopted his stage name early in his professional acting career.) Active on Broadway as well as in vaudeville, she was twice Gershwin's age when the pair toured together. She remembered him affectionately in later years, citing the conscientious way he went about his business. Gershwin made no secret of his aversion to "My Gal Sal." Nevertheless, "there were times when I almost forgot the lyrics, listening to Georgie trying to make that trite melody sound like a beautiful bit of music. . . . It wouldn't have surprised me one bit had he banged the piano one day and walked off the stage. I wouldn't have blamed him too much—but that lovable, shy lad wouldn't have done such a thing."[20]

After New York, Dresser and Gershwin, traveling the Keith vaudeville circuit, played in Boston, Baltimore, and Washington, D.C., where President Woodrow Wilson attended one of their performances. Back in New York after the tour ended, Gershwin took more jobs as a rehearsal accompanist. The first was with *Rock-a-Bye Baby*, produced by Arch and Edgar Selwyn, which opened on May 22. Kern had written the score, and during the show's preparation the two composers renewed their acquaintance. In a mentoring frame of mind, Kern advised the young man to consult first with him if he was ever offered a major creative assignment.[21] Gershwin moved on to a stint as rehearsal pianist for the *Ziegfeld Follies of 1918*, which opened on June 18.[22] His salary was presumably $35 a week, as it had been for *Miss 1917*. Because Max Dreyfus was also paying him the same weekly stipend, the year 1918 must have seen an improvement in the Gershwin family finances.

Between these two Broadway openings, Gershwin sat down one day at the piano with his brother. Ira, yet to be published as a lyricist, had nurtured a hunch that an "American folk song" could make an apt starting point for a musical comedy number. So he wrote an essaylike refrain and worked it over in several drafts. On May 26 he showed his latest draft to George, who responded with a syncopated burst. Ira's opening states the song's premise in an eight-word declaration: "The real American folk song / is a rag." To which George responded, as if via a musical hypodermic: "The

REAL a-MER-i-can FOLK-song is a RAG!!": an explosion both musical and syntactical, demanding an assertive delivery. At a time when such rhythmic disruptiveness was rare on Broadway, a listener may have found the refrain's melody extreme. Yet Gershwin devised two ways to mitigate the beginning's strangeness. One was to follow the explosion with smoother, more restrained melodic motion. The other was to familiarize the syncopation by referring often to it during the rest of his refrain. As Ira explained years later, once he had found a title for a new song, which was sure to appear early in the refrain, he would often "skip to the last line and . . . try to work the title in again with a twist, if possible."²³ And that's what happened here.

Eventually, the brothers' compositional process usually began with George at the piano trolling for music to underline a particular narrative or mood. With "Folk Song," however, their first known collaboration, the opposite was true—up to a point. The words came first, in the form of the lyric Ira wrote for the refrain. George wrote four bars of music to set the first two lines, and then extended them by a mix of melodic repetition and balance to fill out the refrain's form—routinely thirty-two bars long. An adjusted lyric followed, with lines changed and reshaped to fit the new music. The verse came later, presumably invented by George with maximum contrast in mind, and Ira supplying words to fit. George, to be sure, was the composer of what we call the Gershwin songs, and Ira the lyricist of most of them. Yet during the making of these numbers, the line between those roles was not always clear.

SOMETIME during the summer of 1918, vaudeville and Broadway headliner Nora Bayes heard Gershwin play, apparently during a visit to the Harms office, and hired him as onstage pianist for a show soon to go into rehearsal: *Look Who's Here*, renamed *Ladies First* by the time it opened on Broadway. The producer was Harry

Frazee, theater owner and president of the Boston Red Sox (who infamously sold his team's star outfielder-pitcher, George Herman ["Babe"] Ruth, to the New York Yankees). Frazee's creative staff for *Ladies First* was experienced, if old-fashioned. The librettist and lyricist, Harry B. Smith, was perhaps the musical stage's most prolific author, credited with writing the words for over 6,000 songs.[24] Composer A. Baldwin Sloane had scored almost fifty Broadway shows, though his efforts had yet to produce a single hit song.[25] Director Frank Smithson had filled that role for at least three dozen musicals, dating back to the 1890s. The show's chief asset, though, was Bayes, a star high enough in the entertainment firmament to have been ranked among the "Golden Dozen" of vaudeville's single-woman acts.[26] Some numbers were sung with piano accompaniment alone, provided by Gershwin. In addition, he persuaded the show's brain trust to accept three of his own songs: "Some Wonderful Sort of Someone" (lyrics by Schuyler Greene), "Something About Love" (lyrics by Lou Paley), and "The Real American Folk Song."

A long tryout period began early in September, split between Trenton, New Jersey (Ira took the train from New York to experience the thrill of hearing his own words sung from a professional stage), Pittsburgh, Cleveland, Baltimore, Atlantic City, Wilmington, Delaware, and Washington, D.C. One of those tryout performances in Pittsburgh was attended by an eleven-year-old budding musician named Oscar Levant, who years later vividly recalled George Gershwin's accompaniment:

> I don't remember a thing about the performance . . . except that in the second act the show stopped, Bayes came down front and did what amounted to her vaudeville turn. For those who don't remember, her singing was marked by a highly personal treatment of the music and words, in which the piano accompaniments played a very subtle and important part requiring almost constant improvisation. After one chorus of the first song my attention left Bayes and

remained fixed on the playing of the pianist. I had never heard such fresh, brisk, unstudied, completely free and inventive playing—all within a consistent frame that set off her singing perfectly.[27]

Ladies First gave Gershwin his first chance to travel with a professional theatrical company, and he responded with the awareness of a budding professional. After less than two weeks of on-the-road experience, he started to take stock of his situation. "Baldwin Sloane [the composer] told me he received $400 from Trenton & Pittsburg," he wrote Max Abrahamson, a cousin of Lou Paley, from Cleveland on September 12. "Zowie!!! Why didn't I write the show & let him interpolate? He gets 3 percent of the gross." Gershwin was also learning the importance of billing, pleased that Nora Bayes was having his name listed on the program as the composer of interpolated songs. He confided to his friend that he felt ready to write the score of an entire show. "In spite of what J[erome] K[ern] told me, I am getting confidence & encouragement from this show, & B. Sloane (and his royalties). I'm going to make an attempt when I reach N.Y."[28] And he was realizing the importance of the placement of a song in a show, how it was staged, and how it was performed. "It's not merely having good songs that make hits," he wrote to Caesar.[29] "The Real American Folk Song" was being sung *and* staged ineffectively, he felt. In fact, the song disappeared into obscurity until 1958.

Gershwin was thinking hard about the end of his professional apprenticeship. Two-plus years on Tin Pan Alley had made him knowledgeable about current popular song performance and composition. Vaudeville performances, together with experience as a theatergoer, had taught him much about how songs were put over to an audience. Stints as rehearsal pianist for three Broadway shows had instructed him in the school of musical comedy and its stage-craft. And now, watching *Ladies First* take shape, Gershwin had a standard against which he could measure the quality of his own work and his creative potential.

Ladies First opened at New York's Broadhurst Theatre on October 24, 1918. It moved on December 30 to the Nora Bayes Theater, where it ran until March 15, 1919, closing after 164 performances. By the time the show reached New York, however, Gershwin had left the cast, reportedly after an argument with its star. Bayes asked him to change the ending of one of his songs, something she pointed out that both Berlin and Kern had been willing to do for her.[30] The young man refused; he quit the show and returned home. Still, notwithstanding this outcome, his *Ladies First* adventure had given him sufficient experience and confidence, at age twenty, to take a crack at the vocation of Broadway composer.

FROM SYRACUSE
TO NEW YORK (1918–19)

A REVUE FROM THE END OF 1918, *Half-Past Eight*, was the first
show to which Gershwin made a major artistic contribution. Max
Dreyfus was the midwife of the new venture. As Gershwin recalled,

> a chap named Perkins came to Mr. Dreyfus and said he wanted
> to produce a revue. Mr. Dreyfus, who always encouraged young
> producers, offered to help Mr. Perkins by giving him an advance
> and offering to pay for the orchestrations for the show. He also
> told Perkins about a young composer he had signed up recently and
> wondered if it would not be a good opportunity for him. To make a
> long story short, I got the job.[1]

Gershwin and Edward B. Perkins, two theatrical greenhorns linked
by Dreyfus, proved to be collaborators whose careers were headed
in opposite directions: the first setting out on a historic journey
through American music, the second launching a theatrical venture
that would be his first and his last. But the energetic young would-
be magnate had a literary bent; he and Gershwin got together and
wrote five songs for the show.[2] And in rounding up a cast, Perkins

managed to hire Joe Cook, a comedian who had worked in vaudeville since his latter teens, when he advertised himself as a "Master
of All Trades, Introducing in a 15-minute act, juggling, unicycling,
magic, hand balancing, ragtime piano and violin playing, dancing,
globe rolling, wirewalking, talking and cartooning. Something
original in each line."[3] Cook would achieve his first Broadway triumph in a 1923 revue called *Earl Carroll's Vanities*, but had yet to
break into that echelon of the trade.

From start to finish, *Half-Past Eight* was a low-budget operation.
"With Joe Cook and myself, and about $1500 in cash, Mr. Perkins
set up shop and went into rehearsal," Gershwin recalled. "The rest
of the cast consisted of a Clef Club Orchestra of about twenty-five
colored musicians, a bicycle act, [singer] Sibyl Vane and one or two
other people, with no chorus." It is easy to link the Clef Club—a
seminal New York institution whose members were known for their
ability to read music, while also playing in the "hot" improvised
mode of the newest styles—with Gershwin's own musical tastes.[4]

When *Half-Past Eight* opened in Syracuse on December 9, the
curtain went up at 8:45, hardly a promising start given the title.
More ominously, the first act ended at 9:30. Since the advent of the
Ziegfeld Follies of 1907, the Broadway revue had come to be known
as a generous evening of singing, dancing, comedy, drama, spectacle, and topical commentary. If there was a standard knock against
revues, it was that by delivering too much, they tended to leave their
audiences wishing for a little less. *Half-Past Eight* had no such problem. By Gershwin's tally, the intermission lasted half an hour, and
"the final curtain rang down at a quarter to eleven—not much of a
show from the standpoint of running time, you must admit."

By Wednesday afternoon, when the first matinee was scheduled,
some cast members, having already lost faith in Perkins's venture,
were worried about not getting paid at the end of the week. At the
very moment they were confronting Perkins about this matter, an
unshaven Gershwin happened to walk by.

Perkins rushed up to me and said, "You've got to go on—one of the acts just refused to appear and we m[us]t have something to go on while we make a change of scene." I said, "What will I do?" He said, "Play some of your hits." I should have loved to have played my hits—except that I didn't have any. But out I walked on the stage to a very small and innocent audience, and made up a medley right on the spot of some of my tunes. The audience must have thought it very queer. I finished my bit and walked off—without a hand!

Half-Past Eight failed to last out its week in Syracuse. Gershwin was paid just enough to cover his train fare back to New York. He returned home with some rueful memories but also with his confidence undiminished, and carrying the five songs that he and Perkins had fashioned for the ill-fated show.

By 1918, Russian-born Irving Berlin had become an American citizen, and his reputation was secure as a highly successful master of popular songwriting. He was also a resourceful businessman who, early in his career, had become a partner in the firm of Waterson, Berlin, and Snyder, which published his songs. After the war's end, he dissolved his connection with that firm and shortly thereafter offered Max Dreyfus a song called "That Revolutionary Rag."[5] When Dreyfus expressed interest, Berlin told him he needed someone to write the song down for him—his usual modus operandi. Having grown up without formal training, he played the piano by ear and hired a musical secretary to write down his songs as he played, sang, and talked his way through them. By the composer's recollection,

Dreyfus said, "I have a kid here who can do it." The kid, George Gershwin, took the song down, made a lead sheet, and played it for Berlin, improvising to such a degree that Berlin hardly recognized his own song. Yet he could see that the young man was a brilliant pianist. Gershwin had heard that Berlin was looking for a musical secretary and he said he would like the job. Berlin replied that his plans were unsettled and asked him what he really wanted to do. Gershwin said he wanted to write songs. Berlin listened to some Gershwin songs (later to become part of the show *La-La-Lucille*) and said, "What the hell do you want to work for anybody else for? Work for yourself!"[6]

In "That Revolutionary Rag," which Gershwin arranged for Berlin in 1919, the "rag" is not a piece of music but a scrap of calico that Russian revolutionaries dyed red and used as their flag. The subject allowed Berlin, who wrote both lyrics and music, to uncork a fancy rhyme or two—"a tricky, slicky Bolsheviki"—and to tout socialism's threat to the Old Order: "All the royalties / Across the seas / Shake in their BVDs." Known as a craftsman of near-fanatical diligence, Berlin admitted that "That Revolutionary Rag" was "of no importance, except that George took it down for me."[7]

Two songs Gershwin wrote with Irving Caesar in early 1919 suggest the range of professional opportunity now open to the young songwriter. The first, "I Was So Young (You Were So Beautiful)," was unveiled in New York on February 6, as an interpolated song in the Shubert organization's *Good Morning, Judge*, a British import. The sheet music cover to this song, a boy-girl duet for which Caesar and Alfred Bryan joined forces on the lyrics, offers head-shot photos of the performers, Charles and Mollie King—in real life brother and sister, cast in the show as a romantic pair. Gershwin must have known Charles King, a cast member of *Miss 1917*; possibly the request for a song just before the finale of Act I, a key moment in the show, went from the producers, through King, to Harms, who then sent it Gershwin's way. Performance royalties on interpolated songs like this one were most likely negotiated outside the standard agreement between the producer and the show's composer; but even if royalties were small, songwriters and their publishers welcomed Broadway performance as an effective way to boost sheet music sales.

"I Was So Young" radiates a refined elegance belying the composer's youth.[8] The refrain, featuring a rhythmically flexible melody, changes mood from near-dreamy stasis to impassioned memory, all in the space of eight bars. It is hard to think of a later Gershwin song that travels a wider expressive range within so brief a time. "I Was So Young" has been called Gershwin's first hit.[9] Far more enduring, however, was another song from late summer or early fall 1919—"Swanee," written with Caesar alone. From a commercial perspective, it was the most successful song Gershwin ever wrote. True hits being rare in the trade, stories about their genesis tend to survive, and "Swanee" is no exception. Caesar remembered it as an instant success:

> There was a big hit at the time called "Hindustan," a one-step ("Hindustan, where I came to rest my tired caravan"). So I said to George "Why don't we write an American one-step?". . . The idea came quickly, and we wrote "Swanee" very fast up at the Gershwin house on 144th Street. George's father heard it right in the middle of his card game and he went out of the room and came back with a comb wrapped up in tissue paper and he played it and it sounded like a kazoo, and that was the first arrangement the song had. It was sheer inspiration. We wrote "Swanee" in about fifteen minutes or less.[10]

In popular songs of the 1800s and early 1900s, major mode was a norm that was rarely breached.[11] Only something unusual—a distant, imaginary place like "Hindustan," for example—could provide cause for minor-mode music. Like its model, "Swanee" starts with a minor-mode verse, here to sketch a southern ambience that is complex enough to carry a shadow of trouble. The protagonist, a born-and-bred southerner, is aching to return ("I've been away from you a long time / I never thought I'd miss you so"). But as the verse ends, the clouds lift and the refrain dwells on pure positives: devotion to the region and a readiness to forsake the North forever. The sometimes syncopated and always tuneful music is anchored in an exuberantly singable vocal line supported by sunny harmony, yet the tonal shadow dogging the verse hovers over the refrain, too. Not until Gershwin follows the refrain with an entirely new strain—a tuneful trio—do the tonal clouds disappear entirely. In the world of Stephen Foster, "Swanee" suggests a quiet river and a fondly remembered past. Yet Gershwin and Caesar's song, infused with the energy of the one-step, makes room for struggle as well as nostalgia. And the original sheet music, with precise markings of expression and articulation in the piano part, provides a record of Gershwin imagining "Swanee" fully, from large gestures to small details.

In at least one case, the Gershwin-Harms approach to notation did its bit to widen American popular music's global reach. Around 1920, Vladimir Dukelsky, later Vernon Duke, a Russian composer and pianist soon to be a colleague and friend of Gershwin's, bought a copy of "Swanee" in Constantinople, where he lived and worked as a restaurant pianist after fleeing Russia. He remembered:

> Patrons began to request "Hindustan," "Tell Me" and "Till We Meet Again." I promptly purchased all three, also Irving Berlin's earlier successes and a thing mysteriously entitled "Swanee" by a man improbably styled Geo. Gershwin. The Berlins were good in their way, but the Gershwin sent me into ecstasies. The bold sweep of the tune, its rhythmic freshness and, especially, its syncopated gait, hit me hard and I became an "early-jazz" fiend.[12]

Less than half a year after leaving the *Ladies First* company, Gershwin was busy composing the score of a show that actually did succeed on Broadway: *La-La-Lucille!* The key player in this venture was Alex A. Aarons, whose father Alfred also worked in the theater business as a manager, as well as a sometime producer and composer. It is not known when Gershwin and the younger Aarons first crossed paths, but Ira recalled meeting him a few weeks after George did, and soon thereafter witnessing a remarkable scene in Aarons's apartment:

> Alex was fond . . . of at least twenty of George's tunes which had not yet been written up lyrically, so he had no means of calling for any one of them by numeral or title. But he could request what he wanted to hear this way: Whisking his hand across George's shoulder, he would say: "Play me the one that goes like *that*." Or: "Play the tune that smells like an onion." Or: "*You* know, the one that reminds me of the Staten Island ferry." And so on. Though this mutual musical understanding didn't develop between them at their first meeting, it didn't take too long.[13]

Although a project linking a first-time producer and a first-time composer, both in their twenties, *La-La-Lucille!* did not go unnoticed. Even during the planning phase, it captured enough attention to spark a case of generational rivalry. Jerome Kern had had an earlier disagreement with Aarons that had left them on the outs with each other. When Kern, known for having a short emotional fuse, was told of Gershwin's decision to work with Aarons, he responded angrily, and the two composers were estranged for several years—until 1922, when Kern unexpectedly announced his retirement from the stage and, in what seemed a magnanimous gesture, declared that he would transfer his unfulfilled show contracts to Gershwin. Soon, however, he decided not to retire after all, and went on to complete the scores himself. Unlike Berlin, it appears that Kern sometimes found Gershwin's talent and youth threatening. In one of his more ungracious moments, Kern observed of George, "And here's Gershwin, who showed a lot of promise." Ira, who witnessed this rudeness, always wished he had replied, "And here's Kern, who promised a lot of shows."[14]

In *La-La-Lucille!* Gershwin collaborated for the first time with George Garde ("Buddy") DeSylva, with whom he would write more songs than with any other lyricist save Ira. A New York City native, DeSylva grew up in California, where he gravitated toward the world of entertainment as a performer and songwriter. His break came in the summer of 1917, while playing ukulele at Barron Long's Watts Tavern, a spot in Los Angeles frequented by Al Jolson and members of the touring cast of his current show, *Robinson Crusoe, Jr.* A song of DeSylva's called "'N' Everything" impressed Jolson, and before long DeSylva was back in New York writing songs that Jolson made into hits onstage, including 1921's "April Showers" and "California, Here I Come."[15] He also contributed song interpolations for the *Ziegfeld Follies of 1918, Sally* (1920), *Bombo* (1922), and many other Broadway shows. DeSylva became friends with both Gershwin brothers, and shared credit with Ira on a few lyrics. From 1925 until 1930, he belonged to the highly successful songwriting team of DeSylva, Brown, and Henderson, then moved back to Hollywood, where he became a producer at the Fox studios and later executive producer at Paramount. In 1942, he joined with Glenn Wallics and songwriter Johnny Mercer to found Capitol Records.

In the story of *La-La-Lucille!*, John and Lucille Smith are newly married and shadowed by economic difficulties. John's aunt promises to leave him $2 million if he will immediately divorce Lucille; their attorney advises the devoted couple to find a professional co-respondent, divorce, inherit the money, and then remarry. A duet sung by Lucille and her father toward the end of Act I, "Tee-Oodle-Um-Bum-Bo," drew the most critical praise of all the show's numbers. "After it had been sung," wrote one reviewer, "the laughter came much more easily, and unfunny things seemed funny."[16] The words caught critics' attention, but the sheet music points more toward the artistry of the composer, Gershwin, whose command of rhythm, harmony, and musical form lends the song an endearing air of relaxed ease. And its title tune, a fragment just six syllables long, shows up with modest enrichments works as diverse as the *Rhapsody in Blue*, "The Man I Love," and *An American in Paris*.

Act II takes place in the bridal suite of New York's Hotel Philadelphia, site of a comic eruption of shenanigans on the marital front. Here the bridal suite's occupants, newlyweds Britton and Peggy Hughes, sing a duet, "(Oo, How) I Love to Be Loved by You," with lyrics by Lou Paley. Early in the Broadway run, this number was replaced by "Nobody but You," words by DeSylva and Arthur Jackson, which proved a song to reckon with. Key motives prefigure passages of such well-known songs as "But Not for Me" and "Love Walked In," written later with Ira. Sharing the key of E-flat with "Nobody but You," these two songs also have the same formal structure—a pair of sixteen-bar sections that begin with the same melodic material. Direct testimony about Gershwin's creative process is rare, but links like these offer suggestions of how it worked.

Act III starts with an interpolation: a number by Gershwin and Caesar that Vivienne Segal sang in a *Miss 1917* Sunday Evening Concert that year as "There's More to the Kiss Than the X-X-X," revised to "There's More to the Kiss Than the Sound" for *Lucille*. It's sung by Peggy, who is writing a note to her husband to clear up a misunderstanding. At the show's end, after two reprisals of "Tee-Oodle-Um-Bum-Bo," John and Lucille decide to abandon their divorce scheme ("The Ten Commandments of Love"). And the wealthy aunt, who had merely been testing their commitment all along, now stands ready to come through with her bequest.

La-La-Lucille!, marketed as "A New, Up-to-the-Minute Musical Comedy of Class and Distinction," spent more than a month on the road. [17] Starting in Atlantic City on April 21, the company moved south to Washington, then north to Boston, and finally to

New York and Broadway.[18] The tryout process seems to have been eventful, for by the time the company reached Boston, five original cast members, including the leading man and lady, had been replaced. The theater season in New York began on June 1 and ran through May 31; in an age before air conditioning, many theaters closed during the summer months. Few new shows opened then either, and "summer shows" that did were considered the lightest of entertainments. Debuting on May 26, *La-La-Lucille!* was the last musical of the 1918–19 season.

Shows of that day could offer as many as fifteen or twenty musical numbers, and those with the most commercial potential were issued in sheet music form. Once in print, they were marketed for home use, for vaudeville performers, in arrangements for dance orchestras, or as recordings or broadcasts—all part of a process that enabled some show songs to lead separate lives. In contrast, after a production's run ended, so did the sets and costumes; the dancing, singing, and playing; the romancing and the jokes. A musical comedy was ephemeral; even among shows that were counted hits, few were later revived.[19] Once a show had delivered an evening's entertainment for a while, it was discarded to make room for the next one. A musical's songs and reviews offer the best hope of restoring a spark of immediacy to shows long shuttered, and the Gershwin family scrapbook that includes this show contains no fewer than twenty-one different reviews of *Lucille*: five from the tryout run and another sixteen from New York.

Although none of those critics hailed the music as a major force in the show, their take on Gershwin's effort was generally positive. Heywood Broun found the music "spirited rather than melodious," while also commenting on musical comedy's way of "always reminding you of something else, which is usually the one you saw the night before last, which in turn dates back to the one of the Saturday before that." The show proved a modest success at the box office.[20] It had debuted, however, at a time when the Actors' Equity

Association, the legitimate theater's performers' union, was contemplating a labor stoppage against producers, protesting low wages, lack of rehearsal pay, and lack of protection against being stranded when shows closed outside New York. On August 7, Broadway performers launched a successful strike. *La-La-Lucille!* was shut down on August 19, and within two days most of the other theaters were dark. After the strike was settled, the show reopened on September 8 and closed for good on October 11, having totaled 104 Broadway performances.[21]

The summer and fall of 1919 saw Gershwin, now with a successful Broadway show under his belt, active on several fronts. As a Harms staff composer, he continued to write individual songs, and some found their way into stage productions. As a pianist with several years' experience in piano-roll making, he persisted on that front too, now recording more rolls of his own songs, including numbers from *Lucille*.[22] As a twenty-one-year-old musician without formal schooling, he was taking lessons in harmony from Edward Kilenyi. Finally, as an up-and-coming presence in the New York cultural scene, he was meeting influential people and reaffirming friendships with performers he already knew. The writer and cultural entrepreneur Carl Van Vechten remembered meeting Gershwin during the latter half of 1919, at a party where he played "Swanee."[23] Gershwin's social habit of entertaining at the keyboard had by then reached beyond the Paley circle. And Fred Astaire, rehearsing with his sister Adele some time before the October opening of their new show, recalled his surprise one day when, expecting their regular rehearsal pianist in the orchestra pit, he heard a familiar voice call out: "Hey Freddie—you didn't expect to find me here, did you?" Gershwin, filling in that day for a piano-playing colleague, brought them up to date about his first successful musical comedy.[24]

Gershwin also engaged in another common songwriter's practice. In an effort to promote "Swanee," Gershwin, serving as rehearsal pianist for an after-hours show being prepared for the roof of the New Amsterdam Theatre, played and sang his number to entertain "the girls who happened to be up there." Director Ned Wayburn heard the song and wanted to use it in his *Demitasse Revue*, soon to open the new Capitol Theatre, a movie palace. Located at Broadway and West 51st Street, the Capitol seated more than 5,000, and its opening on October 24 was marked by a four-hour show that included a screening of *His Majesty, the American* starring Douglas Fairbanks as well as Wayburn's revue.[25] Caesar found the Capitol opening to be a tremendous send-off for the new song:

> Sixty girls danced to "Swanee;" they had electric lights in their shoes. Arthur Pryor's band played it. Seventy in the band. Everyone on stage sang it. Everyone applauded. There were thousands of copies [published by Harms] in the lobby—but they didn't sell. . . . George and I would hang around the lobby every night and hide behind posts. Occasionally we would try to start the ball rolling and we bought our own music. We thought maybe a line would queue up if we started buying copies, but nothing happened.[26]

A favorable turn took place in December. *Sinbad*, a Shubert production starring Al Jolson, was playing a two-week engagement at a theater in Brooklyn. Jolson gave a party in Manhattan after one performance, and Buddy DeSylva brought along Gershwin, who found his way to the piano and played his repertory of songs, including "Swanee." Jolson, intrigued by the new song, decided to interpolate "Swanee" into *Sinbad* and to include it in his next recording session. His record, made on January 8, 1920, proved a big hit. Thus, in the course of a few months, Gershwin and Caesar's American one-step evolved into a Capitol Theatre production number, a Jolson song, and finally a Jolson *signature* song plugged avidly by Harms. "Swanee" became a marketplace juggernaut. On May 1, *Billboard* noted that it was being "played nightly by the leading dance and hotel orchestras, and numerous leaders have described it as the most novel one-step in the repertoire." And by the middle of May, it was the best-selling song in the country.[27] As of 1931, sales of the sheet music had soared above a million copies and recordings of the song had topped two million.[28]

Sales figures for show tickets, sheet music, and recordings acted as surrogates for the independent critical judgments central to the classical arts, where agreed-upon aesthetic standards separated the best artistic work—the work most likely to endure—from the rest. But in 1924, critic Gilbert Seldes's book *The Seven Lively Arts* broke fresh ground when it singled out certain popular works for critical consideration, as exemplars of popular expression on a high level. Seldes salutes "Swanee" as an artistic achievement, and Gershwin's emotional authenticity as central to that success. "He has taken the simple emotion of longing and let it surge through his music," making real "what a hundred before him had falsified." In a world now prepared to entertain the notion of a "popular classic," Gershwin was already identified as a likely source for such a thing.[29]

ON DECEMBER 26, 1919, *Variety* published a longish article by "Ibee," a regular reviewer, that surveyed theatrical events of the past twelve months.[30] That year was "the most spectacular one in the history of the legitimate stage in America," he asserted, following as it did the end of the war in Europe and the ebbing of the deadly pandemic of influenza. To the latter two international developments Ibee added a third that was peculiar to America: Prohibition, set to become the official law of the land on January 17, 1920. An idealistic effort that still ranks as the country's most ambitious attempt at moral and social reform, Prohibition blocked the legal manufacture and sale of alcoholic beverages. Ibee's article took the line that although New York's restaurants and nightclubs would sustain losses, theaters would gain: "The faster the lovers of the white lights and cabarets discover that an evening at the theatre, even with the lofted admissions, is a lot cheaper than a session in a night cafe, with its poisoned liquor, the greater will be the demand for theatres."

Several months after the law took effect, however, an article in the *New York Times*, "Making a Joke of Prohibition in New York City," offered nothing but bad news for dry advocates. [31] The law may have affected the distribution of alcoholic beverages, but it had hardly curtailed their consumption. Alcohol could be purchased out of taxicabs, in saloons as "soda," in hotel lobbies as "coffee" or "tea," and in restaurants, where waiters proved adept at disguising it. In some nightclubs, customers were allowed to bring flasks of their own liquor. New York had had a vigorous nightlife before, but now that nightlife took on more prominence, thanks in part to a new aura of risk and the overthrow of narrow-minded restrictions. This new sensibility was expressed through jazz (the music and the attitude), uninhibited dancing, occasional racial mixing, and changing gender relations that revolved around the figure of the "flapper," a young woman whose behavior or dress was characterized by daring, freedom, and boldness. The number and variety of nightspots in the city multiplied greatly.

Variety's Ibee was wrong in predicting that the theater would reap an economic bonanza from Prohibition. Yet "the noble experiment" certainly left its mark on Broadway, and on musical comedy in particular. The *Ziegfeld Follies of 1919* included comic songs and sketches on the subject, such as Bert Williams's "Everybody Wants the Key to My Cellar." More and more shows focused on the comings and goings of sophisticated young characters—their habits, values, language, dress, and musical tastes—who lived in a society where violations of the law were commonplace and widely accepted. In *Oh, Kay!*, a 1926 Gershwin show, a Long Island bootlegging operation is conducted by an impoverished English aristocrat. A new generation's normalizing of illegal drinking added excitement to their lives and the cultural activities they supported. As one of the era's leading figures, Gershwin would come to be identified with the fast-paced, youth-oriented culture that Prohibition helped bring to the fore.

SOCIETY, THE MUSIC BUSINESS, AND *GEORGE WHITE'S SCANDALS* (1920)

By the time World War I ended in 1918, the balance of power between the Old World and the New was shifting westward. Yet even before the war, a cultural shift was under way in America that did much to transform the entertainment business in which Gershwin would flourish. During the nineteenth century, gender roles had emanated from the Victorian code, which centered men's lives outside the home and women's activities within it. Women were widely thought to be predisposed toward virtue and restraint, while men's virtue was believed to depend on the moral compass of honorable women. Husbands who sought sexual gratification outside of marriage were not necessarily stigmatized; when stigmatization took place, it was more likely to target "loose" women who did the same. By the early years of the twentieth century, however, that code was eroding.

The 1910s found public entertainment gravitating away from moral affirmation and toward self-expression and personal enjoyment. One result of this development—or was it a cause?—was the so-called dance craze that hit New York around 1911, and soon thereafter swept across the country. Old World dances such as the waltz, schottische, and polka gave way to the fox trot, turkey trot, Charleston, and black bottom, to name a few. Freed from the obligation to execute prescribed steps, dancers now responded to the music through movement that could be restrained or vigorous according to individual choice. The dances were linked to indigenous musical styles: ragtime, which had begun to win popularity even before 1900, and jazz, which reached the public consciousness during the 1910s.[1]

As jazz music and new dancing styles entered the arena of public entertainment, Gershwin became a musician. We have so far seen George, an improviser from the start, show an affinity for new music, whether as a piano pupil whose teacher encouraged his ragging of the classics, or as would-be secretary to Irving Berlin. His expressive approach to the piano, grounded in dance rhythms, had much in common with the way people were learning the new dances. And the world of popular songs and musical comedy on which his sights were set was deeply influenced by the trend toward self-expression and the evolution of gender roles.

The state of the American music business, however, had an economic downside for composers. Piracy was so widespread that no individual author could battle it effectively: hotels, restaurants, cabarets, dance halls, and the like offered music to their customers without compensating the composers or lyricists, which as profit-making ventures they were legally required to do. As a result, early in 1914 the American Society of Composers, Authors, and Publishers (ASCAP) was founded partly in order to give musical creators a way to protect their intellectual property rights. The procedure was simple. Rather than retaining the performing rights conferred by copyright, members assigned them to ASCAP, which in turn collected performance royalties from users of the music, and then paid the creators according to a scheme worked out by the society and its members. The organization faced tough resistance in its early years and was often ignored by proprietors and performers. In 1917, however, the U.S. Supreme Court, overturning a lower court decision, declared that the playing and singing of copyrighted music in restaurants, dance halls, and cabarets—unlike in school glee clubs and church choirs, for example—failed the not-for-profit test, and therefore users must pay royalties when they performed copyrighted works. Thus, by the time Gershwin was hired by Harms in 1918, performance royalties were being channeled directly to composers. Gershwin himself joined ASCAP in 1920.[2]

Another key economic issue for musicians concerned sound recording—the "mechanical reproduction" of music. The first federal copyright law, passed in 1790, had centered chiefly on books. Because much of that era's music was published in book form— sacred tunebooks, anthologies of secular and instrumental pieces— copyright protection of musical works was widespread from the nation's founding. As sheet music sales boomed in the 1800s, most music was copyrighted. But by the twentieth century two questions were growing more urgent every year: Could a musical composition still be considered a copy of a work after it was transferred to a record or piano roll? And if so, did copies constitute a royalty-producing property for the individual who had copyrighted the original? In 1905, when Congress began formal consideration of new copyright practices, income from mechanical reproductions of music was being channeled chiefly to record manufacturers. Most performers were also paid, as Gershwin would be for his work on piano rolls; but the creators made nothing. John Philip Sousa and Victor Herbert were among those who took part in the 1905 hearings, in vigorous support of composers' rights. The 1909 revision was the first law to recognize that a piano roll *could* enjoy copyright protection, though phonograph recordings did not.

The contract drawn up on February 21, 1918, between Gershwin and Harms reveals the relationship between composer and publisher. Its first provision made Gershwin an employee of Harms for one year, hired "to conceive, create, compose, and write music for musical compositions and Numbers." Harms held the exclusive right to "publish, copyright, re-copyright, print, reprint, copy," and sell Gershwin's music and all its lyrics, as well as everything he wrote for "production purposes" (meaning the musical comedy stage). Gershwin assigned copyright to the company in advance for all music created during the contract period, promising not to write music for another publisher, to collaborate on any music to be published by another company, or to allow his name to be linked to any music whose rights Harms did not own. Gershwin, however, still owned the "performing, stage and producing rights" of his "musical plays, musical comedies and operas." For each copy of a published piece sold, Harms paid the composer a royalty of three cents. And the firm agreed to pay him a salary of $35 per week, plus an additional $15, the latter drawn against future royalties. After the contract expired, Harms still held the rights to publish and sell all music written under its provisions, and the composer still collected royalties on the same basis, provided he had complied with the terms of the contract.[3]

By EARLY 1920, Gershwin was gaining public attention. On March 13, *Billboard* magazine published the first of many interviews that Gershwin would give throughout his life.[4] "What do you think the chances are of getting a better type of music in musical comedy?" the interviewer asked. Gershwin thought them excellent, as long as something basic was understood: "A composer doesn't have to be afraid of writing a musicianly score nowadays, if he will only provide melody." Later in the interview, Gershwin steered the conversation back to what seemed to be his idée fixe. "Remember," he insisted, "melody is dominant. Without melody everything will go for nothing. There is a lot of money waiting for the fellow who can write original scores, but once again and always—melody must be dominant." Which prompted the reporter to comment: "From which [I] gathered the impression that, in writing musical comedy, melody is the thing"—and that became the article's headline.

In Gershwin's musical universe, melody was indeed "the thing" around which all else revolved. As a young concertgoer, he devised a technique of "intensive listening" that led him to the piano to revisit and absorb the motifs of the music he had just heard. As a piano student known to "rag the classics," he honed skills as an embellisher of melody that would serve him well as a rehearsal accompanist and an entertaining party guest. As a Tin Pan Alley song plugger, he worked as a salesman with growing expertise on what made a melody sing. As a maker of piano rolls, he engaged with popular songs as an arranger—a framer of melodies that were already or soon to be published. Gershwin's standard improvisational ploy at the piano was to present his own songs with constantly changing embellishments on a still-recognizable melody. When writing classically oriented music, he adorned it with songlike structures and tuneful passagework. For Gershwin, determined to reach listeners, his consciousness of their positive response to what they were hearing helped to direct his creative process.

At the time of his interview, Gershwin was studying harmony with Edward Kilenyi and finding ways to bring technical elements from his classical training into popular songs. "I have used whole tone harmonies a la Debussy in one piece and it was very effective," Gershwin told his interlocutor, adding: "One can write dissonances where a few years ago they would have been torn out of the score instanter." Finally, the interviewer asked whether the young composer had "tried to develop any particular style," to which Gershwin responded,

> Well, I don't know that I have tried, but I think it has naturally come about. I believe that every composer has someone in mind that he makes his idol. Mine was Jerome Kern. I didn't try to imitate him, but I admired his music so much that my early efforts were sub-

consciously similar to his work. Then I think that after one works along he injects more of himself into his work and his style really becomes a remodeling of himself in terms of his idol. . . . I believe that if you are natural you will be different and you will develop your style by just being yourself.

Five years would pass before the first of several articles that Gershwin would write appeared in print. But the *Billboard* interview is a landmark: early proof that as the master of his training, Gershwin relished intellectual engagement with the craft he was practicing. Finding himself in a musical world split into separate spheres, popular and classical, he maintained a staunch commitment to both.

By the time the interview was published in March, Gershwin had missed a chance for another stage credit when *Dere Mable*, a musical comedy based on a book of war letters, flunked an out-of-town tryout in early February. Gershwin and Irving Caesar had interpolated one published song into this theatrical endeavor, a novelty number called "We're Pals," sung by a World War I soldier to his dog. In April, another Gershwin-Caesar interpolation appeared in *Ed Wynn's Carnival*, a successful Broadway show starring the eponymous comedian, author, composer, lyricist, and, in this case, producer. Previously cut from *La-La-Lucille!*, "(Oo, How) I Love to Be Loved by You" featured words by Lou Paley; but it was again replaced by another song soon after the tryout performances.

Interpolations, though, were only a backdrop to a more important event in Gershwin's professional life: being hired as composer for *George White's Scandals*, an annual series of Broadway revues. White, born George Weitz on New York's East Side, was a dancer by trade who, after starting out in vaudeville, worked his way up the Broadway ladder. He filled a secondary role in the *Ziegfeld Follies of 1911*, then won the status of principal player in the 1915 edition, where he danced with Ann Pennington, already a star. The Broadway revue, well established as a genre by the mid-1910s, flourished during the postwar years, and White, along with George Rock and Will Morrissey, all vaudeville performers turned producers, were movers and shakers in its success.

White's first *Scandals*, for which he cowrote the book and lyrics with Arthur Jackson, staged the dances, and performed as a dancer himself, opened on June 2, 1919, a week after *La-La-Lucille!* The composer was Richard Whiting, a midwesterner who had earned his start in the Detroit office of Remick's professional department. Cast members included Ann Pennington, whom White had lured away from the *Ziegfeld Follies*, his chief competitor in the revue business. The story goes that Ziegfeld, stung by his former employee's decision to mount a revue of his own and steal one of his stars, offered White a handsome salary if he and Pennington rejoined the cast of the *Follies*. White supposedly countered with an even more lavish offer to Ziegfeld if he and his wife, actress Billie Burke, left the *Follies* to appear in his *Scandals*.

The first edition of the *Scandals* paid off handsomely for White, thanks to a successful post-Broadway tour. Nevertheless, when he began to consider the 1920 sequel, he decided to change composers, replacing Richard Whiting with Gershwin, an arrangement finalized in late February 1920 when White notified the young composer that he had worked out a deal with Harms to pay Gershwin a weekly stipend of $75, starting with rehearsals and continuing through the duration of the Broadway run.[5] White continued as the cowriter—now with Andy Rice instead of Arthur Jackson, who became the show's lyricist—and took over as stage director, too. He appeared onstage only near the show's end, when he delighted the crowd with his imitations of other famous dance stars. After a brief tryout run in Washington, D.C., *George White's Scandals of 1920* opened in New York on June 7 and ran for 134 performances, matching the Broadway success of its predecessor.

Critical consensus judged the new *Scandals* better than the first, and in some quarters the music was cited as a factor. "The score which George Gershwin has composed for the show," according to the *New York Clipper*, "is not only superior to last year's music in the same show, but it is easily one of the most tuneful now being played on Broadway. Its colorful melodies and piquant jazz strains will not fail of popular rendition in the various cafes and places where orchestras hold forth."[6] The *New York Times*, though leaving the composer nameless, judged the revue "at least twice as good" as the 1919 edition.[7]

One scene in particular, "A Presidential Convention," demonstrated how Gershwin's music supported the timeliness of White's revue. It opened with comedian George Bickel as William Jennings Bryan, three-time Democratic candidate for president and chairman of the convention, welcoming "The Common People," collectively represented by dancing comedian Lester Allen, into the hall. A procession of candidates followed, each rudely dismissed with the help of a down-the-chute contraption of some kind. The convention then turned to a jazz band, the Yerkes Happy Six, for inspiration. With the stage patriotically arrayed in red, white, and blue, Ann Pennington "wafted" onto the scene, and "everybody jazzed it to the curtain," reported Ibee, who reviewed the show for *Variety*.[8] Another song in this scene, "Scandal Walk," introduced a new dance in praise of gossip—celebrating it in a "jazz" idiom that feels up to date. The song made something of a stir in the marketplace, even though its melodic half steps can hardly be called tuneful.

Other songs signal that music in a jazz vein could be ruminative, as well. "On My Mind the Whole Night Long" was Gershwin's first blues song.

We have said "Goodbye."
Too late now to sigh,
Till I feel so blue,
Wearyin' for you, 'cause you are
On my mind the whole night long. . . .

In 1920, the blues as a genre was still in the process of extending its reach beyond southern black communities. A key agent in that process was Alabama-born W. C. Handy, an African American trumpet player, bandleader, composer, arranger, and publisher. As a literate musician who happened upon the local folk practice known as "blues" music, Handy began, early in the 1900s, to write down and arrange melodies from oral tradition as commercial songs, and in the 1910s numbers like "Memphis Blues" (1912) and "St. Louis Blues" (1914) helped to spread the notion of melancholy as a "blue" mood. A very young Gershwin had recorded several rolls reflecting that trend, including "Chinese Blues" by Oscar Gardner and "Honolulu Blues" by James V. Monaco in 1916, and "Hesitation Blues" by Middleton and Smythe in 1917.

Blues numbers came to be marked by a particular set of musical traits: a four-to-the-bar beat, often kicked off by an introduction based on repeated quarter notes; a pitch vocabulary with varying third and seventh scale degrees—"blue notes," sometimes raised, sometimes lowered, sometimes bent; and a phrase structure based on call-and-response, a sung melodic statement followed by an instrumental answer. Sometimes too, blues songs followed a more or less standard twelve-bar harmonic framework: three four-bar phrases, the first centered on a I (tonic) chord, the second split between two bars of IV and a return to I, and the third beginning with a V harmony that resolves to the tonic. The appearance of Kern's "Left All Alone Again Blues" in *The Night Boat*, a musical comedy that opened early in 1920, showed that blues was entering the commercial marketplace and the world of the Broadway stage. "Each time he says 'Good-bye,'" sings the wife of a riverboat captain, "I get those doggone / Left-all-alone-again blues." Blues was gaining acceptance as a way of registering troubles through song, though its rural black roots remained unknown to most.

Although the sheet music for Gershwin's "On My Mind the Whole Night Long" says nothing about blues, nor did the critics, a piano-roll version released in August 1920 labeled it "Blues—Fox Trot." The song does not follow the twelve-bar formal pattern, yet it refers to that pattern while abounding in other blues traits, such as the four-bar intro with repeated quarter notes in the left hand. Gershwin drew upon the richness of this musical idiom to underlie the text's direct, heartfelt sentiment.

At the same time, a song with roots in operetta drew notice for its place in what some critics considered the *Scandals'* outstanding scene. The headline of the *Times* review began "Stunning Chinese Number," referring to the Act II song "Idle Dreams" sung by Lloyd Garrett, Ann Pennington, and a chorus of twenty-two women. Its main verse describes a "China boy" sitting alone beside a stone idol, smoking his pipe. Enchanted by the idol, he calls out to her as if she were a beautiful young woman dancing: "Come my China maid, / I call you from your throne of jade." As the smoker's pipe burns low, the opium-induced image fades. Roused from his reverie, he realizes that the entire scene has taken place in his mind. A piano motive intended to sound Chinese is heard in the introduction, and again as punctuation between phrases of the verse. Based on parallel fifths, it clashes just enough with the underlying harmony to evoke an atmosphere of aural mystery. Gershwin devotes the first two bars of each section of the refrain to a simple melody that, thanks to chromatic voice-leading, is harmonized extravagantly; the effect is one of constantly changing colors.

None of the songs in *George White's Scandals of 1920* have found a place among Gershwin favorites. Yet the three described here— a production-style number, a blues-tinged number, and an exotic fantasy—suggest both the uncommon talent and the practicality of their inventor. The piano accompaniments offer a case in point. Usually made by arrangers, accompaniments were meant for pianists of modest skills; but Gershwin's suggest that he made them himself—or at least had a hand in the process. While still demanding only modest technical skill from the player, their voice-leading—active middle voices between the melody and a decisive line in the bass—gives the pianist a worthy musical role. Buyers of this show's sheet music found themselves in a position to re-create for themselves at least some of the songs' expressive richness.

"ARTHUR FRANCIS" AND EDWARD KILENYI

PURPOSEFUL AND ENERGETIC, by age twenty-one George Gersh-win was a presence in the New York scene. Ira was different: an avid reader from childhood, he was more an observer than a doer, and fond of putting his observations into written form. He gravitated more toward formal education than did George, and to school-sponsored publications that invited him to try on the mantle of humorist and versifier. The brothers both lived at home, but from age fifteen George led his life in the music business, while Ira, after leaving college, worked mostly in family enterprises as he mulled over what kind of writer he might come to be. Even after Ira settled into lyric writing, the brothers' careers remained mostly separate for years—until circumstances persuaded them that their true call-ing was to explore the realm of popular song together. For, whatever their differences in temperament and experience, the Gershwin brothers seem always to have held in common an intuitive and com-patible feel for excellence.[1]

By the summer of 1919, Ira was serving a stint as business man-ager of a circus-style entertainment company. Several months on the road with Col. Lagg's Great Empire Show left him unfulfilled, however, and he returned to New York to continue his existence as "pretty much a floating soul."[2] As Ira floated, George forged ahead, discovering new songwriting opportunities on Broadway and continuing to work with a variety of lyricists.

Early in 1920, another chance for the brothers to collaborate— after 1918's "The Real American Folk Song"—brought forth "Waiting for the Sun to Come Out," their first published song. Producer Edgar MacGregor had put out the word that he was seeking a number for the ingénue of *The Sweetheart Shop*, a show then playing in Chicago and presumably Broadway-bound. George, sensing an opportunity for his brother, enlisted Ira's help and then played their new song for MacGregor. When MacGregor asked about the lyricist, George identified him as a talented but penniless "college boy." MacGregor offered him $250 for the song's performance rights. Later, when the producer continued to delay payment, George advised him that while he could wait for his own share of the money, the college boy was sorely in need of his; this ploy extracted $125 from MacGregor. When Harms found "Waiting for the Sun to Come Out" worthy of publication, Ira, determined not to trade on his younger brother's name, concocted an alias from the names of his other siblings: Arthur Francis. The royalties he received for this song gave him his first taste of the profits that a published lyricist could realize.

"Waiting for the Sun to Come Out" was only the fifth song whose lyrics Ira wrote entirely on his own, and George had composed the music for all five.[3] But this song was a turning point for Ira, and 1920 seems to be when he decided to give lyric writing a serious try. Before the year was out, the brothers wrote two more songs together. Equally significant, if not more so, Ira also began— apparently at his brother's suggestion—to write songs with Vincent Youmans, an up-and-coming composer born just one day after George.[4] In all, Ira wrote lyrics for at least ten songs that year, seven of them for music by Youmans, and all under the name Arthur Francis.

The year was also a busy one for George. His success with *George White's Scandals of 1920* prompted White to hire him for each of the next four *Scandals* editions. In addition to *Broadway Brevities* (which opened at the end of September and for which he composed three songs), Gershwin also contributed to another revue, *Piccadilly to Broadway*, whose Atlantic City tryout started just two days before *Brevities* began its New York run. Produced by E. Ray Goetz, *Piccadilly to Broadway* toured for months, running through several titles, including *Vogues and Vanities* and *Here and There*, but never making it to New York.[5] Yet the lineup of contributors Goetz drew on for this project was extraordinary. A songwriter himself, of both music and lyrics, Goetz joined forces with librettist and lyricist Glen Mac-Donough to supply some of the score. Gershwin wrote three songs, and Ira, as Arthur Francis, may also have contributed three, to music by Youmans; William Daly wrote music and conducted the orchestra; and George W. Meyer, composer of such hits as the 1917 "For Me and My Gal," also contributed music. Ira was in artistically fast company.

In June 1920, Lou Paley married his longtime sweetheart Emily Strunsky, and Gershwin played at the wedding. Soon thereafter the Paleys moved to 18 West Eighth Street, site of their regular Saturday evening open houses. "Ira never missed a Saturday night," Emily recalled, "and George came often. His playing was always a highlight of those evenings." Their house was also a "testing ground" for George's dates: "if one of George's girls didn't like the atmosphere, he gave her up."[6] It would have been difficult for any girl to compete with Emily herself, who, it was generally agreed, was beautiful, gracious, empathetic, and greatly admired by George.

Close friends like the Paleys saw Gershwin as a marvel: charismatic, prodigiously talented, and seemingly always in motion. This view stands behind a note dashed off by Lou in February, inviting George to visit and to bring with him as many friends as he could round up, including Ira, Irving Caesar, and Vincent Youmans.

George,
    I've taken an accurate census of the various theatrical managers, producers, sages, etc. with the following results:

1. Klaw offices	—4 extravaganzas with music to be written by Geo. G.—next Monday—
2. Gest "	—12 pantomimes with incidental music composed by G. Gershwin—next Tues.
3. Shubert "	—1⅓ shows with music—interpolated by Mr. George Gershwin—next Thursday at least
4. Selwyn "	—2,003 Music Review Melodies by Mr. G. Gersh—next Friday—
5. T. B. Harms	17 checks—to be handed to George Gershvin—All next Saturday A.M.

6. Gershwin—familye—26 hours—to be occupied by George (himself) at piano and vicinity for benefit and pleasure of the pop & mom and neighbors—
And
<u>Next Wednesday</u>—At the Paley's
Feb. <u>16</u>, 1921—Bring Caesar—Iz—Vinc.—all & sundry[7]

Gershwin was also involved in one new show at this time. *A Dangerous Maid*, the first and only Gershwin brothers musical comedy for which no libretto is known to survive, began its pre-Broadway tryout at the Apollo Theatre in Atlantic City on March 21. One review found the show highly unconventional, in that "the drama of the plot is sustained," a trait rare in musicals of that day. In fact, the best this critic could say about the music and dancing is that they did not get in the way.[8] Simple arithmetic supports this claim: for a three-act play, George and "Arthur" wrote a score with only eight songs. Director Edgar MacGregor's top priority was to maintain the audience's focus on the story: the spendthrift son of a wealthy family marries a Broadway chorus girl named Elsie, to the chagrin of his family and friends, the latter forming a conspiracy against her, but she proves resourceful and charming enough to win them over.[9]

After Atlantic City, the *Dangerous Maid* company played in Wilmington, Baltimore, Washington, and Pittsburgh.[10] Critical consensus was favorable, with actors playing nonsinging roles receiving the highest praise, affirming the show's emphasis on comedic drama over music and dance. By the time the company reached Pittsburgh, Juliette Day, playing Elsie, had left the cast and was replaced by Vivienne Segal, the star who in 1917 had insisted that her Sunday Night Concert audience recognize Gershwin as someone special. After the final performance on April 16, however, for reasons never spelled out in the press, the show closed and was never seen in the theater again.

By all indications, *A Dangerous Maid* reflected the precepts put forward by Edgar MacGregor in an article published more than a year after its demise. "The musical comedy of the future," he believed, "must have a perfect story, filled with realism, an adequately interpretive score and characters, with unusual ability and talents, if it would prove a success. Art must enter into [its] vivid glamour." Of the show's eight musical numbers, two experienced singers and dancers, Vivienne Segal and Vinton Freedley, sang five. The cast was divided into singing and nonsinging roles, with skilled actors in the latter, and the heroine's role was given to a performer with enough acting ability to play a complex character. Another of MacGregor's ideas was to reduce the size of the chorus to eight and to use it more effectively for dramatic purposes. "Boy Wanted," sung by four female chorus members—Broadway colleagues visiting Elsie—owes its existence to this notion.

The Gershwins' usual practice, once a subject and mood were agreed upon, was for George to compose a melody to which Ira would fit words. However, for a comic song, Ira would occasionally fashion a form and a line or two, or even a stanza, and a gait, and George would come up with music to fit it. "Boy Wanted" seems like a hybrid: a three-syllable cattle call set to George's tune and sung by four female applicants, each with her own wish list. One of Ira's signature traits as a lyricist, evident here, lay in tricky rhymes ("ad**vert**isement / **flirt** is meant") and internal rhyme ("right little **laddie** / I'll make him **glad he** answered"). While the music serves the workmanlike function of carrying the words, the declamation is graceful and airy, with rests in key spots.

In contrast, Ira's lyrics for "Just to Know You Are Mine" are tender. When Elsie sings this number, she is an operetta heroine in the throes of love, untroubled by doubt. George, taking the words seriously, writes a waltz on a grandly expressive scale, and perhaps its vocal demands explain why the operatically trained Vivienne Segal was brought in to play the role of Elsie. The song is written for a singer with a broad range, solid technique, and a secure grasp of operatic expression. Its refrain is filled with rhythmic nuance, and at the end a thunderous climax gives way to an ethereal peroration: a soprano melody floating over the waltz rhythm—"Just to know, just to know, you are mine, mine alone"—as motion and sound melt gradually into a whisper.

"Dancing Shoes," a duet about the joy dancing brings for Elsie and Fred Blakeley, the spendthrift son and her suitor, played by Vinton Freedley, is the score's only jazz-oriented number. Yet Freedley, it turned out, would contribute even more than Segal to the

Gershwin legacy. In 1922, he joined the cast of *For Goodness Sake*, an Astaire show produced by Alex Aarons, with some songs contributed by Gershwin and "Arthur Francis." Two years later, in January 1924, Freedley produced a stage play of his own, entitled *The New Poor*, and shortly thereafter Aarons told the Astaires that he was starting a producing firm in partnership with Freedley. "This was surprising news" to Astaire. "It pleased and amused us a lot that our friend Vinton would now be one of our bosses."[11] Between 1924 and 1933, the firm of Aarons and Freedley would produce no fewer than seven Gershwin musical comedies—including one of the signature shows of the 1920s.

GERSHWIN, though committed to songwriting as a calling, had aspirations that reached beyond that trade. His study with Kilenyi, begun in 1917, continued on and off for roughly five years. In July 1921, Gershwin also furthered his education in a way unprecedented for him: he enrolled in two summer classes at Columbia University, Nineteenth-Century Romanticism in Music and Elementary Orchestration.[12] Kilenyi's instruction followed a textbook, *The Material Used in Musical Composition*, written by Percy Goetschius, a renowned teacher at the Institute of Musical Art in New York, later the Juilliard School of Music. Of his own approach to teaching, Kilenyi commented: "George understood that he was not to learn 'rules' according to which he himself would have to write music, but instead he would be shown what great composers had written, what devices, styles, traditions—later wrongly called rules—they used." He was struck by the zeal with which his student took instruction, and the lad's pleasure in deploying each new harmony to the point of overuse in a new piece. He even recopied exercises after his teacher had corrected them, to produce an elegant-looking manuscript.

Before he began work on *La-La-Lucille!*, Gershwin had sought his teacher's advice on how the score might make use of his lessons, but Kilenyi advised him to "try not to think of anything you learned. Write anything which comes to you spontaneously." Some five months later, a gratified Gershwin reported to Kilenyi that not only had his advice worked, but George had been able to write with less effort.

Among other things, Gershwin's lessons with Kilenyi explored the interconnectedness of harmony and form. They "went through complete classical sonatas and symphonies," where Gershwin learned "to recognize harmonies in their original and complete texts." For lessons on form, Gershwin composed sketches that would later take shape as his piano preludes. But Kilenyi's teaching went beyond the piano. In those days, Kilenyi explained,

> we did not have records and phonographs which could reproduce orchestral instruments with great fidelity. Therefore we went through the discussion of an instrument in our textbooks and looked up characteristic passages from orchestral scores. George wrote out examples and composed some passages himself. Then we engaged a member of a prominent symphony orchestra to play the examples for us. By this time George Gershwin was familiar with the orchestra. He not only attended orchestra rehearsals of his shows but he studied orchestral scores. Subsequently, too, we went over them in his lessons.

As his technical grasp of musical principles and techniques grew, Gershwin seems to have felt more and more at home with their challenges. By Kilenyi's account, in fact, the young composer "often spoke of his desire to quit writing popular music and retire somewhere far away so that he could devote himself to serious music," but Kilenyi found that idea impractical:

> "In a few years," I told him, "you would be forgotten as a Broadway writer. You would face the same difficulty all young Ameri-

cans have to face when trying to have their works performed. You would come nearer your goal if you were to continue your studies and become even a bigger success than you are today. You should attain such fame that conductors in due time would ask you for serious compositions to be performed by them." He saw immediately what I meant.

THIS ADVICE proved prophetic. By 1921, if not before, Gershwin was seeing himself not simply as a composer of musical comedies but as a serious artist contemplating a personal journey across the popular–classical divide. Kilenyi seems to have been an ideal teacher for a young musician who viewed the difference between the two spheres more as a matter of convention and attitude than of artistic quality, and who "had an extraordinary faculty for absorbing everything he observed and applying it to his own music in his own individual ways."[13]

For Gershwin, the *Scandals of 1921*, with Arthur Jackson as lyricist, was that year's top project. The show opened in New York on July 11 and played for ninety-seven performances—a fitting run for a summer show with plans to tour in the fall. The five numbers that survive from this *Scandals* as published songs deserve consideration, although neither the composer nor his work received much notice from critics. The *New York Times*'s terse comment on the score lacked enthusiasm: "not bad, but nothing noteworthy." In a more expansive judgment, Alan Dale of the *New York American* found the music "above the average of the sticky and treacly stuff that adheres to most of our musical shows."[14] If Gershwin's creative contribution seems on the skimpy side, a look at the playbill helps to explain why more new songs were not needed. The star performers—comedian Lou Holtz, Tess Gardella, and Ann Pennington—each appeared with their own signature songs from earlier shows and appearances.

Variety editor and critic Sime Silverman identified "Drifting

Along with the Tide" as the show's intended "plug number" because "it was given two encores in the second act, when everything else had been rushed through." Its status is confirmed by the release, in October 1921, of a piano-roll version by Gershwin, who recorded no other song from the show.[15] The song was introduced in *Scandals* by tenor Lloyd Garrett, with soprano Victoria Herbert, joined onstage by a chorus of female "sailors." In the verse, the male singer and his beloved imagine themselves to be ships on life's vast ocean, carried apart by inexorable tides, and the refrain brings no resolution. But Gershwin's music makes the journey sound like smooth sailing into a mood more wistful than tragic.

"Drifting Along with the Tide" is the only number in the show that carries even a hint of the jazz feel that Gershwin had tapped in both the *Scandals of 1920* and *A Dangerous Maid*. The song is also noteworthy for his command of voice-leading, a staple of classical technique that values the independence of individual musical lines, which manifests in both verse and refrain. Having learned what it meant to realize a figured bass line in the mode of Handel, he fashioned his harmonies in part from an interweaving of contrapuntal lines. The music is grounded in the bass, and a Gershwin bass line's profile tends to be musically robust. Another song, "South Sea Islands," belongs to a scene that critics uniformly enjoyed. It was sung by Charles King, then danced by Ann Pennington, joined by a large female contingent of "South Sea Islanders." The refrain is sung to a melody of impressive breadth—full of sustained notes and virtually rest-free—that attempts to live up to the beauty of a South Sea paradise.

In October 1921, a chance encounter took place in a midtown Manhattan haberdashery that would have a long-term effect on Gershwin's career, though he was not present. Fred Astaire, then costarring with Adele in a musical comedy called *The Love Letter*, wandered into the store, Finchley's, in search of a tie. The clerk knew who Astaire was, and in their conversation he went so far as to advise the twenty-two-year-old dancer that his talents were better suited to intimate musical comedy than revues or operettas. Taken aback, Astaire asked, in effect, what gave him the right to offer such advice. Whereupon the clerk introduced himself as Alex A. Aarons, part owner of Finchley's with plans to enter the musical comedy field full time as a producer.

At that point, the conversation turned to Gershwin, a new composer Aarons said he had signed, and whose music Aarons thought would be a good match for the Astaires. Identifying himself as the producer of *La-La-Lucille!*, Aarons admitted that while that show wasn't much of a hit, "everybody was talking about Gershwin." Astaire, who had been on tour and missed the show, responded that he knew Gershwin pretty well from Remick's. After expressing his belief that *The Love Letter* was in for only a short run, Aarons told Astaire that he would like to sign both brother and sister for his next show.

Before October was out, *The Love Letter* closed as Aarons predicted. Casting about for a new show, the Astaires contacted Aarons and learned that he was eager to feature them in a new musical comedy in which both would have speaking parts. When Astaire learned that Gershwin would not be doing the music—as he was engaged for the *Scandals*—he confessed disappointment. Even so, he and Adele signed on for Aarons's new show, *For Goodness Sake*, which opened on Broadway some weeks into 1922.[16] Thus, more than two years before Aarons and his partner Vinton Freedley brought together the Astaires and George and Ira Gershwin for *Lady, Be Good!*, associations were formed and friendships kindled that would make theatrical history.

SONGWRITER AND COMPOSER (1922)

For Gershwin the songwriter, 1922 began with both a notable number, "Do It Again," and a notable show, *For Goodness Sake*, involving several of his future collaborators. Years later on a radio broadcast during the mid-1930s, he told the story of how the song came to be written. Sometime during the early winter of 1921–22, he happened to be in Max Dreyfus's office when in walked Buddy DeSylva, the lyricist with whom he was to work on the next edition of *George White's Scandals*. "DeSylva said jokingly to me, 'George, let's write a hit!' I matched him by saying, 'O.K.!' I sat down at the piano, and began playing a theme which I was composing on the spot. . . . Buddy listened for a few minutes and then began chanting this title—'Oh, Do It Again!' which he had just fitted to my theme." From that beginning, the two fashioned a thirty-two-bar refrain, and then a verse. No professional assignment was involved.[1]

In this unusual song, a young man and woman who have just met, finding themselves unexpectedly alone, are gripped by mutual attraction. He seizes the initiative by stealing a kiss, triggering a verse that starts with her show of shocked innocence. Then comes the refrain, built around the title line; female desire trumps propriety. "Do It Again" is about a feeling, and that feeling is embodied most of all in the rhythm, starting with the tempo; the sheet music calls for "fox-trot time." The tune conveys a mood at once languid and aroused, as a character tries to hide her surging emotion. That evanescent blend is what DeSylva picked up as Gershwin sat at the piano. The syncopation of the "do it again" motive, and dotted rhythms beneath the sustained notes, hold the song's emotional temperature at a slow boil. The Victorian upbringing of the singer is being challenged by the freedom of the Jazz Age.

Not long after he and DeSylva finished this freestanding song, Gershwin attended a party at the home of one of Manhattan's leading hosts, Jules Glaenzer. Among the guests was actress and singer Irene Bordoni, the wife of producer Ray Goetz, with whom Gershwin had worked on *Piccadilly to Broadway* and other revues. When Gershwin played "Do It Again" for the company, Bordoni, "with a true Gallic flourish, rushed across the room and cried, 'I mus' have that song! It's for me!'" Bordoni, fully aware of the new number's theatrical charisma, sang the song in a show called *The French Doll*—an adaptation of a French play, produced by Goetz as a starring vehicle for his wife. The play opened in New York on February 20, 1922, and ran for 120 performances, and the sheet music for "Do It Again" sold well.[2]

Meanwhile, the evening that followed the onstage debut of "Do It Again," February 21, saw the New York opening of *For Goodness Sake*, a musical comedy with several links to Gershwin's career—past, present, and future. Some of the creative team overlapped with that of *La-La-Lucille!*: Alex Aarons was the producer, the book was by Fred Jackson, and the lyrics were by Arthur Jackson, co-lyricist with DeSylva for *Lucille*. Bill Daly and Paul Lannin composed the score, Daly also serving as conductor. The dance director, Alan K. Foster, would fill the same role the following year in Gershwin's first English show, *The Rainbow*. Above all, what made *For Goodness Sake* tick was that it starred Adele and Fred Astaire, in their fifth Broadway appearance. Fred considered the show something of a breakthrough, as it was around this time that he "started to take hold at creating and choreographing our dances." Robert Benchley of *Life* magazine had little to say about the show "that you couldn't say about most musical comedies, except that the Astaires . . . are in it. When they dance everything seems brighter and their comedy alone would be good enough to carry them through even if they were to stop dancing (which God forbid!)."[3]

Two Gershwin songs appeared in *For Goodness Sake*, "Someone" and "Tra-La-La (This Time It's Really Love)," back to back in the first act. In "Someone," the character Jeff, a lawyer, played by Vinton Freedley, tries to convince Marjorie, played by Helen Ford, that they would make a perfect pair. It's a rare example of a love song in the subjunctive: "If someone like you / loved someone like me, / life would be one long sweet song." The number keeps emotion firmly in check as Jeff addresses a would-be lover in legalese. "Tra-La-La," the playful song that follows, is based on a familiar vocable that registers euphoria. The singer has fallen in love and feels wonderful about it. Few, if any, Gershwin songs are as square-cut as this one. At the same time, his usual attention to harmony and voice-leading is revealed—in the verse's descending chromatic line of whole notes in the accompaniment's middle voice, in the refrain bass line's firm melodic shape, and in the clarity of the overall harmonic plan.

ON MARCH 3, an editorial in *Variety* warned that a technological breakthrough called "radiophony," which enabled sound signals to be transmitted at lightning speed to widely dispersed locations, might change the habits of show business customers. All a listener needed was a reception device—a "radio"—that cost as little as $17 or as much as $200, depending on the distances over which it could receive signals, and entertainment could be brought directly into the home. Few Americans owned receivers yet, but the numbers

were growing, as shown by the appearance of programming sched-
ules in more and more newspapers. Although the showmen who
ruled the theatrical professions had so far paid little heed to the
device, this *Variety* writer thought it was time they did, for its presence would surely divert ticket buyers from the box office.[4]

The 1920s saw commercial radio in America grow from a scat-
tering of independent stations to a vast enterprise with national net-
works as well as local outlets. The expansion took place under the
aegis of the U. S. Department of Commerce, which granted thirty-
one licenses in 1921 and 576 in 1922. During those two years almost
half the stations were owned by manufacturers of electronic equipment, and especially of radios. Others entering the business included
newspaper or magazine publishers (70), educational institutions
(65), and department stores (30), plus auto suppliers, churches, city
institutions, banks, and railroads. Owners were financially responsible for installing and operating their stations. As one historian has
put it, "only the performing talent was free."[5]

With long stretches of time at their disposal, many broadcasters
turned to music as an ideal way to fill them, yet much of the music
they hoped to present was subject to copyright and performance
licensing agreements. As early as 1922, those who controlled performance rights were lobbying for broadcast revenues. At this time,
federal guidelines prohibited the direct advertising of products on
the air. But as technology improved and the medium's commercial possibilities became more evident, that situation changed. By
mid-decade, companies with products to sell could devote advertising monies to the sponsorship of radio programs, and thereby
determine the content of those programs. Sponsors hired performers and paid their salaries. Money from advertising also helped to
resolve conflicts over performance revenues.[6]

During the 1920s, George Gershwin became one of many who
contributed to the growing stock of music available for radio listeners. As a Broadway composer, he added to the repertory of songs

that loomed large in the new medium's offerings—show songs were often performed on such variety programs as the *Eveready Hour* and the *Ipana Troubadours*—and he sometimes played in broadcasting studios. From the early 1920s on Gershwin cultivated a relationship with radio broadcasting that came to be a major avenue for the dissemination of his music. Moreover, as his reputation grew onstage and in the press, radio came to be another medium through which, as an increasingly famous musician with clear and constructive ideas, he joined the public discourse.

A BROADWAY REVUE called *Spice of 1922*, which opened on July 6, featured a song by Gershwin—"Yankee Doodle Blues," with lyrics by DeSylva and Irving Caesar—that was chosen by Harms for aggressive marketing, along with "Do It Again." After an introduction with the quarter notes and four-beat rhythm characteristic of the blues, and a verse outlining its twelve-bar harmonic structure, the song's refrain offers a hymnlike tribute to the singer's feeling for America. This statement is followed by a "patter" section that visits Old World venues—London, Paris, Germany, Russia—and finds them inferior to the New. "Yankee Doodle Blues" was recorded on the Edison label by the Broadway Dance Orchestra as well as by The Virginians, an offshoot of the Paul Whiteman Orchestra. The song's moment in the commercial spotlight continued after a prominent if puzzling notice in *Variety* on September 1 announced that "for the first time since we have been in business," Irving Berlin, Inc., Music Publishers, have taken over from Harms this "outside song," because "every one who has heard this number proclaims it the greatest song ever written for any and every kind of a singing act." "Taking over" a song from another publisher did not necessarily mean transferring its copyright. But the song did enjoy a modest rise in sales that fall.

Gershwin's main work during the summer lay in writing a score for *George White's Scandals of 1922.* In the course of this assignment, he formed a connection with orchestra leader Paul Whiteman that would prove exceptionally rewarding to both men. Whiteman was a classically trained musician; having played viola in the Denver Symphony Orchestra, then the San Francisco Symphony, he conducted a U.S. Navy band during World War I, and after war's end formed his own ensemble on the West Coast and began to experiment with jazz-flavored dance music, hiring composer Ferde Grofé as his top arranger. Whiteman's rise to prominence was swift. After moving east in 1920, his orchestra made its first records for the Victor Talking Machine Company that August. In September, the Palais Royal, New York's largest café and supper club, hired the Whiteman ensemble as its house orchestra. By October, the *New York Clipper* could report that "Whiteman and his orchestra of nine are receiving $2500 weekly, the record price for such an organization."[7]

Whiteman's first Victor recordings with the Palais Royal Orchestra sold extremely well, especially "Whispering" and "Japanese Sandman," both of which topped a million copies. By the fall of 1921, Whiteman, showing an entrepreneurial finesse that kept him atop the music business for many years, had broadened his reach in two directions. One was the establishment of Paul Whiteman, Inc., to book satellite dance bands under the Whiteman aegis for clubs, hotels, and restaurants in New York and elsewhere; by the fall of 1922, more than twenty such groups, including The Virginians, were on the roster.[8] The other project was to make the Whiteman Orchestra a headline attraction in the theater. This effort got rolling with an October 1921 engagement at New York's Palace Theatre, America's premier vaudeville house. *Variety*'s critic observed that "the Whiteman time is dance perfect—his tone is always subdued—his scheme is simple if not intended—he gives drawing room music in a restaurant. It makes you dance, and the more softly played, the greater the desire. . . . Whiteman has made the old feel young; he has made them feel sentiment and he has made them dance."⁹

It was against this background that George White hired Whiteman for an onstage stint in the *Scandals of 1922*, which opened in New York on August 28—the band's first appearance in a Broadway show. Serving as a featured act alongside such stars as W. C. Fields and the Lightner Sisters, Whiteman and his orchestra were assigned the penultimate spot in the first act, performing their specialty—an assortment of compelling instrumental numbers—at center stage. When they finished their set, the Act I finale, a scene labeled "The Patent Leather Forest," commenced: cloths on either side of the orchestra were removed and a pair of white staircases revealed. As Gershwin recalled the scene, the two circular staircases led "high up into theatrical paradise or the flies, which in everyday language means the ceiling."¹⁰ The show's principals took the stage to sing "I'll Build a Stairway to Paradise," joined by a female chorus in shiny black costumes that reflected the spotlights. "Huge palms drop glistening black fronds upon a white staircase draped in the glossy material," noted one critic. "Up and down the stairs and in front of the scene girls in black satin dance and sing one of the piece's musical hits."¹¹

Alexander Woollcott of the *New York Times*, no fan of the new popular music, nevertheless praised White's decision to give "his stage over for a little while to such a festival of jazz as sets the audience to swaying like a wheat field touched by the wind."¹² Sime Silverman of *Variety* wrote, "The Whiteman Band just whanged them. They played high and low, slow and fast, straight and jazzy without faltering at any time. After the curtain came down on them the house orchestra could also have gone home for any more attention they received. There was no music that could follow Whiteman's."¹³ By consensus "Stairway" was the revue's best number, and nobody found it more thrilling than Gershwin. He was captivated not just by the precision and nuance of Whiteman's ensemble but by its energy and drive. "Paul made my song live with a vigor that almost floored me," he said. And the dancers picked up the orchestra's musical electricity. "A dance was staged in the song, and those girls didn't need much coaxing to do their stuff to the accompaniment of Whiteman's music."[14]

"Stairway"'s genesis is no mystery, thanks to Ira's account in *Lyrics on Several Occasions*. One day Buddy DeSylva, then working with George on the *Scandals* score, approached Ira with a question: "I've been thinking about a song you and George wrote, that 'New Step Every Day.' Anything particular in mind for it?" When Ira replied that he considered the song, written a few years back, an unremarkable specimen and had no plan to revisit it, DeSylva's response tickled him: "I think the last line has an idea for a production number. If you like, we could write it up and I think it could be used in the *Scandals*." That last line was "I'll build a staircase to Paradise, with a new step every day," and the young songwriters swung promptly into action. "The next night George and I had dinner in DeSylva's Greenwich Village apartment," wrote Ira, "and about nine p.m. we started on the new song. About two a.m. it was completed, verse included. Outside of the line DeSylva liked, the result was totally different from the simple ditty 'A New Step Every Day'—and even 'staircase' had become 'stairway.' "[15]

The new song, for which DeSylva shared credit with "Arthur Francis," is a celebration of modern dance, and the sanctified spirit achieved through disciplined practice, the right footwear, and the will to battle life's discouragements. The verse, in the manner of blues music, unfolds over the orchestra's repeated quarter notes. But Gershwin complicates the harmony's trajectory and quickens the pace of its modulations. His novel harmonic "steps" support a vocal line that rises over fifteen bars, a semitone at a time, from G to D-flat. The tonal territory traveled is huge, yet each step receives solid underpinning in whole notes. The verse's tonal complexity exceeds that of any song Gershwin had written to date; it is easy to imagine Gershwin's delight in sharing it with Kilenyi.

The shorter refrain then brings other blues earmarks to the fore, including a flatted seventh in the melody. But once the fair skies above the earthly turmoil cited in the bridge are glimpsed, the protagonist's faith in the orderly pursuit of dancing is affirmed: the grip of the blues relaxes, and the final steps to paradise are climbed. Of the seven published songs Gershwin wrote for the *Scandals*, "Stairway" was the most popular. Ira, who had not expected Harms to publish the number, admitted surprise that "the bands around town and some record companies played up 'Stairway to Paradise' more than anything else in the show, and it became a hit—that is, for a revue. (Most hit songs from the stage emerge from musicals rather than revues.)" Ira's earnings from the song were another pleasant outcome: $3,500, "enough to support me for a year."[16]

During July, as the *Scandals of 1922* went into rehearsal, George White faced a decision. As Gershwin recalled in 1931, "DeSylva and I had discussed for some time the possibilities of writing an opera for colored people." They proposed their plan to White, who "thought it was a swell idea and wanted to incorporate it as a small act" in the *Scandals*. By the time the new edition of the *Scandals* was under way, *Shuffle Along*, the top musical hit of the 1921–22 Broadway season, was closing after 484 performances and preparing to tour.[17] Its success owed everything to its African American cast and creative team: Flournoy Miller and Aubrey Lyles wrote the book, Noble Sissle the lyrics, and Eubie Blake the music. White, who expected white performers to apply blackface for his show, told his lyricist and composer to hold back on writing the scene because he wasn't sure how practical it would be for performers to change their makeup as quickly as the revue's projected twenty-one scenes might require. (There is no hint that he considered hiring African American performers.) But around the start of August, White "came to us and said he would like to try it, anyway. So DeSylva sat down with his pencil and I dug down and found a couple of suitable tunes and we began writing. After five days and nights we finished this one act vaudeville opera. It was rehearsed and staged and was thought of highly by those in connection with the show, which included Paul Whiteman and his orchestra."[18]

The "vaudeville opera"—a sketch in operatic style—was set in Mike's Uptown Saloon, a Harlem nightspot. Given the character of the Broadway revue, a comic piece might have been expected, but DeSylva's story was a melodrama: a love triangle involving two men and a woman whose jealousy leads her, through a misunderstanding, to gun down the man she loves. Gershwin's score included a prologue, a blues song, a love song, an aria, a dance, some operatic-style recitative, and, to weave the story together, a good deal of instrumental music. When the music was complete, his friend Will Vodery orchestrated it. Vodery's score labels the work *Blue Monday (Opera ala Afro American)*. Lasting more than twenty minutes, the sketch opened the second half of the *Scandals*.[19]

If we were to seek an early moment in Gershwin's career when a line can be drawn clearly between his songwriting and his composing selves, *Blue Monday* is a good place to start. Gershwin's growing familiarity with the blues idiom enabled him to compose a striking fifty-plus bars of orchestral introduction. A range of blues techniques and earmarks—melodic, harmonic, rhythmic, formal, and expressive—are used in this beginning, but they are subject neither to a continuous accompanimental four-beat rhythm nor to the harmonically defined twelve-bar form. They amount more to a family of tonal affinities than to a structural framework. Indeed, the orchestral beginning suggests a blues fantasy, tapping a vein of inventiveness and lyricism that Gershwin was discovering here and also in "Stairway to Paradise."

Emerging out of Gershwin's bluesified orchestral opening, DeSylva's operatic Prologue announces the imminent tragedy "of a woman's intuition gone wrong." With this prospect in the air, an evening at Mike's Uptown Saloon in Harlem gets under way: the boss orders Sam, the saloon's man-of-all-work, to sweep the floor. Sam responds with a song cast in a blues scale, concluding in two stanzas that he's got "the Blue Monday Blues." A short time later, after the boss calls for more sweeping, Sam picks up his broom and complies with a third stanza. Later, after a crowd has arrived and the dance floor fills with couples, the melody of the "Blue Monday Blues," serving as a theme song of sorts, is heard again in full, this time hummed gently by the dancers.

Vi arrives at Mike's establishment looking for Joe, her man. "Has any of you seen Joe?," she sings, to a melody with a gentle lilt. Although Joe is absent, a musician character named Tom reveals his own interest in Vi, who, in rejecting his advance, flashes a pistol given to her by Joe as protection against overtures from pests like Tom. Once Joe appears, Vi declares her love for him—"my Joe"— to the same melody, even as she reminds him that she counts on his being faithful to her. By this time the audience knows that Joe, who has just won big in a craps game, has a plan for spending the money: a trip south to visit family members with whom he has long been out of touch. In a solemn delivery of eight unrhymed lines set to a sprawling melody, Joe confides to Mike the details of his plan and explains that he needs to hide his departure from Vi, who will surely oppose his leaving. Then, in a rhymed sixteen-bar utterance marked "Dolce" (sweetly), Joe reveals a profound yearning to be in the presence of his mother, ending with a smoothly lyrical melody most likely borrowed from a preexistent but unused song composed for an instrumental piece during Gershwin's study with Kilenyi.

Having notified his mother by telegram to expect a visit from him, Joe awaits a reply while the customers entertain themselves with dancing. During the wait, the conniving Tom tells Vi that the wire Joe is expecting will be "from a woman." When it arrives and Joe moves to keep it out of her hands as he opens it, Vi pulls the revolver out of her purse and shoots him. After falling to the floor, Joe reads the message, from his sister: "No need to come now Joe. Mother has been dead three years. Sis." Horrified by her fatal error, Vi begs Joe for forgiveness, which he grants. Then, with his last breath, he repeats the "Dolce" melody and its maternal tribute in "Grandioso" (majestic) fashion to a more elaborate orchestral accompaniment, including a high B-flat in his penultimate phrase.

George White's Scandals of 1922 was introduced to the public on August 21 at New Haven's Shubert Theatre. After four performances there, the show moved to New York, where it opened on August 28 at the Globe. An all-white cast made up to look black played the *Blue Monday* segment, including Jack McGowan, who sang the Prologue and took a role in the drama, Coletta Ryan as Vi, Richard Bold as Joe, and Lester Allen as Sam. There is no doubt that Gershwin worried about executing the operatic challenge posed by the sketch, for only rarely did he admit to less than full confidence in his creative powers, as he did then. "I can trace my indigestion back to that opening night in New Haven; my nervousness was mainly due to 'Blue Monday.'"[20]

In New Haven, *Blue Monday* made a strong impression on a local critic. "Although Mr. White or any of his confreres may not be aware of it," he wrote, "they will have done one thing which will, or ought to, go down in history: they have given us the first real American opera in the one-act musical piece called 'Blue Monday Blues.' . . . Here at last is a genuinely human plot of American life, set to music in the popular vein."[21] This writer showed an early grasp of issues that would concern composers and critics alike in the years to come. He cited Gershwin's balancing of four homegrown genres: jazz music, used "only at the right moments"; the sentimental song; the blues; and, above all, a new and free ragtime recitative.

By the time the *Scandals* took the stage in New York, however,

George White was having second thoughts about his second-act opener; after the first night's performance, he removed it from the show. Gershwin's response to this decision is not a matter of record. Perhaps he found it a clear disappointment—that would seem to accord with the "composers' stomach" that plagued him later. Or maybe he took it more or less in stride—that would signal an attitude for which he was admired later in life, an ability to place the fortunes of a show above any attachments he might have to his own contributions. The latter may be inferred—has *been* inferred— from the matter-of-fact explanation he gave Isaac Goldberg in 1931: "Mr. White took it out after because he said the audience was too depressed by the tragic ending to get into the mood of the lighter stuff that followed."[22]

Several reviews of the first night's New York performance survive, but perhaps because *Blue Monday* immediately disappeared from the *Scandals*, the most negative has come to be the most often cited. Charles Darnton of the *New York World* judged the scene "the most dismal, stupid and incredible black-face sketch that has probably ever been perpetrated. In it a dusky soprano finally killed her gambling man. She should have shot all her associates the moment they appeared and then turned the pistol on herself."[23]

Yet Charles Pike Sawyer in the *Post* offered a different opinion: "From an artistic point of view, 'Blue Monday Blues' was by far the best number of the twenty." Sawyer found "a little bit of 'La Bohème,' with the liebestod of 'Tristan' to close, burlesqued almost beyond recognition," yet "remarkably well sung and acted."[24] Another testimonial from Merle Armitage, later an important Gershwin booster and friend, recalls its impact on opening night:

> Included in this Scandals potpourri was Gershwin's Blue Monday, now known as his one-act opera 135th Street. The audience had never heard anything like it. The next two or three numbers, comparative froth, made little impression on me. On the way out of the

theater I purchased three tickets for the following night, so that friends might enjoy with me the new mood of Blue Monday: jazz in somewhat operatic form. We waited in vain throughout that second performance. No Blue Monday. The producers had seen the devastating effect of this compelling work upon the rest of their show and had withdrawn it. The other acts could not stand up to the impact of Blue Monday.[25]

The evidence at hand fails to support the idea that *Blue Monday* was cut because it was an inferior piece of work or a poor fit for the show. For White's immediate problem was more practical than artistic. The standard time slot for a Broadway show was 8:30 to 11:15 p.m., and the *Scandals* ended after 11:45. As the longest scene, as well as one that brought a whole different pace to the enterprise, the *Opera ala Afro American* was a logical candidate for removal.

George White's Scandals of 1922 has proven significant mainly for its impact on Gershwin's career. His acquaintance with Whiteman led to a request to write what became the *Rhapsody in Blue*. Yet beyond that, as his first opera-style foray, *Blue Monday* deserves its own place in history. Its full-blooded engagement with African American subject matter expresses an affinity that nourished his music-making throughout his life.

While none of the *Blue Monday* episodes found their way into print, three Gershwin songs from the 1922 *Scandals* did. "I Found a Four-Leaf Clover," sung by Coletta Ryan and an obvious concession to the popular ear, reminded Ira of a Sousa march and his father of the World War I song "It's a Long Way to Tipperary." ("Play me that war song," Morris was known to request of George.) "Across the Sea," also sung by Ryan, accompanied a sea spectacle dominated by fancy costumes and dancing. And in "Argentina," the show's paean to exoticism, Gershwin's music tackles the problem of expression in Latin American music. With its bolero-style vamp and sinuous melody, Gershwin appears to be at home in this Latin style. "Argentina" seeks to mirror the story's elements and passions by juxtaposing changes of meter, between three-beat and two-beat, and mode—minor-major-minor-major. Rather than smoothing rough edges, the music emphasizes them. Gershwin had learned the Latin idiom years earlier when, in December 1917, he served a stint as pianist at the Century Theatre's all-Spanish revue, featuring the music of the Spanish composer Quinito Valverde.[26] He was not an artist to let any experience go to waste.

AMERICANS IN
LONDON (1922–23)

IN MID-SEPTEMBER 1922, AN INTRIGUING ARTICLE written by Dolly Dalrymple for an English audience appeared in the *New York World*: an interview with American pianist Beryl Rubinstein, headlined "Pianist, Playing Role of Columbus, Makes Another American Discovery."[1] Rubinstein's discovery was a musician he considered an unrecognized genius: the composer of the music for New York's *Scandals*. Dalrymple's earlier conversations with Rubinstein had concerned the likes of Liszt, Tchaikovsky, and Busoni, she noted, "so imagine the consternation when Mr. Rubinstein mentioned anything as 'low brow' as the 'Scandals.'"

Yet Rubinstein's claim was based not only on *Scandals* music, but also on the spark of genius and originality he had heard in that composer's "serious" music—presumably piano pieces. "With Gershwin's style and seriousness he is not definitely from the popular musical school, but one of the really outstanding figures in the country's serious musical efforts," he told the interviewer. Rubinstein's remarks indicate that the two men had crossed paths in New York within striking distance of a piano; in 1922, it could have been no simple thing for a classical musician who had heard Gershwin play to describe his music-making to one who hadn't. A discourse grounded in aesthetic, historical, and technical lore was widely shared within the classical sphere, but not in the popular. Because serious music was widely assumed to hold a monopoly on artistic value, popular styles had received little such scrutiny. Rubinstein's experience with Gershwin exposed the limitations of that point of view.

That fall saw Gershwin involved in a new show, eventually named *Our Nell*, in which he shared composing duties with Bill Daly. Beginning its tryout in Stamford, Connecticut, on November 20, *Our Nell* opened in New York on December 4, only to close in January after forty performances. In spite of positive notices, the show proved a gamble that didn't pay off—partly, perhaps, because few cast members had had much prior experience on New York's musical stage.[2] Ira Gershwin wryly summed up the show's character and brief history in a January 12 letter to his cousin Benjamin Botkin:

> To-morrow night I expect our Nell to die. . . . It was a musical travesty on the old mellowdrama which flourished up to about a dozen years ago. The notices in Washington a week before it opened in New York, were marvelous. But she sort of flopped here. She was a good gal while she had it, was Nell, but when she closes to-morrow night, I'm expectin' they'll put a white sheet around her, and call it a season.[3]

As Ira's comment reveals, *Our Nell, or The Villain Still Pursued Her* parodied an old-fashioned dramatic form, unusual for Broadway. It differed enough from regular musical comedy fare, in fact, that some out-of-town audiences were slow to realize that satire was intended, though by the time the show reached New York, the word was out, and the opening-night crowd enthusiastically hissed the villain's first appearance.

Our Nell was first brought to the attention of producers Ed Davidow and Rufus LeMaire by Ray Goetz, who, having decided that a modern sendup of a melodrama had a chance at Broadway success, sponsored the fashioning of one while seeking others to produce it. Goetz's creative team included two stage veterans—playwright A. E. Thomas and lyricist-librettist Brian Hooker—in addition to composers Gershwin and Daly, who also invested in the show. Ira's letter to Botkin confirms that "George had an interest in the show, which adventure in producing will cost him about $3,800. . . . All he can do now is to take it out on his income tax and charge it to experience."

Perhaps Goetz was the one to decide that Gershwin and Daly should work together on the *Our Nell* project.[4] Whatever the catalyst, the friendship that took root during the making of this show proved one of the most important in Gershwin's life, personally and musically.

Born in Cincinnati into a theatrical family, Daly grew up in Boston as a musical prodigy. He studied piano with German-born pedagogue Carl Faelten, who had once headed the New England Conservatory, and his brother Reinhold; before age twelve, he was also studying harmony, counterpoint, and composition. On graduation from Harvard in 1908, he was a self-confessed "musical snob" interested only in the classics, yet averse to making music his profession. In 1909, Daly joined the staff of New York's *Everybody's* magazine, a journal known for investigative reporting, and within two years became managing editor. In 1914, however, the lure of music resurfaced after the eminent pianist and statesman Ignace Jan Paderewski saw him conduct a chorus and recommended him to the director of the Chicago Opera Company, who offered him a contract as assistant conductor. Daly accepted the offer and resigned from *Everybody's*, only to be left jobless when the company canceled its upcoming season.

Finding himself at a crossroads, Daly relaxed his musical standards and found work in the Broadway theater, hiring out as an orchestra pianist while teaching himself how to orchestrate. In 1915, he conducted the Broadway musical *Hands Up*, a Shubert production with a score by Sigmund Romberg and the versatile Ray Goetz,[5] and he went on to conduct more shows in the years that followed, including two featuring the Astaires.[6] Along the way, he also tried his hand at songwriting, contributing to Goetz's ill-fated *Piccadilly to Broadway*. The year 1922 seems to have marked the peak of Daly's career as a Broadway composer: he wrote about ten songs for *For Goodness Sake*, alone or together with Paul Lannin. Then, on November 13, he and Gershwin signed a contract with Hayseed Productions to write the score of *Our Nell*, for which they would each earn a royalty of 1 percent of the weekly box-office receipts.

Set in the fictional Hen's Foot, Connecticut, *Our Nell* featured characters who were rural stereotypes. Much of the show's music has disappeared, but five songs survive: two by Gershwin, one by Daly, and two by both. Brian Hooker wrote the words, and Harms published all but "Little Villages," a Gershwin-Daly number whose focus on Algonquian place names in Connecticut and Massachusetts ("From Missisquoi to Monomoy, from Aspetuck to Kennebunk") made it a poor candidate for publication. A shared sense of humor was one of the traits that brought Gershwin and Daly together, and this song reflects it. The other number whose authorship they shared is "Innocent Ingenue Baby," the only song to outlast the show's closing; it would be heard the following year in Gershwin's first London venture, and later on a song recital he accompanied. There is no way to know which composer contributed what to this song, but the constrained accompaniment, mild harmonic drive, and patterned blue notes suggest that Daly had the heavier hand.

In his January 1923 letter to Ben Botkin, Ira added that George was not working on a new show at the moment but was studying composition with Rubin Goldmark, a figure of consequence in New

York musical circles. A native of New York City, and nephew of Viennese composer Karl Goldmark, he had studied both in Vienna and at New York's National Conservatory while Antonin Dvořák was there in the 1890s. While still a young man, Goldmark headed a music conservatory in Colorado Springs; later, when the Juilliard Graduate School was established in New York in 1924, he was named head of its composition department, a post he held until his death. Between these appointments, he taught harmony and composition privately in New York. His best-known student was Aaron Copland, who respected Goldmark's teaching as thorough and professional but found him unsympathetic to the modern cast of the ideas that captured his own allegiance.

For Gershwin's part, per an article he wrote for the *American Hebrew* in 1929, he considered Goldmark's gift to American composition to be his belief that "the negro spiritual," with its "strong sense for rhythm" and its "sad wails and pathetic groans," could be the foundation of a true American idiom. Goldmark's own contribution to that idiom was *A Negro Rhapsody* for orchestra in 1923, a piece whose significance Gershwin finds more historical than artistic. Still, he argues,

> Goldmark was among the very first to turn his eye towards the negro and to attempt to interpret America through the poignant strains of the spiritual. And since jazz—certainly the most efficacious means, to date, for the creation of American music—has its roots deeply embedded in the negro spiritual, the importance of such a pioneer work as the "Negro Rhapsody" should not be disregarded.[7]

Kilenyi noted in his memoir that Gershwin studied harmony with *him* between 1917 or 1918 and 1922, so Gershwin could not have begun with Goldmark much before the end of 1922. In April 1924, in an encounter initiated by George's mother, Rose, Kilenyi enjoyed a lengthy talk with George, who told him about the instruction he had received since they had parted ways: he had taken three lessons from Goldmark, and he "apologized for not having told me about it." It seems likely that these took place between late 1922 and early 1923. Later, however—probably between May 1926 and mid-1927—he again took lessons from Goldmark, though not for long. The results were positive enough that in the *American Hebrew* article he referred to Goldmark as "my teacher and friend."

In New York on February 8, 1923, Gershwin and English producer Albert de Courville, representing Empire Palace, Ltd., signed a contract securing his services as composer for *The Rainbow*, a revue scheduled for London's Empire Theatre in April. Gershwin, who embarked for London soon thereafter, agreed to deliver a score by March 19, for which he was paid 300 pounds (about $1,500).[8] On Sunday, February 18, having taken up residence in a London hotel, he sat down to write his brother about his first full day on foreign soil:

> A funny thing happened yesterday which made me very joyful & for the moment very happy I came here. The boat was in dock at Southampton & everyone was in line with their passports & landing cards. When I handed my passport to one of the men at a table he read it, looked up & said, "George Gershwin writer of Swanee?" It took me off my feet for a second. It was so unexpected, you know. Of course I agreed I was the composer & then he asked what I was writing now etc. etc. I couldn't ask for a more pleasant entrance into a country. When I reached shore a woman reporter came up to me and asked for a few words. I felt like I was Kern or somebody.[9]

That feeling persisted when, after reaching his hotel, Gershwin fielded a phone call from a reporter for the *Weekly Dispatch*. "He asked my opinion about the possibility of a rag-time opera & when I thought it would come about." Then it was on to the theater for the evening, where a revue called *You'd Be Surprised* was playing: "a fast show, with many scenes from burlesque & music by Melville Morris." The performance left him wondering what music Morris had actually composed, for "all I heard were popular American songs."[10] But "the hit of the show is an orchestra. The Savoy Orchestra. And who do you suppose is the leader? Bert Ralston the sax player who recorded my Mexican Dance with me. He's got a great band and is a riot over here."[11] Gershwin came away from the performance with some ideas about the British musical comedy scene: "From what I can see, America is years ahead of England theatrically, both in wealth of material & money." He also found London "shy of ingenues, leading men, composers, etc.," while granting that good lyric writers abounded.[12]

In his letter to Ira, Gershwin was struck by contrasts he noted with his home turf. "The English are the politest people I've yet met," he wrote, adding that "even the taxi drivers are polite." And he marveled: "how different from the Yellow Cabs of New York," though they "drive on the left of the street which is also a bit befuddling." He had also grasped the essential principle of the currency— "They go by 12ves instead of 10s"—and he was already picking up local speech idioms: "I could go on & tell you more observations of my first 24 hours here but I must trot along to Greys. Did you notice 'trot along?' ... Write heaps & heaps. (Notice? heaps & heaps?)." Finally he referred to the task that loomed ahead. He and lyricist Clifford Grey would start that very afternoon on a show that would begin rehearsals the following Tuesday. Comparing the challenge with that of "writing the Scandals in a month," he imagined that the New York assignment "will seem an eternity compared to the time allotted us."

If George's letter from London displays the energy and high spirits that fueled his rise as a composer, an article written by Ira for the *New York Sun* of April 9 reveals that the composer's less famous brother also brought unusual qualities to the songwriting trade—and a characteristic angle of vision as unique as George's. Ira had come up with a sardonic "questionnaire for poets—beg pardon, for popular song lyricists," designed for a "popular song factory," whose foreman could use it to help assign applicants to the bench or lathe that suited them best. The questions asked:

> What is a mammy?
> What southern state rhymes with mammy?
> What color is inevitably associated with sad and lonely?
> What are the three greatest words in the world?
> Who is your best pal?
> Name three words that rhyme with "home" besides "alone."
> Her kisses taste like what substance from the bees?

Aspirants were then instructed:
> Complete the following with rhymes with the "earl" family:
> > I had a g————
> > She was a p————
> > She put my head in a wh————

And then they were asked:
> Next to your latest, what is the greatest song ever written?

Ira goes on to explain the rationale behind these questions. Although "mammy" is a favorite character in songs about the South, he says he "would like to read a few Tin Pan Alley definitions." The second question is supposed to make readers think of "Alabammy"—until they realize that a lyricist might find "Loosiany" just as acceptable. With the sixth, the author admits that his "home/alone" equivalence is a "subtle and sardonic" move by a writer pretending to think these words actually rhyme. The eighth is a setup: "With a thrill of pride, one would complete the rhyme with the earl family as 'goil,' 'poil,' and 'whoil.'"

Early in 1923, George and Ira Gershwin were still more than a year away from a regular partnership, yet proof of the inventiveness and originality that would stamp their future efforts together lies in what each of them did and said independently during the preceding year. George, working with Clifford Grey, produced a score for *The Rainbow*—the complete revue—in one month. For Ira, the common ground between journalistic humor and lyric writing was that both required an ability to choose a subject, strike a posture, and find words to fit that stance. In this phase of his career his muse was not much moved by dramatic concerns, but he surely continued to cultivate his sense for the sound and rhythm of words.

The score for *The Rainbow* includes nine songs, all published under the joint copyright of Harms of New York and Chappell Music Ltd. of London, an old-line firm that, together with its classical catalogue, published the stage works of Gilbert and Sullivan and other comic operas. Two of these predate the new show: "Innocent Lonesome Blue Baby," based on *Our Nell*'s "Innocent Ingenue Baby," and "Sweetheart (I'm So Glad That I Met You)," which Gershwin and Grey had written in New York for *Flying Island*, a 1921 project organized by Ned Wayburn that was never completed.[13] The other seven numbers, composed between February 18 and March 19, seem to have left no mark outside the show. In some of these, the accompaniment's left hand is conceived chiefly as support for the melody, rather than as the foundation of a multivoice texture; perhaps British popular song, less oriented toward dance rhythms, syncopation, and harmony-based part-writing than Gershwin's customary styles, tended toward a simpler texture than popular song in America.

The Rainbow opened on a Tuesday evening, April 3. Playing thereafter twice a day at 2:30 and 8:30, it remained at the Empire for 111 performances. Reviews were generally positive. British performers made up most of the cast, but some Americans were also featured, including the white singers Grace Hayes and Earl Rickard and a troupe of African Americans: "32 Coloured Singers, Dancers and Musicians from the Southern States of America," with a "syncopated orchestra" under the direction of James P. Johnson.[14] As well as filling a substantial place in the show, a portion called "Plantation Days," this troupe offered longer "cabaret" performances at 5:15 p.m. between presentations of *The Rainbow*, and again at 11:15 after the evening show.

Originating in New York, "Plantation Days" had provided a full evening's entertainment in the United States before and after Johnson became the company's musical director in 1922, enjoying successful stops in Detroit, Pittsburgh, Cleveland, and Chicago before returning to New York in February 1923 with a European tour in the offing. (Hit numbers from Sissle and Blake's *Shuffle Along*, used without authorization, boosted the show's appeal until a formal complaint was lodged and they were removed.) But the company's presence in *The Rainbow*, together with that of the other American performers, sparked a local resentment that boiled over on opening night. A British comedian named Jack Edge used his customary postshow speech to inform the audience that his role as a principal player had been reduced, and suggested that the management had favored American cast members over homegrown talent. A stagehand interrupted Edge's tirade by dragging him, struggling, behind the curtain. When producer de Courville stepped to the footlights to apologize for the incident, his comments drew cheers but also such shouted complaints as "Why don't you give English artists a chance?" and "Send the niggers back."

Shortly thereafter, portions of the show given to Grace Hayes and Earl Rickard were curtailed, while "Plantation Days" was trimmed from twenty-nine minutes to fourteen. Moreover, "the Empire cabaret, announced to open April 5 has been indefinitely postponed," reported *Variety*: "It is said the colored troupe is not believed strong enough to hold it up."[15] Two weeks later, "theatrical, artistic, and social London is becoming incensed over the treatment of the imported American artists by the Empire management."[16] Nevertheless, the "Plantation Days" company managed to survive until the end of the *Rainbow*'s run.[17]

Gershwin seems not to have been involved in these disputes. After fulfilling his contractual obligation to stay in London for a week after the April 3 opening, he traveled to Paris for a visit, then sailed for New York at the end of the month. The nature of the show and his connection to it may explain his nonintervention: rather than an independent production that any playhouse could have staged, *The Rainbow* was a high-end variety show conceived and presented under the Empire's sponsorship. Gershwin held no financial stake in the result beyond the reception of individual songs, and there is no evidence that he felt any particular attachment to the show. Even if the revue proved less than a triumph, it was only the first of his many London engagements during the 1920s. In fact, even as *The Rainbow* approached its opening, a second enterprise was gearing up for what would be a major London hit of the 1923–24 season.

Alex Aarons's *For Goodness Sake* had enjoyed a decent run in New York and a tour through the summer of 1922, sparked by the dancing of Fred and Adele Astaire. At the tour's end, producer Charles Dillingham, who had the pair under contract, exercised his option to present them as stars of *The Bunch and Judy*, a comedy with music by Jerome Kern and lyrics by Anne Caldwell. But when that show opened in New York on November 28, it proved a dud. Aarons soon approached the Astaires with a new plan: "You know this thing is going to fold any week now. I've got a hunch that you two would be a great bet for England. How'd you like to do *For Goodness Sake* in London?" The Astaires liked the idea, and the young producer left for the U.K. to lay the groundwork of his plan.

After *The Bunch and Judy* closed in January, Dillingham declined to pick up the Astaires' options for the next two seasons. "We'll get together a little later on," he told them. "I've got to carry out some other plans for the present. Now, don't go and get too tied up." As Fred Astaire saw it, *The Bunch and Judy* had raised questions in Broadway circles about whether the dancers' talents could actually "carry stardom," and Dillingham's own doubts seemed obvious. In the meantime, though, the Astaires received other feelers, including one from Albert de Courville for *The Rainbow*; perhaps the notion of hiring the pair had been suggested to him by Gershwin. Then a wire arrived from Alex Aarons in London: "CAN ARRANGE ENGLISH PRODUCTION FOR GOODNESS SAKE AS WE DISCUSSED IT. UNDERSTAND YOU'RE CONSIDERING DECOURVILLE REVUE. NO GOOD FOR YOU. DON'T DO ANYTHING UNTIL I SEE YOU NEXT WEEK."[18] When Aarons returned to New York after a quick visit, now in cahoots with the eminent English producer Sir Alfred Butt, he immediately signed Adele and Fred to appear under his aegis, and on March 23, 1923, they sailed for England.

Still bothered by the failure of *The Bunch and Judy* and by Dillingham's flagging support, Astaire later admitted to leaving New York with doubts about the transatlantic adventure. On the way over, however, his confidence got a boost when he and Adele agreed to perform in a charity concert for the Seaman's Fund. On the day of the performance the sea was rough, and by the time the Astaires appeared, their dance floor was pitching and rolling dangerously. The pair adjusted deftly, turning involuntary careenings and pratfalls into comic moments, and charmed fellow passengers with their good grace and sportsmanship. After the performance, an Englishman made them a promise: "I say, you two should make a jolly good hit in London. I shall be there with a party the first night!" From that time on, Fred managed to put his worrying tendency on hold.

Astaire's recounting of the London triumph of *For Goodness Sake*, now renamed *Stop Flirting*, hardly mentions George Gershwin, whose work on the *Rainbow* revue was winding down as the Astaires arrived; when Gershwin's assignment was over, he took a short vacation to Paris, where he visited American friends. Nevertheless, Alex Aarons was surely in touch with Gershwin, for they were now considering a new Astaire project to follow the current one. Gershwin's share in London's *Stop Flirting* would be three-quarters of 1 percent of box-office receipts, but his obligations did not include attending that show's end-of-May London opening; he sailed for New York at the end of April.[19] Since Aarons booked a five-week out-of-town tryout tour—to Liverpool, Glasgow, Edinburgh, and other cities—Gershwin may have attended rehearsals before the tour began. Astaire's only mention of Gershwin in his account of *Stop Flirting*, however, is his comment that "(I'll Build a) Stairway to Paradise," interpolated from the *Scandals of 1922*, had proved one of the show's best numbers.[20]

Toward the end of May, Aarons, having decided that *both* Gershwins were essential for the project he had in his sights, typed a long letter to Ira Gershwin in New York. Confident that a London success would boost the Astaires' appeal at the American box office, he was now preparing his next step. Convinced that in Fred and Adele he had "secured one of the most valuable pieces of property (as far as talent is concerned) on the American musical comedy stage," he recognized that there was no better way for his new stars to display their talents than to have them sing and to dance to the music of the Gershwin brothers. "As George has probably told you," he now wrote to Ira, "I am planning to have him do the score Alone." And the impresario's next words must have felt like manna from above to a young lyricist whose handiwork had so far been published only under a pseudonym. "I believe you know that there is no one I should like so much for the lyrics as you."

Aarons and Astaire were already discussing the type of story, settings, characters, and numbers they wanted for the show following *For Goodness Sake*: a show written to represent the Jazz Age generation. "Of course, everything I am telling you here is strictly in confidence," he warned Ira, "and I should prefer that you discuss it with NOBODY except George. I want to have everything set before I make my plans known to any outsiders." Aarons also asked the Gershwins to "save all your best stuff," adding that "I shall want some numbers that you have already finished but a great amount of new work will be necessary too." For example, "Hang On to Me," a song George had already previewed for Aarons, greatly appealed to the Astaires.[21]

The show that Aarons was hatching was still almost a year and a half away from its onstage debut as *Lady, Be Good!* But the cause for the delay could only have been gratifying to him: the overwhelming success of *Stop Flirting*. The Astaires took the United Kingdom by storm, scoring a triumph with the public, catching the attention of the nobility—even the royalty—and hobnobbing personally with the highest of English society. Not until their show had run for more than a year did Fred and Adele decide it was time to return to the United States and look to the new project that Aarons was cooking up for them.

THE JOB that greeted Gershwin on his return to New York resembled the one he had faced in London: he had about a month to write the score for *George White's Scandals of 1923*. DeSylva was his lyricist again, with Ray Goetz also contributing to a few songs. While Ann Pennington and W. C. Fields, two of the 1922 edition's major stars, did not return, White had recruited a pair of younger vaudevillians, Winnie Lightner and Tom Patricola, who performed specialty numbers with music of their own. There was no Paul Whiteman this year, but Charles Dornberger and his Orchestra, a jazz ensemble of the Whiteman stripe, appeared in the finale of Act II, hoping to send the audience home in an upbeat mood.

The *Scandals of 1923* proved more successful on Broadway than any of its predecessors, opening on June 18 and closing on November 10 after 168 performances. Gershwin's score included twelve songs, seven of which were published. As with the *Rainbow* songs, each of the published numbers has an attribute to recommend it, yet—also like the London revue—none seem to have made a strong impression on the marketplace, the audience, or the critics. By several accounts, the most elegant episode was a scene taking place in a jeweler's shop, with chorus girls impersonating articles of jewelry and single stones: ruby, sapphire, emerald, diamond. As a clerk attends to them, the scene's male protagonist opens his heart to the lovely woman at his side in "There Is Nothing Too Good for You," vowing in the verse to buy the rarest treasures the store has to offer and to lay them at her feet. Perhaps the song's failure to make more of an impact lay partly with the lyrics. The refrain's first two phrases get the rhyming off to a rickety start: "There is nothing too good for you, / Nothing I would not do for you." A real rhyme, like "good for you"/ "would for you," might have encouraged listeners to settle more easily into the moment. And perhaps the song's implication that material treasure wins a woman's heart every time lacked the tenderness to open those hearts.

Another number praised by some critics, "The Life of a Rose," also suffered from clumsy rhyming, as well as the notion that roses bloomed for a single day. "Lo-La-Lo," a Hawaiian-themed song, must have seemed old-fashioned by 1923, though Gershwin tackled this challenge by forging a "Hawaiian" style with near-primitive melody, harmony free of complication, and a retrogressive form: a verse, refrain, and trio.[22] "Throw Her in High," a political song protesting the arrival of Prohibition, was seen by critic Robert C. Benchley as just one more of the *Scandals'* less imaginative quirks:

> Each year there is a strange Messiah-complex manifested at the end of the first act of Mr. George White's "Scandals." He seems to feel that it is his mission, as the producer of a summer revue, to bring some Great Message or other to the world, to bring down his first-act curtain on a scene which will send the audience out into the

lobby shaking their heads and saying to each other: "By George, Moe, I am going to write to Congressman Minnick to-night about this thing." One year it was the Free Passage of American Ships through the Panama Canal to which Mr. White devoted the services of his shapely young ladies. . . . We forget whether or not the Newfoundland Fisheries case has ever been taken up in a serious way by Mr. White. At any rate, this year it is Prohibition.[23]

The quietly beautiful duet "Let's Be Lonesome Together" is built on the poetic concept of "lonesome" togetherness, but an improbable stage setting—a canary in a cage and a goldfish in a bowl who manage to grasp each other's solitary existence—undermined the pensive tune.

In the company of numbers like these, another published song, "Where Is She?," stands out for a premise more suited to the tastes of the time. Written from the perspective of a traveling businessman and in a jazz-tinged idiom, it projects the sincerity of a young man's search for the girl of his dreams. Even from the distance of almost a century, its premise, its lyrics, and the rhythmic inventiveness of the music make it seem eligible for more success than it received.

What we know about Gershwin's two 1923 revue projects suggests a certain similarity between composing for those kinds of productions and employment at the kind of song mill that Ira had mocked in the spring. Broadway had its own industrial-style elements. For both *The Rainbow* and the *Scandals of 1923*, the books for which touched on a variety of subjects, moods, and visual settings—and, not incidentally, musical styles—Gershwin was given around a month to write a complete score of about a dozen songs together with other music. Once the score was delivered, the published songs had to be chosen, arranged, printed, and in the hands of distributors by the time the show opened. Orchestrations had to be made and the music rehearsed by the performers. Individual numbers could be altered or dropped, but not without a cost in time and money. As in a factory, the final product depended on combining many constituent parts under pressure of time, to fit a performance schedule that had been set in advance. Producers could not afford to fuss too much over details. If a "home/alone" rhyme or an awkward bit of melody slipped by, such glitches could always be avoided in the next show. These were the conditions under which Gershwin, between February and June 1923, composed and published at least fourteen new songs, plus perhaps as many as a dozen more that filled their quota but were not judged worthy of publication.

As of that summer, one of those revue songs, "(I'll Build a) Stairway to Paradise," stood out from all the rest: a number, as it happened, whose words were cowritten by "Arthur Francis." It would be an exaggeration to say that that summer the Gershwin brothers were preparing to join forces in the pursuit of song hits. Yet knowing that Alex Aarons, a producer they knew and trusted, had plans to unite them as the songwriting team for a new musical in 1924, they might have had an inkling that George's days as a composer of revues were coming to an end in favor of bigger things.

A RECITAL AND AN EXPERIMENT (1923–24)

ON JANUARY 30, 1924, READERS of the *Boston Transcript* were treated to an astute, open-minded commentary from reviewer Henry Taylor Parker on an unusual concert given the preceding evening in Jordan Hall: a song recital by mezzo-soprano Eva Gauthier, assisted by two accompanists, Frederick Persson and George Gershwin—the latter in his second appearance ever on a concert stage. Gauthier's recital repeated a program she had presented the previous November 1, in New York's Aeolian Hall; instead of Persson, Max Jaffe had assisted then, but Gershwin played at both.[1]

From the start, Gauthier's goal was to make a statement by complementing standard recital fare with something new and different, and she had enlisted music critic Carl Van Vechten to help her plan the program. When he suggested she sing a selection of American songs, "her face betrayed her lack of interest," but when he specified "jazz," "her expression brightened." Gauthier settled on a program she called a "Concert of Ancient and Modern Vocal Music," which included six groups of songs: "ancient," including Byrd, Purcell, and Bellini; and "modern," including Hungarian, German, American,

Austrian, British, and French. The American portion consisted of music from Tin Pan Alley and Broadway. Convinced that a significant moment was at hand, H. T. Parker attended both the New York and the Boston performances.

The American songs were a big success. In Boston as well as New York, Parker reported, the audiences "smiled and stirred and clapped to every one of her seven 'jazz-songs;' would not be stilled until it was obvious that she knew no more." There was a clear connection between jazz music and the world in which present-day Americans live, he noted, and serious concerts ought not "to draw the shades and lock the doors upon a present that happens to intrude from the sidewalk." Simply being serious does not make a human activity meaningful. "'Jazz-songs' are no more 'debasing' in the 'serious' concert-hall than they are when they tootle across the summer air from your neighbor's gramophones; while in the recital-room a Gauthier sings them far better."[2] Parker's view was that if the music was good enough, recitalists should sing it and their audiences would embrace it.

Not only was George Gershwin's role as pianist essential to Gauthier's performance, but he had helped her choose the American songs: Berlin's "Alexander's Ragtime Band," Kern's "Siren Song," Walter Donaldson's "Carolina in the Morning," and three of his own numbers, "Innocent Ingenue Baby," "Swanee," and "Stairway to Paradise." (The pair also prepared a fourth Gershwin song, "Do It Again," as an encore. These seven songs were the extent of Gauthier's popular repertoire, as the audience realized when she repeated her encore number.) And as Parker noted, Gershwin "diversified [the piano parts] with cross-rhythms; wove them into a pliant and outspringing counterpoint; set in pauses and accents; sustained cadences; gave character to the measures wherein the singer's voice was still. As musician, not as song-smith, he played."

Deems Taylor, a prominent composer, and music critic for the *New York World*, wrote that when Gauthier made an offstage exit after the first song groups, she reappeared "followed by a tall, black-haired young man who . . . bore under his arm a small bundle of sheet music with lurid red and black and yellow covers." What happened next startled everyone:

> Eva Gauthier sang "Alexander's Ragtime Band." . . . She just sang it, as seriously and skillfully as she had sung Bartók's "Harom oeszi Koenuycaepp," while young Mr. Gershwin began to do mysterious and fascinating rhythmic and contrapuntal stunts with the accompaniment. And when she had finished she faced a new audience. . . . Here was music they didn't have to think about or intellectualise over, or take solemnly. They didn't have to do anything about it, in fact, except listen to it—which was easy—and enjoy it—which was unavoidable.[3]

Then Taylor summed up his own feelings about the American songs performed in Aeolian Hall on that Thursday evening:

> I hear a good deal of jazz, and of course oceans of "good" music, but I had never before heard a concert singer take jazz in her stride, as it were, placing it beside other contemporary music without comment or apology. And I must say, that jazz group touched something that the other music didn't. It had nothing to do with art, perhaps; it was a more purely human reaction, a thrill of sudden recognition of something native, something of which I was a part. . . . Bartók's Hungarian folk song was "a song of the people" . . . but so is "Ingenue Baby."

Gauthier's program implicitly questioned the divide separating classical and popular music. "If an occasional jazz number should creep timidly into our concert lives," Taylor wondered, "who knows but that American audiences might learn to listen to music AS MUSIC, without bothering about its social position?" And once they have learned "to enjoy good music, even when it is light, they might learn to reject bad music, even when it is heavy."

The concert was greeted as a landmark, especially by Taylor, whose Sunday column, appearing a few days after his review, was one of the first substantial writings to treat Gershwin as an artist. Never before had popular songs been included in a classical recital, nor sung by a singer who performed them as if they were art songs, even as her accompanist emphatically did not. The evening was a tug-of-war for anyone familiar with the world of classical music. On one side stood the recital format's traditional atmosphere: the formality of the surroundings, the presumed dignity of the European repertoire, the singing in four different languages, and the conventions of cultivated vocal technique and text declamation. On the other stood popular songs, familiar enough in idiom, language, and in some cases musical detail to relax the listeners' attitude, or to delight them in what they were hearing, or both. The presence of both forces, and the juxtapositions they introduced—art song and jazz song, singer and accompanist, one mood to another—made for an evening of emotional jolts. The popular–classical split itself became a catalyst for reflection—and, in Gershwin's case, action.

As his first appearance on a concert stage, Eva Gauthier's recital introduced Gershwin to a segment of the public that, even if they recognized his name as the composer of "Swanee," knew nothing of his pianistic talent or physical presence. And the music critics in attendance supplied a fresh kind of feedback for a composer whose work had only been judged publicly, if at all, by drama critics. This jury critiqued what they heard according to standards set by the composers and performers, European and American, who had shaped the traditions of the concert hall. When Deems Taylor or Henry Taylor Parker judged a song, they weighed its merits in a context that included a historical past as well as present-day experience.[4] But this performance, and its reception, proved it was possible for popular music to receive that level of judgment.

In retrospect, Gauthier's recital also brought to mind the possibility that Gershwin the Broadway songwriter could produce a major instrumental composition.

THE UNDERTAKING of the *Rhapsody in Blue* proved so significant that many stories have since been told about its origins, and Eva Gauthier later claimed that her New York concert had been the new work's flash point. Sitting in Aeolian Hall that November evening was Paul Whiteman, who "decided there and then that he too could give an Aeolian Hall concert." Following the performance, Whiteman "came back stage to ask George to write him something for his orchestra, with a piano part which George might play."[5] That work, the *Rhapsody in Blue*, would be premiered in Aeolian Hall on Tuesday, February 12, 1924, just two weeks and a day after Gauthier's recital in Boston.

According to Gauthier, when she, Gershwin, and Persson did some "re-rehearsing" for the Boston concert early in 1924, Gershwin played some of the themes he had developed for his new instrumental piece. Just before traveling from New York to Boston, she invited several musical friends, including Olin Downes, the new music critic of the *New York Times*, and English composer Arthur Bliss, whose music was represented on the program, to her last rehearsal. At the end of their session, she asked Gershwin to play his *Rhapsody* for this select audience to see what their reaction would be. The composer described it as "a new work for Paul Whiteman's concert in a few days, if I can get it finished in time." Gauthier concludes, "And that was really the first performance of the *Rhapsody in Blue*."[6]

Perhaps Gauthier exaggerated her role in the *Rhapsody*'s genesis, but to view it through the prism of her recital brings certain connections to light. On November 1, Gershwin experienced firsthand the popular numbers' transformative impact on Gauthier's audience, which may have taught him something about classical concertgoers. For one thing, like the friends and guests he had entertained at parties, these listeners enjoyed his piano playing, and for another, they relished the American songs. That popular songs could earn attention and foster delight on *musical* grounds in a classical context was no small discovery. Indeed, the expressive linchpin of the *Rhapsody* lay in the variety of its musical materials: its rhythms, sonorities, and most of all melodies, both classical- and jazz-oriented.

That same fall of 1923, Gershwin and DeSylva were occupied with the score for a new Broadway show, to be called *The Perfect Lady* and later changed to *Sweet Little Devil*. Rehearsals started on November 15, scheduled around a move to Boston and Providence for more seasoning before the Broadway debut on January 28, 1924.[7] In the meantime, Gershwin contributed songs to two other shows: *Little Miss Bluebeard*, adapted from a Hungarian original as a starring vehicle for Irene Bordoni and produced by Ray Goetz, and *Nifties of 1923*, a Charles Dillingham revue. "I Won't Say I Will but I Won't Say I Won't," a song written for Bordoni, sounds like a sequel to "Do It Again," this time with "Arthur Francis" assisting DeSylva on the lyric.

Sweet Little Devil, Gershwin's fifth musical comedy after *La-La-Lucille!*, *A Dangerous Maid*, *Flying Island*, and *Our Nell*, was conceived as a vehicle for stage and film star Constance Binney, with producer Laurence Schwab coauthoring the libretto along with playwright and librettist Frank Mandel. The production team included stage director Edgar MacGregor—producer of *A Dangerous Maid* (1921), the Gershwin brothers' first attempt—and dance director Sammy

Lee, a leader in his field through the rest of the 1920s. Even though Ira displaced DeSylva as Gershwin's regular lyricist during 1924, Schwab, Mandel, DeSylva, MacGregor, and Lee were involved, in varied combinations, with fashioning some of the decade's early signature musicals.[8]

In Schwab and Mandel's story, Tom Nesbit, an American mining engineer working in Peru, reads a press agent's article about New York chorus girl Joyce West, said to be as principled and down-to-earth as she is beautiful. Dazzled by the idea of this supposed paragon, he writes her an admiring letter, and receives a reply that seems to confirm every good thing the article said about her. Their correspondence continues, and before long Tom decides to travel to New York to sell a recent invention and meet Joyce in person. But two shocks greet his arrival, both the handiwork of Virginia Arminta Culpepper, Joyce's younger cousin and roommate, and the show's heroine—the "sweet little devil," played by Binney.

It turns out that Joyce, interested only in a suitor's financial prospects and therefore amused by the naïveté of Tom's first letter, consigned it to her wastebasket, from which it was rescued by Virginia, who became Tom's actual correspondent. Then, Tom is shocked anew to discover that a check for thousands of dollars that he expected to receive in New York has failed to appear. Unbeknownst to him, Virginia has intercepted it to keep Joyce from launching a charm offensive when she learns that Tom might get rich after all. Under Virginia's coaching, Tom eventually recognizes Joyce for the gold-digger she is, and takes her to Peru to put her to work in the mines and teach her a lesson. Virginia follows, Joyce hooks up with another, well-heeled young man, and the "sweet little devil" finds enduring romance with her engineer Tom, in the wilds of South America.

Although Constance Binney was *Sweet Little Devil*'s featured star, the performers who actually stopped the show were Ruth Warren, as Joyce's chum, and William Wayne, as a pal who arrives in

New York with Tom. Warren and Wayne, appearing in what was apparently their first and last Broadway production, were a vaudeville song-and-dance team who brought a rough, ready, and athletic approach to dancing and comedy. In the Boston tryout run, one critic called their performance "one of the best burlesque dances of the vigorous type ever seen in this or any other local theatre." For their Act I closer, DeSylva and Gershwin came up with a number called "The Jijibo," named after a modern dance with the rare power to make dancers appear thin or fat, whichever they preferred. It's another Gershwin song in a jazz vein: as the refrain runs through its short list of instructions on changing one's body shape, the music manifests the verve and variety that bring dance-loving customers flocking to the dance floor.

Gershwin and DeSylva wrote at least a dozen songs for *Sweet Little Devil*, and seven were published. Two of these were dropped before the show opened on Broadway: "Pepita," set in Peru and included for local color, and "Mah-Jongg," the last example of the "Chinese" style that Gershwin honed during his years as a composer of revue scores. Of the other published songs, "Under a One-Man Top," written for Warren and Wayne, is a get-away-from-it-all duet for a couple preparing a honeymoon by car. "Hey! Hey! Let 'Er Go!," a song for Wayne with the choristers, amounts to a pep talk: if something is bothering you, hide your melancholy with a show of high spirits. This one-step jumps with a recurrent blue seventh and enough syncopation to sound like a twentieth-century song, if a bit old-fashioned for the century's third decade.

With two exceptions, the songs for *Sweet Little Devil* recall the fruit of Gershwin's labors for *The Rainbow* and *George White's Scandals* earlier in 1923: they are professionally competent and musically inventive enough, yet don't seem to have made much of an impact. The exceptions are the two main numbers written for Binney: "Virginia," which aims to catch the spirit of an irrepressible character and reveals some human complexity, and "Someone Believes in You," a heartfelt duet with Tom. What separates these songs from the rest is how the words and music come together for convincing portrayals of human emotion; both songs seem to hold the potential for a life outside the theater.

The show did well enough, running in New York until May 3, 1924, and racking up 120 performances.[9]

BY THE TIME *Sweet Little Devil* was a thing of the past, the *Rhapsody in Blue* had won Gershwin more public acclaim than anything he had done before. Its February 12 premiere had been part of a concert that, like Eva Gauthier's recital, was supposed to break new artistic ground. But while Gauthier had devoted only portions of her program to expanding the concept of American music, Paul Whiteman's whole Lincoln's Birthday concert aimed to be a lesson on that subject. It is hard to think of another American premiere that realized its artistic potential so fully and publicly.

Whiteman's brand of disciplined jazz music was proving a product of dependable quality, and one that still managed to seem in tune with the ethos of an era known for its impetuous spirit. By 1923, his orchestra stood at the heart of a lucrative business enterprise, and Whiteman was always on the lookout for ways to expand his audience. As 1924 approached, he was determined to demonstrate that the kind of music he and his ensemble played was not just commercially appealing but artistically sound. He hoped to elevate jazz through high-quality performance and an impressively varied repertoire.

Touting his concert as a statement about America's musical identity, Whiteman, or someone on his staff, came up with the title "An Experiment in Modern Music." Regular morning rehearsals began in January, even as the orchestra maintained its daily schedule at the Palais Royal, plus onstage appearances in eight performances of the *Ziegfeld Follies of 1923* every week. The conductor did all he could to control the message he hoped the concert would send, and it was thanks to his promotional persistence—three public rehearsals were held during the runup to the concert, January 22 and 29 and February 5—that many music critics ended up reviewing a performance they might ordinarily have skipped. An elaborate brochure was prepared for audience members, describing the nature and purpose of the "Experiment" and providing program notes by Gilbert Seldes. In the performance hall on February 12, Whiteman's personal manager presided over the occasion with spoken commentary.

And what was the man of the hour thinking as his handiwork took shape? When, in 1926, Whiteman looked back on that first Aeolian Hall concert, what loomed largest was the memory of his own anxieties. "Would we be the laughingstock of the town when we woke the 'morning after'? Would the critics decide I was trying to be smart and succeeding in being only smart-alecky?" As curtain time drew closer, Whiteman's most urgent wish was that he could cancel the performance:

Fifteen minutes before the concert was to begin, I yielded to a nervous longing to see for myself what was happening out front, and putting an overcoat over my concert clothes, I slipped around to the entrance of Aeolian Hall. There I gazed upon a picture that should have imparted new vigor to my wilting confidence. It was snowing, but men and women were fighting to get into the door, pulling and mauling each other as they do sometimes at a baseball game, or a prize fight, or in the subway. . . . I went backstage again, more scared than ever. Black fear simply possessed me. I paced the floor, gnawed my thumbs, and vowed I'd give five thousand dollars if we could stop right then and there. Now that the audience had come, perhaps I had really nothing to offer after all. I even made excuses to keep the curtain from rising on schedule. But finally there was no longer any way of postponing the evil moment. The curtain went up and before I could dash forth, as I was tempted to do, and announce that there wouldn't be any concert, we were in the midst of it.[10]

RHAPSODY IN BLUE
(1924)

WHEN WHITEMAN REQUESTED a new work from him in the fall of 1923, Gershwin at first declined, because of his commitment to *Sweet Little Devil*. Then, early in January, reading a newspaper article about Whiteman's upcoming Aeolian Hall venture, he was surprised to learn that he was—apparently—at work on a symphony for that very concert. "This *was* news," he remembered thinking; but the false report pushed him to reconsider:

> There had been so much chatter about the limitations of jazz, not to speak of the manifest misunderstandings of its function. Jazz, they said, had to be in strict time. It had to cling to dance rhythms. I resolved, if possible, to kill that misconception with one sturdy blow. Inspired by this aim, I set to work composing with unwonted rapidity. No set plan was in my mind—no structure to which my music would conform. The rhapsody, as you see, began as a purpose, not a plan.[1]

Beginning in 1920, as we have seen, Gershwin had composed a number of songs drawing upon blues music for material.[2] But for his first major instrumental work, he now set his sights on a jazz-oriented approach, more varied than a succession of blues-based statements. The concert would give Gershwin a chance to visit broader rhythmic territory, including a variety of tempos. Freedom in that realm, he felt, would call for music more unpredictable and expressive than anything Whiteman and Company—or his competitors—had so far embraced.

Gershwin's first title for his new composition was *American Rhapsody*. It was Ira who came up with a new title reflecting his brother's foray into an unexplored musical zone: a register of sorts, like a key, for a classical composition with dance rhythms, songful theatrical tunes, and a pitch vocabulary grounded in blues music. "Rhapsody in Blue" signified an intent to display in one composition the full spirit of Paul Whiteman's "Experiment in Modern Music."

Later in life Gershwin recalled an extraordinary train trip early in 1924 from New York to Boston, where *Sweet Little Devil* was soon to play, after he had begun work on the *Rhapsody*. Certain sounds along the way struck him, including "the train, with its steely rhythms, its rattle-ty-bang that is often so stimulating to a composer." On this trip, too, something happened that had never happened to him before: "I suddenly heard—and even saw on paper—the complete construction of the rhapsody, from beginning to end." By the time the train reached Boston, he could envision "a definite *plot* of the piece, as distinguished from its actual substance . . . a sort of musical kaleidoscope of America—of our vast melting pot, of our unduplicated national pep, of our blues, our metropolitan madness." By that time most of the new work's themes were already in his head, except for one—his "middle theme," perhaps the piece's most memorable, which had already come to him unbidden as he played the piano at a New York friend's house. "There I was rattling away without a thought of rhapsodies in blue or any other color," he recalled. "All at once I heard myself playing a theme that must have been haunting me inside, seeking outlet. No sooner had it oozed out of my fingers than I knew I had found it."[3]

It would be hard to exaggerate the importance of several decisions that Gershwin acted on after he joined Whiteman's "Experiment." Foremost among them was to compose his first full-fledged instrumental work with a clear purpose in mind: to refute the notion that jazz music was bound to a strict tempo. Presenting five different themes in contrasting keys, timbres, moods, and tempos, the new composition offered listeners a sequence of independently compelling musical events, each of them eminently tuneful, and none of them given a chance to wear out its welcome.

Gershwin also opted to deploy these themes in a concerto-based format, with musical material distributed through dialogue between the ensemble and himself: an accomplished pianist whose personal panache he could trust. This medium fit well into the format of Whiteman's concert, organized in two halves. The first was devoted to short, song-based, jazz-oriented arrangements for the ensemble, and the second to compositions with more ambitious artistic intent, beginning with Victor Herbert's four-movement *Suite of Serenades*. Aware that Gershwin had composed a compelling exemplar of American musical modernism, Whiteman gave the *Rhapsody in Blue* the penultimate place in the concert's order.[4] That strategic placement reflected the music's qualities rather than Gershwin's reputation, for he was then hardly known in the precincts of Aeolian Hall, known as a venue for classical music-making.[5] And the *Rhapsody's* concerto format created an eventful interchange, with a soloist who knew how to project a star's authority to complement the polished professionalism of Whiteman, the conductor, and his musicians.

Gershwin further enhanced this concerto-style invention and technique by casting his jazz-oriented melodies in the mold of popular songs. Rhythmic elasticity from the classical sphere broadens the work's range of expression beyond the conventions of dance-based jazz music, even as Gershwin's command of vernacular melodic invention enabled him to harvest from the plenitude of his songwriting labors. The *Rhapsody's* audience hears a flowing blend of music suited at times to the concert hall, but infused elsewhere with elements from the dance hall and the theater. That discontinuity is balanced by captivating tunefulness.

A masterstroke of another kind was Gershwin's decision to launch the piece with an unexpected sound—not a melody but a surprise: a reedy smear borrowed from the comic realm of jazz novelty. Starting on a low F deep in the clarinet's range, Ross Gorman, Whiteman's premier reed man, played an extended, throaty trill, followed by a seventeen-note sweep up two octaves and a fourth to the first note of the first theme: a concert B-flat. Henry O. Osgood, a New York music journalist who attended at least one rehearsal and the premiere, credits Gorman with figuring out how to make the sound of this takeoff gesture unforgettable:

> Will any one who heard him forget the astonishment he created in that first measure, when, halfway up the seventeen-note run, he suddenly stopped playing separate notes and slid for home on a long *portamento* that nobody knew could be done on a clarinet? It's a physical impossibility; it's not in any of the books; but Ross knew it could be done with a special kind of reed and he spent days and days hunting around till he found one.[6]

The "musical kaleidoscope of America" that had revealed itself to Gershwin on his trip to Boston follows the clarinet eruption, which morphs into the first theme he has chosen for his *Rhapsody*. (It seems clear that he found most of his themes in his tune book, that is, "the trunk.") That thematic unveiling leads into a musical conversation among the composition's three "voices": the piano soloist, the full orchestra, and solo instruments from the latter. As a mix of thematic statements with figuration, transitions, and plenty of free-flowing "tempo rubato," the *Rhapsody*'s opening measures offer a prologue with an unusual richness of thematic substance. But when does this introductory process come to an end? In fact,

not until Gershwin unveils a sustained stretch of complete melodies, in measures 72–130, may listeners feel sure that the piece is
fully under way.

By that time Gershwin has presented three of the *Rhapsody*'s
five themes, each cast to fit the mold of a sixteen-bar popular song
refrain: **aaba**. And the purposeful momentum following the on-
and-off flow of the opening is sustained through a fourth theme,
beginning in measure 138, with a mid-to-low register that provides a contrast with its predecessors. Examples 10.1–10.5 show, in
notated form, the beginnings of these themes, and that of the middle theme too.

10.1

10.2

10.3

10.4

10.5

Gershwin has also introduced a sixth melodic element: a snippet labeled "Tag" here, and heard throughout the *Rhapsody* to complete more than one musical statement.[7]

Having presented four themes as orchestral statements, Gershwin then begins, in measure 172, an extended interlude for the piano. Beginning with a transition, it offers a playful keyboard restatement of Theme 3. Then, behind a dreamy, transparent orchestral return of Theme 1, the pianist moves on to a delicate, dissonant, treble-dominated background of figuration. That interlude continues with vigorous statements from Theme 4, leading into a hushed four-bar preparation, "rubato e legato" (free and smooth), for the dramatic arrival of the *Rhapsody*'s mood-changing middle theme— Theme 5. Marked "Andantino," this lyrical melody for the orchestra introduces a sweeping legato statement fashioned from three arching phrases, each unfolding over a span of twenty-two bars.

Ferde Grofé, a composer himself and the arranger of Gershwin's two-piano score of the *Rhapsody* for Whiteman's ensemble, preserved his recollections of that process, testifying to his own love for that theme. Grofé's memory also offers a rare glimpse of the

Gershwin family at home: Morris, Rose, Ira, George, Arthur, and Frances. At the time they were living in a modest first-floor apartment, with a baby grand piano in the parlor, at the corner of 110th Street and Amsterdam Avenue, across the street from the Cathedral of St. John the Divine.[8]

Aware of the composer's plan to change the pace and mood of the *Rhapsody* well along in the piece, Grofé sensed that Gershwin's first attempt to write an effective "middle" theme had fallen short. But when Gershwin played him another melody in a lyrical vein— the "entrancing middle theme" that had recently come to him at the piano—the arranger found it perfect. He wrote it down, took it home, and returned the next day with that melody in lead-sheet form. Ira advised George that he would be hard pressed to write "another tune as good as this." The dignity and substance of the new theme prompted Gershwin to sound it three consecutive times: twice in the orchestra, the second in "grandioso" fashion, and the third as a memorable piano solo.

But when the pianist shifts abruptly from the long sweep of lyrical melody to a noise of alarm, and a trombone sounds the middle theme in raucous eighth notes, the beginning of the end is nigh. Led by the piano, Gershwin's coda includes a keyboard rendering of the introductory clarinet smear, several iterations of the long-absent tag, and eventually a sudden key change from E-flat to B-flat, wrenching the *Rhapsody* back to its home key. A thundering return of Theme 1 rings out. And as the orchestra sustains the tonic harmony's return, the piano's triumphant sounding of the tag bids farewell.

CRITICAL RESPONSES to Whiteman's "Experiment in Modern Music" provide a range of perspectives on New York's music scene as the decade of the 1920s approached its midpoint. At one end of this purview, though Aeolian Hall was hardly on their regular beat, were two show-business trade weeklies, *Variety* and the *New York*

Clipper. At the other, respected music critics from the daily newspapers formed their own cultural spectrum, taking the concert's aspirations seriously. More than one followed his concert review with a longer piece ruminating further on Whiteman's venture.

The *Variety* review, written by Abel Green—one of the journal's leading reporters, later to become its editor in chief—treated the concert as a subspecies of stage revue, citing a number's catchiness or a lack therof, performance virtuosity, and comments on the audience response. Faced with Gershwin's radically original composition, Green mustered two approving sentences: "Another highlight on the program was George Gershwin's intricate and musicianly 'Rhapsody in Blue,' played by the brilliant young composer to orchestra accompaniment. The arrangement is a gem and forced Gershwin to retire and come back for extra bends three times before permitted to finally depart."[9] A day later, Green wrote another review that offered much more detail.[10] Parting company with "highbrow critics," he remarked on the varied pedigrees of Whiteman's customers: Tin Pan Alley publishers and song pluggers rubbing shoulders with denizens of the cultural elite, Amelita Galli-Curci, Mary Garden, Alma Gluck, Fannie Hurst, Heywood Broun, Walter Damrosch, Jules Glaenzer, Leopold Godowsky, Sr., Jascha Heifetz, Victor Herbert, Otto H. Kahn, S. Jay Kaufman, Fritz Kreisler, John McCormack, Sergei Rachmaninoff, Max Reinhardt, Moriz Rosenthal, Gilbert Seldes, Leopold Stokowsky, Deems Taylor, and Carl Van Vechten among them.The *Rhapsody*, the program's highlight, "was a lengthy number but its intricate arrangement of the clever rhythm made a deep impression. It brings to the fore the native Negro indigo strains mixed with rhapsodical arrangements in a delightfully ingratiating manner." Green was one of few in the critical fraternity who cited "Negro strains" in the composer's mix of styles.

Lawrence Gilman of the *Tribune* compared the *Rhapsody in Blue* with two other song arrangements performed at the concert, "Raggedy Ann" by Jerome Kern and "I Love You" by Harry Archer, however, and found no significant difference between them. The new work sounded to him like just another example of Whiteman's own kind of American dualism: a "paradoxical blend of independence and docility, care-free energy and unadventuresome conformity."[11]

But to Olin Downes, who had recently moved from Boston to New York to take over the *Times*'s music beat, Whiteman's concert brimmed with musical vitality. Downes heard in the players' performance "an abandon equaled only by that race of born musicians—the American Negro, who has surely contributed fundamentally to this art which can neither be frowned nor sneered away." The *Rhapsody*'s

> first theme alone, with its caprice, humor, and exotic outline, would show a talent to be reckoned with. . . . This is no mere dance tune set for piano and other instruments. It is an idea, or several ideas correlated and combined, in varying and well-contrasted rhythms that immediately intrigue the hearer. This, in essence, is fresh and new and full of future promise.

Downes saw the classically inexperienced Gershwin as locked in a struggle with form, but his verdict was positive: "The audience was stirred, and many a hardened concertgoer excited with the sensation of a new talent finding its voice and likely to say something personally and racially important to the world."[12]

W. J. Henderson of the *New York Herald*, who admired the *Rhapsody* greatly, started his review with a bang: "Modern music invaded Aeolian Hall yesterday afternoon." Igor Stravinsky, he imagined, "would have shaken hands with Irving Berlin, Gershwin and Paul Whiteman and shouted (in Russian, of course), 'Great is rhythm! Great is dance! Great are wind instruments! And we are the silver trimmed prestidigitators who know how to use them all!'"[13] And in a later revisiting of what he had heard, Henderson added:

There could be no question about the musical quality of Mr. Gershwin's work. It was as genuine in its field as one of Liszt's Hungarian rhapsodies, and in some respects quite as good. It was too long because it was over elaborated in some rather tenuous spots, and for that reason it was loose jointed in other places. But it was the work of a musician and one of unquestionable talents.[14]

Deems Taylor reviewed Whiteman's concert for the *New York World*'s Wednesday edition, and then, as he had after Eva Gauthier's song recital, followed it on Sunday with a longer piece about issues the concert had raised. As a composer himself, Taylor cared about where this event fit in Whiteman's view of the contemporary scene, not only "jazz as it is to-day, but jazz as it was and may become." To his ear, the *Rhapsody* "possessed at least two themes of genuine musical worth and displayed a latent ability on the part of this young composer to say something of considerable interest in his chosen idiom."

Whatever its faults, the piece hinted at something new. "Mr. Gershwin will bear watching," Taylor wrote; "he may yet bring jazz out of the kitchen."[15]

PART II | IRA COMES ABOARD

ENTER IRA (1924)

WITH 196 BROADWAY PERFORMANCES, *George White's Scandals of 1924* ran longer than any of its five predecessors. By the time it opened on June 30, Gershwin had played the *Rhapsody in Blue* close to a dozen times in public and had recorded it with Paul Whiteman, and the expansive turn his career had taken was current news in some quarters, marking him as a musician to be reckoned with. Yet the fifth *Scandals* proved to be the last revue score he composed for Broadway.

One song from the show registered, however, and it still does. "Somebody Loves Me" bears the stamp of the urban Jazz Age. Buddy DeSylva had help on the lyrics from veteran songwriter Ballard MacDonald, and the two fashioned a courtship number that turns on a simple question: "Somebody loves me, / I wonder who, / I wonder who she can be." The protagonist's words flow easily, carrying a quarter-note–based tune as straightforward as his sensibility seems—especially when the mystery of "who" is emphasized by a sustained blue third in the melody. "Somebody Loves Me" is an early example of what might be called the "Gershwin song," with a lyric revealing character traits through a clear tonal design: a firm establishment of the home key, a move away from it, and then a return. Along with "I'll Build a Stairway to Paradise," it was the only other song out of the almost fifty Gershwin wrote for the *Scandals* to become a hit in the marketplace.

As he pushed to finish his *Scandals* duties while preparing to sail for the U.K. and a new London show, Gershwin got a phone call from a musical friend in need. Vladimir Dukelsky, now residing in New York, called to seek Gershwin's advice about money. "George, with his customary generosity and big-brother kindness to me, told me to come right over," and Dukelsky did, explaining that he hoped to raise funds for a summer stay in Paris to promote his new piano concerto.[1] His timing could hardly have been better. Gershwin, overloaded with work at the moment, needed help with a ragtime number in the *Scandals*; it took Dukelsky only a few hours to come up with the music, for which Gershwin paid him $100. Then he was entrusted with making voice-and-piano arrangements of another six songs.[2] Admitting himself proud of his "fill-ins" for "Somebody Loves Me,'" Dukelsky noted that they also appeared in the orchestration, proof that the arranger "thought them eminently Gershwinesque, which indeed they were." For this work he earned another $120. And Gershwin threw another duty and another $100 his friend's way: arranging the piano solo version of the *Rhapsody in Blue*. When Dukelsky left for Paris, he was supported in part by the work for hire he had done on Gershwin's behalf. It would not be the last such assignment he took on.

By the time the *Scandals* opened late in June, Gershwin himself had sailed to London. There, on the 24th, he signed a contract with Alex Aarons for the musical comedy that would come to be known as *Primrose*.[3] Two weeks later, he wrote Lou and Emily Paley to tell them how much more pleasant this English visit was than his last. He was sharing quarters with Aarons and his wife Ella, "one of the cheeriest flats I've seen anywhere. It looks over Devonshire Gardens, and makes a comfortable place for me to work in." The quarters had already seen visits by such notables as Prince George (the Duke of Kent), Otto Kahn (American financier and patron of the arts), Lord Berners (an English nobleman who was also a composer and writer), and the Earl of Lytton. Gershwin's second London stay seems to have been a mostly enjoyable blend of work and play, at least during its first phase. On top of the socializing, he watched a tennis match at Wimbledon and played a round of golf with Guy Bolton, librettist of *Primrose* and the new Astaire musical scheduled for New York in the fall. ("I believe I shall [take] it up profession-ally," he joked, for golf might be "a good way to knock off some heiress.") Updates about his musical chores were upbeat. He was collaborating on *Primrose* with Desmond Carter, a promising young lyricist on the staff of Chappell, the Harms affiliate in London. "I am most optimistic about this show," he wrote, "because the book seems so good—to say nothing of the score."[4]

Primrose's story revolves around a writer named Hilary Vane who, living on a houseboat, is working on a novel about a character named Primrose. A comely new neighbor, Joan, intrigued by what she can read of the story during a quick visit and fancying her-self mirrored in the title character, sneaks off with the manuscript, and when she returns it, she and Hilary quickly fall in love. But Joan is not free, for her wealthy guardian—Sir Barnaby Falls—has insisted that she marry his feckless nephew, Freddie Falls. Mean-while, Toby Mopham, scion of an aristocratic family, seeks Vane's help in dissolving his entanglement with Pinkie Peach, a romanti-cally aggressive beauty specialist whose muscular big brother stands ready to enforce the matrimonial pledge Toby has made to her. By the time the curtain falls, Hilary and Joan are together, Freddie has found another partner, and Toby and Pinkie Peach stand ready to tie the knot.

Almost three weeks into September, after *Primrose* opened its doors to a warm welcome, poet and critic Edward Shanks appraised the show as a classic example of English musical comedy, though the composer was a twenty-five-year-old American with meager experience writing for London's West End. One reason for that assessment might be the score's several numbers in 6/8 time. In a September 6 newspaper column called "Londoner's Diary," Gershwin explained why he had included them: the English were "a 6–8 nation," he had decided, as it was the rhythm that most closely approached ordinary English speech and the basis of the Arthur Sullivan tradition. America, on the other hand, struck him as "a 4–4 nation" whose musical gait was essentially the fox-trot.[5]

Two 6/8 numbers written for the character of Toby, played by gifted comedian Leslie Henson—"When Toby Is Out of Town" and "Mary, Queen of Scots," a duet with Freddie Falls—are both grounded in comic exaggeration, featuring patter in the mode of W. S. Gilbert. Henson's comedic gifts are also called on for the quick-moving patter song "The Mophams" and "That New-Fangled Mother of Mine," which reveals Lady Sophia Mopham as a fan of liquor and a lover of nightlife. This song bears a definite 2/4 American stamp, although one more from 1910 than 1924: with its moderate pace, strategically placed syncopations, and left-hand accompaniment patterns, it looks back toward ragtime.

"This Is the Life for a Man," another 6/8 number, presents Hilary Vane, played by Percy Heming, as a man's man—a lover of the rural landscape—who happens to be a writer. His last solo number, "Beau Brummel," a drinking song celebrating the British bon vivant of the latter 1700s and early 1800s, allows Gershwin to emulate the pompous cast of British patriotic music. He obviously wrote these two songs with Heming in mind: the singer had made his mark in opera, to which he would eventually return.

Heming also sang two love songs with Margery Hicklin, who played Joan—"Some Faraway Someone" and "Wait a Bit, Susie"—that were less portentous and more subtle. Desmond Carter shared credit for these words with another lyricist: Ira Gershwin.

When George sailed from New York, he carried with him a

backlog of songs he and Ira had already written for possible use in *Primrose*. Indeed, Ira stood ready to provide "second verses and extra choruses," not to mention new lyrics, as needed. In a June 25 letter to George in London, Ira brims with the excitement of a new partner:

> If you haven't already written about it, I want a letter in great detail about the work you're doing and expect to do, who's doing the book [to *Primrose*], who's in it, what lyrics of mine are you using, who's doing the others, what you are getting, what am I getting, what songs are you saving for the Astaires, how about the book for the Astaires, can I get a copy of either or both scripts and start on them, how about the second verses and extra choruses of the songs you have, what new songs do you want, when does *Stop Flirting* stop . . . etc. . . . . Leave out nothing.[6]

One song originally written for *A Dangerous Maid*, "Four Little Sirens," fit comfortably into the London show—it was the only preexistent all-Gershwin number that did. Unrelated to the plot, the song feeds on wordplay for its own sake, revealing its theatrical roots. "We never swim in the sea," confess the four female singers, all dressed in bathing suits, but "still we get along quite swimmingly." Audience members familiar with *The Mikado* would have recognized in this song the comic spirit behind that classic's "Three Little Maids from School."

Another number from *A Dangerous Maid*, "Boy Wanted," sung by four chorus mates in the 1921 show, was reworked for Pinkie Peach alone, who aims her bill of particulars at rich men (the boy of her choice must "own a Rolls Royce"). Desmond Carter, of whom Gershwin thought highly, receives co-lyricist's credit. His role in this and other joint efforts was to start with a lyric written by Ira and revise as needed for the English audience. As George wrote to his brother: "You won't recognize some of your old lyrics but you understand of course, they had to be altered to fit certain situations." These two songs from *A Dangerous Maid* had the effect of adding to *Primrose*'s stock of humorous charm, while highlighting work by the Gershwins that had fallen by the wayside.

One of the ironies of Ira's career was that he won success and respect as a popular song wordsmith in spite of being a staunch antisentimentalist wary of love-song clichés. Most likely his own emotional disposition pressed alternatives upon him, for his body of work abounds in the ambiguity, indirection, self-consciousness, and conditional feelings that real life, courtship included, carries with it. In any event, Ira's emergence as his brother's regular and full-fledged partner was given voice in a burst of conditional love songs. The lyrics of the two new duets sung by Hilary and Joan complicate the show's romantic theme. The dignified "Some Faraway Someone" flows with restrained formality, its rhythm stretching here and there to underline the vocal expression. Joan's words reveal that she is more in love with an image than with a flesh-and-blood man—a premise shared by a far better-known song, "The Man I Love," which the Gershwin brothers had worked on in April in New York, perhaps with the coming Astaire show in mind. "Wait a Bit, Susie," a parable inspired by Hilary's novel-in-progress, was similarly ambivalent: this song's suitor is a "lonely," indecisive man given to "watching" and "waiting," words that echo feelings the young Izzy Gershvin recorded in his diary when romantic inclinations touched his heart.

Primrose had a run of 255 performances, closing in the spring of 1925, and was replaced at London's Winter Garden Theatre with *Tell Me More*, an American import—with a score by Gershwin. But *Primrose* was never revived in London, nor was it produced in America, as the composer had hoped. None of its songs became hits in the U.K.—though "Wait a Bit, Susie" won some popularity—nor did any enjoy much circulation in the United States. The show's significance lay mostly in what it meant for the Gershwins' collaboration: *Primrose*—something of a trial run for the Broadway venture Alex Aarons had been planning for more than a year—marks the functional start of the regular Gershwin partnership that flourished until George's death. From now on, every show or movie for which George wrote the music, with one exception, also included lyrics by his brother, now working under his own name.

Primrose was also the first Gershwin show whose music was published in a piano-vocal score, in addition to the half-dozen songs issued separately. Under the imprint of Harms in New York and Chappell in London, nineteen numbers were engraved and bound together consecutively in a 113-page volume containing, together with the songs, the act openers, dance music, and finales. In later years other Gershwin musical comedies would appear in score form, too, preserving a much more detailed version of the show than what the songs alone could provide.

In mid-September 1924, Adele and Fred Astaire arrived in New York Harbor, where tales of their hobnobbing with the nobility in London had preceded them. "We were pleased to find that we had not been forgotten during our long stay abroad," Astaire wrote later: the reporters who greeted the ship "knew all about what we had been doing over there and were eager to get some statements from Adele about her experiences dancing with the Prince of Wales."[7] Standing on deck, the Astaires also spotted their new producers, Alex Aarons and Vinton Freedley. "While we were going through customs," Aarons "was telling us the plot for our new show," then called *Black-Eyed Susan* but soon to be renamed *Lady, Be Good!* The Astaires signed their contracts on the lid of a trunk while the customs men were going through their baggage. Their joint salary was $1,750 a week in New York and $2,000 on the road.[8]

With barely a month to go before rehearsals started, brother and sister settled into life in New York City, scoping out the theatrical competition. Gershwin, who had preceded the Astaires back to the States, took them to shows that "looked mighty good to us." In fact, Fred admitted, "we started to worry about what we would do in ours"—but their doubts were eased when Gershwin played through the new musical's songs for them. They also learned from Gershwin that the two-piano team of Victor Arden and Phil Ohman would be featured in the orchestra. Ohman, who had served a stint with the Paul Whiteman Orchestra in 1922–23, was currently teamed up with Arden to play popular music in clubs and theaters, and *Lady, Be Good!* was their first Broadway engagement. Their flashy song arrangements would provide yet another way for Gershwin's music to be circulated.[9]

Guy Bolton, collaborating with Fred Thompson, devised a book for *Lady, Be Good!* about a coterie of mostly well-to-do young New Englanders and their entanglements, romantic and financial. The main characters are a sister and brother, Susie and Dick Trevor (played by the Astaires), who, though born to wealth, have come upon hard times: their landlord has evicted them for nonpayment of rent, and they vow to replenish the family coffers. A wealthy young woman named Josephine who fancies Dick eagerly awaits his proposal of marriage—a move that would solve the Trevors' problem if Dick weren't already in love with Shirley Vernon. For her part, Susie falls for Jack Robinson, a hobo just arrived from Mexico—who has inherited his rich uncle's estate but has yet to learn of his windfall. The various plot twists involve lawyers, especially J. Watterson Watkins—"Watty," the comic lead—who works doggedly to cut deals for the Trevors that will line his own pockets. In the end, Jack's inheritance is announced, allowing him to marry Susie and Dick to tie the knot with Shirley. Watty prospers, too, by snaring Josephine.

When Aarons laid his plans in 1923 for a new kind of Broadway musical, he started not with this book or even a story, but with a wish list. He wanted the show to reflect the sensibilities of his generation's creative artists and performers, and his trump card would be the Astaires. Having taken English theatergoers by storm in *Stop Flirting*, they now repeated their triumph in New York, dancing and singing to a score written with their talents specifically in mind. The nimble, bubbly Adele, in the role of a flapper with a deft comic touch, was the duo's star, and for the first time in his Broadway career, Fred stepped beyond the confines of the duo and created a tap routine of his own—to "The Half of It, Dearie, Blues," which he sang with Shirley.

For another dance, Fred got an assist from an enthusiastic social dancer with a sure feel for what worked onstage: Gershwin himself.[10] Shortly before the company headed to Philadelphia for the show's tryout run, Fred and Adele found themselves stuck at the end of a tricky number, "Fascinating Rhythm." "We had the routine set, but needed a climax wow step to get us off," said Fred. "For days I couldn't find one. Neither could dance director Sammy Lee." Then George Gershwin

> happened to drop by and I asked him to look at the routine. We went all through the thing, reaching the last step before the proposed exit and George said, "Now travel—travel with that one." I stopped to ask what he meant and he jumped up from the piano and demonstrated what he visualized. He wanted us to continue doing the last step, which started center stage, and sustain it as we traveled to the side, continuing until we were out of sight off stage. The step was a complicated precision rhythm thing in which we kicked out simultaneously as we crossed back and forth in front of each other with arm pulls and heads back. There was a lot going on, and when George suggested traveling, we didn't think it was possible. It was the perfect answer to our problem . . . and it turned out to be a knockout applause puller.[11]

Astaire, sometimes called "moaning Minnie" by his sister, tended to take a dim view of his shows' prospects as the day of reckoning drew near. However, "from the very beginning," it seemed to him, "*Lady, Be Good!* was one of those naturals that jelled." Opening night in Philadelphia, at the Forrest Theatre on November 17, went without a hitch, and "the audience laughed and applauded everything we had counted on. It didn't matter, that weak plot. Somehow there was an indefinable magic about the show."[12] The mercurial Aarons, known for panic attacks on opening nights—he customarily spent the evening in the men's room—appeared backstage after the first act in a buoyant mood. "This thing is a cinch," he told Astaire. "I just made a deal for six months with the ticket brokers in New York. We're sold out already." The company headed for New York's Liberty Theatre on a wave of optimism, while still trying to guard against overconfidence.

But *Lady, Be Good!* clicked on Broadway as well. "The whole thing had a new look to it, a flow," Astaire wrote.

> Even after the final curtain many of the audience would linger around the orchestra pit to hear Ohman and Arden playing the exit music with the orchestra. Often too, when the exit music was completed, Phil and Vic would put on an impromptu concert for the fans who refused to go home. This happened many times and I was convinced that the new sound of Ohman and Arden's two pianos in the pit had a lot to do with the over-all success of *Lady, Be Good!*[13]

Critical reception in both cities could hardly have been better. Much of the approval centered on the Astaires, especially Adele, whose dancing and comedy skills won many hearts, though Cliff Edwards, a singer already known to many audience members from cabaret and vaudeville as "Ukulele Ike," received the most enthusiastic response. In New York, Frank Vreeland of the *Telegram and Evening Mail* attributed much of the show's momentum to Gershwin's music, which "tugged at the feet and plucked at the roots of the hair."[14]

Perhaps the most sophisticated review was a Sunday piece by Linton Martin of the *Philadelphia North American*, who judged *Lady, Be Good!* nothing less than a "vital contribution to American music." Gershwin had

> combined the musical heritage of his eastern antecedents with the syncopated sounds of Forty-second and Broadway in rhythmic and harmonic effects so bizarre as to bow confidently at Stravinsky, and thus arrive at originality. . . . Bach selling flamboyant sheet music about June moons in the lobby on the way out could hardly be a more startling or unexpected spectacle. . . . This is music that one may listen to time and again, elusive, subtle, individual, piquant and plaintive. It is also jazzy, elementary, even uncouth.[15]

Just as the *Rhapsody in Blue*, with its prescriptive notation and classical references, reflected Gershwin's emergence as an accomplished composer, so did the songs he had written for this landmark show. And three of them—"Oh, Lady Be Good!," "Fascinating Rhythm," and "The Man I Love"—not only made an impression at the time, but became standards. "Swanee" and "Stairway to Paradise" had already turned into independent hits, and "Somebody Loves Me" was showing signs of doing the same, but each of these old songs came from a different show, all of them revues, and had a different source of words. In contrast, the songs from *Lady, Be Good!* were all the work of the same lyricist and belonged to the same theatrical context. The Gershwin brothers were now engaged more fully with each other's imagination and craft, opening up a new era of songmaking with a fresh stamp.

Linton Martin was among the first to identify the blues as one of the most effective arrows in Gershwin's compositional quiver for *Lady, Be Good!*[16] By this date blues music was characterized by any or all of four traits: (1) the use of "blue notes"; (2) repeated quarter-note rhythms in the bass register, sometimes called the "blues bass," or even "quarter-note throb"; (3) melodies based on call-and-response; and sometimes (4) a twelve-bar refrain structure. The title song of the show, although it cannot be called a blues number, does show the composer drawing on blues music to give it a distinctive cast: acting the part of a near-helpless male, Watty pleads with an ingénue as if she were his only romantic hope in the world. In the space of thirty-two bars, the petition "Lady be good" is sung four times to a four-note gesture, often completed as "Lady, be good . . . to me." Gershwin's music offers an aural whiff of the "blue" feeling asserted in the lyrics.

The second standard from *Lady* is about a rhythm disruptive enough to threaten a person's sanity. (The idea that popular music could be dangerous was not new to songdom, for it reaches back at least into the ragtime era, with Berlin's 1911 "That Mysterious Rag.") "Fascinating Rhythm" had its beginning in London during the summer of 1924, when George wrote eight bars of music that seemed weirdly promising. "Alex Aarons, who was with him, and who is one of the keenest judges of a smart tune among the managers, told him to develop it for the next show," Ira recalled. The rhythmic opening of this tune was tricky: six eighth notes plus an eighth-note rest, to be repeated in 4/4 time. That incongruity, George noted with satisfaction, ensured that each repetition would start with a new emphasis.

With rhythm and meter out of sync by design, it was up to Ira to reconcile seven-syllable lines—the last "syllable" being silent—with duple-time accents, while meeting the comprehensibility test of a show-song lyric. His first breakthrough was a masterful phrase, "fascinating rhythm [rest]," that fit the music of George's opening gesture while naming the very thing the gesture embodied. His second was to find two more lines of identical length that would make sense following the first. And his third breakthrough was to invent, for the fourth line, a five-syllable clincher ("I'm all a-quiver") suggesting why such music posed a risk to listeners.

Despite the technical complexities the brothers faced, their goal was to make this song irresistible—a show-stopper. And in that they succeeded. "If you saw the show," said George, "you remember that 'Ukulele Ike' sang the verse and chorus, followed by a miraculous dance by Fred and Adele Astaire. The song was played by an orchestra which featured Ohman and Arden in the pit." These things together turned the technically formidable "Fascinating Rhythm" into a crowd pleaser.[17]

Musically, "Fascinating Rhythm" holds two elements in common with the blues. The regular minor-key pulsing of the verse's bass line combined with a flatted third in the melody gives more than a hint of blueslike sound, and in the refrain's **a** section, the melody's rhythmic complications are supported by a stable harmonic background reflecting blues chordal practice. The **b**, or contrasting, sections offer much more harmonic change, as well as a syncopated rhythmic turn based on the popular dance step known as the Charleston.

But perhaps the most enduring of the three standards in *Lady, Be Good!* is one that was cut from the show before it reached New York.

In the spring of 1924, the brothers were working on a song long since forgotten, and after Ira had finished his words for its refrain, George composed a verse to go with it. Both brothers took a liking to this "definite and insistent melody." But because the music didn't seem "light and introductory enough" for a verse, they "upped its importance to the status of a refrain," which Ira then fitted with new words. Once the brothers gave *this* melody a verse of its own, "The Man I Love" was complete.

Two standard elements of blues music are present here as well: a blue seventh prominent in the refrain's melody, and references to the bass-line throb in the verse. What Ira considered the song's insistent quality lies in the refrain's repetition of a melodic figure that comes in both a six-note and a four-note form, the latter a postcadential sign-off known as "Good evening, friends"; listeners familiar with the *Rhapsody in Blue* may recognize it as the first music played by the piano when it enters with the work's final melodic statement.[18] "The Man I Love" stands out for the sober dignity of the music supporting the singer's determined imaginings. And when *Lady, Be Good!* opened in Philadelphia, Adele Astaire sang it charmingly, Ira recalled. But during the tryout run it became clear that this song, by far the show's weightiest, added nothing essential to the plot. Its solemnity seemed lost among the dancing duets and novelty numbers. It may be, too, that for all of Adele's talents, they did not include taking herself seriously enough as a singer to dramatize "The Man I Love" to a theater audience.[19] After a week, the ballad was withdrawn.

As the show's only self-identified blues number, "The Half of It, Dearie, Blues" offers a more direct example of Broadway's approach to blues music.[20] This is a duet for Dick and Shirley, who, though they have just officially broken up, still love each other. Blues elements fly thick and fast once the title is introduced: a blue third on a strong beat, the quarter-note bass throb, a melody built around call-and-response, and a harmonic move from tonic to subdominant. At the end, Astaire completes the confessional by swinging into his solo tap dance. Real feelings lie behind this "blues" number, but it's also rich in parody.

The only blues element in the show's first song, "Hang On to Me," sung and danced by the Astaires after their characters have been evicted and find themselves out on the sidewalk, occupies just one fleeting moment—a quote from the first phrase of W. C. Handy's "St. Louis Blues" ("I hate to see the evenin' sun go down"). But the show's remaining published song, "Little Jazz Bird," like "Fascinating Rhythm," testifies to the irresistibility of modern popular music at its best. A songbird happens to fly into a cabaret where jazz is being performed, and likes what he hears. After heading home, he tells the other birds that their songs are hopelessly out of date and it's time they learned to syncopate; "a little jazz bird is in heaven when it's singing blue." It appears that Gershwin wanted to put a stamp on the songs of *Lady, Be Good!* that would reflect their American provenance while also identifying them with the Jazz Age generation—and blues music, which could carry either a serious or a comic effect, was coming to be a distinctive marker of the time.

Lady, Be Good! proved a major success, with 330 performances in a forty-one-week run on Broadway, followed by a national tour. In 1926, the show was produced in London with some changes, but still featuring the Astaires, and it enjoyed a lengthy run there as well. Aarons and Freedley's intent was made clear by the contract Gershwin signed on September 30, 1924: "Whereas the Managers desire to secure the services of the Composer, for the purpose of composing the complete score for a Musical Comedy, in which the Managers desire to present Fred and Adele Astaire." No title or librettist is mentioned, just the stars. George Gershwin was paid $250 to sign the contract; once performances began, he received 2 percent (Ira's take was 1 percent) of the weekly box-office receipts, less than half of what each Astaire earned. Whatever the take-home pay, Aarons and Freedley's *Lady, Be Good!* had brought to Broadway two pairs of transcendent, family-based talents whose artistry set a new standard on the musical stage for years to come.

A YEAR IN THE LIFE, PART I (1924–25)

LESTER DONAHUE, A CLASSICAL PIANIST with connections to New York City's café society, wrote a brief recollection in 1938 looking back on a friendship with George Gershwin that had begun some fifteen years earlier. Donahue named 1924 as the year when the composer became a household name, thanks to "the *Rhapsody* heard 'round the world." In some of those households, the man himself was entertaining such English guests as Beatrice Lillie, Gertrude Lawrence, and Noël Coward—and "George's *Rhapsody* became the theme-song for all these occasions." The range of talents Gershwin drew upon in the salons of New York may be seen as both a reflection of his professional work and a template for its future.[1]

On November 15, two nights before *Lady, Be Good!* began its tryout run in Philadelphia, Paul Whiteman and his orchestra played for an overflow audience in Carnegie Hall, their concert again including Gershwin and his *Rhapsody in Blue*. Local critics had weighed in on the piece nine months earlier, but on this occasion a respected voice from overseas was also heard. The British music critic Ernest Newman, serving a stint at the *Evening Post* while on leave from London's *Sunday Times*, singled out the concert's only substantial piece:

> Mr. Gershwin's Rhapsody is by far the most interesting thing of its kind I have yet met with; it really has ideas and they work themselves out in a way that interests the musical hearer. Perhaps it is better not to prophesy. What is at present certain is that Mr. Gershwin has written something for a Jazz orchestra that is really music, not a mechanical box of tricks.[2]

Gershwin's multitasking continued into December. On the 1st *Lady, Be Good!* opened in New York, and on the 4th Whiteman's musicians performed at Symphony Hall in Boston, with the composer himself playing his *Rhapsody*. Henry Taylor Parker's Boston review highlighted the " 'devil-may-care' spirit which should be spice and life to American jazz. . . . For the hour, [Gershwin] is the beginning, and also the end, of the jazz-music that deserves to be."[3] Like some critics before him, including Deems Taylor, W. J. Henderson, and Henry O. Osgood, Parker was intrigued by the artistic potential an orchestra like Whiteman's held for American music, and for modern music as a whole. So far, however, Gershwin seemed the only composer able to seize with authority the artistic freedom that Whiteman's ensemble proclaimed.

As the world of musical comedy and the tiny fiefdom of symphonic jazz continued on their separate paths, a new artistic prospect came to public notice. On November 18, the day after *Lady, Be Good!* opened in Philadelphia, the *New York Evening Mail* reported, with an eye-catching headline—"Wanted: Jazz Grand Opera"— that investment banker Otto Kahn, chairman of the board of New York's Metropolitan Opera, had raised the possibility of a jazz opera. It would be produced at the Met, and three composers were under consideration: Jerome Kern, Irving Berlin, and George Gershwin. Kern, the trio's senior figure, did not rule out Kahn's idea, nor did he rise to the bait. Berlin, while warmly embracing the notion of such a project, declined to take part. "I have talked syncopated opera a long time," he was quoted in the article, "and I'd give my right arm to be able to do it. But I don't feel that I'm equipped for the work."[4]

Gershwin, on the other hand, found Kahn's proposal both appealing and thought-provoking. While Kern had little experience composing instrumental music or orchestrating for the stage, and the self-taught Berlin required a musical secretary to notate his songs, Gershwin, during the past half-dozen years, had been learning the technical skills that classical composition demanded. Kern and Berlin, both in their late thirties, had settled into lucrative careers as songwriters; Gershwin, having established himself as a songwriter, had recently made an impact as a composer-pianist, too. If, as he prepared for the debut of *Lady, Be Good!*, he had found time beyond that to contemplate his professional future, Kahn's call for a jazz opera gave him more to think about.[5]

On November 26, Ira Gershwin closed a letter to Lou and Emily Paley with a plea for a long reply. He got one—a nine-page typewritten dispatch, dated January 10, from Paris. Lou had taken a sabbatical from his teaching job in Manhattan, and the couple were spending the academic year in Europe, chiefly in France. An avid wordsmith, song lyricist, jokester, lover of puns, and self-styled intellectual, Lou Paley was the author of this remarkable document: a travel journal of sorts, written in the ranting voice of an eccentric devoted to exaggerations and lies worthy of a picaresque novel. The letter offers a window on the kind of banter that must have flowed over the years at the Paleys' Saturday evening get-togethers.

On the subject of his shipboard journey, Paley explained how dietary preparation had enabled him to avoid abdominal troubles:

Alors, as I was saying in my impeccable French, the trip thus far
has been . . . a wow, or any multiple thereof. D'abord (there I
go again) I was immune to seasickness, thanks to my Jewish
training. Kugel, Tzmiss, Borscht, Schav, Chulunt, Blintzes,
Miltz (just like mother's), Laahx (who asked you?), Bub, Hayse
Arbess, and a slew, a cold slew, so to speak, of Yiddish trainers
had conditioned me and made me fit.

The ship docked in the port of Cherbourg, where the Paleys
observed

> whores, prostitutes, harlots, strumpets, demireps, trollops, baggages,
> cocottes, courtesans, and a fair sprinkling of street walkers. Real
> bargains—but I refrained, saving my shopping for Paris where the
> selection is greater. We left Cherbourg in the company of several
> Catholic priests, who also were going to do their shopping later.

The scenic trip from Cherbourg to Paris was revisited in a stream
of gag lines (the group had seen "little donkeys on the hillsides" and
gotten "a real kick" out of them). Finally, "Paris at last!"

> I hesitate to write about that glorious city. Dostoevsky has done it
> so much better in "Brothers Karamazov" and in "Crime and Pun-
> ishment"; Karl Marx so beautifully in "Das Kapital"; and Carl
> Sand[burg]—so photographically in "Chicago Poems"; not to speak
> of those others, —Sholem Ash, in his "Motke Goneff." . . . And yet
> I feel somehow, that they all missed something. Dare I say it? Yes, I
> dare. They all held out in their various writings, on the poignancy of
> Paris. . . . They did miss its poignancy, even if it was only by a hair. I
> got it, of course, because I have no hair to miss it by.

Paley's letter continues in a posturing vein for several more pages.
Then, at the very end, the writer assumes a new tone, lyric and sincere.

Blinding sun on yellow, pink and white stucco houses; villas, brilliant facades of splendid hotels; beautiful gals, girls, and gels; automobiles, Rolls Royces, Hispano-Suizas, Sizaire Berwicks, Voisin, and Panhards; Tunisian rug-sellers; shops, Poiret, Patou, Lanvin, and Molyneux; Rajahs, Dukes, (Grand Russian) Dukes, (Grand Street) and their entwhoreage; scandals, fortunes won and lost; and suicides; bands of music in the open, kiss in the open, piss in the open and that and this in the open; The Blue Mediterranean throbbing continually a seaside accompaniment to it all; . . . and threaded through this fantastic embroidery of new scenes is the memory of loved friends. Emily and I keep praying that we are hemstitched even slightly in your memory.[6]

It took Ira until June to respond to Lou's letter.

Dear Lou and Em (and vice versa),
If you haven't heard from me up to now, it's your own fault. That novel, which you modestly called a letter, discouraged me. Ev'ry (excuse it, please—that comes from writing songs)—Every time I wanted to write you (and I have wanted to write almost every other day for the past six months), a vision of fourteen pages of typewriting floated before me. In the time it would have taken me to write a not altogether unworthy response (that is, of course, if I could), I could have done two shows. Well, the answer is, I didn't write, and Tell Me More! was the result. However, after seeing some weekly box office statements of the same, I know I should have written you.[7]

Composing the score for the new musical comedy *Tell Me More*, which opened on Broadway in April and shortly thereafter in London, was only one of a variety of fronts on which George Gershwin was active in the early months of 1925. On February 3, he signed a two-year contract with the Aeolian Company that called for nine recordings per year. A decade earlier the Standard Music Roll Company had paid him $5 per roll; now for each recording he would receive $166.67. Aeolian's main stake in this arrangement lay in its desire for a recording of the *Rhapsody in Blue*. Part II of the *Rhapsody*, issued in May, was the firm's first Gershwin release.

In April Gershwin also accepted a commission from the New York Symphony Orchestra, conducted by Walter Damrosch, to write and perform a new concerto for piano and orchestra. The contract specified that Gershwin was to supply a complete orchestral score; this time, every element of the composition would be his own. That same month Gershwin expounded his thoughts about writing an opera, which by then had taken a decisive turn, in an article published in *Musical America*. He envisioned a wholly original "Negro opera. . . . Negro, because it is not incongruous for a Negro to like jazz. It would not be absurd on the stage. The mood could change from ecstasy to lyricism plausibly, because the Negro has so much of both in his nature." Opera singers with conventional classical instruction and experience could not sing such music, he believed, but African American singers could. Eighteen months before encountering DuBose Heyward's novella *Porgy*, Gershwin had pondered Otto Kahn's idea of an American jazz opera and decided that such a work should be centered upon and performed by black Americans—and rather than in an opera house, it ought to be produced in a theater for musical comedy.[8]

For all the opportunities Gershwin explored early in 1925, musical comedy had been the keystone of his career for some time, and so it remained. As *Lady, Be Good!* had been a vehicle for Adele and Fred Astaire, so *Tell Me More* was designed for Lou Holtz, a comic actor from vaudeville who had enjoyed success on Broadway. The new show's contract reflects Gershwin's rising status, paying him $500 at the outset plus 3 percent of the box-office receipts. Ira, who shared the duties of lyricist with Buddy DeSylva, received a $250 signing fee, and the two men split the lyricist's share of 1 percent of the box-office take.[9] There were other continuities with Gershwin's previous musical theater work: the show's producer was Alfred E. Aarons, father of Alex, first involved with Gershwin in *La-La-Lucille!* In London, a West End version of *Tell Me More* replaced *Primrose* and had the same English producers—George Grossmith and J. A. E. Malone—and music director—John Ansell—as well as several of the same stars, including Leslie Henson and Heather Thatcher. Fred Thompson, coauthor with Guy Bolton of *Lady, Be Good!*'s book, shared credit for the new show's libretto, this time collaborating with William K. Wells; Felix Edwardes served as stage director for both *Lady, Be Good!* and the London production of *Tell Me More,* and Sammy Lee directed ensembles and the dancing for both.

A brief tryout for *Tell Me More* began on April 6 at Nixon's Apollo Theatre in Atlantic City, and the Broadway opening at the Gaiety Theatre took place a week later. (The show's original title, *My Fair Lady,* was changed because it sounded too much like *Lady, Be Good!*) Generally speaking, most of the characters are cut from the same cloth as those in the preceding show—here, meeting at a New York masked ball, a Fifth Avenue millinery shop, and a fancy hotel in Newport, Rhode Island—and the plot once again traces the romantic ups and downs of three couples. Polo-playing Kenneth Dennison and once-wealthy Peggy Van de Leur taste love at first sight, then hit a bump in the road, but rediscover the magic just before the curtain falls. Peggy's brother Billy Smith and a plain shop girl named Bonnie marry offstage toward the end. The millinery's fast-talking, outrageous, and conspicuously Jewish manager, Monty Sipkin, played by Lou Holtz, and the aging heiress Jane Wallace maintain a partially hidden, hard-to-explain romantic connection despite the doubts of the other characters, and their own.

Holtz supplies much of the show's comedy. He introduces himself in "Mr. and Mrs. Sipkin," a song of self-celebration in 6/8 time sounding like a remake of *Primrose*'s "When Toby Is Out of Town." Holtz had made his mark in show business playing ethnic characters, whether a minstrel "darky" in blackface or a Jewish funny man, and his comic song—barely linked to the plot—in Act II, "In Sardinia on the Delicatessen," places him in the latter role, impersonating a Jewish waiter in Newport. Seemingly tailored for a New York audience and never published, the song is a flowing waltz about a town on the banks of the Delicatessen River, where, favored by breezes "spicy and balmy," the citizens can take their leisure by strolling "through the fields of salami."

Gershwin's score for *Tell Me More* drew general approbation from critics but no hint that it rivaled that of *Lady, Be Good!* Robert Benchley commented in *Life* magazine that "Mr. Gershwin's second-best is so much better than most others' best that there should be no complaint." He also noted that two of the show's numbers were based on folk songs. One, "My Fair Lady," sung by a male chorus, is beholden to "London Bridge Is Falling Down." The other is borrowed from a ballad—"I know a boarding house, far, far away, where they have pork and beans three times a day"—that Mark Twain had cited as far back as 1892.[10] While "My Fair Lady" has little to do with the plot, "Three Times a Day" furthers the romance of Kenneth and Peggy: meeting by chance at the masked ball, they immediately fall in love, but a skittish Peggy flees from that encounter, leaving her mask behind. After tracking her down, and explaining that he must leave New York for Newport, Kenneth vows that after his return she may expect his presence on her doorstep "three times a day," and maybe even four. With its arching phrases, the song supports a lyric promise with music conveying true affection.

The show's first number, "Tell Me More," taps an emotional vein—that of memory—more akin to operetta than musical comedy. At the masked ball, Kenneth and Peggy confess a déjà vu sense of having shared each other's company before. The title phrase embodies the empathy they share from the moment they meet. Introduced memorably in this first song, the three-note "tell me more" motive is reprised often thereafter, as a way of signaling assent between characters.

The show's most explosive song is the rhythm number "Kickin' the Clouds Away," sung and danced toward the end of Act I by Monty and Jane, plus a female chorus. Jane, preparing to leave New York for a vacation with her parents in Newport, has been stewing about how to include Monty in the vacation party. Her plan is to invite Peggy and then have Monty drop by, pretending to be Peggy's brother. "Do you think you could be British?" asks Jane, and Monty quickly assures her that he can. (As will become clear later, he mistakenly thinks she said "Yiddish.") He and Jane celebrate the moment with a lively song and dance. By the time the refrain is delivered, audience members have already heard its melody twice: first in the overture, and then, as the curtain rises on the masked ball, from the dance floor. Critic Alexander Woollcott dubbed this song one of Gershwin's "rhythmic anarchies."[11]

As well as being a rhythm number, "Kickin' the Clouds Away" is the only song in *Tell Me More* grounded in the blues—indeed, it embodies the therapeutic idea that this music can dispel glum feelings. The refrain is a sophisticated and musically complex entity built around a blues bass and a syncopated melodic figure that infuses many 2/2 ragtime melodies: an eighth note on the downbeat followed by a quarter note and another eighth note, and then a half note. Short repeated figures like this one have come to be known as riffs in jazz parlance. As Berlin's "Alexander's Ragtime Band" summoned folks to "come on and hear" some compelling music, and then to "come on along" to meet the bandleader, so Gershwin's refrain—though with different declamation—urges: "Come on along! / You can't go wrong! / Kickin' the clouds away." Like "Fascinating Rhythm" in *Lady, Be Good!*, the song serves to display the dancing energies of the cast.

In Monty and Jane's later duet "Why Do I Love You?," Jane admits in the verse that her once rosy view of romantic passion has faded. Based on Monty's response, not to mention the plot of the entire show, Jane's life would be simpler if she had fallen in love with somebody else. She's anxious about Monty's shortcomings as a suitor, and he gives no hint that the quality of their relationship interests him much; his self-regard, fed by a childlike blend of charm and carelessness, protects him from worry. Gershwin's peppy music, seeming not to take this love affair seriously, reflects Monty's attitude more than it does Jane's. The effect is one of mismatched lovers.

On April 18, only a few days after the show's Broadway debut, Gershwin sailed for England to help oversee the London production of *Tell Me More*, scheduled for a May opening. His trip marked the third consecutive year that a theatrical project had drawn him there. As he settled into the customs of London's musical theater scene during these years, he also made an impression in the city's social circles, where he was accepted as a uniquely gifted artist whose talents enriched the theater and whose fondness for entertaining at the piano made him a valued and congenial guest.

As it happened, Eva Gauthier was also in London at the time, and on May 22 Gershwin joined her in a recital repeating the program she had sung in 1923 in New York and early the next year in Boston. After the concert, cousins of King George V, Lord and Lady Carisbrooke, threw a party. "It was Gershwin's first meeting with royalty," Gauthier wrote later, "and it was as if he had always belonged there. With his charm and talent he made the party alive and interesting and had everyone around the piano as he sang and played all his latest songs and dance hits." She also noted that the dose of Tin Pan Alley in her recital's musical mix was rather "too much of a jolt for the English—too radical an innovation. . . . It took nine recitals before I could make them forgive me."[12]

With a run of 264 performances, *Tell Me More* proved a greater success in London than in New York, where it had closed in July after just 100. Gershwin changed relatively little in the score, but he did write three new songs for the London version: "Have You Heard," a song for Monty to replace "In Sardinia"; and two waltzes, "Love, I Never Knew," a soliloquy for Peggy, and the comic "Murderous Monty (and Light-Fingered Jane)," a list song devoted to criminal services. These were two very different approaches to waltz time. "Love, I Never Knew," with its Viennese rhythmic inflections, harmonic richness, and flexible declamation, proved an apt way to deliver a statement with its share of emotional complexity. "Murderous Monty" achieved its comic purpose through a strict oom-pah-pah beat and steady streams of quarter notes, with nary a dotted rhythm within earshot.

A YEAR IN THE LIFE, PART II (CONCERTO IN F)

When Paul Whiteman's orchestra premiered the *Rhapsody in Blue* in February 1924, Walter Damrosch was one of many luminaries in the audience. Toward the end of the piece he is said to have sat with his hands ready to clap the moment the music stopped, and then was the first to call out a hearty bravo. But however much he may have been impressed by the *Rhapsody*, he also had an ulterior motive.

Damrosch, a native of Breslau, Germany, bore a proud musical pedigree. His father Leopold, an accomplished violinist and conductor, had founded New York's Oratorio Society in 1873 and then an orchestra of his own, the New York Symphony Society, in 1878, both of which Walter took over after his father died. From 1903, he led a restructured New York Symphony, which in 1928 merged with the New York Philharmonic, then led by Arturo Toscanini.[1] Violinist Winthrop Sargeant, who joined the Symphony in 1926 and later became music critic for the *New Yorker* magazine, left an indelible portrait of the orchestra in its last years of existence, when the musicians often played "one-night stands of symphonic music in prairie towns, mining camps and smaller cities where the local idea of concert music was otherwise represented by the tooting of the town band." Sargeant characterized Damrosch as a unique figure: a consummate musician possessed of "an absolute imperturbability" to the point that "if the theater blew up, it could be confidently predicted that he would be found somewhere in the wreckage calmly waving his baton."[2]

In retrospect, Damrosch's decision to commission from George Gershwin what became the *Concerto in F* seems a canny maneuver. By the 1920s, faced with the task of holding its own against tough competition, his orchestra was programming a greater variety of music than the rival Philharmonic, and a modern piece that might spark public excitement could be something of a coup. In 1925, Gershwin was the ideal composer-pianist to bring attention and a touch of glamour to the ensemble's season. At the same time, risks were involved. How technically well prepared was he to write a multi-movement, classically oriented composition? Was his command of harmony solid? Could he handle the formal demands of a concerto, and could he really compose for a symphony orchestra—would he not need to learn more about orchestral instruments and the art of orchestration?

Determined to meet these and other challenges, Gershwin found time for further study and plenty of composition during the months before April 1925, when he accepted Damrosch's commission. In an article for the March issue of *Vanity Fair*, Carl Van Vechten refers to two large-scale works Gershwin was already working on at that moment: a cycle of twenty-four piano preludes and a tone poem for orchestra, tentatively entitled *Black Belt*.[3] Gershwin's own words about the concerto's composition show that he was confident but realistic: "I started to write the Concerto in London, after buying four or five books on musical structure," he reported, "to find out what the concerto form actually was! And, believe me, I had to come through—because I had already signed a contract to play it seven times. It took me three months to compose this Concerto, and one month to orchestrate it."[4]

When Gershwin returned home from the U.K. early in July, he focused on the concerto. Van Vechten's diary for the summer and fall provides glimpses of his progress. On August 27, for example, "Alfred and Blanche Knopf [the publishers] gave a party for Noël Coward . . . and George played several of his tunes, the *Rhapsody* and a long passage (possibly a complete movement) from the *Concerto in F.*" In September he and Bill Daly played two movements of the new piece for the Van Vechtens.[5] And by November 10, Gershwin had completed the orchestration of his first "symphonic work." Sometime in the next ten days he "engaged fifty-five musicians to read it for me. Charles Dillingham generously gave me the use of the Globe Theatre for this private tryout. Mr. Damrosch, Ernest Hutcheson, and several other musician friends were there, and you can imagine my delight when it sounded just as I had planned."[6] Gershwin later pointed to this occasion as his greatest thrill in a career full of noteworthy moments: the first time he had ever heard a symphony orchestra play his own orchestrated music. With Daly conducting the run-through, "I played the piano myself, and was listening, as it were with the multiple ears of the audience." He was not the only delighted listener: "You should have seen Doctor Damrosch when it was played. He was like a child. He liked it."[7]

As November came to an end, the conductor who had commissioned Gershwin's new piece, and would lead its premiere, addressed the public with his own fanciful tale of what the young composer had wrought:

Various composers of to-day have been walking around jazz like a cat around a plate of very hot soup—waiting for it to cool off so they could enjoy it without burning their tongues, hitherto accustomed only to the more tepid liquid distilled by cooks of the classical school. Lady Jazz, adorned with her intriguing rhythms, has danced her way around the world, even as far as the Eskimos of the North and the Polynesians of the South Sea Isles. But for all her travels and sweeping popularity she has encountered no knight who could lift her to a level that would enable her to be received as a respectable member in musical circles.

George Gershwin seems to have at last accomplished this miracle. He has done it by boldly dressing this extremely independent and up to date young lady in the classic garb of a concerto. Yet he has not detracted one whit from her fascinating personality. He is the prince who has taken Cinderella by the hand and openly proclaimed her a princess to the astonished world, no doubt to the fury of her envious sisters.[8]

As New Yorkers ruminated on Damrosch's imaginings, the prince in question was out of town with the cast of his latest musical comedy: *Tip-Toes*, from the shop of Aarons and Freedley. During a rehearsal conversation in Washington, he told a reporter for the *New York World* that the country needed "American forms for American music." He explained, "I wrote this concerto in that form, because Mr. Damrosch was interested in my rhapsody and wanted me to write in a form that could be used by his orchestra. . . . I got out my books and studied up on the 'concerto' style and then wrote." As an orchestrator he aimed to coax original sounds out of standard instruments, as in the second movement's "new combination of three clarinets and a muted trombone that give the effect of steam whistles in the far distance."[9]

During the same interview Gershwin also cited the Great Divide in American music, as he saw it, noting that he had composed only three real "opuses": *Blue Monday*, *Rhapsody in Blue*, and the new concerto. Gershwin's inclusion of the operatic sketch from the *Scandals of 1922* on his (very short) list of works in classical forms affirms his belief in its value, as well as its character—a belief shared by Paul Whiteman, who decided to present it in a new arrangement by Ferde Grofé at a Carnegie Hall concert in December. More to the point, however, is Gershwin's sense of accomplishment in these pieces: "I tell you that it requires real bravery to write works like those and know that one is breaking rules and set forms and that much adverse comment will probably be aroused." It is no surprise that the Globe Theatre run-through of the *Concerto in F* in November left him feeling exhilarated. After composing a sketch performed in a Broadway arranger's scoring, and a rhapsody orchestrated by a conductor's arranging wizard, he now could claim a concerto for piano and symphony orchestra for which he had invented every sound.

DURING 1925, Gershwin's "year that was," witnessing the quantitative peak of his creative output, he also wrote his first article on music. The August issue of *Theatre Magazine* carried "Our New National Anthem": a measured response, he announced, to the "controversy" over the impact of jazz music raging "back and forth" on the American scene.[10]

The author begins by stating that, in fact, jazz is no divisive force posing a threat to musical artistry, but a fresh American idiom likely to be "absorbed" eventually "into the great musical tradition as all other forms of music have been absorbed" into classical Western music. Pointing to his own *Rhapsody in Blue*, he explains that its jazz flavor is employed "almost incidentally, just as I employ syncopation." The *Rhapsody*, he writes, being grounded in "the melody, harmony, and counterpoint as every great composer of the past has employed them," has therefore found a way to express the richness of American life. Denying "the superstition that jazz is essentially Negro," he views jazz music from a broader perspective, as "the spontaneous expression of the nervous energy of modern American life."

The next paragraph of Gershwin's article announces that the jazz impulse has mirrored the evolution of "all dances of the past."

"Beginning with crudity and vulgarity," he writes, "it has gradually been freeing itself and moving towards a higher plane." However, since "we are living in an age of staccato, not legato," the challenge for composers has been to create "something beautiful" without compromising the music's vitality. Citing New York's landscape as an analogy, Gershwin recalls earlier attacks on the "ugliness of the early skyscraper architecture," forgotten now in light of the Woolworth Tower and "the new Hotel Shelton" (now the Marriott East Side Hotel).

Gershwin then moves on to the predicament of bringing music grounded in unwritten practices into an arena where performers are trained to follow musical notation scrupulously. "It is almost impossible to write down definitely, exactly, the effects" that enliven jazz performance, he warns, "with the result that the musicians are only too apt to exaggerate their expression." Therefore, it is up to the conductor to "rule the musicians' fancy with an iron hand":

> Indeed, when a conductor undertakes to direct a work in which jazz plays an important part, he must be even more jealous of the composer's intention than if he were conducting a classical symphony. Once give the musicians their head with jazz, and in a short while they will evolve something which the author himself will fail to recognize as his own offspring.

The outlook of Gershwin's article is sophisticated. Perhaps in the wake of recent stays in London and a visit to France, he had observed parallels between American vernacular music and broader Western traditions. As country dances expressed peasant life in the nations of central Europe, and as the minuet reflected the "stately grace" of lives centered at Versailles, so did popular dances such as the Charleston express the spirit of present-day America, which he found dominated by a "nervous, somewhat unthinking vitality." Jazz music was considered "Negro" music in the United

States, Gershwin granted, but he considered that claim exaggerated. "The Negroes, of course, take to jazz," he conceded, "but in its essence it is no more Negro than is syncopation, which exists in the music of all nations." The "opus" he was starting to compose, he reported, would seek to bring "the nervous energy of modern American life" into a musical realm devoted to the artistry of the cosmopolitan West.

In light of these observations it is no surprise that Gershwin accompanied the *Concerto in F* with his first program note. Brief as it is, it offers a frame for listeners. And it implies that a full-fledged concerto for piano and symphony orchestra can deliver more information and pleasure to listeners who have been alerted to what they're about to hear.

> The first movement employs the Charleston rhythm. It is quick and pulsating, representing the young enthusiastic spirit of American life. It begins with a rhythmic motif given out by the kettle drums, supported by other percussion instruments, and with a Charleston motif introduced by bassoons, horns, clarinets, and violins. The principal theme is announced by the bassoon. Later a second theme is introduced by the piano.
>
> The second movement has a poetic, nocturnal tone. It utilizes the atmosphere of what has come to be referred to as the American blues, but in a purer form than that in which they are usually treated.
>
> The final movement reverts to the style of the first. It is an orgy of rhythm starting violently and keeping to the same pace throughout.
>
> George Gershwin.[11]

Beyond the formality of a written statement, Gershwin was given to commenting about his compositions when asked about them. In a

Washington newspaper article published before the new work's premiere, a reporter covering the tryout run of a new musical comedy
quotes the composer on the proportions of the *Concerto in F*, now
forthcoming. "'The whole work takes thirty minutes to perform,
but I've divided it,' and here he shows the innate sense of the true
showman, 'I've divided it so that the first movement lasts fifteen
minutes, then it comes down to ten minutes for the andante and
only five minutes for the finale.'"[12]

Though never embraced as universally as the *Rhapsody in Blue*,
the *Concerto in F* came to be a landmark in Gershwin's life as a
composer—proof of how his artistic world broadened in the wake
of the *Rhapsody*. For all its cosmopolitan breadth and bravura, the
Concerto teems with rhythms and tunes grounded in the popular song and dance of an American "age of staccato," beginning
with sound and rhythm rather than melody. Gershwin jolts the
ear with a percussive announcement from the timpani, followed by
the Charleston rhythm, a motif often in the air in December 1925.
That unmistakable jazz element then inspires varied melodies that
listeners would hear as Charleston-based. Since he was composing
the score for *Tip-Toes* at the same time, it's no surprise that the concerto's first theme and the song "Sweet and Low-Down" from the
musical reveal clear similarities.

In the second movement, which to Damrosch conveyed the
"dreamy atmosphere of a summer night in a garden of our South,"
blues music is enlisted in the service of melodic beauty. Blue notes
color all the important melodies in this rondo-form (ABACA)
movement, and the twelve-bar harmonic cycle is a telling formal
element. There could hardly be a clearer example of the composer's belief that jazz-based music can take on beauty when refined in
the "laboratory" of his own imagination. The finale that Gershwin
called "an orgy of rhythm," with reprises from earlier movements,
sails by at a swift but less than headlong pace.

. . .

THE CONCERTO IN F premiered in Carnegie Hall on the cold and rainy afternoon of Thursday, December 3, as part of a subscription concert put on by the New York Symphony Orchestra. The hall was packed. The concerto arrived at the end of a program that included Alexander Glazunov's Symphony No. 5 and *Suite Anglais* by Henri Rabaud, comprised of old English music arranged for orchestra. Damrosch and his wife hosted a party that evening attended by, among others, pianist Lester Donahue, who later remembered guests debating whether or not Gershwin should abandon Broadway for symphony and opera. Damrosch thought he should, but "the lure of the lighter forms in which [Gershwin] had become such a master, proved too strong."[13]

Reviews of the concerto were a mixed bag. W. J. Henderson of the *Sun* called the composition

> a direct outcoming of the jazz growth. It shouts the voice of the jazz orchestra. It revels in discord at times and it is bold, boisterous, plangent and even defiant. It has the moods of the contemporaneous dance without their banality. . . . Strangely enough it very frequently reminds one of the frantic efforts of certain moderns. It drops into their language sometimes, but it has more to say.[14]

But Lawrence Gilman of the *Herald Tribune* felt that the concerto had turned out "conventional, trite, at its worst a little dull."[15] Another disappointed critic was Olin Downes of the *Times*, who judged the *Concerto in F* less original than the *Rhapsody in Blue*. "It is not only immature—which need be no crime—but it is self-conscious, lacking the esprit and the felicity of touch that he shows when he is truly in the creative vein." Nevertheless, Downes concluded that it only required "more experience and skill than Gershwin now possesses to accomplish what he attempted."[16] The most enthusiastic critic was the *World*'s Samuel Chotzinoff: "George Gershwin is a genius—perhaps the only one of all the younger men who are trying with might and main to express the modern spirit. . . . He is the present, with all its audacity, impertinence, its feverish delight in its motion, its lapses into rhythmically exotic melancholy."[17]

Gershwin and Damrosch repeated the concert on Friday evening at Carnegie Hall, then the next week in Washington, Baltimore, and Philadelphia. Critical response in these cities prompted a range of opinions as broad as the ones in New York. The critic of the *Philadelphia Evening Bulletin*, comparing Gershwin's percussive tendencies with those of Stravinsky, judged the latter's music "dry, febrile and uninspired," while Gershwin's "fairly bubbles and overflows with lilting themes and ingenious instrumental writing."[18] As for W. G. Owst in Baltimore, he found the very idea of a "jazz concerto" a "degradation" of the art of music, and he managed to squeeze two extreme epithets—"degenerate cacophony" and "nauseous buffoonery"—into his plea that Damrosch's concert would prove to be "the first, last and only attempt" to inflict such noise on the public.[19]

Gershwin's contract with the New York Symphony called for two more concerts in 1926. The first, at the Brooklyn Academy of Music, was given on January 16—and the last, at the Mecca Auditorium in New York, almost a year later, on December 26. On the latter occasion, two critics who had aired their reservations on the *Concerto in F*'s quality after its premiere had a chance to revisit their first responses. Downes now judged the concerto "a solid piece of work," with "very definite ideas, extensively transformed and developed."[20] Lawrence Gilman gave Gershwin's piece credit for having survived a year in the orchestra's repertoire, and he looked forward to the day, two centuries hence, when learned program notes would need to illuminate for listeners "the origin of that archaic dance-form, the 'Charleston.'"[21]

Gershwin played the *Concerto in F* regularly to the end of his days, but, whatever the reason, he never recorded it.

. . .

GERSHWIN'S REPUTATION grew substantially during 1925. A May 6 *Variety* article previewed a series of "Revolutionary Concerts" planned by Paul Whiteman for the 1925–26 season, including the December performance of *Blue Monday*, now renamed *135th Street*. Later in May, a sizable Gershwin report appeared in a New York publication, *Home News*. Headlined "Critics Look to Harlem Composer to Write Music for Opera Portraying American Life," this anonymous piece quoted the composer as saying he was ready to begin work on the new opera as soon as he could find a suitable libretto. And near the end of the month, an unnamed journal carried a long piece by Katharan McCommon entitled "Gershwin, King of the Jazz Composers at 26, Says Piano Made Good Boy of Him."[22] This article places its subject "in the celebrity class," a standing confirmed that summer when Gershwin's picture appeared on the cover of *Time* magazine's July 20 issue. By this time in his career, whatever public statement he might offer, a member of the press corps would most likely be there to report it.

A clever sign of Gershwin's standing with New York's smart set appears in the October issue of *Vanity Fair*: a page of caricatures by Miguel Covarrubias under the heading "Prodigious Figures in the World of Music."[23] Seven are pictured: a patron, Otto Kahn; two violinists, Fritz Kreisler and Jascha Heifetz; two conductors, Leopold Stokowski and Serge Koussevitzky; and two composers, Stravinsky—plus Gershwin. An American, and the only one of those luminaries involved with popular music, Gershwin is the outsider, having drawn upon his talent, youth, and chutzpah to invade a realm seemingly off limits to a child of Tin Pan Alley and Broadway. And he had claimed a freedom from category that no other composer enjoyed. Where might George Gershwin take American music next? From this time forward his compositions were likely to be met with that question in mind.

A YEAR IN THE LIFE, PART III

DURING A THIRTY-FIVE-DAY STRETCH from the end of November 1925 to the dawn of the new year, three new Gershwin works were premiered in New York: the *Concerto in F*, the musical comedy *Tip-Toes*, and *Song of the Flame*, an operetta produced by Arthur Hammerstein. Moreover, *Blue Monday* was revived in new dress as *135th Street*, led by Paul Whiteman in a concert celebrating jazz at Carnegie Hall. Ferde Grofé rescored the orchestration by Will Vodery that in 1922 had been played by the *Scandals'* pit orchestra, and Buddy DeSylva, lacking a complete copy of *Blue Monday*, rewrote the words as best he could remember them. Gershwin's one-two punch of artistic command and audience appeal had proved potent enough to cross the lines dividing his various sponsors, but only a composer with a unique blend of skill and confidence would have undertaken such a schedule. As DeSylva wrote him on November 25, "You are surely on the crest of a wave."[1]

Produced by Aarons and Freedley, *Tip-Toes* is somewhat unusual in being built around a female character, "Tip-Toes" Kaye. Written by Guy Bolton and Fred Thompson, the show centers on the kind of young Americans, searching for love and money, who romp onstage in *Lady, Be Good!* and *Tell Me More.*

The main difference, however, is that Tip-Toes and her two relatives, Al and Hen Kaye, are a vaudeville trio bred from hardscrabble urban stock. Hailing from the seedy environs of New York City ("Greenpoint, near the gas tanks"), the Three Kayes have traveled to Palm Beach, Florida, to entertain at a lavish party. Tip-Toes is played by Queenie Smith, a skilled dancer, adequate singer, and appealing ingénue, and her partners are comedians who dance. (Hen Kaye claims that the soles of his shoes have worn so thin that when he stands on a coin, he knows whether it's heads or tails.) The plot hinges on the Kayes' effort to pass off Tip-Toes as a member of New York high society, in hopes of matching her romantically with an unattached millionaire. Step 1 happens soon enough when Tip-Toes meets Steve Burton, a wealthy young innocent. While Tip-Toes impersonates a rich girl, Steve, eager to be loved for himself and not for his $7 million business, pretends to have lost his fortune. In the end, despite a car accident, the heroine's bout of amnesia, and endless examples of the Kaye family's lack of courtliness, Tip-Toes and Steve embrace their true identities and vow eternal devotion.

Parallels with *Lady, Be Good!* include a star who's primarily a dancer, several effective dance numbers directed by Sammy Lee, and Gershwin's sparkling, energetic score. Beginning its tryout in Washington on November 24, *Tip-Toes* spent a month on the road before opening on December 28 in New York. It clicked in all four tryout cities, enjoyed a successful run on Broadway, toured nationally, and in 1926 crossed the Atlantic and won approval on the London stage.

The show also proved to be Ira Gershwin's personal moment of professional arrival. In *Lady, Be Good!*, Ira judged that he had "adequately fitted some sparkling tunes, and several singable love songs and rhythm numbers had resulted," but he still felt that these songs owed their success mainly to the music. His aspirations ran higher, and it is telling that he took the comic song as the true test of the lyricist's craftsmanship. He singled out one number in particular from *Tip-Toes*, the trio "These Charming People," sung by the Three Kayes as they pretend to be members of the socially lofty Van Rensselaer clan from New York. Though comically inept at impersonating society folk, Tip-Toes, Al, and Hen exude confidence. The verse's words flow with fluent predictability, in an **aabccb** rhyme scheme that invited the audience to respond on cue with a laugh:

> AL: We must make it our ambition
> To live up to our position
> As we take our places in society.
> HEN: When those million-dollar blokes pass,
> I will never make a faux pas;
> I will show them I am full of pedigree.

Beyond such laugh lines, Ira's lyrics also fill in the outlines of the characters cavorting onstage.[2] When the Three Kayes arrive in Palm Beach, they are greeted by Rollo Metcalf, whose wife Sylvia has hired them to entertain at a party in honor of her brother Steve Burton. The unexpected appearance of Tip-Toes jars Rollo, who once made a pass at her up north. Fearing now that Sylvia will learn of his indiscretion, he informs the Kayes that the party has been canceled, but they decide to stay anyway. Tip-Toes sings "Looking for a Boy," a soliloquy reflecting a love life that has so far been unfulfilling and demonstrating the expressive power of legato music.

A more enlivened song, sung by Tip-Toes and Steve together, is "That Certain Feeling," a sequel of sorts to "Looking for a Boy" and one crackling with vitality. The song lives on rests and repeated notes; a short eighth-note rest before some lines in the **a** sections of an **aaba** refrain produces an effect that has been described as "kicking" the rhythm. In the bridge, where the harmony sounds stuck for three bars, Ira has Steve admit that Tip-Toes' easy charm has left him speechless. The couple's final duet takes place on a yacht, after her Van Rensselaer masquerade has been exposed. Steve has hosted a party, and all the guests except Tip-Toes have gone home. Having found separate beds to sleep in, remaining loyal to musical comedy's moral code, the pair sing "Nightie-Night," giving Ira a chance to add lullaby-making to his portfolio.

The show's one full-fledged dance number in the mold of "Fascinating Rhythm" and "Kickin' the Clouds Away" is "Sweet and Low-Down," sung by Denise, a dance teacher hired to coach Steve, her colleague Binnie, and Al Kaye at the Blues Café, where the band plays "nothing but the low down." This song about dancing is steeped in the spirit of modern jazz, with a dose of the Charleston rhythm thrown in. Ira took pride in the verbal twist behind the title phrase. His starting point, "Sweet and Low" by Victorian composer Joseph Barnby, was a classic English lullaby with words by Alfred, Lord Tennyson, well known in the Anglo-American world. The connotative gap between the lullaby's gentle sweet-and-low and the Blues Café's earthy, sensual sweet-and-low-down delivered its own delight. As noted earlier, the song also shares a gesture with the *Concerto in F*—the archlike bassoon opening, whose rhythm is duplicated in such phrases as "Grab a cab and go down."

If *Tip-Toes* marked the end of Ira's apprenticeship, his confidence must also have been fortified by a letter he received several months into the show's New York run. The writer was Lorenz Hart, who had recently won praise for the lyrics of *The Garrick Gaieties*, with music by Richard Rodgers. Ira's lyrics, he wrote,

> gave me as much pleasure as Mr. George Gershwin's music, and the
> utterly charming performance of Miss Queenie Smith. I have heard
> none so good this many a day. Such delicacies as your jingles prove
> that songs can be both popular and intelligent. May I take the liberty
> of saying that your rhymes show a healthy improvement over those in

Lady, Be Good! You have helped a lot to make an evening delightful to me—and I am very grateful. Thank you! And may your success continue![3]

Critical response during the tryout phase was for the most part enthusiastic. The production had "class written all over it, from the costuming to the stage settings—and back again," wrote John J. Daly in a Washington newspaper.[4] Critic Leonard Hall called Sammy Lee the real star of the show for having staged "some of the most elegant dance numbers ever seen under roof, canvas or the blue canopy of Heaven—with the assistance of a super-chorus of active and ambitious pippins." Hall judged Gershwin's music "now pretty, now itchy, with the strange broken rhythms he fancies."[5] In Philadelphia, a critic wrote of "These Charming People" that it possessed "the best lines of any patter song since P. G. Wodehouse stopped turning out lyrics for Jerome Kern's tunes."[6] The show was in Newark when Gershwin premiered his *Concerto in F* in Carnegie Hall, and Queenie Smith took the trouble to send a telegram to the composer from across the river: "NIZE BABY EAT OP ALL THE MUSIC LOVERS HEARTS."[7]

When *Tip-Toes* opened in New York at the Liberty Theatre on December 28, the critics gave it a slightly less unanimous embrace. The *Times* found Gershwin's music "average pretty-pretty," ruled the cast "serviceable," and rapped the librettists for not giving the performers better lines—especially the comedians.[8] But Alexander Woollcott, writing for the *New York World*, saw *Tip-Toes* as "Gershwin's evening" above all else.

Bright and gay and good-looking the new musical comedy which came to the Liberty last night is made altogether captivating by the pretty, rebel, infectious music of George Gershwin—all told the best score he has written in his days in the theatre, all told, I think, the best score any one has written for our town this season.

He praised "These Charming People" for "its unblinking determination to rhyme 'enjoy it' with 'Detroit.'" From his perspective,
however, the show reached a high point "when, to the lisping of a
hundred tapping feet in 'Sweet and Low-Down,' a forest of trombones suddenly added their moans. Then the Liberty Theatre quietly but firmly went mad."⁹

A discovery made in 1982, when many of the orchestra parts
from the show's first run were found in a New Jersey warehouse, has
allowed modern listeners to hear what *Tip-Toes* may have sounded
like in a theater of the day. In 1998, to mark the hundredth anniversary of Gershwin's birth, Carnegie Hall, in cooperation with the
Library of Congress, put on a concert version that amounted to a
reconstruction based on original sources. Rob Fisher conducted the
performance, which was then recorded and commercially distrib-
uted.¹⁰ In a booklet issued with the recording, Fisher describes the
scholarly demands of the reconstruction, which began

> by reconciling original programs and scripts with the existing
> musical materials. The orchestra parts were transcribed into a full
> score, which revealed some places where instruments were missing
> measures. Any blank spots were then filled in. Often, where the
> scoring was incomplete in one part of the show, the missing ele-
> ments were found in another passage.

The orchestra included flute, oboe, two clarinets, bassoon, two
French horns, two trumpets, trombones, two pianos, percussion, six
violins, two violas, cello, and double bass. The piano parts, which
made the timbre unique, were the least complete part of the score.

> In some numbers, a part was found for one or the other of the
> two pianos. Arden and Ohman recorded four of the songs from
> Tip-Toes with their own orchestra, featuring extensive duo-piano
> passages. These were transcribed and used at various points in

the score. There were also recordings of George Gershwin playing some of these songs, which provided pianistic ideas that were incorporated. When there were no clues at all, one of our two pianists, Joseph Thalken, wrote duo-parts that he and John Musto later perfected.

The existence of a recording of the music of *Tip-Toes* by musicians who have enacted the show for live audiences adds a fresh Gershwinian element to the realm of America's theatrical soundscape.

As IF the December calendar to which Gershwin had committed himself was not already hard to imagine, he also signed a contract that month with producer Arthur Hammerstein to complete—with librettist Otto Harbach, lyricist Oscar Hammerstein II (Arthur's nephew), and composer Herbert Stothart—the score for a new operetta, with a huge cast and a European setting. Of the eleven new numbers supplied for *Song of the Flame*, which opened on Broadway before the end of the year, Gershwin and Stothart each composed three, and they shared credit for the remaining five. The score also included folk songs, especially in the arrangements sung by the Russian Art Choir, a New York City chorus more than fifty voices strong. *Song of the Flame* was intended to follow Arthur Hammerstein's highly successful *Rose-Marie*, a 1924 show whose creative team included Oscar Hammerstein II and Otto Harbach as colibrettists and lyricists, and Rudolf Friml and Stothart as cocomposers. Friml was at first on board to help write the score for *Song of the Flame*, but he pulled out of the project, and Gershwin was hired to replace him. How he managed the month of December remains a puzzle, but one truth emerges loud and clear: with half a dozen performances of the brand-new *Concerto in F* on his docket, he was surely free of performance anxiety.

Song of the Flame is a story of the Russian Revolution. Aniuta, an aristocrat posing as a washerwoman, becomes a figure akin to Joan of Arc, with her charismatic presence and idealism inspiring the Russian people to revolt against their rulers; her song of rebellion, "The Song of the Flame," is woven through the story. She falls in love with Volodya, a Russian prince, even though they stand on opposite sides of the divide that sparks the Revolution. Act I ends as open conflict breaks out, and Act II takes place two years later on New Year's Eve in Paris, where many displaced Russians now live, including Volodya. Aniuta, who had remained in Russia, arrives and is reunited with Volodya. The pair vow to return to Russia to fight together for the rights of the people.

Gershwin's involvement marks his only theatrical effort with Oscar Hammerstein, who would become one of musical theater's most influential figures. The Prologue he wrote with Harbach shows the distance between this work's sensibility and Gershwin's usual theatrical turf. The place is a street in Moscow; the time is an evening in March 1917. Konstantin, a revolutionary-minded character, is loudly regaling two men with his belief that a folk song being sung in a nearby hall is irrelevant to the times. "What Russia needs to learn is a new song," he proclaims, "a song that will help us bear the political snows that are chilling the hearts of our people." Aniuta, played by Tessa Kosta, takes over the platform: "Russia has had enough of wailing—she needs to learn a new song of life—of courage and of freedom!" As she begins "The Song of the Flame," her singing inspires her countrymen, who, long mired in oppression, yearn for freedom. The singers appearing onstage in this scene number roughly sixty, most of them members of the Russian Art Choir. As the number of singers grows, so does the song's power to change history.[11] The setting, the subject, the language, and the thinking of the characters—all were foreign to musical comedies of the day.

Out of context and unattributed, Aniuta's "Song of the Flame" seems improbable. With its wide melodic range—an eleventh;

minor-mode tonality; melodies that flirt with exotic augmented-second intervals; a climax marked "con fuoco, quasi eroico" (with fire, and heroically); and a refrain grounded in emotional display, the character of the music is hard to square with earlier melodies by Gershwin. And given that from mid-1924 on, the idea of a Gershwin song came to imply music and words in combination, fashioned by George and Ira, a number delivering such hortatory statements as "On! On! Follow the Flame!" could hardly seem less Gershwinian. Perhaps some of the number's non-Gershwinian traits can be traced to Stothart. More to the point, though, the song belongs to an operetta as opposed to a musical comedy. The composers wrote music in a style that would pass as "Russian," for voices of the Russian choir as well as for the operatic voice of Tessa Kosta. This was not the first time Gershwin had met a challenge along these lines; his revue scores had called for songs in a variety of styles, whether that of a South Sea Island or an oriental shrine.[12]

In another Stothart and Gershwin collaboration, "Cossack Love Song (Don't Forget Me)," sung by Aniuta and Volodya, the verse's lighter character departs from the refrain enough in style to suggest that verse and refrain were composed by different hands: the lilting verse, with each voice in this four-voice arrangement enjoying its own countermelodic moment, by Gershwin; and the forward-driving refrain, with its quarter-note empasis, by Stothart.

Except for Aniuta's brief "The Signal," the operetta's only published number composed by Gershwin alone—a rare chance to visit his family's ethnic heritage—is "Midnight Bells," heralding the arrival of the new year in Paris. Here the music abandons the Russian mannerisms and key of G minor that have pervaded much of the score to this point. As bells ring out across the city, the expatriate Russian community toasts the new year, and Aniuta, newly arrived from the motherland, sings this well-made number. Gershwin starts the verse with vocal onomatopoeia: "Ding Dong Ding Dong," each syllable sustained for four beats. When the refrain arrives, the whole notes move into the orchestra, the squareness of a bell-tolling rhythm softened by a melody line replete with triplets.

Nostalgia for the homeland reappears with a "Blossom Ballet," in which the fifty-three-member American Ballet Company shared the stage with dancer Ula Sharon. Brooks Atkinson of the *Times* described it as perhaps the signature scene of an impressive theatrical performance:

> On the dance floor of a Parisian cabaret whirls an entrancing ballet, symbolic of Russia's long Winter of adversity and the first flush of vernal peace. As soon as the gleaming white costumes of that number have vanished, two segments of the rear settings part, discovering a Russian choir in the rich trappings of the peasantry. And with perfect attack and enunciation they sing folk-tunes of their vast and youthful land. Rarely does "Song of the Flame" blend the elements of music and scenery so effectively.[13]

Half a dozen folk songs were arranged for this climactic performance by the Russian Art Choir: "I Was There," "The Song of Gold," "Song of the Field," "Village Pines," "A Christmas Carol," and "Down the Mother Volga."

Song of the Flame, cited as "a romantic opera," drew positive, often highly enthusiastic reviews. Opening at the 44th Street Theatre on December 30, it ran on Broadway until July 10, 1926, logging 219 performances in all. Frank Vreeland of the *World-Telegram* noted that, with the opening of *Tip-Toes* on Broadway, the days from December 25 to January 1 could be called "Gershwin week just as much as Christmas Week."

BLUE MONDAY's reappearance as *135th Street* at Carnegie Hall on the evening of December 29 was eagerly anticipated. It closed a Paul Whiteman Orchestra concert that, together with the customary novelties, included new works by composer-critic Deems Taylor—a suite entitled *Circus Day: Eight Pictures from Memory*—and by Ferde Grofé—*Mississippi (A Tone Journey)*. *135th Street's* only substantial difference from the 1922 version was the new arrangement for the Whiteman band, which offered greater sound variety—trumpets, trombones, tuba, timpani, strings, banjo, two pianos, and celeste—than had Will Vodery's version for the pit orchestra of the *Scandals*. Aside from the title, however, perhaps the biggest change was the standing of the composer, now a star who had publicly declared an interest in writing a full-length jazz opera. Whiteman had hired a cast that featured Blossom Seeley, a vaudeville headliner, as Vi and tenor Charles Hart as Joe, her lover. Seeley's husband, vaudevillian Benny Fields, played the role of Sam, and Jack McGowan, in the character of Tom, sang the Prologue, the part of the work closest to recitative, as he had in 1922. Racial representation was handled as it had been in the *Scandals*: the all-white cast played their roles in blackface.

A *New York Times* review affirmed that an aura of expectation and fulfillment hovered over the evening: the song Joe sang as his life ebbed away "echoed later in a street full of limousines [that] came surging to the carriage calls."[14] But other witnesses were less impressed. To S. Jay Kaufman of the *Telegram*, the drama seemed "so short that it never really began."[15] The *Sun* critic, probably W. J. Henderson, who had been much impressed by Gershwin's earlier opuses, wrote that the music "served simply as an unimpressive accompaniment for an old hokum vaudeville skit that was hoary with age."[16] Olin Downes of the *Times* heard some good melodies, "genuinely dramatic passages," appropriate uses of dissonance, and he liked the way Gershwin "breaks up his duple rhythms and employs scraps and fragments in a manner that is free, emotional, theatrical." He too found the libretto nothing more than a vaudeville sketch. But for all its flaws, Downes saw in *135th Street* a potential "for more than operetta, which is its main importance to Mr. Gershwin."[17] The Whiteman concert was repeated on New Year's Day 1926, and as far as we know, it marked the last performance of *Blue Monday / 135th Street* during the composer's lifetime.

IN ARENAS OLD AND NEW (1926)

THE END OF FEBRUARY 1926 saw Gershwin back in London again, where rehearsals were under way for a production of *Lady, Be Good!* starring the Astaires. Shortly after his return home, on May 6, he attended a luncheon debate at New York's Town Hall Club, sponsored by the American League of Professional Women's Music Forum. The question at hand was "What Shall We Do with Jazz?" and the debaters were the Reverend John Roach Straton, pastor of Calvary Baptist Church, and singer Marguerite d'Alvarez, formerly of the Manhattan and Chicago opera companies. "Let us curb it; let us put it down; let us outlaw the thing," preached Straton, implacable in his scorn for jazz ("the music of the savage, intellectual and spiritual debauchery, utter degradation"). For her part, d'Alvarez testified that "an honest jazz tune is better than a sermon on prohibiting anything. . . . When I die, play George Gershwin's 'Rhapsody in Blue' at my funeral."[1]

The debate left an impression on Gershwin. He wrote an article called "Does Jazz Belong to Art?," published in the July issue of *Singing*, that took Rev. Straton to task for the vagueness of his fiery denunciation: "The most vicious opponents of jazz bring the impartiality of complete ignorance to their judgment seat." But Mme. d'Alvarez, Gershwin had come to learn, interpreted jazz songs "with fidelity and enthusiasm, not merely the notes, but the spirit and the rhythm of the music. . . . It is marvelous what a really great voice can do, musically speaking, with a good jazz air. The greater the voice, the greater its effectiveness in jazz interpretation, provided only that the singer has a superlative sense of rhythm." In fact, having discovered their mutual interest, Gershwin and d'Alvarez were now planning a program in the mode of Eva Gauthier's Aeolian Hall recital in 1923 for the coming fall in the Hotel Roosevelt. He closed his piece with advice for his fellow musicians that amounted to a vocalist's creed:

> If you are a singer, don't ignore jazz music. Study it, love and cherish it, give it free rein in your heart. It will repay you a hundred fold. It will help you over many tough spots in your classics. It will add a new rhythmic meaning to your whole repertoire, old and new. . . . Live in the musical present, and the past will be even more significant and precious.[2]

Singing continued the debate in the September 1926 issue with an article by composer, publisher, critic, and editor A. Walter Kramer, arguing that "jazz does not belong" to musical art. But in October, "Mr. Gershwin Replies to Mr. Kramer" linked that music to professional responsibility:

> As long as there is such a thing as music known as jazz, which is understood and appreciated by millions of people—some highbrow, but mostly lowbrow—the musician should at least know what it is and what it is all about. His musical education is incomplete if he refuses even to recognize that it exists. When I recommended jazz studies to singers, all that I maintained was that certain numbers written in the jazz idiom would do them a lot of good from the

standpoint of rhythm and accent. Here is a type of material which they can get in no other songs or vocal exercises.

Gershwin's words delivered an affirmative answer to the question "Does jazz belong to art?" in a way that was measured, depersonalized, and practical. And his upcoming recital with Marguerite d'Alvarez was meant to demonstrate that yes, in fact it does.

Singer and pianist performed together on the afternoon of December 4. The program included the *Rhapsody in Blue*, arranged for two pianos, with Gershwin playing the solo part and Isidore Gorn the orchestral accompaniment. Their encore was a two-piano arrangement of the *Concerto in F*'s third movement. D'Alvarez sang a group of French and Spanish songs, all accompanied by Edward Hart. But the part that really won over the audience was the selection of songs accompanied by Gershwin: Kern's "Babes in the Woods" from 1915's *Very Good Eddie*, Gershwin's "Nashville Nightingale" from the revue *Nifties of 1923*, and "The Man I Love" and "Clap Yo' Hands" from that year's *Oh, Kay!* "Oh, Lady Be Good" was the encore.

"Five piano preludes (first performance)" were also listed on the program. Though none were identified by key or tempo, they surely included the three that were published the following year as Three Preludes.[3] As it happens, pianist and composer Kay Swift, whom Gershwin met in 1925—and with whom a romance seems to have blossomed as early as May 1926—was present at the creation, or at least the first writing-down, of Prelude I. "George composed the first *Prelude* in one sitting," she recalled later:

I scored it while he played and he made a finished copy from that. It was not just an improvisation; he already had it worked out in his head. The other two came a little later ... the one he called his "Spanish" prelude because of the rhythms, I think came first. I don't know why he published only three; there were others. But he loved to play the three preludes and included them, whenever he could, on programs that were just a little bit too short![4]

For all their variety, the Three Preludes have in common the use of the blue third in some significant way. Prelude II, in C-sharp minor and marked "Andante con moto e poco rubato" (at a walking pace, with a little flexibility), is a song without words, based on the harmonic structure of the twelve-bar blues. Perhaps no other Gershwin composition is more directly devoted to unadorned basics: a quarter-note pulse that, though inflected here and there by rubato, pauses only once in its sixty-one bars; a four-beat left-hand ostinato (a short musical pattern that is repeated persistently) serving as a foil for a rounded melody's unfolding; a commitment to the organizing power of the blues harmonic progression; and a recommendation that the performer restrain the volume and maintain a legato touch.

Preludes I and III are urgent, energetic, and terse. The first flaunts its blues pedigree from the start, with a two-bar intro announcing a theme in B-flat major containing both the lowered third and the lowered seventh. Cast in ABA form, it apparently earned Gershwin's "Spanish" label for a left-hand rhythm that could have been inspired by the Latin American habanera. The fast-moving Prelude III in E-flat minor is as foursquare in its structure as the second, but in a different way. Built from four-bar phrases, it consists of three statements—in sixteen, twenty-four, and eight bars—of the same antecedent material, but with different consequents, or none at all.

Reviews of the concert indicate that Prelude III began the five-piece group, Prelude I ended it, and Prelude II was fourth. But the reviews centered mainly on the matter of eclectic vocal performance and jazz music's place on the concert stage. Samuel Chotzinoff of the *World* felt that Gershwin's songs "sounded as well in the concert hall as they ever did elsewhere," with the composer's playing between verses making a "stunning" effect.[5] Francis D. Perkins of the *Herald Tribune* judged the concert entertaining but "hardly epochmaking," yet he declared the *Rhapsody in Blue* "at least temporarily a classic, and perhaps the only one" of its kind.[6] Richard L. Stokes of the *Evening World* handed down his own judgment of the performers' cause in the debate with Straton: "The holy musicologist was not present Saturday, but he won a verdict by default."[7] The *Evening Post*'s critic, on the other hand, thought the concert "would have won any debate" through its sound alone: "Here was a beautiful performance vocally from beginning to end."[8]

Abbe Niles, whose extended response to the recital was published several weeks later in the *New Republic*, was a practicing attorney on Wall Street and an aficionado of American vernacular music, especially the blues. (Such specialists were rare in 1920s journalism, and the few who fit that description seem to have earned their keep outside the field.) To Niles, Broadway songs had their own performance practice for singers, and the likes of Gauthier and d'Alvarez were "hopelessly outdistanced" by such specialists as "Miss Gertrude Lawrence and Miss Sophie Tucker." He credits Gershwin with being the only composer to write a jazz-based orchestral work in a classical form, the *Concerto in F*, while pointing out that in the introductory measures of *135th Street* Gershwin had "actually employed the most blatant jazz to carry a premonition of tragedy." But what in the earlier 1920s had seemed a promising trend—composing jazz-styled music for the concert hall—by 1926 was looking like a formula for the success of just one American composer. And for all of Gershwin's remarkable versatility, Niles saw him above all else as a composer of musical comedies, with the new number "Do-Do-Do" from *Oh, Kay!* standing as a "perfect piece of song-making."[9]

WHEN GERSHWIN arrived in London in February, he was ready to devote most of the coming month to preparing *Lady, Be Good!* for its English debut. The company traveled to Liverpool for a try-out run, which began on March 29. Three days later, Gershwin crossed the English Channel to Paris to spend time with American friends, Mabel Pleshette and her husband, Bob Schirmer, of the music-publishing family that ran the New York–based firm G. Schirmer. "You can imagine the excitement, the joy of having him all to ourselves," wrote Bob to Emily and Lou Paley about Gershwin's visit.[10] "Our days consisted of breakfast together . . . then lying around the house, playing the piano, the Victor [phonograph], and our vocal chords till about 2 or 3 P.M." Evenings were spent with friends: Irving Berlin, in Paris with his wife on a working visit; Edwin Knopf, brother of publisher Alfred Knopf and later a film producer; novelist Michael Arlen; and American composer George Antheil. "That young super-radical composer" Antheil "tried to give George an idea of his stuff but since most of it is scored [for] 16 grand-player-pianos, with an obligato by a boiler-factory, why I suppose it wasn't a very fair test." But George played from his own songs, the *Rhapsody*, and the *Concerto*, and "a pleasant evening was had by all." The trio also watched prize fights and steeplechase racing in the Bois de Boulogne.

On April 10, Mabel, Bob, and George arrived in London for a stretch of eventful days. They heard Paul Whiteman give his first concert in Albert Hall, which included the *Rhapsody in Blue*. In the composer's opinion, Schirmer reported, "Whiteman murdered the Rhapsody by playing it in a lot of crazy tempi that were nothing at all like the original performances."[11] At another *Rhapsody*-based event, the dress rehearsal of its adaptation as a ballet, "the pianist stumbled thro the solo passages, the clarinetist cracked at the top of that opening upward slide, the trombone blew sour notes from time to time—but in spite of everything it was very effective indeed and made a big hit." Schirmer also walked the Paleys through a West End premiere and its aftermath:

Wednesday night was the opening of Lady, Be Good!—It was a triumph. . . . Everyone went away whistling the tunes and since that night all the orchestras in London play nothing but Lady, Be Good! music. . . . When the Astaires drove up before the show the police had to break a way thru the crowd to let them get to their dressing-room. When it was over the audience sat in their seats for a full 10 minutes after the final curtain—speeches by the Astaires and Billy Kent—the greatest enthusiasm you can imagine—every entrance and exit was greeted by literal cheering such as I have only heard previously at football and baseball games. . . . After the show [George] took us to a party given by Sir Alfred Butt at the Embassy Club (most fashionable night club of London). . . . We left about 2 A.M., but George was up till 8 we heard! Some evening[!][12]

Reviews of *Lady, Be Good!* leaned toward a consensus: the music was catchy, the dancing energetic and sometimes exciting. And audiences loved the show, thanks chiefly to the Astaires, especially Adele. Reviewers found in her a performer both lovable and hard to predict: "piquant, impish, extraordinarily attractive in a quaint spontaneous way," "quick as mercury." Perhaps the best proof of her stage charisma is that critic after critic sought to describe what made Adele unique. The reviewer for the *Era* included many other writers' themes in his appreciation:

> When she is not dancing with a grace of movement and a beauty of rhythm that are scarcely equalled on the stage, she throws herself infectiously into the comedy. Her enjoyment of the fun is always as great as the audience's, and that is mainly the secret of her success. In everything she does there is a touch of the child; the exhilarating high spirits, the joyful antics, and those funny little squeaks of pleasure spring spontaneously from her nature.[13]

By Fred Astaire's account, "Delly" also gloried in the offstage life that came with stardom, filled with social gatherings and parties.[14] Yet there was another side of Adele Astaire that, behind her onstage persona as every man's sweetheart, marked her as a mature woman in love with a man whose fondness for her seems not to have reached much beyond the professional relationship that they—and her brother—had fashioned together and enjoyed.

THE ARCHIVE of the Ira Gershwin and Leonore Gershwin Trusts, now in the Library of Congress, contains fourteen undated letters from Adele Astaire to George Gershwin, many of them written in the U.K. Their content points to approximate dates, the earliest in 1922–23 and the latest in 1928. Some are responses to letters from George, but none from George to Adele are known to have survived.

On what appears to have been Gershwin's last night in London after the April opening of *Lady, Be Good!* in 1926, he received a short, impassioned letter from Adele's residence at 40 Park Lane:

> Dearest—it is a few minutes after we said good-by, & I miss you already! It's going to be too awful without you. George darling—why do I have to love you, why? Can't help it——
> Please think of me a lot—oh, a terrible lot!
>
> I adore you! / Adele

Two more letters to George, back in New York, followed this one, probably in May:

> I've a terrible cold in my chest & it's a good thing—I don't have to sing your masterpieces for records.
> I've decided I don't love anyone or admire anyone but the "great Gershwin."
>
> Your, Adele

Then came news announcing a foible of her new dog:

Darling nozzle nose—just a few lines of "dirt." . . . Did I tell you I
bought that "Scottie" we admired in the Stafford Kennels? He is so
sweet—& makes the loveliest medallions all over the carpet—such
designs you've never seen! We can't spank him—haven't the heart.
Was yours house-broken?

Business is great—the Prince came in the other night. Fred is "hot
footing" around town with his "gal"—Mrs. Dudley Coates (he has a
mash on her).

Ellen Berlin is going to have a papoose—whoopee!

I love you George (not Jean, i.e. George Jean Nathan) I
love *you*! A.[15]

Adele's romantic feelings for Gershwin seem to have dated back
to the early 1920s. In a 1922 letter to both Astaires, George had
apparently revealed that he planned to be working in the U.K. in
the near future. Adele responded enthusiastically: "George dear. . . .
How we all envy you. . . . Your ears should burn, baby, all the nice
sweet things we've been saying about you. . . . Lots of Love." Just
before signing off, she struck a more personal note, citing a recent
hit song: "Did you know that I love to hear from you? So—'Do
it again.'"

A pattern detectable in this phase of the correspondence is one
of George sending news—presumably to both Astaires—about a
new development in his career, and Adele replying with approval
and encouragement, sometimes adding news of her own. In 1923,
she described from London the crown prince's infatuation with
Stop Flirting.

The most amazing thing has happened—the Prince of Wales was
up in the box again for the fourth time, & with him were Duke &
Duchess of York & Lord & Lady Mountbatten—we were asked up
in the box after the show was over, & the Prince presented us to his
brother & the Mountbattens & invited us to supper with them!! I

danced with [the Prince] the whole evening—& George, he is too divine! Good dancer, too.

He kept humming "Innocence Lonesome Blue Baby"—& said his favorite tune was "Yankee Doodle Blues"—then your *girl frien'* told him all about George Gershwin, & that he was writing our next show—he was frightfully interested—especially when I told him you were very young. George, wish you had been with us—he'd adore you.

Just think, George, he has seen our play four times within two weeks.

I've got a "crush" on his Highness! Ahem!

A P.S. added, "There is so much to tell you that I can't put it all down—am frightfully anxious to see you again."

The frank tone of some of Adele's letters is striking: rare in the Gershwin family correspondence as a whole. For instance, toward the end of 1923 she hit "Georgie, my pet" in New York with this question from London: "What do you want me to bring you from here—something that you haven't got[?]—now, don't get naughty. I don't mean what you mean." And early in 1924, from Hull, where the *Stop Flirting* company was on tour, she began on a doubtful note—"Dearest & most beautiful George—I wanted to write ages ago, but thought perhaps you didn't much care whether I wrote or not." But then she added, "You bet I've got loads to tell you— but it sounds 'flat' in a letter, so wait, babe, I'll be wiggling home, soon. Let's have a 'slap & tickle' when we get back—that's the latest expression over here, for anything." To which she added, turning on a dime: "Would you be angry if I suddenly decided to become Lady 'What-not' or 'Duchess of Flatbottom'—I might—oh well, as long as my [heart symbol] is somewhere else it's hard to accept even nobility."

Adele Astaire seems not to have felt bound by the taboos that set the standard in the Gershwins' world of social communication, which avoided criticizing others. Her lively correspondence with George, brimming with show business news and gossip, also includes negative statements about two influential boosters of the young Gershwin: Paul Whiteman and Jerome Kern. The Whiteman comments, from letters she wrote in London in 1926, had to do with the *Rhapsody in Blue*.

> Paul Whiteman's band is an awful disappointment. No one likes it here, at all. And what a rendition of your glorious "Rapsody in Blue!" It's a crime to allow him to do it! I've never heard anything so "lousy"—I think his band has deteriorated. Fred spoke to him last evening—& Fred said it's no wonder he isn't as good as he use to be—he has a terrible "swell knob"—and thinks every one is wrong but him. . . . I wouldn't let him ruin any more of your work if I were you, babe.

Her musical criticism might have echoed Gershwin's own to some degree. A more personal Whiteman reference suggests a spat, or perhaps something stronger, between two longtime collaborators who, from most appearances, maintained a friendly long-term relationship. Although Gershwin and Whiteman would collaborate again, perhaps in the incident described here Whiteman had caught wind of the composer's disapproval, and blown off steam to Fred Astaire. Adele wrote again to George:

> Paul Whitman got into a fight at the Kit Kat Club last night & was thrown out. He has been acting very aggressive & shooting off that big mouth of his so much—that some-one took offense—he's sore 'cause he's flopping—& started arguments about who won the war etc. He told Fred the other night, he didn't like the way you acted & that he "made" you etc. *Can you beat it!* He is a swine & every one hates him.

As for the redoubtable Kern, evidence of sour feelings appears in a letter Adele sent to George from London in September 1923. "George darling, thought you might like to hear about 'Jerry Kern's' efforts over here! 'The Beauty Prize' at the Winter garden—well—it was 'boo-ed' & 'hissed'—& 'panned'—especially the music—hoo-ray!" Later, describing a postshow get-together with the Prince of Wales and friends, she reported that "Lady Mountbatten says she loves you & asked me to give you her love when I write to you. We all agreed that Jerry K. is a rotten composer, & that you are the best one yet. Take your bow, kid."

Some of this anti-Kern talk may have reflected Gershwin's past up-and-down experience with the composer who had been his first idol. But there was clear reason why, at this juncture, the Astaires were no big fans of Kern. The show that had preceded *Stop Flirting* was Charles Dillingham's production of *The Bunch and Judy*. Although at that stage Fred considered it inspiring to be in a Kern show, this one had a number, "Pale Venetian Moon," that he disliked for several reasons. Its melody felt unnatural to sing; he detested the costume he was forced to wear while performing it; and he found the staging precarious, calling for him and Adele to dance on a narrow table that was lifted overhead by chorus members—an insecure perch for the dancers, who more than once during rehearsals were dumped unceremoniously to the floor. Fred complained repeatedly about the song, but to no avail. The number proved symptomatic of a production that deserved to flop, and it did. Fred's autobiography says nothing more about Kern, but his silence may reflect his feeling that Kern was a composer not much tuned in to the practicalities of performing.

Kern's shows had appeared in London through the better part of two decades by the time the Astaires, and Gershwin, entered the scene. Perhaps at least some members of the public now saw the younger Gershwin, with his jazz-oriented scores, setting a new

direction in musical comedy—an American trend appealing especially to the fashion-conscious and to a younger generation. In
any event, it is hard to imagine Adele offering such sharp-tongued
comments about Gershwin's senior colleague and one-time musical
model had she doubted that he would agree in some measure. Her
letters leave no doubt of her eagerness to win George's approval and
love. Late in 1923, she wrote him that a group of English friends,
including Noël Coward, had been raving about Gershwin: "I'm so
tickled every time I hear lovely things about you—you'd think you
belonged to me." The next year, after she heard Alex Aarons play
portions of the *Rhapsody in Blue*, yet to be published or recorded, she
wrote to George: "It makes me all chilly in the spine. You are such
a genius!!!"

Fred Astaire's autobiography devotes a good deal of space to his
work with Adele, which continued until she retired from show business in 1932, and also to Fred's work with Gershwin. Valuable for the
information and perspective it provides about a long, unique career
in show business, it is written in a tone as circumspect and free
of gossip as most of the correspondence of the Gershwins. Fred's
Steps in Time says nothing about a romantic link between Adele and
George. Her last known letter to Gershwin, written in London
probably in 1928, begins ruefully: "Hey you—why don't you write
to a guy? Just because you have a hit show—don't get 'high-hat,'"
the last a reference to that year's *Funny Face*, the last Gershwin-
Astaire musical. She closes with "Darling George / Adele."

Readers may wonder why this account of the Astaire–Gershwin
correspondence—significant, lively, and extended over six years—
is so one-sided. The reason is that only Adele's letters to George
have survived. It's true that more than once she chided him for slow
responses. But George was a responsible letter-writer. And from
a vantage point more than eighty years in the future there is no
way to know whether he had failed to respond to her letters or that
replies from him were removed or lost after his death.

The latter possibility comes to mind because after George Gershwin died in 1937, Kay Swift, his long-time lover and a musical partner with whom he had corresponded over the years, asked Ira Gershwin, a close friend, to return the letters that she and George had exchanged over the years—a request that George's brother honored. By then, however, Adele Astaire, now the wife of Lord Charles Cavendish and the resident of a castle in Ireland, was far removed from the world of American show business. If Adele was in touch with the Gershwin family at that moment, no evidence survives to support it.

Whatever the reason the Astaire–Gershwin romantic relationship has escaped the historical record, it is revealing. A performer adored by international audiences for her artistry and charm, Adele had learned that the ineffable spirit she could deliver onstage seems to have been conjured best in the environment of music by George Gershwin. Over the years, through the experience of creating musical comedies, she had often worked side by side with him, observing his talent, resourcefulness, and humanity as he and the Astaires reached the pinnacle of public success. Recognizing him as a genius, she had fallen in love with George early in their careers. But for all the regard in which he must have held her artistry, and enjoyed her company, Gershwin chose not to find for Adele Astaire a lasting place at his side.

OH, KAY! (1926)

GERSHWIN RETURNED TO LONDON in June 1926 for the West End production of *Tip-Toes*, which opened on August 31. Before then, back in New York, he and Ira got to work, too, on the score for Aarons and Freedley's third musical, *Oh Kay!*, whose Philadelphia tryout was to begin in October.

For this project, librettist Guy Bolton teamed up again with a longtime colleague who had enjoyed success on both sides of the Atlantic: the English novelist, playwright, and lyricist P. G. Wodehouse. Wodehouse's involvement with the London musical stage reached back to 1905, when he wrote his first lyrics to music by Jerome Kern, then a promising twenty-year-old songwriter who was already working both in the West End and on Broadway. Beginning in 1916, at the tiny Princess Theatre on Broadway, Wodehouse, now living in New York and writing theater criticism for *Vanity Fair* while maintaining a flow of stories and comic novels, joined forces with Kern and Bolton in a series of musical comedies that set a fresh, contemporary tone.

In 1923, Wodehouse and Bolton attended a revue called *Rats*, then playing at the Vaudeville Theatre in London, and were mightily impressed by Gertrude Lawrence, a seasoned performer but not yet a star. As they wrote later in a joint memoir, it seemed to them that Lawrence "had everything"—she was capable of "sophisticated comedy, low comedy, singing every possible type of song, and she looked enchanting."[1] Bolton wrote to Lawrence offering her any kind of Broadway show she might like. The result was that after fulfilling a commitment to costar in New York with Beatrice Lillie in *André Charlot's Revue of 1924* and its sequel, *The Charlot's Revue of 1926*, she signed on for the title role in *Oh, Kay!* Bolton, having debated whether to place her with Aarons and Freedley or with Ziegfeld, who was also trying to get her for a new show, said that "it was George Gershwin's connection with Alex and Vinton that tipped the scale in their favor (and eventually put several hundred thousand dollars in their bank accounts)": Lawrence and Gershwin had met during the first Charlot revue's run in New York, and she was eager to work with him.[2] Thus, at least as the librettists tell the story, *Oh, Kay!* was a writer-inspired show.[3]

The book, a story about Prohibition, treats the U.S. government's attempt to criminalize liquor sales as a farce, and celebrates the entrepreneurial impulse of the bootleggers afoot in "Beachampton, Long Island." The bootleggers' ostensible leader is an ineffectual and penniless—but yacht-owning—English duke, whose charming sister, Lady Kay, played by Lawrence, also belongs to the rum-running enterprise. The duke and his accomplices, having stored a large cache of contraband in the cellar of an apparently vacant mansion, are forced to scramble when the mansion's owner, Jimmy Winter, suddenly returns home. Rich, feckless, and essentially good-hearted, Jimmy spends much of his energy trying to settle his confused marital situation: to complete the annulment of an early, ill-advised marriage to his first wife, Mae; to escape the clutches of his current fiancée, Constance, who, though determined to become Mrs. Winter, shows little affection for him; and ultimately to marry his true love, Kay. It turns out that she and her bootlegging boat had saved him from drowning in Long Island Sound a year ago, and he has never forgotten her.

Bootlegger Shorty McGee, the gang's mastermind, is the show's main comedian. Jimmy has hired domestic servants to serve him and his new bride-to-be when they arrive, but Shorty scares them off and assumes the butler's duties himself; Kay later pretends to be his wife. Shorty also becomes Kay's confidante and partner in her attempt to steer Jimmy away from the dour Constance. He's a crook with a heart of gold, who always does right by the heroine, and with his help—and thanks to Kay's intelligence and moxie—Jimmy and Kay do end up together.

Jimmy was played by Oscar Shaw, a skilled dancer, singer, and comedian who had appeared in several of the Princess Theatre shows, while the role of Shorty was played by Victor Moore, a vaudevillian recommended by the librettists but whose "diffident style, his querulous whine, his fatuous, blundering garrulity" in rehearsal left Aarons and Freedley cold. On October 18, the opening night of the Philadelphia tryout, the producers were so sure that Moore would fail that they had "two comedians watching out front, one of them . . . having been virtually promised the part." But audience and critics both loved Moore's performance, and his "staggering triumph" won over the producers, who went on to hire him for five more shows.[4]

Lady Kay made no triumphal stage entrance. Rather, at the end of a long first scene in which three numbers had already been sung, she appeared in the darkened bedroom of the man of the house. "Miss Lawrence was marvelously modest," wrote Alan Dale of the *New York American*. "She had a first 'entrance' that many a featured 'performer' would have kicked at. In fact, she came on in the dark, when none but the ushers recognized her—and they did! They broke into applause and warned us that Miss Lawrence was there."[5] The sound of gunshots preceded her entrance—she had fired at an

Officer Jansen, who was hot on her trail. The lights came on, and she and Jimmy recognized that they had met before.

Jimmy tells Kay about his youthful marriage and its supposed annulment, and of a second marriage that took place earlier that very day, clouded by a postnuptial revelation of the annulment's delay. As Kay listens to his story ("I suppose there are advantages in being a bigamist"), Officer Jansen bursts in through an open window. Kay, with an airy wave at the suitcases filling the room, introduces herself as the new Mrs. Jimmy Winter. Assured by Jimmy that he's okay with her posing as his wife ("I didn't think one more or less would make much difference to you"), she decides that with the officer lurking on the premises, she'd better spend the night in Jimmy's house. As they prepare to bed down in separate rooms, Jimmy and Kay contemplate the vagaries of love and human destiny in the duet "Maybe."

Wodehouse remembered Ira at this stage of his career as paying little heed to the dramatic context for his songs. He "had no notion of getting a situation and fitting a lyric to it," but rather "just turned up with a bundle of lyrics . . . and expected you to fit the book to them, which you did miraculously."[6] Perhaps "Maybe" was one of those miracles. The number is a rarity, a tender love song about doubt, and it shines in its dramatic context as it helps develop Kay's multilayered character. In the refrain, Jimmy reminds Kay that love, usually portrayed as a matter of yes or no, can also leave room for another possibility: "Maybe soon, maybe late." The couple sing the final section together as if joining to embrace shared uncertainties—or maybe not. "Maybe" unfolds in a dialogue that relies on an echo effect: a bar-by-bar alternation of voice and instruments. In formal terms, such patterning leads to a tightly unified musical structure. In expressive terms, it also proves ideal for driving home a message of ambiguity.

Oh, Kay! boasts three more songs that won success on their own.

"Clap Yo' Hands," a show-stopping dance number in the tradition of "Fascinating Rhythm," "Kickin' the Clouds Away," and "Sweet and Low-Down," gave the company, especially Jimmy's female servants, a chance to shine under Sammy Lee's choreographic direction—drawing on the talents of such dancers as Betty Compton, Constance Carpenter, and especially Harland Dixon, known for his eccentric moves. As bootlegger Larry Potter, Dixon urged the duke to stop worrying and follow "the philosophy of sunshine" that he had learned "at the knee of my old colored mammy."

In "Do-Do-Do," a second romantic duet, the lead characters sing about the joys of kissing: a ploy to convince Officer Jansen, who has reappeared in Jimmy's house, that he and Kay are besotted newlyweds. Ira described the song's origins as follows:

> An hour or so before dinner one evening at our house on 103rd Street I told George that maybe we could do something with the sounds of "do, do" and "done, done." We went up to his studio on the top floor and in half an hour wrote the refrain of the song. (I am certain of the time it took because just as we started to work, my bride-to-be telephoned that she *could* make it for dinner with us; and when she arrived, taxiing in half an hour—less, she says—from Eighth Street, we were able to play her a complete refrain.)[7]

From all appearances, the idea of this song as a parody of honeymoon behavior came from Bolton and Wodehouse.[8] Yet it does fit the blend of music and words that the Gershwin brothers conjured so quickly from the sounds of one-syllable words: "Do, do, do / What you've done, done, done / Before, Baby." The repeated *do*'s and *done*'s establish a tick-tocking motion, to a gently curving melody. And in the last section of an **abac** structure, vocables come to the fore: "My heart begins to hum / Dum de dum de dum-dum-dum," sings Jimmy, to which Kay answers, "My heart begins to sigh / Di de di de di-di-di."

By Act II, Lady Kay has turned herself into Jane ("Jine," in her assumed Cockney twang), the wife of butler Shorty McGee. Jane tells Shorty that she and Jimmy love each other, but that he will never back out of marrying Constance. Then comes her character's only solo song, "Someone to Watch Over Me." According to Ira, the music for this ballad, one of the most touching of all Gershwin songs, was composed early in 1926. "George wrote a rather exciting tune which he played at a brisk tempo," he recalled. "Obviously it was destined to be a stage dance-and-ensemble number." But then "one day, for no particular reason and hardly aware of what he was at, George played the dance tune in a comparatively slow tempo." The result was revelatory. "The melody hadn't reached the half-way mark when both of us had the same reaction: this was really no rhythm tune but rather a wistful and warm one—to be held out until the proper stage occasion arose for it."[9] That occasion, the brothers soon realized, was the moment when Kay confides to Shorty her regret that love is about to pass her by again. Sung at the slower tempo, a passage originally full of rhythmic jolts comes over as a gentle, flexible delivery of tender words.

Ira also revealed that the original idea for the lyrics was not his:

George and I were well along with the score for Oh, Kay! when one morning at six a.m. I was rushed to Mt. Sinai Hospital for an emergency appendectomy. I was there six weeks—this was long before the antibiotics shortened stays. When, after great insistence ("They're waiting for me to finish the lyrics!"), exit was finally per-mitted, I was still weak but able to work afternoons. Then, with rehearsals nearing, and myself a bit behind schedule, a friend and many-faceted talent, Howard Dietz, showed up one day and offered to help out, and did. We collaborated on two lyrics and he was help-ful on a couple of others. Also one day when he heard the slowed-up ex-jazz tune he ad-libbed several titles, one of which stuck with me and which, some days later, I decided to write up.

When *Oh, Kay!* opened in Philadelphia, Lawrence sang the song in the show's first scene, as a prologue: Lady Kay introducing herself to the audience with a tender memory of a man she met a year ago and seemed now to have lost. In its tryout phase, however, the show ran too long. By the time it opened on Broadway, on November 8, the prologue had been cut and "Someone to Watch Over Me" moved to Act II—even though one of the lines in the verse, "haven't found him yet," pertained to Jimmy, with whom Lady Kay had already sung two duets. If this glitch in plot detail bothered anyone, it failed to register with the critics. Percy Hammond of the *Herald Tribune* declared the song an emotional high point: "Voiced beautifully by Miss Lawrence," he wrote, Gershwin's music "wrung the withers of even the most hard-hearted of those present."[10] Brooks Atkinson of the *Times* also singled out the song for making familiar romantic material so effective, and for Lawrence's poignant use of a stage prop: a rag doll given her by Gershwin, to which, dressed in her maid's costume, she sang her wistful song.[11] Enthusiasm could reach into ecstasy during a high-energy ensemble like "Clap Yo' Hands." But here was a moment when, entrusted to the right performer, lyricism could transport a theater audience into a state of enchantment.

In all, eight songs from *Oh, Kay!* were published as the show opened on Broadway: the four discussed so far, plus "Fidgety Feet," "Heaven on Earth," and "Oh, Kay," the latter two with lyrics cowritten by Howard Dietz, as well as a fourth, "Show Me the Town," that had been replaced before the New York opening. "Fidgety Feet," sung and danced by Harland Dixon and Marion Fairbanks, is a second up-tempo dance number whose refrain is based on the trickiness of three-beat units' sudden intrusion into duple time. Its verse raises the specter of a "chronic" physical condition remediable only by the "tonic" of modern dance moves, a favorite therapeutic notion—and rhyme—of Ira's. "Heaven on Earth," for Jimmy and the girls, radiates optimism and trust in the virtue of striving. The show's closest thing to a title song comes near the end as Lady Kay asks the men of the company how she ranks in the charm department. "Like a beautiful pome," they reply, she could "break up any home"; a woman with all of Venus's "charms," plus "two good arms." In a refrain with a boom-chuck beat and a tune whose syncopation has a Sousalike ring, they deliver their verdict: "Oh, Kay! You're O.K. with me!"

The show's reception could hardly have been better, with more than one critic calling it the best of the three Aarons/Freedley/Gershwins productions. Burton Davis in the *Morning Telegraph* closed his review with: "'Oh, Kay!' Hell, it's almost perfect!"[12] Both George and Ira, but especially George, won kudos, and special note was taken of Lawrence's excellence as a singer and dancer, but most of all as an actress who made the multiple faces of Lady Kay vivid and convincing. The orchestra, conducted by Bill Daly and enhanced again by the two-piano team of Arden and Ohman, was cited in a few reviews. *Oh, Kay!* would run into June 1927, for a total of 256 Broadway performances, before going on tour, and even returning to New York for a brief revival as the next year began. Following in the footsteps of *Lady, Be Good!* and *Tip-Toes*, a London run with Lawrence in her starring role began in September 1927.

A 1994 RECONSTRUCTION of *Oh, Kay!* on CD offers a more complete view of what a musical comedy required of its composer than could the show's published songs alone.[13] Act openers had their own customs and possibilities, as shown by "The Woman's Touch," which begins Act I after the overture. And "Bride and Groom," featuring references to both Mendelssohn's and Wagner's wedding marches, serves as the kick-off number of Act II. Both are in a quick 2/4 time, set in bright major keys, and sung chiefly by the chorus. Each is also a multipart composition with at least two full-blown melodies and more than one key level.

It is understandable that discussions of Gershwin's work as a whole dwell on specific songs, instrumental works, and *Porgy and Bess*. But another avenue to explore is the aspect of his show music that may be called part-writing: the texture of bass and inner-voice lines that together create a harmonic foundation to support the melodies he fashioned so expertly. Gershwin melody sounds purposeful in part because it is grounded in strong bass lines that also give rise to countermelodies, especially where melodic pauses need filling. When Robert Russell Bennett, Broadway's top orchestrator, pointed to Gershwin as a composer whose sketches welcomed orchestration, he was referring not only to melodic and harmonic logic, but to the integrity of the voice lines implied by the accompanying parts.[14] Gershwin, who composed at the piano, surely thought contrapuntally, tapping that inclination to enrich his music's melodic flow.

In 1929 Gershwin told an interviewer that, deeming "ordinary harmonies, rhythms, sequences, intervals, and so on" fundamental to his compositional vocabulary, he experimented at the piano with ways to enliven these elements. "I would spend hour upon hour trying to change them around so that they would satisfy me." The voice he commanded in song-making thrived on small adjustments. "See what an effect is achieved by merely flatting the third of the major scale, or the seventh," and "following up this effect with appropriate harmonies":

> To my way of thinking, it isn't the fellow with all sorts of complicated chords up his sleeve who will capture the new audiences. It's the man with a musical vocabulary, so to speak, of simple tonic and dominants—chords built upon the first and fifth notes of the scale, respectively—but who will be able, with these fundamental harmonies, to introduce the vital change, the little twist, which will make the harmonic structure sound rich despite the simple means.

This approach could also "be employed in the rhythms of the music, playing off accents against one another."[15]

The score of *Oh, Kay!*—songs, dance music, ensembles, and all the rest—brims with life, exemplifying Gershwin's principle of "much-in-little, and much *with* little." It is devoted to animated melody cast in verse-and-refrain song forms, almost invariably with thirty-two-bar refrains comprised of four-bar phrases and eight-bar sections, and supported by familiar harmonic progressions. There are seven-bar sections in "Bride and Groom," but they sail by barely noticed unless the listener is counting. Enriched by judicious resorts to small surprises, the music moves ever forward with an air of neat, eventful continuity. Though not uniquely so, *Oh, Kay!* embodies the kind of musical comedy that Gershwin mastered during the mid-1920s: hard-to-resist entertainment with plenty of leeway for the exercise of his skill and ingenuity as a composer.

ONCE *Oh, Kay!* had taken the boards of Broadway's Imperial Theatre, Gershwin devoted substantial energy to cultivating the pianistic side of his musical life. Visiting the studio of Columbia Records in New York on November 8 and 12, he recorded his own versions of four songs in the new show: "Do-Do-Do," "Clap Yo' Hands," "Someone to Watch Over Me," and "Maybe." On December 4, he and Marguerite d'Alvarez presented their joint recital. Over a week later, on December 14, the New York radio station WEAF broadcast a program devoted entirely to Gershwin's music and featuring some of his own playing.[16] The following day, the composer was in Buffalo, where he and d'Alvarez repeated their New York program with a few small changes. To round out his 1926 calendar, on December 26 Gershwin made a return appearance with the New York Symphony under Walter Damrosch to play the *Concerto in F* for the first time since the start of the year. Revisiting a work that had left him doubtful the first time around, Olin Downes of the *New York Times* came away with a more positive impression:

> If the concerto does not entirely reach its goal it is a pleasure to say that it grows upon acquaintance that it may grow more with further hearings and that it may very possibly have been underestimated after the first performances last season. The performance yesterday was a spirited one and there was long applause for the composer.[17]

One value of Gershwin's recordings of *Oh, Kay!*'s signature songs is that they reflect his process of turning theater songs into pianistic songs without words. Each starts with an introduction of varied length and character. All include the verse, but not necessarily on the heels of the introduction. Each also presents the refrain, or portions of it, three times, offering one iteration in a new key and then returning to the original. All were tailored to be approximately three minutes long: the playing time of each side of a 78 rpm record.

In all four recordings, Gershwin decorates the melody line energetically, filling in its gaps—especially at the ends of phrases, where the melodic note is a sustained one. In "Someone to Watch Over Me," the slowest of the four, the melody of the **a** section includes a descending series of half notes, each of which Gershwin embellishes with a quick broken-chord gesture. In "Maybe," responding often to the song's two-bar melodic call is a tuneful answer: an eighth-note figure that, more than two decades later, Richard Rodgers could have borrowed for the start of "Some Enchanted Evening" in his 1949 *South Pacific*. In both these songs, the mood changes when the melody moves from the right hand to the left, turning the right hand temporarily into an agent of chordal support. For Gershwin, composer and pianist, his songs were tractable material, ripe for variation, and always offering spontaneity.

UPS AND DOWNS:
KAUFMAN ON THE SCENE (1927)

By 1927 the English-speaking musical world was coming to
see Gershwin as a force whose outlook and talent challenged artistic boundaries. Early in January, when London critic Francis Toye
wrote a column advocating for critical treatment of music of many
kinds, he cited Gershwin's piano recordings of "numbers from *Tip-
Toes*": "I have attended many social functions, where he was present.
So were other musicians, some of them with the most famous names
in the world of music. When Gershwin played his tunes on the
piano (he was always asked to do so) all of them, violinists, pianists,
composers, crowded around and listened with evident delight."[1]
When Gershwin and several friends traveled that same January to
cross the border to Montreal for a winter vacation that included
tobogganing, ice skating, and skiing, critics from local newspapers
visited his hotel and interviewed him as a composer who seemed to
be remapping the musical scene. Their questions centered on the
composer's view of jazz music. "There is jazz and jazz; good and
bad, as in everything else," he told them, granting that he probably
saw "this thing from a different angle to other jazz writers, because

I have studied music, whereas many of them just whistle their tunes or beat them out on a piano."[2]

Back home, a concert staged later in the month in New York's Steinway Hall for the benefit of the MacDowell Colony found Gershwin in a new role: critic. The performers were three prominent amateurs: music critic Olin Downes, author and college professor John Erskine, and the Steinway firm's Otto Urchs. The New York press had chosen two renowned pianists to sit alongside Gershwin as he reviewed the concert, Ernest Hutcheson and Josef Hofmann. The column Gershwin wrote, published in the January 22 issue of the *New York World*, assumes the confident, sometimes jocular voice of a commentator writing from a crossover perspective, before such a thing was common.

Erskine and Downes opened the concert with the two-piano version of Brahms's *Variations on a Theme by Haydn*, leading Gershwin to imagine his own pleasure if "a darn nice chap" of Brahms's caliber were to compose variations on melodies he himself had composed. Erskine then played Mozart's *Coronation* Piano Concerto accompanied by his daughter, a performance Gershwin found to be "an agreeable surprise," noting that to develop a technique with such finesse, "a college professor must have a lot of spare time." When Urchs joined the others for Bach's Concerto in D Minor for three keyboard instruments, the way the performers relayed the themes, "from Erskine to Downes to Urchs," made Gershwin think of baseball, specifically the Chicago Cubs' famous double-play combination, immortalized in the poem "Tinker to Evers to Chance."[3]

On the day that Gershwin's review appeared, the *Saturday Evening Post* published a lengthy article by Gilbert Seldes tracing the history of jazz music as he had experienced it in New York City. Seldes believed that Gershwin's unique place in American music rested on two cornerstones: the early public success of his musical theater songs, and the later public success of the *Rhapsody in Blue*, ratified by the critics' response. "Gershwin has definitely broken with Tin Pan

Alley and cast at least half of his future with the serious symphon-
ists," he wrote. Moreover, "in almost every discussion of jazz opera
his name occurs as the probable winner of the great distinction of
creating a native opera, in the jazz style, for the Metropolitan." In
such ways had jazz offered "one new composer to America."[4]

Less than two weeks after this article appeared, the *Outlook* magazine carried a substantial piece titled "Gershwin and Musical Snob-
bery." Critic Charles L. Buchanan, having panned the *Concerto in F*
in December of 1925, now awarded it "an increasingly clear title to
be ranked the one composition of indubitable vitality, and authentic
progressiveness, that this country has produced." That Gershwin
be encouraged "to grow largely and finely" seemed to Buchanan no
small matter for the future of American music. His article ended
with a plea that the *Concerto in F* be performed more widely. And as
it happened, Fritz Reiner, conductor of the Cincinnati Symphony
Orchestra, agreed, for he invited Gershwin to play both the *Rhapsody in Blue* and the *Concerto in F* in two concerts in Ohio on March
11 and 12. This was Gershwin's first engagement with an orchestra
from outside the orbit of New York, and it would prove a model for
similar engagements in the years to come.

On March 9, Gershwin arrived in town for a Wednesday morning rehearsal with the orchestra, followed by lunch at the Cincinnati Club. Reporter Charles Ludwig described the rehearsal in the
next day's newspaper:

> For the first time in the more than thirty years of its honored clas-
> sical history the orchestra played JAZZ! And they like it—like it
> immensely. Indeed, they came mighty close to "going wild" over it.
> They yelled "Bravo!". . . They clapped their hands when Gershwin
> finished his brilliant performance of his Concerto and his Rhap-
> sody in Blue, the world's most famous jazz works. They stamped
> with their feet and made a noisy cacophony, with their instru-
> ments to voice their approval. "Great!" "Wonderful!" "A marvelous

player!" "Remarkable music!"—the musicians raised on Beethoven and Bach, commented to each other.

Over lunch Gershwin explained that jazz was simply one idiom that he drew on when he composed. "When I write music I do not set myself deliberately to write jazz. I just try to write good music and make use of whatever appeals to me in jazz rhythm and idiom."[5] He also, for the first time in a public forum, linked the phenomenon of blue notes, and blues music, to race: "The 'blues' suggest the sad or 'blue' feeling hidden under the gayety of the negro."[6]

In the wake of the concerts, in which Beethoven's Seventh Symphony and Richard Strauss's *Till Eulenspiegel's Merry Pranks* flanked the two Gershwin compositions, a pair of local reviews offered radically different responses to the challenge Gershwin posed for classical music lovers. One was by Nina Pugh Smith of the *Times-Star*, who declared that "probably no concert ever played in this city will elicit as widely differing opinions as this juxtaposition of jazz and Beethoven." Trying to give Gershwin his due, though personally put off by his music, she described him as "a musician born, a composer born, an original thinker born, and an artistic personality needing to be freed from the artificiality of an environment"—meaning New York City. "If Mr. Gershwin could come out of New York into these broad United States," she ventured, he "could acquire a national, and not a provincial, musical speech."[7]

The lengthy review written by William Smith Goldenburg of the *Enquirer*, on the other hand, recognized that jazz music had now "invaded the symphony concert hall and . . . been received with open arms," which he believed could make it a new force to be reckoned with. Yet, he admitted, "we do not know whether to congratulate 'Jazz' upon its elevation in society or condole with the Symphony for changing the complexion of its associates." Goldenburg wondered: "Who is this George Gershwin and what are his accomplishments that he should be able to . . . cause the musical and non-musical citizens to respond to the phase of art—yes, it's that—which he represents?" The question was one that, decades after he posed it, historians and biographers were still pondering. Goldenburg's conclusion: "He must be headed somewhere."[8]

The early months of 1927 also saw the publication of another article by Gershwin in *Theatre* magazine, this one in the March issue. Each of his earlier written statements had been linked to a particular event or a composition occupying him at the moment. In contrast, "Jazz Is the Voice of the American Soul" reveals the ideas and principles of a composer who hopes to be better understood as an artist. The article's carefully posed photos show Gershwin as a stylish, pensive presence, his hands elegantly displayed.[9] With years of composing behind him, Gershwin allowed that he was not surprised when the likes of Rachmaninoff, Heifetz, and Hofmann "paid me compliments upon my efforts as a composer." What did surprise him, though, was that all these paragons "complimented me upon my piano execution," even though his formal piano study had consisted of

> but four years . . . and those not with teachers of celebrity. . . . My facility had come not from tuition but from a habit I had consciously cultivated since I was in my early teens. I mean my habit of intensive listening. . . . Strains from the latest concert, the cracked tones of a hurdy gurdy, the wail of a street singer to the obligato of a broken violin, past or present music, I was hearing within me. Old music and new music, forgotten melodies and the craze of the moment, bits of opera, Russian folk songs, Spanish ballads, chansons, rag-time ditties, combined in a mighty chorus in my inner ear. And through and over it all I heard, faint at first, loud at last, the soul of this great America of ours.

Having in his 1925 article dismissed as a superstition the notion that "jazz is essentially Negro," he was now perceiving jazz music as "a combination that includes the wail, the whine, and the exultant note of the old 'mammy' songs of the South." Jazz could be described as "black and white," indeed "all colors and all souls unified in the great melting pot of the world," with "vibrant syncopation" as its dominant note.[10]

THERE IS ample evidence that, after writing scores for Aarons and Freedley's three hit musicals, the Gershwins felt ready for shows of a different sort, although several more along earlier lines would continue to appear: 1927's *Funny Face*, starring the Astaires; 1928's *Treasure Girl*, with Gertrude Lawrence; 1929's *Show Girl*, with Ruby Keeler; and 1930's *Girl Crazy*, with Willie Howard, Ginger Rogers, and Ethel Merman. What changed in 1927, though, was that the Gershwins began working for other producers, including Edgar Selwyn, a writer and director as well as producer, and Florenz Ziegfeld—men of an older generation whose subject matter ranged more widely. Indeed, the next Gershwin musical comedy, produced by Selwyn, was based on a libretto by George S. Kaufman, with a tone and subject matter that could hardly have been farther removed from that of the romantic comedies of Aarons and Freedley's productions.

Kaufman, a Pittsburgh native, had been hired by the *New York Tribune* in 1913 as its drama critic. While filling that post—and, from 1917 to 1930, a similar one at the *Times*—he also took classes in acting and playwriting, and in 1918 saw a play of his staged on Broadway for the first time. Two years later, Kaufman and a group of journalistic and show business friends began meeting informally for lunch at the Algonquin Hotel, near the theater district. This congenial crew—their company included Alexander Woollcott, Robert Benchley, Dorothy Parker, Robert E. Sherwood, Franklin Pierce Adams, Heywood Broun, and Marc Connelly, among others—came to be known as the Algonquin Round Table, admired in sophisticated circles for clever pronouncements and the cultural influence they were said to wield in New York and beyond. Kaufman's own brand of humor tended toward the mordant; to advertise a struggling new comedy of his that opened during a flu epidemic, he suggested a campaign built around the slogan "Avoid Crowds. See *Someone in the House*."[11] The success of the 1920 comedy *Dulcy*, written with Connelly as a feature for actress Lynn Fontanne, won for Kaufman a niche among comic playwrights that he sustained in the years to come.

Although claiming little relish for music, Kaufman contributed a sketch to Irving Berlin's *Music Box Revue of 1923*, and later that year, with Connelly, wrote the book for a musical comedy, *Helen of Troy, New York*, starring Queenie Smith and with a score by Bert Kalmar and Harry Ruby; this show logged 191 performances at the Selwyn Theatre. In 1924, Kaufman and Connelly supplied the book and some lyrics for *Be Yourself*, to which Ira Gershwin also contributed. The next year, with Berlin writing words and music, Kaufman provided the script for *The Cocoanuts*, starring the Marx Brothers, which had a run of 276 New York performances.

So when Selwyn commissioned Kaufman and the Gershwin brothers to write *Strike Up the Band* for the 1927–28 season, he had assembled a team with an excellent record of success.

The theme of the United States at war was far from a typical subject for humor less than a decade after World War I's armistice. But the war Kaufman invented for *Strike Up the Band* was an absurdly comic conflict with Switzerland, ignited by a chilly Swiss response to a new U.S. tariff on cheese imports. Sensing a once-in-a-lifetime opportunity, Horace J. Fletcher, proprietor of Fletcher's American Cheese Company of Hurray, Connecticut, talks an advisor of the president into war as a profit-sharing enterprise, with proceeds to come from selling tickets to battles fought in the Swiss Alps.

On a morning during National Cheese Week, the curtain rises on Fletcher's factory, where the workers declare themselves "Fletcher's

American Cheese Choral Society" in solemn four-part harmony, then sing an oath of fealty to the firm, led by their boss. Fletcher's next song affirms his self-infatuation. "Typical Self-Made American," sung to Jim Townsend, himself a farm boy turned reporter for the local newspaper—and the show's hero—is an anthem of self-congratulation, all Fletcher's claims of self-denial and strength of character being seconded by a chorus of workers.

Plant manager C. Edgar Sloane, the show's villain, hopes to marry Fletcher's daughter Joan, though she shows no interest in him. In a conversation between Sloane and Fletcher, the manager threatens blackmail if the boss fails to pressure Joan to be his wife: "I'm sure you wouldn't want anyone—especially the government—to know about that little income tax matter." When a telegram brings news of Switzerland's objection to the cheese tariff, Fletcher reaches for an encyclopedia. " 'Switzerland. A small country in the middle of Europe.' A *small* country. Well!" A military plot starts to take shape.

A coconspirator with access to the levers of power in Washington happens to be visiting Hurray that day to dedicate a mailbox (whatever that ritual might mean): Colonel Holmes, perhaps modeled on a real-life figure, Col. Edward M. House, an influential advisor to former President Woodrow Wilson. His arrival precipitates the show's fifth number, "The Unofficial Spokesman," in which Fletcher dubs Holmes "the unofficial wizard of the age." Holmes, we learn, has always found that he drew attention by remaining silent, and the chorus versifies his philosophy: "He never said a thing that was absurd, / Because, you see, he never said a word." Fletcher offers to pay the war's costs and give the government a quarter of the profits, as long as the war bears his name. And Holmes agrees. A few weeks later, a crowd gathers outside Fletcher's residence. "Fletcher's American Cheese Choral Society" has become "Fletcher's Get-Ready-for-War Choral Society." Their upbeat song, "Patriotic Rally," carries no fear of wartime mayhem, as if a friendly tussle fought with beanbags or pillows were just around the corner.

Jim Townsend and Joan Fletcher cross paths at the rally, and Joan is caught up in the excitement of the moment. But "I'm a peace-loving citizen," Jim tells her. "And I'm supposed to go over there and fight? . . . To make the world safe for Fletcher's Cheese?" Joan replies, "The man I love will want to go—he'll be proud to go." And now the pair joins forces to sing "The Man I Love," the luminous ballad cut from *Lady, Be Good!* Joan, played by Vivian Hart, sings Ira's original words, while Jim, played by Roger Pryor, answers with a second refrain imagining the girl *he* loves. The recycled song works its magic, and the two fall into each other's arms.

Joan loves her father and believes ardently in Fletcher's American Cheese, to the point of thinking war a fair price for protecting its reputation, and Jim's feelings for Joan are strong enough to coax him into the military. But as the martial drumbeat intensifies and patriotic toasts are being proposed, Jim samples the ingredients used in Fletcher's factory and realizes the cheese is the product of Grade B milk. He decides that only one course is open to him: to proclaim the coming war as a fake, an advertisement for cheese manufactured from milk that he, as a dairyman, knows to be substandard. The forum for his stand is the "Finaletto," a public confrontation with Jim on one side and Fletcher, Sloane, and Holmes on the other. Between them stands the chorus, responding to the argument being waged in the arena.

Jim first makes his case in a confident, square-cut melody, and the chorus listens respectfully. The war's proponents answer with driving, agitated-sounding music of uncertain tonality, making a counterclaim with a plausible edge of menace. When Joan weighs in with music radiating trust in her father's integrity, the townspeople's allegiance shifts in her direction, and when Fletcher weighs his own standing against that of the young journalist, the chorus supports his self-endorsement. Jim's lone voice cannot prevail against that groundswell of public opinion. Having begun on a note of controversy, the Finaletto ends with the bumptious unanimity of "Patriotic Rally" music. That this chain of events has unfolded, operalike, among characters who sing rather than speak their words invests the Finaletto with an emotional weight more nuanced and potent than the usual musical comedy temperament.

Jim is dragged off in chains, leaving the stage to Fletcher, Sloane, and Holmes, plus Mrs. Draper, an unattached dowager who shares their goals. ("If there's one thing I like," she assures them, "it's a nice war.") The cabal addresses ideological matters in a meeting of the newly formed "Very Patriotic League," convened as the four of them don Ku Klux Klan–like hoods. Purity of allegiance is deemed essential. Questions are raised about why, for example, *The Swiss Family Robinson* is still available in American libraries. The cabal discusses how upcoming battles may be staged to best dramatic effect and priced for maximum profit. Fletcher invites his colleagues to "imagine a beautiful moonlight night in the Alps—a good battle—music—maybe Paul Whiteman himself."

Brought in to face interrogation by the League, Jim is conscripted into the military, and the show's title song, which serves as the Act I finale, begins. Ira Gershwin remembered vividly the origins of "Strike Up the Band":

Late one weekend night in the spring of 1927, I got to my hotel room with the Sunday papers. . . . I hadn't finished the paper's first section when the lights went up in the next room; its door opened and my pajamaed brother appeared. "I thought you were asleep," I said. "No, I've been lying in bed thinking, and I think I've got it." "Got what?" I asked. "Why, the march, of course. I think I've finally got it. Come on in." . . . He played the refrain of the march practically as it is known today. Did I like it? Certainly I liked it, but— "But what?" "Are you sure you won't change your mind again?" "Yes, I'm pretty sure this time." . . . The reason I wanted assurance was that over the weeks he had written four different marches and on each occasion I had responded with "That's fine. Just right. O.K., I'll write it up." And each time I had received the same answer: "Not bad, but not yet. Don't worry. I'll remember it; but it's for an important spot, and maybe I'll get something better." This fifth try turned out to be it. Interestingly enough, the earlier four had been written at the piano; the fifth and final came to him while lying in bed.[12]

Gershwin's genial military march was just the right fight song for a comic war in which nobody gets hurt. Kaufman would later call it "the best song in any show of mine."[13]

Act II begins in the Swiss Alps. The weather is fine and the crowd is eager to watch a battle, but the Americans' adversaries are nowhere to be found. Jim, relegated to kitchen duty, figures out that when a Swiss general wants his troops to assemble, he summons them with a yodel. Jim proposes that the Americans hide in a particular mountain region while one of their own officers yodels, and then surround the enemy when they answer the call. His plan works like a charm. The Swiss are captured without bloodshed, the war is won, and Jim—Horace Fletcher anoints him "Major James Tecumseh Townsend"—is honored as its hero.

In the show's last scene, back in Connecticut, Jim claims Joan for his bride-to-be, with her father's blessing. He also discovers the culprit who degraded Fletcher's American Cheese from Grade A to B: Sloane, who turns out to be Col. Herman Edelweiss, head of the Swiss Secret Service. Horace Fletcher, who has agreed to marry Mrs. Draper, is vindicated as an innocent party. The way is now clear for the tariff to be repealed, and for him and his company to join an international League of Cheeses, where all cheeses are considered equal.

The ironic subject matter and biting wit of *Strike Up the Band* have worn relatively well into the twenty-first century. Jim Townsend and Joan Fletcher, rather than a juvenile and an ingénue, seem more like a hero and a leading lady; both show strong temperaments tied to moral sensibilities. Fletcher, Holmes, and Sloane are all powerful and flawed. The vacationlike setting in which the show's creators turned the plot into a musical satire is also worth noting. In April 1927, George, with Ira and his wife Leonore, rented a country house near Ossining, New York. The house stood on the forty-acre Chumleigh Farm, allowing the brothers recreational opportunities not readily available on New York's Upper West Side. Guests from the city dropped by for visits, including Kaufman, songwriter Harry Ruby—who brought his baseball glove and a ball so that he and George could play catch—and columnist Franklin Pierce Adams, who took part in a croquet match. It was here, with plenty of daylight hours available and more time than usual on their hands, that the Gershwins were first tempted to take up painting.

One invitee to Chumleigh Farm was composer Charles Martin Loeffler, born in Europe but long a Boston resident, and then living in the eastern Massachusetts town of Medfield. Loeffler had been a teacher of Gershwin's close friend Kay Swift, who, in New York the preceding April, had given a party in Loeffler's honor. Gershwin played the piano at that gathering, and shortly afterward the veteran composer wrote Swift that he had found it a revelation to hear Gershwin "play his Concerto, hear him sing his songs and— to know him." He also found Gershwin a possessor of "that rare something, indefinably lovable."[14] A friendship blossomed between the two composers, and in the coming years Loeffler would attend a number of Gershwin events and Broadway shows. Gershwin invited Loeffler to visit his country retreat, which he was unable to do because of an eye ailment, but a letter he wrote in June testifies to the warmth of his feelings for a younger member of his profession:

> It is needless to say that I have pinned my faith on your delightful genius and on your future. You alone seem to express charm,

grace and invention amongst the composers of our time. When the Anthland and Coptheils *ed tutti quanti* will be forgotten, . . . you, my dear friend, will be recorded in the Anthologies of coming ages! I am looking forward with keenest expectations of consoling delight to your latest work.[15]

The Gershwins' stay at Chumleigh Farm seems to have continued into the latter part of July, when they returned to their New York abode on West 103rd Street.

On August 29, *Strike Up the Band* had its premiere at Reade's Broadway Theatre in the seaside community of Long Branch, New Jersey. A *Variety* critic praised Kaufman and the Gershwins for having constructed an American musical on the model of Gilbert and Sullivan's "Savoy operas," but noted that "satirical musical shows have never been a success in America, though the time may now be ripe. Nor do Americans like to be laughed at on the stage—this seems to appeal only to the English."[16] On September 5, the second phase of the tryout run began, now at the Shubert Theatre in Philadelphia. The critics generally liked what they saw, the *Philadelphia Inquirer* similarly lauding the Gershwin brothers for capturing "the Savoyard mantle."

But although many critics appreciated the artful presentation of a mock war over cheese, the general public had trouble seeing beyond a premise that seemed unpatriotic, hence unfunny. By the time the company reached Philadelphia, key members of the cast had begun to give notice, and attendance fell off quickly. On September 14, barely a week after it opened there, *Variety* pegged the show as a flop and held Kaufman's book responsible. "'Strike Up the Band' won some corking notices, but the clientele did not like it at all" was the diagnosis. "The first string men, who saw it later in the week, waxed even more enthusiastic about it in their 'second thoughts,' but the pungent satire and absence of the usual musical comedy hokum in the George Kaufman book didn't get [over]."[17]

With customers staying away and losses piling up, producer Selwyn closed the show before the "furore" forecast for New York could come to pass. A forlorn memory of *Strike Up the Band*'s last days in Philadelphia probed the chasm between the show's sterling theatrical pedigree and its rejection by theatergoers. It seems that Ira Gershwin, haunted by "the ghosts of D'Oyly Carte"—a reference to Richard D'Oyle Carte, the impresario who brought Gilbert and Sullivan together—was standing with Kaufman and his brother in front of the Shubert Theatre. As they looked disconsolately down the street, a cab drew up and two elegant Edwardian-style clubmen, dressed to the nines, got out, bought tickets, and entered the theater. "That must be Gilbert and Sullivan," Ira commented, "coming to fix the show."[18]

FROM AARONS TO ZIEGFELD (1927)

BEFORE *STRIKE UP THE BAND* OPENED in August 1927, the Gershwins had begun work on their next musical, *Funny Face*, originally named *Smarty*—a return to type. Produced by Aarons and Freedley, the show had a tryout run of six weeks during October and November before bursting onto the New York scene as a hit in the mold of its predecessors. It was a high-stakes enterprise, elected to open a new 1,400-seat theater built for Aarons and Freedley, with a name—the Alvin—fashioned from the first syllable of each of their first names.[1] To mark the milestone the producers hired a potent assemblage of talent: the Gershwins, Fred and Adele Astaire, and Robert Benchley of *Life* magazine as librettist in collaboration with Fred Thompson. And in the end, *Funny Face* succeeded where *Strike Up the Band* had failed—even though at first it seemed a lost cause.

Fred Astaire found the plot "one of those things that wouldn't work—even at rehearsals,"[2] and Ira remembered that "everyone concerned with the show worked day and night, recasting, rewriting, rehearsing, recriminating."[3] After some five weeks of rehearsals in New York starting on September 6, the company left for Philadelphia and the Shubert Theatre, where *Strike Up the Band* had expired a month before. The dress rehearsal, which ran until 1:30 a.m., went so badly that Freedley called the performers and crew together for a reality check. "We don't see how it will be possible to open tomorrow night with the show as ragged as this," he told them. "I know it'll be tough, but I am going to ask you to run through the whole thing again without stopping, otherwise we'll have to postpone the opening." Another three-hour rehearsal followed, keeping the company onstage until 4:30 a.m.

The Philadelphia opening took place on October 11. "The numbers went well," Astaire thought, "but the comedy missed." Aarons decided to keep the show on the road for enough weeks to rewrite most of it, though his plan made for an exceedingly difficult time. Benchley resigned and was replaced by a known "play doctor," Paul Gerard Smith. Bad reviews in Philadelphia kept the crowds small as the company remained in town much longer than originally planned. Observers arrived from New York and returned with such glum forecasts that ticket brokers there declined to order seats for the Broadway opening. Morale ran low as *Smarty* moved on to Washington for a week, then to Atlantic City for another week. All the while, Astaire recalled, "we were playing one version while rehearsing another." The arrival of a new cast member, Victor Moore, whose comedic talents had sparked *Oh, Kay!* a year earlier, provided some encouragement, but the sense of being in limbo persisted.[4] With audiences so small, noted Astaire, "we couldn't tell how the changes were working out because there was never enough of an audience to give us a reaction."

The tour's last stop was Wilmington, where the show opened on November 14 with a newly added dance number for the Astaires, "The Babbitt and the Bromide." "It went in on a Thursday or Friday night," wrote Ira, "when the audience consisted of no more than two hundred—mostly pretty and young and pregnant Du Pont matrons (my wife's observation)." The new number "was introduced at 10:50 and concluded with Fred and Adele doing their famous 'run-around'—to show-stopping applause—and suddenly, with all the other changes, the show looked possible."[5] Astaire, too, sensed that the tide may have turned in Wilmington. "It seemed better, but we didn't know."

When *Funny Face* opened in New York on November 22, they knew. Astaire, who had been dreading certain humiliation, was pleasantly amazed: "the over-all something was there."

> Having gone through such a series of mishaps and revisions on the road, we simply didn't know what we had. Adele sang "'S Wonderful" with Allen Kearns; I did "High Hat" with an all-male chorus, also "My One and Only" with lovely Gertrude MacDonald. Betty Compton had a good specialty dance. Adele and I did "The Babbitt and the Bromide" with the old run-around once more. We discovered we had many high spots both in Victor Moore's and Billy Kent's comedy.

The New York reviews offer no hint of the difficulties that had plagued the company on the road. They are almost uniformly enthusiastic, while saying little about the plot cobbled together by Thompson and Smith. Alexander Woollcott of the *World*, having called the book "singularly perishable," proved his point by staying mum on the matter. John Anderson of the *Evening Post* was more informative: *Funny Face* was "the one about a girl and a tenor, or, to put it more brutally, the [one] about the stolen jewels. . . . They are stolen accidentally by the right people while the real burglars make off with a diary."[6]

Woollcott sensed a rare rapport at the heart of *Funny Face*. "I do not know whether Gershwin was born into this world to write rhythms for Fred Astaire's feet or whether Astaire was born into this world to show how the Gershwin music should really be danced. But surely they were written in the same key, these two." Though he was no music critic, Woollcott had reviewed Gershwin musicals for the better part of a decade, and his comments on the music stand among the most sound-oriented of any to appear in the wake of the Broadway premiere:

> For "Funny Face" Gershwin has written a clever, sparkling, teasing score. I can imagine that there are many who would find such a *sauce piquante* of odd dissonances and stumbling measures a little trying as steady fare, like a whole meal made out of Worcestershire sauce. But it is tickling music, all of it, and for once in a way the Brothers Gershwin . . . have the satisfaction of hearing their songs sung. . . . You hear such lusty volume and such harmony and such loving swipes as seldom reward our songwriters until their songs have reached the campus.

Adele and Fred Astaire, having cut their teeth as vaudeville performers, had tailored their talents to fit that environment. Neither had anything like a stentorian voice, able, like that of Al Jolson or Tessa Kosta, to be heard over the orchestra in a space built for 1,400. Songs the Gershwins wrote for the two of them ran toward the easy conversational tone of "Hang On to Me" or the tricky declamation of "Fascinating Rhythm," rather than ones more reliant on sustained tones and vocal resonance. Still, surviving recordings show that Fred's and Adele's voices had a focused timbre that must have been audible in the theater, if not thrilling for their ring. Fred's vocal production, in particular, reflected his stage persona: a relaxed-sounding performer with considerable resonance from the bottom to the top of his tenor range and the ability to project tones without signs of strain. The result was a clarity of line aided by his keen ear for pitch, apt sense of phrasing, and distinct but unfussy declamation of words—all of it grounded in the rhythmic mastery that made him a superior dancer. Once he began his movie career, Fred eventually won a reputation as a unique vocal stylist.

In *Funny Face*, Astaire plays Jimmy Reeve, guardian of three lively young women: Dora, played by Betty Compton, who has both a boyfriend and a roving eye; June, played by Gertrude McDonald, a model of feminine intelligence and virtue; and Frankie, played by Adele, a charming contrarian and inveterate liar. Much of Jimmy's energy is spent trying to extricate Frankie from trouble. But partway through Act II, he realizes that June is "My One and Only," the only song Woollcott singled out for comment, and fitting his description of "odd dissonances and stumbling measures." The verse stumbles repeatedly, for in each of the first six bars the downbeat is marked by a rest—giving Astaire opportunities to put his brand of understated virtuosity as dancer, singer, and master of rhythm on display. Another Astaire number, "High Hat"—the first time he appeared on Broadway in full evening dress, which came to be seen as his signature costume—strikes a different tone. Jimmy advises a corps of young men how to win the hand of the girl they fancy: give her "the high hat," striking a pose of superiority and indifference. The 2/4 meter forges ahead in the manner of a turn-of-the-century one-step, with syncopations that feel marchlike.

Astaire was involved in three more songs in *Funny Face*, each a duet with Adele, but only the last a full-fledged dance number. The first, the show's title song, concludes an interchange between Jimmy and Frankie that shows how exasperating life as her guardian can be. A police sergeant has given Frankie a speeding ticket; she tells the officer that Jimmy has been rushed to the hospital with a broken leg. But after visiting Jimmy at home and finding him intact, the policeman, who has dealt with Frankie before, forgives the ticket and offers her guardian his sympathies. Jimmy then questions her about a recent public incident, in which an aviator named Peter Thurston, played by Allen Kearns, landed at the local airfield and Frankie made a spectacle of herself by rushing up alone to kiss him. And then there is the matter of Frankie's diary, which includes false accounts of her lunching with Babe Ruth, joining Mayor Jimmy Walker of New York on a trip, meeting heavyweight champ Gene

Tunney, and taking a walk with President "Cal" Coolidge. Jimmy announces, over Frankie's protests, that he intends to lock the diary up in the family safe. Nevertheless, Jimmy realizes, too, that he is touched by the sheer life force of the young woman who lives so restlessly under his roof, and the song he sings now owns up to a genuine fondness. "Funny Face" offers a smooth, serene melody in appreciation of what she has brought into his life: spontaneity, imagination, and a sense of play.

By the last scene, each of the Astaires had done an ample amount of dancing, but the pair had yet to share the stage in a show-stopper. That moment arrived with "The Babbitt and the Bromide," a free-standing novelty number launched into after Jimmy learns that Frankie is engaged to marry Peter Thurston. The marking at the start of the music, "Allegretto humoroso," is unique in the Gershwin songbook.

Ira's tale begins: "A Babbitt met a Bromide on the avenue one day," Babbitt referring to a conventional, small-minded businessman and a bromide being a conventional, commonplace, and tiresome person.[7] The first refrain reproduces their exchange, a stream of clichés ("What's new? / I'm great! / That's good! / Knock wood!"); the two dullards have recognized each other on the street and stopped, but neither one can remember anything about the other, so they fake it. The second stanza depicts a replay: a chance encounter ten years later. Having anticipated "an awful lot to talk about," they return to what they'd said a decade ago. In the third stanza—twenty more years have passed—the Babbitt and the Bromide meet within "Saint Peter's gate." Each now wears wings, carries a harp, and sports a few extra pounds. Other than noting their weight gain and proposing to meet someday to have a drink, the best they can manage is a recap of their original refrain.

Given the song's storytelling form and comic character, it's likely that in this case Ira came up with the idea, mapped out the words, and George set them to music. Each refrain ends with an instrumental tag, to which the Astaires danced their signature "run-around" maneuver, ensuring that the number, and the show, would close on a high note.

Funny Face also features examples of a kind of speech that has been dubbed "flapperese": "I'm worried stiff," "I mean," "don't be ridic."[8] Conspicuous examples are found in "'S Wonderful," one of two numbers sung by Frankie and Peter Thurston. Having thrust herself into Peter's triumphant landing at the airfield, she has decided that a visit to his home is in order. After hearing a confusing story about wanting Peter to steal her diary from Jimmy's safe, he suggests that Frankie go home, which prompts her charge that he's a coward. Stunned by that challenge, Peter vows to do whatever Frankie's bidding may be. "Life has just begun," he intones, to the simplest of motives: four repeated quarter notes plus a whole note. In the verse that unfolds, transfixed by the rightness of that motive, he sings it repeatedly while moving up the scale, a step at a time, and then back down. Frankie's language in her response does the aviator one better, with its flapperesque clipping of syllables, rhyming "fash" (fashion) and "pash" (passion), and following with "emosh." In the refrain of "'S Wonderful" a depth of feeling is registered not through emphatic expression but through musical restraint.[9] The song's deft portrayal of unbidden, unconditional love has enabled it to outlive *Funny Face* by far.

Frankie and Peter's other duet, "He Loves and She Loves," is a substitute for the smoky "How Long Has This Been Going On?," introduced during the last week of the show's tryout. It follows a squabble over an auto accident that is mostly her doing. The refrain—"Slowly, with sentiment"—reflects the mood of a singer determined to preserve his romance with a partner whose unreliability could discourage even the most avid suitor. If "'S Wonderful" registers the feelings of a pair in the throes of new love, "He Loves and She Loves" reveals emotions being tested by time and experience. The refrain requires the singers to turn a melody based on disjunct ups and downs into a musical line. Perhaps the effort of making tunefulness from disjointed pitches mirrors the challenges of romantic love, likely to loom in Frankie and Peter's future.

Funny Face opened in the Alvin Theatre on November 22 and ran for more than six months. Audiences considered the Astaires as a duo, with Adele perhaps the more vivid star. Her ability to bridge the contradictions in a role like that of Frankie proves her uncanny onstage charm.

A FEW MONTHS before the new show opened, George Gershwin took part in a historic concert in Lewisohn Stadium on the campus of the City College of New York, where the New York Philharmonic offered a regular menu of outdoor concerts. On July 25, on a program bookended by Berlioz's Overture to *Benvenuto Cellini* and Rimsky-Korsakov's *Capriccio espagnol*, Gershwin played his *Concerto in F* and *Rhapsody in Blue*, marking his first performance with the city's foremost orchestra, and the first time he had played both works on the same program in New York. The concert was reviewed as a newsworthy event, in large part because of the huge size of its audience—around 16,000. "That cheering multitude must have taken George Gershwin's breath away," fancied Robert Garland of the *New York Telegram*. "Perhaps even he hadn't realized how many men enjoy both music and cigars."[10] Charles Pike Sawyer of the *Evening Post* was convinced that "Gershwin grew greatly between the rhapsody and the concerto and he is going further."[11] An unsigned review in the *Times* found that the *Concerto in F* grows on listeners "with repeated hearings, has characteristics of solid musical worth, and may well achieve a place among the significant works of contemporary American composers."[12] The stadium concert was a celebration of musical artistry that seemed to welcome everyone. No other American musician of the day could have filled a 16,000-seat stadium.

Gershwin was soon to make the aquaintance of an even more celebrated American: the real-life Peter Thurston. After his transatlantic flight the previous May, Charles Lindbergh had returned home from France to a hero's welcome. During highly publicized travels, including a tour of the West Coast, attention grew so unremitting that he dropped out of sight for a time to escape the spotlight. In the fall, as he lay low in a New York apartment, a wealthy banker named Schuyler Parsons organized a bachelor dinner party in Lindbergh's honor. The guests included inventor John Jay Hammond; aeronautical engineer Grover Loening; Charles Lawrence, who had designed the engine of Lindbergh's plane, *The Spirit of St. Louis*; theatrical producer Dwight Taylor; British writer and socialite Beverley Nichols; Charlie Hanson Towne, editor of *Harpers Bazaar* magazine; and, from the world of music, George Gershwin.

Some three decades later, Taylor published an account of the gathering, according to which Nichols, known as a raconteur, took over the conversation and dominated it through an opening round of drinks and much of the dinner that followed. Despite the best efforts of the host and others, Lindbergh was excluded from the conversation. But after the meal, Gershwin took a seat at the piano, and Lindbergh sat next to him on the bench. As Gershwin began to play the *Rhapsody in Blue*, Taylor noticed the aviator hunch forward,

> peering like a puzzled child at the lively fingers as they traveled up and down the keyboard, while Gershwin leaned back, a freshly lit cigar in the corner of his mouth, losing himself in the melancholy intricacies of his composition. The rest of the company remained silent and attentive, fully aware of the drama of the moment, in which these two idols of the contemporary scene were caught together for a brief period in time, never to be forgotten. When Gershwin had finished, the men applauded, but Lindbergh leaned forward and struck a few spasmodic notes on the piano, as if some conjuring trick had been performed, the secret of which, through

the proper research and investigation, he might possibly reveal. For the second time that evening he had found himself in . . . second place, but I think that Gershwin, aware of the atmosphere of tension which had been created by Nichols, had decided to pre-empt the floor solely to engage the guest of honor in other interests, the better to relieve him of his embarrassment.[13]

When Gershwin finished, Lindbergh asked him to play something else. But instead, the composer took the cigar out of his mouth and asked a question—the one that had been on the minds of most of the company all evening. "Tell me, Mr. Lindbergh—weren't you *afraid*?" The rest of the guests burst out in hearty laughter. "Why no!" Lindbergh answered. "Flying's my business. And I'd started out for this Le Bourget field in France." Gershwin, having broken the ice, then questioned Lindbergh in detail about how he felt during the flight.

Among the accomplished men at Parsons's dinner party that night, only he and Lindbergh knew what it felt like to be adored for doing their job: for having accomplished something extraordinary that immense throngs of Americans could appreciate and wholeheartedly admire. That evening, the aviator and the artist sat side by side on the piano bench as peers.

HAVING COMPOSED two musical comedies for production during the second half of 1927, Gershwin was then tapped for a third. *Rosalie* was a project of the foremost theatrical producer of the age, Florenz Ziegfeld, who in February had marked another milestone in an illustrious career when he opened the Ziegfeld Theatre. Born in Chicago to a family devoted to classical music—his father headed a conservatory there—Ziegfeld won his reputation as a purveyor of light theatrical entertainment, and a man whose producing talents owed more to his eye than his ear. The *Ziegfeld Follies*, whose first edition was staged in 1907, made their mark from the start as visual spectacles: dazzling in their colors and sheer profusion, and with meticulous attention to detail, from the top quality of costume materials to the painstaking care taken to create onstage "pictures" made from deftly positioned cast members. Most of all, Ziegfeld built his career around his skill at presenting feminine beauty onstage to striking effect. He ballyhooed his pageantry as part of "the Glorification of the Ziegfeld Girl."

Although raised in a musical household, Ziegfeld claimed no particular interest in music, and especially not the classical kind. On the other hand, well aware that the theater's best-known composers would enhance his shows' appeal, he worked with the likes of Victor Herbert, Irving Berlin, Rudolf Friml, Sigmund Romberg, Jerome Kern, and Richard Rodgers as well as Gershwin. These men and all his other creative personnel had to deal with a boss who controlled his productions like a dictator. Ira Gershwin credited Ziegfeld with a "hypnotically persuasive manner" manifesting "great charm until a contract was signed."[14]

George Gershwin had met Ziegfeld a decade earlier, when he accompanied dancers for *Miss 1917*. As far as can be traced through correspondence, the start of his connection with Ziegfeld the producer dates from shortly before July 22, 1927, when Gershwin wrote him about a forthcoming project:

> When I spoke to you about the Marilyn Miller show [*Rosalie*], I had no idea that the Astaire show [*Funny Face*], which I was scheduled to do, would be postponed until September. That means that the Astaire show will open in October, which would be the same time you would like to start rehearsals on the Marilyn Miller show. It is only right for me to tell you at once that I cannot see how it will be possible for me to give you the best that is in me. This is particularly unfortunate for me, as I so admire Marilyn Miller and Jack Donoh[u]e and would like so much to write for them.[15]

Ziegfeld's reply, showing him in aggressive persuasion mode, arrived the next day by telegraph. The producer asked if Gershwin could give him three or four numbers at least, "as Marilyn is so very anxious to have something from you to dance to and to sing and as you promised me you would do that show only asking me not to announce it for reasons of your own."[16]

When *Rosalie* opened in Boston on the evening of December 5, the score included several songs by the Gershwin brothers. The production that took the Broadway stage on January 10, 1928, had risen from "three or four" musical numbers by Gershwin to nine.[17] In musical comedy history, *Rosalie* has been overshadowed by Ziegfeld's near-simultaneous production: on December 27, *Show Boat*, with book and lyrics by Oscar Hammerstein II and a score by Jerome Kern, opened at the producer's own Ziegfeld Theatre. Not only did *Show Boat* continue into the spring of 1929, on the way to 572 performances, but it also won classic status as a work whose skillful integration of music and drama set a new standard for musical comedy. While *Rosalie* has enjoyed no such afterlife, some critics of the day set it side by side with *Show Boat* as another example of the master touch that Ziegfeld alone could provide.

For *Rosalie* he had certainly assembled a talented crew. The book was drafted by playwright William Anthony McGuire, who cobbled together a detailed scenario that he dispatched via Ziegfeld's medium of choice, the telegram; this one ran to forty-two pages. Ziegfeld liked what he read enough to seek out a second librettist as a collaborator—the experienced, dependable Guy Bolton. Sigmund Romberg composed ten songs for the score with lyrics by P. G. Wodehouse, plus a ballet and incidental music. Indications are that five of the nine Gershwin songs were composed for *Rosalie*, and the other four came from his trunk of unused songs written for earlier shows, including *Funny Face*.

The story was inspired, again, by Charles Lindbergh's trans-atlantic flight, plus another well-publicized event: a visit to North

America in the fall of 1926 by Queen Marie of Romania and her daughter. In *Rosalie*, American pilot Lieutenant Dick Fay lands in the Balkan kingdom of Romanza (rhymes with "stanza") after his solo crossing. There, at a peasant festival, he falls in love with a beautiful young woman, Rosalie, he had danced with at a ball in Paris the year before, only to learn that she is a princess forbidden to marry a commoner. Shortly after Dick returns to the Military Academy at West Point, where he is stationed, the Romanzan royal family pays a visit there. The queen does all in her power to keep her daughter and the aviator apart, but Rosalie manages to reconnect with Dick, and they declare their intention to marry. The final scene takes place in Paris, where the king of Romanza— flirtatious, henpecked, and bored with his job—abdicates. His act makes Rosalie a commoner, free to marry the man she loves.

In a show set in both Europe and America, the Hungarian-born Romberg, a master of operetta, supplied most of the martial and all the Old World dance music, while Gershwin's offerings were cast in more modern and New World styles. Ira wrote the lyrics for most of his brother's music, as Wodehouse did for Romberg's. Neither the credits nor manuscripts surviving from the show indicate that the composers collaborated on any songs, though the lyricists did so on three of them.

Because Marilyn Miller was a famous and accomplished dancer— Ira remembered her as "Broadway's biggest musical star"—and was eager for new music by Gershwin, it is no surprise that four of his nine songs were written for her character. Three are duets, one of which was with Dick Fay, played by Oliver McLennan, sung at the peasant festival in Rosalie's homeland. "Say So!" is a tender exchange between a young man and woman who, believing themselves to be profoundly in love, are actually meeting for only the second time. Gershwin's verse music adds a legato countermelody that brings a textural richness to a tune fashioned around repeated quarter notes. Then, a hint of eroticism in the more dancelike refrain affirms the romantic destiny of the princess and the American commoner.

Miller's other two duets are sung with Jack Donahue in the role of Bill Delroy, Dick Fay's best buddy and Rosalie's coconspirator in her quest to join her destiny with Dick's. In "Let Me Be a Friend to You," the two endorse their personal link in a number that went unpublished and whose music has not survived. Their second duet is a genial and innocent show-stopper that won success outside the theater, "Oh Gee!—Oh Joy!," with lyrics by Wodehouse and Ira. Here, two-syllable exclamations—"gee whiz!," "heigh-ho!," and others—salute love as one of life's best rewards, sung to music with an inexorable, exuberant flow.

One beneficiary of Ziegfeld's recruitment of Gershwin was Bobbe Arnst in the role of Mary O'Brien, Bill Delroy's girlfriend, who is visiting Romanza. Where Miller received new material that displayed her talents mostly alongside others', Arnst was assigned three solo songs, including two written for earlier shows and already in print. "Show Me the Town" had been composed for *Oh, Kay!* but then removed, owing to a change in the script. As the first song in *Rosalie*, it introduces Mary as a spunky American party girl who is game for whatever the locals have in store. Later, she sings "How Long Has This Been Going On?," a potent love song cut from *Funny Face*. Written and published as a duet for Mary with Bill, it was transformed, by the time of *Rosalie*'s New York debut, into a number for her alone to fill an entire short scene in a secluded West Point rendezvous. Now that Mary has met Bill Delroy and taken his measure, the song testifies, she has learned why the physical side of romance has sparked so much enthusiasm. Set in a bluesified four-beats-to-the-bar rhythmic environment, Mary's confession celebrates an innocent's entrée to the realm of erotic loving. Addressing her absent mentor with wonder, this young woman declares her readiness to double down on lessons learned under his romantic tutelage. According to critic Leonard Hall in New York,

"How Long Has This Been Going On?" leaves its mark on the show through the persona of "Little Bobbie Arnst," whose performance as "one of those amazing young lumps of original sin that break out these days, is singled out."[18]

Arnst's personal success mirrored that of the show as a whole. *Rosalie* succeeded at the box office, running from January until October 27, 1928, for 335 performances.

AMERICANS IN EUROPE (1928)

EARLY IN 1928, Gershwin alerted Mabel Schirmer and Ira's wife
Leonore to the trip they would soon be taking to the Old World:

> We sail on the Majestic on March 10th, going straight to London,
> and expect to stay in London from a week to ten days. Then we are
> coming to Paris. . . . I expect that we will stay in Paris for about two
> weeks and then go someplace where the climate is right, and where
> I can do some work. If, however, I find somebody to study with in
> Paris, I may take a place on the outskirts of Paris and stay there most
> of the time.[1]

While the transatlantic junket would be the first for his fellow travelers, it was George's sixth, and it represented a new stage in his
composing career. He had begun work in January on *An American
in Paris*, and his hope of finding a teacher there—a regular quest
through much of his life—persisted as the thought of a prolonged
stay in Europe became reality.[2]

Gershwin met one famous possibility even before setting sail:
Maurice Ravel, visiting North America for the first time. Ravel's

stay in New York included attending a performance of *Funny Face*—which left him "enchanted"—and a fifty-third birthday party given for him on March 7 by Eva Gauthier. Gershwin, one of her evening's guests, "played the *Rhapsody* and, in fact, his entire repertoire, and fairly outdid himself," remembered Gauthier, who acted as interpreter. "It was an unforgettable evening, the meeting of the two most outstanding composers of the day, the young man just beginning to scale the heights, the other at the very pinnacle. (That was before the *Bolero*.)" Ravel professed himself astonished by "the facility with which George scaled the most formidable technical difficulties and his genius for weaving complicated rhythms and his great gift of melody."[3]

Gershwin was anxious to work with him, yet both agreed that such a connection could prove dangerous, in that "it would probably cause him to write bad 'Ravel.'" In a sign that Gershwin had impressed him deeply, Ravel wrote the celebrated teacher Nadia Boulanger in France the next day:

> Here's a musician endowed with the most brilliant, the most captivating, perhaps the most profound qualities: George Gershwin. His universal success is not enough for him any more. He aims higher. He knows that for that he needs something he doesn't have. But were we to teach him what he wants to learn, it might destroy him. Will you have the courage, which I dare not have, to take on this terrible responsibility?[4]

In Paris, Schirmer accompanied Gershwin to visit Boulanger, who told him "she would not take him as a pupil because he had a natural musical talent that she wouldn't dare disturb for anything."[5] But given his successes as a self-directed musician on a path essentially his own, the idea that Gershwin's creative spirit might prove too impressionable to stand up against the influence of even a prestigious teacher like Ravel or Boulanger seems far-fetched.

The Gershwins sailed at 11 a.m. on March 10 and arrived on the morning of March 16. If there had been doubts about the brothers' standing overseas—at least in English-speaking regions—they disappeared when the *Majestic* landed at Southampton. A staff member from Harms-Chappell met the party, shepherding them through customs and into a private compartment on the boat train. "We ordered champagne & biscuits & got to London shortly after 9 [a.m.]," Ira wrote about his first day on British soil.[6]

The Gershwins quickly found themselves part of an elite circle. On March 19, they attended a runthrough of *That's a Good Girl* starring Jack Buchanan, a show for which Ira had written some of the lyrics, collaborating with Desmond Carter and Douglas Furber, both Englishmen, with a score by the Americans Phil Charig and Joseph Meyer. The next day turned into "strictly a Harms affair," as Ira saw it: a gathering of the boss, Max Dreyfus; composers Jerome Kern, Vincent Youmans, and Phil Charig; lyricist Leo Robin; arranger Robert Russell Bennett—who had orchestrated the *Good Girl* score—and the Gershwin brothers. Two nights later, George and Frances attended a Noël Coward revue, *This Year of Grace*, which they enjoyed so much they saw it again the next night. March 24 found the party attending the last night of the Gershwins' *Oh, Kay!* at His Majesty's Theatre, with Gertrude Lawrence in the title role. Ira was impressed with the supper they were served afterward in George's hotel room: "A lovely meal with plenty of wine and cocktails, smoked salmon, consommé, filet of sole, duck, apple sauce, asparagus, sweet, coffee, cigars, brandy—swell."

Sandwiched in among these events was "George Gershwin Night" at an emporium called the Kit-Kat Club. The evening featured a *Rhapsody in Blue* ballet for three dancers, the composer taking a bow at the end; a pair of London singers performing "The Man I Love"; and two songs from *Oh, Kay!* sung by Lawrence, with Gershwin at the piano. "Usually the piano accompanies the voice," wrote one critic of this last turn, "but Gertie Lawrence, realizing that everybody wanted to hear Gershwin, played her part so modestly that the song became an accompaniment to the piano—and a very remarkable piece of piano playing it was, too."[7]

This European excursion, a blend of luxury, privilege, and discovery, was at least partly a celebration of the Gershwins' success. But as the trip proceeded, a theme beyond tourism came to the fore: the artistic standing of a twenty-nine-year-old American composer and pianist, recognized in capitals as varied as London, Paris, Berlin, and Vienna as a significant presence in music. The Gershwins traveled under the banner of Harms, which maintained close ties with European music publishers. Visiting cities where musical life flourished, they received warm greetings upon their arrival, introductions to local musicians, especially composers, and invitations to performances and social events. The gregarious George reveled in doing what he always did. Making friends wherever he stopped, he enlivened many a social occasion, as in New York, by playing his music and captivating listeners as he won the respect of fellow musicians. In a later era, the tour might have been organized on a career-boosting schedule. In the event, however, the trip proved to be a family adventure during which George worked on his new orchestra piece while exploring possibilities for enhancing the classical side of his work. The excursion has left little impact on the historical record, yet—in part due to the diary Ira kept—it offers a clear view of how musicians outside the United States responded to Gershwin and his music.

Leaving London on March 25, the party traveled to Paris, where they settled into the Majestic Hotel for a four-week stay. France would be the family's main stomping grounds through much of their overseas stay, proof that George was convinced that there was no better place to sample the lessons and delights of Old World civilization.[8] Not only was he composing a work set in Paris, he quickly found common ground with other musicians in the city. As Ira saw it, the travelers "were profoundly impressed with the high

regard conservative Frenchmen had for American jazz composers."
While in New York "the only evidence of a writer's popularity is in
his weekly earnings," in Paris "serious composers gather about him,
ask to hear his songs, and send him copies of their scores to read."

American friends in Paris included Josefa Rosanska, a pianist
from New York who had studied with Edward Kilenyi at the same
time as Gershwin. The day after the family's arrival, George's
room was filled with visitors: "Josie" Rosanska played the piano that
had been moved in, and the New Vienna Quartet, led by violinist
Rudolf Kolisch, a student of Arnold Schoenberg, played the first
movements of Schoenberg's String Quartet No. 2 and Schubert's
Quartet in D Minor, subtitled *Death and the Maiden*. Also on the
scene and ready to help entertain the Gershwins was their French
publisher, Salabert.[9] Its store was managed by a Monsieur Fekerte,
and after borrowing a phonograph from the store, George enlisted
Fekerte's help on a personal search he had undertaken on this trip:
a determination to acquire a copy of every piano composition by
Claude Debussy.

On March 29, after treating George and Ira to a meal, Fekerte
led them back to Salabert's, where he acted as interpreter while a
local journalist interviewed George. Back at the hotel around 7:30
p.m., with Rosanska already there, Leopold Godowsky, Jr. arrived
with his mother and father—Leopold, Sr., a world-famous pianist who also composed. The younger Godowsky, a chemist as
well as a violinist, would gain notoriety as coinventor, with musician Leopold Mannes, of the process of color photography known
as Kodachrome—and, two years younger than George, he would
marry Frances Gershwin two years later. On this rainy evening,
with eight hungry mouths to be fed, the Gershwins ordered in from
the hotel kitchen. After dinner, two more couples joined the party:
American pianist Herman Wasserman and his fiancée, and Mr.
and Mrs. Alexander Tansman. Another musical evening was in the
offing. As Ira noted, "Godowsky [Sr.] played—played for 3 hours

almost without stopping. His collar wilted during the 1st piece he played—a Pasacaglia (?) he had just finished—44 variations without pause—on the 1st 8 bars of Schubert's Unfinished [Symphony]. His technique held his auditors spellbound if I may make so hackneyed." It seems that nobody wanted the gathering to end. "The Godowskys (Mrs., that is) had expected to be in bed by 11:30 but the party didn't break up until 2:30—so it must have been good. A lovely evening. To bed at 3:30."

Two days later the Gershwin brothers found themselves at a Saturday concert of the Pasdeloup Orchestra at the Théâtre Mogador that began with Franck's Symphony in D Minor and closed with the *Rhapsody in Blue*. By now Ira was an old hand at listening to his brother's best-known composition, but the Pasdeloup rendering set its own standard. "I alternately giggled & squirmed during this performance; it was at times almost unbelievably bad." The solo piano part had evidently proved too difficult for the soloist, Jean Wiener, who divided the part with an "assistant" who had apparently been told "to oompah." At least one of the harmony players charted a rogue course on a banjo, playing "the same chord almost all thru the piece." Nevertheless, when the middle Andante theme arrived, Ira stopped squirming as he realized that this portion of the *Rhapsody* "couldn't be spoiled." It now occurred to him that the audience members might actually be enjoying the piece; since most of them had never heard this music before, perhaps they had taken the "sour notes as a true reading" and were finding it an interesting kind of modern music. His hunch proved right for, as the performance ended, spontaneous applause resounded "all over the house & lots of cheers & bravos."

George had left for the bar as the performance was winding down, but when Ira "saw Wiener on the platform looking over the audience & then gesticulating to the conductor, I knew they wanted George. So I called him & he was rushed back stage—and on his appearance the house gave him another big hand." As an encore, Wiener and pianist Clement Doucet played a verse and three polished choruses of "Do-Do-Do" from *Oh, Kay!*, this number evidently having been practiced. The conductor, Rhené-Baton, later apologized to George, explaining that an orchestra version of the *Rhapsody* had been cobbled together from the published piano arrangement, and the musicians had had only half an hour's rehearsal.[10] Even so, and "despite the almost laughable performance, George was thrilled by the reception."

As the travelers settled into the Majestic Hotel, George's work on *An American in Paris* resumed in earnest. On April 3, he and Mabel Schirmer went shopping for the Parisian taxi horns whose sound would add local flavor to the piece. Not long after this excursion, Gershwin received a visit from two young pianists, Mario Braggiotti, American-born, and Jacques Fray, a French native, who had teamed up at the Paris Conservatory. They had learned from the newspaper that a musical hero of theirs was visiting Paris and one morning showed up at his door. "There was a Steinway piano right in the middle of his room," Braggioti recalled,

> and I noticed on the piano a collection of taxi horns—from those old-fashioned taxis they used in the Bataille de la Marne. There were about twenty of them lying there. I hadn't been to New York for a few years, so I thought this was some new American eccentricity or fad. I didn't know what to make of it. "Oh," [Gershwin] said, "you're looking at these horns. Well, in the opening section of *An American in Paris* I would like to get the traffic sound of the Place de la Concorde during the rush hour, and I'd like to see if it works."

In the music he had just sketched, a pair of taxi horns would sound an A-flat and an F-sharp, Gershwin explained. "Now, I'll sit down and play, and when I go this way with my head, you go 'quack, quack, quack' like that in that rhythm." "So we took the horns," continued Braggioti, "and there we stood, nervous and excited, and for the first time we heard the opening bars of *An American in Paris*—a lanky American walking down the Champs-Elysées." When the moment for the horn parts arrived, "he nodded and we came in." Braggioti marveled at Gershwin's creative touch in this passage: "He captured the atmosphere, the feeling, the movement, the rhythm so perfectly."[11]

Vladimir Dukelsky dropped by on April 6, having recently won success in London with a musical comedy called *The Yellow Mask*. Dukelsky had spent years in Paris during the 1920s and knew the scene well:

> True to my 1928 form, I paid them a call attired in [a] gunmetal creation (now a little tight for me), a pale-yellow Sulka shirt, an orchid in my buttonhole, the whole structure supported by a magnificent eighteenth-century walking stick, a Christmas present from myself, purchased in Bath. So staggering a façade didn't fail to render the Gershwins speechless; they stared at me, then at one another, then back at me, and had good enough manners not to laugh out loud.

George played him portions of *An American in Paris*, which Dukelsky found "somewhat saccharine in spots."[12]

Frances Gershwin later spoke of the 1928 trip as "the first time something . . . happened to me." The main thing happened during the hours when George and Ira wanted to play poker, and Leo Godowsky would take her off to a café to chat. "I was so shy that I didn't have any idea he was interested in me." But something happened on another front, too: "Frankie" had musical talent as well as good looks, and in Paris she was asked to sing at a party given by Elsa Maxwell. George accompanied her for a roomful of listeners that included Cole Porter. On April 21, as the Gershwins were preparing to leave Paris for an excursion to German-speaking lands, Porter joined them for lunch and asked Frankie if she would be interested in going on the stage. She was very interested, and Porter called the manager of his soon-to-open show, *La Revue des Ambassadeurs*, making an appointment for 10 p.m. That evening the Gershwins and Godowskys dined at the home of ballerina Albertina Rasch and pianist Dmitri Tiomkin. Just before ten, George and Frankie left to see the manager, returning around 1 a.m. with a contract. "How much?" Ira asked, to which George answered unsentimentally that it "might have been better." But when Ira saw the agreement, he could hardly believe it—"$200/wk for an unknown." This coup for the little sister called for a celebration, including more drinking and music-making that lasted until 3 a.m.

The next day, the Gershwins boarded a train for Berlin—leaving Frankie behind to prepare for her show—and arrived on the morning of April 23, taking rooms at the Hotel Esplanade. George was met at the hotel by Fritz Wreede, head of the literary agency Felix Bloch Erben and a man who did business with Louis Dreyfus, brother of Max, who oversaw Harms's European interests. After arranging for a Steinway piano to be delivered to Gershwin's room, Wreede transported him to a meeting of the International Congress of Authors and Composers, a performing rights society. The evening's main activity proved to be within walking distance of the Esplanade: a piano recital at the Salle Bechstein by Josie Rosanska.[13]

Ira stepped out for a while the next morning, April 24, and returned to find George in conversation with a young German composer named Kurt Weill, who had stopped by the hotel.... That evening, at the Grosses Schauspielhaus, the Gershwins attended their first German operetta—*Mme. Pompadour*, by Viennese composer Leo Fall, in a production that Ira found "Ziegfeldian."[14] Lunch the next day, with Fritz Wreede and the eminent operetta composer Franz Lehár, was followed by a meeting of another performing rights organization, this one called GEMA, a German equivalent of ASCAP. Here the composer, introduced as "George Gershwin, a big shit from America," addressed questions about how royalties were figured and dispensed in the United States. In the evening, with Rosanska and Henrietta Malkiel, a New York journalist friend, the Gershwins attended a theatrical performance that affected them deeply: a musical show that Ira identified as *"Die Reise Benjamins des Dritten"* (*The Journey of Benjamin the Third*) presented by the Moscow Jewish Academy. The show impressed Ira more than any other he attended on the trip:

> The direction was absolutely sensational, and never have I seen such acting on the stage. . . . The songs in the production were not delivered in the American manner with verse and choruses. Instead, there were snatches rendered. The music, while Yiddish, was absolutely different from the Yiddish music of Rumshinsky on Second Avenue in New York, who obviously emulates the style of the Broadway tin-pan alley scriveners.

On the morning of April 28, as an overnight train carried the Gershwin party eastward toward Vienna, the Paris edition of the *New York Herald* published a piece based on an interview Gershwin had given in Berlin. In the interview, the composer expressed his view that jazz, as heard on phonograph records, was taken more seriously in Germany than in the United States. Since it loomed so large in the popular marketplace, few American composers found its artistic potential promising; but in Germany, jazz music as a distinctive, imported style offered an intriguing modernity for local composers to explore. "Perhaps next year I shall be able to come over to Germany for a year," Gershwin said.[15]

The Gershwin group, now comprised of George, Ira, Lee, and Henrietta Malkiel, arrived in Vienna on the 28th and was escorted to the Hotel Bristol by Hungarian-born composer Emmerich Kálmán. At lunchtime, Kálmán—joined by two librettists and a pair of newspaper reporters—took them to the Café Sacher; as the party of nine arrived, a jazz band struck up the *Rhapsody in Blue*.

Evening found them at the Theater an der Wien, where Kálmán's newest operetta, *Die Herzogin von Chicago* (*The Duchess of Chicago*), was enjoying the early weeks of a long run. The composer's eagerness to have the Gershwins see this work was no mystery, for, as Ira noted, the music reflected a distinct American influence. It also "took on the aspects of a Wagnerian opera" in that the show began at 7:30 and ended after 11, when the group gathered at a Hungarian restaurant for dinner.

Around 1 p.m. the next day, Kálmán came by the hotel to visit George, who played for him for an hour and then, along with Ira, joined him for lunch at his apartment—where they met playwright and novelist Ferenc Molnár, as well as Albert Sirmay, a Hungarian composer and editor who had moved to New York five years earlier to become a leader of Harms-Chappell music.[16] Determined to offer his guests the ultimate in hospitality, Kálmán had asked his cook to prepare blue ice cream in honor of the *Rhapsody*. Many attempts to reproduce the color failed, however, so they served ice cream studded with American flags instead.

The afternoon at Kálmán's, which lasted until after 5 p.m., was filled with music and conversation. Kálmán's knowledge of the New York stage astonished Ira—knowledge partly gleaned from *Variety*, "which he reads from cover to cover." From their host the brothers learned, too, why American musical comedies had gained little popularity in German-speaking lands: by the time a production such as the 1924 Broadway operetta *Rose-Marie* reached a German city, the music had preceded it and the songs were old-hat. Ira observed with interest that Kálmán and Lehár were "treated like Babe Ruths and Gene Tunneys." Wherever they went, "they are followed by crowds, their countrymen are always taking their photographs and constantly asking the composers for their autographs." And their earning potential benefited from the decentralized network of theater companies in Austria and Germany, where a successful show could be performed in over fifty houses at once.[17]

That evening found the Gershwins at the Vienna Opera House to see Ernst Krenek's *Jonny spielt auf* (*Johnny Strikes Up the Band*), a work much discussed and debated—sometimes under the label of "jazz opera"—since its premiere in 1927.[18] Their presence led to a chance meeting. In the lobby at intermission, a member of the audience was overheard launching a diatribe in English against this "phony" artistic attempt, insisting that "if such an opera were to be done effectively it should be by George Gershwin." The critic—who turned out to be Lester Donahue, currently in Vienna on a concert tour—was startled to hear a reply in that very composer's voice: "Oh yeah?"[19]

Personally and artistically, the stay in Vienna was rewarding for Gershwin. He "could understand a little German," remembered Kálmán, "though he could not speak it, and we both knew a little French. . . . We could not talk much in words, so we talked in music."[20] The two musicians struck up a warm friendship nevertheless, and before leaving Vienna on May 6, Gershwin inscribed a picture of himself: "To my great friend Kálmán with ardent esteem. George."[21]

More consequential, though, was Gershwin's encounter with Alban Berg, whom he visited at his home on May 3, probably in Josie Rosanska's company. Although he did not jump at the chance to play for Berg, whose music differed so greatly in style from his own, after the Viennese modernist encouraged him with a comment along the lines that music is just music, Gershwin did oblige, to the pleasure of those present.[22] "George big hit with Berg," wrote Ira; "even Josie is impressed." On May 5, George's last full day in Vienna, he was treated to some of Berg's latest music. Ira's diary notes: "Kálmán came up [to the hotel], then half an hour later George & Josie returned from Kolisch's where they had heard Alban Berg's string quartet [the *Lyric Suite*] with Berg one of the auditors." Gershwin also brought back with him an autographed photograph of Berg, incorporating a three-bar excerpt from the score: "Mr. George Gershwin in friendly remembrance of [excerpt from the *Lyric Suite* in musical notation], the 5th of May, 1928, and of Alban Berg."[23] The ground had been laid for the Viennese composer's later influence on Gershwin, especially through his opera *Wozzeck*.[24]

WHEN THE GERSHWINS left Vienna the next day, George returning to Paris and Ira, Lee, and "Henry" heading east to Budapest, several more weeks of their European trip remained. At the Ambassadeurs Café in Paris on May 10, Cole Porter's *La Revue des Ambassadeurs* had its official opening, with a mostly American cast. George was on hand to accompany Frankie, whose role took the form of a specialty number. But Porter's revue did not work out for her. As Frankie explained to Ira and "the girls" when they returned to Paris on May 22, "practically nothing could be heard above the dishes," so the management had decided to go in for "a visual, rather than aural show."

The Parisian musical event of Tuesday, May 29, was a concert at the opera house featuring works by Weber, Liszt, Copland, and, for the first time on the European continent, Gershwin's *Concerto in F*. Vladimir Golschmann conducted, and Dmitri Tiomkin was soloist in both concertos. Russian-born and -trained, Tiomkin had lived and worked in the United States from 1925, championing both modern and American music, before marrying choreographer and ballerina Albertina Rasch in 1927.

In the audience that evening were three Russians—two composers and an impresario. "I took both [Serge] Diaghilev and [Sergei] Prokofiev to hear Gershwin's piano concerto," Vladimir Dukelsky reported later in his autobiography:

Diaghilev shook his head and muttered something about "good jazz and bad Liszt," whereas Prokofiev, intrigued by some of the pianistic invention, asked me to bring George to his apartment the next day. George came and played his head off; Prokofiev liked the tunes and the flavorsome embellishments, but thought little of the concerto (repeated by Gershwin), which, he said later, consisted of 32-bar choruses ineptly bridged together. He thought highly of Gershwin's gifts, both as composer and pianist, however, and predicted that he'd go far should he leave "dollars and dinners" alone.[25]

Most critical response to Gershwin's concerto was positive. Emile Vuillermoz, a leading critic in Paris and friend of Debussy and Ravel, felt that every "musician of good will" should "realize that syncopated music has now taken its degree, that it is not a frivolous pastime and that the Old World will be singularly unwise if it does not hastily seize the opportunity to renew its youth by taking a plunge into this fresh river, which might well be a fountain of youth for some of our rather bored artists." The *New York World* reported that "after the concerto the whole audience rose and thundered ovation after ovation for the pianist and conductor and composer." When Tiomkin and Golschmann "bowed their recognition to Gershwin, he was compelled to come to the front box as the hero of the greatest manifestation of enthusiasm seen at the Paris Opera for a long time past."[26] After the performance, wrote Ira,

> we went to Laurent's on Avenue Gabriel where we found in the garden under an awning a crowd of 30 or so; let me see—Cole Porter, Clifton Webb, Mr. Honegger, Frances Hunter, Bea Lillie, Jules & Kendall (looking beautiful), Tansman, George and some countess, our hostesses Elsa Maxwell, Grace Moore, Fray & Braggiotti and others. Had supper and then all adjourned to the dance room where were two Steinways whereon Fray & Braggiotti played, then Porter, Lillie, Moore and George entertained in turn. We left about 2:30.

Informal music-making marked the Gershwins' remaining days in Paris. On May 30, the evening after Tuesday's concerto performance, a musical gathering took place at the home of violinist Samuel Dushkin. As Ira summarized it: "a Concerto for two violins by Bach, then Vladimir Horowitz played, then George. Nice formal people there and a nice formal party. Later Horowitz played his study on Carmen, a marvelous technical accomplishment. Dushkin also played Short Story & Blue Interlude accompanied by George."27 On Thursday after breakfast a musical confluence in George's room consisted of "Josie, the [Kolisch] Quartet, the Tansmans and George playing for a critic who I learned was [London-based] Ernest Newman." That evening, May 31, saw a party in honor of the Gershwins at the home of Mrs. Ernest Byfield, a wealthy American living in France. Ira reckoned the size of the gathering at around 200: "We got there about 11 (Lee, Bob, Mabel & I); Frankie & Golschmann about 11:30 and George, who had been at a party at Baron Rothschild (which one I don't know), about 12." The list of other guests he spotted was varied:

> Blythe Daly, Bea Lillie, Deems Taylor, Margot & Ernie Goldfinger, Helen Laidow, Fray & Braggiotti, some counts and barons, Nadia Boulanger, Dushkin, Russell Bennett, Orloff, George Slocombe, Arthur Moss, a couple of guys with monocles and dirty shirts, a band, 8 caterers, Madame Andre (Boskowitz), Tansmans, Man Ray, Lawrence Vail, Sylvia Beach, the Tiomkins, Mike Shepard, Dersow, Mrs. Marx, Josie, Kolisch, Alex Aarons & Gilbert Kahn & wives, Arthur Kober, Elsa Maxwell, etc. etc.

Dawn was breaking as he and Lee "got into a car with Deems Taylor and Henry" Malkiel and headed back to the hotel.

George left Paris for the U.K. before the rest of the party. On June 3, Ira "went to George's room about 2 and found Lee, Mabel and Henry helping him pack to go to London. Alex [Aarons] came up and Tiomkin and Golschmann and Dagmar [Godowsky] and Dushkin and Riviere and the Tansmans and and and." Five days later, Gershwin visited the Columbia studio in London to record the Three Preludes and the slow theme from the *Rhapsody in Blue*, and on June 13 the family sailed for home.

BACK IN THE U.S.A.:
AN AMERICAN IN PARIS (1928)

DURING HIS GANGPLANK INTERVIEW after the *Majestic* landed in New York Harbor on June 18, 1928, George Gershwin reached into one of his dozen suitcases, pulled out a Paris taxi horn, and honked it. "This is to be part of the scenery and atmosphere in my new 'American in Paris,'" he told the reporters. Then he waved the manuscript of his composition in progress. "It begins in 2/4 time," he declared, "very gay, the atmosphere of Paris," and he identified other national gaits while he was at it—Vienna was 3/4, New York 4/4, London 6/8, and Russia 5/4. After some remarks about the Paris performance of his *Concerto in F* and his admiration for Alban Berg (he had been "all over Europe talking about Berg"), Gertrude Lawrence walked by, and he noted that he'd write a new musical for her as soon as "a good book with a plot" could be found. *Strike Up the Band* would be resurrected, he added. The public could expect a "Rhapsodie in Blue No. 2" too, and "after that a Rhapsodie in Red, but not radical."[1] Comments like these made it clear that the European trip had done nothing to change Gershwin's commitment to both the Broadway stage and the concert hall.

Indeed, the complexity of his creative horizon had increased, for,

together with his references to Berg, he wrote that summer to introduce himself to Charles Henry Meltzer, a British dramatist, critic,
and opera librettist, to ask whether he might have a libretto ready
to go, or an idea for one.[2] Expressing "agreeable surprise," Meltzer asked Gershwin what he had in mind. The composer replied
on August 3:

> I have seen two performances that appeal to me as much as anything
> I have ever seen from the standpoint of operatic possibilities; one
> was DuBose Heyward's "Porgy" and the other was "The Dybbuk."[3]
> "Hansel and Gretel" is another type of opera that appeals to me. I
> must tell you, though, that foremost in my mind at present is sym-
> phonic orchestration, and I expect to do some more work for sym-
> phony orchestras before attempting an opera. Still there is no harm
> in our getting together to talk it over.

Meltzer replied that something like "Porgy" seemed the more likely
choice because of its subject: "Americans would love to hear one big
opera dealing with America." However full Gershwin's slate for
the future might be, the operatic challenge posed by Otto Kahn
in his November 1924 interview had claimed an abiding place in
his plans.

During the late summer and early fall of 1928, Paul Whiteman
recorded an arrangement of the *Concerto in F* that he had commissioned from Ferde Grofé with Roy Bargy, the Whiteman Orchestra's regular piano soloist; both Gershwin and Bill Daly attended
retake sessions that were deemed necessary. The new arrangement
was unveiled to the public at Carnegie Hall on October 7, as part of
Whiteman's "Third Modern American Music Concert."[4] Although
the concert drew an overflow crowd, critics disagreed about Gershwin's concerto. Samuel Chotzinoff of the *New York World* reaffirmed
his belief that the *Concerto in F*, even in this arrangement, was "one
of the two most important works composed in the last ten years,"

the other being the *Rhapsody in Blue*.⁵ But Olin Downes of the *Times* found Grofé's "excessive instrumentation" to be no improvement to a composition that in the first place was "a serious effort, but on the whole, a poor one."⁶

The musical comedy score Gershwin wrote that summer for Gertrude Lawrence was *Treasure Girl*, produced by Aarons and Freedley in hopes of repeating her success with *Oh, Kay!* The show seems to have had an uneventful tryout period, but after opening on November 8 in the Alvin Theatre, it closed early in January after only sixty-eight performances. The notion that this show could flop seemed improbable, considering its charismatic star, successful producers, gifted songwriting team, and corps of skilled dancers. And in fact, the critics found things to praise besides the star: Joseph Urban's sets, the superior costuming and production values, and the contributions of dance director Bobby Connolly, not to mention a few strong musical numbers by the Gershwin brothers. Other cast members too—especially comedian Walter Catlett and the secondary couple, Mary Hay and Clifton Webb—won kudos. But from the start, *Treasure Girl* flunked musical comedy's ultimate test: it failed to entertain the audience. Robert Benchley, writing for *Life* magazine, found the experience deadly: "There is a general atmosphere of a lost cause about the whole thing which depresses the cast as well as the audience."⁷

Most agreed that the libretto by Fred Thompson and Vincent Lawrence deserved much of the blame. Attempts at humor, wrote Richard Lockridge of the *Sun*,

fell and struck the stage and did not perceptibly stir thereafter. "It was a heritage from my grandfather," he says bravely, as he hands her the diamond ring. "Oh, it must have been grandpa's glass eye," she comes back promptly. And then they wait. "What does 'four' stand for?" he asks. "'Four' stands for a quartet," says the other he. And they wait. There is no need to go on; no necessity even to point out that some of the lines are better than these, since it must be apparent that few could be worse.[8]

Brooks Atkinson of the *Times* accused the book's authors of taking "the unforgivable liberty of presenting the accomplished Miss Lawrence in a disagreeable light. When she is not too uncritical of herself Miss Lawrence embodies most of the qualities that make for versatility and splendor in musical comedy stars—slender, fresh beauty, a lilting style of dancing, fullness and sweetness of voice, infectious mirth, a trick or two of clowning, subtle coquetry and a gift for dramatic acting." However, "handicapped by a book that pictures her as a malicious liar and a spoiled child generally . . . she rather overdoes her clowning and coquetry."[9]

The romance in *Treasure Girl* between Ann Wainwright, played by Lawrence, and Neil Forrester, played by Paul Frawley, was rarely delightful to behold. The treasure hunt around which the show revolves is a commercial scheme cooked up by real estate mogul Mortimer Grimes to sell properties on land he is trying to develop: Grimes's hope is that by staging a competition with a princely prize, he will lure prospective customers to his property. Neil is Grimes's manager, recovering from the end of his romance with Ann, who claims to be wealthy but is being hounded by a process server for unpaid debts. In the course of searching for the treasure, Ann finds her way to the cottage where Neil lives. Having once shaken hands on the premise that, for the two of them, "love is a wash-out," they sing a number steeped in wistfulness, regret, and irony: "I Don't Think I'll Fall in Love Today." (Ira doubted that this title would have come to him if he hadn't read G. K. Chesterton's poem "A Ballad of Suicide," which features the refrain "I think I will not hang myself to-day.")[10] When Ann tries to lure Neil away so that the hunters can search for buried treasure on his property, the emotional current latent between them boils to the surface in an impassioned love song, "Feeling I'm Falling," with lyrics filled with a flood of f-words—fooling, feeling, falling, fatal, flutter, felt, flame—mostly in three-syllable lines. But when Ann then rejoins the competition, Neil retreats into his cottage in disgust.[11] And rather than delivering a traditional high-energy first-act finale, the librettists left Lawrence poignantly alone onstage to portray her character's inconstancy: a mimetic challenge that flopped. It is no wonder that as the Act I curtain came down on opening night, applause was brief and tepid. Nor is it surprising that the score for this finale has been lost.[12]

Ann eventually finds the treasure, a box full of money, and engages in an unpleasant fight with Neil. The last scene features the two-piano team of Victor Arden and Phil Ohman, elevated to the stage from the orchestra pit, accompanying Ann in her only solo song, "Where's the Boy? Here's the Girl." She has apparently been transformed, by a process akin to that of Shakespeare's taming of the shrew, and realizes that she needs Neil by her side. When he announces that he has decided to move to Mexico, Ann takes a now-or-never risk: "I have found the treasure of all the treasures," she announces to the crowd that has gathered to celebrate her winning of the prize. "Neil Forrester has just asked me to be his wife and I have accepted him." Dazed at first by her claim—"So you love me that much?"—Neil ends up taking Ann in his arms. Normally, no better result is possible in a musical comedy, yet *Treasure Girl* ends on a skeptical note. In one of the script's more telling exchanges, after Hopkins, the process server, addresses Neil with "Mr. Forrester, my congratulations! This is the happiest day of your life," Neil responds, "No it isn't. I'm going to be married tomorrow." To which Hopkins replies: "That's what I say. *This* is the happiest day of your life."

An early January closing proved the end of the road for *Treasure Girl*. No tour for the company followed, nor did a London production.

Wedding photograph of Morris and Rose
Gershwin, New York City, 1895.

George Gershwin, ca. 1913.

George Gershwin in Atlantic City, ca. 1916.

Paul Whiteman and his Palais Royal Orchestra, ca. 1924.

Fred and Adele Astaire celebrate their famous run-around dance in a publicity photograph for *Lady Be Good!* (1924).

George Gershwin's inscribed photograph
of Rosamond Walling, ca. 1928.

George Gershwin posing with James Rosenberg and Richard Crooks and the *American in Paris* taxi horns, Cincinnati, February 1929.

Frances Gershwin, New York City,
July 1929. In 1930 she married
Leopold Godowsky.

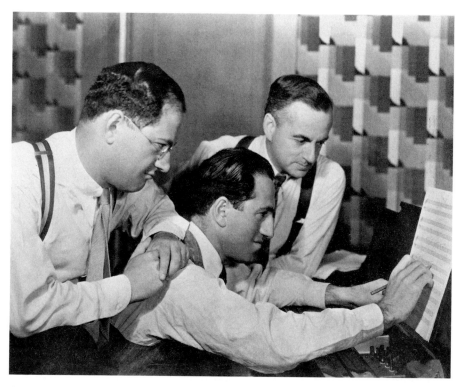

George and Ira Gershwin with *Delicious* scriptwriter Guy Bolton, Hollywood,
December 1930.

George Gershwin with Serge Koussevitzky, posing with the score of the Second Rhapsody before its premiere in Boston, January 1932.

George Gershwin with Bill Daly in Gershwin's penthouse apartment at 33 Riverside Drive, New York City, ca. 1932.

George Gershwin, ca. 1934.

Craps game in Catfish Row, *Porgy and Bess*, Act I, scene 1.

John W. Bubbles as Sporting Life entertains the people of Catfish Row in *Porgy and Bess*, October 1935.

Porgy and Bess opening-night curtain call, Alvin Theatre, New York, October 10, 1935. Behind George Gershwin, from left to right, are: Georgette Harvey (Maria), Ruby Elzy (Serena), Todd Duncan (Porgy), Anne Brown (Bess), Rouben Mamoulian (director), DuBose Heyward, Warren Coleman (Crown), and, probably, Helen Dowdy (Lily/Strawberry Woman).

Kay Swift, ca. 1936. Photographed by George Gershwin.

The last known photograph of George Gershwin, taken during a performance at RKO Studios, June 16, 1937.

. . .

AS DISAPPOINTED as Gershwin may have been by his first Broadway venture after the European trip, by then other opportunities had materialized. On August 14, the *New York Post* reported that he had received an offer of $100,000 from the Fox Movietone Company to write music for a "talking moving picture." But two more years would pass before he and Ira were ready to tackle this new medium; the offer arrived as George completed the orchestral composition he'd been working on since January.

In an article by Hyman Sandow in *Musical America* on August 18, based on a long conversation in the Gershwin domicile on West 103rd Street, the composer explains the nature and purpose of *An American in Paris*, a piece of orchestral program music whose title signals its departure from traditional orchestral fare:

> My purpose is to portray the impression of an American visitor in Paris as he strolls about the city, listens to the various street noises, and absorbs the French atmosphere. . . . Our American friend, perhaps after strolling into a café and having a few drinks, has suddenly succumbed to a spasm of homesickness. The harmony here is both more intense and simple than in the preceding pages. This 'blues' rises to a climax followed by a coda in which the spirit of the music returns to the vivacity and bubbling exuberance of the opening part with its impressions of Paris. Apparently the homesick American, having left the café and reached the open air, has downed his spell of the blues and once again is an alert spectator of Parisian life. At the conclusion, the street noises and French atmosphere are triumphant.[13]

As a world capital, Paris had a rich and distinctive musical legacy for a composer to draw upon, but for *An American in Paris* Gershwin introduced his own musical tradition to complement the

French one. He emphasized that contrast through tempo: walking music played off against nonwalking—café—music. These two realms of musical contrast—French versus American, mobile versus stationary—aided the composer in shaping his ABA^1 form. The statement (A) is designated by a tuneful and absorbing flow of musically related moments experienced during a tourist's city walk, while the contrasting portion (B) is ruminative, addressing listeners with a stately and memorable blues theme, which is interrupted briefly by the effervescent strut of jazz-based dance music. The return of A^1 material, brief enough that Gershwin calls it a coda, reconciles the contrast somewhat by bringing portions of A and B into proximity with each other. As Deems Taylor wrote, characterizing the end of the work on Gershwin's behalf: "The blues return," but the orchestra "decides to make a night of it."[14]

On December 8, 1928, a guide suggesting the narrative that unfolds during the orchestra's performance of *An American in Paris* was published in the *New York Evening Post*. "This analysis was prepared on behalf of Mr. Gershwin," the statement explained, by Deems Taylor, "after going over the score and hearing a rehearsal."[15] At the premiere concert in Carnegie Hall, a slightly longer version of Taylor's scenario was distributed:

> You are to imagine . . . an American, visiting Paris, swinging down the Champs-Elysées on a mild sunny morning in May or June. Being what he is, he starts with preliminaries, and is off at full speed at once, to the tune of the First Walking Theme, a straightforward, diatonic air, designed to convey an impression of Gallic freedom and gaiety.
>
> Our American's ears being open, as well as his eyes, he notes with pleasure the sounds of the city. French taxicabs seem to amuse him particularly, a fact that the orchestra points out in a brief episode introducing

four real Paris taxi horns (imported at great expense
for the occasion). These have a special theme allotted
to them (the driver, possibly?), which is announced by
the strings whenever they appear in the score.

Having safely eluded the taxis, our American apparently passes the open door of a café, where, if one is to
believe the trombones, *La Maxixe* is still popular. Exhilarated by the reminder of the gay 1900s, he resumes
his stroll through the medium of the Second Walking
Theme, which is announced by the clarinetist in French
with a strong American accent.

Both themes are now discussed at some length by
the instruments, until our tourist happens to pass—
something. The composer thought it might be a
church, while the commentator held out for the Grand
Palais, where the *Salon* holds forth. At all events, our
hero does not go in. Instead, as revealed by the English
horn, he respectfully slackens his pace until he is
safely past.

At this point, the American's itinerary becomes
somewhat obscured. It may be that he continues on
down the Champs-Élysées; it may be that he has turned
off—the composer retains an open mind on the subject.
However, since what immediately ensues is technically
known as a bridge passage, one is reasonably justified
that the Gershwin pen, guided by an unseen hand, has
perpetrated a musical pun, and that when the Third
Walking Theme makes its eventual appearance our
American has crossed the Seine and is somewhere on
the Left Bank. Certainly it is distinctly less Gallic than its
predecessors, speaking American with a French into-
nation, as befits the region of the city where so many
Americans foregather. "Walking" may be a misnomer,

for despite its vitality the theme is slightly sedentary
in character, and becomes progressively more so.
Indeed, the end of this section of the work is couched in
terms so unmistakably, albeit pleasantly, blurred, as to
suggest that the American is on the *terrasse* of a café,
exploring the mysteries of an Anise de Lozo.

And now the orchestra introduces an unhallowed
episode. Suffice it to say that a solo violin approaches
our hero (in soprano register) and addresses him in
the most charming broken English and, his response
being inaudible—or at least unintelligible—repeats
the remark. The one-sided conversation continues for
some little time.

Of course, one hastens to add, it is possible that a
grave injustice is being done to both author and protagonist, and that the whole episode is simply a musical transition. The latter interpretation may well be
true, for otherwise it is difficult to believe what ensues:
our hero becomes homesick. He has the blues; and
if the behavior of the orchestra be any criterion, he
has them very thoroughly. He realizes suddenly, over-
whelmingly, that he does not belong to this place,
that he is the most wretched creature in the world, a
foreigner. The cool, blue Paris sky, the distant upward
sweep of the Eiffel Tower, the bookstalls of the *quai*,
the pattern of the horse-chestnut leaves on the white,
sun-flecked street—what avails all this alien beauty?
He is no Baudelaire, longing to be 'anywhere out of the
world.' The world is just what he longs for, the world
that he knows best; a world less lovely—sentimental
and a little vulgar perhaps—but for all that, home.

However, nostalgia is not a fatal disease—nor, in this

instance, of overlong duration. Just in the nick of time the compassionate orchestra rushes another theme to the rescue, two trumpets performing the ceremony of introduction. It is apparent that our hero must have met a compatriot; for this last theme is a noisy, cheerful, self-confident Charleston without a drop of Gallic blood in its veins.

For the moment, Paris is no more; and a voluble, gusty, wisecracking orchestra proceeds to demonstrate at some length that it's always fair weather when two Americans get together, no matter where. Walking Theme Number Two enters soon thereafter, enthusiastically abetted by Number Three. Paris isn't such a bad place after all: as a matter of fact, it's a grand place! Nice weather, nothing to do till tomorrow. The blues return, but mitigated by the second Walking Theme—a happy reminiscence rather than homesick yearning—and the orchestra, in a riotous finale, decides to make a night of it. It will be great to get home; but meanwhile, this is Paris!

The December 13 premiere featured in the first season of the newly merged New York Symphony Orchestra, led by Walter Damrosch, and the venerable New York Philharmonic. To mark Gershwin's debut with New York's foremost orchestra, a gathering in his honor followed at the home of Jules Glaenzer, where Gershwin was presented with a brass humidor engraved with the names of many admirers. An accompanying speech by Otto Kahn, widely reported in the press and published in January, likened the composer's character and achievements to those of another heroic American from the same generation: Charles Lindbergh.

As for the critical response to the premiere performance, Edward

Cushing of the *Brooklyn Eagle* praised Gershwin's composition as something new,

> received with a demonstration of enthusiasm, in contrast to the conventional applause which new music, good and bad, ordinarily arouses. . . . Here is music made of materials that are not thread-bare, that have not been worn thin and defaced by centuries of careless usage, music that is spontaneous and fertile of ideas, whose energy is real and not the product of brain sweat, and whose expressive power in the use of a musical idiom peculiar to the present, and valid as art, cannot be seriously questioned.[16]

Herbert Peyser of the *Telegram*, however, found the American traveler boorish: "a familiar and deadly type" resistant to the cultural riches of a storied city. And as for the music, "Mr. Gershwin's latest 'effusion' turned out to be nauseous claptrap, so dull, patchy, thin, vulgar, long-winded and inane that the average 'movie' audience would probably be bored by it into open remonstrance."[17] The review by Oscar Thompson of the *Evening Post*, however, took a more even-handed approach to music that had engaged the audience:

> The honks have it. Four automobile horns, vociferously assisted by three saxophones, two tom toms, rattle, xylophone, wire brush, wood block and an ensemble not otherwise innocent of brass and percussion, blew or thumped the lid off in Carnegie Hall last night. . . . For those not too deeply concerned with any apparently outmoded niceties of art, it was an amusing occasion. Audience, orchestra, the composer himself, smiled, chortled or laughed aloud as the work was being played. They found its musical buffoonery good fun in spite of, or perhaps because of, its blunt banality and its ballyhoo vulgarity. But after all, this is the twentieth century, and what is a little banality and vulgarity between friends?[18]

Other New York critics judged the new piece in the context of Gershwin's previous classical compositions. Three in particular, who had attended the premieres of the *Rhapsody in Blue* in 1924 and the *Concerto in F* in 1925, command attention as contributors to a body of opinion taking shape around a unique figure on the American scene. W. J. Henderson of the *Sun*—a fierce champion of the *Rhapsody* as a statement of American modernism—credited the new work with a similar "rollicking spirit," "engaging candor," "much cleverness," and a first walking theme that was "aptness incarnate."[19] According to Olin Downes of the *Times*, *An American in Paris* resembled the *Rhapsody* more closely than it did the concerto, which had struck him as a bit too conventional. He found the new work replete with modern influence, if still within the orbit of Broadway. Downes also believed that Gershwin had used his automobile horns to good effect and "in a really witty way."[20] As for Samuel Chotzinoff of the *World*, he judged the new work "harmoniously modern," "alive in every way," and "easily the best piece of modern music since the Concerto in F."[21] In fact, once he had read and digested the responses of a wide swath of his fellow critics, he devoted his next Sunday column to that subject.[22]

GEORGE GERSHWIN's first instrumental composition had been inspired by a specific purpose of his own: to demonstrate that jazz music ranged beyond the strict dance rhythms that had vitalized the American vernacular in the years after World War I. In 1924 Paul Whiteman's groundbreaking "Experiment in Modern Music" had introduced the *Rhapsody in Blue* to the public as an exemplar of home-grown artistry for an audience drawn to concert halls. His second instrumental work, 1925's *Concerto in F*, was a sequel to the *Rhapsody* in that its origins also lay in the agenda of a conductor. Its perpetrator was Walter Damrosch, who, having witnessed the impact of the *Rhapsody*, commissioned the concerto so that he could claim the virtuosity and artistic brilliance of George Gershwin for his own orchestra, and for the concert-hall stage at large. As for *An American in Paris*, however, composed three years later, it was the composer's own idea. Set in a foreign place that Gershwin knew firsthand, the music tells a good-natured story, as the composer put his growing command of the art of orchestration on public display.

The experience of a traveler's walk is reflected—or traced, or implied, or signified, or hinted at—in a composition for symphony orchestra. The music's unfolding creates an aural canvas reflecting what the traveler could encounter as he walks, responding now and then to what he sees and experiences. As a songwriter, Gershwin was practiced at inventing music to express or signify the feelings and doings of human characters. Moreover, as a composer he was engaged in a lifelong process of interweaving musical repetition and contrast over time in order to fashion musical structures balancing variety and coherence. *An American in Paris* offers listeners a story told in a succession of five themes, woven together by a gifted hand. But beyond the story too lay a more strategic goal. As he had explained to the librettist Meltzer that summer, with an opera in his long-term sights, he was determined to gain more experience as a composer of orchestral music to underlie dramatic scenes.

Adding *An American in Paris* to his repertory—his third major composition outside the theater, and the only one not to feature a piano soloist—also encouraged Gershwin to take up the art of orchestral conducting. Within a year of the piece's completion, after coaching with New York musician Arthur Bodansky, the composer was including performances of *An American Paris* in his public career as a maker of music.

IN MIDCAREER
(1929)

ON JANUARY 9, 1929, soon after its premiere, *An American in Paris* was broadcast on the radio by the RCA Victor Symphony Orchestra, conducted by Nathaniel Shilkret, who followed up with a recording on February 4. Gershwin had a hand in the recording, as Shilkret recounted:

George called me and gave me a list of instrumentalists needed to record *American in Paris* the next day. He would bring the score and parts. What he forgot was to mention a celesta player. The next morning Gershwin was at the recording studio, and we started to play the manuscript. As we ran over the number, George kept suggesting this and that for about fifteen minutes. I finally turned to him and said, "George, please get lost for about one hour. This is a new work for me and the orchestra. Let us get acquainted with the score. I'll understand you, but not until then." George went off, but I was sure that he stayed in the hall, where I could not see him. When he returned, I said, "George, you forgot to let me know that a celesta player was needed." He was sorry and said, "I'll play the celesta." We recorded the *American in Paris*, but George was so excited that, in one place, he did not play the celesta.[1]

The end of February found him in Ohio for a performance of the new work by the Cincinnati Symphony Orchestra. Local columnist Charles Ludwig wrote a memorable description of a morning rehearsal: as the session began, Gershwin joined conductor Fritz Reiner on the podium, telling the orchestra what had been on his mind as he composed his new work and throwing in a quick seminar for the percussionist assigned to play the taxi horns. Even after the orchestra swung into action, he stayed at the conductor's side.

> As [Reiner] directed the work, Gershwin, overflowing with enthusiasm, joined in. He was caught up in the lilt and swing of his own jazz music and waved his body and moved his feet and hands with the dance rhythms, pointing to the musicians of different sections of the orchestra as a cue as each, in turn, joined in the performance. And all the while Gershwin smoked his long pipe. It was a rare picture: a dancing young composer smoking a pipe, swinging his body, tapping his feet on the floor in dance time and waving his hands to different parts of the orchestra.[2]

As in New York, the Cincinnati audience welcomed *An American in Paris* warmly, while the critical reception was mixed. Robert Aura Smith of the *Commercial Tribune* wrote that "the audience understood its terminology from first to last and had a wonderful time," but William Smith Goldenburg found the music out of place in a concert hall—a clear case of "Class C goods on a Class A counter."[3]

The winter and spring of 1929 saw Gershwin promoting his new orchestra piece and working on two different Broadway scores— *East Is West* and *Show Girl*, both for Ziegfeld—while significant changes also took place in his personal life. The Gershwins sold the five-story residence on West 103rd Street where they had lived since 1925. By early spring, George had rented a penthouse atop a seventeen-story apartment building at Riverside Drive and 75th Street, while Ira and Leonore moved into an adjoining penthouse. On the heels of this move, word went out in the press that the composer, who in recent years had shown a growing interest in the visual arts, had taken up painting in earnest. His painter cousin Henry Botkin, visiting from Paris, was quoted in the *New York Sun* on April 10: "George only took up painting recently, but he has a natural ability that is absolutely remarkable. He also wants to start a modern picture collection, and to give him a better understanding and appreciation I suggested that he study painting seriously."[4]

The next month, the *New Yorker* magazine published a profile of Gershwin by S. N. Behrman entitled "Troubadour," which conveyed something of the magic of a social gathering when the composer sat down to play:

> You get the sense of a complete mastery, a complete authority—the most satisfactory feeling any artist can give you. . . . He sings. He makes elaborate gestures. When he comes to a line in "My Little Ducky"—"Gloria Swanson is hot for me, / Look at the pin she got for me"—hand flies to his tie to convey the better Miss Swanson's magnanimity. Described, this sounds grotesque, but actually it is as beautifully interpreted as a clever harmony. Gershwin becomes a sort of sublimated and transplanted troubadour, singing an elemental emotion, an unabashed humor.

"He told me once," Behrman continued, "that his mother had cautioned him against playing too much at parties. With engaging candor Gershwin admitted that there might be some truth in this; but . . . 'You see, the trouble is, when I don't play, I don't have a good time.'"[5]

By the spring the long, lucrative run of the current Ziegfeld success was nearing its end. The epic *Show Boat* was going to complete its year-and-a-half run on May 4, and, not wanting to let his Ziegfeld Theatre go dark, the producer needed a replacement. The Gershwins had set to work on *East Is West* as early as January, but when librettist William Anthony McGuire failed to deliver a script by March, Ziegfeld postponed it and pointed the Gershwins toward *Show Girl*. George filled in some of the circumstances for a radio audience in 1934:

> I'll never forget *Show Girl* because it was the greatest rush job I've ever had on a score. I was working on another show for Mr. Ziegfeld, when he suddenly decided to drop that one and produce *Show Girl* immediately. He often did those things. Mr. Ziegfeld called me down to his office one day and said, "George, I'm going to produce J. P. McEvoy's *Show Girl* and you must write the score for it. We go into rehearsal in two weeks!" I said, "But Mr. Ziegfeld, I can't write a score in two weeks. That's impossible." Mr. Ziegfeld smiled up at me and said, "Why, sure you can—just dig down in the trunk and pull out a couple of hits." Flo Ziegfeld had a way of getting what he wanted. . . . Well, the show went into rehearsal with half the score finished and about one third of the book completed. [6]

His comments were made to introduce a broadcast performance of one of *Show Girl*'s most enduring songs, and they led to an anecdote that is hard to forget:

> Mr. Ziegfeld said, "I would like to have a minstrel number in the second act with one hundred beautiful girls seated on steps that cover the entire stage." This minstrel number was to be sung and danced by Ruby Keeler. So we went to work on a minstrel number and wrote "Liza." The show opened in Boston—and I think the last scene was rehearsed on the train going up. The first act went along fine. The second act came and the attractive and talented Ruby Keeler appeared to sing and dance "Liza." Imagine the audience's

surprise, and mine, when without warning Al Jolson, who was sitting in the third row on the aisle, jumped up and sang a chorus of "Liza" to his bride! Miss Keeler and he had just been married. It caused a sensation, and it gave the song a great start!

After this surprise during the Boston tryout, the same thing happened at the Broadway premiere, and virtually every review written in both cities mentioned it.[7]

The character of *Show Girl* and the philosophy of its producer help to explain the speed with which the production—a combination of musical comedy and revue—was thrown together. McGuire's Cinderella-story libretto is centered on Dixie Dugan, an eighteen-year-old from Brooklyn, and how she realizes her ambition to star on Broadway in a Ziegfeld show. The real Ziegfeld placed *Show Girl*'s Dixie, played by a tap dancer who could also sing and act, in both the main narrative and a show-within-a-show purporting to be an edition of the *Ziegfeld Follies*. This allowed him to insert special acts and episodes as he saw fit; discontinuity was the result.

Among the best revue-style episodes involved a trio of nightclub entertainers, all making their Broadway debuts: comedian-singer-pianist Jimmy Durante, dancer Lou Clayton, and minstrel-style singer and strutter Eddie Jackson. Cast as stage crew members, they added comic antics to their professional duties. Durante brought much of his own material to the show, reducing the workload of both librettist and songwriters; Ziegfeld had already taken a step in that direction by adding lyricist Gus Kahn to the songwriting team.[8] Nick Lucas, a singer who accompanied himself on guitar, made two appearances as a specialty act. A decision was also made to start the second act with *An American in Paris*, refashioned as a mix of pantomine, song, and ballet, created by Albertina Rasch and featuring ballerina Harriet Hoctor; during the last week of June, when *Show Girl* was enjoying its tryout run in Boston, *An American in Paris* was simultaneously having its local premiere with the Boston Pops Orchestra under Alfredo Casella. Finally, Ziegfeld added a rising African American jazz ensemble known as Duke Ellington and His Orchestra to the cast. Featured in two spots—Act I's cabaret scene, which included the act-closing "Harlem Serenade," and an Act II "minstrel scene"—Ellington and his musicians completed their *Show Girl* turns early enough in the evening to allow them to fill their regular engagement at Harlem's Cotton Club.

Rather than being "written" by librettist McGuire, *Show Girl* was assembled by interweaving a stage drama with varied specialty stuff. Because Ziegfeld hired the talent, made the decisions, and shaped the whole as it evolved, he acted as the show's architect and its artistic conscience. As if to remind the audience of that fact, the character of "Mr. Ziegfeld" maintains an offstage presence, referred to by characters as a powerful figure whom they strive to please.[9]

Dramatizing a 1928 novel centered on the Broadway theater, the show begins, improbably, with the final scene from a purported Ziegfeld production called *Magnolias*, set on a Colonel Witherby's plantation during the Civil War. The scene features a duel between suitors for the hand of the colonel's daughter, then shifts to the backstage lives of the young working women whose looks and talent make such spectacles possible. Despite its flimsy connection to the main body of *Show Girl*, Ziegfeld continued to work on the lavish opening even after the Broadway run had begun. A specialty for dancers was cut, and a Finaletto for the ensemble by the Gershwins and Kahn was replaced by a new song, "Mississippi Dry," by songwriters not otherwise connected to the show: music by Vincent Youmans, lyrics by J. Russel Robinson. This new number, an African American love lament grounded in the blues, was sung by the Jubilee Singers, a bona fide black chorus. The opening thus introduces the audience to the pagentry of race in the American South. Even before adding the number by the Jubilee Singers, Ziegfeld had Jimmy Durante, blacked up as if in a minstrel show, playing that scene as a servant who delivers mint juleps to Colonel Witherby, responding to his every order with a servile "Yes, Massa."

The critic for the *Boston Herald* cited moments when Durante and his two cohorts "set the house in an uproar of laughter."[10] Moreover, when *Show Girl* reached New York, Brooks Atkinson felt that "Durante's sizzling energy can galvanize any audience," although "his spluttering, insane material does not melt gracefully into a musical comedy book. His personality, however, batters its way through all barriers."[11] Perhaps the admirer most in thrall to Durante's art, and Ziegfeld's too, was Gilbert Seldes, who in the *New Republic* named *Show Girl* his favorite of all Ziegfeld's productions. Durante, he wrote,

> easily "runs away with the show"—but stops short of spoiling it because he manages to make whatever he does contribute to the affairs of Dixie Dugan and her lovers, and, what is more important, to the affairs of the chorus and the stage manager and Mr. Ziegfeld. He tells bad jokes and good ones with complete confidence in their wit or lack of it—and makes them equally amusing.[12]

Ruby Keeler left the cast for reasons of health, but even though she played Dixie Dugan for only a week in Boston and three more in New York, the positive reviews she received, plus the story of her famous husband serenading her, secured her place in the show's history.[13] Atkinson caught hints of erotic complexity in her performance, "a prospect of sin."[14]

Show Girl, touted as "a good summer show," closed on October 5 after 111 performances. Nevertheless, the musical carries historical significance if for no other reason than that it marks the first and only time that Gershwin and Duke Ellington, iconic figures of twentieth-century American music, worked together. As Ziegfeld's show opened in New York, Gershwin was approaching his thirty-first birthday, while Ellington had recently turned thirty. Gershwin was establishing himself as a presence in the classical as well as the popular sphere. Ellington, also a composer-pianist as well as an orchestra leader, was coming to be recognized as a leading and original voice in the New York cabaret and dance hall, and one whose jazz-based music was circulating widely through broadcasts and recordings. If Gershwin was an avid student of music, always ready for more instruction, Ellington was self-taught, apparently by design. Showing uncanny skill at borrowing and synthesizing material from members of his orchestra plus a wide range of other musicians, through his long career he remained wary that formal training might compromise the uniqueness of his musical voice. Considered strikingly fresh in their own day, the music of both composers hardly seems less so today. Indeed, the identification of both Gershwin and Ellington with jazz music, and the differences between their approaches, suggests the breadth of the American musical landscape's creative possibilities in the 1920s.

Even looking beyond the divide that, in 1929, still discouraged interracial collaboration in a metropolis as dominating as New York, the protocols of Broadway musical comedy left little chance for artistic engagement between these two paragons. Both were working for Ziegfeld and were subject to his artistic decisions—and some of those decisions amounted to a waste of Ellington's "magnificent" ensemble in the view of critic Abbe Niles, who felt they had been assigned a role that an ordinary band could have filled just as well.[15]

THE FIRST published Gershwin song from *Show Girl* is sung by Dixie at her audition for the *Ziegfeld Follies*: she's trying out for the role of an innocent who has never kissed the same man more than once. Having recently received a kiss whose clarifying impact lingers in her bones, in "Do What You Do" she sings of being hungry for more of the same. The show's second published song introduces her boyfriend Denny, a traveling greeting-card salesman, played by Eddie Foy, Jr. After opening a glowing letter from Dixie about her upcoming audition, an idea he abhors, Denny shows a genuine strain of lyric tenderness for her in "So Are You." Dixie's next song, "I Must Be Home by Twelve O'Clock," is set in the New York penthouse of John Milton, a rich playboy who is throwing a "pajama party" for the showgirls of *Ziegfeld's Follies*. Dixie, surprised to find herself on a couch next to Milton, together with a gaggle of pajama-clad and crapshooting girls, proclaims over and over that she's absolutely *got* to leave this party. Here the Gershwin brothers—and Gus Kahn—wrote a song whose discontinuities model the workings of a confused mind. The number reveals the dark side of a glamorous social scene, and shows Dixie to be sensible, observant, and no easy mark for a man on the make.

The Act I finale, "Harlem Serenade," is sung by Dixie and the ensemble at the Club Caprice, with Duke Ellington and his orchestra accompanying. This pure revue number is built around the notion of a nightspot featuring music that gives white customers a taste of what was passing there for Africa. Nor was it new to Ellington's musicians, whose regular venue, the Cotton Club, was the kind of establishment where "jungle" scenes and "jungle music" were standard fare.

The remaining new song in *Show Girl*, "Liza (All the Clouds'll Roll Away)," is sung in the Act II "minstrel scene" that, from the start, had loomed large in Ziegfeld's conception of the show. "Liza" is something of a second-act counterpart to the opening plantation number. As the scene was originally conceived, it opens with "Follow the Minstrel Band" sung by Eddie Jackson "in One," meaning in front of the curtain, apparently accompanied by the Ellington Orchestra. After a verse and refrain, the curtain rises on a full stage where the female chorus repeats "Follow the Minstrel Band" and then dances to it. "Liza," sung by Nick Lucas, follows with a nostalgic glimpse of a romantic evening in the antebellum South.

The male protagonist pictures a "moon shinin' on the river" and a "breeze singin'" through the trees.

On the heels of the minstrel band number, the song's parade of racially tinged markers—the chorus of "minstrel girls"; a belle called Liza, a common name for black female characters; the colloquial diction of the lyrics; and the easy informality of the marriage proposal being delivered—give the flavor of a blackface number for white performers.[16] "Liza," a song with a thirty-two-bar refrain, was soon embraced by jazz musicians, partly on the strength of a harmonic plan in **aaba** form that lent itself to theme-and-variation improvising—as the number's composer himself soon learned.

A BREAKUP
AND A REDO (1929–30)

By ALL INDICATIONS, whatever goodwill existed between the
Gershwins and Ziegfeld ran out before the summer of 1929 was
over. According to one report, the producer, dissatisfied with the
music for *Show Girl*, pressed the brothers for more songs. When
they declined, Ziegfeld's lawyer wrote to say that other songwriters
would be called in "to do your work" at the Gershwins' expense.
As a result, Youmans and Robinson's "Mississippi Dry" was added
early in August, and the Gershwins' royalty payments from the
box-office proceeds were apparently discontinued, prompting them
to begin legal proceedings to claim their contractually agreed-to
share.[1] George recounted a final meeting with Ziegfeld in a letter to
Rosamond Walling on October 10, five days after *Show Girl* closed:

> Ziegfeld (the rat) sent for me. On arriving in his office he immedi-
> ately threw both arms around me & only my great strength kept
> him from kissing me. He informed me he was "so sorry" we had a
> disagreement & was anxious to make up—send me a check for back
> royalties—& be friends. I consented but as yet no check has arrived.
> Funny guy, heh?[2]

As it happened, Gershwin's and Ziegfeld's fortunes would soon take opposing turns. The producer's theatrical enterprise was dealt an irreparable blow when, on October 29, the stock market crashed, wiping out his financial base. Although he managed to produce several more shows before his death in 1932, he could not maintain, in the new decade's straitened economy, the mix of free spending and scrupulous care for details that had made his lavish style of stage production possible. Gershwin's escape to fresh ground was highlighted barely a week after the hugging episode in Ziegfeld's office, when the *New York Evening Post* announced that the next step in his musical evolution would likely be the composition of a grand opera on a Jewish theme, to be called *The Dybbuk*. "I am not by any means giving up Broadway," Gershwin assured the reporter. "I am working on a revival of 'Strike Up the Band,' which will be produced this winter." And he added: "I will probably do more musical comedy this season and perhaps a movietone,"[3] the latter his word for cinema with music, which by the end of the 1920s was established as a popular entertainment medium.

Events in the days after *Show Girl* closed offer glimpses of the varied strands in Gershwin's musical life. On October 8, in Milwaukee the local Philharmonic Orchestra performed the *Concerto in F* with a pianist from Chicago.[4] The following evening, a new play, *June Moon*, by George S. Kaufman and Ring Lardner, opened at New York's Broadhurst Theatre; its subject was the Tin Pan Alley songwriting trade, and in one scene the action freezes in awe at the news that George Gershwin has just walked into the office. Moreover, the performing rights to the *Rhapsody in Blue* had just been sold to Universal Pictures for use in a movie featuring Paul Whiteman, earning Gershwin $50,000, the largest price ever paid for such rights.[5] In addition, on October 28 conductor Serge Koussevitzky wrote to Gershwin to invite him to compose a piece for the Boston Symphony Orchestra on the occasion of its fiftieth anniversary.[6] Two days later Gershwin signed a contract with the Metropolitan Opera to write a score for *The Dybbuk* (though it was an agreement that proved null and void when another composer announced that he had a contract for the same work). On November 10, in a concert by the Manhattan Symphony Orchestra, Gershwin conducted a performance of *An American in Paris* at the Mecca Auditorium on West 55th Street; he also served, on that occasion, as a musical commentator.

In November, a journal called the *American Hebrew* published an essay entitled "Fifty Years of American Music: Younger Composers, Freed from European Influences, Labor Toward Achieving a Distinctive American Musical Idiom."[7] The byline was George Gershwin's, but evidence of another voice, or maybe an earnest editor, can sometimes be detected. American music, the author declares, "must express the feverish tempo of American life." The foremost pioneer cited in this mission is Irving Berlin, who has produced "the first germ of an American musical idiom," and in "Alexander's Ragtime Band" the first "real American musical work."[8] "Gershwin" then cites Leo Ornstein and Ernest Bloch for their work in idioms other than jazz, and two younger compatriots, Aaron Copland and Louis Gruenberg, the latter the composer of *Daniel Jazz*, for exploring jazz in works for the concert hall, though the writer finds something vital lacking from the results:

> All of these musicians were trained by Europeans. Men like Bloch and Ornstein have been taught to think in terms of idioms employed by Brahms and Richard Strauss; Copland has been trained to think along the lines of Stravinsky and Schönberg. The result, when they attempt to compose American music, is that their training sticks to them and their American music becomes diluted with their European traditions.

In contrast, the article continues, "neither Irving Berlin nor I were taught by European masters—and so we were the free men whereas all others were slaves. We could plunge wholeheartedly into this new culture that is America, we could absorb the spirit and tempo of American life and, at last, we could express it, more or less, in our music because our music was as yet virgin and uninfluenced."

Whatever the value of its thesis, the article departs significantly in tone from all other writings published under Gershwin's name. Some of the vocabulary—"autochthonous" and "nympholeptic" are two arcane word choices—is foreign to Gershwin's discourse. More-over, the phrase "virgin and uninfluenced" stands at odds with the facts of Gershwin's own training: for European-born and -trained Edward Kilenyi gave him a thorough schooling in part-writing, fig-ured bass, and other skills drawn from the classic masters, and that instruction was built on a foundation laid by concertgoing and years of piano lessons. Finally, the article's last paragraph reads as if some-body else made it up. Gershwin's other articles reveal that he had a voice as a writer, but not this one:

> Fortunately, more and more of the younger American compos-ers are realizing the wisdom of freeing themselves from Euro-pean influences—and so we have an increasing number of young men who, quietly and patiently, labor toward achieving American music. . . . And, now that we have almost reached our destination, we realize that the goal is a glorious one, beckoning us resplen-dently: that it is infinitely worth striving for; and that all of our past efforts and labors have not been in vain.

If, at the end of the 1920s, a trend did exist among young American composers to free themselves from European influence, it's improb-able that Gershwin would have left them all unidentified except for Irving Berlin.[9]

FOR ALL THAT Gershwin found on his classical docket in the fall of 1929, he and Ira had work to do for Edgar Selwyn, who was planning a revised version of *Strike Up the Band*, scheduled to reach Broadway early in 1930. Kaufman's 1927 book had been reworked by Morrie Ryskind, toning down the antiwar and antibusiness themes held to be responsible for the show's initial failure. Horace J. Fletcher returns now as the proprietor of Fletcher's American Chocolate Company. In the wake of a newly imposed tariff on chocolate, protested by Switzerland, Fletcher fears the undoing of his livelihood by Swiss hands. This time, both the political crisis that erupts and the military adventure that follows take place in a dream of Fletcher's. Ryskind's new version maintains much of the original production's material, but it also soft-pedals the notion that unscrupulous American leaders eager to line their own pockets are responsible for leading the country into war.

Eight musical numbers were cut from the original score, and the Gershwins composed eight new ones, each calling for two or more singers. As before, the hero and heroine are newspaper reporter Jim Townsend and Joan Fletcher, the latter torn between loyalty to her father and love for the ethically principled Jim. In the first version, the reporter struggles to win Joan's trust and love, succeeding in the end only after devising a plan to defeat the enemy, and the couple sing three duets, including "The Man I Love." In the new version, however, Jim and Joan are reduced to one romantic duet: "Soon," with a refrain built around a poignant melodic statement from the 1927 Finaletto of Act I, which returns in the new version in intensified form. "Soon" is the show's most powerful declaration of love, and it leaves no doubt that these two are committed to each other from the beginning.

Ryskind's reworking seems curiously shaped, at least on paper. Where Jim and Joan have been cut back to a single duet, Timothy Harper—Fletcher's foreman—and Anne Draper—the cheeky young woman determined to marry him—have been assigned three catchy new numbers, each leading into a dance. Jim and Joan, a couple cast in an operetta mold, now share the stage with a pair who embody the lighthearted ways of musical comedy lovers. Anne and Timothy's first duet, "I Mean to Say," is an adroit piece of songmaking. It takes a verse and refrain to elicit a romantic confession from Timothy, and even then the words come out in question form, and from the mouth of Anne: "You mean you love me?" The dance that follows seals the deal.

As the war clouds in Fletcher's dream darken, Anne wants to marry before combat begins, but Timothy prefers to wait until the war is won. The Gershwins weave the emotional fallout into "What's the Use of Hangin' Around with You?," a spirited song of frustration. Their third duet, "I've Got a Crush on You," composed originally for *Treasure Girl*, was apparently revived because it fit the talents of the two actors, Doris Carson and Gordon Smith.[10] Timothy is now stationed in Switzerland, and Anne has visited him, hoping to take in a battle or two. In the verse, Anne marvels at how she has managed to win Timothy's affection. Apparently he wonders that, too ("it's not that you're attractive"), but he admits that when Anne appeared, "I fell, and it was swell."

The indefatigable Mrs. Draper was played by the veteran trouper Blanche Ring, who brought the skills of a comedian to her performance. After failing to win Horace Fletcher's affections at the start of the show, she makes a play during his dream for Colonel Holmes, who shows up in town with his sidekick Gideon, having already conspired with Fletcher to foment "The Horace J. Fletcher Memorial War." One of producer Selwyn's better ideas was to hire the comedy team of Bobby Clark, who played Holmes, and Paul McCullough, who played Gideon, a pair of vaudevillians already successful on Broadway and in Hollywood. By incorporating their manic brand of slapstick comedy, Selwyn moved his show another step further from its antipatriotic roots.

Another new duet, "If I Became the President," follows a conversation in which Mrs. Draper flatters Holmes by urging him to run for president. Ira took special pleasure in a rhyme he engineered to end the third refrain. Having imagined a bearded Holmes as another Lincoln ("I'm thinkin'"), Mrs. Draper draws from him a promise not to "go as far afield" as had a trio of lesser statesmen ("Tyler, Polk, or Garafield"). Bobby Clark figured correctly that the audience would demand encore stanzas, and he did Ira the dubious favor of inventing new lyrics for such moments. Ira found the results "pretty terrible" (one egregious example: "And just to show we're home-like / We'll bathe in the Potomac"). Yet "imperfect rhymes or not," he confessed, "I am unhappy to report that his lines received as many chuckles as did mine."[11]

After much fretting about her mother's prospects for marriage—Mrs. Draper has decreed that Anne can marry only after she herself has found a husband—Anne brightens up when Timothy offers a solution. He tells Gideon that Mrs. Draper is worth $3 million, though in fact she is close to penniless. When Gideon passes that factoid on to Holmes and Fletcher, her romantic prospects take a giant leap forward. All three court her attention avidly, figuring that if she accepts one of them, they can split her fortune three ways. The fawning suitors' song, "How About a Boy Like Me?," breaks out in a vein the Gershwins were known to tap in situations calling for exposition: a 2/4 melody in a one-step rhythm over an oom-pah bass. A brief dance completes a number that is generic and jolly, though dramatically inconclusive.

Anything but generic, though, is another new song involving Holmes and Gideon, "Mademoiselle in New Rochelle." Dressed in absurd military garb, they strike up a conversation with two pretty Swiss misses, identifying themselves as prominent soldiers in a war soon to erupt, who have left their "mademoiselles" in places as remote from the Swiss Alps as New Jersey. Gershwin's bouncy 6/8 refrain—forty bars long—is repeated often, in more than one key, and the vocal portion is followed by an extended dance with other Swiss peasants joining in. The result is a folklike number with souped-up harmony in the bridge of the refrain.

The show's last new number comes when the scene shifts back to the office of the Fletcher American Chocolate Company, where the boss, awakened from his slumber, writhes in pain, convinced that he's still in Switzerland and that Richard Sloane—in his guise as the spy Edelweiss—has shot him. Joan appears and calls for a doctor, and gradually Fletcher realizes that he's safe in his own office. Sloane is still the plant's general manager, Holmes has returned to Washington, no war has broken out, and Edelweiss is a figment of Fletcher's imagination. Moreover, he admits that he has proved a selfish father and grants his permission for Joan to marry Jim.

The closing scene is set in a ballroom in Fletcher's house, where three couples have just been joined in matrimony: Jim and Joan, Timothy and Anne, and Horace and Mrs. Draper. The scene opens with a chorus singing "Ding Dong" at a spirited 2/4 clip, adding to the festive mood. In a final comic touch, Holmes and Gideon crash the party, ogle the bridesmaids, and deliver a telegram. Russia, it appears, has just reduced its tariff on caviar, leaving Fletcher, who only a day earlier had invested heavily in American caviar stock, to rally his guests with a challenge: "Are we going to stand by and let a lot of Bolsheviks tell us what we're going to do?" Vowing to quash this new threat, he proposes sending the president a wire to that effect, as the sound of the show's anthem, "Strike Up the Band," builds in the background.

Two strategic changes helped Ryskind to transform *Strike Up the Band* from a flop into a success, if not a spectacular hit. The first was to smooth over, though certainly not to remove, the politically based satire that had originally given offense. The second was to increase the stock of standard musical comedy ingredients, by making it funnier—for example, bringing in Clark and McCullough—and emphasizing romantic connections more. The score was enriched with duets and ensembles, many of them involving dance, enabling a colorful assortment of characters to interact in sometimes unexpected ways.

The tryout run opened at the Shubert Theatre in Boston on Christmas Night 1929, with the composer conducting. On the days that followed, the look, feel, and pace of Selwyn's production won enthusiastic praise from Boston critics, as did the Gershwin brothers' music and words. Henry Taylor Parker, who oversaw music as well as drama criticism for the *Evening Transcript*, heard in Gershwin's music "a finer skill with neat little points in the voices and instruments; a new aptness in the fitting of phrase, accent, rhythm and melody to Ira's more intricate and sharp-edged verses; an ingratiating suavity with the sentimental numbers that never oozes into dribble; a jazz that insinuates itself at need into the orchestra rather than rips out of it; a more sensitive hand, quicker humor, readier gayety." At the same time, Parker felt that even the revised show included moments when patriotic notions sacred to many Americans veered close to ridicule.[12] The critic of the *Boston Globe*, who also liked the show very much, similarly believed that if *Strike Up the Band* should fail to win "a widely popular success it will be because its satire will not be pleasant to those who suffered from the Great War. It is perhaps too soon to make a joke of patriotic fervor."[13]

As in Boston and again in New Haven, Gershwin conducted the first Broadway performance on January 14, 1930. Robert Littell of the *World* called the show "one of the few musicals that you must see":

> Last night was particularly memorable, because the leader of the orchestra which played some of the best tunes he has ever written was George Gershwin himself, who seemed to be enjoying things hugely, as well he might. You could see him—and sometimes hear him—singing along with the chorus, and every once in a while a certain pursing of the lips indicated that he was no longer singing but whistling, as many others will do from now on, for such tunes as "Strike Up the Band" and "War Bride," not to speak of half a dozen others, are about as good as tunes can be.[14]

Gilbert Gabriel of the *American* described the show as "an enormously funny, whip-snapping, keen-edged jamboree, musically the town's present best—and pretty nearly Gershwin's best, too."[15]

However, several critics expressed disappointment that the energy of the musical's beginning was not sustained throughout. Burns Mantle in the *Daily News* felt that "the first hour is so exciting the second hour must, by contrast, seem less than completely satisfying. But satirists detest sentiment, so there are no interludes and no ballads, and none of the scene contrasts that do so much for the 'Rose Maries' and the 'Sweet Adelines.'"[16] Richard Lockridge of the *Sun* also found the first and second halves of the show a disappointing match. "It is, for one act surely, a prancing show, festive and almost reckless of the consequences," but "somewhere in the long road this musical traveled before it reached Times Square, there crept up a gray cloud of caution. The shadow of that cloud lies plainly over everything."[17] In a more political vein, Robert Benchley of the *New Yorker* magazine called the first act "about as devastating satire as has been allowed on the local boards for a long time." He felt that "all members of the National Security League, an ultrapatriotic organization (1914–19), should be made to attend 'Strike Up the Band'—and not laugh. In fact, those who have a right to laugh are only those who laughed (or cried) at the same things in the days when we were planning a war of our own."[18]

New York's critics knew their Gilbert and Sullivan, and they found echoes in *Strike Up the Band*. Brooks Atkinson of the *Times*, who admired the book less than did some of his colleagues, praised Gershwin's gift for appropriating traditional forms and conventions to fresh effect. "The Gregorian chant effect of the invocation to Fletcher's American Chocolate Company, the wry humors of the 'Typical Self-Made American,' the elaborate opera bouffe of the discussion about the quality of milk in the Fletcher chocolate have a true Gilbert and Sullivan flavor."[19] Perhaps the most adroit summary of all came from Robert Garland of the *Telegram*, who found a clever way to announce the show's contradictory character. "A couple of musical comedies have found their simultaneous way into the Times Square Theatre," he began his review. "One is boisterous, bitter and satiric. The other is plodding, sugary and commonplace. And the name of the musical comedies is 'Strike Up the Band.'" The new musical, he has decided, "tries its best to be two things at the same time. And comes pretty near succeeding."[20]

BOYFRIEND, SONGWRITER, MUSICAL CITIZEN

TWO WEEKS AFTER THE SUCCESSFUL REOPENING of *Strike Up the Band* in mid-January 1930, Gershwin received a warm letter from a young woman with whom he had been keeping company. Rosamond Walling was a student at Swarthmore College, near Philadelphia and far enough from New York to make their encounters sporadic. But they bridged the gap by writing letters; more than sixty survive from 1928 to shortly before her marriage to Rafit Tirana in June 1932. The letters trace a relationship between a man and a woman who, although twelve years apart in age, were linked by affinities of interest and personality and, it seems, by the confidence that a sense of personal worth can foster: for him, musical talent that had already won international fame and success; for her, the pedigree of an affluent, cosmopolitan family, at ease in the company of high achievers in politics and the arts.

Walling wrote the letter, dated January 29—her twentieth birthday—in her dormitory room, after glancing up from the book she was reading to look "at *You*":[1]

Your picture just came to life and smiled at me—and I put down my book and had quite a long talk with you. You were really *darling*—and we both had a grand time.—except that I did far too much of the talking. . . . I really think that your Picture-self just gave me an excuse to write to you, because I wanted to tell you that I've been thinking of you a lot lately, and I've wanted *very* much to be with you. You know I'm not in my 'teens any longer, and to-night I've discovered several secrets about myself. I feel so old, and so very *wise*! Many things that you discovered in me I have found too, at last.

Walling, a first cousin of Emily Paley and Leonore Gershwin, was the daughter of novelist and Socialist activist Anna Strunsky—who had once been linked artistically, and romantically, with author Jack London—and William English Walling, a wealthy Kentucky-born political activist who championed Socialist causes and in 1909 helped to found the National Association for the Advancement of Colored People (NAACP). Rosamond and George first met at Emily and Lou Paley's wedding in 1920, when he was twenty-one and she ten years old.[2] "After a while George decided that as I was the closest he could get to our adored Emily, I might turn out to be the right wife for him," she later related to an interviewer. What he was looking for was "a good girl, preferably at least half Jewish, and with sense, like his mother. . . . 'It's nice about your father, because I like the English and Southerners and Westerners,' George said. 'But thank God your mother is Jewish.' . . . He liked the idea of the combination."

Walling had enrolled at Swarthmore in the fall of 1927. She wrote her family that October that Ira and Lee had taken her to see *Funny Face*, just then beginning its tryout run in Philadelphia. "Leonore has been WONDERFUL to me—I spent a night with them and saw the show—George is so sweet and modest—I can't imagine anyone more deserving of the sort of fame he's getting.—his music for this show is great. 'S'wonderful, 'S'marvelous'— . . . I laughed pains into both my sides."[3] The next June, she happened to be visiting her Strunsky cousins in Greenwich Village on the day they were meeting the ship carrying the Gershwins back from Europe;

> We all went to 103rd Street afterwards. There were many groups that I didn't know: a pinochle game of Mr. Gershwin's downstairs, pianos and noises upstairs, eating, greeting everywhere. Feeling very much a country cousin, I rode myself up and down in the elevator cage. George got in too, eventually.
>
> "I've been looking for you," he said. Then, as always, because he admired my capacity, "Aren't you hungry?"
>
> "Perhaps some pickles?"
>
> "With a touch of pastrami and salami and two or three pounds of raw beef, a quart of milk and an onion. Come, we'll find something to nibble on. And then there's a surprise for you. I brought you a present from France. In fact, two presents."
>
> The first present was the first "modern art" object in my life. It was a fine cigarette case, in black and white, with an eggshell inlay in cubist design. I was thrilled, especially at the recognition of my dignity—a cigarette case!
>
> He fastened the second treasure on my left wrist. It was very delicate—emeralds, rubies, and little pearls set in old gold.
>
> "I found it in an antique store in Paris. It reminded me of you—it looks as if it has a Russian soul."

"George was always the youngest of the young to the whole world," she continued, "but there were twelve years that made him seem very old to me then."[4]

Soon after this meeting, Rosamond left for summer school at Cornell University in Ithaca, New York. "I wish that I could come down to New York," she told him, "and stand at the door to your music-room armed with a fly-swatter or some other worthy imple-ment to keep out the annoyances"—to keep out anything prevent-ing him from his work on *An American in Paris* and *Treasure Girl.* In another fanciful touch, she closed her letter with a cartoonish drawing of a bone for Tinker, George's dog.[5] In mid-August, Wall-ing joined her family on vacation in the Adirondack region of New York State, where she typed a confident and playful letter show-ing that, although claiming no predilection for music, she had the empathy and background to appreciate the stakes that a musical career held for him:

> I had most uncollegiate hysterics over Ira's Gilbertian rhyme—I'm dying to hear the tunes that could have inspired the titles—they're simply apple.[6] I'll bet that the new show [*Treasure Girl*] is the best yet—and whatever the heat does to Walter Catlett, you have the inimitable and perfect Gertrude, so who cares? . . . Are you going to California? Its a tremendous offer, but what will happen to your study and to the possible "Porgy" or "The Debouk" if you do? I cant help hoping that someday you will write a most wonderful Opera.[7]

On January 19, 1929, Gershwin let Walling know that "the new show & the apartment [on Riverside Drive] are keeping me very busy these days, but I seem to thrive on it as I haven't felt better in a long time. . . . I've chosen all the materials & colors for the apartment & also the silver. All that remains now is to choose the china. It is really exciting, all this business. I went to the factory yesterday & saw my furniture being made. The detail of the whole thing amazes me."[8] Gershwin had recently sent Rosamond a desk set. "Is the writing set I sent you a practical one," he asked, "or is it a peacock—Just there for looks?"[9] Her reply, started ten days later, must have pleased him: "My room has turned Peacock entirely: but who wants Bread when she can have Cake—if you see what I mean." That teasing response—part of the letter written on her twentieth birthday—led into her acknowledgment of what he had just sent her, his own drawing of a likeness of himself: "Dear Artist: I think that Mr. George Porgy Gershwin should keep to one art: your portrait, George, is an exact image—but a little something is lacking. It's *much* better than the darn Times picture of a few weeks ago—that was a crime I thought. You wait till I paint you!"[10]

Gershwin's relocation to Riverside Drive coincided with his burgeoning interest in drawing and painting, and Walling's encouragement likely played a role. Soon after his move, the two of them went on a shopping spree:

> George went nuts in the paint store. He bought a huge empty box and filled it with a complete assortment of Grumbacher or Malfa oils, whichever cost most, in the biggest tubes. Then he chose sable brushes, a palette, and some big canvas boards. We walked all the way back to his new apartment. . . . I had always painted and, as I knew absolutely nothing about music, was very happy at George's deep interest in painting.

In fact, she revealed later that she "nearly married him" after his move "because he said I could have the downstairs apartment and we'd make an inside staircase; so I would have privacy and could paint."[11]

Courting a college student like Rosamond also gave Gershwin a link to the world of books. On February 2, she quoted a passage she had discovered in a new novel called *Mamba's Daughters* by DuBose Heyward. "Someone is talking about a marvelous new Negro musician," she explained. Another character objects:

> "For Heaven's sake don't label it. That's the trouble with us. What we can't label we damn. Can't you see its new—different? Can't you feel that it's something of our own—American—something that Stall-

ings and Harley got a glimmer of in 'Deep River'[12]—that the Theatre Guild caught the pictorial side of in *Porgy*; that Gershwin actually got his hands on in spots of his 'Rapsody in Blue'? It's epoch making, I tell you." Read the Book, George dear—you'll like it. This is page 302.[13]

Letters written in the coming weeks seem to affirm the pair's mutual attraction. In Cincinnati, after the evening performance on February 28 of his newest orchestral work, the composer repaired to his hotel room to write Rosamond about it. "I have just come from Emery Auditorium, where the symphony played 'An American in Paris.' Fritz Reiner conducted it & it seemed to go over with a bang. It made me very happy."[14] In her reply she confessed that she had felt "terribly depressed" that evening, but then "I locked my door and turned off the lights and played your Rhapsody. George dear—it brought me such happiness and comfort!"[15]

Come spring, the pleasure Gershwin was taking in drawing and in his living quarters—"The Hudson River & the sunsets over the Palisades, the little tugboats & the ocean liners, the funny looking phut-phut-phutters, the graceful birds & the imitating aeroplanes— an ever changing picture"—remained fulfilling, but still he looked to her to add something more. "I have already drawn Lou, Emily, Pop Gershwin, Bill Daly, Mabel & Bob Schirmer, Martin Loeffler, cousin Botkin & a dozen others. How about you? Enclosed is a picture of my first lesson on the penthouse roof."[16] A few weeks later, when preparations for Ziegfeld's *Show Girl* were "so far behind that we are not even ready for pandemonium": "I am very keen to do a picture of you in water color & try & capture your lovely face with its rosey colors. That would be quite a task but there is nothing like trying."[17]

Gershwin's correspondence with Walling brought out a personal side he was not in the habit of revealing. In early October, he told her that her letters have a way of making me happy, and, for a long time after receiving them the feeling persists. For example, the other morning I awoke, not feeling too 'hot' & was handed a stack of mail. One after another I opened the letters with the mechanical precision and expression of a robot. Then your letter loomed up and then—a smile—a sitting up in bed—a slight quickening of the pulse—a careful reading of your sweet letter and the day was made for me. . . . Now that you know how to make a fellow happy, what will you do about it? love, George.[18]

Several weeks later, after Rosamond had visited New York to watch him conduct, Gershwin reported that "the market has gone sensible again, everything seems to be settling back to normal, Ira is working, Lee is playing rummy, Mother is going to Lakewood for a stay, Frankie feels fine & still sees Leo Godowsky, Arthur is in good shape, Pop's still playing pinochle and I miss you."[19]

In April 1930, Rosamond and George together attended a Philadelphia concert including both Stravinsky's *Rite of Spring* and music by Arnold Schoenberg. Her letter a few days later, on Easter Saturday, describes her room, now filled with flowers and the sound of music emanating from the radio George had given her for her twentieth birthday. "Isn't a world that creates Radios and Roses and Easter quite *wonderful?*," she muses, relishing her good fortune at having heard on the same program both Schoenberg ("fascinating") and Stravinsky, who "created *real beauty*." She continues,

> Reading, exercise out-doors, painting. I don't resent lon[e]liness: at this time in my life I love it.
>
> Oh, this music is lovely. . . . I'm now listening to [Saint-Saëns's] "the Swan"—a most delicate, sad thing from some French composition. I must learn more about music! George dear, someday could you send me a little list of books on musicians—criticism—of course I realize how little music can be taught, and no one could love

just *listening* more than I no matter how much they read—but I'd like to have a deeper understanding. . . . With all this glory of flowers and music I really don't care if I *never* leave this room![20]

A few days later, Gershwin sent a reply that "I hope will contain some of the warmth my visit to Philadelphia & your last letter made me feel for you." Her "response & understanding of the extra modern music you heard" had left him "more than delighted. . . . You looked your beautiful self, & my friend Hammond kept reminding me (needlessly) how nice you were. And the talk afterwards. . . . I felt you knew me much better because of it. Did you?"[21]

That summer, however, his travels and working schedule, and her sojourn with her family in New England, kept them apart. In July, a rhapsodic letter from Rosamond arrived in George's mail from Provincetown, Massachusetts, on Cape Cod:

> Truly this is a corner of Paradise: a crazy colorful, ancient
> little Sailor-town; three wonderful, changeful faces of the magic
> ocean; vast sand-dunes, most lovely; forests, lakes, flowers and All
> Loveliness. The other night I walked over the miles of dunes in the
> moonlight. It was like walking on the strange, silver face of the moon
> itself—misty pale sand, reaching Forever away in the distance, to
> the silver-grey ocean. . . . I've painted and drawn, and written a few
> poems. In the evening we talk to friends, or read, or I walk alone.[22]

He met her lyrical report playfully, with a missive from an invented hamlet of his own.

> Every morning when I walked to the village I would stop at the post
> office & inquire for mail. "Any mail from Miss Walling?" Old Jen-
> kins, who knew me when I was born, would look over his glasses &
> say in a very old, kind voice "Nope. Guess she's havin' too good a
> time with those artist men up thar in Provincetown to write to an

old fogy like you. Heh, heh. You know she's a durn purty gal, full o' life & she's kept busy with adorin' males around her & she's so busy adorin' nature herself you're lucky if she sends you s'much as a post card. Heh heh. Nope. Nothin' today. Come 'round day after tomorrow when next mail comes in, maybe better luck then."[23]

But Gershwin's correspondence with Walling declined during her last year at Swarthmore, 1930–31. If the matter-of-fact signoff of his summer letter—"So long Rosamond. George. Regards to your family"—signals any cooling in their relationship, his plans for the upcoming theatrical season may help to explain it. He and Ira were committed to spend much of the fall and winter in Hollywood, writing the music for the Fox studio's film *Delicious*. That assignment also gave him an opportunity to draft a new classical work, the Second Rhapsody for piano and orchestra. After returning to New York in March 1931, it seems to have taken him some time to resume his connection with Rosamond, and by the time he did, she had decided to mark the end of her college days with an extended stay in Europe. Her departure marked the end of their romantic relationship. Traveling that summer with a friend named Anna Friede, she moved from London to Paris and then Geneva, and by fall was settled into the life of a student in London.

The two remained on friendly terms, however. On September 26, Gershwin celebrated both his thirty-third birthday and the publication of Isaac Goldberg's biography, *George Gershwin: A Study in American Music*. He sent Walling a copy soon after, and on October 21 she wrote to thank him:

How sweet of you to send me the Book and to inscribe it so beautifully! I read it last night—in front of my fire, in my charming-flower-filled sitting-room. I had many thoughts about you while I was reading the book—some even severe ones. It's pages showed such a picture of your life, the entanglements about you! What has your Fate in store for you—your promised fulfillment, Opera, your own great music,—or Memories, and parties and Shows? Maybe Both?? No one is wishing the *Highest* for you more than I, George![24]

Six months later, Rosamond wrote to express concern for the precarious state of Morris Gershwin's health, conveyed to her by a mutual friend. The letter ends with news of her upcoming wedding, which she delivers with affection and humor:

Do come soon: I've a new friend for you whom you'll <u>adore</u>—Rifat Tirana. <u>If</u> you can keep a secret (ssh—!)—I'll whisper something grand—I'm going to marry him. . . . !!! You win all the bets we made about my 'eart and 'ead, George dear. I won't try to describe him— only I can promise you that you'll love him (not a Pansy!) and thank me for bringing him into the Holy Family! You're all sorts of Bum for not hav[ing] written for so long, but I love you anyhow.[25]

Not long before her wedding in Paris, Rosamond reached out to George again, upon his father's death on May 14, 1932. "I wish I could go to you and tell you how much I feel for you all in your great loss. . . . It's <u>terrible</u> to realize how little we can say or do to help those we love! You've always been the one to give, so that often I longed for you to <u>need</u> something I might do for you. Now when there might be the chance of showing you my understanding there is an ocean between us!"[26]

Decades later, in an interview published in 1973, Walling revisited that same issue:

We made hay in separate fields while the sun shone, waiting for me to acquire some sense and years. We spent what time we could together and we wrote letters in between. But I did not marry George Gershwin. Despite his heavenly eyes, he never made me feel needed. He didn't need me. He had reached the dizzy heights of fame and fortune without me. He would go on to always greater achievement. Sometimes I wanted to dedicate my life to helping him; but often I did not like the idea of missing romance. "It's your Russian soul," he'd say. "You want a poor painter or poet or scholar to suffer with." He knew that a poor painter or poet or scholar my own age seemed more glamorous to me.

By Rosamond's testimony, sex was never part of their courtship.

Whenever I could get away from Swarthmore College, I'd join George in New York, or Atlantic City, or Philadelphia. I would stay with Leonore and Ira, as George was always absolutely correct in his behavior—in fact, fastidious. When he felt romantic—which did happen as time went on and I grew older and we were alone in various paradises—he never in any way tried to influence me. Given a moon, June, and myself in blue (because of the Rhapsody, of course), we might go for a long walk, holding hands, and sometimes dancing— he'd tap-dance at the slightest provocation—conversing on all sorts of subjects in delicious agreement. George might stop me and say, "You could be good for my stomach," or "My friends like you," or "If you could learn to keep your stockings straight and get those run-down heels changed, you might be glamorous. But not in that dress. It's terrible. The skirts are longer now, haven't you read?"[27]

One subject on which no agreement was reached was marriage. "Let's have four children to begin with," George would propose, "and bring them up in the country. You can teach them to ride. . . . We'll get six horses to start with." But for Rosamond, this notion "absolutely lacked charm: I hoped never to see Westchester County again and didn't get around to wanting children for a good ten years." A striving for accomplishment, knowledge, and enrichment of personal experience is hard to miss in Walling's letters. Perhaps the goal of that striving was to make herself a powerful feminine force—akin to that of her mother?—on which the man she would marry could rely. Had she become Mrs. George Gershwin, Rosamond might well have sought to steer him in the direction of the enduring (opera, "the Highest"), rather than the more heralded ephemeral, during the five years of life that remained to him.

IN FEBRUARY 1930, with *Strike Up the Band* running smoothly—it would log almost 200 Broadway performances in a shaky economy—Gershwin took a brief vacation in Florida, splitting his time between Palm Beach and Miami, where his mother Rose was sitting out the north's winter cold. Then he flew back to New York to take part in an unusual radio broadcast: a joint recital with Jesse Crawford, organist at New York's Paramount Theatre. The program, heard on New York's WABC, was broadcast from the Paramount Building on Sunday, March 2, at 10 p.m. Devoted to Gershwin's music, it presented a medley of tunes from *Strike Up the Band* and hits from earlier shows, some sung by tenor Paul Small, and the *Rhapsody in Blue*, played as a piano-organ duet.[28]

The *Rhapsody* all but took over Gershwin's life in early May, when for a fee of $5,000 he took part in a blitz of live performances that many tens of thousands attended. He described the project to Rosamond on April 24: "I have agreed to play at Roxy's Theatre for the week of May 2nd with Whiteman's orchestra. The picture 'The King of Jazz' will have its premier on that day. The feature of the picture is 'Rhapsody in Blue,' which is the why & wherefor[e] of the hook up. Means I've got to start practicing the piano again." The film, a biopic about Paul Whiteman, opened on May 2 with five showings, each followed by a live stage show featuring Whiteman, the Roxy Theatre's orchestra and chorus, and the composer's performance of the *Rhapsody*.

Gershwin's scrapbooks include a *New York Sun* backstage interview after one performance that stands out for the spontaneity of his remarks alone. The reporter seems to have caught him fresh from the keyboard, with applause ringing in his ears, and savoring the thrill of having dodged another bullet. "Gee! But it's hard to play," he admitted. "I don't set myself up as a pianist, although I'll bet I can play that piece better than anybody you can name. But what I have to do! I have to practice ten minutes before I go on. That's to get my fingers limber." (According to Oscar Levant, Gershwin's custom was to warm up with "endless repetitions of the first Cramer study," from a well-known book of piano etudes.) When the interviewer asks about the meaning of the piece, Gershwin replies that it's "so abstract in my mind that it can mean almost anything to anybody." Then he takes off in another direction entirely: "It is all New York, all America. It is a picnic party in Brooklyn or a dark-skinned girl singing and shouting her blues in a Harlem cabaret. I try to depict a scene, a New York crowd."[29]

Yet what may have loomed largest in Gershwin's mind in that moment was what he was learning from his pianistic marathon. Playing that work five times a day for a week, "before twenty or thirty thousand people daily," and to see and feel the audience responses, was proving to be a "wonderful" experience. The *Rhapsody* was growing on him, too, and he didn't really know why, "unless it is because people seem to give it back to me in a mysterious way." The *Rhapsody in Blue* remained the best example of Gershwin's ability to attract listeners who rarely attended concerts, and during the half-dozen years since the work's composition, he had played it countless times in public. His back-to-back-to-back at the Roxy that week, in the service of publicizing *The King of Jazz*, gave further proof of the *Rhapsody*'s undiminished power to hold the attention of a vast and diverse audience, not to say the veneration of the man who composed it.

During that same week, on May 4, the *New York Sunday World* carried an article about songwriting by Gershwin called "Making Music," in which he explained why he preferred to write serious music:

A serious composition is either a success or a failure because of what the composer does to it. I may write a good score for a musical comedy, but if the book or cast is poor my work registers a flop. A symphony, on the other hand, lives or dies according to its real worth. While popular music may be tricked very easily, serious music offers so many more interesting problems in construction, in orchestration, in other details. For a long time—as far back as my eighteenth year—I have wanted to work at big compositions. I am glad I can do it now. [30]

Even so, he judged that the abundance of songwriters on the present scene made it a good time for an experienced practitioner like himself to address the subject of popular music. On the face of it, writing a thirty-two-bar **aaba** refrain should be simple, he explained, but it isn't. "There are times when a phrase of music will cost me many hours of internal sweating. Rhythms romp through my brain, but they're not easy to capture and keep." In the public imagination, composers are thought to conquer creative challenges through inspiration ("an unconscious something that happens within you which makes you do a thing much better than if it were done self-consciously"), but in real life that rarely happens. Two or at most three songs may emerge fresh from his unconscious in the course of a typical year; but with such odds in play, he has learned to rely on "invention":

I see a piece of music in the form of a design. With a melody [i.e., a song] I can take [in] the whole design in one look; with a larger composition, like a concerto, I have to take it piece by piece and then construct it so much longer. No matter what they say about "nothing new under the sun," it is always possible to invent something original. The songwriter takes an idea and adds his own individuality to it; he merely uses his capacity for invention in arranging bars his own way.

To Gershwin, the study of musical technique was indispensable. "Many people say that too much study kills spontaneity in music, but I claim that, although study may kill a small talent, it must develop a big talent." He advises the aspiring composer to "write something every day, regardless of its length or quality." Failure is the norm, and facing failure down is part of the songwriter's daily lot. "Perhaps the tenth—or the hundredth—song will do the trick."

GERSHWIN'S SCHEDULE in the spring and summer of 1930 included another August concert with the New York Philharmonic in Lewisohn Stadium, where he played both the *Rhapsody in Blue* and the *Concerto in F* and conducted *An American in Paris*—the first time he had conducted a symphony orchestra in a concert.[31] The concert was also heard on the radio, marking the growing presence and influence of a medium that had barely existed a decade earlier.

During the runup to the previous December's opening of *Strike Up the Band*, Gershwin had taken the affirmative side in a "debate" over the impact of radio—upholding the medium's virtues as the putative "King of Jazz," while a "Progressive Woman Educator," Dr. Blanche Colton Williams, head of the English Department at Hunter College, deplored the effects of the broadcast medium. No judges were there to declare a winner, nor was an audience present—just Gladys Oaks of the *New York World*. The exchange was held in a nearby theater during a rehearsal of Gershwin's current show.

The composer began the conversation on an unambiguous note:

I think that the radio is the greatest thing that has ever happened to the American household. Look at the little backwater towns from Kankakee to Oskaloosa. What could they know of the gorgeous rush of new things, which is the most important gift of our modern civilization, except for the radio? . . . Think of all the people in the cities, too, who can't afford what the cities have to offer. There is a new kind of culture in the world, and particularly in America. A culture of abundance, of many quick entertainments— ball games, prize-fights, jazz, preaching, science, symphonies, the sharing of adventure with men like [Admiral Richard E.] Byrd and [Charles] Lindbergh. And the voice, the instrument, the supreme interpreter of this new culture is the radio, without which few of us could acquire it!

BCW: You may call it culture, but I feel the word is a little high-falutin. Children trying to study over the clamor, people attempting to sleep while competing, loud-speakers blare in neighboring apartments. In many families the instrument is left on from the time papa comes home, sometimes from the time mama gets up. I was a guest the other night at a home where the radio "went" all evening. Conversation was simply impossible. After a few shrieking interludes, I gave it up. It becomes—

At this point, reported Gladys Oaks, "with the most graceful gesture in the world, Mr. Gershwin interrupted her."

That's simply bad manners, . . . not anything wrong with the radio. Of course we don't expect people to keep it going in the children's study hours, or while their guests are discussing the universe. The beauty of the thing is that you can have just as much of it as you want by merely shifting a dial! . . .

BCW: The thing I really object to most about it is that it standardizes the American audience and the American youth, which is the hope of our future art and our future evolution. . . . Taste is not the product of Gilbert and Sullivan in snatches, political speeches that are indistinct, both in thought and enunciation, symphonies and static. . . .

GG: You should get a good radio. Speeches over my loud-speaker are distinct as possible. And personality comes over with the words, as you'd never get it in a newspaper. When Al Smith says "boid," for example, it does not come out "bird." And suppose it does standardize! Isn't a high standard of citizens better than a low one with a few great minds? . . . The art that represents us must be, I think, a crowded art, an art that expresses the dozens and hundreds of things that are always knocking at us and inviting. The radio is the very symbol of this life-enriching.[32]

Gershwin's remarks on this occasion were consistent with the common sense and clarity that underlie his published articles. Finding modern life rich as well as distracting, he welcomed that quality in modern art, at least in principle. Phrases that evoke modernity—"crowded art," "dozens and hundreds of things that are always knocking at us and inviting"—shed light on his attitude as an artist. And they complement his equally strong belief that artists must study and learn from masters of the past.

GIRL CRAZY

(1930)

BY SPRING 1930, the Gershwin brothers were at work on a show for Sam Harris that was never finished, surviving only as a few references. More important, in April they signed a contract with Fox Film Corporation to write the music for a feature-length film for $125,000—a "signal recognition of the future of films with music, and a notable victory for the Fox organization, as big producers have been angling for the Gershwins for the past year," as the *Hollywood Filmograph* touted it.[1]

Gershwin had recently made the acquaintance of a composer who had been hired by another Hollywood studio, Warner Brothers: Vienna-born Oscar Straus. Straus had come to New York in January to see a revival of his classic 1912 operetta *The Chocolate Soldier*, and meeting Gershwin, he said, was the highlight of his visit. The two composers attended the first performance of the operetta together. Afterward, Straus recalled,

> Gershwin took me to his very modernistic penthouse apartment, where we remained until half-past two in the morning, playing the piano and talking. First my host would play, and then I would play;

and then we would talk about the things that are of eternal interest to men who compose music. On many subjects we did not agree—nor did we pretend that we agreed. We were both honest—the very best, and indeed the only foundation for friendship. And we both love music. It was one of the most delightful evenings I have ever known. Gershwin's music is not my music, but he is a genuine artist. We understood each other.[2]

The evening with Straus brings to mind occasions when Gershwin struck up friendships with such composers as Ravel, Kálmán, Berg, and Prokofiev—all of whom likewise knew they had met a true artist. By contrast, although some of the leading American composers of his own generation lived in New York City, Gershwin found no kindred souls among them. Brooklyn-born Aaron Copland, for example, heard much about Gershwin during the 1920s, he granted. But the two men didn't meet until around 1932, and when they did cross paths, "we had nothing to say to each other."

Copland admitted in his 1984 autobiography how curious it was that he and Gershwin had had so little contact, attributing the gap to the structure of American musical life in those days, when "the lines were more sharply drawn between popular and classical musics." He pointed out that the *Rhapsody in Blue* was introduced by Paul Whiteman and his band, while Serge Koussevitzky and the Boston Symphony Orchestra had premiered Copland's own Piano Concerto. Gershwin came from Tin Pan Alley and Broadway musicals, he then noted, whereas his own theatrical taste ran toward "serious drama." When they met a second time at another social gathering, "We weren't together very long before [Gershwin] was at his piano and playing me his latest composition." Copland implies that, given that this composition was likely a popular song, he would have preferred conversation. The two met one final time in Hollywood in June 1937, when Gershwin praised one of Copland's recent compositions—*The Second Hurricane*, an opera for young performers—and helped him join ASCAP. Copland stopped short of expressing any collegial feelings, nor does his autobiography mention that within weeks of that meeting, Gershwin was dead.[3]

The distance between these two Brooklyn-born composers was also signaled in Gershwin's 1929 article "Fifty Years of American Music," which argued that a European orientation and training had complicated Copland's attempt to catch the spirit of America in a homegrown modernist idiom. And in *Our New Music*, published in 1941, Copland named fifty-one composers, most of whom were active before 1930, who had benefited from two organizations founded to help composers present their work to the public: the International Composers' Guild and the League of Composers. His roster seems to include every consequential figure of the time except Gershwin, whose *Rhapsody in Blue* was by far the most famous American composition of the age—perhaps because Gershwin's music had won audiences without support from the composers' organizations.

The supply of music from the generation of Virgil Thomson, Roger Sessions, Walter Piston, Roy Harris, Henry Cowell, and Copland exceeded listener demand for it by far—but Gershwin's dual musical identity put him in a different category. Already renowned as a songwriter, he succeeded as a composer who had found a way to the hearts and the ears of concertgoers, whether in North America or overseas. That helps to explain why, even as classical composers with European backgrounds welcomed Gershwin as a talented and unique artist, their American counterparts were less inclined to warm to him and his music. Where many from overseas found his music-making vital and distinctive, more than a few of his countrymen—tending to see him more as a crowd-pleasing rival than as a colleague on modernism's straight and narrow—were likely to judge his work slick, facile, and unserious.

Had Copland, meeting Gershwin at a party, made a point of walking him to a piano and playing some of the music he was then working on, chances are that Gershwin would have been genuinely engaged. But it appears that the reverse was not true. After all, the music Gershwin was likely to unveil could well be just another popular song.

THE GERSHWIN BROTHERS devoted much of the summer of 1930 to a new show for Aarons and Freedley called *Girl Crazy*. The libretto was the joint work of Guy Bolton and Jack McGowan, an actor and singer who was turning his attention to the writing side of the musical comedy business. The story they concocted is set in America's Wild West and revolves around Danny Churchill, a New York playboy. Danny has proved so unreliable on his home turf that his well-heeled father, owner of Buzzard Ranch near the remote settlement of Custerville, Arizona, banishes him there to grow up, thinking that avoiding female company—the cause of his son's present downfall—will be easy there. For Custerville has only male residents. However, just outside the town's limits lives the local postmaster, Molly Gray, a spirited young woman played by Ginger Rogers in her first leading role on Broadway. Danny's pursuit begins the moment he lays eyes on her.

Male-female romance, the standard stuff of musical comedy, takes on the flavor of Custerville's geography and rough-and-tumble ways; once a sheriff is elected, for example, his life expectancy takes a nosedive. And the landscape leaves its mark on the Gershwins' score, too, which begins with a musical sketch of inaction, in a song both slow and uneventful. The idea came from a stanza Ira had written for a school newspaper in his college days:

A desperate deed to do I crave,
Beyond all reason and rhyme:
Some day when I'm feeling especially brave,
I'm going to Bide My Time.

"Bidin' My Time" is a study in slow motion. The intro quotes from a languid version of the fiddle tune "Turkey in the Straw," harmonized over a chromatically descending line that, even as it signals the tune's familiar roots, undermines its muscular drive. The refrain then affirms tempo as the song's subject—shortened from **aaba** to **aba**, the better to sustain a "lazy, lethargic mood."[4] To complement "I'm bidin' my time," Ira came up with "'cause that's the kinda guy I'm."

On the heels of this drowsy number comes the first of several songs highlighting cowboy masculinity. "The Lonesome Cowboy" is ready to seek a wife, even as his buddies deliver a warning, citing marriage's "ball and chain for life!" Now Danny, played by Allen Kearns, arrives in a cab he hailed some days ago in New York at the corner of West 48th Street and Broadway. The sound of gunfire signals the current sheriff's demise—a crime for which cab driver Gieber Goldfarb, who has wandered off in search of gasoline, is charged. On the brink of being hanged by local vigilantes, Goldfarb is saved only after Danny intervenes. For the role of Goldfarb, Aarons and Freedley originally had Bert Lahr in mind, hoping to build their new production around the talents of an established comedian, as well as up-and-coming ingénue Rogers. But the George White production in which Lahr was currently starring ran longer than predicted, and he was unavailable. His replacement was veteran comedian Willie Howard, known for vaudeville imitations of famous performers.

Molly Gray then appears, carrying her mailbag and clearly well briefed about Danny and his Arizona exile: "News travels fast in Custerville," she tells him. So that he will have a place to take Molly dancing, Danny decides to turn Buzzard Ranch into a "dude ranch," including the bright lights and excitement of Broadway. He sings the show's first courtship number, "Could You Use Me?"— a song based on a four-note syncopated motive listing his talents ("tie your shoeses / chase your blueses"). But Molly already fancies a local cowboy, and her sung reply finds Danny functionally useless, though after the song Kearns and Rogers break into a dance.

Danny's dude ranch has drawn assorted guests, especially female ones, to Custerville. Patsy West, whom Danny has hired as the hotel's switchboard operator, strikes up a romance with Goldfarb, who has stayed in Custerville to manage the hotel's "motor service." Another guest is Tess Harding, an old flame of Danny's. A couple wanders in, too, looking for work: "Frisco Kate" Fothergill and her husband Slick. He is answering Danny's ad for a manager of the ranch's gambling room; she's a "café singer" in the mode of Diamond Lil, a racy Mae West character. When the company learn that Kate and Slick hail from the Barbary Coast, one of California's most notorious vice districts, Patsy admits that she comes from there, too, and sings about that district's sleazy energy in "Barbary Coast."

Each of the songs so far is a novelty number linked to the show's western customs, and three of them, including the latest, are vehicles for dancing. In this context, plenty of emotional space is left open for the next musical number, a ballad sung by Danny and Molly, which makes its mark through an expression of tenderness far removed from anything *Girl Crazy* has yet offered.

The Gershwins had written "Embraceable You" two summers earlier for the defunct *East Is West*. But now it was enlisted to narrow the emotional gulf enacted in Danny and Molly's "Could You Use Me?" Ira had taken special pleasure in rhyming "embraceable you" with "irreplaceable you," not to mention "silk and laceable you." The refrain is marked "Rhythmically," and it is in the pervasive rhythm, beginning on an afterbeat, that the heart of this melody's appeal lies.[5] Molly admits that, whereas his advances left her cold at first, "now I completely burn up when you're slow to start."

A new guest arrives in Custerville from New York City: Sam Mason, come to foil Danny's new business venture and win the attention of Molly Gray. In Act I's final scene, Danny and Molly's relationship takes a turn for the worse, despite the romantic progress they've made, and Danny's rivalry with Sam sharpens. Meanwhile, Gieber Goldfarb, who has been elected sheriff, is forced into hiding, surviving on bits of leftover ham sandwiches, and Slick and Kate Fothergill have complicated life in Custerville.

This scene proved to be more than just the Act I finale, though. For it marked a historic milestone: the Broadway debut of twenty-one-year-old Ethel Merman.

IN SEARCH of a singer to perform the three songs the Gershwins had written for Frisco Kate, producer Vinton Freedley had been tipped off that he should listen to a young vaudevillian then appearing in Brooklyn. After catching Merman's act at the Paramount Theatre, Freedley arranged for her to meet Gershwin. Merman—née Zimmermann—later recalled, "I sang two or three of the swing numbers I'd been doing in night clubs and vaudeville. . . . It was the first time I'd met George Gershwin, and if I may say so without seeming sacrilegious, to me it was like meeting God. Imagine the great Gershwin, sitting down and playing his songs for Ethel Agnes Zimmermann, of Astoria, Long Island." When Gershwin introduced her to "I Got Rhythm," he explained, "if there's anything about this you don't like, I'll be happy to change it." In fact, "there was nothing about that song I didn't like, but that's the kind of guy he was." She responded with a smile and a nod but no words. In truth, she was "flabbergasted" by the composer's interest in what she might think. Merman was hired to sing the three songs while appearing in only a few scenes. Yet once she began to rehearse and demonstrate her feel for comedy, the role of Kate was expanded to include spoken lines.

The first song Merman sang on a Broadway stage was "Sam and Delilah," a cautionary fable directed toward men who live and work in the wide-open spaces. As she recalled:

It's very hard for me to stand back and take a cold, calm look at that first night of *Girl Crazy*. It's still thunder in the back of my head. I didn't know what was happening to me. When I did my first number, opened my mouth, and let out: "Delilah was a floozy," everybody screamed and yelled, and there was so much noise that I thought something had fallen out of the loft onto the stage.[6]

Aside from the ringing sound of her voice and the clarity of her diction, the musical form of her song and the style of its accompaniment—a sixteen-bar refrain of bluesified narrative—proved convincing, due in large part to the orchestra supporting her in the pit. This ensemble, billed as Red Nichols and his Orchestra, included a remarkable corps of young instrumentalists, all of them white, who were making a reputation as jazz musicians: trumpeters Nichols (age twenty-five) and Charlie Teagarden (seventeen), trombonist and arranger Glenn Miller (twenty-six), reedmen Benny Goodman (twenty-one), Pee Wee Russell (twenty-four), and Babe Russin (nineteen), and drummer Gene Krupa (twenty-one).[7] The string section was headed by Joseph Smith, who for years had led the orchestra at the Plaza Hotel.

Up until this point in the show, the musicians had presumably played the accompaniments as Gershwin had invented them and as Robert Russell Bennett had orchestrated them. But the bluesified "Sam and Delilah" invited a different approach. The song began with an extended four-to-the-bar rhythmic emphasis unlike anything in the score so far, while the structure of its melodic phrases left space open for end-of-phrase fills by players who knew how to improvise as the spirit moved them. By the time Merman proclaimed "Delilah was a floozy," the orchestra already had the audience on a slow boil. What's more, during the intermissions "they'd really turn the band loose," according to a jazz aficionado who attended several performances of *Girl Crazy*. "You should have heard the hot stuff they played."[8]

The dramatic pretext for Kate's second song is flimsy at best. Having watched her husband work a possible romantic angle with another woman, Kate declares that Slick, like other men, is never satisfied with what he's got. But Slick reclaims her trust, and Kate's lyric outburst, "I Got Rhythm," radiates self-assuredness. The number is melodically short-winded and harmonically repetitive to the point of plainness, but it's alive with rhythmic energy. The melody is based on a syncopated rhythmic figure with an accent coinciding with only one of the four beats it fills, and this loose-jointed yet precisely accented pattern drives the whole song. It took a while, though, before cast members could square the notes on the page with a performance that conveyed the song's syncopated rhythmic drive. Bennett described the first day of rehearsals, when Gershwin, as he normally did, played through the score for the company:

> Alex Aarons and I were standing at the back of the empty theater as George played "I Got Rhythm" through twice. Then Earle Busby, the music director, lifted his arms and said, "Okay—everybody sing it!" Gershwin played the . . . two-bar introduction . . . and the hall rang with "I Got Rhythm!" and Alex said in my ear, "Sixty liars!"[9]

Merman's first Broadway performance of "I Got Rhythm" made an instant impact. No more than one stanza was needed for this number; she explained,

> As I went into the second chorus of "I Got Rhythm," I held a note for sixteen bars while the orchestra played the melodic line. . . . By the time I'd held that note for four bars the audience was applauding. They applauded through the whole chorus and I did several encores. It seemed to do something to them. Not because it was sweet or beautiful, but because it was exciting.

When she finished the song, she "still didn't get the meaning of what happened." What she did perceive was that "people were beating their hands together and I had to sing encore after encore":

> I've heard honest—and even intelligent—people describe that first time they heard "I Got Rhythm" as a "high point in the theater." It was the kind of thing that happened when Mary Martin sang "My Heart Belongs to Daddy." During the intermission George Gershwin came up to me and said, "Ethel, do you realize what's happened to you?" "No," I told him. . . . George gave me a funny look and told me, "Don't ever let anybody give you a singing lesson. It'll ruin you."[10]

As "I Got Rhythm" found its way over time into the popular music repertory, musicians discovered that the song's harmonic structure was an ideal playground for fresh melodic invention. Gershwin's scheme balanced tonal stability with tonal freedom in a proportion that proved ideal for a thirty-two-bar **aaba** structure—in this case with a two-bar tag. Jazz instrumentalists seized quickly on the harmonic plan, eventually dubbed "Rhythm Changes," as fertile ground for improvising and composing melody lines free of the one Gershwin wrote. There was no copyright protection for a song's harmonic structure—but Gershwin's inventiveness in that regard, paired with Merman's talent, made "I Got Rhythm" into a hit.[11]

ACT II OF *GIRL CRAZY* begins on a south-of-the-border note with "Land of the Gay Caballero": the company has traveled to Mexico to watch horse-racing. Gershwin's Mexican-style music for this number registers the cultural shift in a variety of ways, including sound (castanets), melody (sinuous and flowing), harmony,[12] and Latin dance rhythms.

Each of the Fothergills is assigned a solo song in the second act. Slick's "Treat Me Rough" invites a gaggle of young women to invade his personal space; in marked contrast, Kate's song, "Boy! What Love Has Done to Me," conveys her despair as the spouse of a manipulative man whose mix of charm and helplessness has proven both irresistible and ruinous to her. Although she knows she's a "sap to love him so," she can't help it. And knowing how it feels to love unwisely touches on a strain of blues sensibility—through quarter-note repetitions and tonal shadings from the blues vocabulary—that lends stature to her character.

Later, Molly and Sam Mason join a group of dancers in the hotel ballroom, but as he grows more and more inebriated, she leaves him on the dance floor—only to spot Danny, who greets her with kindness and understanding. Assuming that she has chosen Sam, Danny urges Molly before he exits to be good to his successful rival. Goldfarb then discovers Molly in tears. "I've found out I'm in love," she tells him, but the man she loves has just bowed out of her life. She distills this moment into "But Not for Me," a serene, reserved, and beautiful lament, fashioned from two-bar gestures until the last phrase. Goldfarb lightens her mood by repeating her refrain first in the Frenchified style of Maurice Chevalier, and then as other contemporary entertainment personalities might deliver it—Eddie Cantor, Al Jolson, Will Rogers—a comic specialty of actor Willie Howard's.

The show's last scene back in Custerville takes place outside the ranch. Sam Mason has received his comeuppance and lost all credibility with Molly. Kate and Slick Fothergill are reunited, though in a less-than-triumphant spirit. Molly appears on Custerville's main drag in a stylish new dress like the ones popular with New York girls, while Danny shows up in western regalia. As he proposes to Molly, the company sings a bit of "Embraceable You," followed by a chorus of "I Got Rhythm."

Girl Crazy's tryout run began at Philadelphia's Shubert Theatre on September 29, 1930. The show opened on Broadway at the Alvin Theatre on October 14 and ran until the following June, logging 272 performances. Two days after the New York opening, a delighted Gershwin wrote to Isaac Goldberg:

> I am just recuperating from a couple of very exciting days. I worked very hard conducting the orchestra at the rehearsal and dress rehearsal and finally at the opening night, when the theatre was so warm that I must have lost at least three pounds, perspiring. . . . Everybody seemed to enjoy the show tremendously, especially the critics. I think the notices, especially of the music, were the best I have ever received.[13]

In view of the critical praise *Girl Crazy* received for virtually all its particulars, it surely gave Gershwin special pleasure to see his score singled out as the linchpin of a hit show. Robert Garland wrote in the *Telegram*: "Despite the excellence of many another thing—the excellence, for instance, of Miss Ethel Merman, who combines much that is best in Miss Helen Morgan and Miss Libby Holman, with much that is best in her own gifted self—is the zestful and imaginative score which Mr. George Gershwin has written for 'Girl Crazy,' which lifts its head and shoulders above any other eye-and-ear divertissement in town."[14]

Alison Smith of the *World* described the show as "robust and exhausting—and unforgettable." Merman's impact "on an already hysterical audience" during "I Got Rhythm" was such, she found, that they seemed ready to make her sing it all night, which would end the plot "then and there."[15] Writing in the *Daily Mirror*, Robert Coleman was one of the few critics to acknowledge the Red Nichols Orchestra, even though he emphasized Gershwin's conducting more than the group's playing.[16] In the *Herald Tribune*, Arthur Ruhl called the show "a sort of mixture of Wild West, Negro spirituals and Broadway 'blues' and in every way out of the ordinary."[17] Sime Silverman of *Variety* found the young Ginger Rogers an even better singer than dancer, while calling Merman a diamond in the rough who needed to "lose her automaton style and give the ballads or rags more expression."

But "the strength of 'Girl Crazy' lay in its balance," he wrote. "While the first act ran over 90 minutes the opening evening, there was nothing in retrospect to cut out. The performance ended at 11.30, with the same verdict. It has music, lyrics, comedy and people, all worth listening to."[18]

HOLLYWOOD
AND THE SECOND RHAPSODY (1930–31)

ON NOVEMBER 2, 1930, FRANCES GERSHWIN married Leopold
Godowsky in George's Riverside penthouse. The next day, Gershwin conducted a performance of *Girl Crazy* at the Alvin Theatre,
and two days after that, George, Ira, and Leonore, along with
librettist Guy Bolton, left New York bound by train for Hollywood.

Arriving on November 9, they stayed at the Beverly-Wilshire
Hotel while the house the Gershwins had rented, at 1027 Chevy
Chase Drive in Beverly Hills—formerly occupied by Greta Garbo—
was being readied for them. Some days later, George described the
scene in a letter to Ethel Merman:

> Well, here we are old Hollywoodites although we've been here about
> a week. It gets you. We're booked for dinner at a different house
> every night this week. And always the same routine. First cocktails,
> then picture [movie] talk. Dinner is served starting with soup which
> is immediately followed by picture talk. Then fried fish or lobster . . .
> with picture talk and onions. That continues until after dessert and
> then demitasse is served in the living room and then the butler leans

over a little and says, "I'll tell you what's wrong with those musical talkies."

For Gershwin, the environment seemed "a fine contrast to the way we wrote *Girl Crazy* that big New York hit with Ethel Merman and lyrics by Gershwin and music by Gershwin. . . . Is the show holding up? I mean the performance. How is Merman behaving?"[1]

The contracts George and Ira signed with Fox studios for a picture titled *Delicious* covered six weeks of work before the Christmas holiday and eight weeks after. When it turned out that the screenplay by Bolton and Sonya Levien called for only half a dozen vocal numbers, and that three of them could be fashioned from songs already in existence, the Hollywood engagement became something that—for Ira, if not for George—must have felt like a paid vacation. For George, it brought a chance to exercise his ingenuity as a showman, and the way he responded is a story in itself.

Once the three Gershwins were settled in their Beverly Hills house—George slept in Greta Garbo's bed, which "hasn't helped my sleep any," as he wrote to Isaac Goldberg—news on the work front proved to be good. Before Christmas he and Ira had read and played through the songs they had written for the film's producer, Winfield Sheehan, and its director, David Butler, and both men seemed pleased. In his letter to Goldberg Gershwin also slipped in the news that the score would include music that had gone unmentioned in the original plan: "a Manhattan Rhapsody— or Fantasy—which I am going to write for it." He then added a musical request: "Please write me about any new music the Boston Symphony Orchestra is giving these days."[2] In the fall of 1929, Serge Koussevitzky had invited him to compose a new work for the orchestra's fiftieth anniversary celebration, planned for 1931; Gershwin had declined then, pleading other obligations, but his query to Goldberg suggests he was thinking about possible uses for the "Rhapsody" or "Fantasy" he had decided to compose for *Delicious*.[3]

The plot of *Delicious*, which Bolton apparently originated, centers on a romance between a Scottish immigrant girl, played by Janet Gaynor, and a wealthy American, played by Charles Farrell. Gaynor's character, Heather Gordon, is a lone traveler who expects to be met in New York Harbor by a relative, and Larry Beaumont, Farrell's character, is a socially prominent Long Islander returning from an overseas trip with his girlfriend and her mother. The movie's opening scene takes place on an ocean liner steaming westward across the Atlantic. From first class, affluent passengers look down on the steerage deck below, teeming with immigrants who are entertaining themselves with dancing and singing.[4] Larry enjoys what he sees, unlike his condescending girlfriend Diana. Among the passengers in steerage is a family of Russian-born musicians on their way to an engagement at the "Russian Café" in New York City. Sascha, played by Raul Roulien, is a composer and pianist who has taken a fancy to Heather and has written a song about her. Eager to hear it, she leads him up a stairway to the first-class deck in search of a piano, but they are spotted by a steward and flee in different directions. Heather finds herself in the ship's horse stalls, where she meets Larry, a polo star, who is tending his favorite pony.

Their conversation is interrupted when Sascha calls out to Heather, who leaves to join him. The two immigrants resume their search for a piano, which they locate in the ship's saloon. Sascha can now sing the first Gershwin number in the show, to an audience of four: Heather, Larry, Diana, and her mother, Mrs. Van De Berghe. He explains that the song's origins lie in the charm of a mispronunciation by Heather: "You're so de-lic-i-ous," followed by "cap-ri-ci-ous," "am-bish-i-ous," and "re-pe-tish-i-ous."[5] As Sascha sings and plays, Larry is transfixed by the young woman he has just met. He has already proposed marriage to Diana, but, though inclined to accept him, she has asked for time to think it over. Mrs. Van De

Berghe cautions her daughter that Larry may be "thinking it over" too. In a performance lasting a bit more than three minutes, "Delishious" reveals the artistry of Sascha, affirms the magnetism of Heather, and casts her in a light appealing to Larry. "As the song ends," reads a cue in the shooting script, "Heather and Larry have forgotten that it is Sascha's song."

The scene that follows takes place below deck, where Heather confesses her attraction to Larry to Sascha's sister, Olga. Falling asleep, Heather dreams of being welcomed to New York with a lavish ceremony, in which "Mr. Ellis," proprietor of Ellis Island, presents her with a giant key to the city.[6] But when she actually disembarks the next morning, she finds herself a fugitive from justice, sought by U.S. immigration officials for deportation back to Scotland. She escapes from her pursuers in a truck transporting a polo pony to its owner's estate on Long Island—coincidentally, the estate of Larry Beaumont. Larry's valet Jansen, who knows Heather from the ocean voyage, hides her in an upstairs guest room.

Heather has rejected a marriage proposal from Sascha, whom she admires but does not love. And now she sings a reflective song, "Somebody from Somewhere," affirming her faith that someday she will find the real thing.[7] The song owes much to her Scottish identity,[8] with a verse that quotes Robert Burns's classic song "Comin' through the rye."[9] Although the refrain melody is spare, the harmonies show enough richness—especially in their use of secondary dominants—to reflect Gershwin's compositional touch. When Larry learns that Heather has found her way to his estate, and that a friendly note he wrote her before leaving the ship was never delivered, he greets her warmly, offering her a place of refuge until her immigration trouble is resolved. But she slips away during the night, not wanting to live on his charity, and assuming that his kindness to her stems from pity.

Now the scene shifts to Lower Manhattan and the Varick Street flat where Sascha and his extended family live in a state of artistic penury. Heather has found her way there, and she is offered a pantomimed role in the act the family is preparing for the nearby Russian Café. On the evening of her debut, Larry is sitting at a table with Diana and her mother. Sascha and his musician colleague Toscha announce a new comic number: "Katinkitschka," a slapstick folk song about a Russian peasant couple who are having trouble with their daughter Katinka, played by a mute Heather. Here, Ira invokes the broad comedy of a suffix run wild to mock parents whose spirited daughter has flaunted their house rules by falling for a soldier boy instead of marrying a banker's son. But in the end, the sight of Katinka's "wedding ringitchka" inspires her "Popitschka" and "Momitschka" to "laugh and singitchka."

To Larry's astonishment, after the show Diana's mother announces an engagement party for him and her daughter, to be held during the coming week. In light of that news, a subdued Heather accepts Sascha's second proposal of marriage. Back in the Varick Street flat, Jansen joins a family effort to compose a wedding song, mostly on vocables like the title—"Blah, blah, blah"— with an occasional word of endearment appearing when a rhyme is required. Everyone but the bride-to-be is caught up in the tide of good spirits that the new song fosters.[10]

On Sascha and Heather's wedding day, after the family troupe has left for the Russian Café, Heather turns on the radio only to learn that Larry Beaumont has suffered a nasty fall in a polo match. She rushes out to Long Island to be by his side, offering her services as a nurse and obviously raising his spirits. But when the local police learn of her whereabouts, they show up to arrest her, and she barely manages to escape. Returning to Sascha's flat, she finds wedding decorations still hanging on the walls and the cake standing untouched on the sideboard. Sascha, sitting at the piano, is playing the soaring slow theme from the "New York Rhapsody" he has just completed, a theme that Gershwin referred to as "Brahms-like."

After greeting Heather, Sascha guides her through his new composition, citing different aspects of New York City: its towers, noise, riveters, nighttime silence. As the other musicians return to the apartment, they join in immediately with Sascha to play music from his new rhapsody. An immigration officer has been spotted in the neighborhood, and Sascha hopes the music will distract him as Heather finds a place to hide. But by now discouraged, exhausted, and not wanting to get her friends into trouble, Heather leaves the premises through a window onto the fire escape. And at this point, the musicians' on-screen music-making yields to the sound of a symphony orchestra.

Unrelated to any of the film's other songs, Gershwin's symphonic music represents the metropolis, its people, and the urban landscape through which Heather walks, deep into the night, with no comfort or haven to be had. Much of this scene's drama lies in the interaction between cinematic images of Heather and the surroundings she encounters, with the expressive, often forceful orchestral music that underlies them. Gershwin's contemplated "Manhattan Rhapsody— or Fantasy," now realized, provides a dramatic complement to a remarkable episode.[11] Heather's nocturnal wanderings finally bring her to a police station, and the music, through a final reprise of the solemn and heroic Brahmsian theme, comes to a climactic cadence as she approaches the front desk and gives herself up.[12]

The end of the picture is brief and frenetic. Larry Beaumont, his head still wrapped in bandages, learns that Heather will be deported on the *Majestic* later that evening. Having learned, too, that Diana had been the one who summoned police, he speeds through the night, sprints up the ship's ramp, and claims his true bride just in time, to the strains of "De-li-ci-ous."

After an advance screening of *Delicious* in December 1931, several reviewers pointed to the "New York Rhapsody" scene as an original and noteworthy aspect of the new film. A critic for the *Motion*

Picture Herald called it "one of the finest, if not the finest, musical composition originally conceived for motion pictures."[13] Where the idea for such a blend of action and music originated is not known—from Gershwin himself, or from conversations involving him and others in the brain trust of *Delicious*: Bolton, Butler, or Sheehan. Once sound film had been introduced in the late 1920s, the idea of this kind of coordination—editing a film to fit the structure and style of preexisting music—had been in the air, though more among European and Soviet filmmakers than those in the United States. *Delicious* marks the first such attempt in Hollywood, followed only a decade later by Walt Disney's *Fantasia*.[14]

One witness on the scene as Gershwin was composing music for the young refugee's nocturnal adventure was Hugo Friedhofer, later in life an award-winning film composer and arranger. In 1931 he was a staff musician at the Fox studio and, as it turned out, eager to help Gershwin realize his plan for another orchestral work that could stand alongside the *Rhapsody in Blue* and *An American in Paris*. He recalled:

> We became quite close, because George loved to have some-body around when he was writing. . . . I used to take his original—what were really piano parts, or two-line sketches, and blow them up. In the case of the Second Rhapsody, originally called Rhapsody in Rivets, I laid out the first orchestral sketch on it, from sitting alongside him and discussing orchestration as we went along.[15]

After returning to New York early in March, well before *Delicious* was filmed, Gershwin spent several months completing and orchestrating his Second Rhapsody, drawing on music he had composed in Hollywood. A read-through of the score took place on June 26, an occasion he described to his close Hollywood friend Aileen Pringle:

I hired fifty-five men last Friday to play my orchestration of the new Rhapsody, and the result was most gratifying. In many respects, such as orchestration and form, it is the best thing I've written. It was a bit longer than I expected, lasting about fifteen and one-half minutes. The National Broadcasting Company, whose studio I used, are connected by wire with the Victor Recording Laboratories so the studio, as a great favor to me, had a record made of the rehearsal. I shall get it tomorrow. Good idea, eh?[16]

A possible return trip west for the film's shooting remained on Gershwin's mind through the summer, even though by July he and Ira were already at work on a George S. Kaufman musical comedy named *Of Thee I Sing*. "If there was any possible chance," Gershwin wrote George Pallay in California on July 30, "I would love to come as I am more than anxious to have a hand in the making of DELICIOUS. I hope to Heaven that the picture will be made right and will prove a big hit. There is nothing that would please me more than to come out to California next year to do another musical picture."[17]

Delicious opened at New York's Roxy Theatre on Christmas Day 1931, to mixed reviews.[18] *Of Thee I Sing*, on the other hand, opened on Broadway the very next day and was an instant hit. But for the Gershwin brothers, the release of *Delicious* was a letdown; by then the experience of creating the picture's score—in California, and the better part of a year in the past—had surely faded. And George was less than pleased with the result, as he admitted in a New Year's greeting to Pringle: "I was very disappointed in the picture we wrote. . . . It could have been so swell but imagination in producing it & cutting it was lacking." But there was no time to wallow in regret: in spite of his disappointment, *Delicious* would "come near breaking the all time record at Roxy's. They expect to do $130,000 this week," he told Pringle. Moreover, he added, the "Boston Symphony will finally play the new Rhapsody on Jan 29 & 30th in Boston & Feb. 5 in New York."[19]

GERSHWIN's Second Rhapsody for Orchestra with Piano was premiered on January 29, 1932, by Koussevitzky and the Boston Symphony Orchestra. After the Boston premiere, several critics described the work as an expansion of a sequence of music written originally for *Delicious*, and their claim remained part of the composition's lore into the twenty-first century.[20] But in Gershwin's mind, the Rhapsody, more than the movie score, was the primary artistic takeaway from his first Hollywood stay. "Nearly everybody comes back from California with a western tan and a pocketful of moving-picture money," he claimed airily to Goldberg. "I decided to come back with both those things, and a serious composition—if the climate would let me."[21] In an interview in the *Boston Evening Transcript*, he contrasted the new piece's genesis with that of the *Rhapsody in Blue*:

When I started on the earlier work, I had exactly five weeks to the time of performance. So I wrote it in three. I turned over page after page, knowing it was not as good as I would have liked it to be. But I knew also that it had to be finished and that I could waste no time on revisions. I kept saying to myself, "Never mind, I'll fix that after the concert." But the *Rhapsody in Blue* was a success and its weak spots have never been fixed.

For the Second Rhapsody, he had had seven weeks:

The parties and the night-life of Hollywood did not interest me in the least. They bored me in fact. Here was my chance to do some serious work. Seven weeks of almost uninterrupted opportunity to write the best music I could possibly think of. What a chance! The main theme came out of the picture, of course. . . . The picture was not to be released until Christmas, and I was requested not to bring out the Rhapsody until after the picture had been launched. All the while I have been revising and polishing. I have even made minor changes since coming to Boston. In this piece I have had the opportunity of doing pretty nearly what I wanted.

And the result had offered its own reward, for Koussevitzky "brings out things, and makes them sound like a million dollars," he added, "that I hardly knew were there!"[22]

The sounds of the Rhapsody's first section—industrial riveting, jazz-oriented dancing, and discordant harmony—reflect an urban landscape. Gershwin's inventiveness shines in the metamorphosis of the percussive "rivet theme" from a succession of repeated eighth notes to a tidy, propulsive eight-bar tune that helps to unify the first section. A middle section, arriving about halfway through with a dignified mien, invites the listener into a more contemplative space, where melodic emphasis comes to the fore. Its "Brahms theme," introduced by the orchestra, was cited years later by Robert Russell Bennett as "the best tune Gershwin ever wrote." This soaring melody unfolds over an archlike bass line, with strategically placed blue notes lending a modern aura to the sound.[23] "Middle" implies a three-part form along the familiar lines of ABA, but in fact the third section proves shorter and quicker than the first, with a pianistic display that brings the piece to an end with a flourish.

Those distinctive final measures apparently came about thanks to Edward Kilenyi, one of the musicians Gershwin had invited to his orchestral runthrough in June 1931. One evening not long after that session, Gershwin invited his former teacher to dinner and showed him the finished orchestration of his new work, written on extra-large score paper to accommodate all the lines he needed. "When he expressed anxiety about the form of the work," Kilenyi recalled,

I suggested that he play and explain it to me while I followed the orchestral sketches. I could not find anything to suggest except a change in the closing passage. This was an orchestral tutti with the piano soloist not playing at all! I lightly remarked that perhaps audiences might expect the soloist to continue to play after the orchestra stopped. He agreed with my comment and asked help in creating an effective ending. I suggested that he use the main motif for brass and piano, giving it fortissimo. He sat down and changed the ending accordingly. When . . . Bill Daly arrived, he warmly announced to him: "Look, Bill, what new ending Edward suggested!"[24]

The new work's premiere, six weeks after the successful Boston debut of *Of Thee I Sing*, sparked much local excitement. Moses Smith in the *Evening Traveler* deemed the Rhapsody a triumph, and Gershwin's compositional skill remarkable—especially for a composer who claimed to shun musical "traditions."[25] "Through out, there is a conciseness of formal development, a neat way of saying something and then going on with other matter. Now and then the expression becomes unduly sentimental or bombastic. But this is the exception: for the most part Gershwin displays the taste, the intellectual command of the artist."[26] For Warren Storey Smith of the *Post*, no fan of Gershwin, the piece was "much better made, from the technical standpoint, than its famous predecessor." Beyond that, however, "his musical speech is still predominantly that of Tin Pan Alley. . . . Most of the new rhapsody calls out for a musical comedy setting. At a symphony concert it is as out of place as a one-piece bathing suit."[27] Henry Taylor Parker recalled that to hear Gershwin play his *Rhapsody in Blue* was to feel as if the music was "springing anew from the mind and temperament that created it." But he perceived a different approach at its successor's unveiling. "Mr. Gershwin . . . proceeded cautiously; took thought, as it seemed, of every measure and every tone; was sedulous with each accent, each shading." The idea that inhibition could be "inherent in the music itself" troubled this seasoned critic.[28]

A week after the Boston premiere performances, Koussevitzky led his orchestra in a pair of Carnegie Hall concerts that introduced the new Rhapsody to listeners in Gershwin's home city. *Times* critic Olin Downes felt that "with all its immaturities, the *Rhapsody in Blue* is more individual and originative than the piece heard last night. . . . We have had better things from Mr. Gershwin, and we expect better in time to come."[29] W. J. Henderson of the *Sun* also thought the new Rhapsody suffered in comparison with its predecessor:

> It is likely that most music lovers will believe that the first rhapsody expressed America and its musical inclinations even better than this one. Mr. Gershwin possesses a unique talent and his endeavors to put jazz in the artistic category are interesting and commendable. He was heartily applauded last evening after he and the great orchestra had performed his work with extraordinary brilliancy.[30]

After its second New York performance, more than six months went by before the new piece was heard again—as part of an unprecedented all-Gershwin concert in Lewisohn Stadium on August 16, 1932. Moreover, only two more performances of the work have been documented during Gershwin's lifetime, neither of which involved him: on November 4, 1932, as part of Paul Whiteman's fourth "Experiment in Modern Music" concert in Carnegie Hall—Ferde Grofé's arrangement, with Roy Bargy at the piano;[31] and on March 20, 1933, performed by Hamilton Harty and the London Symphony Orchestra, with Solomon Cuttner as soloist.[32]

Gershwin came away from the first performances with a positive impression of his new composition. Talking with Boston's music critics during rehearsals, he had spoken approvingly about the "revising and polishing" that seems to have continued almost until the eve of the premiere. He apparently came to cede his artistic judgments more than usual to the process of rethinking that circumstances had offered him. Perhaps some of the confidence in his first inspirations through years of composing to a deadline had eroded as he continued to polish details in the Second Rhapsody.

Of his five performances under Koussevitzky, two seem to have involved moments of uncharacteristic nervousness. Boston critic Moses Smith's review cited an unspecified pianistic glitch early in the first performance, attributing it to "a slight attack of nerves at the opening of the rhapsody." And a week later, Gershwin's piano-playing friend Oscar Levant, sitting with him backstage in Carnegie Hall before the first New York performance, urged him to relax by playing through a few of his own songs, only to incur Gershwin's ire when the onstage call was unexpectedly delivered. Gershwin blamed Levant for distracting him from his systematic warmup.[33] These mishaps contradict Gershwin's usual public persona, known for offering performance as a way to share with others the delight he took in his artistry and music-making. "It may be that this new Rhapsody," H. T. Parker suspected, "was written subduing himself to reflection, bending too long and considerately over music-paper before he set down the just and final note," a process "at odds with the natural, the essential play of his creative instinct."

OF THEE I SING
(1931)

As the story goes, on January 15, 1930, the night after the revised *Strike Up the Band* opened on Broadway, the two men who wrote the book—George Kaufman and Morrie Ryskind—watched the performance from the back of the theater with mixed feelings. Producer Edgar Selwyn joined them in a triumphal mood. Changes that had softened what some had found unpatriotic about the first version, he told them, explained the audience's enthusiastic reception. But the playwrights took his opinion less as a compliment than as a challenge: the next time they should "do one just for ourselves," with the Gershwins again on board.[1]

By the time the authors came up with a workable idea, George and Ira had signed on for the screen and *Delicious*. But when the brothers headed west, they took with them Kaufman and Ryskind's fourteen-page scenario for a new show, which enabled them, during spare moments in California and after their return home, to work on at least some ideas. With fingers crossed, the authors also sent their scenario to producer Sam Harris, who wired them back that "it's certainly different," which Kaufman rightly took as a yes.[2] By July 1931, the first-act script of the new show, apparently first called

The Big Charade, was in the Gershwins' hands, and conversations were taking place about where the plot might need songs and which music should go where.

Meanwhile, in London on July 27, the BBC Symphony played a program in Queen's Hall as part of the International Society for Contemporary Music's Ninth Festival. Six orchestral works were performed, each by a composer from a different nation, and the concert ended with *An American in Paris*, conducted by Alfredo Casella.[3] Gershwin's composition drew neither enthusiastic plaudits nor scornful dismissals from the critics, though more than one found the taxi horns overdone. The London *Times* critic found that "like all musical jokes, it went on too long, repeated a good joke (that of the motor-horns, for example) too often, and between the jokes relapsed into platitudes."[4]

As the ISCM explored present-day inventiveness in the U.K., in New York City the Philharmonic was introducing a conductor new to the orchestra to lead a two-week series of summer concerts at Lewisohn Stadium. Fritz Reiner, erstwhile music director of the Cincinnati Symphony Orchestra, was now on his way to a new post as assistant conductor of the Philadelphia Orchestra. Reiner had just returned from a European trip, and he singled out George Gershwin as "the only American composer who has a popular following in Europe," where "critics and public alike respect his work."[5] The last concert in his Lewisohn series was to be an all-American affair scheduled for Monday, August 10. But that plan was foiled by rain, which lasted until the 13th, by which time Reiner had left to fulfill an engagement in Philadelphia.

Despite the delays, that concert proved a source of satisfaction for Gershwin. "Who do you suppose I got to conduct for me?" he wrote Rosamond Walling, who by then was in Europe. "None other than my good-looking Irish pal Bill Daly. It will be his first performance as symphony conductor & we're all excited about it."[6] In a letter to George Pallay the day after the concert, he left no doubt that the evening's highlight had been Daly's debut as symphonic conductor. "I believe I have told you about Bill being probably my best friend. Well, I got him to conduct the Rhapsody and also Russell Bennett's March for Orchestra and Two Pianos. It was the general opinion that the Rhapsody had never been heard to better advantage, even when Whiteman played it." Nor was Gershwin alone in his appreciation. Francis Perkins of the *Herald Tribune* considered that the *Rhapsody in Blue* blossomed under Daly's approach to sonority:

> Mr. Gershwin, as a rhapsodist in blue, is well known to Stadium audiences, but the orchestral colors of the work were set forth with unusual brilliance, the jazz had an unusual warmth in last night's performance under the spirited, able leadership of Mr. Daly. . . . Under his direction the orchestra gave probably the most Whit[e]manesque performance of its career.[7]

September 26 saw the publication of Isaac Goldberg's biography, the outcome of a personal connection that had begun in the summer of 1929, when the two men met after an *American in Paris* concert in Boston. Since then, the scholarly Goldberg had become a friend of both George and Ira, as well as a close student of George's music and career. Deems Taylor advised his readers:

> If you want to read the life story, so far, of an authentically talented musician, who began his career as a fifteen-dollar-a-week song plugger in Tin Pan Alley . . . a young man who still rides with one foot on the back of the bucking bronco of musical comedy and the other on that of the milk-white steed of symphonic music, and has not been thrown yet; all told by a chronicler whose unabashed devotion to his subject matter is not the least attractive feature of his work—where were we? If memory serves, there was an "if" somewhere in the misty beginning of that sentence. Anyhow, try the book. It will, I think, amuse and interest you.[8]

A month later, Ira was informing Pallay in Los Angeles that "we are up to our necks in 'Of Thee I Sing' which goes into rehearsal in a couple of weeks. We're a little stale on it just now and, for the past three weeks, I give up trying to get ideas, and forget the show, on the slightest invitation to a cross word puzzle or backgammon. But as it's been that way with every show in the past, I'm not particularly worried. We'll probably get a lot done at the last minute."[9] By early November, they had finished drafting a score for an endeavor George called "different from anything we've ever done. . . . the music & the book are wedded to such a degree that most of the big situations are done to music."[10]

On November 10 George wrote "Ike" Goldberg to explain his current optimism:

> We are in rehearsal with the principals and chorus of the new show. The principals seem to be thrilled wth the music and the chorus—which started yesterday—also seem pleased. It's a little hard for me to tell you how it is going to turn out but, at the moment, I feel it is the most complete score that Ira and I have ever written. We have taken whole scenes of Kaufman's book and set them to music and lyrics. As I have never written this sort of thing so completely before, I find it difficult to predict its final value. However, I will say that it has a chance, in my opinion, of having some importance in American musical comedy.

In other words, as in the Finaletto to Act I of *Strike Up the Band*, the Gershwins were now creating a musical comedy steeped in operatic dramaturgy.[11]

And two weeks later, in another letter to Goldberg, George confessed that "the last two weeks in Boston" had been "unusual and delightful" because "the show went so well." The cause? "I feel Ira and I had at last become fortunate in the finding of a first rate book."[12]

. . .

A TALE of presidential politics set in Washington, D.C., the plot of
Of Thee I Sing centers on one John P. Wintergreen, played by William Gaxton, nominated before the show begins to fill the highest
office in the land.[13] Wintergreen is the candidate of a political party
that has found no issue to run on. A hint of that problem surfaces
in the opening scene, a torchlit political parade whose marchers
are singing "Wintergreen for President" and carrying banners with
such slogans as "Win with Wintergreen" and "A Vote for Wintergreen Is a Vote for Wintergreen." Lasting barely two minutes,
the arresting scene consists entirely of music delivered in unison
by a mixed chorus with orchestra—mostly in call-and-response
exchanges, and peppered with quotations from patriotic songs.

Scene 2 shows the party's National Committee hammering out
an election platform. The committee's membership numbers five:
Matthew Fulton, owner of a big-city newspaper; two U.S. senators,
one from the South and the other from the West; and two political
bosses—Gilhooley from New York's Tammany Hall, where Irish
political power is centered, and Lippman, who can deliver the Jewish vote. After much palaver and a bit of debate, the members stum-
ble onto an issue: Wintergreen, a bachelor, will run as an advocate
of "love," and his campaign will include a search for a first lady. A
beauty contest will be held in Atlantic City with a contestant from
each of the forty-eight states; if elected, President Wintergreen will
marry the winner.

The convention has chosen a running mate for Wintergreen so
innocuous that nobody can remember his name. In fact, when Alexander Throttlebottom, played by Victor Moore, shows up at the
committee's strategy session seeking to resign from the ticket—he
fears that his mother will learn of his nomination—he is almost
ejected as an interloper. When party leaders learn that he spent
years as a hermit before entering politics, they return him to the

cave where he came from, on the grounds that vice presidents must stay out of sight. But he reappears immediately, having been thrown out by the other hermits.

Scene 3 takes place in Atlantic City, where beauty pageant contestants parade by in bathing suits. In "Who Is the Lucky Girl to Be?," the girls comment on the experience of being in a competition with one winner and forty-seven losers. Wintergreen is introduced to the bevy of beauties as their "future husband." Dazzled at first, he grows uneasy with the prospect of life at the side of the likely winner: Diana Devereaux of Louisiana, a southern belle played by Grace Brinkley with a thick regional drawl. He then strikes up a conversation with a noncontestant: Mary Turner, played by Lois Moran, secretary of the organizing committee, who can, the candidate learns, bake "the best darned corn muffins you ever ate." Sampling one of Turner's glories as Devereaux is declared the winner, Wintergreen rejects the party's political agenda. With apologies to Devereaux, he declares that Turner will be his bride because he loves her *and* her muffins ("Some Girls Can Bake a Pie"). At first, consternation reigns, but eventually Wintergreen carries the day, as Devereaux and the other would-be first ladies protest in agitated counterpoint.

Scene 4, staged shortly before the election, is a political rally—with banners, music, speeches, and, for spectators who find politics a bore, a wrestling match—in New York's Madison Square Garden. In "Love Is Sweeping the Country," an inspirational campaign song, the ensemble predicts that passion will "soon be national," with Gershwin's music supplying the high-octane vitality required for the song to energize Americans to vote for love and Wintergreen. The brisk, 2/4 refrain music, with its bold melodic gestures, persistent syncopation, and fast-moving declamation, embodies exhilaration. The rally's central moment is the appearance of Wintergreen and Turner, who implore the crowd to join in their political quest before Wintergreen leads a rendition of the show's title song. If "Love Is Sweeping the Country" is brash and challenging, "Of Thee I Sing" exudes dedication, fusing romance with love of country. Borrowing a line of text from a patriotic classic originally sung to the melody of the British "God Save the King," it desolemnizes the worshipful gravity of the first two phrases by ending both with the colloquial "baby." The final measures, broadening the tempo, approach anthemlike majesty.

Scene 5, election night, unfolds on a moving picture screen, the melodies of "Love Is Sweeping the Country" and "Of Thee I Sing" providing an aural backdrop. Returns show that Wintergreen has beaten Jefferson Davis in Atlanta, barely edged out Mickey Mouse in Hollywood, and won handily in Richmond over Mason, Dixon, *and* Mason and Dixon. Wintergreen is elected and Throttlebottom refuses to concede his election as vice president.[14]

Act I closes in scene 6 on the steps of the Capitol, where Wintergreen takes his oath of office and promises to be a faithful husband to Mary Turner. A fanfare based on the title song's first phrase introduces the nine Supreme Court justices, who boast that "only we can take a law and make it legal." The president-elect sings a farewell to his bachelor days ("Here's a Kiss for Cinderella"), as the crowd adds a countermelody of its own. Turner arrives, accompanied by music that includes portions of the wedding march from Wagner's *Lohengrin*. As the chief justice administers both the oath of office and the matrimonial vows, the orchestra plays "Of Thee I Sing" softly in the background. But the solemnity is shattered when a strident female voice breaks in: "Stop! Halt! Pause! Wait!" Diana Devereaux has arrived to serve Wintergreen with a summons for breach of promise. "I was the most beautiful blossom in all the Southland," she begins, going on to relate what happened after she was "sent up north" and denied her prize unfairly. Wintergreen then raises the question of the hour: "Which is more important? Justice or corn muffins?" The Supreme Court justices go into a football-team huddle, and suspense builds over background music until they break for their verdict: The muffins have it, the crowd hails the decision, and Act I closes on a note of solemnity.

The curtain of Act II rises in the White House on a his-and-hers presidential office as secretaries show up for work, whistling and dancing to a graceful melody ("Hello, Good Morning"). Fulton from the National Committee, however, informs the first couple that Diana Devereaux's complaint is the talk all over the country. His news prompts the show's third and last freestanding song, "Who Cares?," with a scornful verse. "I love him and he loves me and that's how it will always be so what care we about Miss Devereaux?," the first lady announces on a succession of quarter notes. But now a foreign entanglement looms, in the person of the ambassador of France, whose entourage arrives to walking music borrowed from the composer's *An American in Paris*. He has come to the White House because a grievous wrong has been done to a French descendant.

This notion had struck Ira in Hollywood, when he figured that an important French father for Diana might have comic potential. "Not wishing to use the names of any contemporary personages," he recalled, "I went historical." She would be the "illegitimate daughter of an ill. nephew of Louie-Philippe (or Napoleon)"—and her blue blood would enable Ira to rhyme "Napoleon" with "the old Simoleon" (i.e., the almighty dollar). [15]

"The Illegitimate Daughter," a pompous 6/8 march delivered by the ambassador with mock dignity and pristine clarity, leaves his audience unsettled. To sharpen his case, he has brought the spurned damsel with him, her voice heard first in the distance singing "I was the most beautiful blossom in all the Southland." When the Wintergreens cut her off with an abrupt "We know all that!" the ambassador insists that their marriage be annulled. But Wintergreen stands by his wife, whereupon the politicos, concerned with their own standing, decide to begin an impeachment hearing. The president and first lady sing a reprise of "Who Cares?" softly, with a wispy violin obbligato, substituting steadfast new words for the original defiant ones.

By scene 2, it has dawned on the committee that if Wintergreen is removed from office, Throttlebottom will become president. Wintergreen, however, seems unbothered by that prospect, and he dispenses advice to his vice president: on policy (during the first four years "don't do anything except try to get re-elected"), Congress ("keep them out of Washington"), and speech-making ("only make a speech when you want the stock market to go down"). Scene 3, staged in the Senate, is called to order by Throttlebottom ("The Senator from Minnesota"), who does his best to welcome Wintergreen to his own impeachment: "Won't you sit down, while we kick you out?" The charge against the president is chanted in four parts, each beginning with "Whereas." Diana delivers a new lament ("Jilted") in waltz time about the humiliation she has suffered, while Wintergreen embraces his fate.

But now a cry from the first lady brings the impeachment to a halt. "I'm about to be a mother," she carols, in a lilting waltz-time filled with bold leaps, exuding an aura of vitality and joy. The singing and dancing ensemble agrees that "we can't bother / A budding young father," as the president faints at the bombshell his wife has just dropped. After Throttlebottom notes that "the Senate has never impeached an expectant father," the senators all vote "Not guilty!" As the melody of Diana's well-worn lamentation "I was the most beautiful blossom . . ." echos once more, the Atlantic City girls restate phrases from one of their pageant songs, and the chief justice congratulates the president: "You've done your duty by posterity." His line allows Wintergreen to deliver the title of the next number, "Posterity is just around the corner." A tango rhythm emerges from the orchestra, giving the melody such a lift that the ensemble jumps on board in a flash—the senators are already wielding tambourines—and so does the first lady. "France consents to your having a child," the president is informed in the next scene, but only if the baby is turned over to the French state.

When the curtain rises on the last scene in the Yellow Room of the White House, it unveils a stage full of gifts as everyone wonders whether the baby will be a boy or a girl. The Supreme Court judges, who alone can decide the gender of a sitting president's baby, are announced by fanfare. "By a strict party vote," proclaims the chief justice, "it's a boy." Congratulations are showered upon Wintergreen, who distributes cigars. But then another fanfare is heard. The Court returns, and the chief justice repeats the birth announcement: "This time it's a girl." An outraged French ambassador warns that war is now virtually certain, for the United States has deprived France of not just one baby, but two. Somewhere in the distance, Devereaux may be heard singing, "I was the most beautiful blossom. . . ."

With tension between America and France near the breaking point, it dawns on Wintergreen that it's in circumstances like these that the vice president can replace the president. "I get her!" Throttlebottom gloats. "Article Twelve!" confirms the chief justice. "Monsieur, you are a genius," says the ambassador. "Oh, my God!" Wintergreen exclaims when a third fanfare sounds, relaxing only after the chief justice assures him that it's only "the boys" practicing. As a huge canopied bed comes into view, occupied by Mary Wintergreen with a baby on each arm, the show ends with the entire cast singing the refrain "Of Thee I Sing."[16]

Of Thee I Sing, opening on December 8 in Boston and December 26 on Broadway, proved a near-unanimous success with the drama critics. As one New York reviewer put it, the show was original without sacrificing any of "the virtues of the musical comedy, per se. Beautiful girls, lively music, lovers nearly parted—all these are present," along with a "great generosity of ideas" that put the musical in a class by itself.[17] No critic paid closer heed to the show than Boston's Henry Taylor Parker, who credited Gershwin's compositional approach for "a music that is part and parcel of the narrative. . . . We who are fond and foolish, and so ambitious for the American theater, went home with a warming sense that the new play had enlarged it."[18]

The reviewer for the *Boston Globe* commented that while Gershwin had received great applause as he walked down the aisle to conduct the first performance, Kaufman, Ryskind, and his brother should have been with him. For "happy as Mr. Gershwin's music is, happier indeed are book and lyric," which together "make one of the funniest plays in a long, long time. . . . The lyricist has worked out a style that combines the method of [W. S.] Gilbert with that of the librettists of Italian grand operas—now rapid patters of short, jerky rhymes, now the repetition by the chorus of the statements of the principals, and again the operatic style of tossing a line here and a line there to different sections of the chorus. Extremely effective."[19] A review by Leslie A. Sloper, music critic of the *Christian Science Monitor*, was more measured in its praise, finding "various coarsenesses which are quite gratuitous and which belong to the tradition of a lower type of musical comedy." Nevertheless, "we must not forget to mention that this imperfect operetta is hugely amusing."[20] As the tryout run in Boston neared its end, Parker revisited *Of Thee I Sing* and was more than ever convinced that the show was "original work, American through and through."[21]

A substantial number of New York critics agreed that the show's originality and inventiveness would earn it a place in American theater history. Richard Lockridge's judgment, "the grandest American stage satire I have any knowledge of," was typical.[22] Robert Garland of the *World Telegram* wrote, "I must remember to tell my grandchildren that I was present at its opening."[23] Brooks Atkinson of the *Times* called librettists Kaufman and Ryskind "as neat a pair of satirists as ever scuttled a national tradition."[24] And in the *Eve-*

ning Post, John Mason Brown singled out Victor Moore's triumph in making Throttlebottom "as richly humorous as he is wistfully pathetic."[25]

In the January 2, 1932, issue of the *New Yorker*, E. B. White, after stating that " 'Of Thee I Sing' has the funniest book of any musical comedy you can put your finger on," added that "whatever it is, it is a Step Forward, as anybody feels who has seen the show. . . . The moment never arrives (as it does early in most musical comedies) when the startling clarity of the plot sickens you with the realization that it is going to take another act and a half to get it down on paper. This show really covers ground, and keeps building up and up."[26] On January 3, Atkinson, returning for another performance, saluted the musical's success in presenting entertainment "funnier than the government, and not nearly so dangerous."[27]

Sometime after the opening, a lonely dissenting view came from New York's Franco-American Society, which counted itself unamused by lines that referred jokingly to the weighty war debt owed by France to the United States. On the society's behalf, the Rt. Reverend William T. Manning submitted a resolution asking that the charge be toned down. Kaufman responded that he would gladly remove these offending lines "if Bishop Manning will write a couple for me which will get the same big laughs." The lines remained, and the show ran on Broadway for more than a year, logging 441 performances.[28]

MORE DOWNS AND UPS AND DOWNS
(1932)

ON MAY 3, 1932, THE PULITZER PRIZE for drama was awarded to George Kaufman, Morrie Ryskind, and Ira Gershwin for *Of Thee I Sing*, but the show's composer received no such recognition, for in that day there was no Pulitzer Prize for music. Ira's inclination was to refuse the prize, but George insisted that he accept.[1]

Less than two weeks later, on May 14, Morris Gershwin died of leukemia at age sixty-two. Those who knew George Gershwin well agreed that the death of his father affected him deeply. His aunt, Rose Gershwin's sister Kate Wolpin, witnessed George exclaiming in the hospital, "Papa, I would give everything in the world if I could do something for you to get well," and she remembered his sending "for medication to that big hospital in Maryland, and for special doctors."[2] Friend and pianist Oscar Levant, also saddened by Morris's death, admitted that he lacked the sensibility to engage with others on such matters as sorrow and loss—an incapacity that he and Gershwin, he believed, held in common. Levant could "lay no claim to a special access to [George's] feelings," he recalled later. "We merely had a healthy, extrovertial intimacy, born . . . of mutual interests. Excluding the members of his family," Levant believed, "the only man who could possibly be said to have enjoyed such a special affection from George was Bill Daly."[3]

Another hint of Gershwin's emotional reticence now may be suggested by a letter he wrote to DuBose Heyward just six days after his father died. As part of their correspondence that spring, about the opera the two men had been considering over the past five years, Heyward had written from North Carolina with news that he had finally cleared operatic rights to his novella *Porgy*. Gershwin's brief reply, explaining that he would not be free to start composing the opera until 1933, was all business, carrying no hint of the personal loss he had just sustained.[4]

As success made Gershwin a figure whose doings were followed by the press, perhaps the most persistent question about his personal life was why one of New York's most eligible bachelors—who in interviews avowed his intent to marry when "the right" woman came along—stayed single. Long after her brother died, it seems that Frances Godowsky was still pondering that matter. In a 1983 interview, she recalled his saying that he wanted to live in a setting "with beautiful things in it. He loved glass and beautiful dishes, and he loved paintings. He said 'I want to have a home.' Somehow it never happened." In fact, George, who in 1929 had set up his own household, did surround himself with beautiful things from that time forward. But he found no female companion to share his existence with. Frances could not avoid looking back on her brother's extraordinary life with a certain regret. "George wasn't a happy person," she told an interviewer. "He didn't understand why he couldn't get out of life what he wanted, which was a companion. Somehow there may be something in our background that did that to him."[5]

The list of women with whom Gershwin was romantically involved over the years is long, and many among them were famous in their own right. In addition to Adele Astaire and Rosamond Walling, they include pianists Josepha Rosanska and Pauline Heifetz (sister of violinist Jascha), Countess Nadige de Ganny, Julia

Thomas Van Norman, and actresses Marilyn Miller, Ginger Rogers, Aileen Pringle, Roberta Robinson, Kitty Carlisle, Elizabeth Allan, Simone Simon, Luise Rainer, and Paulette Goddard.[6] But the longest-lasting of his relationships, with pianist-composer Kay Swift, was also the one linked most closely to his musical life.

Born into a musical family in 1897—her father Samuel was a New York music critic—Katharine Faulkner Swift studied piano and composition at the Institute of Musical Art, which later became the Juilliard School of Music. Receiving her diploma in 1917, she married James Paul Warburg, of a prominent New York banking family, a year later. Between 1919 and 1924, the couple had three daughters, even as Katharine continued her musical studies. She was something of a free spirit, and the Warburgs carried on an active social life, filled with entertaining, partygoing, and an apparently relaxed attitude toward marital vows. There were days when the daughters—looked after by a staff of servants—saw their parents only in the evening, dressed to the nines and on their way to a dinner party or the theater. By 1924, the couple had purchased Bydale, a twenty-five-acre farm in Greenwich, Connecticut, that eventually grew to more than eighty acres.

On April 17, 1925, Katharine gave a party honoring Jascha Heifetz, and Gershwin was there in the company of Pauline. He attended another Warburg party in February 1926, and this time, with the premiere of the *Concerto in F* behind him and two shows running on Broadway, he spent much of the evening at the piano, apparently the first time the hostess had witnessed him in action. After some time he rose abruptly from the keyboard and announced, "Well, I've got to go to Europe now," a comment she found rather charming.[7] The next day he did leave for Europe—bound by ocean liner for work on the upcoming London production of *Lady, Be Good!*[8]

Before this occasion, in line with her background and training, Katharine had paid little attention to music outside the classical sphere, and her composing had run to art songs and character pieces for piano. But now she found herself paying heed to the music Gershwin played, and gaining new respect for the popular realm. When Gershwin returned from London early in May—to the disappointment, we have learned, of Adele Astaire—James Warburg was traveling on business, and Katharine and George struck up a friendship, which gave her an escort to the concerts, art exhibits, theatrical parties, and posttheater gatherings that comprised much of her social routine. Their friendship also included sessions at the piano, where Gershwin introduced her to the popular songs of such masters as Irving Berlin and Hoagy Carmichael. Following George's lead, Katharine now began to answer to "Kay."

Kay Swift was an excellent pianist with a quick ear and an uncanny memory, ready to assist Gershwin on such tasks as editing and copying his music. Technical skills that he was still working to master, such as orchestration and counterpoint, lay within her ken. Later that year, as Gershwin was composing short piano pieces to play at a Marguerite d'Alvarez recital, Kay rendered in musical notation the third of the Three Preludes for Piano that he soon published. She also introduced Gershwin into a lofty echelon of New York's café society, and at Bydale she introduced him to horseback riding. It was through Kay and Bydale, too, that he met Charles Martin Loeffler, with whom she had studied composition in earlier days, and who came to be one of the few American composers to give Gershwin encouragement and support.[9] During times when Gershwin needed a hideaway where he could work without interruption, she offered the use of the farm; it was there, in the fall of 1928, that he completed the orchestration of *An American in Paris*.

Kay's relationship with Gershwin alerted her to opportunities in the world of popular music, and she seized them. She joined the musicians' union, worked with stage designer Norman Bel Geddes on a musical comedy project, and was hired in the fall of 1927 as rehearsal pianist for Rodgers and Hart's *A Connecticut Yankee*. Such a job, with its long hours and strict rehearsal schedule, would have been impossible for an on-duty mother with children who were then eight, five, and three years old, but the Warburgs' wealth allowed her to outsource childcare to a household staff. James Paul Warburg proved to be the kind of banker who found the challenges of light verse intriguing. As his wife began to compose popular songs, he began to invent lyrics for them.

By 1928, the songwriting team of "Kay Swift" and "Paul James" had collaborated on a pair of songs worthy of being interpolated into a Broadway show. The next year saw the publication of their first hit, "Can't We Be Friends?," sung by chanteuse Libby Holman in a successful revue called *The Little Show*.[10] And in September 1930, *Fine and Dandy*, a production by Morris Green and Lewis E. Gensler, with a book by Donald Ogden Stewart and songs by Kay Swift and Paul James, opened on Broadway: the Great White Way's first musical comedy with a score composed entirely by a woman, and a most successful one at that, running for 255 performances.[11] But although their marriage continued until 1934, the couple's creative partnership did not. Gershwin and Kay kept frequent company through these years, during which she devoted much of her musical energy to him and his projects. "George was a fascinating but disturbing element at Bydale," Warburg recalled in his autobiography.

> His exuberant vitality and many-sided zest for life knew no bounds. He wanted to learn and experience literally everything that he had not known in a childhood on Manhattan's Lower East Side. He wanted to learn to ride a horse, to buy and wear the right country clothes, to play with young children, and, most of all, to acquire from Kay the techniques of orchestration. He would sit for hours at the piano, experimenting in contagious excitement with a new melody or rhythm while Kay suggested harmonic treatment. Day turned into night and night into day when George was in the throes of creation.[12]

By no means did Gershwin's connection with Kay Swift, which continued until he moved to Hollywood in 1936, preclude attachments to other women. His involvement with Rosamond Walling took place while he and Kay were also spending considerable time together. On his first trip to Hollywood, he formed a close connection with actress Aileen Pringle, coming to feel sufficiently at home in her domicile on Adelaide Street that he did some composing there. Indeed, he and "Pringie" stayed in touch after he returned to New York. Nevertheless, the musical sensibilities and skills that Kay brought to their relationship gave her a unique place among his closest professional colleagues.[13]

Kay Swift was the dedicatee of a unique volume published in May 1932 under the imprint of Simon and Schuster: *George Gershwin's Song-book*, a retrospective compilation of eighteen songs, arranged in chronological order from 1919 to 1931. The book's format and contents mark it as the artistic statement of a songwriter with a distinctive perspective on the musical comedy song. First issued in a deluxe edition with a 300-copy print run, each song came with an illustration by Constantin Alajolov, a Russian-born painter, illustrator, and cartoonist whose covers for such magazines as the *Saturday Evening Post* and the *New Yorker* had made his work familiar. Each first-edition copy was signed by both the composer and the artist.[14]

"With the general increase of technical skill at the piano," Gershwin's introduction announces, "there has arisen a demand for arrangements that shall consider that skill. Playing my songs as frequently as I do at private parties, I have naturally been led to compose numerous variations upon them, and to indulge the desire for complication and variety that every composer feels when he manipulates the same material over and over again." In the *Song-book* he explores the material as his "desire for complication and variety" urges him on—with arrangements that seem invented on the spot. The format is straightforward: first the song's sheet-music version—

introduction, verse, and refrain, with lyrics—and then Gershwin's embellished version of the refrain, without lyrics—intended for the benefit of accomplished pianists "who enjoy popular music but who rebel at the too-simple arrangements issued by the publishers with the average pianist in view."

Because the music now demands it, Gershwin explains, present-day players of popular music are more likely than their earlier counterparts to be accomplished musicians. "As the American popular song has grown richer in harmony and rhythm, so has the player grown more subtle and incisive in his performance of it," he observes. However, he has learned, "our study of the great romantic composers has trained us in the method of the legato," while "our popular music asks for staccato effects, for almost a stenciled style." Classically trained pianists tend to fail "lamentably," he warns, when they play ragtime or jazz, because "they use the pedaling of Chopin when interpreting the blues of Handy."[15]

Gershwin's introduction says nothing about how he has chosen the songs in the anthology, but some of his reasoning is obvious—for example, his desire to represent his achievements as a songwriter from his first hits to the present. The earliest songs, "Swanee" and "Nobody but You," date from 1919, and the latest, "Who Cares?," comes from *Of Thee I Sing*, still running on Broadway. Gershwin also chose to republish songs that had won popularity beyond their original context. They vary in character; most are love songs, but such subjects as the American South, the joy of dancing, life in a modern city, and even wartime activity are represented, too. Each number is a concise instrumental interpretation of a thought or a mood encountered in the urban United States during the years after World War I.

As well as being chronologically ordered, the songs fall into four groups, based on sources, key relationships, and affinities within the trajectory of Gershwin's career:

GROUP 1

"Swanee" (1919; Caesar)	F
"Nobody but You" (1919; DeSylva)	E-flat
"I'll Build a Stairway to Paradise" (1922; DeSylva and Arthur Francis)	C
"Do It Again" (1922; DeSylva)	F

GROUP 2

"Fascinating Rhythm" (1924; Ira Gershwin)	E-flat
"Oh, Lady Be Good" (1924; Ira)	G
"Somebody Loves Me" (1924; DeSylva and Ballard MacDonald)	G
"Sweet and Low-Down" (1925; Ira)	G
"That Certain Feeling" (1925; Ira)	E-flat
"The Man I Love" (1924; Ira)	E-flat

GROUP 3

"Clap Yo' Hands" (1926; Ira)	B-flat
"Do-Do-Do" (1926; Ira)	E-flat
"My One and Only" (1927; Ira)	B-flat
"'S Wonderful" (1927; Ira)	E-flat

GROUP 4

"Strike Up the Band" (1927; Ira)	B-flat
"Liza" (1929; Ira and Gus Kahn)	D-flat
"I Got Rhythm" (1930; Ira)	D-flat
"Who Cares?" (1931; Ira)	C

When played in their published order, the embellished refrains constitute a suite for pianists to include in public performances. *George Gershwin's Song-book* offers a compelling mix of examples of how Gershwin treated some of his best-known songs when the spirit moved him to sit down at the piano and play them. But, further, the composer declares his own song repertory fair game for decoration, offering other pianists exemplars of how they might proceed along similar lines with other songs, including their own.

A LEWISOHN STADIUM concert of the New York Philharmonic Orchestra on August 16, 1932, proved to be a landmark in the composer's career: the music was all by Gershwin, including a world premiere.

I. *Of Thee I Sing*, overture
William Daly, conductor

II. *Concerto in F*
Oscar Levant, piano; Daly, conductor

III. *An American in Paris*
Albert Coates, conductor[16]

IV. *Rhapsody in Blue*
Gershwin, piano; Daly, conductor

INTERMISSION

V. "Wintergreen for President"
Daly, conductor

VI. Second Rhapsody
Gershwin, piano; Coates, conductor

VII. *Rumba* (premiere)
Coates, conductor

VIII. Medley of tunes arranged by Daly
"Fascinating Rhythm," "The Man I Love,"
"Liza," "I Got Rhythm"
Gershwin, piano; Daly, conductor [17]

The next day, Gershwin confided to George Pallay: "This is the morning after a very big night before. . . . It was, I really believe, the most exciting night I have ever had." The attendance set a record. "17,845 people paid to get in and just 5,000 were at the closed gates trying to fight their way in—unsuccessfully." His only comment about the performances themselves was that *Rumba* had gone "very well."[18] A letter later that month to Isaac Goldberg recalled a Gershwin concert with something for everyone:

> It was interesting to hear comments from different sources . . . I was glad to see that almost every piece was 'liked best' by someone—some the Concerto, others the Rumba,—and the Second Rhapsody had quite a number of supporters. Many thought that the American in Paris had its best performance under Coates' direction. Some people enjoyed the popular part of the program more than the serious—and others resented the popular music.[19]

Soon to be renamed *Cuban Overture, Rumba* was the fruit of a vacation Gershwin had taken early in February, after the New York premiere of the Second Rhapsody. His traveling party—including Everett Jacobs, Adam Gimbel, and publisher Bennett Cerf, as well as Ira and Leonore Gershwin—indulged in "two hysterical weeks in Havana, where no sleep was had but the quantity and quality of the fun made up for that."[20] Financier Emil Mosbacher joined the others in Havana for a few days, and saw "George and Bennett chasing after the same girl, each trying to keep [her] from the other."[21] What caught George's composerly interest, though, were the local dance orchestras, "who play most intricate rhythms most naturally."[22]

The novelty and impact of that Cuban music lingered in his consciousness until July, when he drafted a solo piano version of *Rumba*. His orchestration of that piece was finished by August 9. Determined to enliven his thematic material with Cuban rhythms, he called for indigenous percussion instruments to be placed in front of the conductor's stand; he even provided sketches of sticks, bongo, gourd, and a pair of maracas in his "conductor's note."

A program note that Gershwin wrote for his new composition describes it as "a symphonic ouverture" combining "Cuban rhythms with my own thematic material" in a three-part structure. An introduction prefiguring bits of that material leads into a contrapuntal first section, "Moderato e molto ritmato" (relaxed and very rhythmic), with two themes. The composer explains in technical terms what comes next:

> A solo clarinet cadenza leads to a middle part, which is in a plaintive mood. It is a gradually developing canon in a polytonal manner. This part concludes with a climax based on an ostinato of the theme in the canon, after which a sudden change in tempo brings us back to the rumba dance rhythms.
>
> The finale is a development of the preceding material in a stretto-like manner. This leads us back once again to the main theme.
>
> The conclusion of the work is a coda featuring the Cuban instruments of percussion.[23]

Like three of Gershwin's one-movement orchestral compositions that predate it—the *Rhapsody in Blue*, *An American in Paris*, and the Second Rhapsody—the *Cuban Overture* is cast in ABA[1] form.

BY THE FALL of 1932, the hardship caused by the Great Depression was weighing heavily on the musical world. Under the leadership of Walter Damrosch, the Musicians' Emergency Aid had been formed in New York to raise funds for unemployed colleagues, and a group called the Musicians' Symphony Orchestra had staged five concerts during the 1931–32 season, with musicians paid from Emergency Aid funds. Twenty more concerts were given in 1932–33, the first on

November 1 on the stage of the Metropolitan Opera House.[24] The first half of the program that evening was Franck's Symphony in D Minor, led by the group's permanent conductor, Sandor Harmati. The second half was all-Gershwin, beginning with the *Concerto in F*, with Daly conducting and the composer as soloist. Daly then led *An American in Paris*, followed by the second-ever performance of the *Cuban Overture*, which the composer conducted. To close, Gershwin returned to the piano and Daly to the podium to lead the same songs played in the summer's Lewisohn Stadium concert. Later that month, Gershwin and Daly traveled to Pittsburgh for a concert that enabled the beleaguered Pittsburgh Symphony Society to open its season on a high note, drawing a standing-room-only audience of 4,000.[25]

The fall of 1932, however, saw the Gershwin brothers focused on a new musical comedy from Aarons and Freedley: *Pardon My English*, set in Dresden, Germany. Ira deemed the project "a headache from start to finish," and its performance history bears out that verdict: after more than six weeks on the road, the New York run lasted for only forty-three performances. The show's incurable problem lay in the role of the leading man, played by Jack Buchanan, a Scottish actor who had had a successful career in both the U.K. and the United States. The script called for him to play a split personality: Michael Bramleigh, an affluent scion of the British aristocracy; and, after suffering a brain-scrambling head injury in a plane crash, a coarse and thuggish kleptomaniac named Golo. Thereafter, each thump on the head induces a switch to the counteridentity, with no memory of the other one. Golo proved to be beyond Buchanan's range as a performer, and his role evolved into that of a jewel thief. Even so, after weeks of trying, Buchanan gave up and bought his way out of the production.[26]

To replace Buchanan, the producers hired George Givot, who lasted three weeks, and then Joseph Santley.[27] Changes in the Michael/Golo role, and in the casting of it, altered the show considerably. By the end, in a plot now revolving around crime and punishment, the leading male character was a comedian: Commissioner Bauer, head of the Dresden police, played by Jack Pearl. Bauer locks people up and releases them on a whim, walks the streets of Dresden with a dachshund for an attack dog, and allows a continuous craps game to flourish in police headquarters.

The show's female lead, Gita, played by Lyda Roberti, is a blond bombshell with a thick Polish accent, an entertainer by trade and a thief on the side. Devoted to Golo and matching him in toughness, she courts the unmarried Commissioner Bauer under Golo's orders. Both of her solo songs radiate uninhibited exuberance. In the first, a rhythmically aggressive number called "The Lorelei," she likens herself to a seductress in German mythology who casts a spell over sailors and lures them to their doom. The lyrics were considered raw enough to keep the song off the radio; she admits to being "lecherous" (rhymes with "treacherous"), while confiding, "I want to bite my initials on a sailor's neck."[28] Gita sings her second solo number, "My Cousin in Milwaukee," to a contingent of the Dresden police, explaining how and where she got her torrid approach to singing and dancing.

Bauer's beautiful daughter Ilse is the show's other female lead, and another role with a high turnover: Ona Munson played her in Philadelphia, beginning December 2; Roberta Robinson, an ex-girlfriend of Gershwin, in Brooklyn, beginning December 26; and, finally, Josephine Huston on Broadway, beginning January 20. Ilse is the woman with whom Michael Bramleigh falls in love, after he's knocked unconscious by an automobile as Golo. "Isn't it a pity," Ilse and Michael marvel, that "we never met before?" By the third stanza of this ballad of true love sung by a mature man and woman, they have agreed to share henceforth a life worthy of the couple they surely were destined to be.

But when a birdhouse falls on his head, Michael wakes up as Golo and learns that Ilse is soon to be married. Golo and Gita plot to kidnap the bride before the wedding, and he arranges to have a boat ready to spirit Ilse away to an inn up the Elbe River from Dresden. When he shows up to abduct her, she greets him as Michael and, under the impression that they are eloping, joins him in the boat. At the inn they occupy the bridal suite and, after a long colloquy set to music, "Tonight," agree to consummate what for Ilse is a marriage arranged for the next day and for Golo a tactically contrived seduction. The music underlying this drama unfolds in a many-faceted waltz worthy of an opera, showing Gershwin's skill as an inventor of music to support heartfelt emotions. Two different yet complementary melodies—one each for Golo and Ilse—suggest separate identities approaching synchrony, filling almost six minutes with continuous music, all but a small part of it in 3/4 time.

Pardon My English opened in Philadelphia on December 2: the eve of a much-anticipated college football game to be played there. One critic described the festive anticipation and dashed the audience's hopes:

> Since the big Army-Navy show today had attracted visitors from all parts of the country to our city, the theatre was filled to overflowing. The spectators, in smart attire, and high spirits, were eager for entertainment. They watched and waited and displayed resolute patience. When, at odd and infrequent intervals, it seemed as if Jack Buchanan and his associates might possibly snap the slumbering mediocrity into some sort of life, they acknowledged their gratitude by rapturous applause.[29]

By the time the show reached New York, Jack Pearl and Lyda Roberti had emerged as its main stars, Jack Buchanan and Ona Munson were gone from the cast, and the out-of-town difficulties had become part of the show's story. Robert Benchley of the *New Yorker* commiserated with the (unnamed) authors of the libretto, confessing that he had once contributed to a script that was even

worse. "As is usually the case when a show has taken a lot of doctor-
ing on the road," he wrote, the doctors themselves "come down with
the disease and the whole thing turns into a shambles." Benchley
does his best to imagine an audience that might actually enjoy *Pardon My English*. "If you had never heard anything from the Gershwins before, you might not know that this score is definitely not one
of their major works. Very, very young people, who do not remember Miss Roberti . . . would be sufficiently charmed by her presence
to think that everything was going all right. . . . So perhaps we can
recommend 'Pardon My English' after all—to all those who are too
young to remember."[30]

To Gilbert Gabriel of the *New York American*, after all the show's
troubles, "It would be nice deportment on a critic's part, to kiss it on
both cheeks, overlook its faults . . . and bid it welcome." But, "well,
no sir, I can't. . . . The sense of such sheer wastage of [the Gershwins'] musical and lyrical wit makes me nothing except mad."[31] And
John Mason Brown of the *Evening Post* ended his review with a nod
to Jack Buchanan, "a wise man" who, after sampling the wasteful
incoherence of *Pardon My English*, had had the good sense to put as
much distance as possible between it and himself. [32]

THE LAST MUSICAL COMEDY (1933)

Reviewing the premiere of *Pardon My English* in Philadelphia, critic Robert Reiss watched "lantern-jawed and sweet-eyed George Gershwin" conduct the orchestra for the first act, "and then spend the second walking nervously up and down the lobby with his hands behind his back and his chin in a figurative third hand."[1] Reiss's glimpse of an anxious composer is the only known evidence of Gershwin's feelings about a show that failed. Its last performance took place on February 25, 1933. While the failure cannot have pleased the Gershwin brothers, the regrets that Ira expressed later show that they had never had much hope for that one in the first place. Nor, given the success of *Of Thee I Sing*, did they have reason to worry about finances. By the end of its first year, that show's gross intake stood at $1.4 million, and by spring 1933 the same creative team was at work on a Wintergreen sequel.

Let 'Em Eat Cake begins with an overture previewing several of the show's melodies, while also striking a martial note that sets the stage for the events that lie ahead—from comic to grim. The curtain rises on a night scene familiar to anyone who had seen *Of Thee I Sing*: a street in an American city during election season. Supporters of two presidential candidates, carrying placards, march and sing in separate groups. One group touts President John P. Wintergreen ("Keep Love in the White House"), who is running for a second term, and the other supports his opponent, John P. Tweedledee ("More Promises Than Wintergreen"). "Wintergreen for President," sung to the original music for *Of Thee I Sing* but with lyrics updated for the incumbent, quotes familiar melodies—"The Stars and Stripes Forever," "The Sidewalks of New York," "Hot Time in the Old Town Tonight," and "Of Thee I Sing"—as the Tweedledee forces borrow from "Dixie," "The Battle Hymn of the Republic," and "Over There." Moving quickly, this number—a fresh take with densely packed lyrics, a minor-mode cast with a barrage of tune references in major, and a busy orchestral accompaniment—nears the brink of overload. But when the opposing groups converge onstage, the result is more clarifying than anarchic. For Gershwin has composed another double song—a Tweedledee melody singable against the Wintergreen melody. A student of Russian-born composer and music theorist Joseph Schillinger at the time, he had prepared himself for *Let 'Em Eat Cake* by studying counterpoint, which seemed to him "in keeping with the satire of the piece" and an essential tool for executing "what I am trying to do."[2]

The next musical number follows an extended three-part form (ABA) to make its own satirical point. The scene is set in New York's Union Square, where John and Mary Wintergreen—he has lost the election to Tweedledee—have opened a store featuring "Maryblue" shirts to take advantage of the sewing skills of the ex–first lady. Passersby stroll through the square singing a graceful ditty about its merits as a forum where political and social matters are debated in open public discourse. Their serene melody is a rare case in which Gershwin has borrowed from a classical source: the first movement of Schubert's String Quintet in C Major.[3] But the strollers' amiable music is disrupted by a fiery song-within-a-song: "Down with Everyone Who's Up." A radical activist named Kruger leads a fiery attack on "conditions as they are." By his lights, the notion that one plus one makes two is debatable, majorities deserve no deference, and minorities are no less corrupt. As Kruger's litany of society's failures continues, compatriots echo his hit list in a fierce call-and-response exchange that ends in a skirmish among the radicals. This number embodies the social struggle that Kaufman and Ryskind's plot satirizes: the A section, with its relaxed dotted rhythms, is apt strolling music for New Yorkers at peace with their lives, while the frenetic B section deems their satisfaction simply a façade disguising the corruption and exploitation that seethe beneath the surface.

John P. Wintergreen decides that the time to stage a revolution is at hand, and he makes Maryblue shirts his rallying point. "Italy—black shirts! Germany—brown shirts! America—blue shirts!" he declaims.[4] Blue shirts selling for a dollar become a national fad. Alexander Throttlebottom, now a floorwalker in the Maryblue flagship store, joins with coworkers to sing about the future of America: "Comes the revolution, we'll be eating cake!"[5] But even as the Wintergreens are hailed as visionaries, the ex-president's thoughts dwell on his wife. "Mine," the show's only love song, doubles down on Gershwin's attachment to counterpoint. Its main melody relies on sustained notes, to the point that the first phrase requires only four syllables ("Mine, love is mine"), as does the third ("Mine, you are mine"). Because the countermelodic musical voice behind this melody fits the personas of John and Mary equally well, either can sing it alone, both can sing it together, or they can deliver it in alternation. The devoted connection affirmed by the music is built to last—an affirmative sequel of sorts to *Of Thee I Sing*'s "Who Cares?"

Well aware that a revolution needs an army, Wintergreen and Throttlebottom plan a military coup with the Union League, an ultraconservative men's club with military roots, as the core of their force. On arrival at the club's headquarters, however, the conspirators encounter a room of rich, doddering oldsters who claim Rip Van Winkle as their idol and spend their days napping, eating lunch, and reading the *New York Tribune*, which had ceased to exist as an independent newspaper in 1924. The members describe their time-honored way of life in unison singing that evokes a remote past—complete with an extended Handelian melisma. Should the outside world trouble their settled existence, they have a strategy for political engagement ("Don't change horses in the river") and another for combat ("Watch your kidneys, watch your liver!").

When Wintergreen and Throttlebottom spread a rumor among club members that the British are ready to march again on Bunker Hill, the Union Leaguers are jarred from their torpor and begin toning their aging bodies for battle. Soon thereafter, Wintergreen and his "Blue Shirts" begin a march toward Washington, where they expect to meet Gen. Adam Snookfield and the U.S. Army, who have joined forces to depose President Tweedledee. The music they sing on the way is a military march with a brisk gait and a genial tone that affirm two facts laid out in the verse: musical comedy armies march a lot, and when they do, they sing. By marching "on and on and on," down hills (D to G to D) and then up hills (D to G to D), this soldierly corps covers territory "hither and thither and yon."

When Wintergreen and his troops arrive at the White House on the Fourth of July, General Snookfield is nowhere to be seen, having headed off to a party with his girlfriend, Trixie. So Wintergreen cuts his own deal with the troops: "Make me your Dictator, and the war debts are yours!" His forces take President Tweedledee into custody, Independence Day bombs burst in the air, and Wintergreen proclaims a "dictatorship of the proletariat." As Act I ends, he leads the crowd in singing "Let 'Em Eat Cake!," an anthem claiming the legacy of the French Revolution as his own.

Act II begins with the chorus singing "Blue, Blue, Blue," lauding the "sainted" color with which "heaven is painted" as another Wintergreen innovation. Dictator Wintergreen—now dressed in a gaudy uniform, demanding Nazi-style salutes (until they put too much strain on his arm), and striking Napoleonic poses in front of mirrors—has reassembled, in the renamed and redecorated Blue House, cronies from his presidential team and shirt business. A new ritual calls for the Blue House workforce to start their day with a sung tribute to the excellence of "our dictator Wintergreen," set by Gershwin in solemn counterpoint.[6] The boss has also come up with "Who's the Greatest?," a sprightly quiz in 6/8 time for which the staff has all the right answers: chiefly "Wintergreen."

Nine delegates to the League of Nations arrive for a conference on international finance. When questioned about paying their war debts, the League members respond with a sung stew of feigned incomprehension: "No comprenez, no capish, no versteh!" Wintergreen decides to settle the debt on a baseball diamond, pitting the nine Supreme Court justices against the nine debtor nations, with the spoils going to the winners, double or nothing. Improbably, the visitors win on a disputable call by the umpire, with results so financially ruinous to the losing American side that a courtroom trial is convened.[7] The judge in the case is Wintergreen, the prosecutor the renegade Kruger, the plaintiff the army, and the defendant the umpire, Alexander Throttlebottom, who stands accused of taking a bribe from the League of Nations. But once a legal and punitive emphasis shows up in the form of capital punishment, a story brimming with cleverly contrived absurdities curdles in the direction of a sour parable of justice gone amok.

The show's last scene opens on a stage dominated by a guillotine, with beheadings on the day's docket. The crowd joins in a threnody, "Hanging Throttlebottom in the Morning," a solemn blues-tinged processional reckoning the cost of what radical politics has wrought.[8] In the end, however, the story reclaims its comic-opera roots, and the guillotine, looming ominously on the stage, goes unused. As in *Of Thee I Sing*, Mary Wintergreen emerges as the plot's deus ex machina; this time, she represents the fashion consciousness of the women of America, who have had their fill of blue. Behind Mary's invitation to all women to appreciate beauty and style wherever they appear, and in whatever color, sounds the reassuring melody of "Blue, Blue, Blue," undercutting the deadly symbolism of the guillotine that hovers over the scene.[9] The political crisis is resolved and the republic restored, now under the leadership of President Throttlebottom. To celebrate the reconciliation, the entire cast ends the show by singing the refrain of "Of Thee I Sing."

After a run in Boston that began on October 2, *Let 'Em Eat Cake* opened at Broadway's Imperial Theatre on October 21. Some two weeks later Gershwin wrote George Pallay that "the show is going along very well, and I think it has a good chance of running for some time."[10] But the sequel to *Of Thee I Sing* ran only until January 6, 1934—a total of ninety performances—and it closed without touring at all. More than one New York critic, recalling the tide of laughter that had carried *Of Thee I Sing* through a joyous evening in the theater, had anticipated more of the same but failed to find it. Gilbert W. Gabriel of the *New York American* did his best to explain why the sequel's humor flunked the test:

> Funny? Yes, often immensely, occasionally magnificently funny, especially in the greater gusto of the first act. But a brand of funniness which, for all its freedom from the old musical show formula, is apt to make you chaw your fingernails, apologize for living and wonder whether you yourself don't belong up there on the stage below the guillotine's wit-edged blade.[11]

A tour de force of musical craft and dexterity of wit, the satirical *Let 'Em Eat Cake* failed on Broadway: doomed at the end, it seems, by the curdling of its humor, but perhaps too for lack of a hero more commanding than America's President Alexander Throttlebottom.

As LET 'EM EAT CAKE approached its first public performance, George Gershwin turned thirty-five and was reflecting on the course of his career. Now, having made a significant mark in both the classical and the popular spheres, and one of the few American composers whose music aroused interest both within and outside the United States, Gershwin set his sights on a project—the opera with DuBose Heyward—in an arena that he now was sure he was ready to enter.

PART III

COMPOSER IN CHARGE

A TURN IN THE ROAD
(1933–34)

AMONG THE REWARDS OF STUDYING George Gershwin's life in music is the opportunity to behold and trace the course of an artist who, endowed with talent, confidence, and a hunger for learning, never stopped broadening and deepening his command of these gifts. And as we have seen, that artistic sensibility reached beyond the realm of music. On November 10, 1933, Gershwin's growing art collection—paintings, drawings, and sculpture, plus three oil canvases and a watercolor of his own making—went on public display in Chicago's Arts Club gallery, where it remained for two weeks. A brief notice in the *Chicago Tribune* caught the flavor of a keenly anticipated opening: "Never have the galleries been such a crush! Somebody thought it looked like the subway (the one we haven't got) at the rush hour. . . . I glimpsed two amazing Modeglianis [*sic*], but it is a picture show one will go many times to see."[1] The *Chicago Daily News* found that Gershwin "collects pictures as an intelligent painter might—choice little things from this studio or that, with an individuality—a little touch of the unusual that sparkles."[2]

Whatever his achievements in visual art, as a maker of music,

Gershwin was a resourceful manager of his opportunities. From early days he showed a growing awareness of where his talents could contribute to the landscape open to him. On October 3, 1933, the day after *Let 'Em Eat Cake* began its first tryout run, the *Boston Post* carried an interview that, in retrospect, indicates he had already relegated that project to the past.[3] Though he made no such announcement, the view of musical comedy he reveals helps to explain why *Let 'Em Eat Cake* proved to be the brothers' last work in that genre.

Gershwin's first point was that the traditional musical comedy, to which he and Ira had devoted their skills, relied more upon "pretty girls, dancing, and songs" than on the interactions taking place among the characters. In such "Cinderella musicals" the substance of the story mattered little, as long as the song-and-dance moments satisfied the audience. But 1931's *Of Thee I Sing* had been different: enacting an ingenious and appealing story by Kaufman and Ryskind, its music had furthered the plot rather than pausing for interludes of song and dance. With a libretto of the Kaufman-Ryskind stripe, as in its sequel—which offered only one love song and almost no dancing at all—the composer was obliged to "follow the book," applying his skills and artistry to animate the story. Indeed, *Of Thee I Sing*'s artistic and commercial success signaled to him nothing less than "the composer's legitimacy." Its triumph led Gershwin to entertain the notion that a new American audience for a theatrical brand of political satire with sophisticated music was coming into existence.

A second matter addressed in Gershwin's interview has to do with casting. He argued that the quality of performing talent available to the Broadway musical theater was in decline, and decried a shortage of compelling leading men and women, citing Marilyn Miller as the last of the breed. More strangely, he then revisited even more remote days, when composers had had the likes of Julia Sanderson—"the best of them," who had flourished in the 1910s and early 1920s—to bring larger-than-life talents to roles that librettists, lyricists, and composers were then fashioning for the stage. To cast a show in 1933, Gershwin had learned, had become a "difficult" task. By the time *Let 'Em Eat Cake* was ready to open on the road, the composer's plans for the future had already shifted to an arena beyond musical comedy and its limitations.

In fact, before the end of October the artistic venture he'd been planning for years took an essential step toward fulfillment when the parties involved signed a contract for an opera—a work based on the 1925 novel and the 1927 play *Porgy*—for which he would compose the music, author and playwright DuBose Heyward would supply the libretto, and both Heyward and Ira Gershwin would write song lyrics for a production by New York's Theatre Guild.[4] With an opera looming in the near future, the concerns expressed in Gershwin's interview make perfect sense; as a composer now practiced in "following the book" through Kaufman's satires, he must have relished the prospect of engaging with the endeavor he and Heyward had been contemplating for so long. As for the comments about casting in his Boston interview, they acknowledge that the project he was about to undertake would rely upon African American performers whose talents, if unschooled in opera, would bring a freshness of attitude and vitality to the enterprise. Having embraced his "legitimacy" as a composer, he was prepared to "follow the book" in a way that would bring his skills and his artistry into full play.

SEVERAL ASPECTS of DuBose Heyward's background and career made it likely that his tale about an African American community in Charleston, South Carolina, would be culturally and artistically credible. He was a native of Charleston who lived there for most of his first forty years. He grew up in a white household where the customs and lore of the local "Gullah Negroes" were a living presence, and from the time he began to fancy himself a writer, he concentrated on African American life in the South. Approaching that subject through close observation, respect for his characters, and an appreciation of black culture, he found a milieu suited to his talents and the literary environment of his day.[5]

The phrase "too poor to paint and too proud to whitewash" was applied to the Heyward family of Charleston in the late 1800s. DuBose's father, who died when his son was two years old, counted a signer of the Declaration of Independence as an ancestor, and his mother—whose maiden name was DuBose—descended from once-prosperous plantation owners. Before age sixteen, the family's future man of letters dropped out of school to help supplement the meager family income, and some of his jobs brought him into contact with South Carolina's black population. Hired by an insurance company as a teenager, he canvased black neighborhoods to collect "burial money"; during the summers of 1900–1903, he supervised black field hands on the nearby plantation of a relative; and beginning in 1905, working as a cotton checker for a steamship line, he came to know something of stevedore life. Each of these jobs gave the young man a vantage point for observing a people who remained separate from, and imperfectly known by, the white population of Charleston. The racial imbalance of power never claimed much of his attention; what fascinated him was the mystery of cultural difference.[6]

In 1920, Heyward and several writing cohorts founded the Poetry Society of South Carolina, and during the next few years no one in Charleston took their goal of stimulating "an interest in the reading, writing, and critical appreciation of poetry in the community" more seriously than Heyward. As corresponding secretary, he supervised the group's series of guest lecturers, and managed trips to the MacDowell Colony in New Hampshire during the summers of 1921 and 1922. Contacts made through the Poetry Society enabled him to publish poems in such journals as *Poetry*, the

Atlantic, and *Contemporary Verse,* and in April 1924 he quit his job in the insurance business and began a career as a professional writer.[7]

Heyward may have been encouraged in his leap into the unknown by the economic prospects of his wife, playwright Dorothy Hartzell Kuhns, whom he met at the MacDowell Colony and married in 1923, and whose play *Nancy Ann* enjoyed a short run on Broadway in 1924.[8] But more important, by the spring of 1924, Heyward, with no illusions about a poet's career, had settled on a subject for a novel—after years of pondering what he deemed the "secret law" that seemed to animate the lives of the "alien people" of Charleston. He later admitted to a feeling close to envy, having come to see "the primitive Negro as the inheritor of a source of delight that I would have given much to possess. . . . What was the quality in a spiritual sung in the secrecy of some back room that brought the chance listener up short against the outer wall with a contraction of the solar plexus, and lachrymal glands that he was powerless to control?"[9]

The moment that sparked the novel arrived when Heyward spotted an item in a Charleston newspaper: "Samuel Smalls, who is a cripple and is familiar to King Street with his goat and cart, was held for the June term of court of sessions on an aggravated assault charge. It is alleged that on Saturday night he attempted to shoot Maggie Barnes at number four Romney Street. His shots went wide of the mark." On further inquiry, Heyward learned that Smalls had tried to escape in his wagon but had been captured by the police patrol.[10] The incident gave Heyward a fresh window on the life flourishing around him, where an existence like that of Smalls "could never lift above the dead level of the commonplace." Yet this news notice also carried the stuff of personal tragedy that Heyward had previously reserved for white people. On such an imagined character, "I could impose my own white man's conception of a summer of aspiration, devotion, and heartbreak across the color wall."[11] Drafted that summer and published in September 1925, *Porgy* became a best-seller. As a serious portrait of African American life, which most white authors had treated lightly in the past, it was also considered groundbreaking.

Even before *Porgy* was published, Dorothy Heyward was drafting the script for a play based on the novel. Heyward's response to his wife's idea was at first skepticism, but once he saw her script, he realized that it offered a closer approximation of the artistic ideal he had imagined. The challenge was to recruit a black cast, and he was determined to postpone production indefinitely rather than resort to white actors in disguise.

By early 1926, Heyward's career change could be considered a success. Then, in October, after reading Heyward's slim novel at one sitting, George Gershwin wrote from New York City to propose a collaboration on an operatic treatment.[12] The prospect delighted Heyward, and the two men met that fall in Atlantic City to discuss it.[13] Heyward's first impression of his future collaborator was "singularly vivid":

> A young man of enormous physical and emotional vitality, who possessed the faculty of seeing himself quite impersonally and realistically, and who knew exactly what he wanted and where he was going. This characteristic put him beyond both modesty and conceit. About himself he would merely mention certain facts, aspirations, failings. They were usually right. We discussed *Porgy*. He said that it would not matter about the dramatic production, as it would be a number of years before he would be prepared technically to compose an opera. . . . It was extraordinary, I thought, that, in view of a success that might well have dazzled any man, he could appraise his talent with such complete detachment.[14]

The Heywards' play *Porgy*, with its all-black cast, was produced by the Theatre Guild in October 1927 and enjoyed a long run. But although Heyward and Gershwin stayed in touch over the next several years, no further progress was made on their project until the playwright let Gershwin know on May 10, 1932, that rights had been secured for the play script to be turned into an opera libretto. Ten days later, Gershwin sent Heyward a brief letter that left no doubt about his commitment:

> I was very glad to have your letter telling me that the operatic rights of "Porgy" are free and clear. Of course there is no possibility of the operatic version's being written before January 1933. I shall be around here most of the summer and will read the book several times to see what ideas I can evolve as to how it should be done. Any notions I get I shall forward to you. I think it would be wise for us to meet—either here or where you are—several times, before any real start is made.

Heyward visited New York early that fall, and by October he and Gershwin were addressing each other as "DuBose" and "George." A new element that entered momentarily into their planning was singer Al Jolson's approach to Heyward, asking about the possibility of a musical show based on *Porgy*, with him in the title role.[15] On September 3, Heyward asked Gershwin if he thought it would be possible to use Jolson, "and arrange some sort of agreement with him, or is that too preposterous?"[16] Gershwin's reply was sent within the week:

> I think it is very interesting that Al Jolson would like to play the part of Porgy, but I really don't know how he would be in it. Of course he is a very big star, who certainly knows how to put over a song, and it might mean more to you financially if he should do it—provided that the rest of the production were well done. The sort of thing that I should have in mind for PORGY is a much more serious thing than Jolson could ever do. Of course I would not attempt to write music to your play until I had all the themes and musical devices worked out for such an undertaking. It would be more a labor of love than anything else. If you can

see your way to making some ready money from Jolson's version I don't
know that it would hurt a later version done by an all-colored cast.[17]

Heyward replied on October 17 that, although out of financial
necessity he had not flatly rejected Jolson's approach,

> What I would like to be able to afford would be to wait indefinitely
> for your operatic version, and to work with you myself without the
> least thought of the commercial angle. It is not my idea to work in any
> way upon a possible Jolson musical, but merely to sell the story. . . .
> Please let me tell you that I think your attitude in this matter is sim-
> ply splendid. It makes me all the more eager to work with you some
> day, some time, before we wake up and find ourselves in our dotage.[18]

Jolson soon gave up on his *Porgy* idea, and it took another year for a
contract to be signed. But on October 26, 1933, DuBose Heyward,
George Gershwin, Ira Gershwin, and Warren B. Munsell of the New
York Theatre Guild signed a contract for an opera based on DuBose
and Dorothy Heyward's play *Porgy*. And less than three weeks later
Heyward sent Gershwin two copies of the opera's first scene.

Heyward had often insisted that Gershwin would benefit from
firsthand experience of the region where *Porgy* took place, and on
December 2, 1933, the composer acted on that advice. He boarded a
train for Charleston with his friend Emil Mosbacher, whose family
spent the winter months on an ocean-front estate in Palm Beach,
Florida. Apparently alerted by Heyward, the *Charleston News and
Courier* of December 4 reported Gershwin's presence in town:

> Yesterday afternoon he and Mr. Heyward went to a negro church
> and listened to the singing. "I'm sure even Mr. Heyward was sur-
> prised at the primitiveness of this particular service and it gave me
> a lot to think about," Mr. Gershwin said. Mr. Heyward is going
> to conduct the composer around the city. They plan to arrange to

hear as much negro music as possible and Mr. Gershwin is anxious to listen in on some of the fish and vegetable hucksters.[19]

Gershwin and his friend accompanied Heyward "from home to home where the shutters would go up and the houses looked as if they were on stilts," in Mosbacher's account. "George would get the people in the homes to dance so hard that I thought the houses would fall down. I went to church with George, and when they passed the hat, I watched what DuBose put in. He put in a half-dollar, so George and I did the same."[20]

On December 6, the two northerners completed their journey south to Florida. Since the opera would leave him no time for another musical comedy, Gershwin had arranged a concert tour, scheduled to start in Boston on January 14, 1934, with the idea of replacing income likely to be lost. Mosbacher's rented estate included a separate house where the composer could work uninterrupted on a new piece for the tour: Variations on "I Got Rhythm," for piano and orchestra; by the time Gershwin left Florida, on January 2, it was almost completed. He had also had time to share some thoughts on *Porgy*'s progress with the Palm Beach newspaper. Having by then given a careful reading to the first scene, he was wrestling with the matter of recitative: "I have not made up my mind whether to combine speech with singing or what to do," he said. "The problem will work out by itself when I begin work on it in earnest. I like to digest ideas a long time." And then he added: "I am really only happy when I am composing or just finishing something."[21]

MUCH OF THE STORY of Gershwin's tour, managed by Harry Askins in New York (it was Askins who had recommended the nineteen-year-old rehearsal pianist for *Miss 1917* to Max Dreyfus), is embodied in the program distributed at the concerts, and in the demanding itinerary—twenty-eight concerts in twenty-eight days.

Tour Celebrating the Tenth Anniversary of
"Rhapsody in Blue"

PRESENTING

GEORGE GERSHWIN
Composer-Pianist

JAMES MELTON, Tenor
and the
REISMAN SYMPHONIC ORCHESTRA

CHARLES PREVIN, *Conductor*

IN A PROGRAM OF GERSHWIN SUCCESSES
(Program subject to change)

1. Concerto in F   Gershwin

Mr. Gershwin

2. (a) Swanee   Gershwin

Do It Again; Sam and Delilah

Lady Be Good

(b) Mine

Strike Up the Band

Orchestra

3. (a) Hills of Home   Oscar Fox

(b) Home on the Range   [Arr. by] David Guion

(c) Carry Me Back to the Lone Prairie   Carson Robison

[encore, The Last Roundup]

Mr. Melton [accompanied by the orchestra]

4. Rhapsody in Blue   Gershwin

Mr. Gershwin

INTERMISSION

5. An American in Paris   Gershwin

Orchestra

6. (a) Sometimes I Feel Like a Motherless Child   Arr. by Frank Black
   (b) G'wine to Hebb'n   [Arr. by] Jacques Wolfe
   (c) Shortnin' Bread   [Arr. by] Jacques Wolfe

James Melton

7. "I Got Rhythm" Variations (New)   Gershwin

Mr. Gershwin

8. "Wintergreen for President" from "Of Thee I Sing"   Gershwin

Orchestra

9. Medley (a) Fascinating Rhythm   Gershwin
            (b) Man I Love
            (c) Liza
            (d) I Got Rhythm

Mr. Gershwin

Steinway Pianos Used

Sun. Jan. 14	Symphony Hall	Boston, Mass.
Mon. Jan. 15	City Hall Auditorium	Portland, Me.
Tues. Jan. 16	Memorial Auditorium	Worcester, Mass.
Wed. Jan. 17	City Auditorium	Springfield, Mass.
Thurs. Jan. 18	Lincoln Auditorium, Central High School	Syracuse, N.Y.

Fri. Jan. 19	Massey Hall	Toronto, Ontario
Sat. Jan. 20	Music Hall, Public Auditorium	Cleveland, Ohio
Sun. Jan. 21	Orchestra Hall	Detroit, Mich.
Mon. Jan. 22	Shrine Theater	Fort Wayne, Ind.
Tues. Jan. 23	Auditorium	Milwaukee, Wis.
Wed. Jan. 24	West High School	Madison, Wis.
Thurs. Jan. 25	Auditorium	St. Paul, Minn.
Fri. Jan. 26	The Coliseum	Sioux Falls, S.D.
Sat. Jan. 27	Technical High School	Omaha, Neb.
Sun. Jan. 28	Convention Hall	Kansas City, Mo.
Mon. Jan. 29	Shrine Auditorium	Des Moines, Iowa
Tues. Jan. 30	Masonic Auditorium	Davenport, Iowa
Wed. Jan. 31	The Odeon	St. Louis, Mo.
Thurs. Feb. 1	English Opera House	Indianapolis, Ind.
Fri. Feb. 2	Memorial Auditorium	Louisville, Ky.
Sat. Feb. 3	Taft Auditorium	Cincinnati, Ohio
Sun. Feb. 4	Auditorium Theater	Chicago, Ill.
Mon. Feb. 5	Memorial Hall	Dayton, Ohio
Tues. Feb. 6	Syria Mosque	Pittsburgh, Pa.
Wed. Feb. 7	Academy of Music	Philadelphia, Pa.
Thurs. Feb. 8	Constitution Hall	Washington, D.C.
Fri. Feb. 9	Mosque Auditorium	Richmond, Va.
Sat. Feb. 10	Academy of Music	Brooklyn, N.Y.

As the tour's avowed purpose was to mark the tenth anniversary of the *Rhapsody in Blue*, Gershwin made it his program's centerpiece. The orchestra's founder, Leo Reisman, had planned to be on the podium, but when an auto accident left him hospitalized with a fractured hip, he was replaced by Broadway maestro Charles Previn, who had conducted earlier Gershwin musicals, most recently *Of Thee I Sing*. The musicians—five from Boston and thirty from New York, including concertmaster John Corigliano—were joined by traveling manager Herbert Farrar and Paul Mueller, Gershwin's valet. Mueller was on hand to supervise the handling of the musical instruments that players didn't (or couldn't) carry with them, to give Gershwin a daily massage, and to "keep people away, especially women, who tended to overwhelm both George and [tenor James] Melton."[22]

The most meaningful deviations from the printed ordering seem to have taken place at the end of the program. Apparently it dawned on Gershwin early on that there was no good reason to keep the concert's two star performers entirely apart onstage. In Worcester, Massachusetts, critic Dorothy Boyd Mattison described a highlight:

> Probably the most delightful moment of the program came at the very end when Mr. Melton and Mr. Gershwin, tossing aside the final scheduled number, "Wintergreen for President," and silencing the orchestra, got together at the piano. Mr. Gershwin played and Mr. Melton sang "Of Thee I Sing" and a number from Mr. Gershwin's "Oh, Kay!" The informal, parlor-like atmosphere lent zest to the evening, and brought it to a beautiful climax.[23]

As the tour progressed, Gershwin and Melton chose different encores as the spirit moved them. "The audience would have kept both Gershwin and Melton all night after their last number together," wrote a critic in Milwaukee. "You do not often hear such perfect rapport between composer and interpreter in consonance."[24] An honest effort to wrap words around the idea of Gershwin as a jazz composer appeared in a Chicago newspaper the day after a Sunday afternoon concert on February 4. "He catches one's ear, as every good composer of jazz must do, but he also leaves one a little more to guess about [than] what is strictly a jazzist's gift. Indeed, the most musical element in his style seems to me the reticence which jazz never possesses, but which good music, even the most expressive, always does."[25] Three days later, Philadelphia critic Odell Hauser found Gershwin a less-than-expert composer only in his command of musical form. "Time and time again," he displayed a "restless tendency . . . a willingness to cut off abruptly from one figuration and plunge into another" that could lead to an impression of disorder. "However, give him time."[26]

The concert variations Gershwin composed on "I Got Rhythm" bear a musical pedigree far removed from that of swing bands and the jazz tradition. Two differences stand out especially. One is that the Variations' life-blood is found not in the song's harmony or form, but in its melody, which is heard in full, or almost so, in every section of the piece, as well as in recurrent motivic statements. And just as tempo variety and nuance had loomed large in the *Rhapsody in Blue*, this work changes pace from one variation to the next, and also within variations. Gershwin's notation controls every musical moment, including three brief passages in Variation 5 that he composed in "swing" rhythm.

By making a song's melody the basis for an entire theme-and-variations piece for piano and orchestra, Gershwin linked the songwriting and composing sides of his musical persona in an imaginative way—as indeed he was acccustomed to do whenever he performed on-the-spot variations on any of his songs.

However, despite his artistic successes, when the tour ended and the costs and expenses were tallied, the star of the show found himself several thousand dollars out of pocket. Gershwin summed it up in a letter to Heyward:

Well here I am, back again after an arduous but exciting trip of 12,000 miles which took 28 days. The tour was a fine artistic success for me and would have been splendid financially if my foolish Manager hadn't booked me into seven towns that were too small to support such an expensive organization as I carried. Nevertheless, it was a very worthwhile thing for me to have done and I have many pleasant memories of Cities I had not visited before.[27]

In another letter written the same day, this one answering his friend George Pallay's plea for a personal loan, he assessed the state of his finances.

On account of losses of the LET 'EM EAT CAKE company and losses of my tour which was most successful from every angle except the financial one . . . my funds are fairly low at the present time. I don't like to go below a certain bank balance so if $500 will help now I will be glad to send it to you and if you need the other $500 a little later I will let you have that also. I am glad to hear you are going into business and hope it will be the start of a big fortune.[28]

During the fall of 1934—long after *Let 'Em Eat Cake* had run its course and Gershwin was well into his work on the opera—Gilbert Seldes published an article about where this gifted songwriter's career seemed to be headed. "Swanee," now more than a dozen years old, "was just Gershwin writing a Mammy song for Al Jolson," he recalled, "but it was one of the best and it is the sort of thing Gershwin wouldn't be found dead with today. . . . Popular music used to be written to be sung; then to be danced to; and now it is written to be played. . . . No one has ever sung, no one has ever tried, no one was ever meant to try, to sing Wintergreen for President, but who can forget it?" Gershwin now "composes to be heard," he concluded, "not to be sung. He is lucky because we are becoming a nation of listeners, thanks to the radio. But he is losing ground as a pure troubadour. He has stopped singing himself." Still, because his prodigious talent allowed him to produce first-rate results, "he can afford to be spendthrift" with his uncommon abilities.[29]

But the critic's report of the demise of his subject's singing days was premature. For by the time this message appeared in print,

DuBose Heyward's libretto had been completed for almost a year; and George Gershwin had spent more than half of that year contemplating and composing a folk opera whose characters, a cast of African Americans accompanied by a symphony orchestra, would sing the words for him.

MUSIC BY GERSHWIN AND PORGY AND BESS, ACT I (1935–36)

ON FEBRUARY 19, 1934, less than ten days after Gershwin returned to New York from his concert tour, he stepped into a National Broadcasting Company (NBC) radio studio to preside over the first of a series of programs called *Music by Gershwin*, to be aired from 7:30 to 7:45 p.m. on Mondays and Fridays. Experienced showman that he was, Gershwin brought firm priorities to his role as a radio host and performer: "informality and balance." The first was "something that only public reaction can convince us we are getting," he knew, but musical balance was a practical necessity. "When I set out to build a program," he explained in an interview, "Finus Farr, a writer from the William Esty agency, and Edward Byron, the agency production man, drop up to my apartment. I run over a few of the tunes on the piano. Then we'll pick out one of my songs for discussion. Farr very quietly pulls a notebook out of his pocket and starts to [ask] questions about the 'birth' of the song." Taking "Liza" as an example, Gershwin offers the exchange that might follow:

> FARR: What show was "Liza" in?
> GG: It was in Flo Ziegfeld's production of "Show Girl."

FARR: Did it take you very long to write it?

GG: No indeed. It was the greatest rush job I've ever had on a musical score.

FARR: A rush job in writing music—what do you mean?

GG: Well, you see I was working on another show for Mr. Ziegfeld when he suddenly decided to drop that one and produce "Show Girl" immediately.

FARR: That's a funny thing to do, isn't it?

GG: Ziegfeld often did those things. He called me down to his office one day and said, "George I'm going to produce J. P. McEvoy's 'Show Girl' and you must write the score for it!"

FARR: But that's an almost impossible request, isn't it?

The conversation continues until Farr declares, "Thanks—I've got the dope. You just tell it on the radio the way you told me about it, and it'll be good, informal continuity."

Once a song had been settled on, an overture was chosen for the in-studio orchestra of twenty-five, conducted by Louis Katzman. To complement the featured song, the orchestra played something by a fellow composer; this was followed by another Gershwin song, without much commentary. Then, having also settled on a featured song for the next broadcast, he and the orchestra would play a few bars of that in the manner of a movie trailer. At the "dress" rehearsal, with all the commercials added, the show was timed. "It generally runs a minute or two over, so we must go back over the music, page by page, cutting here and there. . . . I'll cut my own stuff, but I never touch the other fellow's." The sponsor left such decisions in his hands, making Gershwin the only performer in radio who bore the ultimate responsibility for each program.[1]

The new job, beginning in February and continuing until June, earned Gershwin a weekly salary of $2,000. As he wrote George Pallay, the sponsor was "the only kind of firm that I would work for—three guesses!—it's a laxative concern! I knew I would make the grade."[2] Once *Porgy and Bess* took the stage Heyward wryly acknowledged the role of the "laxative concern" (a chewing gum called Feenamint) in providing Gershwin the economic means to work on its score. "And with the authentic medicine-man flair," he explained, "the manufacturer distributed his information in an irresistible wrapper of Gershwin hits, with the composer at the piano. There is, I imagine, a worse fate than that which derives from use of a laxative gum. And, anyhow, we felt that the end justified the means, and that they also served who only sat and waited."[3]

Once *Music by Gershwin* was launched, the composer's artistic focus on the opera took hold in earnest. After reading the script for Act II, he wrote Heyward, on February 26:

> I really think you are doing a magnificent job with the new libretto
> and I hope I can match it musically. I have begun composing music
> for the First Act and I am starting with the songs and spirituals first.
> I am hoping you will find some time to come up North and live at my
> apartment—if it is convenient for you—so we can work together on
> some of the spirituals for Scene 2, Act I. Perhaps when the weather
> grows a little warmer you will find time to do this. I cannot leave
> New York to go South as I am tied up with the radio until June 1st.[4]

But before receiving this letter, Heyward had fired off one of his own: "Swell show, George, but what the hell is the news about PORGY!!!!" His patience was wearing thin, and his plea for action reflected a longstanding anxiety that the physical distance dividing the collaborators would work against the regional spirit he had intended for the opera. Approaching the age of fifty and never robust in health, with a wife and a young child, Heyward had maintained something of the comfortable standard of living that his earlier success had made possible—most recently with the help of screenwriting jobs in Hollywood—but he worried that progress on his opera could founder for lack of a committed composer. Two quick visits to Charleston were insufficient to acquaint anyone with the local culture, he felt.

> I am naturally disappointed that you have tied yourself up so long in New York. I believe that if you had gotten down for a reasonably long stay and gotten deep into the sources here you would have done a bigger job. I am not criticizing your decision. I know well what an enormously advantageous arrangement the radio is, and I know, also, how this tour of yours and the broadcasts are rolling up publicity that will be good business for us when the show opens, only I am disappointed. There is so much more here than you have yet gotten hold of.[5]

But the collaborators did finally meet in New York in mid-April, and with Ira joining them, they settled into an effective, congenial partnership.

Included in the opening pages of the script Heyward had sent Gershwin after the contract was signed were lyrics for two songs: the lullaby "Summertime," sung by Clara, the community's young mother figure; and "A Woman Is a Sometime Thing," delivered by her husband Jake, captain of a fishing boat, and his crew. Gershwin made it his first order of business to compose songs to fit those verses. As he and Heyward had agreed, his task was to assign most of the script to one of three kinds of musical material: songs, with melodies that could stand alone; thematic material, which offered recognizable melody and was often linked to a character, a mood, an incident—or even a leitmotif; and recitative, to carry the story forward. It is no surprise that Gershwin started with songs. "I am not ashamed of writing songs at any time so long as they are good songs," he wrote soon after *Porgy and Bess* opened in New York. Having composed many dozens of songs for stage characters in a wide variety of situations, he had no reason to doubt that he could do the same for a drama whose characters sang instead of speaking.

No strategic decision Gershwin made was more important than the one to compose all the opera's music himself. *Porgy* the play had been fitted with authentic Negro spirituals, but Gershwin, rather than accepting the built-in appeal and cultural cover that folk material could bestow, insisted on the music being "all of one piece." The folk expression he fashioned for *Porgy and Bess* was determined not by its sources but by the character and style that Gershwin decided to impart to it.[6]

In June and July, while the radio program was on vacation, Gershwin made an extended trip to South Carolina—to Folly Beach, near Charleston and close to Heyward's Folly Island vacation home, where he moved into a cottage with his valet Paul Mueller and cousin Henry Botkin. There, "bare and black above the waist"—according to a New York newspaper—and with a two-inch beard, he and Heyward spent most afternoons together working on music and lyrics for Act I, as well as attending church services and revival meetings that enabled Gershwin to partake of "the philosophy behind the southern Negro's life" expressed in their music. Sometimes music from Gershwin's rented piano drew "a group of Negroes" to gather "in front of his cottage and beat the sand with their feet." Gershwin explained to the reporter that all of the opera's singing would fall to the "Negroes," for whom "a song expresses an outlet for joy and a valve for sorrow." The opera's few white characters, "more civilized" but "more unemotional" too, would speak their lines. By the end of a five-week stay, the score for the first act was composed.[7]

SET IN the recent past in Catfish Row, an African American neighborhood near the Charleston waterfront, *Porgy and Bess* begins with a burst of energized sound from the orchestra—a high trill followed by eccentrically accented sixteenth notes, with prominent xylophone. The curtain rises on a darkened stage that proves to be the room of one Jasbo Brown who, seated at the piano, is playing a "low-down blues," evoking a climate of restrained eroticism, a facet of life in Catfish Row. Dancers, belonging to a general ambience that grounds the story in the life of a community, sing vocables in response to a persistent melodic call from the piano.[8] Their singing fades gradually as the lights dim on Jasbo—and grow brighter elsewhere to show Clara rocking her baby, to the string music leading into her lullaby.

The song "Summertime" reveals Catfish Row at its most peaceful. It was also a landmark for each of the opera's creators: for Heyward, a published poet, it marked his debut as a song lyricist; for Gershwin, it offered a chance to fit music to words rather than the other way around. And the persuasive result of their collaboration reflects the affinity that drew them to one another's work in the first place.

"Summertime" embodies Gershwin's claim that the characters in *Porgy and Bess* sing "folk music," for both words and music are cast in a convincingly folklike style. Heyward's text consists of a pair of four-line stanzas, producing a short strophic song with words in a colloquial English that evokes regional African American speech. The imagery is of the bounty of nature, soon to be ripe for the harvesting, and the sanguine mood of a mother with blessings to count:

Summertime, an' the livin' is easy,
Fish are jumpin', an' the cotton is high.
Oh, yo' daddy's rich an' yo' ma is good-lookin',
So hush, little baby, don't yo' cry.

For this lyrical structure Gershwin composed a simple four-phrase melody in B minor, the minor mode reinforcing its homespun character, with an orchestral accompaniment that enhances the richness of the harmony. As Clara begins her second stanza,

Gershwin's fondness for varied repetition shines through: she is joined by a female chorus singing two-part harmony (on "ooh") and a soft countermelody in the violins. With a melody so straightforward and indelible, it is no surprise that "Summertime" returns more than once as the opera unfolds.

In roughly a dozen bars of instrumental music, Gershwin's orchestra then moves from the domestic side of Catfish Row to the men of the neighborhood, who, as their work week comes to an end, are ready to unwind on a Saturday night with a craps game. The chattering staccato of string music prefigures the buzz of excitement that pervades the contest:

> *Oh, nobody knows when de Lord is goin' to call,*
> *It may be in the summer time an' may be in the fall,*
> *But you got to leave yo' baby an' yo' home an' all.*

Following Heyward's book, Gershwin sets these lines as a series of solo statements, sung in free rhythm by crapshooters Mingo and Sporting Life. Each solo line prompts a rhythmically flexible choral response, "Roll dem bones, roll!"[9] The men's solemn colloquy is followed by a two-bar melody from the orchestra that Gershwin introduces in order to signify a certain mood, marked "Moderato molto deciso" (relaxed and very decisive).[10] By repeating this motive in parallel situations later, Gershwin turns it into a musical marker that all is well in the neighborhood: lives are proceeding as usual in a community whose customary pace accommodates a mix of varied activity.

Essential to the opera's dramaturgy, too, are leitmotifs linked to particular characters. In the first scene, Porgy, a crippled beggar, and Crown, a formidable stevedore—two men who will vie for the love of Bess—are set up as rivals by the music. Each man makes a conspicuous entrance, and each is announced by a characteristic musical statement—a leitmotif—that accompanies him as the opera proceeds. Porgy appears first, arriving in his goat cart to a leitmotif reflecting stability and dignity, built around the notes of a major triad with a blue third. Here is a member of the community who is obviously held in respect.[11]

Shortly thereafter, Crown and Bess appear in the distance. From the moment the pair are spotted, Porgy has Bess in his sights. Jake, the fishing-boat captain, suggests that Porgy may be "sof' on Crown's Bess," a charge Porgy brushes aside with a curt denial: "I ain' nebber swap two words with Bess." That Porgy sings those words to notes from his own musical mark of identity—the only time his leitmotif is vocalized—seems indication enough that Bess is on his mind.[12] But his past experience has shown that no woman he could love could imagine the crippled Porgy as her lover. Gershwin sets the words "When Gawd make cripple, he mean him to be lonely" to thematic material worthy of a man who has overcome much to win respect on Catfish Row. Porgy perceives his physique within the plan of a benevolent, all-powerful God, and Gershwin's markings—"with free expression" and "colla voce" (with the voice)—give the singer leeway to express the blend of pain, hardship, and acceptance that destiny has imposed on him. He imagines his life as a journey along a "lonesome road," with steps marked in the orchestra by dissonant quarter notes.

If Porgy's motive projects lyricism and calm, Crown's is intrusive—conceived, it seems, to interrupt, making Crown the center of attention.[13] As he demands a pint of whiskey from the bootlegger Sporting Life and joins the game,[14] the bustling music in the string section features clipped, cross-accented, chattering sounds that pause from time to time, as the roller of the dice wishes himself luck. Eloquent in this way is a sequence in which Porgy, chanting with half-closed eyes, envisions the "bones" in his hands as "little stars" rolling "a sun an' a moon" for "dis poor beggar." He manages more than one successful roll, leading Crown, who grows increasingly belligerent, to accuse him of cheating. As Crown grabs

Porgy's arm, two familiar themes sound simultaneously in the orchestra: the burst of treble sixteenth notes on which the opening curtain rose, and a restatement of Porgy's leitmotif. The first is a reminder of Catfish Row's vitality, and the second proves that this crippled beggar is not intimidated by the formidable Crown. Their brief skirmish is followed by a one-bar anticipation of one of the opera's signature songs: "I Got Plenty o' Nuttin'," the "banjo song" in which Porgy will lay out his philosophy of life in Act II.

As the craps game music continues, Crown's motive recurs from time to time, woven into the musical texture yet always audible. Crown has watched a neighbor named Robbins drink deeply from his (Crown's) whiskey bottle, and his mistrust grows. When Robbins hastily sweeps up winnings from a victorious roll, Crown seizes his wrist, and the two men start to fight. Now the percolating craps game music turns into fight music, with interjections of Crown's leitmotif as a reminder of where the aggression has come from. The people of Catfish Row add their voices to the musical mix, imploring the adversaries to stop. With nine different vocal parts in the air, each with its own words and music, plus an orchestra playing its own contrapuntal lines, the score's musical texture is as complex as anything Gershwin ever composed. No one intervenes, though, and Crown's strength and weaponry prevail. When his foe falls lifeless to the floor, Serena Robbins screams and throws herself on her husband's body. Jake shouts, "Jesus, he's killed him!"

Several characters now face altered conditions. The first to act is Bess, who jolts Crown out of his drunken daze with an order to "wake up and hit it out" before the police arrive. Once Crown is gone, Sporting Life approaches Bess, declaring himself "the only frien' you got left." She begs the drug peddler for "a touch of happy dust" to calm her nerves. Then he offers to hide her from the authorities until the two of them can book passage on the next boat from Charleston to New York, where, he assures her, "you an' me will make a swell team." Bess rejects the prospect of selling sexual favors to bolster his success in the drug trade, and Sporting Life beats a rapid retreat.

Bess is now alone on a darkened stage with Serena, who hovers over her husband's body, and Maria, proprietor of the neighborhood cook shop, who now closes up for the evening. With nowhere to spend the night, Bess runs from door to door and finds them all closed to her, as another orchestral return of the fight music reflects her growing anxiety. Reduced finally to begging Maria for a night's shelter, she is refused on the grounds that she's caused trouble enough already. Just one possibility remains unexplored, Maria tells her. But it's Porgy's room, and he's not a man inclined to welcome the likes of her. The sound of a police whistle forces Bess toward Porgy's place. But now the orchestra sends a sweeping lyrical message far removed from the rebuff that Maria has predicted: the poignant music behind Porgy's testimony that the life of a cripple has made it impossible for him to meet a woman to love. It is no surprise, then, when Porgy's door swings open to Bess from within.

THE CURTAIN for scene 2 rises on Serena's room, which is filled with mourners. Robbins's murder will be noticed by the white authorities, bringing the racially separate cultures of Charleston together onstage. The authorities will need to arrest a suspect, and they will insist that the body be dealt with at once. Thus, the murder carries economic consequences as well as legal and emotional ones. Robbins has left his widow impoverished, and a saucer has been placed on his body, inviting contributions for the cost of his burial.

Serena is scene 2's central figure. Yet much of the action is carried out by the other residents of Catfish Row, who grieve at their compatriot's death, donate to his burial fund, pray for his soul, stand with his widow, and rejoice, as the scene ends, in the hope of meeting their comrade again in the Promised Land. Because the neighbors respond collectively to each of these needs, choral music is fundamental to the action. But rather than emphasizing the melody and poetry of rounded compositions, as imported spiritual songs could have done, Gershwin's choral music here tends toward the episodic, changing character to fit each turn of events. "Where is Brother Robbins?" asks an unnamed soprano from the higher reaches of her voice. The company replies that he's "gone, gone, gone, gone, gone, gone, gone," to a descending melody over a rising bass. Other soloists step forward with memories of Robbins, and each draws a similar response from the chorus, as the rendering of "gone" in seven quarter notes becomes a (varied) melodic refrain in itself.

Porgy and Bess, in their first appearance as a couple, now make their way up the stairs to Serena's room. The sight of Bess, shepherding the crippled Porgy as he slowly climbs, sparks the widow's ire, but she accepts Bess's gift of Porgy's money. The mourners urge each other to "fill up de saucer till it overflow," while Porgy launches a prayer to Jesus on Robbins's behalf. But the abrupt arrival of a detective and two policemen halts the scene's exuberant musical flow in its tracks. From the widow the authorities discover that, for lack of insurance, Robbins must be "saucer-buried." From Peter, an elderly honey vendor, they learn that Crown is the killer. From Porgy they can pry loose no information, but after threatening him with jail, they decide instead to jail Peter, the honey man, until Crown turns up. In these exchanges, the white men of the law speak their words into silence, while the black individuals sing theirs, accompanied by an orchestra whose support includes musical gestures related to the characters. Once the police have left with an unhappy Peter in tow, Porgy reflects on the strangeness of a legal system that would leave the husband and father Robbins dead, a killer at large, and the harmless, innocent Peter in captivity. His musings prompt a choral return of "gone, gone, gone," starting softly but swelling, as a fuller orchestra joins the singers in a passionate transition to Serena's lamentation: "My Man's Gone Now."

Porgy and Bess contains no more desolate statement than this aria, grieving a human loss with perfect economy, in four syllables, four words, and a four-note melodic phrase. Gone is the "comp'ny" of a husband and partner whose steps on the stairs she waits to hear at the end of his work day. Gershwin composed this evocation of a suffering heart around an **aaba** melody, in a familiar thirty-two-bar framework, each **a** section starting its lament over lurching, nonlegato drive in the orchestra. After both of the first two **a** sections, Serena sings a wordless, archlike wail, extending her statements by responding to them herself; and she closes with a long rising glissando that seems the very embodiment of her pain. If Serena is emotionally spent as her aria ends, it is at least partly because Gershwin has built into this tour de force of vocalized tragedy a pause for a performer who has given her all to stop and take a bow.[15] He surely knew that this music would create a show-stopping moment.

Now Serena is approached by an undertaker who agrees to see her through so that her husband's corpse can be properly buried, and the chordal "gone, gone, gone" is heard one last time. But as the mood of Catfish Row hangs in the balance, an assertive female mourner—none other than Bess—seizes the moment, starting a new song in a spirit of hope that had faded when donations in the funeral saucer fell short. Her words portray Robbins's soul as already safe in the Promised Land, and reunion with him only a train ride away. "Oh the train is at the station, an' you better get on board, 'cause it's leavin' today," Bess declaims, starting slowly but then picking up speed. Her invitation prompts others to join in, as the music turns the death of Robbins into a shared episode in the life of Catfish Row.

"Leavin' for the Promise' Lan'" is the opera's closest number yet to a spiritual with roots in African American oral tradition, but Gershwin's technical mastery is also on display. The tempo traces the metaphorical journey described in the text, as the train leaves the station, then gains speed gradually and moves forward to a strict clickety-clacking pattern. Once running speed is reached, the riders revel in the momentum, singing out encouragement to "keep that drivin' wheel a-rollin', / rollin', rollin', rollin', / rollin', rollin, let it roll, / Until we meet our brudder in the Promise' Lan'!" Two distinctive musical emphases—contrapuntal display and train-travel effects—have given rise to an energy that allows Gershwin to end the first act on a note of triumph. And it is Bess, at first a social outcast, who has led the people of Catfish Row from shock and grief into the realm of celebration and hope, through an affirmation of their faith and the power of the music pouring from their hearts.

PORGY AND BESS,
ACT II

THE SECOND ACT CURTAIN rises on the denizens of Catfish Row going about their morning business as the orchestra takes up the "normal activity" leitmotif from Act I. Jake and his fishing crew, preparing to head for the blackfish banks, mend their nets while singing about the journey that awaits them. Their song takes a verse-and-refrain form, with the captain singing major-mode verses ("It take a long pull to get there, HUH!") and the crew joining him in the minor-mode refrains ("But I'll anchor in de Promise' Lan'"). As the song ends, a woman calls down from her second-floor window to remind the fishermen that it's a special day, with a parade at ten and a picnic to follow.

Porgy, keeping tabs on the neighbors' doings from his window, takes this moment to sing a song about himself—an occasion missing from Heyward's original libretto, but one that materialized when Ira, George, and Heyward met in George's apartment on East 72nd Street (where he had moved from his Riverside penthouse in the spring of 1933), during one of the librettist's visits to New York, which seem to have begun in April 1934.[1] According to Ira, the song idea came from George, who wanted to give Porgy a chance to sing something "lighter and gayer" than what he had been assigned in Act I. A little improvising at the piano led to

a few preliminary chords and in less than a minute a well-rounded, cheerful melody. "Something like that," he said. Both DuBose and I had the same reaction: "That's it! Don't look any further." "You really think so?" and, luckily, he recaptured it and played it again. A title popped into my mind. (This was one out of only three or four times in my career that a possible title hit me on first hearing a tune. Usually I sweat for days.) "'I got plenty o' nuthin','" I said tentatively.

It took only a moment for the "balance line" to occur to him: "An' nuthin's plenty for me."[2]

Ira's readiness to draft a lyric for George's melody followed naturally from the brothers' usual way of working. This time, though, it drew an unexpected response from Heyward. In Ira's account, he said:

"Ira, would you mind if I tried my hand at it? So far everything I've done has been set by George and I've never written words to music. If it's all right with you I'd love to take the tune along with me to Charleston." I think we discussed generally the mood and even arrived at a couple of lines. Two weeks later DuBose sent me a version that had many usable lines; many, however, looked good on paper but were awkward when sung. . . . So on this song I did have to do a bit of "polishing." All in all, I'd consider this a 50–50 collaborative effort.[3]

Porgy's joyful "I Got Plenty o' Nuttin'," hinting at Act I's craps game and marked "Moderato con gioja (Banjo Song)" in the score, reveals how a month with Bess has improved his disposition. Neighbors, singing in chordal harmony, marvel at how Porgy has grown friendlier and less likely to find their children a nuisance. The song is about familiar things, whether they exist in nature (the sun, the stars, the ocean) or flow from his inner consciousness (his God, his woman, his song). The musical fundamentals seem straightforward, yet Gershwin stretches the phrase structure unpredictably, offering a harmonic plan that visits remote tonal regions, bringing a glow of discovery to the testament of a reflective, solitary man.

The God-fearing community of Catfish Row includes two characters—the stevedore Crown and the bootlegger Sporting Life—who may be judged villains, for different reasons. Crown's outsized strength and appetites have fostered impulsiveness and a lack of restraint; his fellow workers on the Charleston docks give him a wide berth. In contrast, Sporting Life, a peddler of alcohol who deals drugs on the side, is a calculating strategist; he operates, socially and professionally, on the margins. As the opera begins, both men are focused on Bess: Crown because she has been his woman for years and he wants things to stay that way, and Sporting Life because, aspiring to a grander style of life, he sees Bess as the key to his pimping aspirations. From the opera's first scene through its penultimate one, he seeks to corrupt Bess, whose weakness for "happy dust" makes her vulnerable.

In the wake of "I Got Plenty o' Nuttin'," Sporting Life wanders into Maria's establishment, sits down at a table, and pours white powder into the palm of his hand. When Maria grabs his hand and blows the powder away, an infuriated Sporting Life responds with "What you t'ink you doin'? Dat stuff cos' money." But Maria warns him, "I ain' say nuttin', no matter how drunk you get dese boys 'roun here on rotgut whiskey, but nobody ain' goin' peddle happy dust 'roun' my shop." Meanwhile, Frazier, a lawyer who works the Catfish Row district of Charleston, shows up at Porgy's door looking for business. Porgy learns that the idea of a "divorce" from Crown appeals to Bess, and he stands ready to foot the bill. But when a bystander proclaims that Bess "ain' never marry!" the lawyer explains that that complication will demand a higher fee: "it take expert, to divorce woman what ain't marry." By the time the transaction is over, Porgy has bought an official-looking document, Bess has a divorce in writing, and the people of Catfish Row have enjoyed bantering with Frazier in a call-and-response interchange.

Now a white Charlestonian, Mr. Archdale, appears on the scene, wanting to restore honey man Peter's freedom by paying his bail money. But as he explains his mission to Porgy, a buzzard flies low across the stage, terrifying neighbors who have gathered to hear the white man's news. Porgy identifies the carrion-eating bird as a herald of trouble: "Once de buzzard fold his wing an' light over yo' house," he tells the visitor, "all yo' happiness done dead." Taking charge of the situation, Porgy, in an extended aria with support from the chorus, commands the menacing creature not to land on his house ("Buzzard, keep on flyin' over"), and the bird flies off. The presence of two such dissimilar arias in the same scene—the exuberant banjo song and the somber, acerbic buzzard song—testifies to the human scope of the character of Porgy.[4]

As the people scatter to their rooms to prepare for the day's parade and picnic, Sporting Life sidles up to Bess, to a seven-note triplet statement heard earlier in Maria's shop, and offers her a sample of the drug he is sure she craves. But "I's through with that stuff," she protests as he grasps for her hand. At this moment, Porgy reaches out of his hiding place nearby to grab Sporting Life by the wrist, and the two men scuffle briefly. Managing to pull loose, the peddler marvels, "Gawd, what a grip for a piece of a man!" He leaves Bess with a chilling thought before sauntering off in the direction of the picnic: "Yo' men frien's come an' they go, but remember ole Sportin' Life an' de happy dus' here all along."

This episode touches on an element of the opera's story that, while significant, is hardly reckoned with: Porgy's difficulty in walking. We know from Act I that Porgy rides in a goat cart and that stairs are an obstacle for him. Moreover, the current scene gives no hint that he has considered attending the picnic, his disability apparently making such a journey impossible. Yet Porgy's skirmish with Sporting Life reveals physical strength to balance the weakness of his impaired physique. Todd Duncan, who originated the role, recalled the physical demands it imposed. His Porgy, relying on hands and arms to pull the rest of him around, would surely have convinced audience members that a man unable to walk easily could have developed compensating strengths in his arms and hands, enough to make him a physical force to be reckoned with.[5]

Dressed to the nines and with baskets full of food, the people of Catfish Row will soon make their way to the ferryboat that will take them to Kittiwah Island for a picnic sponsored by a church-based lodge. But Porgy and Bess are not inclined to join the celebration. He has just learned that, with Bess in his life, the sight of a buzzard hovering over his room no longer terrifies him. And she, having given full voice to her loathing for Sporting Life's plot for her future, and now "divorced" from Crown, is free to dwell on the emotional world that she and her liberator have fashioned. The orchestral return of Porgy's "night time, day time" melody from the opera's opening scene, on a stage just emptied of everybody else, sets up a duet in which, for the first time, these lovers are able to translate their feelings for each other into an extended song.

"Bess, you is my woman now, you is, you is!" Porgy sings, in the heart of his baritone range, blending calm with energy through downward octave leaps to balance the rising ones. The lovers' song moves through time with the ebb and flow of an aria—a natural pace for a sweeping legato melody laced with blue notes, and sung with openhearted sincerity. The melody of Bess's response in kind repeats Porgy's opening section, and her music addresses his isolation, too. If his physical handicap keeps him from the picnic, then she'll stay there with him.[6] And Bess follows that pronouncement with a full-voiced "Porgy, I's yo' woman now, / I's yours forever." And then, in the gentlest of voices, she affirms her constancy in two bars of chanted eighth notes ("Mornin' time an' evenin' time . . ."), which Porgy echoes note for note. Their ultimate promise to each other seals the pledge in octaves: "From dis minute I'm tellin' you, / I keep dis vow."

At this point the lodge band invades the scene, and the people of Catfish Row pour onto the stage on their way to the picnic. An exuberant number, "Oh, I Can't Sit Down!," dwells on the high spirits of a picnic day, when decorum yields to self-expression, filled with singing, dancing, and more. Maria approaches with a huge basket and, learning to her surprise that Bess will stay behind with Porgy, insists that she join the crowd headed to the ferry and the picnic. When Porgy supports that plan, Bess concurs and bids him a tender farewell. Secure in his woman's word, he reprises the final portion of his song of satisfaction, "I Got Plenty o' Nuttin'," as she departs.

Act II, scene 2 opens on Kittiwah Island with an explosion of African-style drumming, joined soon by other instrumental sounds and cries of revelry. Then, in a spirit of shameless sacrilege, Sporting Life assumes the pose of a preacher exhorting his "congregation" with a tuneful sermon about the improbability of familiar Bible stories. "It Ain't Necessarily So" proves to be the opera's only song based on a leitmotif: a seven-note, blues-tinged triplet gesture introduced in Act II, scene 1. That motive is first heard when Sporting Life, sitting in Maria's eatery, prepares a dose of happy dust that the irate proprietor swats away. And it returns a bit later to mark his failed offer of the drug to Bess—observed by Porgy, whose physical intervention scares the peddler off. Both incidents end with rebukes, outing the peddler as a dealer of fakery. And now the motive becomes the beginning of a song centered on Sporting Life's preoccupation with truth and falsehood.[7]

Supported by a pervasive cross rhythm between the triplet vocal melody and the duple "boom-chuck" of the accompaniment, Sporting Life's song supports the fake preacher's contrarian stance in both sound and meaning. Indeed, by proclaiming Bible stories seen through a skeptic's eye, he transforms the picnickers into a complicit congregation, joining him in a spirited call-and-response rejection of Old Testament lore. There was the youthful "Li'l David," he begins, armed only with a slingshot yet miraculously felling the gigantic Goliath, who lay "down and dieth." Doubtful too, the preacher continues, is the tale of Jonah, who "lived in de whale"—making his home in "dat fish's abdómen." And finally there was Methuselah, said to have survived to the age of 900, although "who calls dat livin' when no gal'll give in / To no man what's nine hundred years?" "It Ain't Necessarily So" stands out in the opera too as a solo turn, or "specialty," in which a star performer puts signature skills on display. Indeed, Sporting Life's time in the spotlight leads into dancing moves, as a musical comedy number will do, but it's interrupted by an irate Serena Robbins, who has her own sermon to deliver.[8]

As Serena's denunciation of Sporting Life's blasphemy pours forth, the ferry's warning whistle sounds, marking the end of the revelry. But when Bess starts toward the ferry, a whistle from the bushes distracts her. She sees that the signal has come from none other than Crown, whose lurching leitmotif now resounds in the orchestra's lower reaches. Having spent the last month hiding on the island, he has waited out the picnic for a chance to talk to Bess. Soon, he informs her, he plans to leave the island and head for Catfish Row to spirit her away on a riverboat bound for Savannah, where they can start a new life together. In the exchange that follows, one of the opera's most dramatic and eventful, the formidable Crown does his best to restart their relationship. But Bess's weeks with Porgy have made her a changed woman. Treating Bess with kindness and love, Porgy has won her heart. Indeed, given that she—that very morning—has embraced in song the role of Porgy's woman, Bess must now explain her change of heart to a formidable, increasingly resentful ex-lover.

Over the orchestra's statement of Porgy's motive, Bess declares her discovery of a new way of life. But when she reaffirms her determination to leave the island without him, Crown responds with disbelief: "You tellin' me dat you'd rather have dat cripple dan Crown?" Bess's plea to let her return only hardens Crown's resolve. As the orchestra begins a driving accompaniment for a melody to be sung "pleadingly with expression and rhythm," she is reduced to begging. "What you want wid Bess?" are the words Heyward gives her for this confrontation, and for them Gershwin invented a syncopated, disjunct, asymmetrical melody veering between major and minor: a tonal thrust fashioned, it seems, on the brink of panic. Bess's driving expression of despair is a song that features neither poetic meter nor a rhyme scheme, and Crown rejects her appeals through vocal counterpoint to her plea. As the ferry prepares to leave the island, Bess tries to escape, but Crown holds her in a firm embrace, and she lacks the strength to resist either his physical dominance or the erotic rush his touch has always awakened "deep inside" her. As the scene on the island draws to a close, it seems questionable that Porgy and Bess can survive as a couple in the wake of this encounter.

When scene 3 opens on predawn Catfish Row a week later, Jake and his crew, preparing to set out for the blackfish banks, sing a stanza of the work song "It Take a Long Pull to Get There." The sound of a troubled female voice issues from Porgy's room: "Take yo' hands off me, I say"—the voice of Bess, to which Serena Robbins may be heard responding that "she still out of her head." Peter the honey man, just released from jail, learns from Maria that Bess got lost on the island after the picnic and missed the ferry, and it took two days for her to find a way back to Catfish Row. Porgy adds that she has been in a delirium since her return. With Porgy's encouragement, Serena sinks to her knees and, in a long, emotive stretch of recitative addressed to "Doctor Jesus," pleads that He "cas' de devil" out of Bess's "afflicted" soul.

Through the hours after Serena's prayer over Bess, she and Porgy wait, hoping that the widow's plea has broken the spell. As they linger, street hawkers of local delicacies pass by, peddling their wares: a woman with a distinctive "strawberry" call, a crabmonger, and Peter, who's got "honey from the comb" to sell.

Later that afternoon, after the church clock strikes the time, Bess is heard offstage singing, "Porgy, Porgy, dat you there ain' it?" He responds to the sound of her awakening with a quiet "Thank Gawd." Bess makes her way onto the stage as the orchestra picks up in the background the theme of "Bess, You Is My Woman Now." To a lightly textured melody, Porgy helps to fill the gaps in her memory of recent events. When he describes Bess's state upon her return from the island—she was unable to even recognize him—the orchestra dwells on the melody for the words "you mus' laugh an' sing an' dance for two instead of one" from their love duet, a theme that taps into Bess's shame at having betrayed Porgy. But he brushes that concern aside, telling her that "I know you been with Crown," citing his cripple's intuition. "He's comin' for me when de cotton come to town," she admits, adding that she has agreed to join him when he arrives. When Porgy replies, "If you wants to go to Crown, dat's for you to say," Bess begins the opera's second love duet: "I Loves You, Porgy." She wants to stay with him, she explains, but she cannot resist the erotic power of Crown's embraces.

The F-major melody to which Bess sings her confession is unlike any that Gershwin had yet invented. Based on a five-note motive built from melodic thirds and shaped into archlike gestures, it suggests a character who, facing a crisis, still manages to choose her words and music with restraint and precision. Porgy's response intones a question in recitative mode: "If dere warn't no Crown, Bess, if dere was only jus' you an' Porgy, what den?" Returning to the first section's music with "I loves you, Porgy," she then begs him to protect her:

If you kin keep me,
I wants to stay here
Wid you forever,
An' I'll be glad.

Porgy resolves that, when Crown comes to carry her away, "that's my business." The duet closes in triumph with a driving repeat of Bess's "I loves you, Porgy." By the time it ends, not only have the lovers' commitments been reaffirmed, but Porgy, in effect, has promised Bess a future without Crown.

After Bess and Porgy leave the stage, Clara hovers at the waterfront waiting for Jake and his crew to return. She senses a storm waiting, "holdin' its breath," and "list'nin' for dat hurricane bell." In Act I, scene 2, the people had gathered in Serena Robbins's room to mourn the outcome of a violent deed. And now, in the second act's fourth scene, they have again gathered there, this time to cope with terror. A standard beginning for a scene like this one could be a songful plea to the Almighty, but Gershwin instead composed a choral prayer that, with barely a hint of tuneful melody, preserves some individuality among the supplicants. As a four-part chorus hums pairs of open fourths, six soloists simultaneously sing their own unmeasured prayer, directed (from top to bottom) to "O Heavenly Father," "Oh, Doctor Jesus," "Professor Jesus," "Oh, Lawd above," "Oh, Captain Jesus," and "Oh, Father." To catch the details would require superhuman aural acuity, for no one voice can be singled out, except perhaps at the very beginning. Rather, the words and voices of the soloists disappear immediately into the babble until just before the end of this unique prayer, when everyone joins in an emphatic, harmonized outcry: "Lawd, hab mercy."

Where did this choral eruption come from? DuBose Heyward recalled a summer night in 1934, when he introduced Gershwin to a local mode of collective praying that he seems to have drawn upon for this scene. As the two of them approached a dilapidated cabin that had been taken as a meeting house by a group of Negro Holy Rollers, George caught my arm and held me. The sound that had arrested him was one to which, through long familiarity, I attached no special importance. But now, listening to it with him, and noticing his excitement, I began to catch its extraordinary quality. It consisted of perhaps a dozen voices raised in loud rhythmic prayer. The odd thing about it was that while each had started at a different time, upon a different theme, they formed a clearly defined rhythmic pattern, and that this, with the actual words lost, and the inevitable pounding of the rhythm, produced an effect almost terrifying in its primitive intensity. [9]

The scene-opening prayer is followed by a unifying spiritual, with Heyward's words of apocalyptic upheaval:

Oh, de Lawd shake de Heavens an' de Lawd rock de groun',
An' where you goin' stand, my brudder an my sister,
When de sky come a-tumblin' down—

Gershwin created a two-part hymn tune (**ab**) that becomes a refrain of sorts for a scene steeped in drama, religious fervor, and superstition, all attributes he deemed fundamental to African American life. "Oh, de Lawd Shake de Heavens," sung "religiously" (the score instructs) and with restraint, has a tuneful continuity that makes it an effective background for individual reactions to the storm raging outdoors. Many believe that Judgment Day has arrived. Porgy tries to console Clara, whose husband ventured out of the harbor with his crew more than a day earlier. Serena's plea for collective prayer draws comment from Sporting Life, who doubts that Judgment Day can truly be at hand. An agitated Clara, baby in arms, peeks through a crack in the shutter, hoping to catch a glimpse of Jake's boat. During a brief lull, she soothes her child with a second stanza of "Summertime." With Crown presumably still on the island as giant waves pound its shore, Bess tells her man, "I guess you got me for keeps, Porgy."

A burst of wind, lightning, and thunder prompts a new spiritual from the chorus: "Oh, Dere's Somebody Knockin' at de Do'," the opera's only song that had also been sung (with the same general outline) in *Porgy* the play.[10] As the chorus repeats the "Knockin'" song, the door is forced open from outside. The result is a shock, registered in the orchestra by the sound of the storm rushing in and the return of a familiar leitmotif. For it is Crown who bursts in, radiating physical strength, the courage of a survivor, and scorn for those who have tried to keep him outside. The sight of Crown is enough to bring about a pause in the continuous singing of hymns. After he approaches Bess to ridicule her choice of a partner, she and Porgy reaffirm their love as the orchestra quotes from "Bess, You Is My Woman Now." Serena warns Crown that his actions risk provoking the wrath of the Almighty, and he responds with a forthright vocal rejoinder, more a proclamation than a song.

Crown's "A Red-Headed Woman," which Gershwin sets in an "Allegretto (tempo di Jazz)" (fast [jazz tempo]), shows a bullying character at his most defiant. As the people of Catfish Row beg the Almighty for protection and mercy, Crown looks to the power of sex, his words paying homage to a proverbial seductress who can drive men wild. The energetic, blues-based song, a blend of power and sacrilege, is so provocative that when he repeats the second stanza, the neighbors add a new choral layer, beseeching God either to ignore Crown's blasphemies or to strike him dead. A scream rings out when, through the shuttered window, Clara spots Jake's boat upside-down in the river. Handing off her baby to Bess, she rushes out the door. As the orchestra plays agitated music in the background, Bess calls for a man in the house brave enough to join Clara's search for Jake. Mocking Porgy for failing to heed her call, Crown plunges into the maelstrom. When the door flies open at his exit, the wind blows hard enough to extinguish the lamp, plunging the room into darkness. Act II ends with the sound of the chorus repeating the entire "Doctor Jesus" prayer, now over an orchestral background that includes a continuous wash of storm sounds.

PORGY AND BESS,
ACT III

ON THE NIGHT AFTER THE HURRICANE, the people of Catfish Row are counting their losses. A subdued celestial prologue that includes the tolling of chimes opens the third act as a Christian community marks the death of beloved residents. Gershwin's artistry distills the mood of the moment into a serene melody as Heyward's text has survivors addressing words of consolation to the souls of neighbors and friends who have drowned in the storm. "Clara, Clara, don't you be down-hearted," a song begins, for in the person of Jesus, "walkin' on the water," God has dispatched a comforting presence to guide souls who are ready to "rise up and follow" Him home. Like most of the opera's spirituals, this one is strophic—two stanzas plus the start of a third. "Clara" also suggests a litany, in that each stanza centers on a different individual who has perished—Clara, then her husband Jake, and then, though for only two bars, even Crown, before an interruption. In music approaching the sublime, Gershwin encourages community members to trust that normal life on Catfish Row will be restored.

But as the chorus begins its third stanza, the sound of raucous laughter interrupts the mourners, proving that at least one hurricane survivor is unmoved by the existential side of the storm's after-math: Sporting Life, linked musically to his leitmotif. Signaling that news of Crown's death may be false, his laughter ridicules the grieving of the widows, drawing a rebuke from Maria. As she enters her shop, and Sporting Life leaves the stage with his ruthless take on human nature echoing behind him, the orchestra plays a brief, lighthearted bit of transition music leading to a glimpse of domestic tranquility—for now Bess appears at the window of Porgy's room with Clara's baby in her arms, reflecting the trust Porgy has won for her in the community. Nothing could signal more clearly Bess's embrace of the role of mother than her delivery of a stanza of "Sum-mertime," as the choristers head back home and night falls.

But a decisive timpani stroke abruptly roils the prevailing calm, and snatches of Crown's leitmotif begin to sound. The darting fig-uration of the fight motive from the first-act craps game joins that melodic gesture, adding rhythmic tension and a premonition of vio-lence. Crown appears in the darkened courtyard, crawling toward the door of Porgy's room, prepared to lead Bess away with him. But suddenly, from inside the room, as stage directions indicate, "an arm is extended, the hand grasping a knife" that stabs Crown in the back. A deathly struggle follows, with Porgy's hands eventually locking on Crown's throat. Mortal combat in the dark is reflected in the savagery of the orchestral music, echoing the struggle between Crown and Robbins. And soon the victorious voice of Porgy calls out that, at last, Bess has got her man. As a quick curtain falls, a soaring statement of Porgy's leitmotif is sounded in the orches-tra. It appears that, on this matter, Charleston's African American community has its own code of crime and punishment. Judging from the triumphant music supporting this scene, local justice has been served.

As scene 2 begins the next day, a bustling Catfish Row is vis-ited by local authorities: a detective and a coroner, investigating the death of Crown. The detective, who earlier took the innocent Peter into custody, considers Serena Robbins his prime suspect, but when he knocks on her window, her friend Annie tells him that Serena has been sick in bed for the last three days. Serena slowly makes her way to the window, repeating the three-days-in-bed excuse, and the detective eventually gives up his interrogation. Determined, however, to find a witness for the coroner's inquest, he kicks open Porgy's door, ordering that he come out for questioning. Sporting Life, who has sauntered unobtrusively onto the scene, hears the white man explain that at a coroner's inquest a witness is required only to identify the body of the deceased. But when Porgy learns that he faces being alone in the room with the body of Crown, he is terror-stricken, his fear underlined by an orchestral outburst of agitated chords and repetitions of his leitmotif. He is in the thrall of an ancient superstition: as Sporting Life explains to the gathering crowd, "When the man that killed Crown go in that room an' look at him, Crown' wound begin to bleed."[1] Porgy's panic over this notion persists until he is dragged off to jail for contempt of court, to the sound of the peddler's laughter.

Sporting Life now speculates loudly on the punishment for contempt of court, alleging a lengthy jail term or worse. Overwhelmed as the growing odds of being separated from her man sink in, Bess buries her face in her hands, which prompts Sporting Life to reach out gently for one of them. She finds to her horror that he has left a dose of his "happy dust" in her hand—but then she clasps her hand over her mouth as the orchestra shouts out three bars of the "ain't necessarily so" leitmotif. "That's the thing, ain't it?," the peddler croons, followed by "there's plenty more where that came from."

"There's a Boat Dat's Leavin' Soon for New York," Sporting Life's second song, is another of Gershwin's Broadway-style numbers with lyrics by his brother.[2] Unlike "It Ain't Necessarily So," this one is dramatically consequential, for it marks the outcome of his quest to bring Bess fully under his control. His sales pitch, steeped in an aura of urban glitz, convinces her to join him in a city where people like them live in mansions—where the women, dressed in "silks and satins in de latest Paris styles," may be seen "struttin'" on the streets of Harlem, "up on upper Fi'th Avenue." The music, with a slithering, snakelike foundation in bass clarinet and bassoon, blends invention and modernity with high spirits. Nevertheless, a still-skeptical Bess orders him away from her door, while the orchestra's frequent repetition of the "ain't necessarily so" leitmotif warns that genuine New York high life is far removed from Sporting Life's fable.

Sporting Life offers Bess another packet of the drug, which she knocks out of his hand—in what proves to be her last gesture of defiance. Pausing at the door of Porgy's room, she hears the peddler's siren call: "Don't want a second shot, eh! All right, I'll leave it here . . . maybe you'll change yo' mind." Whereupon, as a musical turn that proves to be a chromatic cocaine leitmotif sounds eerily in the orchestra's treble range, a stage direction in the vocal score specifies: "He tosses the paper of dope on the doorstep where she can reach it from where she stands. She runs suddenly into the room and slams door behind her." As Sporting Life lights a cigarette and saunters off, the music that takes over in the orchestra is a blaring and *fortissimo* rendering of the last phrases of "There's a Boat Dat's Leavin' Soon for New York." In Heyward's original libretto, the stage directions for the end of this scene read: "Sporting Life exits gate, smiling to himself and blowing smoke rings. After he is gone, Bess opens door, looks out, reaches for small package lying on the step. As she reaches for it—Quick curtain."[3] Scholar and critic Joseph Horowitz credits this idea to the director, finding that "the resulting counterpoint of music and gesture—the grandiose peroration juxtaposed with Bess's pathetic capitulation—is pure Mamoulian, a savage ironic flourish foreign to Heyward and Gershwin both." And the "wicked laughter" in the orchestra that follows "unexpectedly produces one of the opera's saddest moments."[4]

The last scene of *Porgy and Bess* begins a week later, on a Catfish Row that has seen further change since the hurricane roared through, though at first it seems everything is back to normal. The people are engaged in varied wordless stage business while the orchestra plays tuneful music, including morning business-as-usual themes that by now are familiar. New moods follow in a pantomime sequence that has come to be known as the "Occupational Humoresque." The first is a dreamy twenty-bar section labeled "Sleeping Negro." This gives way to a syncopated "Man with broom," then "Man with hammer and man with saw," alternating a sprightly, ragtime-based gesture (hammer) with a lower-register one based on a triplet (saw). Gershwin's anonymous characters start to exchange greetings, paving the way for an exuberant children's chorus, followed by a satisfied expression of "feelin' fine and dandy" from the grownups.

When the orchestra sounds the energetic musical burst that began the opera, the people gather to greet Porgy returning from a week in the jailhouse. His words, sung in recitative, express relief—"Thank Gawd I's home again!"—but the choral response ("we're all so glad you is back again") seems restrained. He reports that at the inquest he outfoxed the authorities by keeping his eyes closed while identifying Crown's body; here Gershwin quotes Porgy's leitmotif in inverted form. And having smuggled his lucky dice into the jailhouse, he has managed to complete his time in detention with more money in his pocket than when he was locked up—which he has used to buy gifts for friends in Catfish Row. Anticipating a settled future for him and Bess, safe from the threat posed by Crown, he has imagined his homecoming as a joyous time of handing out gifts, topped by the red dress and hat he has picked out for Bess.

But Porgy's friends soon realize that he has no inkling of the shock that awaits him, and the spectacle unfolding before them is one that many have no stomach to watch.[5] As Porgy starts to distribute his gifts, with a comment on each one, those who have gathered to welcome him home begin gradually to slip away. After most of the gifts have been displayed and the melody of his banjo song has been reprised, the time for Bess's new red dress to be unveiled has arrived. Since she has not yet appeared, though, Porgy calls out to tell her that he's home, as the orchestra quietly introduces the lead-in to "Bess, You Is My Woman Now." However, when Serena appears with an infant in her arms, Porgy recognizes the child as Clara's. And now it dawns on him that the homecoming he has imagined is a delusion. With bits of his leitmotif sounding in the background, he turns to Maria, demanding, "where's my Bess?" Serena tells him, "you lucky; she gone back to de happy dus'," but Maria blames "dat dirty dog Sportin' Life" for convincing Bess that the authorities could keep Porgy in jail forever. During the heartfelt trio that follows in triple time, the two women weave wordy counterpoint around his raw outcries of distress and pain, while Porgy fails to fully grasp what his friends are telling him. A harmonic vertigo in the trio's middle section reflects the turmoil that has seized him.

Only after the trio ends does Porgy learn that Bess, whom he had feared dead, has left Catfish Row for New York. The news leaves him ecstatic. It tells him that, like a "child what's gone astray," Bess is waiting for him to rescue her.[6] Turning decisively to his friends, he orders them to "bring my goat!" With Porgy's leitmotif sounding in the orchestra, Serena, Maria, and other citizens of Catfish Row do what they can to dissuade him from any such journey. But a determined Porgy, described in the score as "transformed and excited," intones his final declaration:

> Ain't you say Bess gone to Noo York?
> Dat's where I goin',
> I got to be wid Bess.
> Gawd help me fin' her,
> I'm on my way.

The spiritual song that concludes *Porgy and Bess*, "Oh Lawd, I'm on My Way," composed in a standard refrain form (**abab**¹), is remarkable in several ways, none more striking than its brevity. Porgy's journey cannot start too soon for him. Indeed, maybe that's why his farewell stands so literally by its improbable message: "I'm on my way." The melody sung by Porgy and the people of Catfish Row delivers its news over a Charleston-based rhythm in the orchestra, plus a countermelody replete with references to melodies and moments from earlier in the opera.

Closing with a four-bar orchestral tag marked "Grandioso" (majestic), Gershwin revisits the opening statement of "Bess, You Is My Woman Now" and then Porgy's leitmotif. That the final bars of music unite the lovers in sound, even as they seem lost to each other, testifies to Gershwin's affirmation that there could be no richer subject for an American opera than the lives of African Americans, in all their hope, heartbreak, and capacity for dramatic and musical expression.

TEN DAYS after *Porgy and Bess* opened on October 10 at New York's Alvin Theatre, Gershwin introduced his new opera to the public in the Sunday edition of the *New York Times*. The headline of his article, "Rhapsody in Catfish Row," could have applied to a walk-through of how the new work, dwarfing anything he had tackled before, came to be. But his statement, published on October 20, 1935, is an analysis of the opera's elements in sixteen spare, lucid, unlabeled paragraphs—most of them brief.

Genre. He starts with "folk opera," the label carried by *Porgy and Bess*. People in the opera "would sing folk music," Gershwin declares. But borrowing "original folk material" would have compromised his decision to compose a musical score "all of one piece." Therefore, he explains, "I wrote my own spirituals and folk songs"—meaning that *Porgy and Bess* unfolds to spirituals and folk songs by Gershwin, tuned to specific moments in the story.

Subject. The second paragraph turns to the work's subject, claiming "Negro life in America" as fresh territory for the operatic stage. Then Gershwin cites the attributes of that life: drama, humor, superstition, religious fervor, dancing, "and the irrepressible high spirits of the race." Touching these elements, he believes, has enabled him to create "a new form, which combines opera with theater": a blend made from the material he and Heyward have chosen.

Audience. The third paragraph identifies the public Gershwin intends to reach. Rather than following "the usual sponsors of opera in America," he has chosen to develop "something in American music that would appeal to the many rather than to the cultured few."

Locus. Gershwin's fourth paragraph holds that life in an African American community in Charleston, South Carolina, has given him a range of human inclination and behavior from "humor" to "tragedy." "Negroes as a race are ideal for my purpose," he explains, "because they express themselves not only by the spoken word but quite naturally by song and dance."

Humor, Casting, and Performance. The next three paragraphs cite elements fundamental to Gershwin's professional specialty: musical comedy. According to the fifth paragraph, the opera's humor flows "from the story" of *Porgy and Bess*, free of "gags" imported to draw laughs. The sixth cites three performers who play their roles with exemplary skills. They include John W. Bubbles as Sporting Life, a drug peddler "who is likable and believable and at the same time evil," and Todd Duncan (Porgy) and Anne Brown (Bess), who bring "intense dramatic value" to the music. He and his team, Gershwin explains, have been able to find these artists "because what we wanted from them lies in their race. And thus it lies in our story of their race." Then the seventh paragraph points to stage director Rouben Mamoulian and conductor Alexander Smallens: experts in coaching cast members and musicians to deliver their words and their music as if they were true denizens of Catfish Row.

Scale. In effect, the eighth paragraph claims Gershwin's responsibility for making the story of *Porgy and Bess* into an opera rather than a musical comedy or a series of sketches. He explains:

> When I wrote the *Rhapsody in Blue* I took "blues" and put them in a larger and more serious form. That was twelve years ago and the *Rhapsody in Blue* is still very much alive, whereas if I had taken the same themes and put them in songs they would have been gone years ago.

Plot Attributes. Gershwin's ninth paragraph deems *Porgy* as his own idea of an American tale made for the operatic stage. From the start he has found Heyward's novel a unique balance: "100 percent dramatic intensity," he puts it, "in addition to humor."

Medium–Subject Match. The tenth paragraph cites DuBose and Dorothy Heyward's creative engagement with *Porgy* before 1933, when Gershwin joined their project. Both had witnessed the advent and success of *Porgy* as a book (1925) and then as a play, which "audiences crowded the theater" to see over a two-year period: 1927–29.

Music: Songs. Gershwin's eleventh paragraph breaks fresh ground. Engaged so far with the background and properties of the opera, his statement now turns to songs: the core of his own music-making life. Songs, readers are reminded, can infuse the operatic stage with a matchless quality of lyric expression.

Songs: History. Following up on songs, Gershwin cites two examples from the past: the "song hits" in Verdi and in Bizet's *Carmen*. Then he adds a historical reminder: even a well-worn number such as "The Last Rose of Summer" got its start on the operatic stage.

Miscellaneous: Words and Music, Songwriting, Composition, Study. Weighed against the sharp focus of the first dozen paragraphs, the thirteenth is a mix. Starting with praise for American songwriters, Gershwin touts his opera's recitative for being "as close to the Negro inflection as possible," lauding his American colleagues for setting "words to music so that the music gives added expression to the words." Then come a confession and an affirmation of an earlier promise. Granting his use in the opera of "sustained symphonic music to unify entire scenes," he credits that skill to his own "further study in counterpoint and modern harmony."

Song Genres. Gershwin's fourteenth paragraph points to variety in the character of the opera's song lyrics. Two different lyricists, he explains, have written different kinds of words for his melodies: DuBose Heyward for "the native material," and Ira Gershwin for "most of the sophisticated songs."

Song Genres Explained, Attributes. In the last two paragraphs of this introduction, the fifteenth distinguishes "native" songs (folk styles) from "sophisticated" ones (numbers for the stage). And the sixteenth, harking back to the list's second paragraph—citing the work's subject—puts the goal and provenance of *Porgy and Bess* in a nutshell. It's an opera, readers are reminded, delivering "entertainment for the theater, with drama, humor, song, and dance"—all attributes of the African American culture that George Gershwin and DuBose Heyward have portrayed.

.   .   .

AVOIDING technical revelations, sociological claims, and exhortative flourishes, Gershwin's statement is the composer's reckoning of *Porgy and Bess*. Whatever moved him to introduce his magnum opus to the public with a gazetteer of its elements and anatomy, the result is a clarifying lens for regarding an opera fashioned over a decade of pondering, collaborating, studying, composing, and then enacting the results onstage.

33
___

PERFORMING PORGY AND BESS

EVEN AS GERSHWIN TOOK PART in coaching the *Porgy and Bess* players, all of whom had been chosen through auditions in which he had the final say, he stood ready to learn from their ideas. The opera's choral director, Eva Jessye, recalled how she and her chorus came to join the cast:

> My choir had just been barnstorming all through South Carolina, and for not very much money—we were barely making the train fare from town to town—and we'd come back to New York, where I was doing a radio program on South Carolina life. . . . I saw this notice in Film Daily looking for a black choir, and so we all went up and we auditioned. People from the Theatre Guild were there, I remember. We did the shout "Plenty Good Room," and danced all over the stage.

George Gershwin jumped up and shouted: "That's it! That's what I want." Gershwin, she added, "let us do what we knew how to do."[1]

Anne Wiggins Brown, who originated the role of Bess, recalled that Gershwin "never objected to changes in his music." She was in a position to know, having been directly involved in the opera's creation:

> He used me as a guinea pig and he tried everything and he would ask me, "Is this too high for a baritone?" "No, no, not if he doesn't stay up there too long," I would say. "How's this, should I change this note?" "No, no. As a matter of fact, I'd like to do it higher," would be my answer. I even made a few changes in "I Loves You Porgy," notes which fit my voice better and he would say, "That's good, let's use that."[2]

Brown was a twenty-one-year-old student at Juilliard when she read in a newspaper that Gershwin was interviewing singers for his opera. She wrote him a letter and two days later received a phone call inviting her to sing for him. Before the audition, she had the foresight to learn some facts about Gershwin.

> I found myself standing in the foyer of his apartment, bending over to look under the coat rack for a place to put my boots. "What are you looking for?" he asked politely. And then one of those crazy ideas popped into my head. I said without thinking, "Your roller skates!" George Gershwin was quiet for a few moments and then he laughed. He threw back his head and roared. "How did you know about my roller skates?" he said, still laughing. "Well, I read, you know."[3]

Expecting the session to last about half an hour that day, she ended up staying for almost two, singing art songs in French, German, and Russian and a spiritual, "A City Called Heaven." Then Gershwin played as much of the opera as he had composed, singing all the parts. When he asked her to sing "Summertime," "it just rolled out of my throat."[4]

In the weeks that followed, Brown auditioned for the directors of the Theatre Guild and again for Ira and Rose Gershwin. One day

Gershwin called to say, "Annie, I've just finished music for Clara. I want you to come and sing it for me."[5] Sometimes other singers joined Brown in Gershwin's apartment, but more often it was just the two of them, singing "songs, and duets, and trios as soon as the ink was dry on the paper." At the very least, the experience provided "good training for my sight-reading." It also mattered to her that he was investing so much of himself in an opera about black Americans.

> When I went to his apartment . . . he would play through the music. Then I would eat lunch with him, and he would sometimes, once or twice, invite me into his bed. Of course, I never went there. After lunch he would play the whole opera over again on his Hammond organ! And make all sorts of variations on the different themes. He would sing and he would ask me to sing; we had fun! . . . He was so proud of this music, it was his baby. It also expressed his acceptance of all forms, his love for the elements of the rhythm and the harmonies of black men.

When Gershwin offered her the opera's leading female role, Brown recalled,

> I had suspected for some time that he would say just that. Even so, it came as a surprise. "Bess is, in the original story, a very black woman," he said. "But I cannot see any reason why my Bess shouldn't have a *café au lait* complexion. Can you?" "No, no," I answered quickly. And gave him a big hug. Then I asked him, "what will you do if the Theatre Guild insists on engaging another singer for the Bess role?" "They'll have to do it over my dead body," he said.

Some time thereafter, over lunch at a café near the Alvin Theatre, where rehearsals were being held, the composer solemnly informed her that the opera, referred to as *Porgy* in all earlier conversations, would from now on be known as *Porgy and Bess*. Also, he told her that "from the beginning you have harassed me to find a place for Bess to sing 'Summertime.'" "It's the most beautiful melody in the whole opera," I said, "I love it." "Just keep still and listen now. I composed a trio for Lily and Serena and Maria for that spot in Act III but I have decided to drop the trio and let you sing your favorite melody.[6] It's very logical; I don't know why I didn't think of it before. Are you happy now, Miss Brown?" he said. I wouldn't allow myself to cry in front of him, so I said nothing.[7]

Todd Duncan, a decade older than Brown and a voice teacher at Howard University in Washington, D.C., was hired as the show's male lead very differently. According to Brown, she and soprano Abbie Mitchell, who was cast as Clara, were in Gershwin's apartment one day late in 1934 when Mitchell proposed Duncan as a candidate for Porgy. Duncan's classical backround had made him suspicious of Gershwin and what he fancied as "show business stuff," and at first he had no interest. But when Gershwin called to suggest an audition, he found it hard to say no. On a Sunday not long before Christmas 1934, he arrived at the door of Gershwin's apartment with a stack of music under his arm. He asked first to sing an Italian aria, which the composer accompanied from the sheet music.[8] Duncan recalled,

> I sang about eight bars, and I was standing beside him. He said, "Do you know this?" "Yes, I know it." "I want to look at your face when you sing." So I went around in the bow of the piano, and he played it, and looked at me while I was singing—he had memorized it that quickly! I sang the same eight bars, and he stopped me and asked, "Will you be my Porgy?" "Well," I said, "I don't know whether I could or not. I'd have to hear your music." He laughed. "Well, I think we can arrange for you to hear some of my music. Would you come back next Sunday and sing for some other people?"

A week later Duncan returned to New York with an accompanist, as well as his wife Gladys, for what was to be a two-way audition.

Singing for the Theatre Guild's board of directors, Duncan had expected to perform three or four songs but ended up singing much more—opera, Negro spirituals, German lieder, and French chansons. Then George and Ira "stood there with their awful, rotten, bad voices and sang the whole score," and Duncan found himself caught up in the flow of music.

> He just kept playing; they kept singing. He turned around and grinned. The more they played, the more beautiful I thought the music was. By the time twenty minutes or a half hour had passed I just thought I was in heaven. These beautiful melodies in this new idiom—it was something I had never heard.

Early in the run-through of Act II, the composer paused, turned to Duncan, and announced: "This is your great aria. This is going to make you famous." "It was a little ditty," thought Duncan about "I Got Plenty o' Nuttin'," but so infectious and so beautiful. "Well, they finally finished, and when he ended with 'I'm on My Way,' I was crying."

Later Gershwin coached Duncan on singing that banjo song. "This is a bitter song and you have to sing it with tongue-in-cheek; you have to sing it smiling all the time. Because what you're doing is making fun of . . . people who make money and to whom power and position is very important."[9] A pair of lines in the bridge section (lines over which the writers had "labored in pain") were the key: "I got no lock on the door, that's no way to be. / They can steal the rug from the floor, that's okay with me." Beyond the attitude that came with Porgy's role, since he had to sing the entire opera on his knees, Duncan would quickly run out of breath. He found it helped to sing this song lying on his back, "and that used to bring the house down; boy, it sure did! . . . Then I would rise up and they just wouldn't let me stop."

By the time staging rehearsals began in August, Brown and Duncan knew their parts almost perfectly. Duncan and his wife found an apartment near the Alvin Theatre, which allowed him and Brown to rehearse together. "We knew that this was going to be an important opera and we were professionals," he recalled. Most of the cast were highly trained as well, though some proved unschooled in certain ways of the world—unfamiliar, for example, with "happy dust." John W. ("Bubbles") Sublett, who played Sporting Life and who offered the chorus girls marijuana in spare moments, did know about happy dust, but nothing about reading music. When he arrived for rehearsals in August with his part barely explored, and clueless about how to learn it, his sketchy grasp of the role frustrated conductor Alexander Smallens. Infuriating, too, was that Bubbles did not feel bound by the production's rehearsal schedule. According to Oscar Levant, only the composer's presence at a rehearsal one day saved his place in the cast:

> Gershwin shared the opinion of Fred Astaire that the slim, dapper Negro was one of the great performers of the day and a dancer beyond compare. Moreover, he had shaped the part to fit Bubbles's talents. But Bubbles' negligence about rehearsals and promptness almost overbalanced his abilities, and on one occasion Smallens' exasperation caused him to fling down his baton and shout to [director] Mamoulian, "I'm sick of this waiting. We'll have to throw him out and get someone else." Gershwin bounded from his seat. "Throw him out?" he said. "You can't do that. Why, he's—he's the black Toscanini."[10]

Duncan described how Gershwin taught Bubbles "all the notes, all the rhythms, all the cues—with his feet. It was brilliant. And when he learned to dance it, he never made a mistake after that."

Duncan also singled out an unforgettable moment in one of the director's rigorous rehearsals. As Gershwin walked in and headed for the back of the darkened theater, where he usually sat to watch, sometimes eating peanuts or smoking a cigar, Mamoulian and his cast were addressing the moment in Act II where Serena prays over the ailing Bess.[11] The scene called for Porgy to sing the line "I think that maybe she gonna sleep now, a whole week gone and now she ain't no better," and he had to repeat it as many as ten times under the director's relentless scrutiny. The other participants, near exhaustion after what seemed an endless cycle of repetition, found themselves part of "the exact atmosphere required for the prayer," Duncan felt.

> Miss Elzy (Serena) went down on her knees as if her own mother had been ill for weeks; she felt the need of prayer. Two seconds of silence intervened that seemed like hours, and presently there rose the most glorious tones and wails with accompanying amens and hallelujahs for our sick Bess that I ever hope to experience. This particular scene should have normally moved into the scene of the Street Cries, but it did not. It stopped there. The piano accompaniment ceased, every actor (and there were sixty-five of them) had come out of his rest position, sitting at the edge of his seat and [Mamoulian] was standing before us quietly moving his inevitable cigar from one side of his mouth to the other, his face lighted to sheer delight in realization, and then, George Gershwin like a ghost from the dark rows of the Guild theatre appeared before the footlights. He simply could not stand it. He knew then, that he had put down on paper accurately and truthfully something from the depth of soul of a South Carolina Negro woman who feels the need of help and carries her troubles to her God.[12]

A NATIVE of Tiflis in the country of Georgia, Rouben Mamoulian had learned English only after mastering Armenian, Russian,

Georgian, French, German, and Latin. In his youth, as his affluent family moved to Paris and then back to his native city, he also
learned to play the violin. At Konstantin Stanislavsky's Moscow Art
Theater, he learned that drama was best served when the director's
conception of the work touched all its facets—story, music (if any),
movement, pace, visual elements—and blended them into a unified
whole. He embraced the practice of "stylization," in which a distinctive style of expression was devised and followed rigorously by
the players.

Mamoulian directed his first play in English in London in 1922.
The next year, he became codirector of the newly founded Eastman
School of Drama and Dramatic Action in Rochester, New York,
where he met Gershwin late in 1923. Author Paul Horgan, then
attending Eastman, described Mamoulian as a man of wide-ranging
talents who "knew more about the various contributing elements of
a stage production than any of the artists separately charged with
creating each. . . . more of music than the composer, more of painting than the painter, more of acting than the actor."[13]

In the spring of 1927, the Theatre Guild hired him to direct
the Heywards' *Porgy*.[14] Knowing little about the American South or
African American people, Mamoulian and his stage designer paid a
summer visit to Charleston, taking their measure of the place with
the help of contacts provided by DuBose Heyward. What he saw
there reminded him of Tiflis—the music, the hospitality of the residents, and a palpable link to the past. The "Negro life" he witnessed
fit his "favorite idea of stylized, rhythmic composition" for the
stage.[15] After cast members were chosen for the play, Mamoulian
was faced with the task of teaching them a vocabulary of motion
and behavior that he had devised himself. Much of it was "utterly
unrealistic," and it took the players a while to learn. But the director had discovered that "when inner emotions are genuine, then the
correctly stylized position is the most expressive one, and to the
audience it appears to be completely realistic."[16]

Critical reception for *Porgy* was excellent, and James Weldon Johnson wrote years later that the play "loomed high above every Negro drama that had ever been produced."[17] Late in 1933, when the Theatre Guild was choosing a director for the opera, Mamoulian and John Houseman were the leading candidates. By then Mamoulian had made his mark in Hollywood with such films as 1931's *Dr. Jekyll and Mr. Hyde*, 1932's *Love Me Tonight*, and 1933's *Queen Christina*, with Greta Garbo. Houseman, who had directed Gertrude Stein and Virgil Thomson's opera *Four Saints in Three Acts*, with an African American cast, met with Gershwin for two mornings, during which the composer played and sang the score. But as Gershwin wrote to Heyward—who favored Houseman[18]—the Guild decided that Mamoulian knew "more about music than any other [director] and might do a beautiful thing with the musicalization of the book," while Houseman "might be somewhat inexperienced to handle so huge a task."[19] When offered the job, Mamoulian at first expressed shock at the very idea of an opera based on *Porgy*, feeling that "the play was so pure and complete in its form . . . that any attempt to translate it into operatic form might spoil it." But on second thought he decided that if there was any composer who *could* manage such a transformation, it was George Gershwin.

Arriving in New York during the week of May 5, 1935, the director spent his first evening in town in Gershwin's apartment. "The brothers handed me a tall highball and put me in a comfortable leather armchair. George sat down at the piano while Ira stood over him like a guardian angel." Mamoulian remembered the electricity in the air, though each man was "trying to be nonchalant and poised." When George, with Ira sitting next to him at the piano, unleashed the opening burst of instrumental music, Mamoulian found it so exciting—"so full of color and so provocative in its rhythm"—that "after this first piano section was over, I jumped out of my armchair and interrupted George to tell him how much I liked it."

When my explosion was over . . . they both blissfully closed their eyes before they continued with the lovely "Summertime" song. . . . To describe George's face while he sang "Summertime" is something that is beyond my capacity as a writer. . . . It was touching to see how [Ira] . . . would look from him to me with half-open eyes and pantomime with a soft gesture of his hand, as if saying, "*He* did it. Isn't it wonderful? Isn't *he* wonderful?" George would frequently take his eyes away from the score and covertly watch me and my reaction to the music while pretending that he wasn't really doing it at all. It was very late into the night before we finished the opera and sometimes I think that in a way that was the best performance I ever heard.[20]

Not long after this charmed evening, Mamoulian was back in Hollywood. The first vocal rehearsals began early in July in the studio of Alexander Steinert, the musical coach. Gershwin's score proved demanding to learn, but the cast included musicians whose background and training had readied them for an operatic challenge. Also on hand as assistant coach was the veteran composer and songwriter J. Rosamond Johnson, who had helped to supervise the musical side of the play *Porgy*, and Eva Jessye, whose choir had a substantial amount of music to master.[21] Mamoulian's rehearsals began on August 26, with the director in the center of the Alvin Theatre's stage, conductor Smallens to his right, and pianist Steinert next to the conductor. Principals and choristers were seated around these three figures. For seven hours a day during the next two weeks, the director taught the players their movements. The second week of September saw an empty stage turned into a "skeleton" of the Catfish Row set by the Russian designer Serge Soudeikine; the piano was lowered into the pit, Mamoulian and Smallens moved into theater seats, and the cast began to enact the drama.

Music critic Irving Kolodin, who had signed on for a substantial magazine article and was attending rehearsals regularly, was struck not only by Mamoulian's technical grasp of music, but by his deep understanding of what music can communicate. He always had a copy of the score open in front of him at rehearsals, and he showed "a precise concern for measures and accents in the music," as well as for the meaning of the words. As Mamoulian rehearsed the chorus, Kolodin watched each singer learning to act as "a genuine participant in the drama." The director had established

> in the minds of the chorus, the feeling that only an accident of fate kept them from being principal factors, rather than . . . by-standers in the drama. Any one of the men could have been Robbins, slain by a blow from the drunken Crown; any one of the women, the widowed S[ere]na. Not only Jake was drowned in the storm; each of the fishermen might have met the same ending, and the bereavement of Clara was the bereavement of all their wives.[22]

Yet even as he coordinated the movement of large groups of performers, Mamoulian also warned against striking regimented poses and standing around "like a chorus." To the company as a whole, and particularly the principals, Mamoulian said during the early rehearsals: "Do the thing that comes to your mind—if I don't like it, I'll tell you." For example:

> When the drunken Crown is being taunted by his fellow crap-shooters, Crown's interpreter first portrayed his mounting rage by sweeping gestures. Mamoulian suggested that he remain quiet—as though brooding on the thought "Who are these fellows to make fun of me, the invincible Crown?"—before hurling his command to "Shut Up!" The change in effectiveness was amazing, and the performers instinctively cringed under the impact of Crown's transition from silence to fury.

Still, Mamoulian's ideas were always

> susceptible to check or alteration . . . by Smallens, who supervised the tempo of each bit as it was rehearsed. Thus there would be no conflict when the singers became responsible wholly to his baton. But Smallens' function at the rehearsals was by no means confined to tempo. His constant presence permitted him to enforce his ideas—regarding the interpretation of the score, the technical matters of singing difficult passages accurately in pitch and with the rhythmic emphasis he desired—more effectively than he could have in a few general rehearsals crowded into the end of the preparatory period. The capacity of the personnel for absorbing ideas and reproducing them was only exceeded by the complete concentration brought to their tasks by the two directors.

Porgy and Bess had its premiere performance on September 30 in Boston; by then, Mamoulian and company knew that cuts in the score were necessary. The piano-scene opening, for example, came to be judged a distraction from the mood-setting tableau, so the character of Jasbo Brown was dropped and his piano music shortened. Soon after the Broadway opening, that entire interlude was eliminated, so that the orchestral introduction moved directly to "Summertime." Another reason to cut became clear in Boston, when the first performance ran for some four hours.[23]

But perhaps the cast's most unforgettable performance had already taken place before the company moved to Boston, when singers and orchestra performed Gershwin's score for the first time in a private read-through in Carnegie Hall. For Anne Brown, the occasion felt like a dream come true:

> I remember so well that day—after weeks of rehearsals . . . when we had the first full orchestral rehearsal of the finished opera with

soloists and chorus on the stage of Carnegie Hall, hired by the Theatre Guild for just that purpose. When the echoes of the last chords of *Porgy and Bess* had disappeared into the nearly empty hall, we were—all of us—in tears. It had been so moving. . . . George Gershwin stood on the stage as if in a trance for a few minutes. Then, seeming to awaken, he said, "This music is so wonderful, so beautiful that I can hardly believe that I have written it myself."[24]

JUDGING
PORGY AND BESS

IF THERE WAS ANY DOUBT about the New York public's anticipation of *Porgy and Bess*, it was addressed by an article that appeared in the *Times* on October 1, 1935, headlined "Gershwin's Opera Makes Boston Hit":

> Both musically and theatrically, George Gershwin's and the Theatre Guild's new folk opera, "Porgy and Bess," which had its first performance at the Colonial here this evening, was an event. An audience which assembled, uncertain whether they should find a heavy operatic work or something more closely resembling musical comedy, discovered a form of entertainment which stands midway between the two. The immediate response was one of enthusiasm that grew rather than diminished as the evening progressed.

"An extremely approving audience" had made its way to the Colonial Theatre for the premiere, observed an anonymous reviewer for the *Boston Globe*, and "only a few minutes were required to bring waves of spontaneous handclapping, and a phenomenon rare in the theatre: repeated cries of 'Bravo!'"[1] In the *Christian Science Monitor*, L. A. Sloper credited Mamoulian with "welding music, drama, art and dance movement as to enhance the effect of each and to give a single harmonious effect to the whole. . . . This production may point the way to a correlation of the arts, dreamed of by Wagner but never realized by him or by any of his successors. The theater has refused to come to the opera. Perhaps the opera must come to the theater."[2]

Perhaps no Boston reviewer made a more arresting claim for the opera's impact as a theatrical work, though, than Elliot Norton, drama critic of the *Post*. *Porgy and Bess* struck him as

> an effort to transfuse vital, black blood into the somewhat hardened arteries of conventional opera, with the idea that the public at large might like to see that there is life in the lovely old lady. It is an impressive demonstration. There is life there, all right. On the stage of the Colonial the lady sat up, opened her eyes, smiled and capered gaily. . . . The way in which [actors] have been instructed, directed, molded into a vast, responsive unit is little short of thrilling.[3]

Warren Storey Smith, the *Post*'s music critic, took what he judged to be Gershwin's varying musical styles as a sign of artistic immaturity. On the other hand, he had nothing but praise for the performance, which in fact he ascribed more to the singers' ethnicity than to their artistry.[4]

The *Porgy and Bess* that opened in New York on October 10, shortened somewhat from the Boston version, made the Alvin Theatre the focus of a true sense of occasion. New York's critical brain trust, music and drama critics alike, turned out en masse. Pieces were written too for the next Sunday's papers and, in the days to come, for weekly journals like *Time* and *Newsweek*, plus extended articles for such monthly publications as *Stage* and *Theatre Arts*. Beyond this chorus of critical judgments, both Heyward and Gershwin wrote about their opera while it was brand-new. Heyward's statement appeared as a lengthy, engaging tale in *Stage* magazine, tracing how the endeavor had unfolded, and registering admiration for his collaborator's gift for transposing the musical practices of a southern American culture to the operatic stage.[5] As noted, George Gershwin's piece for the *New York Times* was the composer's statement of the elements and properties of *Porgy and Bess*.[6]

Brooks Atkinson, drama critic for the *Times*, reported that even as he wrote his own review, the paper's music critic, Olin Downes, was "beetling his brow in the adjoining cubicle," the sound of "his typewriter clatter" carrying "an authoritative ring."[7] "Let it be said at once," announced Atkinson, "that Mr. Gershwin has contributed something glorious to the spirit of the Heywards' community legend," for music has brought a "glow of personal feeling" to a play short on that quality. Downes judged the operatic Gershwin as good as ever at inventing melodies, crediting him with "an instinctive appreciation of the melodic glides and nuances of Negro song, and an equally personal tendency toward rich and exotic harmony." Indeed, Downes was too close a listener and too conscientious a thinker to share Warren Storey Smith's view that an opera composer who "mixes styles" has committed an artistic misdeed. Rather,

> Here and there flashes of real contrapuntal ingenuity combine themes in a manner apposite to the grouping and action of the characters on the stage. In ensemble pieces rhythmical and contrapuntal devices work well. Harmonic admixtures of Stravinsky and Puccini are obvious but not particularly disconcerting. . . . [Gershwin] makes effective use of "spirituals," not only by harmony sometimes "modal" but by the dramatic combination of the massed voices and the wild exhortations of individual singers. . . . The prayer of Serena for Bess is eloquent, original and the most poetical passage in the whole work.[8]

W. J. Henderson, music critic of the *Sun*, perceived that *Porgy and Bess* broke new ground that deserved recognition as belonging to a true "folk opera":

> Mr. Gershwin is at his best when he is writing songs with a touch of jazz in them, with ragtime rhythms, harmonies that sting, choruses which echo the "shout," the camp meeting hymn and the spiritual. The high level of the jazz rhythm is reached with Porgy's song in the first scene of the second act, "I got plenty o' nuttin." This was without question the "song hit" of the night.⁹

And Lawrence Gilman of the *Herald Tribune* was also impressed and moved. A decade earlier, he had resisted the spell that the *Rhapsody in Blue* cast over many of his colleagues, but now he had no doubt of *Porgy and Bess*'s impact on theatergoers:

> When last night's audience, at the close of Act II, broke into an outburst of applause elicited by the frenzy of the terrified gathering of Negroes shrinking from the storm, praying, shouting, swaying, moaning, beseeching "Captain Jesus," their voices rising on the crest of an infuriated orchestra above the shriek and tumult of the hurricane, it was evident that Mr. Gershwin, in the finest pages of his score, had given us something suspiciously like an authentic folk-opera in an unmistakably American vein.¹⁰

Gilman perceived that up to now Gershwin had "written nothing even remotely approaching the choral passages in this work, the music of anguish and supplication and despair and faith. Here there is music of a dramatic passion and intensity and power which set the climactic passages of the opera in a new organic continuity with the emotional patterns of the play." He took less kindly, however, to such "sure-fire rubbish" as the love duets "Bess, You Is My Woman Now" and "I Loves You, Porgy."

The anonymous review that appeared in *Time* magazine on October 21 made a confident claim for the opera's accessibility: "Negroes were assembled who knew no stuffy traditions, had true feeling for rhythm. Mamoulian's hand was particularly evident in the big mass groupings, in the way he kept the action in pace with the music. The Negroes in prayer suggested an entire down-trodden race. . . . Porgy and Bess is not 'grand,' is not intended for the musical few. . . . Laymen left [the] folk opera humming with satisfaction."[11] A piece in the weekly *Musical America* by its editor, A. Walter Kramer, closed with an expression of gratitude for Gershwin from "all who have been awaiting just such an effort by an American composer":

> With Porgy and Bess he has expressed himself in the terms of a story taken from the life of his own times, in a section of his country, and has pointed the way for other composers to follow. American opera must not be legendary, it must not be anything but illustrative of American life. Porgy and Bess meets that requirement in its libretto. George Gershwin has fulfilled it superbly in his music.[12]

As critics in Boston and New York weighed in, friends and acquaintances sent congratulations to the composer by telegraph and mail. One telegram that Gershwin loved especially, according to his brother, arrived from a pair of cast members on the day of the Boston opening: "MAY THE CURTAIN FALL WITH THE BANG OF SUCCESS FOR YOU AS THE SUN RISES IN THE SUNSHINE OF YOUR SMILE BUCK AND BUBBLES."[13] A letter from Richard Rodgers, not known for emotional displays, must have pleased and gratified his fellow composer for the stage. Before the opera went into production, Gershwin had previewed some of its numbers at the piano for his colleague, and Rodgers lost no time in conveying his response to the whole work the day after it opened:

If you ever got a sincere letter in your life, this is it, and it's a pretty difficult one to write. There's no sense in my telling you how beautiful your score is; you know that. But I can tell you that I sat there transfixed for three hours. I've loved the tunes ever since you played them for us here one night but I never thought I'd sit in a theatre and feel my throat being stopped up time after time. Let them never say that Mr. Gershwin can't be tender; you kicked hell out of me, for one. I won't dribble on. I just want you to know that one of us is very happy this morning over your success last night. Yours sincerely, Dick[14]

Further into its run the new opera was assessed in the November–December issue of *Modern Music*, a forum for contemporary American composers, by Virgil Thomson, whose *Four Saints in Three Acts*, with a black cast, had created a stir during the preceding year.[15] While Thomson found the "astonishingly fine" melodic invention in *Porgy and Bess* "abundant and indefatigable," he found the results weakened by "being tied up with" harmonies from Tin Pan Alley which, to his way of thinking, limited Gershwin's expressive resources. And he missed a crucial distinction in the opera's treatment of race when he wrote that whenever Gershwin "has to get on with the play he uses spoken dialogue," and that "it would have been better if he had stuck to that all the time." He seems unaware too that the white characters in the opera never sing, while the black characters both sing *and* speak.[16] Nevertheless, to this composer-critic "the exciting thing is that after all those years the writing of music is still not a routine thing" to Gershwin. Fancying *Porgy and Bess* as "a real live baby, all warm and dripping and friendly," Thomson likened Gershwin's composition to its hero, "who didn't have a leg to stand on but who had some radiance in his face and a good deal of love in his heart."

Writing for *Stage* magazine, music critic Marcia Davenport began with a warm endorsement of *Porgy and Bess*'s qualities as "an honest-to-God opera," which she defined as a "drama in musical form, realizing itself in an indissoluble integration of music, emotion, and thought." For her, the essential element was Gershwin's melodic flow, infused with "direct, natural, and spontaneous beauty," and fueling his music's "pulsating emotion," realized through "the equipment of a concientious and commanding composer." By her lights the wake scene in Act I was one "to glorify any opera":

> Quite aside from the tension built up by inspired grouping, lighting, acting, and direction, the music pours out a wail of mourning, a torrent of despair. It mounts vitally and tensely, its rhythms Negroid, its soaring, minor cadences yearningly Hebraic, to the point where Serena begins to sing "My Man's Gone Now." And that is the point where this opera can stand comparison with anything written in many, many years. Forbiddingly difficult, Miss Ruby Elzy sings this dirge in a high-piercing soprano voice that embodies every shade of difference between the black throat and white. The burden is a wail, a minor arpeggio for which the composer's direction is *glissando*—something that demands a violin rather than a voice. The singer has it. She distills heartbreak from this extraordinary piece of music.[17]

In the December issue of *Stage*, Isaac Goldberg, who had contemplated George Gershwin's accomplishments in print more analytically and historically than anyone else, ventured that an artistic amalgam so culturally varied could not have been created elsewhere in the world:

> A Russian and [an] Armenian had, respectively, prepared the scenery and the production; two Nordics, man and wife, had provided the novel and the play upon which the libretto was based; two Jews, brothers, had joined talents for lyrics and music, the labor of George being, naturally, the most considerable single expenditure

of energy that had been brought to bear upon the venture. A cast of Negro singers and actors had interpreted this collaborative inspiration. It was an American symbol.[18]

The last review considered here appeared in the January 1936 issue of *Opportunity: A Journal of Negro Life*, a monthly academic publication sponsored by the New York–based National Urban League.[19] The author, Francis Hall Johnson, was a composer, violinist, arranger, and the founder and conductor of a choir known for its interpretation of African American folk song. He was also known for his experience in bringing spiritual singing to the Broadway stage, first as arranger and director of music for the 1930–31 *The Green Pastures*, which enjoyed a 640-performance run, and then as author, composer, and arranger for *Run, Little Children*, a "Negro Folk Drama" with music that ran for 126 performances in 1933.

In *Porgy and Bess*, Hall Johnson found a disproportion between unity and variety. The audience, he believed, was "confronted with a series of musical episodes which, even if they do not belong together, could be made to appear as if they do by a better handling of the musical connecting tissue." Johnson also agreed with a number of New York's other critics in judging Gershwin's use of recitative inept. "The Mendelssohn of *Elijah* or the Strauss of *Salomé* would be excellent school-masters for Mr. Gershwin in this subject of *recitativo*. Even better, for his current needs, would have been a perusal of the freer verse-lines of any of the Negro spirituals, wherein the significance of every word is immeasurably heightened by its tonal investiture." This composer also found Mamoulian's stage direction unsympathetic at every turn:

Will the time ever come when a colored performer on a Broadway stage can be subtle, quiet or even silent? . . . Must the light revues always be hot, fast and *loud*, and the serious pieces always profane, hysterical and *louder?* . . . Why does Clara have to *scream* the lullaby to her baby in the middle of the noisome courtyard of Catfish Row where only a drunk could sleep? . . . Why does Porgy have to *bawl out* his contentment, his new-found, inward happiness,—like a young and fiery captain of Hussars brandishing his sword before his men about to rush into battle?

From Hall Johnson's perspective, the redeeming force in *Porgy and Bess* was "the intelligent pliability of the large Negro cast," who were "able to infuse enough of their own natural racial qualities into the proceedings to invest them with a convincing semblance of plausibility." Johnson cited a basic quality existing in "genuine Negro music," namely "the quality of utter simplicity—in theme and in style."

It is only in the singing of large groups of Negroes that a contrapuntal or harmonic complexity may occasionally seem to be present, and this illusion is due to the simple approach of the individual singers. Each sings his part as he feels it. The result is musical because each contrapuntal part keeps constantly in mind the announced theme; it sounds complicated because the creator of each part is not bothering himself at all about the elaborate improvisation his neighbor may be preferring at the same moment. But the fundamental idea of simplicity is still active.

As Johnson saw it, "It Ain't Necessarily So" proved "so un-Negroid, in thought and structure, that even Bubbles cannot save it." It was impossible to believe that Sporting Life "could be so entirely liberated from that superstitious awe of Divinity which even the most depraved southern Negro never quite loses." But nevertheless in two duets—"Bess, You Is My Woman Now" and "What You Want Wid Bess"—Gershwin, he believed, caught "a real racial strain."

But even considering the encumbrances that "American Folk Opera has had to struggle up under," Johnson, who attended the production four times, ultimately decided that *Porgy and Bess* had "turned out surprisingly well," affording "quite adequate fare for the average uncritical audiences without too much interest either in opera or in Negroes."

COMPOSER OF
PORGY AND BESS

BY THE END OF NOVEMBER 1935, some six weeks after *Porgy and Bess* debuted in New York, Gershwin and three friends were on vacation aboard the Grace Line's *Santa Paula*, a cruise ship bound for the Caribbean. Members of the traveling party included philanthropist Edward Warburg, a cousin of Kay Swift's ex-husband and cofounder of George Balanchine's American Ballet, and Marshall Field III, from the Chicago department store family, an investment banker, publisher, and breeder of horses. The apparent organizer of the excursion was New York psychiatrist Gregory Zilboorg, and—if Gershwin is counted in their number—all three of his companions were patients of his. Russian-born Zilboorg had entered Gershwin's life through Swift, who began therapy with him early in 1934 to help her deal with the complications of her relationship with Gershwin. She had thought highly enough of her psychiatrist to recommend him to the composer, who seems to have welcomed the idea as an opportunity to enhance his self-knowledge as he shouldered the artistic challenge of composing an opera—while also unsure, himself, of where his relationship with Kay would lead. Indeed, during the spring of 1935, with his operatic score complete, and engaged with the task of orchestrating it, Gershwin booked daily sessions with Zilboorg, Monday through Friday, for at least one week in April.[1] A week later, however, the doctor canceled these appointments in a letter of apology to Gershwin explaining why he would "be unable to see you as we planned," and adding that he would not resume his "full schedule until October first." "Should you still wish to try and be analyzed" at that time, he advised, "we shall be in a better position to start working unperturbed."[2]

According to Warburg, mornings aboard the cruise ship began with individual sessions with the doctor, followed by a breakfast meeting at which, in violation of his profession's ethics, Zilboorg openly discussed what each had divulged to him during their "private" sessions. One stop on the group's itinerary was Mexico City, where they attended a party that included prominent Mexican artists—painters David Siqueiros, Miguel Covarrubias, and Diego Rivera, and composer Carlos Chavez—and the Japanese-American visitor Isamu Noguchi, who had sculpted a bust of Gershwin some years earlier. The composer was not called to the piano as often took place during gatherings of this kind. Instead Zilboorg, who was fluent in Spanish, steered the company into an extended conversation about politics.[3]

Gershwin's presence aboard the *Santa Paula* proved newsworthy enough that when the ship docked in New York on December 17, reporters were there to greet them. The *Post* noted the presence of *Porgy and Bess* cast members on the pier, perhaps as a means of luring more customers to the Alvin Theatre: "A band, wearing red uniforms, with a boy beating a huge drum labeled 'Charleston Orphan Band,' burst into Gershwin's own music as the composer crossed the gangplank from the Grace liner Santa Paula, while the entire Negro cast of his folk opera, 'Porgy and Bess,' cheered and sang." Some weeks later Gershwin wrote to Elizabeth Allan, a Hollywood actress he had dated in New York in 1934, that the fall cruise had been "fun and educational":

No, I didn't fight with Eddie or even the Doc. We all got along 'splendid.' Much sight-seeing, traveling for 10 days at an average height of about 500 ft., seeing all the churches (but no synagogues), looking, but in vain, for the Mexican beauties one hears about, listening to the music but finding it difficult to get anyone to play anything away from 6/8 time. Spent a great deal of time with charming fat Diego Rivera & charming lovely Mrs. Diego Rivera [the artist Frida Kahlo]. Made color pencil portraits of them both.[4]

Box-office receipts for *Porgy and Bess* were declining by now. Ticket prices had been reduced from $4.40 to $3.30, and the Theatre Guild had tried to save money by cutting the size of the orchestra, but the musicians' union had balked. Ira, who had a new show almost ready to open—the *Ziegfeld Follies of 1936*, for which Vernon Duke had written the music—offered to waive his royalties for a couple of weeks, and George had already agreed to cut his royalties in half. Finally, on January 25, *Porgy and Bess* ended its 124-performance run in New York. But the company opened two evenings later at the Forrest Theatre in Philadelphia, the first leg in a tour that also took the production to Pittsburgh, Chicago, Detroit, and Washington.

As the new year 1936 arrived, with no desirable musical comedy prospects in sight, Gershwin fashioned a Suite from *Porgy and Bess* for symphony orchestra, a shortened take apparently intended more as a complement to the original than as a condensation of it. Some music cut from the opera in Boston gained new life in the Suite's five movements: "Catfish Row" (a musical précis of Act I, scene 1), "Porgy Sings" (Act II, scene 1), "Fugue" (a slice of the first scene's fight music), "Hurricane" (Act II, scene 3), and "Good Morning, Brother" (mostly material in Act III, scene 3). The Suite was premiered in Philadelphia on January 21 by the Philadelphia Orchestra, conducted by Alexander Smallens. Thus, even as *Porgy and Bess*'s place in the theater was being established, Gershwin had taken a first step to add its music to his concert repertory—and to his conducting repertory, as well. The composer led the Suite himself at its second performance, on February 9 in Washington's Constitution Hall with the National Symphony Orchestra, where he also served as piano soloist for the *Concerto in F.* After a similar concert on March 1 with the St. Louis Symphony, only six more performances of the Suite are known to have taken place during his lifetime.

Elsie Finn of the *Philadelphia Record* had deemed the Suite's premiere historic. To her way of thinking the new composition "bridged the chasm between Duke Ellington and John Sebastian Bach for once and all time." Indeed, this critic fancied that by taking "Harlem by one hand and the world of classical music by the other," Gershwin had joined them "in a marriage that should end their lengthy feud forever."[5] Some ten days later the *Washington Times* reviewer had good words to say about the composer's conducting: "If anyone went to the concert yesterday afternoon at Constitution Hall with any misgivings as to George Gershwin's ability as a conductor because of the published report that 'it's like a croquet player taking up baseball,' this delusion was soon dispelled by the masterly manner in which he conducted the National Symphony Orchestra," the critic reported. And the Suite's "hurricane music, as a purely descriptive piece, is quite vivid, ranking high with the attempts of many other composers in picturing storm scenes."[6] To Ray C. B. Brown, music critic of the *Washington Post*, "this suite is sturdy stuff, essentially music for the theater, highly vitalized and dramatically potent. Its colors are glaring, and its rhythms intense to the point of savagery, yet there is no crudeness in the application of the colors and the instrumentation is consistently skillful."[7]

An article by Marcia Davenport in the March 1936 issue of *McCall's* magazine brings a music critic's judgment and a novelist's engagement with human nature to her view that Gershwin was an "authentic creative musical genius" who, improbably, had "come up through the clattery medium of Tin Pan Alley."[8] Her words offer an engaging sketch of his singular character and artistry:

> It is easy to see in the smartly-tailored, luxuriously-housed darling of the gods the grimy urchin on roller-skates who once belonged to a gang down near Brooklyn Bridge and talked some of the argot you can currently hear in *Dead End*.[9] At the same time you see clearly that the earnest musician speaking of his work, or showing you his collection of Picasso, Derain, Renoir and Utrillo, is passionately devoted to these things, and not a mere acquirer of them as badges of success or from ulterior desires for their luster. . . . He always has time to be cordial, he is perfectly accessible, unlike most people so sought after, and his smiling, blue-jowled face, with its protruding lower jaw and inevitable cigar is to be seen bending over the keyboards in all the houses he visits. And he visits a lot, for he loves life and everything that goes with it. . . . If somebody should steal one of his unpublished ideas he would shrug and write something else.

Early in April, still seeking a worthy Broadway proposition for him and Ira, Gershwin authorized Hollywood agent Arthur Lyons to negotiate on their behalf a songwriting deal with RKO and Universal—a process that wore on for more than two months before a contract with Pandro Berman and RKO was finally agreed to. Whereupon Ira bubbled over with questions for his boyhood pal Yip Harburg, now a lyricist in Hollywood: "Do they work you hard? I see you're on your third picture. Is it fun? What do you do nights? Do you have to report to the studio daily? That's the sort of thing I'd like to know. . . . Write me reams. Well, two pages, anyway—but single space."[10] Any speculation that Gershwin's operatic venture had dampened his own enthusiasm for music less than highbrow was brushed aside in a June 22 telegram to Archie Selwyn of Goldwyn Pictures: "Am out to write hits."[11] By June 26, the Gershwins were committed to writing songs for two films for RKO, each on a sixteen-week contract, with the first earning them $55,000 and the second $70,000. Selwyn, who helped to negotiate the final contract, informed them that a third film would most likely follow, to be produced by Samuel Goldwyn.[12]

But the Gershwins wouldn't be ready to leave New York for the West Coast until August. Moreover, well before the spring of that year, George had reengaged with his painting. On April 22, New York's Society of Independent Artists sponsored a show of new work at Grand Central Palace, in which Gershwin, the best known of the exhibitors, displayed two recent canvases.[13] On May 7, he played the *Concerto in F* and the *Rhapsody in Blue* with the Boston Pops Orchestra led by Arthur Fiedler, and conducted his Suite from *Porgy and Bess*. Journalist Morris Hastings, who attended a rehearsal, wrote that at one point the composer "jumped down from the stage where he had been rehearsing his Piano Concerto with the orchestra" and marveled to Hastings, a total stranger: "that music wears well, doesn't it?" When the journalist, after agreeing, asked him what he was working on now, Gershwin replied that he was "just writing light songs" for a musical. And then he explained that it was "just as difficult to write popular music as it is to write serious music":

> I work hard to find a good theme for a popular song. I try to get one that doesn't sound like all the others, and then I like to put a little twist into the song that will make it "different." . . . I never want to fall into the rut of writing only serious music or only popular music. I do want to be sure, though, that if I'm writing serious music it is serious music, and the other way around.[14]

That summer, the management of Lewisohn Stadium scheduled a pair of all-Gershwin concerts conducted by Alexander Smallens, on the evenings of July 9 and 10. After the orchestra opened with *An American in Paris*, Gershwin appeared as the soloist in the *Con-*

certo in F, and this was followed by the evening's artistic highlight: nine selections from *Porgy and Bess,* sung by Todd Duncan, Anne Brown, Ruby Elzy, and members of the Eva Jessye Choir.[15] The program closed with Gershwin at the piano for the *Rhapsody in Blue.* Reviews of the July 9 concert, which was broadcast, had little but praise for the music and its performance, but the attendance fell far short of expectations—most likely because the temperature that day in New York reached a record 115 degrees. The next day, which topped off at 100 degrees and included a lightning storm during that evening's concert, drew a disappointing crowd of 4,500.[16]

But if the Lewisohn Stadium concerts were less than triumphant, the one remaining engagement on Gershwin's schedule before California proved to be riotous. Taking place on Saturday, July 25, at Chicago's outdoor Ravinia Park, the concert offered an all-Gershwin program with the Chicago Symphony Orchestra: *An American in Paris,* led by Bill Daly, whom Gershwin had brought with him from New York; Gershwin as soloist in the *Concerto in F* and the *Rhapsody in Blue*; and Gershwin conducting the Suite from *Porgy and Bess.* The audience turnout—more than 7,000— overwhelmed the facility. Headlines recount the ruckus: "Ravinia Committee Busy Restoring Flower Beds and Lawn Trampled by Crowds," "Ravinia Crowds Give Up Day to Hear Gershwin / Arrive in Morning to Make Sure of Unreserved Seats; Many Socialites Disappointed," "Tin-Pandemonium" ("the greatest night of Ravinia's history, so far as volume of interest can designate it"). A review in the *Chicago Herald* measured the glut of attendees and gauged their mood:

> It was the largest audience in the park's thirty-odd years of history and the best-humored. For there were seats for only 1,400 in the pavilion and for 2,000 more on the benches. Late comers—and anybody arriving an hour before the time set for the concert's beginning was a late comer—raided the new refectory for chairs to place

in the walks and on the lawns until stopped by the police. Then they broke into the old restaurant and carried off chairs, benches, tables, discarded props of the opera—anything that could be converted into a seat—until these doors too were locked, and youngsters of either sex climbed to vantage points in convenient trees.[17]

Two weeks after the Ravinia concert, on August 8, George, Ira, and Leonore flew to California. George's departure was remembered by Kay Swift as a poignant end to a romantic and musical relationship that had persisted, on and off, since the latter 1920s. "He and Ira went to the airport separately. George and I went in a taxi. We had decided we were not going to see each other or write and see how it went and if it would be a happy arrangement. We kept everything cheery and bright. He laughed and talked about the picture. We said goodbye and he walked up the ramp." George and Ira, each in a natty business suit, were photographed as they boarded the plane. That final glimpse of George included "a mark around his head which was a deep groove from a straw hat that was too small for him." When he waved the hat before boarding, "all I could see," Swift recalled, "was the groove that went around his head like an Indian headband. . . . I knew for sure I'd never see him again. I didn't know why, but I knew that was all. That was it."[18]

HOLLYWOOD SONGWRITER I:

SHALL WE DANCE (1936–37)

ON THEIR ARRIVAL IN CALIFORNIA, the Gershwin brothers' priorities were to start writing songs for an Astaire-Rogers picture that was being called *Stepping Toes,* and to find a place to live. While Leonore went house-hunting, a piano was moved into their suite at the Beverly-Wilshire Hotel, and George and Ira got to work. With no script to guide them—just a story outline—they first took a crack at a number reflecting mindless rapture, "Hi-Ho!" Ira explained the setup: "Fred Astaire sees on a Paris kiosk the picture-poster of Ginger Rogers, an American girl then entertaining in Paris, and immediately feels: THIS IS SHE! He dances through the streets, extolling to everyone the beauty and virtues of this girl whom he has never met, but whose picture he sees pasted on walls and kiosks everywhere." Director Mark Sandrich admired the new number, but costs for the Parisian sets would have been prohibitive, and the idea was scrapped. "So the song has been unknown," Ira recalled, "except to a few of our friends, like Oscar Levant, Harold Arlen, and S. N. Behrman, who were around at the time, and to a few others who in the years since have learned of its existence."[1] George's piano accompaniment for this number is realized in fuller detail than that of almost any Gershwin song published in his day, the right hand answering the singer's exclamations with a playful figure akin to a hiccup of irrepressible joy.

The hotel suite came also to be the worksite for another song in an offbeat vein. A spring evening earlier that year had found the brothers "musically kidding around by exaggerating the lifts and plunges and *luftpauses* of the Viennese waltz" in George's New York apartment. Their antics appealed to Vincente Minnelli, a producer and director friend who had dropped by that evening. Now Minnelli wired them at their hotel to ask if they could complete "the Straussian take-off," which he thought might work in a show he was assembling. Taking a break from their film assignment, the brothers promptly finished the waltz, composed in the voice of a crotchety purist whose love of Strauss waltzes is matched only by his disdain for American popular music. In December 1936, "By Strauss" was performed in New York in Minnelli's revue *The Show Is On*.[2]

Within a week of their arrival, George and Ira had attended their first local ASCAP meeting, and by the second week they had found an appealing house at 1019 North Roxbury Drive in Beverly Hills. To bring the spacious blank walls to life George wired his assistant in New York, Zena Hannenfeldt, asking that favorite paintings in his collection be sent through the Budworth Company, "who are very experienced in shipping pictures so they will not be damaged in any way." His choices included works of Picasso (*Absinthe Drinker*), Gauguin (*Self-Portrait*), Utrillo (*Fishermen Houses*), Modigliani (*Portrait of Doctor* and *Woman's Head*), Rousseau (*Ile de la Cité*), Siqueiros (*Mexican Children*), Thomas Hart Benton (*Burlesque*), Chagall (*Rabbi* and *Slaughter House*), and Max Jacob (*Religious Festival*), along with Gershwin's *Portrait of Grandfather*. His own painting materials followed days later.[3]

George described the paintings' new home approvingly in a letter to Mabel Schirmer:

We finally found a house that is really lovely. It is in Beverly Hills and has many charming things about it, not the least of which are a swimming pool and a tennis court. It is a nice spacious, cheery house with a fine workroom. The living room is very large, white walls and a fine Steinway piano. The furnishings aren't all to our taste but then—you can't have everything, can you?

Ira and I have been doing a little work on some songs, but we haven't really begun to dig in. We are waiting for the script to be put into better shape. However, with the little start that we have, we feel quite confident that we won't be stuck. We've had some very gay times out here already with the Jerome Kerns, Sam Behrmans, Moss Hart, Oscar Levant, Harpo Marx, Yip Harburg and dozens of others of our old cronies. . . . Have you seen Kay? I haven't written to her nor have I heard from her. I should like to know if you ever see her. What's happening around town these days? . . . Have you seen Emilie and Lou [Paley]? Please write to me, telling me all that goes on in little old New York.[4]

A couple of weeks later, he was sharing another range of matters with Mabel, from politics to musical news, including a comment about the new Astaire-Kern pairing on film:

I miss you very much, Mabel, and wish it were possible for you to come out here. This place is just full of people you know and who love you. . . . Of course, there are depressing moments, too, when talk of Hitler and his gang creep into the conversation. For some reason or other the feeling out here is even more acute than in the East. . . . I saw Swing Time out here and liked the picture very much. Although I don't think Kern has written any outstanding song hits, I think he did a very creditable job with the music and some of it is really delightful. Of course, he never really was ideal for Astaire, and I take that into consideration.

Otto Klemperer is playing the "Music for Orchestra and Baritone" by Ernst Toch, next week. It is a concert given by the American Guild for German Cultural Freedom—and I shall be there. Will write you about it.[5]

Male friends to whom George reached out by letter included Gregory Zilboorg, Emil Mosbacher, music editor Albert Sirmay, and Bill Daly. To Mosbacher he observed: "This place has shown a tremendous improvement since we were here six years ago. The studios are really going out for the best talent in all fields and they have learned a great deal about making musical pictures since the last time. Even the food has improved greatly. . . . Ira, of course, loves it out here. He can relax much more out here than in the East—and you know how Ira loves his relaxation."[6]

Letters between Gershwin and Daly were rare, but Daly did write in response to two of them from his friend.[7] "Dear Pincus," he began, using the nickname they had chosen for each other:

Your two letters were like manna from heaven—and so overcome am I that I am breaking all rules by answering them. I [am]
glad to hear that you have gotten into the atmosphere of the place
so quickly—pool, [Lake] Arrowhead, etc. But look out for those
designing females. Of course, I only know what I read in the
newspapers.

Things are so quiet here that you can hear only the taxi-horns.
I may fly out your way in a month or so—and no reasonable
offer refused. Are you contemplating any Gershwin nights at the
[Hollywood] bowl?

I'm sure the orchestra won't be as bad as the one at Ravinia.

I do hope the Porgy & Bess venture goes through [a possible
London production]—I'm sure the English will go for it in a big way.

Give my love to Ira & Lee. And how did they like the ride? Ira
seemed somewhat disappointed that the aeroplane wasn't bigger:

maybe he'd been looking at pictures of the China Clipper [a hot-aircraft of that day].

And give my best—and congratulations,—to Fred Astaire. From what my scouts tell me, he seems to be a hit. Tell him he'll really get some tunes, now. [8]

Daly may well have intended to make the journey west, but on December 4 he died suddenly of a heart attack. Colleagues since the early 1920s, Gershwin and Daly had enjoyed an unusually close friendship. The loss must have touched Gershwin deeply, but his response is not a matter of record.

Gershwin's first exchange with Zilboorg from California—"Dear Grisha" / "My Dear Goish"—reveals two men who have found a comfort zone with each other. After reporting on the climate, the newly rented house, the local food, the parties, and the "series of fantastic and interesting dreams" he's been having, George turns to the subject of therapy. A friend in the Hollywood community, he writes, has confessed that there are "many subjects" about which he can't talk to his therapist. Doubting that such an attitude could lead to successful psychiatric analysis, Gershwin then turns to his relationship with Kay Swift, to whom he bade farewell three weeks ago in a New Jersey airport. That fact leads him to his own state of mind.

> I have not heard a word from Kay nor have I written her. I think about her a good deal & wonder how she is getting along with her work and without me? I wonder if this is really the end of our seeing one another. Who knows? . . . I have many friends here but somehow I feel alone inside quite frequently. I hope that feeling will disappear, but again—who knows?[9]

Later that month an echo from the recent past surfaced when Anne Brown wrote Gershwin from her home in Baltimore. Men-

tioning a possible London production of *Porgy and Bess*, she wrote
with a request in mind:

> Porgy, Serena, Crown, Clara, Sportin' Life, Jake and others all have
> their individual "spots" in the opera. But, there is *not one* for Bess. My
> suggestion is this: That you arrange with the producers to have me (if
> I am Bess in the forthcoming production) to sing "What You Want
> With Bess," alone—as a solo. I have sung it with great success this
> way in concert many times already.[10]

Gershwin found Brown's idea reasonable. "If the London production goes through, it is perfectly okay if you want to try doing it
as a solo for a couple of performances to see how it goes. If it's an
improvement, it can stay that way; if not, it shall go back immediately
to the original." As it turned out, however, the original cast members' salary demands were higher than the London resources could
bear, and no overseas production of *Porgy and Bess* was mounted.[11]

Partway through October, concert impresario Merle Armitage
contacted Gershwin with a proposition for a pair of all-Gershwin
concerts in Los Angeles. Armitage, who had met the composer in
New York during the 1920s, had secured a niche on the West Coast
by helping to establish opera there early in the 1930s. Now he ear-
marked two back-to-back dates in February 1937 for Gershwin at
the 3,000-seat Philharmonic Auditorium, which Armitage managed. The composer agreed to play the *Rhapsody in Blue* and the
Concerto in F, with Alexander Smallens conducting, and to conduct
the rest of the program himself: the *Cuban Overture*, rarely heard
since its debut in 1932, but also excerpts from *Porgy and Bess*, with a
chorus recruited from the local community and soloists brought in
from elsewhere.

During the rehearsal phase for these concerts, Gershwin and
Armitage spent a good deal of time driving together through Los
Angeles. The entrepreneur recalled endless talks "back and forth

from my house to his house, to the Philharmonic Auditorium, to Central Avenue," where they picked up chorus members, as among his "most treasured memories":

> George had a new Cord car, a front-drive vehicle of great chic, one of the earliest streamlined cars. He loved to drive it. My interest, though, was in his conversation, for Los Angeles being a huge sprawling community we spent hours in crossing town to our various engagements. George and I talked art. Or we talked music. One of the things we discussed was the string quartet on which he was working at the time. This was a fascinating subject, as the quartets of Beethoven, of Haydn, Debussy, and Ravel were among my favorites. He talked of the form his quartet would take, a fast opening movement, followed by a very slow second movement, based on themes he had heard when visiting Folly Island off the Carolina coast with DuBose Heyward. The sounds of the dominant themes were so insistent that he had not bothered to write them down. "It's going through my head all the time," George said, "and as soon as I have finished scoring the next picture, I'm going to rent me a little cabin up in Coldwater Canyon, away from Hollywood, and get the thing down on paper. It's about to drive me crazy, it's so damned full of new ideas!"[12]

Even as Gershwin found room in his consciousness for a composition that never reached written form—as one who composed at the keyboard, he presumably had a version of the quartet under his fingers—the work that had brought him to Hollywood proceeded apace. The script for the picture now called *Shall We Dance* was finally submitted partway through October. Moreover, performances with other symphony orchestras were scheduled: with the Seattle Symphony Orchestra on December 15; the San Francisco Symphony, under Pierre Monteux, on January 15, 16, and 17, 1937; and the Detroit Symphony Orchestra on January 20.

. . .

BUT HOW did George and Ira's contract with Hollywood stand when the script finally arrived? With no major work on their docket in the wake of *Porgy and Bess*, the Gershwins had arrived in California with several new songs in hand. And by the end of October, six usable songs had been completed for the RKO movie, with just one more plus a ballet yet to be written. In a long and informative letter George characterized the new songs to Dr. Gregory Zilboorg:

> We played our little efforts to Fred & Ginger Rogers & the direc-
> tor the other day & I must say the reception was an enthusiastic one.
> We have concentrated mainly on light, dancy, comedy songs, & they
> seem just right for Fred.

Then, however, after outlining his plans for the near future, he expressed regret that his psychoanalytic treatment with the doctor had yet to take place in earnest.

> It doesn't look as though I'll get back to New York as soon as I had
> expected. R.K.O. is taking up an option, which was in our contract,
> and Sam Goldwyn also wants us to do a film for him. The thing that
> makes me sad about all this is that it will postpone my seeing you. It
> is a pity that this trip to the coast had to interfere with my analysis,
> however I hope to continue when I get back—that is if you will still
> be interested in taking me on then.

Which led his train of thought to the social activity of a thirty-seven-year-old single man in a town known for its abundance of appealing single women.

> My love life out here has been almost non-existant. I have seen quite a
> number of girls but most of them are fairly insipid & dull. About the

brightest of the lot are two foreign actresses, Simone Simon, French, and Luise Rainer, Austrian (really german but for picture reasons, Austrian). Simon is pert, clever, & makes me laugh. Rainer is serious, solemn, & in love with Clifford Odets.[13] I see more of Simon.

Gershwin then gave Zilboorg a glimpse into his future:

Brother Ira loves it out here & is seriously considering building a house in San Fernando Valley. His wife Leonore shares his enthusiasm. I do not think I would care to settle here as one can become pretty sedentary in this climate, but for the moment it is a solution to my eastern problems.

And then he wondered whether his doctor and friend in New York had news to share about the relationship that had long loomed large in his consciousness.

By the way, do you hear anything about Kay, directly or indirectly? She has not yet written a word to me, as she agreed. I think about her often and, as you can imagine[,] not without a touch of sadness. She is a great girl & I hope with everything I have that she is all right in every way.[14]

Zilboorg's response to Gershwin's letter on November 3 dodged George's query about Kay Swift. Soon he would be leaving on a trip to "distant lands," he reported, including Brazil, Argentina, and Chile, and returning on December 29. And as for the composer's other concerns, "all your friends as far as I know are here, well and crazy as usual." But Gershwin's reply a week later brought decisive news:

I got a letter from Kay the other day for the first time, in which she says she heard I was going to stay out here for a long spell and felt that she had to break the silence to let me know that it looked like fini for us. I haven't as yet answered, but I expect to shortly.[15]

Whether or not George replied to Kay Swift at this time or later, the Gershwins completed their first assignment for RKO before the end of the year, to be enacted, filmed, and released to the public as *Shall We Dance* in mid-May 1937. Thus, by then the brothers were free to begin work on their second picture: RKO's *Damsel in Distress*, whose score was to be finished by early in May.

Gershwin's new year began, however, with a report of two personal discoveries, cited in a letter to Emily Paley in New York. The first one addressed his fascination with the filming of the picture he'd been working on through the fall. Instead of starting 1937 with *Damsel in Distress* in mind, he seems to have split his attention between the RKO studio, watching *Shall We Dance* being turned into a movie, and rehearsing for his concerts in January and February. His second discovery involved the state of his bodily self.

Recently my masseur suggested a hike in the hills. I acquiesced & have become a victim to its vigorous charm. For the past week, every day, hot or cold, we walked back in the hills & really Em, I feel as tho I have discovered something wonderful. It is so refreshing & invigorating. Better than golf, because it eliminates the aggravation that inevitably comes with that pastime.[16]

A letter to Zilboorg partway through February shows that the routine with his "masseur" had taken hold. At that point it involved "five or six days a week" of hiking in the hills of "truly beautiful & rugged country . . . on the average of four or five miles."

But that letter closes with Gershwin's account of the final chapter of his romantic relationship with Kay Swift:

About Kay. When she heard that our option had been taken up she wrote a letter, saying she realized finally that I was planning my life without her. She knew it was no criticism of her, but that I couldn't do otherwise. I answered, telling her, her realization was right. I was not planning to come back to her as I was incapable of supplying the assurance of a future together. The fault, if any, was mine, not hers. A few weeks ago a letter was handed me at the lunch table. It was from Kay. I read it & although its contents were logical, I received quite a shock. She stated frankly the [*sic*] she was going to marry Ed Byron & wanted to tell it to me before I heard it from anyone else. Appreciating her fine consideration I nevertheless had to do some mental contortions to realize that at last the finish had come. It was painful. However, the pain was mixed with some sort of happiness for her. No one is more deserving of getting a good break than Kay. She is, as I have told you a thousand times, a great person. She asked for my blessings. She received my blessings. She has left an indelible mark. Now, as to my future? I believe I have matured to a point where I can & will make decisions. A great change has come over me & think that I can at last have an opportunity to find my true level. If I decided on anything in the way of a radical change, you can be assured I shall let you know. In the meantime please write me anything you may know that would be of interest to me in this matter.

Dear Doc, I'm glad you miss me, & I hope you stay well. Please give my greetings to your family & to our mutual friends.

Yours, warmly,

George G.[17]

Gershwin's lengthy last paragraph, explaining to his psychiatrist the breakup of a longtime romantic relationship, displays his study and learning about the workings of his mind and heart, as we have observed him learning throughout his life about the art of music. In this engagement, as one of a duo of accomplished musicians with a strong and deep emotional attraction to each other, he has nevertheless shown himself through the years to be "incapable" of giving Kay Swift "the assurance of a future together." Having coped with that incapacity for years, she has now shocked him by announcing a decision to marry another man. His response? Pain that her intimate presence will now be lost to him, and perhaps an anticipation of justice served, if in the future she is spared the heartbreak of his falling for another woman. Thus in California, extending his quest to understand himself, Gershwin has remained in touch with his psychiatrist in New York. And what he seems to have learned from the doctor is that he must "make decisions" about his "love life," then act upon them, and finally learn from the results.

As for the picture titled *Shall We Dance*, its elements were combined and integrated during the early months of 1937, and released for public distribution in May, as the Gershwins' second feature film, following 1931's *Delicious*.

Shall We Dance opens in Paris, where the "Russian" ballet dancer known as Petrov, played by Astaire, has fallen hard for a less highbrow dancer, Linda Keene, played by Rogers. She is about to sail for New York, and he arranges to get his ballet troupe booked on the same crossing. Exposed onboard as an American, Petrov borrows a dog so he can join Linda in a daily promenade to "Walking the Dog" music, and they grow friendly. The picture's first song, "Slap That Bass," is performed by Astaire in an ocean liner's bright, tidy engine room. The crew members there, fifteen African American men dressed in white T-shirts, comprise a chorus and several instrumentalists, including a double-bass player who flaunts what could be called a slaphappy technique on his instrument. One vocalist sings the verse, while another supplies wordless instrumental effects between his phrases, most tellingly delivering a break in the style of a Duke Ellington growl trumpeter.[18] This number advises keeping spirits high even when "the world is in a mess." After an introductory "Zoom-zoom! Zoom-zoom!," the lyrics find consolation in the "zoom" of popular music's rhythmic vitality. "Dictators would be better off," the singer declares, "if they zoom-zoomed now and then." Once Astaire takes over the song, he climbs deftly up an intertwined arrangement of stairs, pipes, and platforms to a balcony of sorts. Orchestra music gives way to rhythmic machine sounds, the soundtrack now consisting of Astaire's more and more elaborate tapping as he moves along catwalks and varied contraptions provide a churning sonic background. He ends his dance with a flourish, bowing to applause from the engine-room crew on the floor below.

The next number, "(I've Got) Beginner's Luck," takes place on deck, as Petrov marvels to Linda at his good fortune: "The first time I'm in love / I'm in love with you." The song ends abruptly, however, as though recognizing that all will not be smooth sailing for Petrov. An ex-luminary of the Russian ballet company, Lady Carrington, is determined to snare him for herself, though he wants nothing to do with her. His ballet master, played by Edward Everett Horton, knowing the situation, has told Lady Carrington before the ship sailed that Petrov is a married man—but she doubts this is true. Calling his bluff, she starts a rumor that Petrov and Keene are secretly married. Once Linda, who in fact is engaged, realizes that everyone on board seems to believe this rumor, she leaves the ship on a mail plane.

Back in New York, Linda, her fiancé Jim, Petrov, and his ballet master are seated at a fancy club run by Linda's manager, played by Jerome Cowan. She's invited to sing "They All Laughed" for the customers, accompanied by the house orchestra. The song's refrain cites historical figures who have made transformative discoveries in the face of skepticism: Columbus, Edison, the Wright brothers, and Marconi. Likewise, her story concludes, people also laughed at "me wanting you," but "who's got the last laugh now?" The crowd greets Linda's performance warmly—but then, to her surprise, Petrov bounds onto the stage, having been encouraged to do so by her manager, who wants to keep Linda gainfully dancing rather than marrying Jim. The dance that follows starts as a gauntlet-throwing challenge. To the ballet master's arsenal of classical moves Linda responds with a brief sequence tap-danced in an American vein; Petrov returns promptly to ballet steps, which he tops off with an adept flourish of tapping, in an I-can-do-what-you-can-do spirit. His mastery sparks Linda's combative juices, and from here to the end of the orchestra's jazz-oriented rendering of the song, they join in a captivating, increasingly virtuosic tap dance that ends with the two of them perched side by side on the harp end of a grand piano. Both they and the audience have learned that Keene and Petrov are an artistic match, and maybe an emotional one too.

The roots of "They All Laughed" lay in Ira Gershwin's past, in the commercial world of the 1920s—a time, he recalled, when "the self-improvement business boomed":

> One correspondence-school advertisement, for instance, featured "They all laughed when I sat down to play the piano." Along this line, I recall writing a postcard from Paris to Gilbert Gabriel, the drama critic, saying: "They all laughed at the Tour d'Argent last night when I said I would order in French." So the phrase "they all laughed" hibernated and estivated in the back of my mind for a dozen years until the right climate and tune popped it out as a title.

The brothers, indeed, had previewed this song for playwright George S. Kaufman, who happened to be in Hollywood at the time, even though they knew he was no fan of love songs. Having listened through the verse plus almost half a refrain, Kaufman interrupted at the line "they told Marconi / wireless was a phony" by commenting: "Don't tell me this is going to be a love song!" When the next line was sung—"They laughed at me wanting you"—Kaufman "shook his head resignedly, commenting: 'Oh well.'"[19]

As Linda and Petrov continue to be plagued by rumors that they are married, encouraged by Linda's manager as well as Lady Carrington, they try to escape a press corps that has staked out their hotel. During an afternoon in Central Park, having rented rollerskates, they review their situation. When Linda admits to having no inkling of how to solve their predicament, Petrov replies, "Nyther do I," which she greets with an icy "The word is neether." Thus is launched another improbable love song ("You like potato and I like potahto / You like tomato and I like tomahto") and an exhilarating dance on rollerskates that leads to their careening off the rink to a soft landing on a grassy knoll. Because the subject of "Let's Call the Whole Thing Off," written earlier in New York before the Gershwins' trip to Hollywood, has more to do with diction than with passion, it must have emerged from the brain of Ira—especially since he traced it to another early memory:

> I still clearly remember the story our 6B teacher in P.S. 220, New York, told the class when she digressed for a moment in a spelling session. It concerned an American and an Englishman arguing about the correct pronunciation of "neither," with the American insisting on "neether," the Englishman on "nyther." They called on a bystander to settle the dispute: Was it "neether" or "nyther"? "Nayther!" said—who else?—the Irishman.[20]

But now Linda has an idea about their predicament: they should marry, and then file immediately for a divorce. So they travel by boat to New Jersey to seek out a justice of the peace. It's dark by the time the ferry begins its journey back to Manhattan. Holding a white flower her new husband has bought her, a pensive Linda admits to never having imagined how dispiriting marriage can be. Petrov, who from the start has hoped to marry Linda, consoles her with a tender ballad, the film's most enduring song: "They Can't Take That Away from Me." A man tasting true love for the first time in his life sings about his feelings for her so convincingly that Linda cannot help but be moved. The script and the Gershwin brothers have portrayed the character of Petrov as an artist who perceives Linda as a true artist herself, whereas Jim, a playboy proud to flaunt the trophy companion he has singled out, shows no more interest in Linda's accomplishments than she does in his company.

Some songs in this picture—"Let's Call the Whole Thing Off" and "Slap That Bass," for example—have melodies that reflect the meter, with phrases consistently beginning on downbeats. But in the regretful aura of "They Can't Take That Away from Me," phrases usually start on upbeats and afterbeats, avoiding metrical accents more often than they jibe with them. As a result, the refrain tends to linger, savoring the nuanced memories of a romance nearing an end. Petrov's words and music visit endearing things about Linda that he will miss: the way she dons her hat, the look of a knife resting in her hand, her gift for singing off-key and getting away with it. In fact, the motive at the heart of the refrain's melody, built around five repeated short notes and a long one, settles into a regular call-and-response exchange between voice and orchestra. "George had an idea for a melody," Ira recalled, based on three eighth notes and one quarter note. "If you can give me two more notes in the first part," Ira suggested, "I can get 'the way you wear your hat.' George tried that," and "liked it" (he "was always obliging that way").[21]

The film's last scene opens in a New York theater, where Petrov is featured as the architect and ultimately the star of a lavish presentation combining classical ballet with show-business dance and song. The stage is filled with some twenty female ballet dancers, soon joined by Harriet Hoctor, an accomplished Hollywood ballerina, in an extended solo turn, and eventually Petrov as a ballet master.[22] The finale he has conceived is based on a song for the entire company, "Shall We Dance?" Petrov has made it known to manager and friends alike that he had hoped to include Linda as his partner in this extravaganza. But, convinced by what she reads as a slight—again through no fault of the innocent Petrov; Lady Carrington had made her way into his suite, where Linda surprised them together—she has refused to join him onstage. As the finale gets under way, Linda and Jim appear in the audience, she determined to deliver personally to Petrov a legal summons for divorce.

As the couple settles in to watch from a box seat, her manager tells Linda of Petrov's vow that if he can't feature Linda Keene in the show, he'll end it dancing with a stage filled with likenesses of her. Accordingly, each of the dancers in the finale, "Shall We Dance?," carries a mask of Linda's face. Ira's lyrics combine threat (must we surrender to despair?) with gaiety (or should we give in to revelry?). And to Ira's ear, George's "distinctive tune" brought "an overtone of moody and urgent solicitude" to this climactic number. Linda is enchanted by what she sees onstage. Whether moved most by the spectacle of her own presence, or by the esteem and love for her that Petrov's gesture reflects—or by perceiving on the spot what she can add to this performance—she orders her manager to escort her backstage.

Onstage the set has been turned into a semicircular row of niches, each with its living facsimile of Linda Keene. As Petrov makes the rounds, a familiar voice speaks a purportedly Russian word that has cropped up before during the course of the film, "Chichornia." Rapidly lowering the mask of each dancer in turn, Petrov finally finds Linda, animated and aglow with affection and joy. Now a couple whirling across the stage to conclude "Shall We Dance?," they move together toward the audience and bring the performance and the picture to a close with a triumphant question borrowed from "They All Laughed": "But ho, ho, ho! Who's got the last laugh now?"

HOLLYWOOD SONGWRITER II:
A DAMSEL IN DISTRESS (1937)

CRITICAL RESPONSE TO HIS December 1936–January 1937 concerts in Seattle and San Francisco, as well as in Detroit, leaves no doubt that West Coast audiences warmed to the approach Gershwin brought to the concert stage. " 'Tired business men' by the hundreds patted juba to the captivating rhythms," fancied a reviewer of the *Porgy and Bess* Suite in the *San Francisco Call-Bulletin*;

> The banjo, it seems was the final straw. Messrs. Beethoven, Brahms and Bach may have, for all we know, turned over in their graves. But we think not, remembering that they, too, were chroniclers of their times. Listening in some Valhalla, they probably chuckled and commented upon the fact that Gershwin was making more money than they did when they wove folk songs into symphonies.[1]

En route to the Bay Area, Gershwin had enjoyed the hospitality of Sidney and Olga Fish at their Palo Corona Ranch on the Monterey Peninsula. Accompanying him were supporters "up from L.A. to hear me play & see the sights & new bridge.[2] They are, Mother, Ira & Lee, Jerome Kern, wife & daughter, Dorothy Fields

& brother Herbie & sweetheart Felix Young & several others."[3] At the same time, the ranch hosted a working conference for key players in the Gershwins' second RKO picture, *A Damsel in Distress*— among them director George Stevens, who had directed the earlier Astaire-Rogers film *Swing Time*, and producer Pandro Berman.

For Merle Armitage's sold-out concerts in Los Angeles on February 10 and 11, Gershwin was rejoined by conductor Alexander Smallens during the *Rhapsody in Blue* and *Concerto in F*, and Todd Duncan for the *Porgy and Bess* excerpts. (Marguerite Chapman, a local white soprano, sang the role of Bess.) *Los Angeles Times* critic Isabelle Morse Jones felt that in *Porgy and Bess* Gershwin had "taken popular song writing into a new field and won recognition for it on its merits," and Florence Lawrence of the *Los Angeles Examiner* judged the program "unquestionably one of the most novel and interesting ever heard in Philharmonic."[4] But Richard D. Saunders of the *Hollywood Citizen-News* deemed the performance an evening of Gershwin overkill, complete with "garish orchestrations" and harmony sprinkled with seconds and fourths in the hope of hiding the music's sentimentality. "It was obvious that a large number had never been in the Philharmonic Auditorium before," he wrote. "Anyway, they saw some movie stars."[5]

Movie stars there were. After the second concert, Armitage hosted a party at a Sunset Strip night spot, where

George was in great spirits, and the whole group, exclusively celebrities, seemed to have been electrified by what they had heard. As he chatted with me, Jack Benny, the old maestro, said, "Armitage, you have a lot of nerve, this thing was too damn good for Hollywood." Dining with George, Ira, and a few of their friends, our enthusiasm running high, I proposed that the next year we do Porgy and Bess on the coast, and take it across the country for a second New York engagement. George tempered his enthusiasm by a word of caution. "It's devilishly expensive, Merle. The Theatre Guild lost money. Do you dare?" My reply was positive, possibly more positive than my reservations warranted.

The entrepreneur also revealed a brief mishap at the February 11 performance:

> At the second concert, unknown to a single person in the audience, George had suffered a black-out while playing the Concerto in F. He said afterward that everything suddenly went black and he missed a few bars. Smallens covered this nicely. George regained complete control and continued the performance brilliantly.

Whether or not the memory slip had anything to do with it, Gershwin notified Zena Hannenfeldt a week later that he would play no more concerts until he had finished writing the songs for his two remaining films.

And he had fallen a bit behind schedule. At least since early January, Gershwin, deeply interested in the process of movie-making, had been an avid observer on the *Shall We Dance* set. "The Astaire picture is being 'shot' & is most interesting to watch," he wrote Emily Paley. "It fascinates me to see the amazing things they do with sound recording, for instance. And lighting and cutting and so forth."[6] On March 19, having used up more than two months of a sixteen-week contract to compose songs for *A Damsel in Distress*, he confessed to Mabel Schirmer that he had "spent so much time watching the first picture being shot that Ira & I are a little behind on the second one."[7]

George and his brother were eagerly anticipating the first picture's release, scheduled for May 7. "There is a real excitement about the opening of a film that compares favorably with a Broadway opening of a show," he wrote Isaac Goldberg as that date approached.

In fact, it's really much bigger, for example, "Shall We Dance," our first Astair[e] opus, will be playing in probably a hundred cities at the same time, including a large theatre in London during the Coronation. Also, all the record companies record the numbers before the picture is released—on Broadway sometimes you have to wait months before the numbers are recorded.[8]

But his verdict on the finished film included some reservations once it was released: "The picture does not take advantage of the songs as well as it should. They literally throw one or two songs away without any kind of a plug," he wrote Goldberg. "This is mainly due to the structure of the story which does not include any other singers than Fred and Ginger and the amount of singing one can stand of these two is quite limited."[9]

Critics, however, had few reservations. Frank S. Nugent of the *New York Times* called the movie "one of the best things the screen's premier dance team has done," and Gershwin's score "the one we intend to ask for if ever the critics have to make good their promise and actually go dancing through the streets."[10] And *Variety's* critic saw the "underproduced" nature of the songs as more a virtue than a flaw. "They Can't Take That Away from Me" was "merely given a verse and one chorus. No reprise, no plug. Almost a once-over-light but it's smart and it helps curtail footage."[11]

As 1937 ARRIVED, Gershwin wrote hopefully to Mabel Schirmer that this might be "their year":

A year that will see both of us finding that elusive something that seems to bring happiness to the lucky. The pendulum swings back, so I've heard, and it's about due to swing us back to a more satisfying state. 1936 was a year of important changes to me. They are too obvious to you to mention here. So, sweet Mabel, lift your glass high with me & drink a toast to two nice people who will, in a happy state go places this year.[12]

One fundamental change for him, of course, was the absence of Kay Swift, a presence in Gershwin's life for more than a decade. George's cousin Henry Botkin, at that time a frequent visitor to Southern California, told biographer Robert Kimball:

> The last year of his life was an awful year. Did you know about the awful loneliness he had? I remember once he came out with it and said, "Harry, this year I've GOT to get married." Just like that. Like saying he had to write a new opera or something. The truth is George wanted the most beautiful gal, the most marvelous hostess, someone interested in music. What he wanted and demanded just didn't exist. He would have loved to have a son or a daughter or two. George was very soft. I could never get over that.[13]

Emil Mosbacher also recalled that "in the last years George was increasingly restless. Even more than before, he needed people to share things with. He was lonely in many ways and would call me up at all hours, as I'm sure he called others, just to talk and get something off his chest."[14]

Come spring, Gershwin seems to have felt he had finally met that "most beautiful gal." In mid-March, he attended a particularly enjoyable evening at the home of Edward G. Robinson and the film star's wife Gladys, along with his mother Rose, visiting from New York, and Igor Stravinsky, among others. "The whole evening was memorable," he reported in a letter to Emily Paley:

> Stravinsky was the guest of honor & was charming. He asked if he & [violinist Samuel] Dushkin could play for the group. They

played seven or eight pieces superbly. Stravinsky & mother got on famously. Isn't Hollywood wonderful? . . . Gladys sat me next to the most glamorous & enchanting girl in the west. Paulette Goddard. She is a really exciting creature. Gladys knows my taste better than I thought. The whole evening was grand, what with those pictures, Stravinsky, Miss P.G., Frank Capra & thoughts & talk about you.[15]

From this evening forward, Gershwin harbored a romantic interest in Goddard, even though the actress was married at the time to Charlie Chaplin. The social connection that blossomed between them that spring was caught in a photograph that shows them dressed in shorts and relaxing in lawn chairs, in what seems to be the yard of the Gershwins' house on North Roxbury Drive. Most of what we know about Gershwin's feelings at that time is gleaned from his correspondence with Emily, Mabel, his sister Frances, and his mother. Two months after their meeting, addressing a question about "Miss P." in a letter from Rose, he replied that "there is nothing new to tell you about her. I see her less frequently than I did. She seems very well and asks about you often. There is a possibility of her appearing in the picture 'Gone with the Wind.' That's about all the news there is to tell about her."[16] A letter written the same day to Mabel Schirmer offers more on the subject; New York columnist Walter Winchell had apparently reported a romantic connection between the two:

About your reference to Winchell's item concerning Miss Goddard and myself, it is only partly true. For your own information, I met Miss Goddard a couple of months ago and found her the most interesting personality I've come across since arriving in Hollywood. You would be crazy about meeting her as she has one of the most alert minds you could possibly imagine. On the other hand, she is married to the "famous Charlie" and under such circumstances I am not allowing myself to become too involved.[17]

A few days later, Gershwin ended a letter to Frances with a P.S.: "It is true that I took the young lady out a couple of times and found her most attractive, but whether it goes any farther than that, I doubt."[18]

Since returning home from California in April, Rose Gershwin had consulted her personal network in and around New York, where Paulette Goddard had been born and raised. "You know that she is a Jews girl," she wrote her son in June, "and was married before." Adding in her unique style, she continued: "Dagmar is a friend of her's the name was Levy but that does not meet a thing, you steel love her. Write me all about wath is going to happen . . . tell me the true, do you mees me, a little?"[19] George replied immediately, on June 10:

> It was a most pleasant surprise to get your nice fat letter with so much news in it. Your writing is certainly improving and if you don't watch out some Hollywood studio will sign you up—I think I've got something there because the only thing the Gershwin family lacks is a book writer and it would be simply wonderful if the posters read—Book by Rose Gershwin—Lyrics by Ira Gershwin—Music by GG—and we've got to get Arthur in somewhere, so let's say—Entire Production staged by Arthur Gershwin.

But, he told his mother, he had not seen Goddard "for about a week as she went to Palm Springs for a rest." However, he continued, "she phoned yesterday and said that little Blumenthal was in town and asked if she could come over for lunch with him, so either today or tomorrow I expect to see them both. There's nothing more to tell you about her at this time."[20]

To songwriter Harold Arlen, a neighbor of the Gershwins in Beverly Hills, George made it no secret that he had imagined Goddard as part of his future. But Arlen expressed his doubts about Gershwin and marriage:

You know, he wanted to marry Paulette Goddard. We sat by his pool talking about it. She was a great girl, but George's life style was very free-wheeling. I knew that marriage would tie him down, so I told him that he would have to give up some of the freedom he had. He didn't say anything, because I knew—all of us knew—that he wanted to get married. But George was the kind of guy who would go first to one house and play a few songs, then go on to another house and play some more, then to another and so on. He knew he couldn't do that if he were married. Yet there was that warmth and wistfulness in him too, and it all made for great internal conflicts. So it would have been hard for George to change his life style from work, party-going, tennis, golf, long fast walks in the mountains. He always was so God-damned excited, and the glory road had to be his.[21]

Further evidence that Gershwin had been smitten by Paulette Goddard at the Robinsons' party appears in a detailed doctor's report from an examination of the composer's health. That report noted on June 9 that he had experienced insomnia "four months ago" in mid-March, "when the patient was in love."[22]

THE GERSHWIN brothers had finished their songs for *A Damsel in Distress* by May 17, when George sent them to Henry Botkin in New York with instructions to have them copyrighted in the composer's name and then put away "where nobody can see them," for it would be "at least several months before they can be made public."[23] On May 25, the brothers had a visit from Fred Astaire, who "for the first time listened to the second score that we wrote for him," George wrote to Frances. "He made us very happy by apparently liking the entire score immensely. There wasn't one number he could find fault with."

In *A Damsel in Distress*, Astaire plays Jerry Halliday, a famous

American entertainer who has arrived in England accompanied by George Burns, his press agent, and Gracie Allen, Burns's secretary. The film's first song, "I Can't Be Bothered Now," enacted on a London street, reveals Jerry as a man who lives to dance. Shortly before this number, Jerry, mobbed by adoring fans, has hopped into a cab, only to be startled when a lovely young woman—played by Joan Fontaine—opens another of the cab's doors and dives into his lap, with a polite request to hide her. She is Lady Alyce, daughter of Lord John Marshmorton of Totleigh Castle and a niece of Lady Caroline Marshmorton. Lady Alyce has come to the city to visit an American man with whom she suspects—wrongly, as it happens—she may be in love, and is being trailed by a servant sent by Lady Marshmorton. Her choice of a husband has sparked such keen interest within the Totleigh household staff that they have set up a sweepstakes on which of her suitors she will prefer. One staff member, guessing that Jerry Halliday is the American she fancies, forges a love letter from her to Jerry, who has fancied Alyce from the moment she landed in his cab.

At Totleigh Castle, Jerry sneaks onto the premises in the guise of one of a group of madrigal singers. These choristers have specialized in old English music, an emphasis that brought out the scholar in Ira Gershwin. In "The Jolly Tar and the Milkmaid," the Gershwins tried for "the feel of an English eighteenth-century light ballad," so Ira threw in phrases—"with a hey and a nonny" and "a down-a-derry"—that the *Oxford English Dictionary* revealed had been sung since the 1500s. For this number George fashioned a sportive 6/8 tune, moving with the easy coherence and swing of a Gershwin melody but with major/minor modal freedom, giving the harmony an archaic flavor.

Jerry, imagining that Lady Alyce is smitten with him, has rented a cottage near the castle grounds with Burns and Allen. Learning that Alyce plans to attend a "fun fair," perhaps with another suitor, Jerry and his colleagues decide to go there, too. He follows her into a Tunnel of Love and tries to kiss her in the dark, only to get a slap in return—whereupon the three Americans sing and dance to "Stiff Upper Lip," celebrating the vaunted refusal of Englishmen to complain, no matter how vexing the setbacks they may face. The words are set to a catchy melody, in tune with the good-natured setting of a fun fair. Ira borrowed some of the song's lingo from P. G. Wodehouse—who had adapted his novel for the screenplay—and some from show business of the day. "Whether Englishmen actually greeted each other or not with 'old bean' or 'old fluff' or 'old tin of fruit' didn't matter frightfully," he granted later, but "we had been conditioned by vaudevillians and comic weeklies to think they did."[24]

The first love song in *A Damsel in Distress* is sung by Jerry to Lady Alyce, on the grounds adjacent to his cottage. A heart-to-heart conversation with her father, who has found Jerry likable and trustworthy, convinces Alyce of the American's merits, and she admits her attraction to him. Jerry responds with "Things Are Looking Up," sung to music with a rich harmonic palette and an unsyncopated flow mirroring his respect for her dignity and candor. Joan Fontaine was known as neither a singer nor a dancer—Burns and Allen are Astaire's dancing partners in this picture—but she and Astaire move gracefully through two orchestral statements of this melodious refrain.

That evening at the castle ball, the madrigal group performs "Sing of Spring" as guests arrive. The lyrics of this part song, composed some years earlier for a number called "Back to Bach" that had never found its way onstage, also include vocables of yore— "Spring is here / Sing 'Willy-wally-willo!' "—but its music avoids the "Jolly-Tar" effect of more ancient vintage. Now, however, in an act of social sabotage, a servant who in the suitor sweepstakes has bet against the American makes sure that Lady Alyce sees an inflammatory article smearing his character. Jerry, the article claims, has broken the hearts of no fewer than twenty-seven would-be lovers, and *she* is marked to be his twenty-eighth victim. Outraged by this charge, Alyce orders the staff to bar Jerry from the castle. Then she storms up to her room, where she looks out a window and sees him walking about the grounds, apparently in contemplation. In the evening mist, Jerry sings about wandering the streets of London on "A Foggy Day."

Ira's account of how the song came to be written reveals it as one of the few that Gershwin attributed to inspiration:

> We had finished three or four songs. One night I was in the living room, reading. About 1 a.m. George returned from a party . . . took off his dinner jacket, sat down at the piano. . . . "How about some work? Got any ideas?" "Well, there's one spot we might do something about a fog . . . how about *a foggy day in London* or maybe *foggy day in London Town*?" "Sounds good. . . . I like it better with *town*" and he was off immediately on the melody. We finished the refrain, words and music, in less than an hour. . . . Next day the song still sounded good so we started on a verse. . . . All I had to say was: "George, how about an Irish verse?" and he sensed instantly the degree of wistful loneliness I meant.[25]

The protagonist of this song has spent a solitary, misty day wandering city streets when a transformative moment arrives. "Suddenly I saw you there"—a phrase that reflects the meeting of Jerry and Lady Alyce, with the adverb at the peak of the melody—and out comes the sun. A quarter-note loop to the tune of Big Ben's clock (*mi-do-re-sol*) fills out the melody of the refrain, as if the first encounter of a couple-to-be has brought the music into synchrony with time as it is measured in London town.

With the help of Lord Marshmorton, the servant's mischief is revealed and the romantic misunderstanding resolved in time for the castle's social gathering that evening. Again Jerry shows up as a cheeky chorister, now in a didactic number called "Nice Work if

You Can Get It"—touting the rewards bestowed upon true lovers, from hand-holding by starlight to being welcomed home at the end of a working day. (On this reward, Ira quotes himself in a line borrowed from "I Got Rhythm": "Who could ask for anything more?") Sung by a choir perhaps to Lady Alyce and Jerry, a couple ready to embark on the road of matrimony, the advice the singers deliver takes a cautionary turn at the end of the refrain, warning that "if you get it, won't you tell me how?"

As for the song's title, Ira counseled songwriters in later years that "in lyric-writing it's nice work when you get hold of a seemly title, for that's half the battle. But what follows must follow through in the verse and refrain, whether the development is direct or oblique. In short:

> *A title*
> *Is vital.*
> *Once you've it—*
> Prove *it.*[26]

The madrigal singers perform "Nice Work" with Jerry conspicuously among them, calling attention to himself, in a parody of a self-regarding choir member. The end of the choral singing finds Jerry in a virtuosic encounter—partly danced—with a drum set, to the strains of the new song. And that caper extends into a finale in which he and Lady Alyce march arm in arm out of Totleigh Castle, presumably with more nice work and a new life together in their sights.

Once the Gershwins had finished the music for *A Damsel in Distress* on schedule in mid-May, they started immediately to write music for the last project on their contract: Samuel Goldwyn's *Goldwyn Follies* (1938), for which they were able to complete only part of the musical score.

GONNA RISE UP SINGING

IN THE FIRST OF HIS MEMOIRS, Oscar Levant reveals that he was one of the few listeners who noticed Gershwin's memory slips during his two Los Angeles performances in February 1937. "Though he had played the 'Concerto' dozens of times in public with great fluency I noticed that he stumbled on a very easy passage in the first movement. Then, in the andante, in playing the four simple octaves that conclude the movement above the sustained orchestral chords, he blundered again." The next evening, Gershwin mentioned that while conducting another number, "he had experienced a curious odor of some undefinable burning smell in his nostrils . . . and a sudden headache." Nobody, least of all Gershwin, attached significance to these lapses, experienced by a man who radiated good health and vitality.

When the headaches recurred more frequently later on, some friends saw them as a neurotic response to working conditions in Hollywood, but Levant found that line of thinking "plainly fallacious." Gershwin's interests were expanding; his musical life in Hollywood was going well, and "his mental outlook was altogether healthy."

He took a great interest in the contemporary music that was being played in Los Angeles at the time, where, contrary to the usual opinion, the musical atmosphere was a sharp and bracing one. Stravinsky made a guest appearance with the Los Angeles Orchestra, conducting his own works; there were the Schoenberg quartet concerts, the WPA Schoenberg-and-pupils concert; the presence of Ernest Toch and Aaron Copland on the coast—all these things interested and stimulated him. The freshness of these contacts, indeed, aroused George to the contemplation of renewed work in large forms, which had not engaged his attention since *Porgy* more than two years before. From his conversation I believe this would have been in the field of ballet or, possibly, a string quartet.[1]

As mentioned earlier, Levant's first exposure to Gershwin had been in 1918 in Pittsburgh, at a performance of *Ladies First*, where the "completely free and inventive playing" of the accompanist left a lasting impression tainted by envy.[2] After moving to New York in the early 1920s, the classically trained Levant had learned that the only work available to him lay in the field of dance music, most of which he held in a state of "unhealthy contempt." But the songs that awakened his professional envy often proved to be the work of Gershwin, who had begun to loom in his mind's eye as "a contemporary worthy of my most zealous dislike."[3]

Early in 1925, Levant received an emergency morning phone call from conductor Frank Black at the Brunswick studio. An orchestra had been assembled there to record the *Rhapsody in Blue*, but the piano soloist had failed to show up. Could Oscar fill in? He could and he did, forgetting in the excitement to negotiate a larger-than-usual fee for having saved Brunswick's and Black's venture. Discovering later that he had been paid at union scale, he decided to seek "consolation in a word of praise from the composer," whom he had yet to meet, and phoned him. Yes, he had heard the Brunswick recording, Gershwin told him, but he preferred his own version with the Victor recording label—a judgment that Levant came to share. Levant's mother, noting that from then on the *Rhapsody in Blue* seemed to be the only music her son was ever invited to perform, often registered disappointment on his behalf. When, without mentioning repertory, the pianist told her that the prestigious Roxy Broadcast radio program had hired him to perform on the air, she was thrilled. But when he called home after the broadcast, "she remarked not too cryptically, 'Again the "Rhapsody"!'" a phrase that came to be a punch line for Gershwin and Levant when either spotted a redundancy in his life.[4]

The first face-to-face meeting of these two composer-pianists took place later in 1925, when Levant dropped by the 110th Street apartment where the Gershwin family then lived. George was at work on the *Concerto in F*'s first movement, with Bill Daly playing the orchestra part on a second piano, and the encounter was short but sour. "Bristling with inarticulateness," the best Levant could manage when the music stopped was a remark "graceless" enough to annoy Gershwin, who promptly "returned to his work."[5] Several years went by. Then, in a coincidence inviting more unfavorable comparison, *Ripples*, a Broadway show for which Levant had composed the music, was playing across the street from the Selwyn Theatre, where the revised version of Gershwin's *Strike Up the Band* was holding forth. "As quickly as the score of *Ripples* palled on my audience, it palled on me more," Levant recalled. "Hypnotically, I would find myself at the rear of the Selwyn, resentfully transported by the fresh rhythms and humors of the Gershwin lyrics and music." At a matinee performance one day, drinking in Gershwin's music from the back of the theater, he felt a tap on the shoulder from a young woman who asked how his show across the street was going. The tapper was Leonore Gershwin, whom he had met once before. At intermission, Levant invited her to have a look at *Ripples*. They watched a few numbers, she escorted him back to *Strike Up the Band*, and then she invited him home with her.[6]

Thus it was that, beginning early in 1930 with Leonore's ice-breaking gesture, the Gershwin brothers' adjoining penthouses on Riverside Drive evolved into the unofficial headquarters of Oscar Levant, then a single man who called a New York hotel home.

> Leonore was a gracious hostess and the first person to tolerate my unresolved social dissonances. With this encouragement, I flowered as a buffoon, warmed in the sun of this amiable household.... From the first day's supper I worked up to having four and five meals a day with the Gershwins, eating my way through the composition of the music and lyrics for *Delicious* and *Girl Crazy*.... Between the two households I emerged as a penthouse beachcomber.

Levant's pianistic skills made him a valuable musical collaborator for George, who would sketch his large instrumental works for two pianos before he orchestrated them. Both the Second Rhapsody in 1931 and the *Cuban Overture* in 1932 were composed in this way, with Levant at the second piano.[7] He also made an engaging witness to the lively environment of work and play at the Gershwin household early in the 1930s:

> Surrounding the music in the two apartments (Ira had a fondness for singing George's settings of his lyrics) both from the pianos and the phonographs, was a sporadic stream of talk embracing prize fighting, music, painting, football and sex. The Gershwin enthusiasm for ping-pong was communicated to me along with the scores, and we spent hours at the game. Amid this constant activity there was recurrently a recess for food, variously disguised as lunch, dinner, supper or midnight snack.

At the same time, Levant found his own efforts as a composer submerged in the tide of Gershwin's energy and his talents: "He had such fluency at the piano and so steady a surge of ideas that any time he sat down just to amuse himself something came of it."[8]

By the time the Gershwins arrived in Hollywood in the summer of 1936, Levant and his first wife, whom he married in 1932, were settled there. Levant was then studying composition with Arnold Schoenberg, who shared with both Gershwin brothers a passion for tennis.

> The meeting of Schoenberg and Gershwin was an affectionate one and resulted, among other things, in a standing invitation for the older man to use the Gershwin court on a regular day each week. He would arrive with an entourage consisting of string-quartet players, conductors, and disciples. . . . One of the most memorable experiences I have ever had in music occurred during that California visit, when Mrs. Elizabeth Coolidge sponsored the performance of the four Schoenberg quartets and the last group of Beethoven, played by the Kolisch ensemble. George, Ira and I were overjoyed by this opportunity, and all of the music impressed us deeply.[9]

Levant also learned of Gershwin's appetite for jazz music. For example, of the many recorded versions of "Oh, Lady Be Good," the composer was especially fond of the one by the Benny Goodman Trio, with Gene Krupa on drums and Teddy Wilson on piano. And a special favorite among performers was Art Tatum, whom Gershwin had invited to his New York apartment before leaving for California, to play for company that included pianist Leopold Godowsky. Tatum enjoyed displaying his keyboard virtuosity by inventing strings of variations on certain jazz standards, including "Liza" and "I Got Rhythm." At one point later, in a "small, dingy, badly lighted room" in the Los Angeles area, Levant and Gershwin heard Tatum play "virtually the equivalent of Beethoven's thirty-two variations" on "Liza." When that prodigious adventure was over, Gershwin's response was to ask for more.[10]

. . .

GERSHWIN SPENT the last weeks of his life at work on "a super, super, stupendous, colossal, moving picture extravaganza which the 'Great Goldwyn' is producing," as he announced to Isaac Goldberg.[11] After thirty-two weeks of song-making for RKO and the supportive Pandro Berman, the brothers found themselves in a far less welcoming environment. In an ironic twist of fate, their new project was based on a show business tradition started by Ziegfeld: the most overbearing and least trustworthy producer they had worked for—until now. One industry executive described Sam Goldwyn as "the kind of man who, if he understands what you tell him, thinks he thought of it himself."[12] From the start, the Gershwins' venture with him was fraught with complication and mistrust beyond what would come to be recognized as a decline in George's health.

Gershwin began his new assignment with a sense of having been overextended, longing for a break from the pressures of songwriting. A letter on May 19, 1937, to Mabel Schirmer, who had written to tell him of the European trip she was planning for June and July, was far from upbeat about the artistic grind the brothers faced:

> Ira and I have had to literally drag ourselves to work the last few days as we have just finished the second Astaire score and have to start right in on the "Goldwyn Follies." Even the Gershwins can't take that kind of routine. It's too bad our contracts followed one another so closely as we both could use a month's rest. Anyway, the silver lining on this cloud is that after the "Goldwyn Follies" we are going to take a long vacation, come to New York and perhaps I may even go to Europe.[13]

A week or so later, George received a letter from Frances Godowsky informing him that she and Leo and their ten-month-old daughter would soon be off on a European trip of their own. He answered her the same day, detailing his plan to return to New York once the *Follies* music was done, and stated the brothers' determination to limit themselves in the future to one picture per year. He also applauded Goldwyn's decision to film the picture in Technicolor. "Still, our health is good and our brains seem once again to be functioning," he assured her, "so we are getting some pretty good starts of songs for the 'Follies.'"[14]

But early in June, he revealed concern about his health—in what proved to be his last letter to his mother.

> Of late I haven't been feeling particularly well. Yesterday I put myself in the hands of a Dr. Segall and he is going to try to find out the reason for the slight dizziness I get every once in a while. He examined me yesterday and told me not to worry about it as he was convinced that it was nothing of a serious nature but that he would like to investigate it further to make sure about the cause of it.[15]

During his last contact with Gregory Zilboorg, with whom Gershwin had recently kept in close touch via correspondence, the psychiatrist had urged him to see Ernst Simmel, a Los Angeles psychiatrist and highly regarded pupil of Freud. After examining Gershwin, Simmel felt that his medical history suggested an "organic disorder" and referred him immediately to Gabriel Segall.

Gershwin was convinced that the headaches he was having were psychosomatic, caused by exhaustion from a heavy work schedule. Nor did the thorough examination conducted by Dr. Segall in the house on North Roxbury Drive reveal physical abnormalities. But during the next two weeks his headaches grew worse, particularly in the morning. Sometimes they were accompanied by nausea and dizziness, and the sensation of a foul odor (in medical terms, "olfactory hallucinations"). On June 23, Dr. Segall admitted Gershwin to Cedars of Lebanon Hospital, calling in a neurologist, Eugene

Ziskind, who found some light sensitivity but no tangible evidence of organic disease. A diagnostic spinal tap was recommended, but Gershwin refused it, fearing that such a test would aggravate his headaches. Three days later, on June 26, he was discharged from the hospital at his own request; the final note on his chart stated "most likely hysteria."[16] In the days after his discharge, Simmel paid daily visits to his patient at home, and a full-time psychiatric nurse remained at Gershwin's side.

On Saturday, July 3, Sam Behrman arrived from New York to attend the Los Angeles opening of his play *Amphitryon 38*. He was shocked to see his always-vital friend in such a diminished condition. "He was very pale. The light had gone from his eyes. He seemed old. He greeted me mirthlessly. His handshake was limp, the spring had gone out of his walk." Did he feel like playing the piano? Behrman asked, prompting "the first refusal I'd ever heard from him." As for whether he would be attending the premiere on Monday, Gershwin shook his head.

> "I had to live for this," he said, "that Sam Goldwyn should say to me: 'Why don't you write hits like Irving Berlin?'" There was silence. . . . He looked at me with lusterless eyes. I had a sinking feeling: he is no longer one of us.[17]

On July 6, Segall and Ziskind, joined by Carl Rand, a local neurosurgeon, reexamined Gershwin. This time a spinal tap was performed, and the result proved consistent with the presence of a brain tumor.

Since the onset of George's symptoms, Leonore Gershwin, arbiter of the household's day-to-day activity, had shown little sympathy for her brother-in-law's uncharacteristic behavior, suspecting that his actions reflected emotional self-indulgence. But once medical experts convinced her that George faced a delicate, specialized operation, she launched a national search for the surgeon best qualified to perform it; her chief collaborator was the well-connected Emil

Mosbacher. Through a White House aide, an attempt was made to enlist the eminent Walter Dandy of Johns Hopkins Hospital in Baltimore. But Dandy turned out to be vacationing on a yacht in Chesapeake Bay, and by the time he was located and ready to make the journey west, Gershwin's declining condition demanded immediate surgery. Carl Rand undertook that task, beginning shortly after midnight on July 11 as family and friends gathered in a waiting room. They were briefed periodically by George Pallay, acting as a messenger from the operating room. After the skull was opened,

> a large cyst was found on the right side of the brain that compressed the left ventricle and shifted the right ventricle across the midline. The family was heartened by the news of a large cyst (as opposed to a tumor) that could be removed, but no mention was made of the trauma to the brain tissue that occurred as a result of its herniation and shift past the midline. The cyst was opened but revealed a mural nodule located on its medial side. It was presumed to be malignant. Both the cyst and the nodule were removed and the wound closed. The family, now subdued, all left the hospital around 6 a.m., after completion of the surgery.[18]

But after Gershwin was returned to his hospital room, his body temperature climbed to an unsustainable level, his heart rate sped upward, and so did his rate of respiration. At 10:35 that morning he died without regaining consciousness.[19]

ABOUT a month later, Dr. Dandy, having reviewed Gershwin's medical records, wrote to Dr. Segall:

> I do not see what more you could have done for Mr. Gershwin. It was just one of those fulminating tumors. There are not many tumors

that have uncinate attacks that are removable, and it would be my impression that although the tumor in a large part might have been extirpated and he would have recovered for a little while, it would have recurred very quickly since the whole thing fulminated so suddenly at the onset. I think the outcome is much the best for himself, for a man as brilliant as he with a recurring tumor would have been terrible: it would have been a slow death.[20]

Gershwin's body was transported by train to New York City, and his funeral took place on July 15 at two o'clock on a rainy afternoon at the Temple Emmanu-El in Manhattan, attended by 3,500 mourners; 1,000 more were turned away. He was buried at Westchester Hills Cemetery in Hastings-on-Hudson. At the same time on the same day, another thousand attended a morning service at Temple B'nai B'rith in Los Angeles, where Oscar Hammerstein served as eulogist:

> We remember a smile that was nearly always on his face, a cigar that was nearly always in his mouth. He was a lucky young man, lucky to be so in love with the world, and lucky because the world was so in love with him. It endowed him with talent. It endowed him with character. And, rarest of all things, it gave him a complete capacity for enjoying all his gifts.[21]

A spoken memorial broadcast from Los Angeles the day after George died included this tribute from Arnold Schoenberg:

> Music to him was the air he breathed, the food which nourished him, the drink that refreshed him. Music was what made him feel, and music was the feeling he expressed.
> Directness of this kind is given only to great men, and there is no doubt that he was a great composer. What he achieved was not

only to the benefit of a national American music but also a contribution to the music of the whole world.[22]

Those who knew him personally, and the multitudes who loved
his music, found themselves struggling to adjust to a world without George Gershwin in it. As writer John O'Hara registered the
impact, "George died on July 11, 1937, but I don't have to believe it
if I don't want to."[23] Still feeling the loss years after the fact, Oscar
Levant railed in his memoir against the "cliché panegyrics whose
one unison refrain was: 'But his music lives on.' . . . I detest this self-
derived omniscience . . . the survival of music is not determined by
such tea-leaf fortunetelling." For this friend and musical colleague,
no amount of music by Gershwin "could compensate for the loss
of his corporeal presence, the cessation of his creative being—
especially when we could have had both."[24]

Press accounts of the passing of an American icon show that both
of the musical spheres that Gershwin had served—as songwriter
and as composer—valued him as an artist of true consequence.
On Monday morning, July 12, the *New York Times* measured the
breadth of his accomplishments:

> In the tempo of jazz he jabbed at the dignities of American life,
> while he won the plaudits of the musical élite with the classic qual-
> ities of "A Rhapsody in Blue." With his brother Ira and that master
> of gentle satire George S. Kaufman[25] he set the nation laughing at
> the foibles of its government; but, in more serious mood, he found
> time to write music that the great conductors of his time were glad
> to present. Mr. Gershwin was a child of the Twenties, the Age of
> Jazz. In the fast two-step time of the years after the war he was to
> music what F. Scott Fitzgerald was to prose. . . . He had turned out
> tunes with all the tricks of the dove that rhymed with love. He had
> woven the cadences of Broadway into his songs and he had given
> America the plaintive Negro music of Porgy and Bess.[26]

The same day, the *Boston Herald* celebrated Gershwin's uniqueness and the infectious delight he brought to his music-making, whether as a composer or a pianist:

> As a delineator of the hard, brittle rhythms of contemporary America in the hundreds of songs which he wrote for musical comedies he was unexcelled. His score for "Of Thee I Sing" . . . was musical inventiveness of the deftest sort. Who, for instance, can ever forget the tingling tomfoolery of the music for the torchlight parade which opened the show, "Wintergreen for President"? . . . Whatever Gershwin may have done to introduce jazz to the concert hall is little compared to the happiness which he gave—and still gives—to the millions who sing, whistle, or dance to his tunes.[27]

In contrast, a July 13 piece in the *New York Herald Tribune* centered on Gershwin's compositions, with hardly a word about his songwriting self:

> For the first time in its long and ultra-respectable history American music became something that the man in the street delighted to hear. It had ceased to be essentially Colonial music, derived from European models, and had become a relatively new thing, full of native character and wit and charm, and with its sentimental prettiness artfully concealed. . . . Not only was he the most popular of American composers, he was perhaps the only American composer whom the Europeans took seriously. It is said that when Mr. Gershwin requested the great Stravinsky to give him some lessons in composition. Mr. Stravinsky asked Mr. Gershwin what his yearly income was, and was told $100,000, or something of the sort. "Oh," said Mr. Stravinsky, "well, then, I think you had better give me lessons in composition." . . . In his last important work, the opera "Porgy and Bess," there were indications of a growing mastery and

power that might eventually have yielded an even more important contribution to American music.[28]

On July 15, the *New Republic* struck a note more acquiescent than bereaved. Its farewell, titled "The Man I Love," began with an announcement from jazz critic Otis Ferguson: "Last Sunday night, the word came over the radio that George Gershwin was dead at the age of thirty-eight, and almost everywhere in the country people must have stopped for a moment. They knew him well, for they had sung his songs." And then the critic judged Gershwin in America's landscape of music-making as a giver of gifts that would long outlive him.

> He made the idea of jazz—as opposed to jazz itself, of course— acceptable to those who must get their music over a shirtfront and would otherwise be oblivious of anything in America that spoke without a thick accent to this day. . . . When you think back to the strange running sadness of "The Man I Love," or "Soon," and when you don't have to think back to "Somebody Loves Me" because Jack Teagarden . . . recorded it again a year or so ago; or to "Lady Be Good," because it is still to be found in the books of the first bands after these eleven years . . . you don't have to think any farther. . . . So he's gone, and let him go, and God bless him. And if there is any requiem at all, it should be a glad one, playing tonight in the swinging phrases of, say Benny Goodman's current arrangement of that title tune for "Lady Be Good."[29]

Ira Gershwin stands on the written record as a shadowy figure during his brother's decline. Said to have been numbed by grief in the wake of George's passing, he appears, during the course of his brother's illness, to have ceded to his wife whatever domestic responsibilities may have fallen to him. But after the funeral, he returned to Beverly Hills as a man with a legacy to manage.

The first thing Ira had to deal with was a disagreement over the memorial concerts being planned for Los Angeles in early September. "There were two groups working against each other," he wrote Rose Gershwin on July 31: ASCAP and the Hollywood Bowl, planning concerts within two weeks of each other. Ira suggested "that ASCAP hire the Hollywood Bowl and the Los Angeles Symphony and run the entire concert and the Bowl organization cooperate and get 25% of the proceeds for their deficit. So far they have bowed to my judgement in every respect and I'm hoping there will be no more trouble."

The uncompleted film contract, though, was more vexing. Sam Goldwyn had hired a musical collaborator, Vernon Duke, to flesh out the *Follies* score. Nevertheless, Ira explained,

> it now develops that Goldwyn thought he was hiring Duke to help me finish the score and that he doesn't want to pay any more money than he has to. Yesterday I gave Duke a lead sheet of a waltz of George's to go ahead with for a dance that [George] Balanchine wanted. Today I called Duke and explained the situation and he agreed not to work on the waltz, but would put in one of his own.
>
> As you probably know, George and I signed a contract as a *team*, so that when George was through I was through. Goldwyn wants me to come to work Monday to help Balanchine and Duke on an idea for the opening. I told [Arthur] Lyons to ask for at least two week's [*sic*] guarantee for me, but I couldn't even get that. His (Goldwyn's) attitude is that I ought to be able to finish it in a week. . . . I'll probably go to see him, but frankly I've found him a great disappointment, to put it mildly, and personally I don't care if I go on with it at all.[30]

With Russian-born choreographer and dancer George Balanchine as a key collaborator in an enterprise featuring ballet dancer Vera Zorina, his wife, it had been agreed from the start that the Gershwins' score would include a new ballet for Zorina. Ira and George had decided to write the songs first, leaving time in their sixteen-week contract to spend on the ballet. They had completed five songs and drafted material for one more before George's symptoms overtook his capacity to compose. To compensate, Gershwin had offered Goldwyn free use of the score of *An American in Paris*. Goldwyn had agreed, but the result he witnessed toward the end of July failed to please him—"too highbrow."

As for Balanchine, his first encounter with the Gershwins had begun awkwardly; his English was poor, and he had had trouble understanding George's New York accent. But the choreographer had come to expect a "very enjoyable" association:

> We met a few times and then I heard George was sick. I went to visit him and found him lying in bed in a dark room with all the shades drawn. He had a towel against his head and he obviously was in great pain. In that dark room he said to me, "It is difficult for me to work now, but I'll be all right." He knew I was trained in music, so he also said, "Do what you must. I know it will be good." He had more confidence in me than Goldwyn did then. "And when I'm all better, we'll do our ballet just the way you want it."[31]

The Gershwins' first new song to appear in the *Goldwyn Follies*, "Love Walked In," was written with tenor Kenny Baker, playing a short-order cook, in mind. The melody was not new, having been sketched in a manuscript tunebook dating from the days of *Girl Crazy* (1930). The refrain's flowing, legato, wide-ranging (an octave plus a fifth), and rhythmically graceful theme was another that George referred to as "Brahms-like." Indeed, if he had a specific source, it could have been the theme of the fourth movement of Brahms's First Symphony. And as for Ira's notion of a "completely new" world revealed by the beloved's arrival, it shows that, for all his emotional reserve, he could deliver when George walked in with a melody demanding warmth. "Love Walked In" made plenty of "noise" in the marketplace—Harold Arlen's word for commercial success—rising to No. 1 on the *Hit Parade* radio program in the spring of 1938.[32]

"I Was Doing All Right," the *Follies'* second number, is sung by a secondary character played by Ella Logan, whose comfortable life has been disrupted by a lover who sets her physical person "tingling all through." The music of Gershwin's refrain disconnects her complicated present from a simple past, back when she was "doing all right." "I Love to Rhyme," a light-hearted number introduced by comedian Phil Baker and ventriloquist Edgar Bergen working with his dummy, "Charlie McCarthy," dwells on rhymers and their talents—mountaineers, for instance, driven to climb, and criminals who prefer "to crime." The song glories in the sounds of rhymes, whether in one syllable ("gay, day, may, hey"), two ("chuckle, knuckle"), or more ("variety, society, propriety"). But would it not be "sublime," the protagonist wonders, "if one day it could be / That you rhyme with me?"

"Just Another Rhumba," an ambitious, extended number with a fully realized piano accompaniment whose rhythmic motor channels that of the *Cuban Overture*, went unused in Goldwyn's picture.

But as for "Love Is Here to Stay," it's a song that George did not live to complete in written form: it was finished according to his wishes by Ira and Oscar Levant.[33] As a song with an existential subject, it stands as a rarity in the Gershwin canon: a view of romantic love that professes permanence on an epic level. Trading conviction for eloquence, a plain truth—"our love is here to stay"—is sung word-for-word in three of the refrain's four sections, linked each time to the melody's only syncopated turn. Never had the gist of a Gershwin love song been stated more persistently.

More than half of the lyric Ira came up with for George's "start" dwells on a world in which "nothing seems to be lasting." His first examples point to human ingenuity and the quickening of social change wrought by gadgets: phones, radios, even the cinema. Then, however, he turns to the stability of nature at its most monumental (Gibraltar, the Rocky Mountains). Nothing short of the song's protagonists' faith in their love could have brought such exemplars of permanence to mind. The sentiment expressed here rang true as Ira and a devoted musical friend completed "Love Is Here to Stay" from the nine bars of melody that comprise the last music Gershwin committed to paper, plus Ira and Levant's recollection of what he had suggested or played for them to fill unfilled places.

As those nine bars of "Love Is Here to Stay" took shape, the composer's last days were at hand. Gershwin received a cable from Paris on July 6 inviting him to appear in a number of concerts later that year. But by the time that invitation arrived George's vitality had ebbed to the point that "Ira had had his brother and himself taken off contract" with the Goldwyn studio.[34] George was also too ill to learn that he had been elected an honorary member of the Academy of Santa Cecilia in Rome, Italy's highest award to musicians.

For all the achievements and success of George and Ira Gershwin's partnership, their move to Hollywood in the summer of 1936 opened, by the end of the year, a divide between the musician and the wordsmith, based on the lives they each preferred to lead. At first, taken by the attractions of the setting—for work and for play—George may have given serious thought to making Beverly Hills a permanent home. But by the end of October, he had learned that "one can become pretty sedentary in this climate," and his future was more likely to flourish elsewhere.[35] Conversations with Leo and Frances Godowsky, who visited her brothers during the 1936 holiday season, revealed that George had come "out here to make enough money with movies so I don't have to think of money any more. Because I just want to work on American music: symphonies, chamber music, opera. This is what I really want to do. I don't feel I've even scratched the surface." He told Leo, Frances later said, that he wanted to start on a string quartet. This was the last remark he made to us. We left and I never saw him again because we were in Europe when he died.[36]

Centered more on composition than on songwriting, George's inclinations for the future leaned toward New York, whose quicker pace and wealth of resources he missed in Hollywood.

In the meantime, as the brothers invented songs whose treatment on the screen lay in the hands of others, Ira, a master at biding his time, had "permanently succumbed" to Southern California's climate and to the "geographical remoteness that protected him from the business pressures of New York." He and Leonore would spend the rest of their lives within the orbit of Hollywood.

But if Ira had found a life that he and his wife savored, George had broader vistas to explore. The European trip he'd been contemplating since the family junket in 1928 might have enabled him to perform on concert stages overseas as a pianist and conductor, to compose music he had imagined writing for some time, and to enrich his life as an art collector and painter. Indeed, perhaps the task uppermost in his mind was the composition of a string quartet, whether the one sparked by his visit in 1934 to Folly Island, or another inspired in Hollywood after he heard all four of Arnold Schoenberg's exemplars.[37]

At the moment when fate brought George Gershwin's life to an end, his collaboration with Ira was poised to enter a new phase, which would most likely have seen his brother settle into a house in Beverly Hills, perhaps with a "studio-cottage" for George, who would be based in New York. George would presumably have returned to his apartment on East 72nd Street, free to travel, but also to host Ira when the next promising project beckoned, be it a musical comedy, an opera, or another project that called for lyrics.

THE END of the 1800s and the beginning of the 1900s saw the birth of three composers of varied background and persuasion who loom large in the annals of America's musical history. Duke Ellington, who was born in 1899 and died in 1974, left behind a vast legacy of jazz-based music composed, played, and recorded over five decades. A lifetime of satisfying customers while experimenting with the varied worlds of sound explored by his ensemble won for him the distinction of being named the century's foremost maker of American music: of "music that illuminated the unprecedented conditions of modern life."[38] Aaron Copland, who was born in 1900 and died in 1990, was long thought of as the foremost American composer of the age for a more symbolic reason: his recognizably homegrown composition in the Eurocentric, "classical," and academic camp of a professional world in which popular music seemed a sphere separate from music to be taken seriously.

And then there was George Gershwin, who lived from 1898 to 1937, and who, after a life shorter by far than those of Ellington and Copland, was mourned by multitudes: by those who "had sung his songs" and heard him on the radio; and by generations drawn to the theater, the concert hall, and the stadium to enjoy music as fullfilling and varied as the *Rhapsody in Blue, Lady, Be Good!,* and *Porgy and Bess.* For the few who knew him best, life could never be the same in the absence of so irreplaceable a presence. But in the Western world at large, his music had already won a valued place in the lives of listeners and institutions, and in the hearts and habits of performers, professional and amateur alike. Welcomed in his youth as a fresh voice of the Jazz Age, George Gershwin maintained the flavor and conviction of that voice through the better part of two decades. His days on earth were limited to the summertime season of life. But the music he left behind, endowed with his extraordinary inventiveness and intellectual curiosity, has yet to cease thriving as an evergreen gift to the world.

ACKNOWLEDGMENTS

EARLY IN THE 1970S, as the Bicentennial anniversary of the United States of America approached, the relatively small group of scholars conversant with the history of this country's music-making found themselves in demand. As part of that crew, I met individuals I never would have met otherwise. One was Martin Williams, a jazz critic whose work I had admired for years. In person, he turned out to be the kind of friend who told you what he thought you should be doing. And it didn't take long to learn that Martin's belief in his musical opinions was firmer than was mine about my own. Before long he took to sending me cassette tapes of jazz-oriented music that had caught his ear. And pretty much everything he sent found its way into my Again-and-Again Playlist—a sign, I realized, of a true critic's talent. As we discussed American songs early in the 1980s, he commented that George Gershwin was a composer who deserved a biography that a person like me should tackle. And that notion planted a hearty seed in my mind.

This book's Introduction has already reported how Williams's advice came to pass. And in fact, once I started compiling the chronology in which my story of Gershwin is grounded, I found myself in a new place. In the past, my research and writing on American music as a scholar had centered on musicians in the days of yore, serving the needs of Protestant worship grounded in British and Germanic traditions. In fact, when, early in the 1990s, Michael Ochs of W. W. Norton invited me to write a history of American music, I accepted his invitation, on the grounds that at least I had an idea of how to begin such a project. Having been focused on organized music-making taking root on these shores, I'd moved on in *America's Musical Landscape* (1993) to investigate this country's musical historiography by studying a succession of exemplars, from George Hood's *History of Music in New England* (1846) to Charles Hamm's *Music in the New World* (1983). That exercise prepared me to take on Mike Ochs's offer. And toward the end of 2001, *America's Musical Life: A History* was published by W. W. Norton.

Having completed a history whose sweep spans four centuries, and having retired from the classroom in 2003, I relished the notion of narrowing my focus. Free to chart a new course, this author found years of investigating musical practices and trends over time yielding to the notion of centering my attention on a single American musician. Convinced by now that George Gershwin was the American musician I most wanted to study, I began to make a chronology of a life lived as fresh rhythmic vitality was marking the present with a musical label: the Jazz Age. That setting invited me to learn how Gershwin's skills and imagination had thrived as he nourished his popular music-making with techniques from the classical sphere while, on occasion, fashioning his own kind of classical works.

George Gershwin hailed from a family of Russian immigrants who had no history of musical talent. But once he and his brother

Ira won success in the world of musical entertainment, other members of their family embraced their achievements. Ira, deeply aware of the excellence of George's music, had seen to it from the start that his manuscripts were saved. The family, we recall, lived together under one roof until 1929, and by the time George died in 1937, the Library of Congress in Washington, D.C., had already established its own Gershwin Collection. By 2003, when I began to compile my Gershwin chronology, sources covering the composer's activities were readily available. Indeed, by the time I took that project as far as it needed to go, I had gathered so much data that I began to wonder whether a two-volume biography was in the offing. (The publication in 2005 of Howard Pollack's monumental biography [884 pages] eventually put that notion to rest.)

Once my chronology reached the end of Gershwin's life, I began to write a story that I hoped would describe the man and artist he was, and what his effort meant to his contemporaries. Still in touch with H. Wiley Hitchcock, my first mentor and now an éminence gris of American musical history who had long ago moved to New York City, I sought his advice on who might act as a reader of what I was writing about my subject. He recommended Robert Kimball: an expert on American musical theater, who had written extensively on the Gershwins and knew Ira well. Through the months and years that followed, I gradually mailed my draft to Robert, chapter by chapter. And each time, after he'd read the next chapter, the two of us had a conversation on the telephone. Kimball had not known George Gershwin, but throughout the writing of my forty-chapter draft I had the good fortune to be in touch with a reader whose appreciation and depth of knowledge of my subject helped to steer me in what felt like the right direction. Conversations with another New York friend, Joseph Horowitz, helped me to situate Gershwin's work in that milieu during the 1920s.

A unique helpmate whose advice has enhanced this book considerably is Wayne Shirley, a staff member of the Library of Congress's Music Division. A scholar whose first article on Gershwin dates from the 1970s, Wayne is still at work, as *Summertime* goes to press, editing the score of Gershwin's magnum opus: the folk opera *Porgy and Bess*, whose enduring success has only in recent years won for it a version of Gershwin's score that deals with the changes he made while he was still alive. Readers of my account of that composition will encounter Wayne Shirley's contribution to my outlook on the opera whose place in the story of Gershwin's life and work looms large.

Thanks to a family connection—Amy Crawford, a daughter living and working in California—my go-to source for documents began in 2005 to be the archive of the Ira and Leonore Gershwin Trusts in San Francisco: a mecca for me until 2012, when its contents were added to the Gershwin holdings in the Library of Congress. That archive, managed by Michael Owen, a significant contributor to this biography, was built around the materials saved, gathered, and kept by Ira, who, once the brothers left New York for Hollywood in 1936, had remained in Southern California until his death in 1983. The story of how these holdings found their way to San Francisco is beside the point. But the archive, professionally run and informally welcoming, was a place whose ambience and clientele gave a reader a taste of the Gershwin family's legacy: pride in its artistic past, respect for people who appreciated that past, and a readiness to aid and abet their needs and desires. I was able to visit the archive often, and its holdings added much data to my chronology. On the home front, I added to my modest store of Gershwin scores a gift from conductor and friend Gustav Meier: his well-worn copy of the *Porgy and Bess* vocal score.

Graduate students at the University of Michigan during my latter teaching years have proved to be helpful in gathering Gershwiniana on my behalf. Especially active early on were Todd Decker and Joshua Duchan. Eric Saylor also helped on that front, as did Sara Suhodolnik later on. Special thanks are due to Mark Clague, a Michigan undergraduate who later joined the faculty, is now a dean there, and who was instrumental in bringing the Gershwin Initiative to the Michigan campus. A couple of years ago Mark taught a course on Gershwin's music, which he invited me to address. After that encounter I got to know Kai West, a graduate student who assisted me during the summer and fall of 2018, and then participated in a fortunate scholarly transaction. Visiting the Library of Congress that summer, he was told by Ray White, curator of the Music Division's Gershwin's Collection, that letters acquired recently had yet to be seen by Gershwin scholars, including me. One batch added to that of the collection's correspondence was between Gershwin and Isaac Goldberg, his first biographer. The other batch preserved an exchange with Gregory Zilboorg, who became Gershwin's psychiatrist in 1935 and proved to be a trusted friend. The Zilboorg letters add significantly to what we know about the love life of a man who, engaged over the years with many different women, failed to find the life partner for whom he yearned. Ray White's heads-up and Kai West's delivery to my doorstep of copies of "new" Goldberg and Zilboorg letters have enabled me to weave fresh information into the story near the end of its telling.

Editors at Norton have assisted me in the fashioning of this biography. Maribeth Payne shepherded the project before retiring in 2017. Susan Gaustad, who had edited *America's Musical Life*, took charge of a still-swollen manuscript and exercised her gift for finding in it the clearest and most engaging story the author had managed to offer. After Helen Thomaides gave the manuscript a final editorial polish for a trade audience, Harry Haskell applied his musical knowledge plus a sharp-eyed and rigorous command of the scholarly trade's formal conventions.

Finally, I thank three long-term Ann Arborites for help in other realms of furtherance: Jamie Abelson, a fan of music and dance in the neighborhood who, through many years of morning dog-walking, has always been ready to discuss my Gershwin venture since it was hatched; Professor Glenn Watkins, a musicological colleague at the University of Michigan since the 1960s, for his friendship and his outlook on the job each of us had taken on, including encouragement from the start to read each other's work-in-progress; and this book's dedicatee, my wife Penelope Crawford, an accomplished pianist whose presence, brain, and ingenuity have enabled the author to complete a book almost guaranteed to be his last.

—Easter Sunday, April 21, 2019

NOTES

CHAPTER 1. THE GERSHWINS: MORRIS AND ROSE AND FAMILY

1. Howard Pollack, *George Gershwin: His Life and Work* (Berkeley: University of California Press, 2006; henceforth Pollack), 1.
2. Edward Jablonski and Lawrence D. Stewart, *The Gershwin Years* (Garden City, NY: Doubleday, 1973; henceforth Jablonski and Stewart 1973), 31.
3. Harold Meyerson and Ernie Harburg, *Who Put the Rainbow in "The Wizard of Oz?": Yip Harburg, Lyricist* (Ann Arbor: University of Michigan Press, 1995), 16.
4. On 1 March 1916, a contract was issued for George's first published song, "When You Want 'Em, You Can't Get 'Em; When You've Got 'Em, You Don't Want 'Em," with words by Murray Roth, issued by Harry Von Tilzer music publishers. The seventeen-year-old composer signed his name as "George Gershwin," and that is how it appeared on the song when it was published in May. Robert Kimball and Alfred Simon, *The Gershwins* (New York: Bonanza Books, 1973; henceforth Kemball and Simon), 12. They report: "George had always admired Ed Wynn, the comedian, and so changed the 'vin' ending to 'win' in honor of his idol." The Perfection Music Company's March 1916 advertisement for the first piano rolls made by the composer also lists him as "George Gershwin." However, when Ira began his diary in September 1916, he signed his name "I. Gershvin," and he continued to do so for some time after. The family's adoption of the now-standard spelling was a gradual process.
5. Isaac Goldberg, *George Gershwin: A Study in American Music*, supplemented by Edith Garson, with Foreword and Discography by Alan Dashiell (New York: Frederick Ungar, 1958; first published 1931; henceforth Goldberg), 57–58.
6. Ira Gershwin (henceforth IG) Diary, Fall 1916, Library of Congress, Washington, DC, Gershwin Collection (henceforth DLC GC), 2 Oct. 1916.

7. Jablonski and Stewart, 31.
8. The Gershwin scrapbooks in DLC GC abound with interviews of George.
9. Goldberg, 20–21.
10. S. N. Behrman, "Troubadour," *New Yorker*, 25 May 1929: 28. See also Merle Armitage, *George Gershwin* (New York: Longmans, Green & Co., 1938), 211–18.
11. Oscar Levant, *A Smattering of Ignorance* (Garden City, NY: Garden City Publishing Co., 1942), 172.
12. Goldberg, 52.
13. Ira Gershwin, *Lyrics on Several Occasions* (New York: Alfred Knopf, 1959), 31; henceforth cited as IG, LoSO. A later printing with a Preface by John Guare and an Envoi by Lawrence D. Stewart (New York: Limelight Editions, 1997) supplies the references in this book.
14. Levant 1942, 174.

CHAPTER 2. A PIANO IN THE HOUSE, AND ELSEWHERE

1. Kimball and Simon locate this address in the East New York section of Brooklyn, between Sutter and Belmont Avenues. The house, they report, "had a front room, a dining room, a kitchen, and a maid's room on the ground floor; upstairs there were three or four bedrooms, one of which was rented" to a boarder (2–3).
2. Ira Gershwin, ". . . But I Wouldn't Want to Live There," *Saturday Review*, 18 Oct. 1958: 27, 48.
3. Goldberg, 54. The image of a barefoot boy on 125th Street has yet to spark a question from biographers.
4. Ibid., 58. As Max Rosen, Maxie Rosenzweig would become a noted professional concert violinist. According to Alberto Bachmann, *Encyclopedia of the Violin* (New York: Appleton, 1925), he was born in Rumania in 1900, "came to New York in infancy, and studied under Mannes, Sinsheimer, Auer, and Hess. Made his debut in Christiana and toured Denmark, Norway, Germany and Sweden; made his New York debut with the Philharmonic Society in 1918; since then has been concertizing in the US" (395). Thanks to Mark Katz for the reference. According to Edward Jablonski, *Gershwin* (New York: Doubleday, 1987), 7, Max Rosen died in 1956.
5. Goldberg, 55–56. Jablonski reports that the friendship between the two boys included talk about music, and plenty of wrestling. George, Jablonski writes, "took boyish pleasure in throwing the huskier, heavier Maxie in their wrestling matches" (7–8).
6. Meyerson and Harburg, 8.
7. Deena Rosenberg, *Fascinating Rhythm: The Collaboration of George and Ira Gershwin* (Ann Arbor: University of Michigan Press, 1997), 11; quoted from Ira Gershwin, *The George and Ira Gershwin Song Book* (New York: Simon and Schuster, 1960), Foreword.

Edward Jablonski, *Gershwin* (New York: Doubleday, 1987; henceforth Jablonski 1987), 8, gives a more explicit and extensive memory: "I remember being particularly impressed by his left hand. I had no idea he could play and found that despite his roller-skating activities, the kid parties he attended, the many street games he participated in (with an occasional resultant bloody nose) he had found time to experiment on a player piano at the home of a friend on Seventh Street."

8. Jablonski mentions Miss Green on p. 9. Beyer gets an entry in *The New Grove Dictionary of Music and Musicians*, 2nd ed., ed. Stanley Sadie (London: Macmillan, 2001).

9. Goldberg, 59–60.

10. Ibid., 67. Goldberg quoted these words about "intensive listening" from an article Gershwin published in *Theatre* magazine, March 1927.

11. Ibid., 60. Gershwin's piano lessons began in 1912, when the family bought a piano. His first interview—in *Billboard*, 13 March 1920—fixes that date. But the chronology of his piano lessons remains vague. We know, however, that his concertgoing began in earnest in December 1912 and that he heard his future teacher, Charles Hambitzer, play a piano concerto by Anton Rubinstein with the Waldorf-Astoria Orchestra in April 1913. Later Gershwin reckoned the length of his pianistic training as four years.

12. Walter Monfried, "Charles Hambitzer Was My Greatest Influence, Says 'Rhapsody' Writer," *Milwaukee Journal*, 28 Jan. 1931. This article was an important source of information on Hambitzer and his family. Hambitzer's sister, Mrs. Ernest Reel, wife of a successful businessman, is said to have been musically gifted, able at age four to play Sousa marches on the piano after just one hearing. "But my brother Charles was the real genius of the family," she assured Monfried.

13. Nathaniel Shilkret, *Nathaniel Shilkret: Sixty Years in the Music Business*, ed. Niel Shell and Barbara Shilkret (Lanham, MD: Scarecrow Press, 2005), 29–30.

14. Ibid., 30.

15. Pollack, 26, gives Hambitzer's dates as 1878–1918.

16. Goldberg, 60–61.

17. Shilkret, 32.

18. Kimball and Simon, 7; also David Ewen, *George Gershwin: His Journey to Greatness* (Englewood Cliffs, NJ: Prentice-Hall, 1970), 19.

19. Rosenberg, 12–13.

20. The song was "Since I Found You," with lyrics by Leonard Praskins, a friend of Ira's from the neighborhood. See Pollack, 219. Goldberg questioned George about this number, reporting: "He laughs as he recalls how, having begun the refrain of this song in G major he found himself suddenly at sea in F, unable to regain the shore" (67). "Ragging the Träumerei" was apparently a rhythmically extemporized classic. The first number does not survive; only the music of the second is extant.

21. Goldberg, 70. Moses Edwin Gumble (1876–1947) was a songwriter who became known for his effectiveness as a song plugger. See David A. Jasen, *Tin Pan Alley* (Donald I. Fine, 1988).

22. This story was reported personally by Berlin in the 1970s, after the publication of Kimball and Simon, *The Gershwins*, in 1973. Author's phone conversation with Robert Kimball, July 2006.

23. Jablonski and Stewart 1973, 48. They add that Gershwin "later made more money when he performed at parties with Fred Van Eps, the banjo player."

24. Another reason to believe that Gershwin's song-plugging career began in the fall rather than the spring is that, in later interviews, he refers to his stint at the Remick firm, which ended on March 17, 1917, as having lasted two and a half years, or sometimes just two, but never three or "almost three." Also, when mentioning his age when he started, he was likely to say sixteen, or even seventeen. He turned sixteen on 26 September 1914. From that birthday to the day he left Remick's was almost two and a half years. In 1938, the year after his death, Ira Gershwin, usually meticulous about factual accuracy, wrote that George had begun his Tin Pan Alley career at fifteen. If that and the Irving Berlin story are both true, he must have started plugging songs in late August or early September: after his return from the Catskills but before his sixteenth birthday. (See Armitage 1938, 17, for Ira's statement.)

25. See Jasen on the Remick firm's early days.

26. This number, an inspirational British song from the World War I era, with words by Douglas Furber and music by A. Emmett Adams, reveals a protagonist praying fervently for the safe return of an absent lover.

27. The plugging function referred to here was that of a publisher's employee who, by singing songs in public settings, advertised them for sale. For example, in a vaudeville house, a standard ploy was for a pianist to begin a targeted number onstage, prompting a song plugger planted in the audience to rise and sing it, doing all he could to urge audience members to join in. (A sheet with the song's words was sometimes distributed beforehand; copies of the sheet music were likely to be for sale on the premises, or nearby.) Sometimes, if he had a voice that could carry throughout the house, the singer might be the piano player himself. There are no accounts, however, of George Gershwin in either role. Whatever plugging he did seems to have been at the piano. Goldberg writes: "Remick's, nightly, sent forth to the cafés of New York City a corps of some eight pluggers, accompanied by song-and-dance artists who would sing and hoof the new tunes into the popular ear. George was one of the fleet" (75).

28. Kimball and Simon, 12.

29. Goldberg writes that during his years at Remick's, Gershwin came to consider both men his musical heroes (80–82).

30. *The Girl from Utah*, with a book by James T. Tanner and lyrics by Percy Greenbank and Adrian Ross, had a score primarily by English composers Paul Rubens and Sydney Jones. Kern's songs were additions to the score. The show opened in New York on 24 August 1914.

31. Ewen, 26.

32. "Recollections of Irving Caesar," Kimball and Simon, 24.

33. Caesar's words were: "Since there were ten composers for one lyric writer, George welcomed me around him." Ibid.

34. Ibid., 23.

35. Glenn Watkins, *Proof through the Night: Music and the Great War* (Berkeley: University of California Press, 2002), 246.

36. Fred Astaire, *Steps in Time* (New York: Harper & Brothers, 1959; this paperback version, Perennial Library, New York: Harper & Row, 1987; henceforth Astaire 1959), 55; quoted in "Recollections of Fred Astaire," Kimball and Simon, 10.

37. Kimball and Simon, 286–90, carries a Gershwin "Piano Rollography" compiled by Michael Montgomery.

38. Michael Montgomery, Trebor Jay Tichenor, and John Edward Hasse, "Ragtime on Piano Rolls," in Hasse, ed., *Ragtime: Its History, Composers, and Music* (New York: Schirmer Books, 1985), 90–91.

39. These selections are found on a compact disc, *George Gershwin: The Piano Rolls*, vol. 2, realized by Ardis Wodehouse (Nonesuch 7559-79370-2), first issued in 1995.

40. *The ASCAP Biographical Dictionary of Composers, Authors, and Publishers*, 2nd ed., ed. Daniel McNamara (New York: Thomas Y. Crowell, 1952), 381.

41. Pollack, 97–98.

42. Rosenberg, 41 (interview with Mabel Schirmer, 11 May 1978).

43. "Harry Von Tilzer," *ASCAP Biographical Dictionary*, 516. See also Isaac Goldberg, *Tin Pan Alley: A Chronicle of American Popular Music*, Introduction by George Gershwin (New York: Frederick Ungar, 1961; first published 1930), 170–73.

44. Goldberg, 84–85. Later that year, the composer made a piano roll version.

45. Sigmund Romberg (1887–1951) was then the Shubert brothers' chief staff composer. "Mr. Simmons" was Ernest Romayne ("Ma") Simmons (1865?–1954), who served as the Shuberts' casting director from 1912 into the 1940s. According to Foster Hirsch, *The Boys from Syracuse: The Shuberts' Theatrical Empire* (New York: Cooper Square Press, 2000), 141–42, Simmons auditioned "almost every singer and dancer who ever appeared in a Shubert show."

46. Hirsch, 137–38, offers details about Atteridge's professional duties on Broadway: "Atteridge typically would write lyrics for about thirty-five songs, at least ten of which would be cut during the rehearsal period. Often on the first day of rehearsal, he would have five times more material than would actually end up in the show on opening night. Atteridge attended every rehearsal, where he would take suggestions from the director, the leading performers, and the composers."

47. "Edward Kilenyi," *The New Grove Dictionary*, vol. 13, 590. E. Kilenyi: *Gershwiniana: Recollections and Reminiscences of Times Spent with My Student George Gershwin* (n.p., 1963).

48. "Schoenberg's Harmony" by Kilenyi appeared in the *New Music Review* 14, nos. 6 and 7 (September and October 1915): 324–28, 360–63. "The Theory of Hungarian Music" appeared in the *Musical Quarterly* 5 (1919): 39. On a more practical level, Kilenyi wrote the piano accompaniments for a folk song collection compiled and edited by Eleanor Hague, *Folk Songs from Mexico and South America* (New York: H. W. Gray, 1914).

49. IG Diary, 17 March 1917.

50. Susan E. Neimoyer, "*Rhapsody in Blue*: A Culmination of George Gershwin's Early Musical Education" (Ph.D. diss., University of Washington, 2003), 72.

CHAPTER 3. A SONGWRITER EMERGES (1917–18)

1. The story as told here is a conflation of Isaac Goldberg's account, 88–90, and the version that appeared in the *New York American*, 2 Jan. 1932.

2. In a letter written to a cousin on 21 September, Ira, reporting on George's new job, noted that his brother had "met Victor Herbert, Jerome Kern, & P. G. Wodehouse . . . the other day." IG to Benjamin Botkin, 21 Sept. 1917. DLC GC.

3. William Henry Bennett ("Will") Vodery (1884–1951), an intriguing figure, is the focus of Mark Tucker's research in an entry in the *International Dictionary of Black Composers*, ed. Samuel A. Floyd, Jr. (Chicago: Fitzroy Dearborn Publishers, 1999), vol. 2, 1166–68.

4. Kimball and Simon, xxiii. This claim, which does not appear in William Bolcom and Robert Kimball's *Reminiscing with Sissle and Blake* (New York: Viking Press, 1973), is made in an introductory essay on the Gershwins by jazz critic John S. Wilson.

5. According to Joan Peyser, *The Memory of All That* (New York: Billboard Books, 1998), 40–41, Roberts told "Harlem historian Delilah Jackson," whose work seems not to have found its way into print, "that George came to his apartment and watched him play." Peyser continues, though without documentation: "Eubie Blake claimed Roberts visited him, sat next to him, and copied what he did. Roberts told Delilah Jackson that Gershwin did something like that with him." According to Pollack, 721, Robert Kimball, in an interview with him, "recalled Roberts saying that Gershwin came to his apartment for 'lessons in styling.'"

6. Jablonski and Stewart 1973, 50.

7. Scott E. Brown, *James P. Johnson: A Case of Mistaken Identity* (Metuchen, NJ, and London: Scarecrow Press and Institute of Jazz Studies, Rutgers University, 1986), 112.

8. The first of the several Princess Theatre shows, *Nobody Home*, premiered in New York on 20 April 1915. Kern wrote the music and Bolton the book, but the lyrics were the work of several different writers. Gerald Bordman, *Jerome Kern: His Life and Music* (New York: Oxford University Press, 1980), Chapters

7 and 8 (106–42), gives detailed accounts of several of the shows. The term of choice for the interweaving of music and plot has been "integration."

9. See Marjorie Farnsworth, *The Ziegfeld Follies* (New York: Bonanza Books, 1955), which describes the shows and includes many pictures.

10. According to Armond Fields and L. Marc Fields, *From the Bowery to Broadway: Lew Fields and the Roots of American Popular Theater* (New York: Oxford University Press, 1993), 366–67, *Miss 1917* received good reviews and, at first, a favorable audience response, but fell victim to a general slump in attendance that wartime conditions brought to the theater business as 1917 came to an end.

11. P. G. Wodehouse and Guy Bolton, *Bring on the Girls: The Improbable Story of Our Life in Musical Comedy* (New York: Limelight Editions, 1984; first published 1953), 82–83.

12. David Ewen, *George Gershwin: His Journey to Greatness* (Englewood Cliffs, NJ: Prentice-Hall, 1970), 85–86.

13. Ibid., 41.

14. Peyser, 47–48. Caesar's story, however, suggests excessive naïveté about the publishing business. After more than two years on Tin Pan Alley, could Gershwin really have believed that it would take a $250 payment to get this song into print?

15. Goldberg, 91.

16. David Jasen and Trebor Jay Tichenor, *Rags and Ragtime* (New York: Seabury Press, 1978), 5. Also Russell Sanjek, *American Popular Music and Its Business: The First Four Hundred Years*, vol. 3: *From 1900 to 1984* (New York: Oxford University Press, 1988), 93–96.

17. Richard Rodgers, *Musical Stages: An Autobiography* (New York: Jove/HBJ, 1975), 86–88.

18. *Billboard*, 13 March 1920.

19. In the liner notes to a four-record set produced by RCA Victor, *Fascinating George* (LM 6033, LPM-6000, 1955), composer Arthur Schwartz wrote the following: "Max Dreyfus, dean of music publishers, gave [Gershwin] his first big victory, a composing contract—thirty-five dollars a week—and no specified hours. . . . Every producer of musical shows considered him headquarters for new talent. . . . To have him give you a contract! That meant you were IN. George Gershwin, now aged nineteen, was unequivocally in." Quoted from Rosenberg, 30.

20. Jablonski and Stewart 1973, 54–56. Dresser's comment about his continuing efforts to make the music of "My Gal Sal" shine is further proof that Gershwin's piano accompaniments, rather than fixed, tended to be shaped to fit the occasion.

21. Gerald Bordman, *Jerome Kern: His Life and Music* (New York: Oxford University Press, 1980), 174–78. The *Rock-a-Bye Baby* cast included Louise Dresser. (Kern is said to have been displeased by Gershwin's failure to follow this advice

when, in 1919, he accepted an invitation to score *La-La-Lucille!*, produced by Alex A. Aarons.)

22. There is some confusion about when Gershwin began that assignment. Kimball and Simon, 18, print an undated entry of Ira's diary, between one for 25 February and another for 22 May 1918. It begins: "George played Baltimore, Boston and Washington with Louise Dresser," a trip that ended after the week of 4 March. It ends: "At present he is rehearsal pianist at the New Amsterdam Roof Garden where the 1918 Ziegfeld Follies is in preparation." Chances are that this duty began in mid- to late May, after *Rock-a-Bye Baby* was made ready for its opening on the 22nd, and lasted until the *Follies* opened in mid-June.

23. Ira Gershwin, "Which Comes First?," *New York Telegram*, 25 Oct. 1930.

24. Gerald Bordman, *American Musical Theatre: A Chronicle*, 2nd ed. (New York: Oxford University Press, 1992), 93.

25. A historian of the Broadway musical stage, in a comment about Sloane and his colleague Raymond Hubbell of the same generation, judges them "extreme mediocrities" and "hacks." Ibid., 388.

26. The accolade was bestowed by vaudeville historian Joe Laurie, Jr., in his *Vaudeville*. Others in the group were Maggie Cline, Bonnie Thornton, Lillian Russell, Eva Tanguay, Vesta Victoria, Alice Lloyd, Irene Franklin, Florence Moore, Helen Morgan, Fanny Brice, and Irene Bordoni. "Nora Bayes," Laurie writes, "was the 'class' of all the single women—a truly great artist who did everything with class gestures" (53–54). Joe Laurie, Jr., *Vaudeville: From the Honkey-Tonks to the Palace* (New York: Holt, 1953).

27. Levant 1942, 148. Levant's uncle, Oscar Radin, was the show's conductor, indicating why the youngster attended the performance in the first place.

28. George Gershwin (henceforth GG) to Max Abrahamson, 12 Sept. 1918. DLC GC.

29. GG to Irving Caesar, late September 1918. DLC GC.

30. Jablonski and Stewart 1973, 61. According to Goldberg, who provides more detail, on the tour "whatever went wrong was laid at Gershwin's door. He was the target of continual reprimands. But he had his artistic revenge. Once when Miss Bayes (née Dora Goldberg) asked him to change the ending of a certain song, he met her with adamantine resistance. 'You're a mere kid!' she exclaimed. 'Why Irving Berlin or Jerome Kern would make the change for me at the mere suggestion. Who are you to hold out like this?' 'I'd be glad to do it if it were any other song,' countered George. 'But this ending cost me plenty of time and effort. Besides, I like it as it stands.' Later, Nora and George became the best of friends, and remained so until her untimely death" (93–94).

CHAPTER 4. FROM SYRACUSE TO NEW YORK (1918–19)

1. GG to Isaac Goldberg, 15–16 June 1931. Harvard Theatre Collection. This letter forms the basis for the account of the show's history published in Goldberg, 95–98.

2. Perkins's lyrics were ascribed to a nom de plume, Fred Caryll.

3. Quoted from Abel Green and Joe Laurie, Jr., *Show Biz from Vaude to Video* (New York: Holt, 1951), 32. Cook's ad appeared in a 1909 issue of *Variety*.

4. Eileen Southern, *Biographical Dictionary of Afro-American and American Musicians* (Westport, CT: Greenwood Press, 1982) cites the Clef Club on p. 73.

5. Robert Kimball and Linda Emmett, eds., *The Complete Lyrics of Irving Berlin* (New York: Alfred Knopf, 2001), 174.

6. Kimball and Emmett, xv, quoted from Kimball and Simon, 20. Copyrighted on 20 February 1919, "That Revolutionary Rag" was published by Harms. Later that year Berlin began to publish songs through his new publishing company, Irving Berlin, Inc. (Kimball and Emmett, 174). "Lead sheet," pertaining to jazz and popular music, means "a shorthand score or part. It may provide melody and chord symbols." *Harvard Dictionary of Music*, 459.

7. This comment, made in 1973, is quoted in Kimball and Emmett, xv. Elsewhere in that volume, Kimball notes that, in his own dealings with Berlin in old age, Gershwin would sometimes be mentioned, and Berlin "wanted to be certain I knew how great George Gershwin and his brother Ira were" (xix).

8. Born in 1895, Caesar was twenty-three when the number was written. His collaborator, Alfred Bryan, was of an older generation. It seems fitting, however, to think of this song as a Gershwin-Caesar number, since the two worked together from 1916 or 1917 to 1924; there is no record of collaboration between Gershwin and Bryan.

9. Howard Pollack calls it "the hit of the show, which translated into sheet-music sales and increased name recognition." He also says it was "widely singled out by the critics," citing one newspaper clipping of a review of *Good Morning, Judge*. The "hit" claim seems to have come from Irving Caesar, who called it "a hit of sorts" (230–31 and footnotes). Pollack also reports that English composer William Walton (1902–1983), a Gershwin fan, was especially fond of "I Was So Young" (138).

10. "Recollections of Irving Caesar," Kimball and Simon, 23–24.

11. Music in major mode is made from melodies and harmonies fashioned from a major scale, exemplified on a piano keyboard from middle C to the C eight notes above it. The core of minor mode lies in the white keys between middle A and the E above it; but the last three steps offer three alternatives, hence a broader range of expressive possibilities.

12. Vernon Duke, *Passport to Paris* (Boston: Little, Brown, 1955), 77.

13. IG, LoSO, 66. Ira also reported having learned a word for what Aarons was doing: synesthesia, meaning "a process in which one type of stimulus produces a secondary subjective sensation, as when a specific color evokes a specific smell sensation" (67).

14. Jablonski and Stewart 1973, 63–64.

15. "'N' Everything" was published in 1918 with "words and music by Bud DeSylva, Gus Kahn, and Al Jolson."

16. Alan Dale, "'La-La-Lucille' a Comic Uproar with No Intent but to Amuse," *New York American*, 27 May 1919.

17. This characterization appeared on the sheet-music covers of the published songs from the show.

18. Opening in Atlantic City on 21 April, the company then moved to Washington, DC, on 27 April 27, to Boston on 12 May, and to New York on 26 May.

19. Operettas were the musical shows most likely to be exceptions to this rule.

20. "Drama" / 'La-La-Lucille!' Has Its First Performance at the Henry Miller." Unidentified New York paper carries review by Heywood Broun. *Variety*, 18 July 1919, commented as follows on *La-La-Lucille!*, then in its eighth week at Henry Miller Theatre: "Will probably stick out the summer season. Show undoubtedly handicapped by location off Broadway. Is about breaking even, with the takings a little over $7,000" (14). According to Pollack, Gershwin signed a contract with DeSylva, Arthur Jackson, and Alex Aarons in March giving him 1.5 percent of the show's gross box-office receipts (232). If the receipts were $7,000 per week, his take would amount to $105.

21. Information on the strike comes from Sanjek 1988, 47, and Bordman 1992, 107.

22. On rolls of songs by other composers, such as Irving Berlin's "Mandy," or Kenbrovin and Kelette's "I'm Forever Blowing Bubbles," from *The Passing Show of 1919*, he was now billed as "George Gershwin, composer of *La-La-Lucille*."

23. Edward Jablonski and Lawrence D. Stewart, *The Gershwin Years* (Garden City, NY: Doubleday, 1958), 21.

24. Astaire 1959, 71–82. The Astaires' new show was an operetta, *Apple Blossoms*, composed by violin virtuoso Fritz Kreisler and produced by Charles Dillingham, which opened on 7 October 1919.

25. Pollack, 236. Also appearing in the Capitol Revue, starting on 17 November, was the sixteen-year-old soprano Jeanette MacDonald, later an operetta star. See Edward Baron Turk, *Hollywood Diva: A Biography of Jeanette MacDonald* (Berkeley: University of California Press, 1998), 31.

26. "Recollections of Irving Caesar," Kimball and Simon, 24.

27. Edward Foote Gardner, *Popular Songs of the Twentieth Century: A Charted History* (St. Paul, MN: Paragon House, 2000), vol. 1: *1900–1949*, 82.

28. Goldberg, 105, credited "Swanee" in 1931 with launching "2,250,000 records."

29. Gilbert Seldes, *The Seven Lively Arts* (Mineola, NY: Dover Publications, 2001; first published 1924), 75.

30. "Ibee," "The Year in Legit.," *Variety*, 26 Dec. 1919: 9.

31. "Making a Joke of Prohibition in New York City," *New York Times*, 2 May 1920.

CHAPTER 5. SOCIETY, THE MUSIC BUSINESS, AND *GEORGE WHITE'S SCANDALS* (1920)

1. The classic study of the process cited here is Marshall and Jean Stearns, *Jazz Dance: The Story of American Vernacular Dance* (New York: Macmillan, 1968).

2. Sanjek 1988, Chapter 4, "Inside the Popular-Music Business," 32–44, chronicles the industry's workings between 1900 and 1920, including copyright law, the treatment of recordings, and the founding of ASCAP.

3. Contract between GG and T. B. Harms, 21 Feb. 1918. DLC GC.

4. "Melody the Thing, Young Composer Declares; George Gershwin, Writer of Musical Comedy Hits, Says Better Music Is in Demand," *Billboard*, 13 March 1920.

5. George White to GG, 27 Feb. 1920. DLC GC.

6. "'Scandals of 1920' Has All Essentials for Summer Hit," *New York Clipper*, 9 June 1920.

7. "George White's New Revue Is a Good Summer Show of Diverse Scenes," *New York Times*, 8 June 1920.

8. Ibee, *Variety*, 11 June 1920.

CHAPTER 6. "ARTHUR FRANCIS" AND EDWARD KILENYI

1. I think they shared a sense of how expressive popular song in this idiom could be. George, with his mastery of melody and spirit, and his evolving engagement with harmony and counterpoint, composed songs whose music brimmed with shades of expression. Ira, though unschooled in musical technique, was a deeply musical being able to sense and to find words for George's musical responses, once a song's mood and subject were determined.

2. Goldberg, 174. When "Waiting for the Sun to Come Out" (see below) came out, the disparity in experience between the brothers was large. Before he and George wrote the new song, Ira had written lyrics for only six songs; and on two of the six, he had joined forces with more experienced hands: Lou Paley on "Beautiful Bird" (1917) and B. G. DeSylva on "Kitchenette" (1919). In contrast, by then George had written more than fifty songs before he and Ira fashioned "Waiting for the Sun to Come Out," and twenty-three of them were published. A majority of his songs—thirty-four of the fifty-two, in fact—were written for stage productions, so the range of his experience included work as a Tin Pan Alley songsmith, a vaudeville accompanist, and both a rehearsal pianist and a composer of Broadway shows. George had by then also worked with at least a dozen different lyricists, including his brother.

3. For the record, George had also composed at least three instrumental numbers, including two for piano—"Tango" (1914) and "Rialto Ripples" (1917) in collaboration with Will Donaldson—and one for string quartet, "Lullaby" (1919).

4. Apparently, George was known to call Youmans "Junior," or other such diminutives, while Youmans called Gershwin "old man." Pollack, 159.

5. On 9 October 1920, *Billboard* magazine noted that E. Ray Goetz's production *Piccadilly to Broadway* was "expected to go into New York in about three weeks' time" (26). More than a month later, the same journal carried a notice dated New York, 18 November, and announcing that the show, still on the road, was

about to undergo further revision. "At the termination of its engagement at Providence, R.I., last week," the notice read, *Piccadilly to Broadway* was to be "closed for reconstruction and restaging, under the direction of Ned Wayburn. Next week it will reopen at Springfield, Mass. The piece will be renamed, and, after the Springfield engagement, will go to the Majestic Theater, Boston, for a run, with a New York showing to follow." Several new cast members were also named (26).

6. Kimball and Simon, 30.
7. Jablonski and Stewart 1973, 79.
8. What the critic actually wrote was that they were not allowed "to obtrude irrelevantly upon the main scheme of conveying a human story of love and sentiment."
9. *Variety*, 25 March 1921.
10. The tally of dates is Atlantic City, 21–23 March; Wilmington, 24–26 March; Baltimore, 28 March–April 2; Washington, DC, 4–9 April; and Pittsburgh. See Robert Kimball, ed., *The Complete Lyrics of Ira Gershwin* (New York: Da Capo Press, 1998; first published 1993), 12.
11. Astaire 1959, 122.
12. Jablonski and Stewart 1973, 69.
13. It should be noted, too, that although Gershwin's lessons with Kilenyi ended early in 1923 at the latest, the relationship between the two men continued throughout the 1920s and into the 1930s. More than once, when Gershwin found himself in need of specialized advice relating to a problem he faced with classical music, he sought it from Kilenyi. In the late 1920s, for example, when Gershwin was hired not only to play in a summer concert at Lewisohn Stadium in New York, but to conduct the New York Philharmonic-Symphony Society there, Kilenyi helped him to prepare for that assignment. And in Hollywood in the early 1930s, as he was completing his Second Rhapsody, his former teacher claimed to have helped him solve a problem relating to the end of that composition. Edward Kilenyi, "George Gershwin . . . as I Knew Him," *Etude* 68, no. 10 (October 1950): 11–12, 64.
14. Alan Dale, "'Scandals' Opens July, Meat for Entire Year," *New York American*, 12 July 1921.
15. Michael Montgomery, "George Gershwin's Piano Rollography," in Wayne Schneider, ed., *The Gershwin Style: New Looks at the Music of George Gershwin* (New York: Oxford University Press, 1999), 225–53. This was the last roll Gershwin made until 1925.
16. Information from Astaire 1959 85–88.

CHAPTER 7. SONGWRITER AND COMPOSER (1922)

1. Jablonski and Stewart 1973, 76–78.
2. According to Gardner's log of popular songs, "Do It Again" reached No. 17 by mid-June 1922. Gardner, 86–87.

3. The show is discussed in Astaire 1959, 88–92. Benchley's encomium in *Life* magazine appears on p. 92.

4. "Radiophone Opposition," *Variety*, 3 March 1922.

5. Sanjek 1988, 77.

6. Ibid., chap. 8, pp. 74–90, traces that process in some detail.

7. Don Rayno, *Paul Whiteman: Pioneer in American Music*, vol. 1: *1890–1930* (Lanham, MD: Scarecrow Press, 2003; henceforth Rayno 2003), 45.

8. Rayno 2003, 50, lists the following, compiled from the pages of the *New York Clipper*, 1921–24: Eddie Elkins and his Pavilion Royal Orchestra; Barney Rapp and his Broadwalk Orchestra; Irving Weiss's Romance of Rhythm Orchestra; the All Star Trio—F. Wheeler Wadsworth (alto sax), Victor Arden (piano), and George Hamilton Green (xylophone); Joe Raymond and his Little Club Orchestra; Clyde Doerr and his Club Royal Orchestra; Arnold Johnson (and later Jimmy Guest) and the Vernon Country Club Orchestra; the Carlton Terrace Orchestra in Cleveland; the Hotel Sinton Orchestra in Cincinnati; the New Ocean House Orchestra in Swampscott, MA; Maurice Swerdlow and his Orchestra; the Whiteman Piano Quartette (Zez Confrey, Victor Arden, Phil Ohman, and Al Mitchell); the Whiteman Saxophone Sextette; the Russian Balalaika Orchestra, directed by Harry Mogiloff and Charles Weinberg; Charles Dornberger's Orchestra; the Zez Confrey Orchestra; Paul Whiteman's Collegians; The Virginians, led by Ross Gorman; Al Mitchell and his Arcadia Orchestra; Joe Gibson and the Moulin Rouge Orchestra; Eddie Davis and his Orchestra; Charles McLean and his Orchestra; Jimmy Caruso and his Orchestra; Louis Rizzo and his Orchestra; and Alex Hyde's Orchestra.

9. Quoted from ibid., 49.

10. GG, "(I'll Build a) Stairway to Paradise," Kimball and Simon, 33–34.

11. Unidentified critic, "Scandals 1922 Outscandals Everything / New White Production at Globe a Wonderful Collection of Scenery and Jazz, Mostly Jazz," unidentified New York paper, 29 Aug. 1922.

12. Alexander Woollcott, "A Dancer's Revue: 'George White Scandals of 1922,'" *New York Times*, 29 Aug. 1922. "All the good music in the *Scandals* was written for something else—some of it before young Mr. White was born," Woollcott wrote, referring to quotations of earlier favorites—"'Neath the Shade of the Old Apple Tree" was one—in certain scenes. It should be noted that while the Whiteman band was a special onstage attraction, a pit orchestra conducted by Max Steiner accompanied the other numbers of the show.

13. Sime Silverman, review of *George White's Scandals of 1922*, *Variety*, 1 Sept. 1922.

14. GG, "(I'll Build a) Stairway to Paradise," Kimball and Simon, 33–34.

15. IG, LoSO, 294–96.

16. Ibid., 296.

17. *Shuffle Along* closed on 15 July 1922.

18. GG to Goldberg, 15–16 June, 1931. Harvard Theatre Collection. Whiteman

and his orchestra had been hired by White to perform a specialty in the first act's penultimate slot, and also to accompany the finale of Act I.

19. The most far-reaching and detailed account of this work is John Andrew Johnson, "Gershwin's *Blue Monday* (1922) and the Promise of Success," in Wayne Schneider, *The Gershwin Style* (New York: Oxford University Press, 1999), 111–41. See also Wayne Shirley's brief article in the *ISAM Newsletter*, Spring 1982. Howard Pollack's account of *Blue Monday* (1922) and its later incarnations is also valuable; see pp. 269–75 of his biography.

20. Known throughout his life as a healthy, vigorous, and athletic physical specimen, Gershwin was nevertheless known to be sometimes plagued with an unsettled stomach. No hard evidence advanced until later in his life, I believe. See Pollack 206–07.

21. W.S., "White's Scandals of 1922 Score Triumph," unidentified New Haven newspaper, 22 Aug. 1922.

22. Quoted in Goldberg, 123.

23. Charles Darnton, " 'George White's Scandals' Lively and Gorgeous," *New York World*, 29 Aug. 1922.

24. C.P.S., " 'Scandals of 1922' Is Most Pleasing," *New York Post*, 29 Aug. 1922.

25. Merle Armitage, *Gershwin: Man and Legend* (New York: Duell, Sloan and Pearce, 1958), 26–27.

26. Jablonski and Stewart 1973, 50.

CHAPTER 8. AMERICANS IN LONDON (1922–23)

1. *New York World*, 16 Sept. 1922. A handwritten note in the Gershwin scrapbooks dates the article Sept. 6, perhaps referring to its original publication in the U.K. The portion of the article that mentions Gershwin is reprinted in Robert Wyatt and John Andrew Johnson, eds., *The George Gershwin Reader* (New York: Oxford University Press, 2004; henceforth *Gershwin Reader*), 41–42.

2. Information about the careers of cast members comes from Richard C. Norton's three-volume *Chronology of American Musical Theater* (New York: Oxford University Press, 2002).

3. IG to Benjamin Botkin, 12 Jan. 1923. DLC GC. There is a small discrepancy of dates here; official records of *Our Nell* have the show closing in New York on 6 Jan. 1923.

4. *Hitchy-Koo of 1917*, a revue coproduced by Raymond Hitchcock and E. Ray Goetz, had been conducted by Daly. Like Gershwin, he also contributed songs to *Piccadilly to Broadway* (1920).

5. According to the interview, Frank Saddler, then Broadway's leading orchestrator, knew Daly by 1915 and played a leading role in his landing that conducting job.

6. Data on William Daly is quoted by the author from memory of a lost clipping from an unidentified Cincinnati, Ohio, newspaper of the early 1930s.

7. George Gershwin, "Fifty Years of American Music . . . Younger Composers, Freed from European Influences, Labor Toward Achieving a Distinctive American Musical Idiom," *American Hebrew*, 22 Nov. 1929. Quoted from *Gershwin Reader*, 115–16.

8. The contract of George Gershwin, composer, and Albert de Courville, producer and coauthor with Edgar Wallace and Noel Scott of *The Rainbow*, may be found at DLC GC.

9. See Norton, *Chronology*.

10. Morris (1888–1987), a New York native and a charter member of ASCAP, was a composer and pianist who worked for a time playing piano at the Jerome H. Remick music publishing company where Gershwin worked. (He composed "Kangaroo Hop," of which Gershwin made a piano roll released in 1916.). He also accompanied Al Jolson and Blossom Seeley in vaudeville. Later in 1923, he returned to the United States to work for Paul Whiteman's organization as a booker for his satellite band business. See Rayno 2003, 314. "You'd Be Surprised" was the title of a 1919 Irving Berlin song. Gershwin's comment about American popular songs in the score suggests that these were songs already familiar in the U.S.

11. A native of Minnesota, Bert Ralton (Gershwin added an "s" to his name) had started his career in 1918, when he joined the Art Hickman Orchestra in San Francisco as a saxophonist. He traveled to New York, apparently with the Hickman band, and that is where he and a banjo player on 20 July 1920 joined with Gershwin to record two sides for the Victor label. After a stop in Havana, Cuba, Ralton landed that same year in London. As one report has it, he "created a sensation with his many eccentricities, one of which was smoking a cigarette and playing a clarinet at the same time." Ralton and his ensemble were headquartered at London's Savoy Hotel when Gershwin saw them in *You'd Be Surprised*. They also made recordings in London.

12. GG to IG, 18 Feb. 1923. DLC GC. Jablonski and Stewart 1973, 81–82, affirms its significance by reproducing the entire letter in facsimile.

13. The music of the first song, a Gershwin–Daly collaboration, remained unchanged, but the lyrics were refashioned by Grey for *The Rainbow*. As we shall see, the original American version was sung later in 1923 by mezzo-soprano Eva Gauthier as part of a song recital at Aeolian Hall, in which she included a group of American popular songs with George Gershwin accompanying her on the piano. As for the second, refashioned as "Baby" and with new lyrics by DeSylva, it eventually appeared in the 1925 Gershwin show *Tell Me More*.

14. Quoted phrases are from the playbill. For the earlier Gershwin and Johnson link, see Chapter 3.

15. *Variety*, 12 April 1923.

16. *Variety*, 26 April 1923.

17. Brown, 153–56.

18. Astaire 1959, 101–02.

19. Charles Schwartz, *Gershwin: His Life and Music* (Indianapolis and New York: Bobbs-Merrill, 1973), 51, cites Gershwin's April encounter in Paris with a prostitute, engineered by Jules Glaenzer and Buddy DeSylva.

20. Aarons is said to have taken Fred and Adele to the premiere performance of *The Rainbow*, which took place on 3 April, and about which they had reservations. *Steps in Time*, however, makes no mention in this notice of Gershwin or his involvement with the show.

21. See Alex Aarons to IG, 19 May 1923, Library of Congress, Washington, DC, Ira and Leonore Gershwin Trusts (henceforth DLC IGLG Trusts), for the plan, written in London, envisioning a collaboration in New York between the Astaires and the Gershwin brothers.

22. Benchley's review in *Life* (7 July 1923) called the song "a Hawaiian Hula-Hula number right out of the files of 1921–22." Harms also published "On the Beach at How've-You-Been," a parody of "Lo-La-Lo" with comic lyrics, e.g., "Ev'ry time you come across a bunch of native blokes / They say 'Hicky-wicky-y-woo!' which means how are the folks!" It's also worth noting that in the middle 1910s, DeSylva, who was attending the University of Southern California, participated in a Hawaiian band that played in a club around Los Angeles.

23. Benchley, *Life*, 7 July 1923.

CHAPTER 9. A RECITAL AND AN EXPERIMENT (1923–24)

1. Carl Van Vechten, Introduction, Jablonski and Stewart 1973, 22.

2. Henry Taylor Parker, "Jazz Enlarges Mme. Gauthier's Newest Harvest," *Boston Transcript*, 30 Jan. 1924.

3. Deems Taylor, "Eva Gauthier," *New York World*, 2 Nov. 1923. The *New Grove Dictionary* gives the title of Bartók's song as "Három őszi könnycsepp."

4. Deems Taylor, column on Eva Gauthier's recital, *New York Sunday World*, 4 Nov. 1923.

5. Whiteman's presence at the concert is confirmed by his biographer, Don Rayno, who writes that the recital "served to reinvigorate his plans to perform an entire program of modern American music in a concert hall setting" (Rayno 2003, 76). He does not mention, however, any tendering of an offer to Gershwin on that occasion. See also Eva Gauthier, "Personal Appreciation," Armitage 1938, 194–95.

6. Gauthier in Armitage 1938, 194–95.

7. Pollack, 289.

8. One such success was *The Gingham Girl* (1922–23), codirected by McGregor and choreographed by Lee, which ran for 322 performances.

9. A review of *Sweet Little Devil* for *Variety* found the show's principal strength the spirited dancing conceived by Sammy Lee. The three-act script, however, was deemed "transparent," and Gershwin's score "average," with only one (uniden-

tified) song a potential hit. As for Constance Binney, who played the lead role and had been "allotted a vast majority of the vocal numbers," she apparently rendered them "none too convincingly." Moreover, "provided with ample opportunity to dance, including a brief episode of toe work," the reviewer reported that she had had to rely chiefly "upon pleasing magnetism and a winsome appearance." "Skig," review of *Sweet Little Devil, Variety,* 24 Jan. 1924.

10. Paul Whiteman and Mary Margaret McBride, *Jazz* (New York: J. H. Sears, 1926), 98.

CHAPTER 10. *RHAPSODY IN BLUE* (1924)

1. Goldberg, 138–39.
2. Our discussion of *George White's Scandals of 1922* in Chapter 7 notes Gershwin's delight in the Whiteman Orchestra's performance of "Stairway to Paradise," and that number's reliance on blues elements. In his article "Toujours Jazz," Gilbert Seldes also praises Whiteman's "incredible mingling of 'A Stairway to Paradise' with the 'Beale Street Blues'" in his performance, reproduced on his recording of that number. See Gilbert Seldes, *The 7 Lively Arts,* with a New Introduction by Michael Kammen (Mineola, NY: Dover Publications, 2001; first published 1924), 83–108.
3. Goldberg, 139–40.
4. Edward Elgar's ceremonial march *Pomp and Circumstance* closed the program.
5. Shortly before the concert, Whiteman invited music critics Leonard Liebling, Henry O. Osgood, and Pitts Sanborn to a morning rehearsal of the new piece by "this young fellow Gershwin," predicting that it would be "a knockout success." Liebling remembered asking Osgood at the time, "Who's Gershwin?" and learning "that Gershwin had written several 'song hits' in current revues and musical comedies." He also recalled that he and Osgood were "captivated" by the *Rhapsody* when they heard it that day. Quoted by Goldberg, 141–42, from Liebling's article in the *Musical Courier,* 17 May 1930: 27.
6. Henry O. Osgood, *So This Is Jazz* (Boston: Little, Brown, 1926), 190.
7. A tag is a melodic sign-off. In the *Rhapsody* it's a melodic snippet sounded to complete a musical statement or section.
8. "I got to be a member of the family," Grofé recalled, "because I was down there all the time, naturally. They taught me how to drink Russian tea and introduced me to a lot of dishes and asked me to stay for dinner. I practically slept there. . . . I lived in uptown New York, above 180th Street, so I was constantly going between the two places. I had a car and I'd drive down, pick up the music and go back again. Back and forth, back and forth. I would orchestrate the music as fast as he wrote it." Grofé interviews, Reel 115. See Rayno 2003, 77–78.
9. Abel Green, "Paul Whiteman's Brilliant Recital Says Jazz Craze Will Never Die," *Variety,* 14 Feb. 1924.

10. Abel Green, "Whiteman's 'Jazz' Recital," *New York Clipper*, 15 Feb. 1924. Both *Variety* and the more venerable, but soon-to-expire, *Clipper* were by this time issued by the same publisher.

11. Lawrence Gilman, "Paul Whiteman and the Palais Royalists Extend Their Kingdom," *New York Tribune*, 13 Feb. 1924.

12. Olin Downes, "A Concert of Jazz," *New York Times*, 13 Feb. 1924.

13. W. J. Henderson, "Paul Whiteman's Concert Reveals the Rise of Jazz," *New York Herald*, 13 Feb. 1924.

14. W. J. Henderson, "Paul Whiteman Shows Things Beyond the Tin Pan Alley Vision / Victor Herbert and George Gershwin Aid in Demonstration—Jazz and Ragtime Described—Importance of the Instruments," *New York Herald*, 17 Feb. 1924.

15. Deems Taylor, "Mr. Whiteman Experiments," *New York World*, 18 Feb. 1924.

CHAPTER 11. ENTER IRA (1924)

1. Duke, 102–03. Dukelsky (later Vernon Duke) had shown his concerto to pianist Artur Rubinstein, who was impressed, and who recommended Paris as a place he might arrange performances.

2. Ibid., 103–04. "The songs I 'arranged,'" Dukelsky recalled, "were the ever-popular 'Somebody Loves Me,' 'In Araby,' 'Kongo Kate,' 'Tune in on Station J-O-Y,' 'Year after Year,' and a rhythm song, the name of which escapes me."

3. *Primrose* was produced by George Grossmith and J. A. E. Malone, proprietors of London's Winter Garden Theatre (not to be confused with its New York namesake). Because Gershwin was under contract to Alex A. Aarons, he and his new producing partner, Vinton Freedley, were also listed on the show's credits, as extenders of an arrangement through which the show was appearing. Contract signed on 24 June 1924 by GG and Alex Aarons. DLC GC.

4. GG to Emily and Lou Paley, 8 July 1924, reproduced in facsimile in Kimball and Simon, 38.

5. "A Londoner's Diary," unidentified English newspaper, 6 Sept. 1924. DLC GC.

6. IG to GG, 25 June 1924. DLC GC.

7. Adele's response steered clear of any hint of gossip. "The Prince of Wales and other members of the Royal Family were very kind to my brother and me," she told the reporters, adding: "I'm not talking about it for publicity purposes." Astaire 1959, 124.

8. Ibid., 124–25.

9. According to the show's playbill, Arden and Ohman filled the penultimate slot in Act I.

10. The show's credits identified Sammy Lee as director of dances and ensembles, but Fred Astaire, though he never claimed the title, served as the team's choreographer, as shown in his autobiography.

11. Astaire 1959, 134–35.

12. Ibid., 126–27.

13. Ibid., 129.

14. Frank Vreeland, "The Astaires, Catlett, and Gershwin All Win," *New York Telegram and Evening Mail*, 2 Dec. 1924.

15. Linton Martin, "When Musical Comedy Lifts Its Highbrows," *Philadelphia North American Sunday Review*, 23 Nov. 1924.

16. Rosenberg, *Fascinating Rhythm*, devotes pp. 84–104 to expressive affects in several songs from *Lady, Be Good!*

17. Ira's statement is quoted from Goldberg, 201–02. See also IG, LoSO, 173.

18. David Schiff, *Gershwin: "Rhapsody in Blue"* (Cambridge: Cambridge University Press, 1997), 13, refers to the two-part, twelve-note "tag" as "the familiar 'good evening friends.' " In this author's experience, the tag's first gesture was sometimes sung to "without a shirt."

19. IG, LoSO, 5.

20. The phrase "you don't know the half of it, dearie" was popularized in entertainment circles by Bert Savoy, a well-known female impersonator of the day. Wikipedia.

CHAPTER 12. A YEAR IN THE LIFE, PART I (1924–25)

1. Armitage 1938, 172.

2. Quoted from Jablonski and Stewart 1958, 23. Whiteman's concert took place on Saturday, 15 November, and the show's debut on Monday, 17 November.

3. *Boston Evening Transcript*, 5 Dec. 1924. Early in January, music critic Francis Perkins, in an article titled "Jazz Breaks into Society," noted the "conservative" stylistic leaning of most jazz-oriented works. Citing concerts in 1924 by both Whiteman and Vincent Lopez, he wrote: "Two dozen concerts of Whiteman or Lopez will roll up fewer discords than one evening with the International Composers' Guild." *Boston Independent*, 3 Jan. 1925. His critique holds that only Gershwin's *Rhapsody* carries promise for the future.

4. "Wanted: Jazz Grand Opera / O. H. Kahn Would Produce at Metropolitan American Play with Modernized Music," *New York Evening Mail*, 18 Nov. 1924.

5. Otto Kahn, George Gershwin, and Mr. and Mrs. Alex A. Aarons had been fellow passengers on the ship that returned Gershwin to New York after *Primrose* opened in London in September. It was on that voyage, in fact, that Kahn heard "The Man I Love" for the first time, apparently played (and sung?) by Gershwin in a shipboard concert. Ira later reported that it was on the strength of that experience that Kahn agreed to invest $10,000 in *Lady, Be Good!* IG, LoSO, 5.

6. Lou Paley to IG and GG, 10 Jan. 1925. DLC IGLG Trusts.

7. IG to Lou and Emily Paley, 8 June 1925. DLC IGLG Trusts.

8. Henrietta Malkiel, "Awaiting the Great American Opera: How Composers Are Paving the Way," *Musical America*, 25 April 1925. See also Richard Crawford,

"Where Did *Porgy and Bess* Come From?" *Journal of Interdisciplinary History* 36, no. 4 (Spring 2006): 697–734; see especially 728–29.

9. The contract was signed on 25 Feb. 1925. DLC GC. According to Jablonski 1987, 95, DeSylva was brought in on the job under pressure of time.

10. The melody linked to this reference, sometimes known as "Happyland," contains four sections, like Gershwin's song. The four-note gesture to which "three times a day" is sung is the same in both the earlier song and Gershwin's melody.

11. Alexander Woollcott, "Gershwinisms at the Gaiety / 'Tell Me More' a Summer Show Full of Sweet Sounds," *New York Sun*, 15 April 1925.

12. Armitage 1938, 196–97.

CHAPTER 13. A YEAR IN THE LIFE, PART II (*CONCERTO IN F*)

1. See George Martin, *The Damrosch Dynasty: America's First Family of Music* (Boston: Houghton Mifflin, 1983) for biographical background.

2. Winthrop Sargeant, *Geniuses, Goddesses, and People* (New York: E. P. Dutton, 1949), 42, 64.

But according to Deems Taylor, *Of Men and Music* (New York: Simon and Schuster, 1937), Chapter 13, "Godfather to Polymnia," 144–53, Walter Damrosch was also a talented and faithful servant of American music-making during the twentieth century's first several decades.

3. Carl Van Vechten, "George Gershwin: An American Composer Who Is Writing Notable Music in the Jazz Idiom," *Vanity Fair*, March 1925: 40, 78, 84.

4. "Concerto in F (1925)," Kimball and Simon, 52, cites the composer as the source.

5. Carl Van Vechten, Introduction to Jablonski and Stewart 1973, 24.

6. GG, "Jazz Is the Voice of the American Soul," *Theatre Magazine*, March 1927. Reprinted in *Gershwin Reader*, 91–94.

7. The last sentence of this paragraph is quoted from Jessie M'Bride, "The New Prophet of American Music," *Washington News*, 24 Nov. 1925.

8. "Gershwin's Work Feature of the Week / New York Symphony, via Walter Damrosch, Scores Signal Victory," *New York World*, 29 Nov. 1925.

9. Ibid.

10. Gershwin, "Jazz Is the Voice of the American Soul" (cited above).

11. *New York Herald Tribune*, 29 Nov. 1925. See also Jablonski and Stewart 1973, 105.

12. This claim is found in an unidentified Washington newspaper printed as the composer was overseeing the tryout of *Tip-Toes* in that city, from November 24 to 28.

13. Lester Donahue, "Gershwin and the Social Scene." Quoted in Armitage 1938, 173.

14. W. J. Henderson, "Gershwin Concerto in F Played," *New York Sun*, 4 Dec. 1925.

15. Lawrence Gilman, "Mr. George Gershwin Plays His New Jazz Concerto with Walter Damrosch," *New York Herald Tribune*, 4 Dec. 1925.

16. Olin Downes, "The New York Symphony," 4 Dec. 1925.

17. Samuel Chotzinoff, "New York Symphony at Carnegie Hall," *New York World*, 4 Dec. 1925.

18. "New York Symphony / Damrosch Plays Gershwin Concerto at the Academy," *Philadelphia Evening Bulletin*, 11 Dec. 1925.

19. W. G. Owst, "Damrosch Conducts Orchestra at Lyric—GG, Composer-Pianist, Is Soloist," unidentified Baltimore newspaper, 11 Dec. 1925.

20. Olin Downes, "Sibelius and Gershwin Mingle," *New York Times*, 27 Dec. 1926.

21. Lawrence Gilman, "A New Work from Sibelius at the Symphony Concert," *New York Herald Tribune*, 27 Dec. 1926.

22. Neither of these two published articles found in a Gershwin scrapbook dated 1925 can be identified further, but both—especially the one by McCommon, in which Gershwin, age twenty-six and working on the London production of *Tell Me More*, is interviewed at some length—are well informed.

23. *Vanity Fair*, October 1925: 47.

CHAPTER 14. A YEAR IN THE LIFE, PART III

1. B. G. DeSylva to GG, 25 Nov. 1925. DLC GC.

2. IG, LoSO, 119–20.

3. Undated letter from Lorenz Hart to IG, quoted in Kimball and Simon, 55.

4. John J. Daly, "Tip-Toes a Winner in National Premiere," unidentified Washington newspaper, 25 Nov. 1925.

5. Leonard Hall, "A Thorobred," *Washington Daily News*, 25 Nov. 1925.

6. Arthur B. Waters, " 'Tip-Toes,' an Ingratiating Show with Charming Cast," unidentified newspaper [*Variety*?], 13? Dec. 1925.

7. Smith's telegram to GG is quoted in Kimball and Simon, 52.

8. Anonymous reviewer, "Tip-Toes Here with Tunes," *New York Times*, 29 Dec. 1925.

9. Alexander Woollcott, "Mr. Gershwin's Latest," *New York World*, 29 Dec. 1925.

10. Issued by New World Records, 80598-2/2/DIDX # 071577, this reconstruction presents sixteen tracks from the Carnegie Hall concert production, conducted by Rob Fisher. A booklet with information about the endeavor and lyrics accompanies the recording.

11. The show's playbill, p. 19, contains the following note: "The character of 'The Flame' and the story which surrounds her are frankly legendary and not based on fact, except in so far as the Russian Revolution of 1917 is used as a background."

12. Also included should be the *Rainbow* revue he wrote for London in 1923.

13. Brooks Atkinson, "An Operatic Spectacle," *New York Times*, 31 Dec. 1925. "Paul Whiteman Gives 'Vivid' Grand Opera / Jazz Rhythms of Gershwin's '135th Street' and Deems Taylor's 'Circus Day' Delight," *New York Times*, 30 Dec. 1925.

15. S. Jay Kaufman, "Whiteman-ey," *New York Telegram*, 30 Dec. 1925.

16. "Paul Whiteman at Carnegie Hall," *New York Sun*, 30 Dec. 1925.

17. Olin Downes, "Paul Whiteman's Novelties," *New York Times*, 31 Dec. 1925.

CHAPTER 15. IN ARENAS OLD AND NEW (1926)

1. "Pastor and Singer Debate Over Jazz," *New York World*, 7 May 1926.

2. George Gershwin, "Does Jazz Belong to Art?," *Singing*, July 1926: 13–14.

3. Robert Wyatt, "The Seven Jazz Preludes of George Gershwin: A Historical Narrative," *American Music* 7/1 (Spring 1989): 68–85.

4. Kay Swift, interview with Robert Wyatt, 10 Jan. 1987. Ibid.

5. Samuel Chotzinoff, "Gershwin and Alvarez," *New York World*, 5 Dec. 1926.

6. Francis D. Perkins, "Gershwin Gives His First Public Performance of Year," *New York Herald Tribune*, 5 Dec. 1926.

7. Richard L. Stokes, "Realm of Music," *New York Evening World*, 5 Dec. 1926.

8. H.B., "Mme. d'Alvarez and George Gershwin," *New York Evening Post*, 6 Dec. 1926.

9. Abbe Niles, "The Ewe Lamb of Widow Jazz," *New Republic*, 29 Dec. 1926.

10. Robert Schirmer to Emily and Lou Paley, written after 15 April 1926. Quoted in Kimball and Simon, 63–64.

11. It didn't help the visitor's mood either that "during the concert someone stole George's hat and overcoat which were hanging up in the back of the box we were in. I had to lend him my cane," wrote Schirmer, "so that the poor boy wouldn't look absolutely naked walking around the streets." Ibid.

12. Robert Schirmer to Lou and Emily Paley, after 15 April 1926. DLC GC.

13. "Lady, Be Good!," *Era*, 21 April 1926.

14. G.F.M., " 'Dance—Cold Bath—Ride, Says Adele Astaire,' a Gallery Girl Writes," unidentified London newspaper, 1925. This item is centered on habits of healthy exercise and diet, and what they could teach the British—females especially. Gershwin scrapbooks, DLC GC.

15. In another letter to Gershwin from 1923, Adele names George Jean Nathan, prominent New York drama critic and author, as a possible romantic rival for her affections. "George Jean Nathan has been with me for the past three weeks," she announced, "& left today for N.Y. on the Mauretania." Early in 1924 she cited Nathan as a frequent correspondent and a perpetual source of New York gossip. "George Jean N. supplies me with all the 'dirt' of B'way—get loads of letter[s] on every boat."

CHAPTER 16. *OH, KAY!* (1926)

1. Wodehouse and Bolton, 209.
2. Pollack, 379, cites an affinity between Gershwin and Lawrence that began in 1923.
3. Information here and below comes from Wodehouse and Bolton.
4. Wodehouse and Bolton, 236.
5. "Dale Finds Much Good in 'Oh, Kay!,'" *New York American*, 9 Nov. 1926.
6. Quoted from Pollack, 384, based on a letter to Bolton in 1973. The song titles mentioned in Wodehouse's letter pertain to numbers in *Oh, Kay!*
7. IG, LoSO, 261. In 1925 the Gershwins had moved to a house on 103rd Street.
8. Ira's note, published in 1959, stated: "As I recall it, Jimmy (Oscar Shaw), meeting Kay (Gertrude Lawrence) for the first time, kissed her that evening, with no resultant How-dare-you. Here they meet again" (260). In fact, their first kiss took place during *this* meeting, their second. It was prompted by the sudden appearance of Officer Jansen, for whom they trotted out their newlywed impersonation; honeymooners would hardly have postponed their first kiss until the morning after their wedding night. Ira's "as I recall" shows that, though usually meticulous about factual details, he had not checked the script before writing this note.
9. Ira Gershwin, "Marginalia," *The George and Ira Gershwin Songbook* (New York: Simon and Schuster, 1960), xi–xii. Quoted in Philip Furia, *Ira Gershwin* (New York: Oxford University Press, 1996), 58; also IG, LoSO, 111.
10. Percy Hammond, "Miss Gertrude Lawrence in a Clean, though Pleasing and Pretty Musical Comedy, Entitled 'Oh, Kay!,'" *New York Herald Tribune*, 9 Nov. 1926.
11. Brooks Atkinson, "Bootlegging Bedlam," *New York Times*, 9 Nov. 1926.
12. Burton Davis, "'Oh Kay' a Hit at the Imperial," *New York Morning Telegraph*, 9 Nov. 1926.
13. Issued on the Nonesuch label, 79361-2, via Roxbury Recordings, the recording of numbers from *Oh, Kay!* delivers twenty tracks with singers including soprano Dawn Upshaw plus the Orchestra of St. Luke's, conducted by Eric Stern. A booklet with brief essays and the lyrics is also included.
14. George Ferencz, ed., *The Broadway Sound: The Autobiography and Selected Essays of Robert Russell Bennett* (Rochester, NY: University of Rochester Press, 1999), 115–17.
15. These quotes come from an interview with Gershwin found by Kai West in unused manuscript extracts of Isaac Goldberg's biography. A typescript of these extracts was supplied to Ira Gershwin by Jack Neiburg in 1956. Currently in DLC IGLG Trusts.
16. "Gershwin to Play Own Compositions for Radio / Young Composer to Be Centre of Eveready Hour Devoted to 'Classics' of Twentieth Century," *New York Evening World*, 11 Dec. 1926.
17. Olin Downes, "Sibelius and Gershwin Mingle," *New York Times*, 27 Dec. 1926.

CHAPTER 17. UPS AND DOWNS: KAUFMAN ON THE SCENE (1927)

1. Francis Toye, "Jazz—Good and Bad," London *Morning Post*, 5 Jan. 1927.
2. "Jazz to Survive, Says Gerschwin [*sic*]," *Montreal Daily Star*, 6 Jan. 1927. "Jazz No Worse Than the Auto," *Montreal Herald*, 6 Jan. 1927, identifies producer Alex A. Aarons as one of the vacationers.
3. George Gershwin, "Critic Artist, Artist Critic in This Review of Concert / Musician Given Chance of a Lifetime to Get Back at Traditional Enemy and Leaps to It with Right Good Will," *New York World*, 22 Jan. 1927. Franklin Pierce Adams's well-known verses for the Tinker-Evers-Chance trio were written about the 1914 World Series between the Chicago Cubs and the New York Giants.
4. Gilbert Seldes, "What Happened to Jazz / Rejected Corner Stones," *Saturday Evening Post*, 22 Jan. 1927.
5. Charles Ludwig, "Banjo, up from Georgia, Elbows Lordly 'Cello When Gershwin Rehearses with Symphony Orchestra / And Trumpet, Wearing Derby Hat, Sits Down Near Harp and Bassoon / 'King of Jazz' Compliments Cincinnati on Fine Musical Organization," *Cincinnati Times-Star*, undated but published after 11 March 1927. The column, which opens with two four-line stanzas of verse in praise of Gershwin, quotes Fritz Reiner at length on the subject of Gershwin's creative and musical prowess.
6. Though direct evidence is lacking, there is good reason to connect this statement to the publication of W. C. Handy's groundbreaking *Blues: An Anthology*, with an introduction by Abbe Niles (New York: A. and C. Boni, 1926); Handy reviewed Gershwin's music in the *New Republic* in December. The first page of Niles's forty-page introduction states that the blues "began as a form of Afro-American folksong—a 'form' since they were distinguished primarily by their peculiar structure," and that W. C. Handy "wrote the first (and many more) published blues, commencing a revolution in the popular tunes of this land comparable only to that brought about by the introduction of ragtime" (Handy, 1). Later, Niles characterizes Gershwin as "a pioneer" among composers for his use of the blues—not for its "over-and-over" twelve-bar form but as an "insistent experimenter" who found in blues music "material fit for building on a larger scale" (Handy, 21).

   Moreover, the last seven pieces in the anthology, grouped together by Niles under the heading "The White Viewpoint" (Handy, 38), include complete blues songs by Cliff Hess, Irving Berlin, and Jerome Kern, followed by an excerpt from John Alden Carpenter's jazz ballet *Krazy Kat*, and then three Gershwin selections: the song "The Half of It Dearie Blues" from *Lady, Be Good!*; the first page of the *Rhapsody in Blue* in a solo piano version; and three pages of a short-score arrangement of the *Concerto in F*, second movement. In Cincinnati, Gershwin told his lunch companions that in the *Concerto in F*, "the 'blue' or sad melody" in the second movement "is different from the ordinary 'blues' in that for the first time I have given it a distinctly nocturnal atmosphere."

7. Nina Pugh Smith, "Beethoven and Jazz Each Has Day in Court," *Cincinnati Times-Star*, 12(?) March 1927.

8. William Smith Goldenburg, "George Gershwin, Jazz King, Attracts Capacity Audience to Regular Symphony Concert," *Cincinnati Enquirer*, 12 March 1927.

9. George Gershwin, "Jazz Is the Voice of the American Soul," *Theatre Magazine* 45, no. 311 (March 1927). The striking photographs are credited to Nicholas Haz.

10. Ibid., printed in *Gershwin Reader*, 91–94.

11. Another Kaufman quip that made the rounds was the epitaph he suggested for one of the waiters in the Algonquin dining room, who were known for inattentiveness: "God finally caught his eye." In 1991 Elektra Nonesuch issued through Roxbury Records (79273-1 & 2) a reconstruction of *Strike Up the Band* (1927 version) conducted by John Mauceri, plus a booklet with essays. See Laurence Maslon, "George S. Kaufman: The Gloomy Dean of American Comedy," 27–31, in the booklet.

12. IG, LoSO, 22–25.

13. By way of contrast, Alec Wilder, *American Popular Song: The Great Innovators, 1900–1950* (New York: Oxford University Press, 1972), 138, has nothing good to say about "Strike Up the Band," holding that its survival "outside the marching bands is a mystery to me. For no matter how reverent is the public's memory of Gershwin, this song might as well have been written by any capable hack writer and, having no characteristic of Gershwin's style that I can find, does nothing to enhance his creative reputation." Wilder's interest in this book as a whole, however, lay in songs not as word–music combinations, nor as expressions of characters, but as musical compositions in the context of the composer's output.

     An admirer of the song, or at least of the refrain's harmonic plan, was Duke Ellington, who based a 1941 instrumental flagwaver he named "The Giddybug Gallop" on Gershwin's chord progressions for "Strike Up the Band."

14. Ellen Knight, *Charles Martin Loeffler: A Life Apart in American Music* (Urbana and Chicago: University of Illinois Press, 1993), 236.

15. Charles M. Loeffler to GG, 27 June 1927. DLC GC. "Anthland" and "Coptheil" are a play on the names of composers George Antheil and Aaron Copland, the switch of syllables suggesting a lack of distinctiveness in their modernist musical styles, at least when Loeffler compared them with Gershwin's. The letter announcing his eye problem, dated 17 July, includes the following: "My specialist will not allow me to get out of the reach of him for another few weeks. I have his promise that I may go to N.Y. for your 'Strike up the Band' show."

16. Austin, "Plays Out of Town, Strike Up the Band," *Variety*, 7 Sept. 1927.

17. Implying that two hits had been expected, a headline had proclaimed: "Only One Smash So Far in Philly," *Variety*, 14 Sept. 1927. *Manhattan Mary*, a musi-

cal comedy produced by George White with lyrics and a score by DeSylva, Brown, and Henderson, had a successful tryout in Philadelphia before a September 26 opening in New York, launching a run of 264 performances.

18. The anecdote, presumably first told by Ira Gershwin, is attributed to Lawrence Stewart in Jablonski and Stewart 1973, 124–26. By 1914 nearly 200 British theatrical companies were producing Gilbert and Sullivan operas, leading to an agreement that henceforth amateur companies would follow the D'Oyly Carte Opera Company's staging, using its prompt books. And these policies were then imposed on non-British companies.

CHAPTER 18. FROM AARONS TO ZIEGFELD (1927)

1. Alexander Woollcott, "George Gershwin and Fred Astaire," *New York World*, 23 Nov. 1927. "The managerial partnership between Alex A. Aarons and Vinton Freedley, which has busied itself of late years with the crass business details behind the Gershwin harlequinades," he began, "solemnized the union last evening by inaugurating a brand new playhouse, recently flung to the stars in a desperate effort to relieve the theatre famine in this unfortunate city."

2. Astaire's recollections of *Funny Face* provide the narrative of the show's origins and tryout run, with interjections from Ira Gershwin.

3. IG, LoSO, 28, 280, 277, 251.

4. Also added to the cast were comedian Earl Hampton and juvenile Allen Kearns. The latter, who had costarred with Queenie Smith in *Tip-Toes* (1925), arrived in early November from England. See "Astaire Show Stays Out for More Fixing," *Variety*, 9 Nov. 1927.

5. Ira's remarks in LoSO, 24. Edward Jablonski, *Gershwin: A Biography* (New York: Doubleday, 1987), 145, attributes the Astaires' "run-around" maneuver, a crowd-pleasing way to get offstage at the end of a dance routine, to dance director Edward Royce and *The Love Letter* (1921), an earlier musical in which they had appeared. Adele, he notes, would "put out her arms, as if grasping the handlebars of a bicycle and, with a blank face, begin circling the stage as if looking for a place to go, around and around. At about the third circuit, Fred would join her, also expressionless, to reiterative *oompahs* from the pit. After several runarounds they would trot into the wings with great applause."

6. John Anderson, "The Play: The Alvin Theatre Opens with the Astaires in 'Funny Face,'" *New York Evening Post*, 23 Nov. 1927. A much later summary gives a fuller idea of the plot, while leaving Act II to the imagination. This one takes the jewel robbery as the show's central event. "Jimmy Reeve [Fred Astaire] has three wards: Frankie [Adele Astaire], June [Gertrude McDonald], and Dora [Betty Compton]. When Jimmy takes Frankie's diary (she has been filling it with nasty lies about him), Frankie enlists a pilot she worships (Peter [Allen Kearns]) and Dora's boyfriend (Dugsie [William Kent]) to steal it back.

But while Peter and Dugsie are carrying out their mission, two real crooks—Chester [Victor Moore] and Herbert [Earl Hampton]—break into Jimmy's home to purloin the family jewels. The diary and the jewels (both kept in blue envelopes) get switched; second-act mayhem is the result." Tommy Krasker and Robert Kimball, *Catalog of the American Musical* ([New York:] National Institute for Opera and Musical Theater, 1988), 115.

7. Lewis's *Babbitt*, published in 1922, was named after its main character. The "bromide" in the song may have been inspired by a book by Gelett Burgess, *Are You a Bromide?* (1907).

8. See Philip Furia, *Ira Gershwin: The Art of the Lyricist* (New York: Oxford University Press, 1996), 65–66.

9. Ira recalled hearing Walter Catlett, who played the comic lead in *Lady, Be Good!*, "clipping syllables" from words, and he tried it himself in a song called "Sunny Disposish," written with composer Phil Charig for *Americana* (1926). IG, LoSO, 252.

10. Robert Garland, "Well—What of It? / Hats, No Hats, Orchestras, Gershwin and the Empress Josephine," *New York Telegram*, 26 July 1927.

11. Charles Pike Sawyer, "Gershwin Music by Philharmonic," unidentified New York newspaper [*Evening Post?*], 26 July 1927.

12. "Stadium Throng Gives Gershwin a Welcome," *New York Times*, 26 July 1927.

13. Dwight Taylor, *Joy Ride* (1959) carries the story of this encounter.

14. IG, LoSO, 30.

15. GG to Florenz Ziegfeld, 22 July 1927. DLC IGLG Trusts.

16. *New York Telegraph*, 23 July 1927.

17. The Boston run of *Rosalie* was extended to four and a half weeks. "Good Grosses Keep Up in Beantown," *Variety*, 11 Jan. 1928. Before *Of Thee I Sing* (1931), no musical comedy with music by Gershwin ran longer on Broadway than did *Rosalie*.

18. Leonard Hall, "Flo's Latest Beauty Has Marilyn and Jack," *New York Telegram*, 11 Jan. 1928.

CHAPTER 19. AMERICANS IN EUROPE (1928)

1. GG to Mabel Schirmer, 28 Feb. 1928. DLC GC.

2. Sketches for a new instrumental composition are dated "January 1928." *Gershwin Reader*, 317.

3. Eva Gauthier, "Personal Appreciation," Armitage 1938, 199.

4. Maurice Ravel to Nadia Boulanger, 8 March 1928. Quoted from Jérôme Spycket, *Nadia Boulanger*, trans. M. M. Shriver (Stuyvesant, NY: Pendragon Press, 1992), 71–72.

5. Interviewed in the 1970s, Mabel Pleshette, who dropped her married name after she and Bob Schirmer divorced, remembered Gershwin seeking out Bou-

langer in Paris in the spring of 1928. "Recollections of Mabel Schirmer," Kimball and Simon, 90.

6. Ira's diary of the family trip, from which the quotes in this section are taken, is found in DLC IGLG Trusts. See also Jablonski 1987, 153–81, for a detailed account of the family trip in Chapter 19.

7. "A Gershwin Night," London *Daily Sketch*, 24 March 1928.

8. It seems likely that the Gershwins' choice of Paris in particular, and France in general, was influenced by their close friends Lou and Emily Paley, who had spent Lou's sabbatical year 1924–25 in Paris and the south of France.

9. Salabert published some of Gershwin's songs in Paris with French texts. Ira confessed that he had been "surprised to find upon his arrival here that the 'Funny Face' numbers were already popular and were being sung. Not only were they sung, but when he picked up a Victrola record at a small shop he was amazed to find that it contained a number from the musical show which had been discarded because it wasn't considered good. And here in France it was sufficiently meritorious to be recorded on a phonograph disc." It is not known whether the *Funny Face* sheet music carried the standard English texts of Harms or Chappell or were Salabert publications with French texts.

10. In 1924 Harms published a solo piano arrangement of the *Rhapsody in Blue*, which seems to have eluded Wiener, Doucet, and the Pasdeloupers in Paris.

11. "Recollections of Mario Braggiotti," Kimball and Simon, 95.

12. Duke, 206–07.

13. Josefa Rosanska (1904–1986), an American pianist who lived and worked from 1925 to 1939 in Europe. Associated with protagonists of the Second Viennese School, she was the first wife of Rudolf Kolisch (1933–42), founder of the Kolisch Quartet. Her papers are in the library of Harvard University. Her program on 23 April included Alban Berg's Piano Sonata.

14. On 11 Nov. 1924, producers Charles Dillingham and Martin Beck staged an adapted version of this show in New York. It ran for only eighty performances, however, closing in January.

15. "Germany Taking Jazz Seriously, Gershwin Finds / American Composer in Berlin Lunches with Viennese Lehar / (Special Correspondence)," *New York Herald*, Paris edition, 28 April 1928.

16. After immigrating to the United States, where for many years he worked for Max Dreyfus in New York at the Harms-Chappell publishing firm, Sirmay (1880–1967) was involved with many Gershwin publications and became a close friend of the composer.

17. By way of comparison, Ira said in his later interview: "In Vienna, a show can be kept running for a long time, if it grosses $10,000 a week. In New York few legitimate shows can make a profit with those receipts." That interview is quoted in Alan Hutchinson, "A Song-Writer Listens to Some Foreign Melodies / In Which an Impressionable Young Man from Tin-Pan-Alley Says His Say on What He Saw," Paris *Comet*, July 1928.

18. Though Gershwin had not yet visited Austria or seen *Jonny spielt auf* when he told the Paris *Herald* reporter that jazz was taken "seriously" in Germany, perhaps he had that work in mind as an example.

19. Armitage 1938, 174.

20. Pollack, 81–82. Kálmán is said to have been Jewish, which suggests that he was familiar with Yiddish, which is grounded in German, apparently his native tongue. Occasionally George, and more often Ira, used a Yiddish word in a letter or in speech. But had George been fluent in that language, it seems possible that he and Kálmán would have communicated in it, which they did not. It should also be noted that Kálmán read *Variety* regularly, so although he did not speak English well, he must have read it fluently.

21. Pollack, 82.

22. Ibid., 144–45. In Lawrence Stewart's bibliographical essay at the end of Jablonski and Stewart 1973, he explains: "George had been playing for Berg when he suddenly realized the onesidedness of the situation and its intellectual, as well as social imbalance. 'Mr. Gershwin, music is music,' reassured the composer, who was fascinated by George's pianism." See pp. 394–95.

23. The original inscription reads: "Mr. George Gershwin zur freundlichen Erinnerung: an [the *Lyric Suite* quotation], den 5. Mai 1928 und an Alban Berg." Thanks to Dorothea Gail for the translation.

24. Pollack, 145. Christopher Reynolds's article "*Porgy and Bess*: 'An American Wozzeck' " (*Journal of the Society of American Music* 1, no. 1 [2007]: 1–21) points out similarities between Alban Berg's opera *Wozzeck* and Gershwin's *Porgy and Bess*, revealing that the meeting of the two composers during the Gershwin family's European trip in 1928 introduced a fresh element to George's "jazz opera" ruminations.

25. Duke, 209.

26. "Special Cable to the World / Gershwin Triumphs at Opera," *New York World*, 3 June 1928.

27. Early in 1925, at Dushkin's request, Gershwin composed a brief violin and piano piece in ABA form, which he and Dushkin premiered on 8 February. It was published later that year by Schott under the title *Short Story*. Pollack, 337–38.

CHAPTER 20. BACK IN THE U.S.A.: *AN AMERICAN IN PARIS* (1928)

1. "Gershwin Finds Great Opera Artist / Returning on Majestic Composer Tells of Thrills Abroad," *New York Morning Telegraph*, 20 June 1928.

2. Gershwin wrote on 25 July, Meltzer replied on 28 July. This and the letters quoted below are found in DLC IGLG Trusts.

3. Early in the fall of 1929 Gershwin signed a contract with the Metropolitan Opera Company to compose an opera, *The Dybbuk*, based on a play by Szymon Ansky.

4. Rayno 2003, 213–14.

5. Ibid., 213.

6. Olin Downes, "Whiteman's Jazz," *New York Times*, 8 Oct. 1928. "The first title on Mr. Whiteman's list," Downes complained, "was 'Yes, jazz is savage.' Our objection is that it was not 'savage' at all! It was anything but savage. It merely wore clothes more pretentiously cut than ever before, and tried to use long words, with a learned accent."

7. Robert Benchley, review in *Life* magazine, 30 Nov. 1928; cited in Pollack, 429.

8. Richard Lockridge, "And Now Gertrude Lawrence: 'Treasure Girl' Brings Her, in Whirl of Color, to the Alvin Theatre," *New York Sun*, 9 Nov. 1928.

9. Brooks Atkinson, "Gertrude Lawrence Returns," *New York Times*, 9 Nov. 1928.

10. IG, LoSO, 36.

11. Robert Kimball, editor of *The Complete Lyrics of Ira Gershwin* (1993), in his section on *Treasure Girl* on p. 32 writes that the first-act finale was originally conceived as a mixture of dialogue and song for Ann, Neil, her team compatriots (Larry, Nat, and Polly), and the ensemble, followed by Lawrence's act-ending turn. At some point, however, that earlier portion was cut. No music for the omitted section has survived.

12. Ibid., 134, presents the text of the finale: "Where's the Boy? Here's the Girl!"

13. Hyman Sandow, "Gershwin Presents a New Work," *Musical America*, 18 Aug. 1928.

14. *Gershwin in His Time: A Biographical Scrapbook, 1919–1937*, edited, with an Introduction, by Gregory R. Suriano (New York: Gramercy Books, 1998), 61–62.

15. The article is reproduced on the New York Philharmonic's digital archive: https://archives.nyphil.org/index.php/artifact/f08aa3f0-c460-4f1e-85ec -4dd6d1bc0d09-0.1/fullview#page/6/mode/2up.

16. Edward Cushing, "Mr. Gershwin's New Orchestral Piece, 'An American in Paris,' Has Its Premiere at a Concert of the Philharmonic-Symphony Orchestra, Mr. Damrosch Conducting," *Brooklyn Eagle*, 14 Dec. 1928.

17. Herbert Peyser, "Damrosch Introduces 'An American in Paris' at Philharmonic-Symphony," *New York Telegram*, 14 Dec. 1928.

18. Oscar Thompson, "Gershwin's 'An American in Paris' Played for the First Time by the Philharmonic-Symphony Orchestra," *New York Evening Post*, 14 Dec. 1928.

19. W. J. Henderson, "Philharmonic Plays Novelty: Gives First Performance of Gershwin's Work 'An American in Paris,'" *New York Sun*, 14 Dec. 1928.

20. Olin Downes, "Gershwin's New Score Acclaimed," *New York Times*, 14 Dec. 1928.

21. Samuel Chotzinoff, "The Philharmonic Plays Gershwin," *New York World*, 14 Dec. 1928.

22. Samuel Chotzinoff, "A Suggestion to Mr. Gershwin," *New York Sunday World*, 23 Dec. 1928.

Having read many reviews of "An American in Paris," Chotzinoff, striking a good-humored tone, takes issue with what he finds an unwarranted dismissal of what Gershwin had accomplished. His response? To devise an experiment involving audience members.

"At the second performance of 'An American in Paris,'" he explains, "I placed myself at one of the exits of Carnegie Hall and stopped every sixth subscriber with the query: 'Did you think Mr. Gershwin's piece meaningless twaddle?'" The answers he got revealed that those who had heard twaddle were offended less by Gershwin's music than by what that music was said to signify. A number of naysayers deemed the score unworthy of respect, he discovered, because the story told in the program was undignified for a Philharmonic crowd. How could such an audience possibly care about an American who, according to Mr. Taylor, sets out deliberately to partake of the grosser pleasures and aspects of the French? In other words, the notion that the traveler depicted in Gershwin's new composition was a drinker of alcohol, and may have crossed paths with prostitutes in Paris, was beyond the pale for a respectable concertgoer.

Tongue in cheek, Chotzinoff goes on to propose a counterstory far removed from the one suggested by Gershwin, then written and polished by Deems Taylor. In his Plan B, the protagonist, an American in the mold of Walt Whitman, revels in the human vitality afoot in Paris, and his day ends in Montmartre, where he regales the city's demimonde with tales of kindred spirits who are alive and well in America.

CHAPTER 21. IN MIDCAREER (1929)

1. Nathan Shilkret, *Sixty Years in the Music Business* (Lanham, MD: Scarecrow, 2005), 99.
2. Charles Ludwig, "Four French Taxicab Horns Furnish Symphony 'Music' / Lend Touch of Paris to Gershwin's New Production," *Cincinnati Times-Star*, 1 March 1929.
3. Both Robert Aura Smith's and Goldenberg's reviews, the latter titled only "Symphony Concert," were published on 2 March 1929.
4. *New York Sun*, 10 April 1929.
5. *New Yorker*, 25 May 1929. See also Suriano, 64–67.
6. "Music by Gershwin" program, 2 March 1934. DLC GC. Copy from DLC IGLG Trusts.
7. In fact, Al Jolson and Ruby Keeler were married in September 1928. At the first performance of *Show Girl* in the Boston tryout on 25 June 1929, "Liza" was introduced with unusual elaboration. As described in Herbert Goldman, *Jolson: A Legend Comes to Life* (New York: Oxford University Press, 1990; first published 1988), 191–92, a male singer, Frank McHugh, delivered the song's scene-setting verse, which then gave way to Ruby Keeler's softshoe-style

dance to the serene, lyrical refrain of "Liza," to be followed by her singing of that melody. In the debut performance, however, as McHugh's verse came to an end, Jolson, seated in the second row of the audience, rose to his feet and, "at the top of his lungs," sang the refrain. His unexpected gesture drew an encore from the opening-night crowd. (See Katharine Lyons's review of *Show Girl* in the *Boston Traveler*, 26 June 1929.)

8. German-born Gus Kahn (1886–1941) lived in America from early childhood, publishing his first song lyric in 1908. After a stretch in vaudeville, he established himself as a musical comedy lyricist in 1925, moving to Hollywood in 1933.

9. O. O. McIntyre, in a theater column in *Life* magazine, 30 August 1929, exclaims: "What a marvelous self-exploiter, this irrepressible Ziggy! The play deals more with Ziegfeld and his theatrical activities than with the tribulations of a show-girl but with the adroit skill that is fascinating."

10. W.E.G., "Show Girl," *Boston Herald*, 26 June 1929.

11. Brooks Atkinson, "Behind the Scenes with Ziegfeld," *New York Times*, 3 July 1929.

12. Gilbert Seldes, "Summer Shows: *Show Girl*," *New Republic*, 24 July 1929.

13. According to Ira Gershwin, Doris Carson, already a cast member, took over for Keeler during the weeks of 22 July and 29 July, and was then replaced by Dorothy Stone, who played Dixie Dugan from 5 August until the show closed. Kimball, *Complete Lyrics of IG* (1993), 142. The nature of Keeler's ailment has not been noted.

14. Visiting the show later, Brooks Atkinson, in "Summer: In Theatrical Memoriam," *New York Times*, 25 Aug. 1929, judged the "ardent" dancer Dorothy Stone a less effective Dixie Dugan than Ruby Keeler.

15. Abbe Niles's lengthy article "Enter the Musical Shows: Jazz, Its Artists, Wits, and Humorists," *Theatre Guild Magazine* (November 1929), includes two negative judgments: "It murders Gershwin's musical fancy, *An American in Paris*"; and "it gives Duke Ellington's magnificent orchestra the material of an ordinary band."

16. Such numbers as "Sweet and Low-Down" from *Tip-Toes*, "Clap Yo' Hands" from *Oh, Kay!*, and even "Harlem Serenade" in *Show Girl* have roots in minstrelsy too, although all of them are played by white performers. Their subject, however, is vigorous and jazz-oriented, involving uninhibited dancing, whereas "Liza" (not to be confused with Maceo Pinkard's earlier revue song), is a love song that leads into dancing of a different character. The script calls for Dixie Dugan to do a "tap and soft shoe dance" to this number.

CHAPTER 22. A BREAKUP AND A REDO (1929–30)

1. Pollack, 460–61, reports these details and quotes from a letter written to Gershwin by "Ziegfeld's lawyer," but does not give the source of the letter.

The summer of 1929 saw the beginning of George's connection with Isaac

Goldberg, who was already gathering information for the biography he would publish in 1931. Here is what Goldberg wrote about the end of the *Show Girl* venture: "Ziegfeld retired to his chambers, and wrote plethoric epistles, sent long telegrams to Gershwin, less than a mile away. There were disputes,—the sort that Ziggy habitually has with his composers. The Gershwins were compelled to sue for royalties. *Show Girl*, from the first, had had no show. It was too bad, for McEvoy's book had the makings of a good take-off on the modern sweetie and modern salesmanship. The music, amid the general mix-up, went unnoticed" (Goldberg, 246).

2. GG to Rosamond Walling, 10 Oct. 1929. DLC GC. Although the contract between the Gershwin brothers and Ziegfeld does not survive, it is likely that the unpaid royalties were the weekly percentage of the gross box-office receipts that producers agreed to pay members of the creative team, including composers and lyricists.

3. *New York Evening Post*, 16 Oct. 1929.

4. Alfred F. Pahlke, "Our Orchestra Wins Applause," *Milwaukee Journal*, 9 Oct. 1929. Harriet Pettibone Clinton, "New Philharmonic Orchestra Is Plum to Be Picked for Greater Glory of Musical Milwaukee," *Milwaukee Leader*, 9 Oct. 1929. R.E.M., "Acclaim 2nd Philharmonic," *Wisconsin News*, 9 Oct. 1929.

5. GG to Rosamond Walling, 10 Oct. 1929. DLC GC. The movie, called *The King of Jazz*, was released in 1930.

6. Serge Koussevitzky to GG, 28 Oct. 1929. DLC GC.

7. Published on 22 November 1929, on pages 46 and 110. Reprinted in *Gershwin Reader*, 114–19.

8. A column signed "Mephisto" in *Musical America*, 25 Dec. 1929, took strong exception to this opinion. "Lest there be any doubt about it, let me say that I am second to none in my admiration for what amounts to little short of genius in the case of Mr. Berlin," the writer explains. "I think he has written popular songs for a decade and a half which have an extraordinarily strong appeal, and I count 'Say It with Music,' 'Blue Skies,' 'Tell Her in the Springtime,' 'How About Me?' and 'The Song Is Ended' among the outstanding tunes of their kind. But to confuse a pronounced gift for this kind of music with a prodigious genius like that of Franz Schubert is not only to mislead innocent readers of one's opinion but to indict oneself as a musician without critical standards. Surely the very talented composer of the 'Rhapsody in Blue,' now that he has entered the concert halls, would not have us think that about him. How about it, George? Asks your / Mephisto."

9. A likely candidate for the role of editor/writer of this item is David Ewen, who knew Gershwin personally and wrote during this period for the *American Hebrew*. My guess is that the writer decided to publish an article based on a conversation with the composer. How this piece came to be published under Gershwin's name is unknown, but it's impossible to imagine him approving all of its wording and contents.

In later years Ewen published two biographies of Gershwin. But in 1973, Lawrence D. Stewart, coauthor of *The Gershwin Years* (1958; 1973), omitted these titles from his bibliographic essay in the latter edition, on the grounds that the quality of Ewen's research was less than "serious." See p. 391.

10. Ira Gershwin later remembered "I've Got a Crush on You," in 2/4 meter and marked "Allegro giocoso" (fast and playful) being performed pleasantly in the older show by Mary Hay and Clifton Webb. But more vivid in his mind was the memory of Carson and Smith's rendering, "danced in about the fastest 2/4 I ever heard." Apparently the publisher was slow to see commercial promise in the song, for it was not published until February 1930, according to Kimball, 128–29.

11. IG, LoSO, 39.

12. Henry Parker Taylor, "Triple Event for Boston in Musical Comedy / Clark and McCullough Plus 'Strike Up the Band' and George Gershwin," *Boston Evening Transcript*, 26 Dec. 1929.

13. "Wartime Satire in Musical Gayety / 'Strike Up the Band' on the Shubert Stage," *Boston Globe*, 26 Dec. 1929.

14. Robert Littell, "War with the Swiss Helps to Deliver the Words and Music of 'Strike Up the Band,'" *New York World*, 15 Jan. 1930; quoted in Kimball, 158.

15. Gilbert Gabriel, "'Strike Up the Band' / Mr. Selwyn Thinks Better of It and Brings in Some Great Words and Music," *New York American*, 15 Jan. 1930.

16. Burns Mantle, "'Strike Up the Band' Go Bobby Clark [and] Blanche Ring / They Strike Up the Band and Keep It Going," *New York World*, 15 Jan. 1930.

17. Richard Lockridge, "With 'Strike Up the Band' at Times Square Theater," *New York Sun*, 15 Jan. 1930.

18. Robert Benchley, "Satire to Music," *New Yorker*, 25 Jan. 1930.

19. Brooks Atkinson, "In Ridicule of War," *New York Times*, 15 Jan. 1930.

20. Robert Garland, "War and Tired Business Man Targets of Its Cutting Satire / Song-and-Dance Show Close to Being a Pair of Musical Comedies, Says Reviewer of Premiere," *New York Telegram*, 15 Jan. 1930.

CHAPTER 23. BOYFRIEND, SONGWRITER, MUSICAL CITIZEN

1. Rosamond Walling to GG, 29 Jan. 1928. DLC, GC. The photograph in her room was most likely Edward Steichen's portrait of Gershwin in formal dress, seated at the piano. On 29 November 1928, he inscribed a copy of that likeness: "To Rosamond with admiration and affection / George," adding in musical notation the start of the Andantino theme from his *Rhapsody in Blue*. Reproduced in "Recollections of Rosamond Walling Tirana," Kimball and Simon, 136–39.

2. Quoted from ibid., 136.

3. Rosamond Walling to her parents, 20 Oct. 1927. DLC GC.

4. "Recollections of Rosamond Walling Tirana," Kimball and Simon, 136.

5. Rosamond Walling to GG, 9 July 1928. DLC GC.

6. In the idiom that Walling occasionally used with her sisters and friends her own age, "apple" meant perfect, or hunky-dory.

7. Rosamond Walling to GG, 15 Aug. 1928. DLC GC. Walter Catlett played the comic lead in *Treasure Girl*; Gertrude Lawrence was the show's star.

8. GG to Rosamond Walling, 19 Jan. 1929. DLC GC.

9. GG to Rosamond Walling, 13 Jan. 1929. GLC GC.

10. The reference here is to an article by B. J. Woolf, *New York Times Magazine*, 20 Jan. 1929: "Finding in Jazz the Spirit of His Age / George Gershwin, a Product of New York's East Side, Holds Art Must Always Express the Contemporaneous." The page features a large bust of Gershwin captioned: "GG / Drawn from Life by B. J. Woolf."

11. Rosamond Walling to GG, 29 Jan.–2 Feb. 1928. DLC GC.

12. *Deep River*, billed as "a Native Opera in Three Acts," had a book and lyrics by Laurence Stallings and music by Frank Harling. Produced by Arthur Hopkins, it opened on Broadway on 4 October 1926, and closed on 30 October, after thirty-two performances.

13. Rosamond Walling to GG, 2 Feb. 1929. DLC GC.

14. GG to Rosamond Walling, 1 March 1929. DLC GC.

15. Rosamond Walling to GG, 9 March 1929. DLC GC.

16. GG to Rosamond Walling, 29 April 1929. DLC GC.

17. GG to Rosamond Walling, 19 May 1929. DLC GC.

18. GG to Rosamond Walling, 10 Oct. 1929. DLC GC.

19. GG to Rosamond Walling, 21 Nov. 1929. DLC GC.

20. Rosamond Walling to GG, 19 April 1930. DLC GC.

21. GG to Rosamond Walling, 24 April 1930. DLC GC.

22. Rosamond Walling to GG, 10 July 1930. DLC GC.

23. GG to Rosamond Walling, 17 July 1930. DLC GC.

24. Rosamond Walling to GG, 21 Oct. 1931. DLC GC.

25. Rosamond Walling to GG, 26 April 1931. DLC GC.

26. Rosamond Walling to GG, 4 June 1932. DLC GC.

27. "Recollections of Rosamond Walling Tirana," Kimball and Simon, 138–39.

28. Two clippings from unidentified New York newspapers in Gershwin's program books supply the information, one dated 1 March 1930, and headlined "Gershwin and Crawford on WABC Tonight," the other dated March 2 and headlined "Why Gershwin Flew."

29. "Gershwin Plays His Rhapsody / Declares New Yorkers Like Famous 'Blues' Composition as Interpreting Their Life," *New York Sun*, 7 May 1930.

30. George Gershwin, "Making Music," *New York Sunday World*, 4 May 1930. Reprinted in Suriano, 74–77.

31. The date was 28 August. In a letter the next day to Rosamond Walling, Gershwin reported the size of the crowd as more than 12,000. GG to Rosamond Walling, 29 Aug. 1930. DLC GC.

32. "RadioCulture," *New York World*, 9 Dec. 1929.

CHAPTER 24. *GIRL CRAZY* (1930)

1. "Films Attract Gershwin / Signs Contract to Compose Music for a Fox Production," announces that the Fox Film Corporation has signed a deal with Gershwin, *New York Times*, 20 April 1930. And early in May, a Hollywood newspaper reports "Gershwin, Famous Composer, to Fox / Creator of 'Rhapsody in Blue' and His Lyricist Brother, Ira, Sign Contracts," *Hollywood Filmograph*, 10 May 1930.
2. *Screenland* magazine, May 1930.
3. Aaron Copland and Vivian Perlis, *Copland: 1900 through 1947* (New York: St. Martin's / Marek, 1984), 271.
4. IG, LoSO, 271.
5. Though not in the original sheet music, "Rhythmically" appears in the full score of the show published in 1954.
6. Ethel Merman, as told to Pete Martin, *Who Could Ask for Anything More?* (Garden City, NY: Doubleday, 1955), 78–79.
7. Twenty-five tracks of music from *Girl Crazy*, conducted by John Mauceri, were recorded in 1990 by Elektra Nonesuch, 79250 2, via Roxbury Records. The album includes a booklet of ninety-four pages with seven essays and lyrics. No attempt was made to find a singer to match the style or sound of Ethel Merman.
8. That booklet's essay by Richard M. Sudhalter (51–55), titled "And You Should Have Heard The Hot Stuff They Played," identifies the aficionado as Warran Scholl, a pioneer in "the field of jazz record reissues."
9. George J. Ferencz, ed., *"The Broadway Sound": The Autobiography and Selected Essays of Robert Russell Bennett* (Rochester, NY: University of Rochester Press, 1999), 115.
10. Ethel Merman, as told to Pete Martin, *Who Could Ask for Anything More* (Garden City, NY: Doubleday, 1955), 82–83.
11. The story of "I Got Rhythm" offers an example of a show song that, in the hands of jazz instrumentalists, has survived its time in another sphere. Beginning in the early 1930s, the song's tonal architecture, with its repeated use of the ii-V-I chord progression in the refrain's (a) section, played off in the bridge (b) against the circle-of-fifths progressions in other keys, made "I Got Rhythm" an ideal vehicle for jazz improvisation in thirty-two-bar form (in this number plus a two-bar tag). The tonal structure Gershwin fashioned proved to be so logical and inviting that, in a way analogous to the blues progression in twelve-bar cycles, it became the foundation for a host of other musical compositions in that widespread form.

    On how Gershwin's song fit into the jazz repertory of its day, see Richard Crawford and Jeffrey Magee, *Jazz Standards on Record, 1900–1942: A Core Repertory*, CBMR Monographs, No. 4 (Chicago: Columbia College, Center for Black Music Research, 1992). See also "George Gershwin's 'I Got Rhythm'" (1930), Chapter 6 in Richard Crawford, *The American Musical Landscape* (Berkeley: University of California Press, 1993), 217–35, 336–44.

12. One instrumental interlude includes the distinctive progression I-^{b}VII-^{b}VI-V.

13. GG to Isaac Goldberg, 16 Oct. 1930. Harvard Theatre Collection.

14. Robert Garland, "Gershwin's Score for 'Girl Crazy [cut off] / Lilt and Punch of Songs Carry Audience Along," *New York Telegram*, 15 Oct. 1930.

15. Alison Smith, "An American in Arizona," *New York World*, 15 Oct. 1930.

16. Robert Coleman, "'Girl Crazy' Musical Delight, One of Best Town Ever Saw," *New Daily Mirror*, 15 Oct. 1930.

17. Arthur Ruhl, "'Girl Crazy' / Gershwin Melodies Offered in New Musical Comedy at Alvin," *New York Herald Tribune*, 15 Oct. 1930.

18. Sime, "Plays on Broadway / *Girl Crazy*," *Variety*, 22 Oct. 1930.

CHAPTER 25. HOLLYWOOD AND THE SECOND RHAPSODY (1930–31)

1. GG to Ethel Merman, quoted from Ethel Merman, with G. Eells, *Merman: An Autobiography* (New York: Simon and Schuster, 1978). The nightclub where she was appearing was the Casino.

2. GG to Isaac Goldberg, 22 Dec. 1930. Harvard Theatre Collection.

3. Goldberg replied to Gershwin's letter immediately. On this subject, he wrote: "The Boston Symphony has been having a raft of new stuff, most of it conventional celebration music. The Stravinsky Concerto, however, marvelously played by [José] Sanroma, is fine and has some good jazzical passages. His setting of several psalms is also quite impressive, for mixed voices and a very peculiar orchestra. (No violins, five flutes, and so on.) But he achieves new effects. At this concert I saw Copland sitting with Madam Koussevitzky; he is a wild Stravinskian. I had no chance to talk with him." The first work mentioned here is Stravinsky's Concerto for Piano and Winds (1925), and the second his *Symphony of Psalms*. Isaac Goldberg to GG, 26 Dec. 1930. DLC IGLG Trusts.

4. This quotation and later explanatory ones are taken from the shooting script, dated December 1930. Copy in DLC IGLG Trusts.

5. That pronunciation may have had a real-life model. It is said that Albert Strunsky, the father of Ira Gershwin's wife, had a habit of saying "de-li-ci-ous" when he sat down to a meal.

6. In the shooting script dated December 1930, Heather's dream continues in a more elaborate direction, and in midtown Manhattan. The key she has been given is used to open the door to "the great Cathedral on Fifth Avenue." Suddenly aware that she is dressed in a bridal gown, Heather realizes too that "in formation around the Cathedral are crowds of Indians, cowboys," and "girl graduates in cap and gown . . . singing the counter melody to 'Delicious.'" A solemn ceremony is afoot: a wedding, in fact, that involves her. But who is the groom? Now she realizes that there are two of them: Larry and Sascha. Meeting her at the altar, each pledges his love for her with a ring, one for each hand. When the rings are in place, the minister announces: "I pronounce you *men and wife*," whereupon Larry and Sascha serenade her with "Delishious."

7. The attitude she strikes is parallel to that of the female voice behind "The Man I Love," composed by the Gershwins half a dozen years earlier. But the two musical statements vary profoundly in their degrees of elaboration.

8. Here and there in the shooting script, and occasionally in Janet Gaynor's pronunciation, evidence can be found that Scottish dialect—a distinctive mode of pronunciation known as the Scottish "brogue"—was attempted. To the ear of an author whose paternal grandparents were Scottish Lowlanders, and whose father often used the brogue he inherited from them to humorous effect, the attempt was realized with only modest consistency. On the other hand, Gaynor did employ what might be called a Scottish cadence: a rise and fall of the voice, and a rhythm of speech, that distinguishes her from the other characters, whose ways of speaking English include several different dialects. In this cinematic tale of immigration, the native Russian speakers include Sascha, his sister Olga, and his brothers Toscha, Yascha, and Mischa, who is married to Mamushka. Jansen's accent is Swedish. O'Flynn was born an Irishman.

9. Burns's "Comin' through the Rye" was first published in 1782.

10. The melody for "Blah, Blah, Blah" had been composed in 1928 for a Ziegfeld operetta, and then tried in his *Show Girl*, from which it was cut. Characterizing it as "a good ballady tune," Ira Gershwin traced its history in his anthology of lyrics. See IG, LoSO, 151–53.

11. Granting that in the silent film era, which ended in 1927, it was common for "wordless action" to be underlaid by orchestral music, that technique disappeared when "sound-on-film recording technology" enabled sounds and images to be recorded simultaneously on the same reel of film stock. Not until 1933 did the technique of orchestral "underscoring" become common. Yet underscoring, as in background music, does not describe what goes on during this episode. See James Wierzbicki, "The Hollywood Career of Gershwin's Second Rhapsody," *Journal of the American Musicological Society* 60, no. 1 (Spring 2007): 152–54.

12. Paraphrased from ibid., 163–64.

13. *Motion Picture Herald*, 12 Dec. 1931: 35–36; quoted from Wierzbicki.

14. Wierzbicki, 176.

15. Irene Kahn Atkins, "Oral History with Hugo Friedhofer," 90; quoted in Danly, Hugo Friedhofer, 49.

16. GG to Aileen Pringle, 30 June 1931. DLC GC.

17. GG to George Pallay, 30 July 1931. Wierzbicki reports that filming began on 29 August.

18. See Wierzbicki, 178.

19. GG to Aileen Pringle, 31 Dec. 1931. DLC GC.

20. The work's "genesis myth" is discussed at some length in Wierzbicki, 134–40.

21. Goldberg, 273. Goldberg documents neither the claim on p. 271 nor this one.

But the latter has been traced to a letter from Gershwin to Philip Hale, 30 June 1931. Hale was the program annotator for the Boston Symphony Orchestra.

22. "As Gershwin Makes Ready His Rhapsody / Forward the Backward with the New Piece through a Manifold Morning," *Boston Evening Transcript*, 28 Jan. 1932.

23. Pollack, 492, refers to the work's final cadence as a "minor" version of Stephen Foster's melodic turn in "Old Folks at Home." More likely to my ear is that, rather than quoting Foster, the phrase continues on the theme's path, marked with blue notes. Bennett's encomium on Gershwin's "Brahms theme" is also cited on the same page.

24. Edward Kilenyi, "George Gershwin as I Knew Him," *Etude* 68, no. 10 (Oct. 1950): 11–12, 63.

25. The last chapter of Goldberg's biography begins with an epigraph: "Stretto: 'I Am a Man without Traditions,'" which may explain why the critic is raising the point here.

26. Moses Smith, "Gershwin at the Symphony," *Boston Evening Traveler*, 30 Jan. 1932.

27. Warren Storey Smith, "Gershwin Plays Own Rhapsody / Symphony Gives Taylor's 'Alice' Suite," *Boston Post*, 30 Jan. 1932.

28. H. T. Parker, "Symphonic Saturday," *Boston Transcript*, 31 Jan. 1932. Eugene O'Neill's *Mourning Becomes Elektra* had opened in October 1931.

29. *New York Times*, 6 Feb. 1932.

30. *New York Sun*, 6 Feb. 1932.

31. This version, with Bargy at the piano, was recorded in 1938, the year after Gershwin's death.

32. Pollack, 496.

33. Oscar Levant, *The Memoirs of an Amnesiac* (Hollywood, CA: Samuel French, 1989; first published, 1965), 122.

CHAPTER 26. *OF THEE I SING* (1931)

1. Malcolm Goldstein, *George S. Kaufman: His Life, His Theater* (New York: Oxford University Press, 1979), 194ff.

2. Ibid., 196–97.

3. The Gershwin scrapbooks in DLC also include a copy of an extensive article from an English periodical, *Music and Youth*, headlined: "'An American in Paris' / A Work for Orchestra by George Gershwin, the famous American Composer / Hear This Work Broadcast from London at 8 O'Clock on July 27th." The article lays out the work's program and notes that a recording exists, giving the record number. It then offers five notated themes from the work and continues with a more or less blow-by-blow musical analysis of the composition's events from a listener's point of view.

4. London *Times*, 29 July 1931.

5. George Britt, "Reiner Tells of Gershwin's Fame Abroad and Plans to Conduct Classics at Stadium," *New York World-Telegram*, 28 July 1931.

6. GG to Rosamond Walling, 3 Aug. 1931. DLC GC.

7. The references in this paragraph are found in the *New York World-Telegram*, 14 Aug. 1931, and the *New York Herald Tribune*, 14 Aug. 1931. The critic's "Whitmanesque" refers to Paul Whiteman, not Walt Whitman.

8. *New York American*, 7 Oct. 1931.

9. IG to George Pallay, 17 Oct. 1931. Copy in DLC IGLG Trusts.

10. GG to Aileen Pringle, 23 Nov. 1931. DLC GC.

11. GG to Isaac Goldberg, 10 Nov. 1931. DLC GC.

12. GG to Isaac Goldberg, 24 Dec. 1931. DLC GC.

13. "I once asked George Kaufman what the P. in John P. Wintergreen stood for," Ira Gershwin wrote almost three decades after the show. "His answer: 'Why, Peppermint, of course!' with a look that could mean only that any child knew *that*." IG, LoSO, 337.

14. *Kaufman & Co., Broadway Comedies* (New York: Library of America, 2004), contents selected and notes written by Laurence Maslon. *Of Thee I Sing* excerpts from pp. 408–13.

15. IG, LoSO, 331–32.

16. *Kaufman & Co.*, 468.

17. Richard Lockhart, *New York Evening Sun*, 28 Dec. 1931.

18. H. T. Parker, "Musical Play That Is Event Upon Our Stage / New Field, Matter, Manner in Kaufman and Gershwin's 'Of Thee I Sing,'" *Boston Evening Transcript*, 9 Dec. 1931.

19. *Boston Globe*, "Majestic Theatre / 'Of Thee I Sing,'" 9 Dec. 1931.

20. L. A. Sloper, "Theaters," *Christian Science Monitor*, 9 Dec. 1931.

21. H. T. Parker, *Boston Evening Transcript*, "Plays and Players / Day's Garner from Boston Playhouses / Reply of a Chidden Spirit Over 'Of Thee I Sing,' Plays Next Week," 24 Dec. 1931.

22. Richard Lockridge, "The Stage in Review: Mr. Wintergreen for President," *New York Evening Sun*, 28 Dec. 1931.

23. Robert Garland, "More About That Comic Opera Classic," *New York World Telegram*, 28 Dec. 1931.

24. Brooks Atkinson, "The Stage in Review: Mr. Wintergreen for President," *New York Times*, 28 Dec. 1931.

25. John Mason Brown, "Of Thee I Sing, a Jubilant and Immensely Enjoyable Satire of Politics and High Office in America," *New York Evening Post*, 28 Dec. 1931.

26. E. B. White, "Theatre: 'Of It We Sing,'" *New Yorker*, 2 Jan. 1932.

27. Brooks Atkinson, "Of Thee I Sing," *New York Times*, 3 Jan. 1932.

28. Pollack, 512–13. Reported in *New York Times*, 18 Dec. 1932.

CHAPTER 27. MORE DOWNS AND UPS AND DOWNS (1932)

1. Pollack, 513.

2. Vivian Perlis and Libby Van Cleve, *Composers' Voices from Ives to Ellington* (New

Haven and London: Yale University Press, 2005), 209. Kate Wolpin, OHAM (Yale University, Oral History of American Music) interview with Perlis, 30 Jan. 1986, Pompano Beach, FL.

3. Sam Kashner and Nancy Schoenberger, *A Talent for Genius: The Life and Times of Oscar Levant* (Los Angeles: Silman-James Press, 1994), 124. As it happened, Daly himself predeceased Gershwin, and the latter's records contain no indication of his friend's passing.

4. GG to DuBose Heyward, 20 May 1932. DLC IGLG Trusts.

5. Perlis and Van Cleve, 195. Frances Gershwin Godowsky, OHAM interview with Vivian Perlis, 3 June 1983, New York City.

6. Pollack, 110.

7. Vicki Ohl, *Fine and Dandy: The Life and Work of Kay Swift* (New Haven and London: Yale University Press, 2004), 48–50.

8. Ibid., 51.

9. Ibid., 55.

10. Ibid., 56–58.

11. Ohl's Chapter 4 is devoted to *Fine and Dandy*.

12. James P. Warburg, *The Long Road Home* (Garden City, NY: Doubleday, 1964), quoted from Ohl, 113.

13. Frances Godowsky's 1983 interview claims that Kay "was mad for him, but George was never in love with her. He was very flattered by Mrs. Warburg— George was flattered by things like that. He was a little more like my mother that way, in that he was impressed by people with money. He had a lot of friends in all circles, but Kay was a very good musician and a good composer. They had a lot in common, and she just adored him." Perlis and Van Cleve, 203.

   In the 1970s his close friend Emil Mosbacher recalled that Gershwin had "great admiration" for Kay Swift, "and both talked to me about marriage— separately, mind you—and I had one answer to both of them. I said that I wasn't going to open my mouth, I wasn't that crazy. From George I'd get it every day. He was nuts about her." Kimball and Simon, 151.

14. Once the deluxe edition's print run ran its course, a plainer edition of the *Song-book* was published without the illustrations. In a letter to Isaac Goldberg, Gershwin judged Alajolov's pictures "uncommonly good." GG to Isaac Goldberg, 5 Aug. 1931. DLC GC.

15. *George Gershwin's Song-book* (New York: Simon and Schuster, 1932), Introduction.

16. The orchestra's custom for the summer schedule at Lewisohn Stadium was to hire a different guest conductor for each week. Albert Coates, an English conductor, was in charge of the orchestra during the week when the Gershwin concert was scheduled. This event marked the first time that a Lewisohn Stadium concert had been devoted entirely to the music of a single American composer.

17. Jablonski 1987, 234–35.

18. GG to George Pallay, 17 Aug. 1932. Copy in DLC IGLG Trusts.

19. GG to Isaac Goldberg, 28 Aug. 1932. DLC GC.

20. GG to George Pallay, 8 March 1932. Copy in DLC IGLG Trusts. The visit also prompted a postcard to Isaac Goldberg from Havana. It reads in full: "Hello Ike—If you are interested in Sunshine, bathing, liquor, rhythmic music, & marvelous shaking of hips & buttocks Havana is the place. Regards to the Mrs & yourself. George." 29 Feb. 1932. DLC GC.

21. "Recollections of Emil Mosbacher," Kimball and Simon, 151.

22. GG to Pallay, 8 March 1932. DLC GC.

23. Jablonski and Stewart 1973, 181.

24. Olin Downes, "Helping the Unemployed," *New York Times*, 30 Oct. 1932.

25. Ralph Lewando, "Symphony Buries Blue Laws, Hangs Up S.R.O. at Recital," *Pittsburgh Press*, 20 Nov. 1932.

26. Ira Gershwin estimated the cost to the actor of that move as $20,000. See IG, LoSO, 325.

27. *Variety*, 6 Dec. 1932 (Philadelphia); Kimball, ed., *Complete Lyrics of IG*, 192; *Variety*, 31 Jan. 1933.

28. According to Oscar Levant, "The Lorelei," which he considered a "fine old-fashioned jazz tune," failed to win popularity "because its text was too purple for radio." Oscar Levant, *A Smattering of Ignorance* (Garden City, NY: Garden City Publishing Co., 1942), 208.

29. Unidentified Philadelphia newspaper, 3 Dec. 1932.

30. Robert Benchley, review of *Pardon My English*, *New Yorker*, 28 Jan. 1933.

31. Gilbert W. Gabriel, "'Pardon My English' / Jack Pearl and Friends in This Year's Gershwin Show," *New York American*, 21 Jan. 1933.

32. John Mason Brown, "Aarons and Freedley Present 'Pardon My English' at the Majestic with Jack Pearl and Lyda Roberti," *New York Evening Post*, 21 Jan. 1933.

CHAPTER 28. THE LAST MUSICAL COMEDY (1933)

1. Robert Reiss, unidentified Philadelphia newspaper, 3 Dec. 1932.

2. Elizabeth Borton, "'Must Let One's Ego Flower to Do Creative Work'— Gershwin," *News Service*, [mid-October] 1933.

3. Levant 1942, 191–92.

4. During World War I, army personnel of Italy (black) and Germany (brown) wore shirts with these colors.

5. The melody for this number, a thirty-two-bar two-halves structure (**abac**) in 2/4 time, was borrowed from *Pardon My English*, where it was sung to words beginning "Hail the Happy Couple!" at an engagement or wedding party.

6. The notion of choral praise for a boss, or even a product, was relished by George Kaufman, who in *Strike Up the Band* had a morning ritual for the workers in praise of Horace A. Fletcher of Fletcher's American Cheese.

7. The total spending of federal, state, and local governments of the United States during 1933, the year when *Let 'Em Eat Cake* appeared on the Broadway stage,

was $12.6 billion. In contrast, the trial of Alexander Throttlebottom accuses him of having lost the nation more than $286 billion.

8. No explanation has been given for the lyric of "Hanging Throttlebottom in the Morning," sung in the shadow of the guillotine imported from France to carry out the beheadings mandated by Kruger and his kangaroo court. Other than artistic license, it's not easy to imagine why hanging was the chosen mode of execution, unless the song was written before the guillotine was decided on, and the original words and music fit so well together that the mismatch was dismissed as a technicality.

9. John Anderson, reviewing the show for the *New York Journal*, included a cautionary note to self: "Item: a guillotine, however decked out for the musical comedy stage, is not funny." "Of Thee I Sing Sequel Staged Sumptuously," *New York Journal*, 23 Oct. 1933.

10. GG to George Pallay, 9 Nov. 1933. DLC IGLG Trusts.

11. Gilbert W. Gabriel, "Let 'Em Eat Cake: Kaufman, Ryskind, Gershwin and Gershwin Oblige Us with a Sequel," *New York American*, 23 Oct. 1933.

CHAPTER 29. A TURN IN THE ROAD (1933–34)

1. "Art Lovers Shove and Push to See Gershwin's Collection," *Chicago Tribune*, 19 Nov. 1933.

2. C. J. Bulliet, "Gershwin in His Role of Art Collector," *Chicago Daily News*, 11 Nov. 1933.

3. Grace Davidson, "More Serious Things Replace Love Songs and Dances Now, Says Composer Gershwin," *Boston Post*, 3 Oct. 1933.

4. The contract for the opera on *Porgy* was signed on 26 October 1933. DLC GC.

5. Heyward's mother, Jane Screven ("Janie") Heyward, an energetic researcher into local customs and lore, had made the Gullah Negroes, whose culture she grew to admire, a focus of her interest and a presence in the family's everyday life. By the 1920s, she was appearing as a dialect recitalist. Her stories sometimes focused on the emotional and cultural kinship between white and black women across the racial divide. Therefore, the "aristocratic white" background that DuBose Heyward brought to his poetry and fiction after World War I was grounded in a long, sympathetic, and multifaceted engagement with local African American culture. See James M. Hutchisson, *DuBose Heyward: A Charleston Gentleman and the World of Porgy and Bess* (Jackson: University Press of Mississippi, 2000), 6–9, which supports Janie Heyward's involvement in Gullah culture, DuBose's experience with local black folks, and his artistic decision to write about them.

6. Ibid., 9–10.

7. Ibid., 11–13, 20–24, 39–42, 50. The Poetry Society's guest list in 1921 included Carl Sandburg, Harriet Monroe (editor of *Poetry* magazine), Jessie Rittenhouse (founder of the Poetry Society of America), Robert Frost, John Crowe

Ransom, Vachel Lindsay, Louis Untermeyer, and Stephen Vincent Benet. See ibid., 28–33 for the early days of the Poetry Society and Heyward's role in it.

8. Gerald Bordman, *American Theatre: A Chronicle of Comedy and Drama, 1914–1930* (New York: Oxford University Press, 1995), 229, documents the opening of *Nancy Ann*. Hutchisson, 60.

9. DuBose Heyward, Introduction to Dorothy Heyward and DuBose Heyward, *Porgy: A Play in Four Acts* (New York: Doubleday, Doran & Co., 1928), ix–x.

10. Ibid., xi.

11. Ibid., xi–xii.

12. Frank Durham, *DuBose Heyward: The Man Who Wrote "Porgy"* (Columbia: University of South Carolina Press, 1925), 108, 119.

13. Heyward and Heyward, xii–xiii.

14. DuBose Heyward, "Porgy and Bess Return on Wings of Song," *Stage*, October 1935; quoted from Suriano, 103–07.

15. According to his biographer, Jolson's plan was to play Porgy in whiteface, using an all-black cast. Herbert G. Goldman, *Jolson: The Legend Comes to Life* (New York: Oxford University Press, 1988), 289.

16. DuBose Heyward to GG, 3 Sept. 1932. DLC IGLG Trusts.

17. GG to DuBose Heyward, 9 Sept. 1932. DLC IGLG Trusts.

18. DuBose Heyward to GG, 17 Sept. 1932. DLC IGLG Trusts.

19. Article in *Charleston News and Courier*, 4 Dec. 1933.

20. "Recollections of Emil Mosbacher," Kimball and Simon, 219.

21. Lillian Harlow Holley, "'Palm Beach Ideal Spot for Composers,' Says Gershwin," *Palm Beach News*, 29 Dec. 1933.

22. Jablonski and Stewart 1973, 208–09. The authors elaborate on what they learned from Mueller: "Many stops for the orchestra were sponsored by local music clubs or other culture groups, whose membership was largely made up of women, who made a point of meeting the train upon arrival. In St. Paul, for example, a mob of women met them at the station. As Paul and James Melton had left the train before George, they led the way through the crowd with George trailing diffidently behind. Paul carried the practice keyboard. Soon he and Melton were surrounded. A woman threw her arms around Melton, kissed him, then turned to Paul, saying 'Welcome to St. Paul, Mr. Gershwin!' and planted a kiss on his cheek." "This was generally the tenor of the tour. In Kansas City the concert was held in the Armory and backstage Paul encountered a dowager who announced, 'I'm looking for my niece, have you seen her?' No, he had not, but she was soon discovered in Melton's dressing room—and forcibly, but gently, evicted." For more on Melton, see Pollack, 563–65, 648.

23. Dorothy Boyd Mattison, "Gershwin and Melton Share Musical Honors / Audience of 2000 Enjoys All-American Program," unidentified Worcester, MA, newspaper, 16 Jan. 1934. The song from *Oh, Kay!* may have been "Maybe," which had been sung the preceding evening.

24. C. Pannill Mead, "Gershwin, as Pianist, Wins Praise, Melton Scores Hit," unidentified Milwaukee newspaper, 24 Jan. 1934.

25. Review of concert on 4 Feb. 1934, by unidentified writer in unidentified Chicago paper, 5 Feb. 1934.

26. Odell Hauser, "Gershwin Plays His Own Music / Composer Heard at Piano with Orchestra in Varied Program at Academy," unidentified Philadelphia newspaper, 8 Feb. 1934.

27. GG to DuBose Heyward, 26 Feb. 1934. DLC IGLG Trusts.

28. GG to George Pallay, 26 Feb. 1934. DLC IGLG Trusts.

29. Gilbert Seldes, "The Gershwin Case," *Esquire*, October 1934.

CHAPTER 30. *MUSIC BY GERSHWIN* AND *PORGY AND BESS*, ACT I (1935–36)

1. George Gershwin, as told to Charles Earle, "Making an Hour Click with Gershwin Music," *Radio Guide*, 7 April 1934: 7, 12.

2. GG to George Pallay, 13 Jan. 1934. DLC IGLG Trusts.

3. DuBose Heyward, "Porgy and Bess Returns," *Stage*, October 1935, 104–05. See Suriano, 104–05.

4. GG to DuBose Heyward, 26 Feb. 1934. DLC IGLG Trusts.

5. DuBose Heyward to GG, 2 March 1934. Copy in DLC IGLG Trusts.

6. Note, however, some exceptions, e.g., the street cries, and the simultaneous prayers that begin and end Act II, scene 4—both simulations of Gershwin's on-site experience with indigenous "folk" material.

7. *New York Herald Tribune*, 8 July 1934.

8. A vocable is a nonsyntactic "word" made from sounds.

9. *The Theatre Guild Presents "Porgy and Bess" / Music by George Gershwin / Libretto by DuBose Heyward* (New York: Gershwin Publishing Corporation, 1935), vocal score, 18–21.

10. Vocal score, rehearsal 30, p. 21.

11. Vocal score, rehearsal 70ff., p. 45. Porgy has enjoyed a profitable day of begging and, as he assures his friends, he's willing to risk it in the game he is there to play. As the men talk, the orchestral background sounds Porgy's motive three more times in full. See vocal score, 45–47.

12. The pitches emanate from the motive's second gesture, in its second and third bars.

13. See vocal score, 52–53, beginning at rehearsal 83 for lead-in, with the motive itself two bars before rehearsal 84.

14. See vocal score, 56, beginning at rehearsal 90, for the single-note lead-in without the motive itself. Here the single note is sounded no fewer than three dozen times.

15. Anne Brown, the first actress to play Bess, cited the first actress to play Serena—Mississippi-born, conservatory-trained soprano Ruby Elzy—as one who, after Gershwin heard her spontaneous embellishments of his vocal line in

an Act II prayer enactment, was told by the composer to leave them in. Gershwin, Brown observed, "never objected to changes in his music" if made by the performers. *Gershwin Reader*, 221.

CHAPTER 31. *PORGY AND BESS*, ACT II

1. DuBose Heyward to GG, 2 March 1934 (copy in DLC IGLG Trusts), accepts in principle Gershwin's invitation to work together on the score in New York, figuring that mid-April might find him free. Within the week, Gershwin replied that, having begun to compose, he was "skipping around" in the libretto, citing a number in Act II that had caught his eye (GG to DuBose Heyward, 8 March 1934; copy in DLC IGLG Trusts). Thus the new song for Porgy could have been composed as early as April.

2. IG, LoSO, 359–60.

3. Ibid., 358–60. The story is told in Kimball, ed., *Complete Lyrics of IG*, 236.

4. The "Buzzard Song" was cut from the original production, and later productions have sometimes omitted it, too.

5. See the interview with Todd Duncan in *Gershwin Reader*, 224.

6. It seems worth noting that, as with Gershwin's musical comedy scores, the publisher—in this case his own Gershwin Publishing Corporation—issued some numbers from the opera independently in sheet-music form. Although the piano accompaniment for this version is somewhat simplified from that in the opera's vocal score, the lyrics, with their references to the characters in the opera, including the matter of going or staying, remain the same.

7. As will appear later, however, in the case of "Bess, You Is My Woman Now," the beginning gesture of a prominent song sometimes acts as a leitmotif referring to her attractiveness.

8. In an eight-page commentary to Richard Crawford dated 9 April 2014, Wayne Shirley interprets the stop marked in the bar preceding rehearsal 137 as signaling the end of "It Ain't Necessarily So," followed by applause, and then the dance as the start of an encore. He points out that the "formal end" of the song is thereby marked, while making it possible for Serena "to interrupt the final cadence." This move, he points out, is "[also] in the musical-comedy tradition of putting in a small dance to end a comic number" (5).

9. See Heyward's "Porgy and Bess Return on Wings of Song," *Stage*, October 1935; quoted from Suriano, 105–06.

10. See vocal score, 402–03, for the stage direction at this moment: "Convinced that nobody is knocking, Maria opens the door herself."

CHAPTER 32. *PORGY AND BESS*, ACT III

1. Thanks to Wayne Shirley for his explanation of this "ancient superstition."

2. See Ira Gershwin's note on this song in LoSO, 82–83, where he explains that

the wording of the title is not simply an inconsistency but an indication of his use of dialect in the opera.

3. Heyward's original libretto may be found in DLC GC.

4. Joseph Horowitz, *"On My Way": The Untold Story of Rouben Mamoulian, George Gershwin, and "Porgy and Bess"* (New York: W. W. Norton, 2013), 131.

5. In the vocal score from rehearsal 128 to 152, stage directions direct the movements of the characters.

6. "Rhapsody in Catfish Row," *New York Times*, 20 Oct. 1935.

CHAPTER 33. PERFORMING *PORGY AND BESS*

1. "Recollections of Eva Jessye," Kimball and Simon, 184.

2. *Gershwin Reader*, 232.

3. Isaac Goldberg's biography had described Gershwin as a boy growing up on the streets of New York, and being a "champion" rollerskater in his neighborhood. See Goldberg, 53. That Brown had read up on him before her audition delighted Gershwin.

4. The date of Brown's audition is not known, but it could not have been before the late summer or early fall of 1934. We know too that "Summertime" was the first song composed for the opera, and that Gershwin's letter of 26 Feb. 1934 to Heyward reports that composition of the score had recently begun.

5. "After meeting my mother and hearing her call me Annie, he always called me Annie," Brown told the interviewer. *Gershwin Reader*, 230.

6. In a letter to Richard Crawford sent on 1 August 2014, Wayne Shirley writes that either Brown is "misremembering this description, or Gershwin is misremembering the duet for Bess and Serena which he'd cut from earlier in Act III Scene 1." He explains: "The two women's parts in the trio 'Bess, Oh Where's My Bess?' were originally to be sung by Serena and Maria; when Maria proved to be unable to manage her part it was given to Lily. That may be why Brown remembers Lily in the context of a trio."

7. *Gershwin Reader*, 232.

8. Duncan's interview with Robert Wyatt quoted above dates from 1990 and is found in the *Gershwin Reader*, 221–28; see especially 221–22. An earlier interview by Robert Kimball picks up the story from here: "Recollections of Todd Duncan," Kimball and Simon, 180–81.

9. *Gershwin Reader*, 224–25. See also *Along This Way: The Autobiography of James Weldon Johnson* (New York: Viking, 1968; first published 1933), 120–21, for extended comment on the attitude of the southern black "masses" early in the twentieth century. "For one thing," Johnson wrote, "they learned the white man with whom they had to deal. They learned him through and through; and without ever completely revealing themselves. Their knowledge of the white man's weaknesses as well as his strength came to be almost intuitive. And when they felt it futile to depend upon their own strength, they took advantage of his

weaknesses—the blind side of arrogance and the gullibility that always goes with overbearing pride."

10. Levant 1942, 179–80.

11. See Act II, scene 3, rehearsal 187–88, pp. 334ff. of the vocal score for Serena's prayer as written.

12. Todd Duncan, "Memoirs of George Gershwin," Armitage 1938, 59–60.

13. Paul Horgan, *A Certain Climate* (1988), 206. Quoted in Horowitz, 74.

14. Ibid., 29.

15. Ibid., 30.

16. In 1958 Mamoulian recorded an interview now housed at Columbia University's oral history archive. References from that interview are cited in ibid., 34–35.

17. Quoted from ibid., 39–40.

18. James Hutchisson, author of a biography of Heyward, writes that the librettist had found Mamoulian "hard to work with in 1927—too mercurial and too harsh a taskmaster on cast and crew," and thought Houseman would be a better choice. Hutchisson, 153.

19. GG to DuBose Heyward, 17 Dec. 1934. DLC IGLG Trusts.

20. Armitage 1938, quoted from Rouben Mamoulian, "I Remember," 47–50.

21. Anne Brown remembered in an interview during the 1990s that Johnson, who also played the part of Lawyer Frazier, had been effective in a coaching role. *Gershwin Reader*, 233.

22. Irving Kolodin, "*Porgy and Bess*: American Opera in the Theatre," *Theatre Arts*, November 1935: 855–56.

23. Charles Hamm, "The Theatre Guild Production of *Porgy and Bess*," *Journal of the American Musicological Society* 40, no. 3 (Autumn 1987): 495–532. Page number for the footnote is 514. This article is a report of the cuts made in *Porgy and Bess* in Boston and New York as the opera was being unveiled during September and October 1935.

24. Interview in *Gershwin Reader*, 232. Note also that Mamoulian recalled a late-night phone call that evening in which Gershwin confessed: "After listening to that rehearsal today, I think the music was so marvelous—I really don't believe I wrote it myself!" Armitage 1938, 51.

CHAPTER 34. JUDGING *PORGY AND BESS*

1. "Porgy and Bess," *Boston Globe*, 1 Oct. 1935.

2. L. A. Sloper, "Mr. Gershwin Writes an Opera," *Christian Science Monitor*, 1 Oct. 1935.

3. Elliot Norton, "Premiere of 'Porgy and Bess' / Opera at the Colonial Able and Brilliant Experiment," *Boston Post*, 1 Oct. 1935.

4. Warren Story Smith, "Gigantic Task / Gershwin Starts Out Ambitiously and Music in Final Act Shows Real Craftsmanship—Thereafter Mixes Styles—Singing Excellent," *Boston Post*, 1 Oct. 1935.

5. DuBose Heyward, "Porgy and Bess Return on Wings of Song." *Stage*, October 1935; reprinted in Suriano, 103–07.
6. George Gershwin, "Rhapsody in Catfish Row," *New York Times*, 20 Oct. 1935.
7. Brooks Atkinson, "Dramatic Values of Community Legend Gloriously Transposed," *New York Times*, 11 Oct. 1935.
8. Olin Downes, "Exotic Richness of Negro Music and Color of Charleston, S.C., Admirably Conveyed in Score of Catfish Row Tragedy," *New York Times*, 11 Oct. 1935.
9. W. J. Henderson, "'Porgy and Bess' Heard Here," *New York Sun*, 11 Oct. 1935.
10. Lawrence Gilman, "George Gershwin's New Opera, Porgy and Bess," *New York Herald Tribune*, 11 Oct. 1935.
11. "Folk Opera," *Time* magazine, 21 Oct. 1935.
12. A. Walter Kramer, "Gershwin's Porgy and Bess Hailed in New York," *Musical America*, 25 Oct. 1935: 6.
13. IG, LoSO, 83. Buck and Bubbles were a vaudeville team. In the opera "Bubbles" played the role of Sporting Life and "Buck" appeared as Mingo.
14. Rosenberg, 318–19.
15. Virgil Thomson, "George Gershwin," *Modern Music*, November–December 1935: 13–19. Because the quotations used here appear in a sequence parallel to the article's text, only the most extensive ones are documented.
16. See ibid., 18. Black characters sing most of the time but, as Wayne Shirley shows in a six-page inventory headed "Lines spoken rather than sung by black characters in *Porgy and Bess*," sent to Richard Crawford on 8 September 2014, passages in which they speak their lines are not rare. Shirley also cites one instance where a white detective sings a brief portion of a line to imitate a black character who has just sung. He ascribes the broad declamatory spectrum open to the black characters to Gershwin's admiration for Alban Berg's opera *Wozzeck*.
17. Marcia Davenport, "Rhapsody in Black: Porgy and Bess, as an Opera," *Stage*, November 1935; quoted from Suriano, 118.
18. Isaac Goldberg, "Score by George Gershwin / In the Music for *Porgy and Bess* Mr. Gershwin Richly Expands and Intensifies the Original *Porgy*," *Stage*, December 1935.
19. Francis Hall Johnson, "Porgy and Bess: A Folk Opera," *Opportunity*, January 1936: 24–28.

CHAPTER 35. COMPOSER OF *PORGY AND BESS*

1. The proposed dates were 15–19 April, at 3:15 or 5:30 in the afternoon. Secretary to Dr. Zilboorg to GG, 4 April 1935. DLC GC.
2. Gregory Zilboorg to GG, 11 April 1936. DLC GC. Since the production of *Porgy and Bess* would be having its tryout run at that time, and its debut in New

York would be at hand, 1 October would find Gershwin occupied. But once the opera opened in New York on 10 October, he would presumably have been free. Perhaps between mid-October and mid-November one or more sessions between Gershwin and Zilboorg were arranged with the cruise in mind. But a professional connection does seem to have been under way by the time the Gershwin party embarked on the *Santa Paula*.

3. Peyser, 254; Walter Rimler, *George Gershwin: An Intimate Portrait* (Urbana and Chicago: University of Illinois Press, 2009), 118–20.

4. GG to Elizabeth Allan, 23 Jan. 1936. DLC IGLG Trusts.

5. Elsie Finn, "Gershwin Delights in 'Porgy' Premiere / Philadelphia Orchestra Wins Plaudits of Composer and Audience," *Philadelphia Record*, 28 Jan. 1936.

6. "World of Music," *Washington Times*, 9 Feb. 1936.

7. Ray C. B. Brown in *Washington Post*, 9 Feb. 1936.

8. Marcia Davenport, "An Earful of Music," *McCall's* magazine, March 1936.

9. *Dead End*, a play by Sidney Kingsley, is set in the East Fifties of New York City. A new luxury high-rise overlooking the East River had gone up across the street from tenement houses, where crime flourished. The play, which opened on Broadway in October 1935 and ran for more than 600 performances, became a Hollywood movie in 1937. See Gerald Bordman, *American Theatre: A Chronicle of Comedy and Drama, 1930–1969* (New York and Oxford: Oxford University Press, 1996), 124.

10. IG to Yip Harburg, 12 June 1936. DLC IGLG Trusts. Quoted in Rosenberg, 323, 325.

11. The charge is found in a telegram from Archie Selwyn to GG, 12 June 1936. Quoted in Pollack, 667.

12. Jablonski and Stewart 1973, 247–50, traces the brothers' process of agreeing to write songs for a Fred Astaire movie for RKO, taking an option on a second one.

13. "Few Nudes in This Year's Independent Artists' Exhibition," *Boston Globe*, 24 April 1936.

14. Morris Hastings, "Confident Gershwin," *Microphone*, 16 May 1936.

15. For the most part, the music was performed in operatic order: "Summertime" by Anne Brown and chorus; "Gone, Gone, Gone" by chorus; "My Man's Gone Now" by Ruby Elzy and chorus; "Train Song" by Anne Brown and chorus; "I Got Plenty o' Nuttin'" by Todd Duncan; "Bess, You Is My Woman Now" by Duncan and Brown; the "Storm" by the orchestra; the "Buzzard Song" by Duncan; and "I'm On My Way" by the whole company.

16. Rimler, 127–28.

17. Glenn Dillard Gunn, "Audience Hails King of Jazz as Conductor / Gershwin Interprets Popular Idiom to Perfection, Says Gunn; and Orchestra Too," *Chicago Herald*, 26 July 1936.

18. "Recollections of Kay Swift," Kimball and Simon, 200.

CHAPTER 36. HOLLYWOOD SONGWRITER I: *SHALL WE DANCE* (1936–37)

1. "Recollections of Ira Gershwin," Kimball and Simon, 203. Ira's statement ended by noting that, while "Hi-Ho!" had never been published, it was about time for it to be. The copyright date on the music is 1967.
2. *The Show Is On*, billed as a musical revue, opened in New York on 25 December 1936 and closed on 17 July 1937, after 236 performances. "By Strauss," sung by Gracie Barrie and Robert Shafer, opened Act II of the show. A dancer was also involved.
3. "They might come with all the pictures; however, if the pictures have already gone out I wish you would have a package made up of my painting parapher-nalia, including perhaps some of the unpainted small canvases that are lying around, and send it to me. If it doesn't cost too much to send it, perhaps you can include my new easel in the package too." GG to Zena Hannenfeldt, 11 Sept. 1936. DLC GC.
4. GG to Mabel Schirmer, 1 Sept. 1936. DLC GC.
5. GG to Mabel Schirmer, 18 Sept. 1936. DLC GC.
6. GG to Emil Mosbacher, 11 Sept. 1936. DLC GC.
7. William Daly to GG, 13 Sept. 1936. DLC IGLG Trusts, Miscellaneous File D.
8. Ibid. For the record, the orchestra at Ravinia had been the Chicago Symphony Orchestra.
9. GG to Gregory Zilboorg, 1 Sept. 1936, DLC GC.
10. Anne Brown to GG, 1 Sept. 1936. DLC IGLG Trusts, Miscellaneous File B.
11. Warren Munsell to GG, 30 Sept. 1936. DLC IGLG Trusts. According to the manager, both Brown and Todd Duncan, invited to play Porgy, demanded a salary of $500 per week, which was out of proportion with the English theater's resources. For Gershwin's reply and more on a projected musical comedy, see GG to Warren Munsell, 6 Oct. 1936. DLC IGLG Trusts.
12. Merle Armitage, *George Gershwin: Man and Legend* (New York: Duell, Sloan and Pearce, 1958), 77.
13. Clifford Odets (1906–1963) was an American playwright, screenwriter, and director then working in Hollywood.
14. GG to Gregory Zilboorg, 26 Oct. 1936. DLC GC.
15. GG to Gregory Zilboorg, 11 Nov. 1936. DLC GC.
16. GG to Emily Paley, 4 Jan. 1937. Quoted in Jablonski and Stewart 1973, 272–73.
17. GG to Gregory Zilboorg, 19 Feb. 1937. DLC GC.
18. Todd Decker, *Music Makes Me: Fred Astaire and Jazz* (Berkeley: University of California Press, 2011) offers a detailed description of "Slap That Bass" on pp. 278–88. The author cites Ellington and Bubber Miley's "East St. Louis Toodle-oo" as a possible reference in this arrangement, but to my ear that minor-mode statement recalls the opening tune of "St. James Infirmary."
19. IG, LoSO, 258–59.
20. Ibid., 265.

21. Jablonski 1987, 302. See also Pollack, 187.
22. Shilkret, 172–74, includes an account of the lengthy ballet preceding the "Shall We Dance?" finale.

CHAPTER 37. HOLLYWOOD SONGWRITER II: *A DAMSEL IN DISTRESS* (1937)

1. Marie Hicks Davison, "Novel Recital Given by Gershwin," *San Francisco Call-Bulletin*, 16 Jan. 1937.
2. At this time San Francisco's Golden Gate Bridge, completed in 1937, was being built.
3. GG to Emily Paley, 9 Jan. 1937. DLC GC. Facsimile in Jablonski and Stewart 1973, 272–73.
4. Isabella Morse Jones, "Gershwin's Concert at Philharmonic Auditorium. Brilliant Event," *Los Angeles Times*, 11 Feb. 1937; Florence Lawrence, "Gershwin Scores Triumph," *Los Angeles Examiner*, 11 Feb. 1937.
5. Richard D. Saunders, "Screen Celebrities Put Show on as Gershwin Symphonic Fare Heard," *Hollywood Citizen-News*, 11 Feb. 1937.
6. GG to Emily Paley, 9 Jan. 1937. DLC GC. Facsimile in Jablonski and Stewart 1973, 272–73.
7. GG to Mabel Schirmer, 19 March 1937. Copy in DLC IGLG Trusts. See also Kimball and Simon, 214.
8. GG to Isaac Goldberg, 13 April 1937. DLC IGLG Trusts.
9. GG to Isaac Goldberg, 12 May 1937. Copy in DLC IGLG Trusts.
10. Frank S. Nugent, "The Screen: 'Shall We Dance,'" *New York Times*, 14 May 1937.
11. "Sid," "Shall We Dance (Musical)," *Variety*, 12 May 1937.
12. Kimball and Simon, 205, prints a facsimile of this letter in Gershwin's hand. It also shows a facsimile of a telegram he sent Schirmer on 31 December 1936: "FOR THE NEW YEAR LOVE AND KISSES HEALTH AND HAPPINESS / GEORGE."
13. "Recollections of Henry Botkin," Kimball and Simon, 216.
14. "Recollections of Emil Mosbacher," ibid., 218.
15. GG to Emily Paley, 16 March 1937. DLC GC.
16. GG to Rose Gershwin, 19 May 1937. DLC GC.
17. GG to Mabel Schirmer, 19 May 1937. DLC GC.
18. GG to Frances Gershwin Godowsky, 27 May 1937. DLC GC.
19. Rose Gershwin to GG, 6 June 1937. DLC IGLG Trusts.
20. GG to Rose Gershwin, 10 June 1937. DLC GC.
21. "Recollections of Harold Arlen," Kimball and Simon, 204.
22. The report by Dr. Gabriel Segall of Los Angeles of his examination of Gershwin on 9 June 1937 fills five double-spaced pages. It is preserved in DLC GC, with a cover letter addressed more than a year later to Dr. Gregory Zilboorg, 12 October 1938.
23. "Henry Botkin" is the "Harry Botkin" to whom Gershwin had usually referred as "my cousin Botkin, the painter" (1896–1983). Botkin had advised Gershwin

in his art-collecting endeavor and helped his cousin learn to paint. He had an exhibit of his own work in Southern California during the time George and Ira were settled in Beverly Hills.

24. IG, LoSO, 157.

25. Ibid., 65–66.

26. Ibid., 97. Ira recalled seeing the title-line in an article about cartoons rejected by *Punch* magazine. "Two charwomen are discussing the daughter of a third, and the first says she's heard that the discussee 'as become an 'ore. Whereat the second observes it's nice work if you can get it."

CHAPTER 38. GONNA RISE UP SINGING

1. "My Life or the Story of George Gershwin," Levant 1942, 198–200.

2. Ibid., 148.

3. Ibid., 150.

4. Ibid., 151–52.

5. Ibid., 153.

6. Levant's recollection of self-abasement continues. Ibid., 154–57.

7. Ibid., 157–59.

8. Readers will know, however, that when describing his approach to songwriting in his 1930 article "Making Music," Gershwin cited the creation of a refrain melody as the toughest part of the process. Levant, who surely overheard his friend in the throes of songful invention—"making music" was a handle Gershwin sometimes used for that task—may not have been exaggerating in the claim made about Gershwin's fluency. But by the composer's own testimony, melodies that satisfied him often took him considerable labor to arrive at. See *Gershwin Reader*, 133–36.

9. Levant 1942, 187.

10. Ibid., 195–96.

11. GG to Isaac Goldberg, 12 May 1937. DLC IGLG Trusts.

12. A. Scott Berg, *Goldwyn* (New York: Ballantine, 1989), 198, 201.

13. GG to Mabel Schirmer, 19 May 1937. DLC GC.

14. GG to Frances Gershwin Godowsky, 27 May 1937. DLC GC.

15. Rose Gershwin's response to George's news prompted a conversation with Dr. A. M. Garbat, her doctor in New York, in which she complained that George's regime of hiking and dietary restrictions seemed to be bad for his health. Whereupon the doctor dashed off a dutch-uncle style of letter to the composer, warning those who become "faddists" about diet and exercise to practice moderation on these fronts. The doctor's counsel offers a light moment in a trend that grew darker as the days passed. A. L. Garbat, M.D., to GG, 30 June 1937. DLC IGLG Trusts.

16. Mark Leffert, "The Psychoanalysis and Death of George Gershwin: An American Tragedy," *Journal of the American Academy of Psychoanalysis and Dynamic Psychiatry* 39 (2011): 424–52.

17. S. N. Behrman, *People in a Diary* (Boston: Little, Brown, 1972), 253–54.

18. This report is quoted from the Leffert article cited above.

19. Thanks to surgeon—and longtime friend—Dr. Theodore G. Dodenhoff for advice on the medical facts cited in this chapter. His help includes an explanation in a message to me that "herniation" means that "the malignant tumor had protruded against brain tissue." Herniation, he writes, is simply "a structure (cyst, clot, tumor, etc.)" that, "due to enlargement," pushes against other tissues and "applies pressure" to them.

20. Quoted from Leffert, n. 443.

21. "Coincident with Services Held in New York Yesterday," *Variety*, 16 July 1937: 37. Quoted from *Gershwin Reader*, 271–72.

22. Levant 1942, 209–10. The broadcast took place on 12 July 1937.

23. Reported in "An American in Memoriam," *Newsweek*, 15 July 1940. See Pollack, 117.

24. Levant 1942, 210.

25. The writer must have intended irony in calling Kaufman's satire gentle.

26. "George Gershwin, Composer, Is Dead," *New York Times*, 12 July 1937.

27. "George Gershwin," *Boston Herald*, 12 July 1937.

28. "George Gershwin," *New York Herald Tribune*, 13 July 1937.

29. "The Man I Love," *New Republic*, 21 July 1937. For an article centered on the business side of the composer's career, see also "Gershwin Reminiscences," *Variety*, 14 July 1937.

30. IG to Rose Gershwin, 31 July 1937. DLC GC.

31. "Recollections of George Balanchine," Kimball and Simon, 222.

32. IG, LoSO, 139–40.

33. Ibid., 284; Pollack, 687. Although the song's published version bears the name "Love Is Here to Stay," a title that survives in *The Songs of George and Ira Gershwin*, A Centennial Celebration (Miami: Warner Bros. Publications, 1998), each of the phrase's use in the song declares, "Our love is here to stay." Perhaps Ira maintained the title written in George's sketch as a gesture of respect so that this final song of George's carried a title applied by him. The number's copyright in July 1937 as an unpublished song bore the title "It's Here to Stay." See Kimball, ed., *Complete Lyrics of IG*, 276. (Perhaps George's heading for the sketch was a placeholder for "the song about love is here to stay.")

In several measures (mm. 1–2, 8) the composer added a second voice to the melody line, signaling a harmonic choice he deems essential to his new song's character at that moment. Another bar (m. 7) suggests that, before deciding to end his second phrase with a whole-note A, he toyed with the idea of continuing the melodic figure in the preceding measure (m. 6). Finally, in bar 9 he considers anticipating the second beat with a tied eighth note before deciding to place the second note directly on that beat. Gershwin's "start" points to the form his refrain will take. The last three notes in m. 8, leading into a new section, signal that the melody he has in mind will be structured in two halves: in **abac** form, in fact, whose last section begins with a reference to **b** music and ends with the title-line sung to new cadential material.

34. Jablonski and Stewart 1958, 264, is the source for this quotation, and for the rest of the material quoted here. Readers may be reminded that this biography is based on materials in Ira's personal archive of Gershwin sources. I have cited that book in Chapter 1 as the Gershwin biography most closely incorporating Ira's thinking on the subject.

35. GG to Gregory Zilboorg, 26 Oct. 1936. DLC GC.

36. Frances Gershwin Godowsky, in Vivian Perlis and Libby Van Cleve, *Composers' Voices from Ives to Ellington* (New Haven and London: Yale University Press, 2005), 204–05.

37. Jablonski and Stewart 1958, 264.

38. David Schiff, *The Ellington Century* (Berkeley: University of California Press, 2012) makes this claim in its preface.

INDEX